THE BORZOI ANTHOLOGY
OF LATIN AMERICAN LITERATURE

Volume II

THE BORZOI ANTHOLOGY OF LATIN AMERICAN LITERATURE

**Volume II
The Twentieth Century—from
Borges and Paz to Guimarães Rosa
and Donoso**

**Edited by
EMIR RODRÍGUEZ MONEGAL**

*With the assistance of
THOMAS COLCHIE*

Alfred A. Knopf   New York   1986

THIS IS A BORZOI BOOK
PUBLISHED BY ALFRED A. KNOPF, INC.

Copyright © 1977 by Alfred A. Knopf, Inc.

Library of Congress Cataloging in Publication Data

Main entry under title:

The Borzoi anthology of Latin American literature.

    CONTENTS: v. 1. From the time of Columbus to the twentieth century.—v. 2. Twentieth century.
      1. Latin American literature—Translations into English. 2. English literature—Translations from Spanish. 3. English literature—Translations from Portuguese. I. Rodríguez Monegal, Emir. II. Colchie, Thomas.
PQ7087.E5B6   860'.8   76–19126
ISBN 0–394–73301–0 pbk. (v. 1)
ISBN 0–394–73366–5 pbk. (v. 2)

Manufactured in the United States of America

Published July 21, 1977
Reprinted Once
Third Printing, November 1986

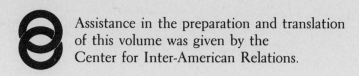 Assistance in the preparation and translation
of this volume was given by the
Center for Inter-American Relations.

The following selections are reprinted in this volume by the kind permission of the publishers, authors, and individuals hereinafter acknowledged:

"The Aleph" by Jorge Luis Borges. From *The Aleph and Other Stories 1933–1969* by Jorge Luis Borges, edited and translated by Norman Thomas di Giovanni in collaboration with the author. English translation Copyright © 1968, 1969, 1970 by Emece Editores, S.A. and Norman Thomas di Giovanni. Reprinted by permission of E. P. Dutton & Co., Inc. and Jonathan Cape Ltd.

"El Señor Presidente" by Miguel Angel Asturias. From *El Señor Presidente*, translated by Frances Partridge. Copyright © 1963 by Victor Gollancz Ltd. Reprinted by permission of Atheneum Publishers, Inc. and Victor Gollancz Ltd.

"Journey Back to the Source" by Alejo Carpentier. From *War of Time*, translated by Frances Partridge. Copyright © 1970 by Victor Gollancz Ltd. Reprinted by permission of Alfred A. Knopf, Inc. and Victor Gollancz Ltd.

"Jacob and the Other" by Juan Carlos Onetti, translated by Izaak A. Langnas. From *Prize Stories from Latin America*, edited by James Alberse. Copyright © 1963 by Time, Inc. Reprinted by permission of Doubleday & Company, Inc. "A Dream Come True" by Juan Carlos Onetti, translated by Ines de Torres Kinnell. From *Doors and Mirrors: Fiction and Poetry from Spanish America, 1920–1970*, edited by Hortense Carpentier and Janet Brof. Copyright © 1972 by Hortense Carpentier and Janet Brof. Reprinted by permission of Grossman Publishers, a division of The Viking Press, Inc.

"Alone" by Vicente Huidobro. From *El Ciudadino del Olvido* ("Solo"). Copyright © 1963 by Empresa Editora Zig-Zag, S.A., Santiago, Chile. Translated by David Guss. "Poem to Make Trees Grow," "Alert," "Announcement," "Ars Poetica," "New Year," "Altazor: Canto III" by Vicente Huidobro. From *Altazor*. Translated by Eliot Weinberger. Copyright © 1963 by Empresa Editora Zig-Zag, S.A. Reprinted by permission of the publisher.

"Human Poems" by César Vallejo. From *Poemas Humanos/Human Poems*, translated by Clayton Eshleman. Copyright © 1968 by Grove Press, Inc. Reprinted by permission of the publisher.

"You Come in the Night with the Fabulous Smoke of Your Hair" by César Moro, translated by H. R. Hays. From *An Anthology of Latin American Poetry*, edited by Dudley Fitts. Copyright 1942 by New Directions Publishing Corporation. Reprinted by permission of the publisher.

"Death Without End" by José Gorostiza, translated by Rachel Benson. From *New Poetry of Mexico*, edited by Mark Strand. Copyright by Siglo XXI Editores, S.A. English translation Copyright © 1970 by E. P. Dutton & Co., Inc. Reprinted by permission of the publishers.

"Angel-Nocturne" by Xavier Villaurrutia, translated by Dudley Fitts. From *An Anthology of Latin American Poetry*, edited by Dudley Fitts. Copyright 1942 by New Directions Publishing Corporation. Reprinted by permission of the publisher. "Rose Nocturnal" and "Cemetery in the Snow" by Xavier Villaurrutia, translated by Donald Justice. From *New Poetry of Mexico*, edited by Mark Strand. Copyright by Siglo XXI Editores, S.A. English translation Copyright © 1970 by E. P. Dutton & Co., Inc. Reprinted by permission of the publishers.

"Kiln-stone" and "Arrival" by Nicolás Guillén. From *El Son entero*, translated by Stephan Schwartz. Reprinted by permission of *Mundus Artium*, Vol. 3, No. 1 (Winter, 1969).

"Dead Gallop," "Ars Poetica," "Ritual of My Legs," "The Widow's Tango," "Entrance to Wood," "Josie Bliss" by Pablo Neruda. From *Residence on Earth*, translated by Donald D. Walsh. Copyright © 1973 by Pablo Neruda and Donald D. Walsh.

Reprinted by permission of New Directions Publishing Corporation and Souvenir Press Ltd.

"Memory" and "Descent into Oblivion" by Enrique Molina. From *Poemas*, translated by Thomas Hoeksema. Reprinted by permission from *Mundus Artium*, Vol. 3, No. 1 (Winter, 1969).

"Paradiso" by José Lezama Lima. From *Paradiso*, translated by Gregory Rabassa. Translation Copyright © 1974 by Farrar, Straus & Giroux, Inc. Reprinted by permission of the publisher. "Summons of the Desirer" and "An Obscure Meadow Lures Me" by José Lezama Lima, translated by Nathaniel Tarn. From *Mundus Artium*, Vol. 3, No. 1 (Winter 1969). Reprinted by permission of the publisher and the translator. "Boredom of the Second Day," "Now Has No Weights," "The Cords" by José Lezama Lima, translated by Elinor Randall. From *Tri-Quarterly* No. 13–14, Fall/Winter issue, 1969. Copyright © 1969 by *Tri-Quarterly*, Evanston, Illinois. Reprinted by permission of the publisher.

"Salute to Recife" by Manuel Bandeira, translated by Dudley Poore. From *An Anthology of Latin American Poetry*, edited by Dudley Fitts. Copyright 1942 by New Directions Publishing Corporation. Reprinted by permission of the publisher. "The Cactus" and "The Sky" by Manuel Bandeira, translated by Giovanni Pontiero. From *New Directions in Prose and Poetry #20*, edited by J. Laughlin. Copyright © 1968 by New Directions Publishing Corporation. Reprinted by permission of Giovanni Pontiero. "Deeply" and "The Dead Ox" by Manuel Bandeira, translated by Thomas Colchie. Permission granted by the translator and by the poet's widow, Sra. Maria de Lourdes Heitor de Souza.

"Ballad of the Esplanade Hotel" and "Sentimental Memoirs of João Miramar" by Oswald de Andrade, translated by Thomas Colchie and Jack E. Tomlins. From *Memorias sentimentais de João Miramar*. Copyright © 1973 by the Estate of Oswald de Andrade. Reprinted by permission of Editora Civilizacao Brasileira, S.A.

"São Bento Street," "Landscape I," and "Nocturne" by Mário de Andrade. From *Hallucinated City (Paulicea Desvairada)*, translated by Jack E. Tomlins. Copyright © 1968 by Vanderbilt University Press. Reprinted by permission of the publisher. "Jungle-Mother Ci" by Mário de Andrade, translated by Barbara Shelby. From *Macunaíma*, reprinted by permission of the publisher, Livraria Martins Editora S.A.

"The Big Mystical Circus" by Jorge de Lima, translated by Dudley Poore. From *An Anthology of Latin American Poetry*, edited by Dudley Fitts. Copyright 1942 by New Directions Publishing Corporation. Reprinted by permission of the publisher.

"To a Hotel Scheduled for Demolition" by Carlos Drummond de Andrade, translated by Thomas Colchie. Reprinted by permission from *The Hudson Review*, Vol. XXV, No. 2 (Summer 1972). Copyright © 1972 by The Hudson Review, Inc.

"The Third Bank of the River" by João Guimarães Rosa. From *The Third Bank of the River and Other Stories*, translated by Barbara Shelby. Copyright © 1968 by Alfred A. Knopf, Inc. Reprinted by permission of the publisher.

"Blanco" by Octavio Paz, translated by Eliot Weinberger. From *Configurations* by Octavio Paz, published by New Directions Publishing Corporation. Translated and reprinted by permission of the publishers, New Directions Publishing Corporation and Laurence Pollinger Ltd., and of the translator.

"Nineteen-Thirty" translated by Miller Williams, "The Viper" translated by W. S. Merwin, "The Individual's Soliloquy" translated by Lawrence Ferlinghetti and Allen Ginsberg, "Clever Ideas Occur to Me" translated by Miller Williams, "Women" translated by Denise Levertov, "Test" translated by Miller Williams, and "I Take Back Everything I've Said" translated by Miller Williams, all by Nicanor Parra. From *Poems and Antipoems*, edited by Miller Williams. Copyright © 1967 by Nicanor Parra. Reprinted by permission of New Directions Publishing Corporation and Laurence Pollinger Ltd.

"The Myth of Orpheus and Eurydice" by Adolfo Bioy Casares. From *Guir-*

nalda con amores, translated by Suzanne Jill Levine. Reprinted by permission of the author and the translator.

"The Other Heaven" by Julio Cortázar. From *All Fires the Fire and Other Stories,* translated by Suzanne Jill Levine. Copyright © 1973 by Random House, Inc. Reprinted by permission of Pantheon Books, a division of Random House, Inc.

"Report on the Blind" by Ernesto Sabato, translated by Stuart M. Gross. From *Tri-Quarterly,* No. 13–14, Fall/Winter issue 1969. Copyright © 1969 by *Tri-Quarterly,* Evanston, Illinois. Reprinted by permission of the publisher.

"The Pigeon" by Carlos Martínez Moreno, translated by Giovanni Pontiero. From *Short Stories in Spanish,* edited by Jean Franco. Translation Copyright © 1966 by Giovanni Pontiero. Reprinted by permission of Penguin Books Ltd. and Alfo Libreria Editorial.

"Luvina" by Juan Rulfo. From *The Burning Plain and Other Stories,* translated by George D. Schade (1970). Reprinted by permission of University of Texas Press.

"The Dog Without Feathers" by João Cabral de Melo Neto, translated by Thomas Colchie. Reprinted by permission from *The Hudson Review,* Vol. XXIV, No. 1 (Spring 1971). Copyright © 1971 by The Hudson Review, Inc.

"Didactic Elegy" by Lêdo Ivo, translated by Thomas Colchie. From *Elegia Didática,* published by Livraria São Jose. Reprinted by permission of the author and the translator.

"Two Concrete Poems" by Haroldo de Campos. From *Concrete Poetry: A World View,* edited with an introduction by Mary Ellen Solt. Copyright © 1970 by Indiana University Press. Reprinted by permission of the publisher.

"The Passion According to G. H." by Clarice Lispector *(A Paixao Segundo G. H.,* 1964), translated by Jack E. Tomlins. Reprinted by permission of the author and the translator.

"The House of Passion" by Nelida Piñon *(A Casa da Paixao,* 1972), translated by Gregory Rabassa. Reprinted by permission of the author and the translator.

"Epistle to Hieronymus Bosch" by Alberto Girri. From *Latin American Writing Today,* edited and translated by J. M. Cohen. Copyright © 1967 by Penguin Books, Ltd. Reprinted by permission of the author and the publisher.

"Widower's Monologue" and "The Wanderings of the Tribe" by Ali Chumacero, translated by William Carlos Williams. From *Evergreen Review,* Vol. 2, No. 7, Winter, 1969. Copyright © 1959 by Florence H. Williams. Reprinted by permission of New Directions Publishing Corporation for Mrs. William Carlos Williams.

"The Dispossessed" by Cintio Vitier, translated by Tom Raworth, and "The Light on Cayo Hueso" by Cintio Vitier, translated by Nathaniel Tarn. From *Con Cuba, An Anthology of Cuban Poetry of the Last 60 Years,* edited by Nathaniel Tarn (1969). Reprinted by permission of the publisher, Cape Goliard Press.

"Poems" by Ernesto Cardenal, translated by Eduardo González, Quincy Troupe and Sergio Mondragón. Reprinted by permission from *Mundus Artium,* Vol. 3, No. 1 (Winter, 1969).

"The Things I Say Are True," "In the Mirror," and "The Observer" by Blanca Varela, translated by Donald Yates. Reprinted by permission from *Mundus Artium,* Vol. 3, No. 1 (Winter, 1969).

"Bach's Music Moves Curtains" and "Smashed" by Jaime Sabines, translated by Paul Blackburn. From *Evergreen Review,* Vol. 2, Winter, 1969. Copyright © 1976 by Joan Blackburn. Reprinted by permission of Joan Blackburn.

"O Cybernetic Fairy" by Carlos Germán Belli, translated by Clayton Eshleman. From *Tri-Quarterly,* No. 13–14, Fall/Winter issue 1969. Copyright © 1969 by *Tri-Quarterly,* Evanston, Illinois. Reprinted by permission of the publisher.

"The Defeat" and "The Good Old Days" by Enrique Lihn, translated by William Witherup and Serge Echeverría. From *New Directions in Prose and Poetry,* edited by J. Laughlin. Copyright © 1971 by New Directions Publishing Corporation. Reprinted by permission of the translators.

"The Milky Way" and "Poem in Nanking" by Fayad Jamis, translated by David Ossman and Carl Hagen. From *Con Cuba, An Anthology of Cuban Poetry of the Last 60 Years,* edited by Nathaniel Tarn (1969). Reprinted by permission of the publisher, Cape Goliard Press.

"Travelers" and "Important Occasions" by Heberto Padilla, translated by Paul Blackburn. From *The New York Review of Books,* Vol. XVI, No. 10, June 3, 1971. Copyright © 1976 by Joan Blackburn. Reprinted by permission of Joan Blackburn.

"Theory re Daniela Rocca" by Juan Gelman, translated by Patrick Morgan. From *Tri-Quarterly,* No. 13–14, Fall/Winter issue 1969. Copyright © 1969 by *Tri-Quarterly,* Evanston, Illinois. Reprinted by permission of the publisher.

"The Elements of Night" by José Emilio Pacheco. From *Latin American Writing Today,* translated by J. M. Cohen. Copyright © 1967 by J. M. Cohen. Reprinted by permission of the publisher. "For Some Time Now" by José Emilio Pacheco, translated by Elinor Randall. Reprinted by permission from *Mundus Artium,* Vol. 3, No. 1 (Winter, 1969).

"Five Poems" by Homero Aridjis, translated by Eliot Weinberger. Reprinted by permission from *Mundus Artium,* Vol. 3, No. 1 (Winter, 1969).

"The River" by Javier Héraud, translated by Paul Blackburn. From *Tri-Quarterly,* No. 13–14, Fall/Winter issue, 1969. Copyright © 1969 by *Tri-Quarterly,* Evanston, Illinois. Reprinted by permission of the publisher.

"The Dead Conquerors," "Tupac Amaru Relegated," and "Three Testimonies of Ayachcho" by Antonio Cisneros. From *The Spider Hangs Too Far from the Ground,* translated by Maureen Ahern, William Rowe, and David Tipton (1970). Reprinted by permission of the publisher, Cape Goliard Press.

"Legitimate Games" by José Donoso. From *This Sunday,* translated by Lorraine O'Grady Freeman. Copyright © 1967 by Alfred A. Knopf, Inc. Reprinted by permission of Alfred A. Knopf, Inc. and A. M. Heath & Co., Ltd.

"The Doll Queen" by Carlos Fuentes. From *The Doll Queen,* Copyright © 1974 by Antaeus. Reprinted by permission of Brandt & Brandt.

"One Day After Sunday" by Gabriel García Márquez. From *No One Writes to the Colonel and Other Stories* by Gabriel García Márquez, translated from the Spanish by J. S. Bernstein. Copyright © 1962 by Universidad Veracruzana, Vera Cruz, Mexico. Copyright © 1968 in the English language translation by Harper & Row Publishers, Inc. Reprinted by permission of the publisher.

"Three Trapped Tigers" ("I Heard Her Sing") by Guillermo Cabrera Infante. From *Three Trapped Tigers* by Guillermo Cabrera Infante, translated by Donald Gardner and Suzanne Jill Levine. Copyright © 1965 by Guillermo Cabrera Infante. English translation Copyright © 1971 by Harper & Row Publishers, Inc. Reprinted by permission of the publisher and the author.

"The Buenos Aires Affair" by Manuel Puig, translated by Suzanne Jill Levine. Reprinted from Chapter VII, pages 98–115 of *The Buenos Aires Affair: A Detective Novel.* Copyright © 1974 by Manuel Puig; English translation Copyright © 1976 by E. P. Dutton & Co., Inc. Reprinted by permission of the publisher.

"The Green House" by Mario Vargas Llosa. From *The Green House* by Mario Vargas Llosa, translated from the Spanish by Gregory Rabassa. Copyright © 1965 by Editorial Seix Barral, S.A., Barcelona. Copyright © 1968 in the English language translation by Harper & Row Publishers, Inc. Reprinted by permission of the publisher.

"The Entry of Christ into Havana" by Severo Sarduy. From *Triple Cross* by Carlos Fuentes, José Donoso, and Severo Sarduy. English translation by Suzanne Jill Levine. Copyright © 1972 by E. P. Dutton & Co., Inc. Reprinted by permission of the publisher.

CONTENTS

Preface to the Second Volume

For too long, Latin Americans suffered from a feeling of having come too late to the world's banquet-table—from an ingrained conviction that everything had been said or done, that there was nothing new to invent, no new books to write. Their fate, or so it seemed, was always to repeat what had already been done better in Europe or the United States. In the present century, however, they gradually began to acquire confidence in their ability to play an active and influential role in the affairs of the world; and this new mood of self-affirmation (though not without some fits and starts) took a progressively firmer hold as the decades passed. By 1950 the Mexican poet Octavio Paz was proclaiming, in his *Labyrinth of Solitude*, that "For the first time in our history, we are contemporaries of all mankind."

In the literary world, the first impulse was provided by Darío and the modernists around the turn of the century. But though many of these writers managed to attract attention abroad, and even for a time exerted a significant influence on literary developments in Spain, things began after a while to revert to "normal." The ponderous classical tradition quickly regained its predominance in the mother country, and some scholars even attempted to prove that modernism had been simply a passing fashion. Darío's impact in France (where he resided during several periods of his life) was negligible. The modernists presumably felt themselves to be contemporaries of all mankind, but the rest of mankind failed to take sufficient notice.

It was with the diverse avant-garde movements that a genuinely radical change occurred. Spanish poetry was updated by the combined efforts of the Chilean Vicente Huidobro and the Argentine Jorge Luis Borges, who brought to the mother country what they had learned and practiced in Paris and Geneva. In the thirties, the publication in Spain of some of the outstanding Spanish American novels of the time—Azuela's *The Underdog*, Gallegos's *Doña Bárbara*, Rivera's *The Vortex*, Güiraldes's *Don Segundo Sombra*, and Guzmán's *The Eagle and the Serpent*—as well as of a volume of tales by South America's leading storyteller, Horacio Quiroga, served to acquaint the metropolitan Spanish reader with a narrative tradition that was to become in two more decades one of the most important in the world. At the time, however, Spanish was still a language of secondary importance in the general scheme of things, and the linguistic barrier restricted the expansion of the good news.

The final breakthrough took place in the sixties, and was signaled by the award in 1961 of the international Formentor Prize to Jorge Luis Borges (jointly with Samuel Beckett). The award both reflected and embodied, in some measure, a definitive acknowledgment of Latin American fiction as a literary movement of the first rank.

The breakthrough had its roots in the new international situation existing at the close of World War II. The end of colonialism, and the emergence of new nations in Africa, Asia and Oceania, compelled the Western world to adapt to new political and cultural realities. It also helped to overturn the ingrained logocentrism of the Western world-view, its basic disposition to equate culture with rationalism and advanced technology. A new curiosity about forms of culture based on other assumptions and values; the awareness (rather late, to be sure) that even within the Western fold there had long existed minorities which did not share in whiteness of skin, the Christian faith, or capitalistic affluence; the related realization that from its very beginnings the West itself had survived and prospered through the assimilation of alien cultures; the re-emergence of China and the Arab world as powers to be reckoned with—all these factors have helped to abolish the rather naïve image of a unified Western culture, happily autonomous and self-sufficient.

These new perceptions in the West have found a parallel in the discovery by the nations of the so-called Third World that high culture is not the privilege of any given race or country, that it exists in many forms, and, moreover, that one method of producing an original culture in a colonized society is by thoroughly parodying—and thus destroying, and thus re-creating—the culture of the colonizers.

To the performance of this task Latin Americans have brought, and bring, obvious advantages. For nearly four centuries their writers and thinkers have devoted themselves, with the help of Indians, Blacks, and assorted Europeans, to the production of a new Iberian culture on this side of the Atlantic. They succeeded in creating their own variety of Baroque, and anticipated their peninsular counterparts in adapting to their own purposes the techniques and insights of parnassianism, symbolism, and naturalism. In this century, they became involved in the work of the international avant-garde, in the development of the *nouveau roman,* and even in the founding of a new school of criticism. Latin Americans have, at long last, become true contemporaries, if not in fact the vanguard, of all mankind.

Borges (his legend as much as his actual work) represents precisely this contemporaneity. But his is not an isolated case—there are many Latin Americans who have helped to produce this breakthrough. Some of their names and works will be found in the present volume. But in truth the task has been carried forward by a whole continent of men and women, in both Brazil and Spanish America, for the greater part of a century. On their shoulders rests not only the Latin American literature of today but that of the future. Their collective production may well be read as a map of that future.

Part Four

THE MODERN MASTERS

Whereas romanticism, realism, naturalism, and symbolism traveled slowly to the New World, and in some cases took decades to reach it (see introductions to Parts Two and Three), the European avant-garde movement of the first thirty years of this century almost immediately found an echo in the growing urban centers of Latin America. By the turn of the century the emerging nations had produced a strong cultural elite. This elite was still heavily dependent on Europe for its nurture, but European developments and influences were largely received through intermediary, and sometimes unreliable, sources. It was about this time, however, that the relative affluence of several Latin American countries (Mexico, Brazil, Argentina, Uruguay, Chile) permitted some members of their intelligentsia to travel to Europe, either to complete their education or just to participate as faithful followers in the cultural revolution of the avant-garde. Futurism, Dadaism, cubism, expressionism, and, later, surrealism were for them simply different aspects of a unified though complex movement toward modernity, which had arisen in the second half of the nineteenth century and was now approaching its culmination.

A major task of this movement was to construct a coherent aesthetics for the new culture. Within its fold were various distinct and even opposed groups, which shared, nonetheless, one common aim: a freeing of arts and letters from the dead weight of academic tradition, a freedom that would allow them to participate imaginatively in the second great technological revolution then beginning. The avant-garde sought artistic means of expressing the changes brought about in their world-view by Marx, Freud, Einstein. It would demand the abolition of museums and libraries; it exalted the motorcar and the airplane, symbols of a newly discovered sense of speed; it espoused the cause of socialism and the Russian Revolution; it explored man's labyrinthine subconscious. It sought to free painting and sculpture from the conventions of mimetic representation; to free literature from the nineteenth century, and the values of the despised bourgeoisie. "A free art in a free society" was its motto.

The avant-garde had its beginnings in a number of European cities—Zurich, Moscow, Berlin, Rome, London—but eventually found its international capital in Paris, where it flourished vigorously during the first two decades of this century. While Braque and Picasso were discovering cubism and African art,

Marinetti was busy editorializing about the art of the future, Apollinaire was publishing his graphic poems in little magazines, Stravinsky was outraging bourgeois sensibilities with *Le Sacre du printemps;* Joyce and Pound were just arriving in Paris while Breton was avidly reading one of the few extant copies of Lautréamont's *Chants de Maldoror.* The scene was set for the great confrontation of the 1920s.

The Chilean Vicente Huidobro arrived in Paris in 1916. He would later claim that he had discovered the avant-garde while still in Chile, and had even invented a new ism, creationism, while lecturing in Buenos Aires. Perhaps so. What is indisputable, in any event, is that very soon he was contributing some clumsy French texts to the experimental magazines published in the late 1910s by Apollinaire, Max Jacob, and Pierre Reverdy. While Huidobro was in Paris, the Argentine Jorge Luis Borges (selection 1), was quietly finishing high school in Geneva and becoming acquainted with German expressionism. In 1918, Borges and Huidobro met, for the first time, in Spain. Borges, notwithstanding his aversion to assuming any sort of leadership role among his colleagues, became a guide for the new Spanish poets through the maze of conflicting tendencies within the avant-garde. Huidobro, on the other hand, tried to bully everyone into acknowledging him as the master and prime mover of the new literature. He failed, and went back to Chile. Borges stayed in Spain until 1921, helping to develop ultraism—a branch of futurism characterized by an obsessive concern with the magical effects of imagery and metaphor. While he was still there, Huidobro returned to Spain, but only to face the continuing hostility of the ultraists, who accused him of having stolen creationism from Pierre Reverdy. Once more he went back to Chile, to devote himself to the publication of silly manifestoes and strikingly beautiful poems. By then, Borges had also gone home, rediscovered his native city, Buenos Aires, and helped Oliverio Girondo (selection 13) and other poets to develop an Argentine form of ultraism, less concerned with airplanes and machine guns than with the hidden poetry of ordinary things. Borges returned to Europe in 1923, for a tour of France, England, and finally Spain, once again, where he consolidated his position among the younger poets. On his return, he settled in Buenos Aires. (In the early sixties he was to return to Europe again, now no longer a young iconoclast but a master.)

But Huidobro and Borges were not the only South Americans to be actively engaged in Europe. Two young Peruvian poets left for Paris in the 1920s: César Vallejo in 1923, never to return home (selection 7); César Moro in 1925, to stay until 1933 (8). But their respective attitudes to the avant-garde were radically different: Moro not only contributed to surrealist magazines, but wrote the largest part of his poetry in French; Vallejo rejected surrealism for political reasons. Already in the late twenties, Breton had become disillusioned with the Soviet Union and was moving toward Trotskyism, while a group of his comrades (Aragon, Eluard, Desnos) continued to support Stalin. The break was not exclusively political; it also reflected changes in Soviet cultural policy. After brutally liquidating or silencing the futurists and formalists in the Soviet Union, Stalin had established socialist realism as the official revolutionary aesthetic.

For Breton, this development represented a reversion to the sort of academic, bourgeois art he despised. Vallejo, a dedicated Communist, reacted differently: After two trips to the USSR, the promised land, in 1928–29, he wrote a propaganda novel about a strike at the tungsten mines in Peru (1931). Another South American poet, the Chilean Pablo Neruda (12), briefly visited Spain and France in 1927, on his way to the Far East. He later claimed to have found a total lack of understanding for his poetry among the Spanish ultraists.

An anthology published in Buenos Aires in 1926 helped to promote the names of some of these new poets among the "happy few." It was called *Index of the New Spanish American Poetry* and was edited by the Peruvian Alberto Hidalgo. Two of its introductory critiques were signed, respectively, by Huidobro and Borges. Among the contributors were ultraists from the River Plate area, creationists from Chile, and even stridentists (a local branch of the avant-garde) from Mexico. Vallejo and Neruda, though not adherents of any certified literary ism, were also included. This collection turned out to be a dress rehearsal for a larger, and more academic, enterprise: the *Anthology of Spanish and Spanish American Poetry (1882–1932)*, published in Spain in 1934 by Federico de Onís, professor at Columbia University. In it he assembled, in impeccably chronological order, the best representatives of modernism, postmodernism, and the avant-garde. Thus was signaled at last the acceptance (or neutralization) of the iconoclasts. Now each one of them had a "dossier."

The publication of this anthology coincided with a new gathering of Spanish American poets in Spain. Neruda had arrived the same year, and immediately became the leader of a new group of Spanish poets, more politically and socially oriented. He published in 1935 the second and best edition of *Residence on Earth*, the most important book of poems in contemporary Spanish. Vallejo had been visiting Spain regularly since 1930, and had also become involved with the left-wing writers there. He wrote there some of his *Humane Poems* (published posthumously in 1938), a work some critics even prefer to Neruda's. The outbreak of the Civil War in 1936 would bring them together again in Paris and Madrid. Huidobro and the Cuban Nicolás Guillén (selection 11) would also come to Spain, as well as a young Mexican poet, Octavio Paz (he was only twenty-three), who participated with his elders in the task of defending the cause of freedom. The collapse of the Republic dispersed them again. With the exception of Vallejo, who died in Paris in 1938, they all returned to Latin America to continue the fight against fascism. By that time, the European avant-garde movement had been stopped dead by the outbreak of World War II. Most of the Spanish American poets felt themselves to be part of that war. Some, like Borges, would come to the defense of England; others, like Neruda and Guillén, would devote themselves to the writing of politically committed, antifascist verse. Huidobro would fluctuate between uncompromising experimentalism and left-wing political involvement. Only Moro would remain steadfastly faithful to surrealism, actively promoting its diffusion in Peru and Mexico. Paz followed a different course of development. He actually belonged to a later avant-garde group, and would come to accept surrealism after 1950.

logic and theory of causation, intolerant of loose ends and, in fact, more rigorous than the system of the natural or "scientific" world. (Here his ideas were close to what Lévi-Strauss would later define as the "savage mind.") In addition, Borges anticipated the structuralists in viewing literature also in systemic terms, as an integrated collection of interrelated texts with its own autonomous development.

In the forties, Borges published his two most important volumes of stories: *Ficciones* (1944) and *The Aleph* (1949). He also collaborated with a younger Argentine writer, Adolfo Bioy Casares (Five, 3), in writing some detective stories, *Six Problems for Don Isidro Parodi* (1949), in a Chestertonian vein, but with a freedom of language that was reminiscent of the avant-garde. These books became the foundation of a new Spanish American narrative. They influenced writers as diverse as Onetti (Four, 5), Cortázar, Sabato, Fuentes, García Márquez, Cabrera Infante, Puig, Sarduy, Sáinz, and Arenas (Five, 4–5, 13–16, 18–20), to name only those included in this anthology.

Of Borges's most recent books, three titles are outstanding: *Dreamtigers* (1960), a collection that further blurred the distinction between prose and verse; *The Book of Imaginary Beings* (1968), which combined a witty rewriting of some well-known myths with some newly invented ones; and *Dr. Brodie's Report* (1970), in which he attempted to disguise his labyrinthine twists and turns under the conventions of realistic narrative.

Although Borges has always been highly appreciated as a lyrical poet —a poet of a metaphysical turn, elegiac in mood, deeply concerned with memory and oblivion, and with the myths of dream and death—his international reputation is chiefly based on his rather brief and tantalizing stories and essays. In them, he has postulated the existence of a planet invented by a secret society of encyclopedists and later rather clumsily interpolated into mere reality (this negative Utopia is called, "Tlön, Uqbar, Orbis Tertius"). He has also invented a chance game whose blind laws, like fate, rule all men ("The Lottery in Babylon") and an infinite collection of books that ends up by becoming the world ("The Library of Babel"). He has told time and again the story of a man who is all men ("The Immortal") or who is nobody ("The Circular Ruins"); that of the hero who is also a coward ("The Form of the Sword," "Theme of the Traitor and the Hero," later adapted by Bertolucci in his 1970 film *The Spider's Stratagem*), or that of the traitor who is a god ("Three Versions of Judas"). He has invented all manner of puzzles, from the lucid enigmas of personal identity ("The Theologians," The Dead Man," "The Other Death") to the obscure quest for the monster who lies at the center of the labyrinth ("The House of Asterion"). He has explored the incestuous drives that compel two brothers to kill the woman they both love ("The Intruder") or that keep some men outside the seemingly magic rite of immortality ("The Sect of the Phoenix"). In his essays, collected in *Other Inquisitions* (1952), he has also attempted to prove, unsuccessfully, that time does not exist and neither do we ("New Refutation of Time," 1947); that reality is incomprehensible except through metaphors ("The Wall and the Books"); that readers, not writers, are the real authors of the texts they read ("The Flower of Coleridge," "Kafka and His Precursors").

The labyrinths that appear so often in his short stories and poems are merely ironic symbols of the total labyrinth of his writings: a paper labyrinth in which there is no depth and no center, only the surface of a text that circularly refers back to itself. But Borges's labyrinths do not always assume a complex form. A good part of his work aspires to simplicity. There is no contradiction, however, between labyrinth and line. As Zeno proved, and Borges recalled, the perfect labyrinth is the straight line. On that simple line, Achilles will never overtake the tortoise. In one of Borges's most famous detective stories ("Death and the Compass"), the protagonist and his rival discover, too late, the possibility of another straight-lined labyrinth. Other tales hide this same view of the abyss beneath an apparent simplicity.

Perhaps the most nearly perfect example of this type of story is "The Aleph." Borges has explained the strange object that gives the story its title in notes to the American edition: "What eternity is to time, the Aleph is to space. In eternity, all time—past, present, and future—coexist simultaneously. In the Aleph, the sum total of the spatial universe is to be found in a tiny shining sphere barely over an inch across." He also has commented on those critics who have praised the story's complexities: they "have detected Beatrice Portinari in Beatriz Viterbo, Dante in Daneri, and the descent into hell in the descent into the cellar. I am, of course, duly grateful for these unexpected gifts." Borges's ironical humility notwithstanding, it is by no means impossible to read the story as a parodic précis of *The Divine Comedy*. Times have changed, of course, and we do not have Dante's central faith. What we do have is an extremely shy character called "I" (not to be confused with the author), hopelessly in love with an unworthy woman named Beatriz. We also have a guide to the cellar, the poet Carlos Argentino Daneri, who is as ambitious as Vergil in his desire to write a supreme national poem—but who is also a fool. And we have the Aleph. More despairing, more willing to confront and accept defeat, Borges attempts here to describe what Dante kept to himself: the unbearable ubiquity of God. To this end, he uses a method borrowed from another of his masters, Walt Whitman: "The setting down," as Borges explains in his notes, "of a limited catalogue of endless things"—a seemingly "chaotic enumeration" in which "every apparently haphazard element has to be linked to its neighbor either by secret association or by contrast." The Aleph, like God, is also a word—the first letter of the Hebrew alphabet. That word is the key to a verbal labyrinth: the world. The story also suggests to its readers another possible meaning. The Borges *aficionado* will immediately recognize in Beatriz Viterbo, beautiful and unfaithful as she is, the archetype of those women, half seen, half dreamt, who brand Borges's texts with a mark of despair. These women are the Aleph too, but one made only of desire, of horror, and the acceptance of failure. It is works such as this that have secured for Borges his place among this century's masters of the word.

The Aleph

From The Aleph and Other Stories, *translated by Norman Thomas di Giovanni and the author (New York: E. P. Dutton, 1970), pp. 15–30.*

O God! I could be bounded in a nutshell, and count myself a
King of infinite space. . . .

Hamlet, II, 2

But they will teach us that Eternity is the Standing still of the
Present Time, a *Nunc-stans* (as the Schools call it); which neither
they, nor any else understand, no more than they would a
Hic-stans for an Infinite greatness of Place.

Leviathan, IV, 46

On the burning February morning Beatriz Viterbo died, after braving an agony
that never for a single moment gave way to self-pity or fear, I noticed that the
sidewalk billboards around Constitution Plaza were advertising some new brand
or other of American cigarettes. The fact pained me, for I realized that the wide
and ceaseless universe was already slipping away from her and that this slight
change was the first of an endless series. The universe may change but not me,
I thought with a certain sad vanity. I knew that at times my fruitless devotion
had annoyed her; now that she was dead, I could devote myself to her memory,
without hope but also without humiliation. I recalled that the thirtieth of April
was her birthday; on that day to visit her house on Garay Street and pay my
respects to her father and to Carlos Argentino Daneri, her first cousin, would be
an irreproachable and perhaps unavoidable act of politeness. Once again I would
wait in the twilight of the small, cluttered drawing room, once again I would
study the details of her many photographs: Beatriz Viterbo in profile and in full
color; Beatriz wearing a mask, during the Carnival of 1921; Beatriz at her First
Communion; Beatriz on the day of her wedding to Roberto Alessandri; Beatriz
soon after her divorce, at a luncheon at the Turf Club; Beatriz at a seaside resort
in Quilmes with Delia San Marco Porcel and Carlos Argentino; Beatriz with the
Pekinese lapdog given her by Villegas Haedo; Beatriz, front and three-quarter
views, smiling, hand on her chin. . . . I would not be forced, as in the past, to
justify my presence with modest offerings of books—books whose pages I finally
learned to cut beforehand, so as not to find out, months later, that they lay around
unopened.

Beatriz Viterbo died in 1929. From that time on, I never let a thirtieth of April go by without a visit to her house. I used to make my appearance at seven-fifteen sharp and stay on for some twenty-five minutes. Each year, I arrived a little later and stayed a little longer. In 1933, a torrential downpour coming to my aid, they were obliged to ask me to dinner. Naturally, I took advantage of that lucky precedent. In 1934, I arrived, just after eight, with one of those large Santa Fe sugared cakes, and quite matter-of-factly I stayed to dinner. It was in this way, on these melancholy and vainly erotic anniversaries, that I came into the gradual confidences of Carlos Argentino Daneri.

Beatriz had been tall, frail, slightly stooped; in her walk there was (if the oxymoron may be allowed) a kind of uncertain grace, a hint of expectancy. Carlos Argentino was pink-faced, overweight, gray-haired, fine-featured. He held a minor position in an unreadable library out on the edge of the Southside of Buenos Aires. He was authoritarian but also unimpressive. Until only recently, he took advantage of his nights and holidays to stay at home. At a remove of two generations, the Italian "S" and demonstrative Italian gestures still survived in him. His mental activity was continuous, deeply felt, far-ranging, and—all in all —meaningless. He dealt in pointless analogies and in trivial scruples. He had (as did Beatriz) large, beautiful, finely shaped hands. For several months he seemed to be obsessed with Paul Fort—less with his ballads than with the idea of a towering reputation. "He is the Prince of poets," Daneri would repeat fatuously. "You will belittle him in vain—but no, not even the most venomous of your shafts will graze him."

On the thirtieth of April, 1941, along with the sugared cake I allowed myself to add a bottle of Argentine cognac. Carlos Argentino tasted it, pronounced it "interesting," and, after a few drinks, launched into a glorification of modern man.

"I view him," he said with a certain unaccountable excitement, "in his inner sanctum, as though in his castle tower, supplied with telephones, telegraphs, phonographs, wireless sets, motion-picture screens, slide projectors, glossaries, timetables, handbooks, bulletins. . . ."

He remarked that for a man so equipped, actual travel was superfluous. Our twentieth century had inverted the story of Mohammed and the mountain; nowadays, the mountain came to the modern Mohammed.

So foolish did his ideas seem to me, so pompous and so drawn out his exposition, that I linked them at once to literature and asked him why he didn't write them down. As might be foreseen, he answered that he had already done so—that these ideas, and others no less striking, had found their place in the Proem, or Augural Canto, or, more simply, the Prologue Canto of the poem on which he had been working for many years now, alone, without publicity, without fanfare, supported only by those twin staffs universally known as work and solitude. First, he said, he opened the floodgates of his fancy; then, taking up hand tools, he resorted to the file. The poem was entitled *The Earth;* it consisted of a description of the planet, and, of course, lacked no amount of picturesque digressions and bold apostrophes.

I asked him to read me a passage, if only a short one. He opened a drawer of his writing table, drew out a thick stack of papers—sheets of a large pad imprinted with the letterhead of the Juan Crisóstomo Lafinur Library—and, with ringing satisfaction, declaimed:

> Mine eyes, as did the Greek's, have known men's
>   towns and fame,
> The works, the days in light that fades to amber;
> I do not change a fact or falsify a name—
> The *voyage* I set down is . . . *autour de ma chambre*.

"From any angle, a greatly interesting stanza," he said, giving his verdict. "The opening line wins the applause of the professor, the academician, and the Hellenist—to say nothing of the would-be scholar, a considerable sector of the public. The second flows from Homer to Hesiod (generous homage, at the very outset, to the father of didactic poetry), not without rejuvenating a process whose roots go back to Scripture—enumeration, congeries, conglomeration. The third—baroque? decadent? example of the cult of pure form?—consists of two equal hemistichs. The fourth, frankly bilingual, assures me the unstinted backing of all minds sensitive to the pleasures of sheer fun. I should, in all fairness, speak of the novel rhyme in lines two and four, and of the erudition that allows me —without a hint of pedantry!—to cram into four lines three learned allusions covering thirty centuries packed with literature—first to the *Odyssey*, second to *Works and Days*, and third to the immortal bagatelle bequeathed us by the frolicking pen of the Savoyard, Xavier de Maistre. Once more I've come to realize that modern art demands the balm of laughter, the scherzo. Decidedly, Goldoni holds the stage!"

He read me many other stanzas, each of which also won his own approval and elicited his lengthy explications. There was nothing remarkable about them. I did not even find them any worse than the first one. Application, resignation, and chance had gone into the writing; I saw, however, that Daneri's real work lay not in the poetry but in his invention of reasons why the poetry should be admired. Of course, this second phase of his effort modified the writing in his eyes, though not in the eyes of others. Daneri's style of delivery was extravagant, but the deadly drone of his metric regularity tended to tone down and to dull that extravagance.*

Only once in my life have I had occasion to look into the fifteen thousand alexandrines of the *Polyolbion*, that topographical epic in which Michael Drayton recorded the flora, fauna, hydrography, orography, military and monastic history of England. I am sure, however, that this limited but bulky

---

*Among my memories are also some lines of a satire in which he lashed out unsparingly at bad poets. After accusing them of dressing their poems in the warlike armor of erudition, and of flapping in vain their unavailing wings, he concluded with this verse:

> But they forget, alas, one foremost fact—BEAUTY!

Only the fear of creating an army of implacable and powerful enemies dissuaded him (he told me) from fearlessly publishing this poem.

production is less boring than Carlos Argentino's similar vast undertaking. Daneri had in mind to set to verse the entire face of the planet, and, by 1941, had already dispatched a number of acres of the State of Queensland, nearly a mile of the course run by the River Ob, a gasworks to the north of Veracruz, the leading shops in the Buenos Aires parish of Concepción, the villa of Mariana Cambaceres de Alvear in the Belgrano section of the Argentine capital, and a Turkish baths establishment not far from the well-known Brighton Aquarium. He read me certain long-winded passages from his Australian section, and at one point praised a word of his own coining, the color "celestewhite," which he felt "actually *suggests* the sky, an element of utmost importance in the landscape of the continent Down Under." But these sprawling, lifeless hexameters lacked even the relative excitement of the so-called Augural Canto. Along about midnight, I left.

Two Sundays later, Daneri rang me up—perhaps for the first time in his life. He suggested we get together at four o'clock "for cocktails in the salon-bar next door, which the forward-looking Zunino and Zungri—my landlords, as you doubtless recall—are throwing open to the public. It's a place you'll really want to get to know."

More in resignation than in pleasure, I accepted. Once there, it was hard to find a table. The "salon-bar," ruthlessly modern, was only barely less ugly than what I had expected; at the nearby tables, the excited customers spoke breathlessly of the sums Zunino and Zungri had invested in furnishings without a second thought to cost. Carlos Argentino pretended to be astonished by some feature or other of the lighting arrangement (with which, I felt, he was already familiar), and he said to me with a certain severity, "Grudgingly, you'll have to admit to the fact that these premises hold their own with many others far more in the public eye."

He then reread me four or five different fragments of the poem. He had revised them following his pet principle of verbal ostentation: where at first "blue" had been good enough, he now wallowed in "azures," "ceruleans," and "ultramarines." The word "milky" was too easy for him; in the course of an impassioned description of a shed where wool was washed, he chose such words as "lacteal," "lactescent," and even made one up—"lactinacious." After that, straight out, he condemned our modern mania for having books prefaced, "a practice already held up to scorn by the Prince of Wits in his own graceful preface to the *Quixote.*" He admitted, however, that for the opening of his new work an attention-getting foreword might prove valuable—"an accolade signed by a literary hand of renown." He next went on to say that he considered publishing the initial cantos of his poem. I then began to understand the unexpected telephone call; Daneri was going to ask me to contribute a foreword to his pedantic hodgepodge. My fear turned out unfounded; Carlos Argentino re-marked, with admiration and envy, that surely he could not be far wrong in qualifying with the epithet "solid" the prestige enjoyed in every circle by Álvaro Melián Lafinur, a man of letters, who would, if I insisted on it, be only too glad to dash off some charming opening words to the poem. In order to avoid igno-miny and failure, he suggested I make myself spokesman for two of the book's undeniable virtues—formal perfection and scientific rigor—"inasmuch as this wide garden of metaphors, of figures of speech, of elegances, is inhospitable to the least detail not strictly upholding of truth." He added that Beatriz had always been taken with Álvaro.

I agreed—agreed profusely—and explained for the sake of credibility that I would not speak to Álvaro the next day, Monday, but would wait until Thursday, when we got together for the informal dinner that follows every meeting of the Writers' Club. (No such dinners are ever held, but it is an established fact that the meetings do take place on Thursdays, a point which Carlos Argentino Daneri could verify in the daily papers, and which lent a certain reality to my promise.) Half in prophecy, half in cunning, I said that before taking up the question of a preface I would outline the unusual plan of the work. We then said goodbye.

Turning the corner of Bernardo de Irigoyen, I reviewed as impartially as possible the alternatives before me. They were: *a)* to speak to Álvaro, telling him this first cousin of Beatriz' (the explanatory euphemism would allow me to mention her name) had concocted a poem that seemed to draw out into infinity the possibilities of cacophony and chaos; *b)* not to say a word to Álvaro. I clearly foresaw that my indolence would opt for *b.*

But first thing Friday morning, I began worrying about the telephone. It offended me that that device, which had once produced the irrecoverable voice of Beatriz, could now sink so low as to become a mere receptacle for the futile and perhaps angry remonstrances of that deluded Carlos Argentino Daneri. Luckily, nothing happened—except the inevitable spite touched off in me by this man, who had asked me to fulfill a delicate mission for him and then had let me drop.

Gradually, the phone came to lose its terrors, but one day toward the end of October it rang, and Carlos Argentino was on the line. He was deeply disturbed, so much so that at the outset I did not recognize his voice. Sadly but angrily he stammered that the now unrestrainable Zunino and Zungri, under the pretext of enlarging their already outsized "salon-bar," were about to take over and tear down his house.

"My home, my ancestral home, my old and inveterate Garay Street home!" he kept repeating, seeming to forget his woe in the music of his words.

It was not hard for me to share his distress. After the age of fifty, all change becomes a hateful symbol of the passing of time. Besides, the scheme concerned a house that for me would always stand for Beatriz. I tried explaining this delicate scruple of regret, but Daneri seemed not to hear me. He said that if Zunino and Zungri persisted in this outrage, Doctor Zunni, his lawyer, would sue *ipso facto* and make them pay some fifty thousand dollars in damages.

Zunni's name impressed me; his firm, although at the unlikely address of Caseros and Tacuarí, was nonetheless known as an old and reliable one. I asked him whether Zunni had already been hired for the case. Daneri said he would phone him that very afternoon. He hesitated, then with that level, impersonal voice we reserve for confiding something intimate, he said that to finish the poem he could not get along without the house because down in the cellar there was an Aleph. He explained that an Aleph is one of the points in space that contains all other points.

"It's in the cellar under the dining room," he went on, so overcome by his worries now that he forgot to be pompous. "It's mine—mine. I discovered it when I was a child, all by myself. The cellar stairway is so steep that my aunt and uncle forbade my using it, but I'd heard someone say there was a world down there. I found out later they meant an old-fashioned globe of the world, but at the time I thought they were referring to the world itself. One day when no one was home I started down in secret, but I stumbled and fell. When I opened my eyes, I saw the Aleph."

"The Aleph?" I repeated.

"Yes, the only place on earth where all places are—seen from every angle, each standing clear, without any confusion or blending. I kept the discovery to myself and went back every chance I got. As a child, I did not foresee that this privilege was granted me so that later I could write the poem. Zunino and Zungri will not strip me of what's mine—no, and a thousand times no! Legal code in hand, Doctor Zunni will prove that my Aleph is inalienable."

I tried to reason with him. "But isn't the cellar very dark?" I said.

"Truth cannot penetrate a closed mind. If all places in the universe are in the Aleph, then all stars, all lamps, all sources of light are in it, too."

"You wait there. I'll be right over to see it."

I hung up before he could say no. The full knowledge of a fact sometimes enables you to see all at once many supporting but previously unsuspected things. It amazed me not to have suspected until that moment that Carlos Argentino was a madman. As were all the Viterbos, when you came down to it. Beatriz (I myself often say it) was a woman, a child, with almost uncanny powers of clairvoyance, but forgetfulness, distractions, contempt, and a streak of cruelty were also in her, and perhaps these called for a pathological explanation. Carlos Argentino's madness filled me with spiteful elation. Deep down, we had always detested each other.

On Garay Street, the maid asked me kindly to wait. The master was, as usual, in the cellar developing pictures. On the unplayed piano, beside a large vase that held no flowers, smiled (more timeless than belonging to the past) the large photograph of Beatriz, in gaudy colors. Nobody could see us; in a seizure of tenderness, I drew close to the portrait and said to it, "Beatriz, Beatriz Elena, Beatriz Elena Viterbo, darling Beatriz, Beatriz now gone forever, it's me, it's Borges."

Moments later, Carlos came in. He spoke drily. I could see he was thinking of nothing else but the loss of the Aleph.

"First a glass of pseudo-cognac," he ordered, "and then down you dive into the cellar. Let me warn you, you'll have to lie flat on your back. Total darkness, total immobility, and a certain ocular adjustment will also be necessary. From the floor, you must focus your eyes on the nineteenth step. Once I leave you, I'll lower the trapdoor and you'll be quite alone. You needn't fear the rodents

very much—though I know you will. In a minute or two, you'll see the Aleph
—the microcosm of the alchemists and Kabbalists, our true proverbial friend, the
multum in parvo!"

Once we were in the dining room, he added, "Of course, if you don't
see it, your incapacity will not invalidate what I have experienced. Now, down
you go. In a short while you can babble with *all* of Beatriz' images."

Tired of his inane words, I quickly made my way. The cellar, barely
wider than the stairway itself, was something of a pit. My eyes searched the dark,
looking in vain for the globe Carlos Argentino had spoken of. Some cases of
empty bottles and some canvas sacks cluttered one corner. Carlos picked up a
sack, folded it in two, and at a fixed spot spread it out.

"As a pillow," he said, "this is quite threadbare, but if it's padded even
a half-inch higher, you won't see a thing, and there you'll lie, feeling ashamed
and ridiculous. All right now, sprawl that hulk of yours there on the floor and
count off nineteen steps."

I went through with his absurd requirements, and at last he went away.
The trapdoor was carefully shut. The blackness, in spite of a chink that I later
made out, seemed to me absolute. For the first time, I realized the danger I was
in: I'd let myself be locked in a cellar by a lunatic, after gulping down a glassful
of poison! I knew that back of Carlos's transparent boasting lay a deep fear that
I might not see the promised wonder. To keep his madness undetected, to keep
from admitting that he was mad, *Carlos had to kill me.* I felt a shock of panic,
which I tried to pin to my uncomfortable position and not to the effect of a drug.
I shut my eyes—I opened them. Then I saw the Aleph.

I arrive now at the ineffable core of my story. And here begins my
despair as a writer. All language is a set of symbols whose use among its speakers
assumes a shared past. How, then, can I translate into words the limitless Aleph,
which my floundering mind can scarcely encompass? Mystics, faced with the
same problem, fall back on symbols: to signify the godhead, one Persian speaks
of a bird that somehow is all birds; Alanus de Insulis, of a sphere whose center
is everywhere and circumference is nowhere; Ezekiel, of a four-faced angel who
at one and the same time moves east and west, north and south. (Not in vain
do I recall these inconceivable analogies; they bear some relation to the Aleph.)
Perhaps the gods might grant me a similar metaphor, but then this account would
become contaminated by literature, by fiction. Really, what I want to do is
impossible, for any listing of an endless series is doomed to be infinitesimal. In
that single gigantic instant I saw millions of acts both delightful and awful; not
one of them amazed me more than the fact that all of them occupied the same
point in space, without overlapping or transparency. What my eyes beheld was
simultaneous, but what I shall now write down will be successive, because language is successive. Nonetheless, I'll try to recollect what I can.

On the back part of the step, toward the right, I saw a small iridescent
sphere of almost unbearable brilliance. At first I thought it was revolving; then
I realized that this movement was an illusion created by the dizzying world it
bounced. The Aleph's diameter was probably little more than an inch, but all

space was there, actual and undiminished. Each thing (a mirror's face, let us say) was infinite things, since I distinctly saw it from every angle of the universe. I saw the teeming sea; I saw daybreak and nightfall; I saw the multitudes of America; I saw a silvery cobweb in the center of a black pyramid; I saw a splintered labyrinth (it was London); I saw, close up, unending eyes watching themselves in me as in a mirror; I saw all the mirrors on earth and none of them reflected me; I saw in a backyard of Soler Street the same tiles that thirty years before I'd seen in the entrance of a house in Fray Bentos; I saw bunches of grapes, snow, tobacco, lodes of metal, steam; I saw convex equatorial deserts and each one of their grains of sand; I saw a woman in Inverness whom I shall never forget; I saw her tangled hair, her tall figure, I saw the cancer in her breast; I saw a ring of baked mud in a sidewalk, where before there had been a tree; I saw a summer house in Adrogué and a copy of the first English translation of Pliny—Philemon Holland's—and all at the same time saw each letter on each page (as a boy, I used to marvel that the letters in a closed book did not get scrambled and lost overnight); I saw a sunset in Querétaro that seemed to reflect the color of a rose in Bengal; I saw my empty bedroom; I saw in a closet in Alkmaar a terrestrial globe between two mirrors that multiplied it endlessly; I saw horses with flowing manes on a shore of the Caspian Sea at dawn; I saw the delicate bone structure of a hand; I saw the survivors of a battle sending out picture postcards; I saw in a showcase in Mirzapur a pack of Spanish playing cards; I saw the slanting shadows of ferns on a greenhouse floor; I saw tigers, pistons, bison, tides, and armies; I saw all the ants on the planet; I saw a Persian astrolabe; I saw in the drawer of a writing table (and the handwriting made me tremble) unbelievable, obscene, detailed letters, which Beatriz had written to Carlos Argentino; I saw a monument I worshiped in the Chacarita cemetery; I saw the rotted dust and bones that had once deliciously been Beatriz Viterbo; I saw the circulation of my own dark blood; I saw the coupling of love and the modification of death; I saw the Aleph from every point and angle, and in the Aleph I saw the earth and in the earth the Aleph and in the Aleph the earth; I saw my own face and my own bowels; I saw your face; and I felt dizzy and wept, for my eyes had seen that secret and conjectured object whose name is common to all men but which no man has looked upon—the unimaginable universe.

I felt infinite wonder, infinite pity.

"Feeling pretty cockeyed, are you, after so much spying into places where you have no business?" said a hated and jovial voice. "Even if you were to rack your brains, you couldn't pay me back in a hundred years for this revelation. One hell of an observatory, eh, Borges?"

Carlos Argentino's feet were planted on the topmost step. In the sudden dim light, I managed to pick myself up and utter, "One hell of a—yes, one hell of a."

The matter-of-factness of my voice surprised me. Anxiously, Carlos Argentino went on.

"Did you see everything—really clear, in colors?"

At that very moment I found my revenge. Kindly, openly pitying him,

distraught, evasive, I thanked Carlos Argentino Daneri for the hospitality of his
cellar and urged him to make the most of the demolition to get away from the
pernicious metropolis, which spares no one—believe me, I told him, no one!
Quietly and forcefully, I refused to discuss the Aleph. On saying goodbye, I
embraced him and repeated that the country, that fresh air and quiet were the
great physicians.

Out on the street, going down the stairways inside Constitution Station, riding the subway, every one of the faces seemed familiar to me. I was afraid
that not a single thing on earth would ever again surprise me; I was afraid I would
never again be free of all I had seen. Happily, after a few sleepless nights, I was
visited once more by oblivion.

Postscript of March first, 1943—Some six months after the pulling
down of a certain building on Garay Street, Procrustes & Co., the publishers, not
put off by the considerable length of Daneri's poem, brought out a selection of
its "Argentine sections." It is redundant now to repeat what happened. Carlos
Argentino Daneri won the Second National Prize for Literature.* First Prize
went to Dr. Aita; Third Prize, to Dr. Mario Bonfanti. Unbelievably, my own book
The Sharper's Cards did not get a single vote. Once again dullness and envy had
their triumph! It's been some time now that I've been trying to see Daneri; the
gossip is that a second selection from the poem is about to be published. His
felicitous pen (no longer cluttered by the Aleph) has now set itself the task of
writing an epic on our national hero, General San Martín.

I want to add two final observations: one, on the nature of the Aleph;
the other, on its name. As is well known, the Aleph is the first letter of the
Hebrew alphabet. Its use for the strange sphere in my story may not be accidental.
For the Kabbalah, that letter stands for the *En Soph*, the pure and boundless
godhead; it is also said that it takes the shape of a man pointing to both heaven
and earth, in order to show that the lower world is the map and mirror of the
higher; for Cantor's *Mengenlehre*, it is the symbol of transfinite numbers, of
which any part is as great as the whole. I would like to know whether Carlos
Argentino chose that name or whether he read it—applied to another point
where all points converge—in one of the numberless texts that the Aleph in his
cellar revealed to him. Incredible as it may seem, I believe that the Aleph of
Garay Street was a false Aleph.

Here are my reasons. Around 1867, Captain Burton held the post of
British Consul in Brazil. In July, 1942, Pedro Henríquez Ureña came across a
manuscript of Burton's, in a library at Santos, dealing with the mirror which the
Oriental world attributes to Iskander Zu al-Karnayn, or Alexander Bicornis of
Macedonia. In its crystal the whole world was reflected. Burton mentions other
similar devices—the sevenfold cup of Kai Kosru; the mirror that Tariq ibn-Ziyad

---

*"I received your pained congratulations," he wrote me. "You rage, my poor friend, with
envy, but you must confess—even if it chokes you!—that this time I have crowned my cap with the
reddest of feathers; my turban with the most *caliph* of rubies."

found in a tower (*Thousand and One Nights*, 272); the mirror that Lucian of Samosata examined on the moon (*True History*, I, 26); the mirrorlike spear that the first book of Capella's *Satyricon* attributes to Jupiter; Merlin's universal mirror, which was "round and hollow . . . and seem'd a world of glas" (*The Faerie Queene*, III, 2, 19)—and adds this curious statement: "But the aforesaid objects (besides the disadvantage of not existing) are mere optical instruments. The Faithful who gather at the mosque of Amr, in Cairo, are acquainted with the fact that the entire universe lies inside one of the stone pillars that ring its central court. . . . No one, of course, can actually see it, but those who lay an ear against the surface tell that after some short while they perceive its busy hum. . . . The mosque dates from the seventh century; the pillars come from other temples of pre-Islamic religions, since, as ibn-Khaldun has written: 'In nations founded by nomads, the aid of foreigners is essential in all concerning masonry.' "

Does this Aleph exist in the heart of a stone? Did I see it there in the cellar when I saw all things, and have I now forgotten it? Our minds are porous and forgetfulness seeps in; I myself am distorting and losing, under the wearing away of the years, the face of Beatriz.

2

MIGUEL ANGEL ASTURIAS

Miguel Angel Asturias embodied, almost too perfectly perhaps, a certain model of what a Latin American writer ought to be: one deeply rooted in his native soil, committed to the anti-imperialist cause, high-sounding and even prophetic in his style. His winning of the 1967 Nobel Prize—the second to be awarded a writer of this area (see Part Three, 19, IV)—seemed to confirm the validity of this model. The paradox in this is that Asturias had discovered his own path to his Latin American roots—in Paris, and under the dual guidance of a French authority on Central American religions, and of some surrealist poets.

Born in Guatemala, in 1899, of a well-to-do family of mixed ancestry (he was always proud of his Mayan features), Asturias lived the first twenty-one years of his life under Estrada Cabrera's brutal dictatorship. It was a fitting preparation for a man who would become famous for a brilliant satire on Latin American dictatorships, *El Señor Presidente*.

Cabrera's downfall in 1921 did not, however, bring democracy to Guatemala. In 1923 (after he received his law degree with a thesis on *The Social Problem of the Indians*), Asturias decided that it was healthier to go to London to study political economy. At the British Museum, he discovered the splendors of Mayan art (rather neglected in his native country); less welcome was his discovery of the rigors of the English winter. A quick visit to Paris, to attend the popular festivities on the Fourteenth of July, was soon transformed into a permanent residence. At the Sorbonne, he took courses on Central American mythology given by Professor Georges Raynaud. With a Mexican friend, Asturias translated into Spanish, from the French of Raynaud, some of the oldest texts of Mayan literature. He was soon in touch with Paris's small but brilliant colony of Spanish American writers (Introduction to Part Four). He also became acquainted with a number of surrealist poets, especially Robert Desnos, who quit the Breton group in 1930 to follow the Soviet line.

Although Asturias had already published some work in his native country, it was in Paris that he began to write in earnest. Apart from his translation of the *Popol Vuh,* the sacred book of the Mayas (1925), he wrote many tales in a poetic prose: *Legends of Guatemala* (1930, with an enthusiastic preface by Paul Valéry), and he began the preliminary work on *El Señor Presidente.* A short story, "The Political Beggars," written then but not published, was the nucleus of the book. It presented a brutal murder in a sort of Goyaesque atmosphere; later it would become the first chapter of the book, excerpted here. But the novel would not be completed until some twenty years later.

In the meantime, Asturias had returned home in 1933 to find another dictator in charge. Asturias shelved the novel and devoted his energies to a radio program, "The Newspaper of the Air," which he founded in 1937. The dictator's downfall allowed him to resume his novel in peace. He finished and published it in Mexico in 1946. A second, larger edition came out in Buenos Aires in 1948. By then, Asturias was living in Argentina as a representative of the democratic government of Juan José Arévalo.

If the Mexican edition had passed almost unnoticed, the Argentine one was a continental success. The critics proclaimed it the best Latin American novel of its time. Only a few dared to point out that some twenty years earlier, the Spanish writer Ramón María del Valle Inclán had published a similar book, *Tirano Banderas* (1926). Asturias claimed that he read that novel only after the resemblance to his own book had been pointed out to him. This is certainly possible. The similarities are of a general nature: both works present through satire and caricature the squalor and corruption of an unidentified Latin American dictatorship; both use avant-garde style and techniques. But while Valle Inclán's novel was more consistent in tone—maintaining a grotesque mood and atmosphere throughout—that of Asturias was less disciplined, and even resorted here and there to naturalistic devices. Another difference: Valle Inclán always kept his cool; Asturias got angry, and sometimes sentimental. For the Spanish writer, Latin America was a fabulous, alienated, and alienating landscape that he peopled with puppets; for Asturias, it was the anguished scene of his formative experience.

His second novel, *Man of Maize* (1949), was more compact in structure, and composed of a series of interconnected tales about a land in which the ancient Mayan myths were as alive as contemporary social and political conflicts.

This brilliantly written work was his most important contribution to the new Latin American narrative that Borges, Carpentier, and Uslar Pietri (selections 1, 3, 4), among others, were already producing. Although the use, and sometimes abuse, of native words made it hard to read, *Men of Maize* was Asturias's masterpiece. His subsequent fiction either followed the same fantastic pattern, but with less grace and skill (*Mulata*, 1963), or sought to blend it, unsuccessfully, with anti-imperialistic propaganda: *Strong Wind* (1950), *The Green Pope* (1954), and *The Eyes of the Buried* (1960), a popular trilogy about the banana industry; and *Week-end in Guatemala* (1956), a collection of short stories dealing with the CIA coup that overthrew the legitimate left-wing government of Jacobo Arbenz.

All these works were highly celebrated by the Latin American intelligentsia, who proclaimed Asturias a model and mentor. Less celebrated was his willingness to represent his country in 1966 as ambassador to Paris, at a time when the government was crushing revolutionary guerrillas with U.S. assistance.

Although Asturias also wrote poems and plays, it is as a novelist that he will be best remembered. Pressed to define his aesthetic credo in a 1972 interview with Rita Guibert, he resorted to an old avant-garde formula—magical realism—to which he gave his own twist: "There are no boundaries between reality and dreams, between reality and fiction, between what is seen and what is imagined. The magic of our climate and light gives our stories a double aspect —from one side they seem dreams, from the other, they are realities." This definition was closer to what Alejo Carpentier had earlier called the "marvelous real" than to the slogan originally coined in 1924 by the German art critic Franz Roh. But this is a minor point. What matters is that with this somewhat clumsy formula, and his early fiction, Asturias had firmly pointed the way out of the trap of socialist realism, demonstrating that it was possible to write politically committed works that transcended mere propaganda. It was a useful lesson for the confused fifties.

El Señor Presidente

From El Señor Presidente, *translated by Frances Partridge (New York: Atheneum, 1969), pp. 7–11.*

In the Cathedral Porch

"Boom, bloom, alum-bright, Lucifer of alunite!" The sound of the church bells summoning people to prayer lingered on, like a humming in the ears, an uneasy transition from brightness to gloom, from gloom to brightness. "Boom, bloom, alum-bright, Lucifer of alunite, over the somber tomb! Bloom, alum-

bright, over the tomb, Lucifer of alunite! Boom, boom, alum-bright . . . bloom
. . . alum-bright . . . bloom, alum-bright . . . bloom, boom."

In the frozen shadow of the cathedral, the beggars were shuffling past
the market eating-houses as they made their way through the ocean-wide streets
to the Plaza de Armas, leaving the deserted city behind them.

Nightfall assembled them, as it did the stars. With nothing in common
but their destitution, they mustered to sleep together in the Porch of Our Lord,
cursing, insulting and jostling each other, picking quarrels with old enemies, or
throwing earth and rubbish, even rolling on the ground and spitting and biting
with rage. This confraternity of the dunghill had never known pillows or mutual
trust. They lay down in all their clothes at a distance from one another, and slept
like thieves, with their heads on the bags containing their worldly goods: left-over
scraps of meat, worn-out shoes, candle-ends, handfuls of cooked rice wrapped in
old newspapers, oranges and rotten bananas.

They could be seen sitting on the steps of the Porch with their faces
to the wall, counting their money, biting the nickel coins to see if they were false,
talking to themselves, inspecting their stores of food and ammunition (for they
went out into the streets fully armed with stones and scapularies) and stuffing
themselves secretly on crusts of dry bread. They had never been known to help
each other; like all beggars they were miserly with their scraps, and would rather
give them to the dogs than to their companions in misfortune.

Having satisfied their hunger and tied up their money with seven knots
in handkerchiefs fastened to their belts, they threw themselves on the ground and
sank into sad, agitated dreams—nightmares in which they saw famished pigs, thin
women, maimed dogs, and carriage wheels passing before their eyes, or a funeral
procession of phantom monks going into the cathedral preceded by a sliver of
moon carried on a cross made of frozen shinbones. Sometimes they would be
woken from their deepest dreams by the cries of an idiot who had lost his way
in the Plaza de Armas; or sometimes by the sobs of a blind woman dreaming that
she was covered in flies and suspended from a hook like a piece of meat in a
butcher's shop. Or sometimes by the tramp of a patrol, belaboring a political
prisoner as they dragged him along, while women followed wiping away the
bloodstains with handkerchiefs soaked in tears. Sometimes by the snores of a
scabby valetudinarian, or the heavy breathing of a pregnant deaf-mute, weeping
with fear of the child she felt in her womb. But the idiot's cry was the saddest
of all. It rent the sky. It was a long-drawn-out inhuman wail.

On Sundays this strange fraternity used to be joined by a drunk man
who called for his mother and wept like a child in his sleep. Hearing the word
"mother" fall more like an oath than a prayer from the drunkard's lips, the idiot
would sit up, search every corner of the Porch with his eyes and—having woken
himself and his companions with his cries—burst into tears of fright, joining his
sobs to those of the drunkard.

Dogs barked, shouts were heard, and the more irritable beggars got up
and increased the hubbub by calling for silence. If they didn't shut their jaws the
police would come. But the police wanted nothing to do with the beggars. None

of them had enough money to pay a fine. "Long live France!" Flatfoot would shout, amidst the cries and antics of the idiot, who became the laughingstock of the other beggars in the end, simply because this scoundrelly, foul-mouthed cripple liked to pretend to be drunk several nights every week. So Flatfoot would pretend to be drunk, while the Zany (as they called the idiot), who looked like a corpse when he was asleep, became more lively with every shriek, ignoring the huddled forms lying under rags on the ground, who jeered and cackled shrilly at his crazy behavior. With his eyes far away from the hideous faces of his companions, he saw nothing, heard nothing, and felt nothing, and fell asleep at last, worn out with weeping. But it was the same every night—no sooner had he dropped off than Flatfoot's voice woke him again:

"Mother!"

The Zany opened his eyes with a start like someone who dreams he is falling into space; he shrank back with enormously dilated pupils as if mortally wounded and the tears began to flow once more; then sleep gradually overcame him, his body became flaccid, and anxious fears reverberated through his deranged mind. But no sooner was he thoroughly asleep than another voice would wake him:

"Mother!"

It was the voice of a degenerate mulatto known as the Widower, sniveling like an old woman, amidst bursts of laughter:

". . . Mother of Mercy, our hope and salvation, may God preserve you, listen to us poor down-and-outs and idiots. . . ."

The idiot used to wake up laughing; it seemed that he too found his misery and hunger so amusing that he laughed till he cried, while the beggars snatched bu-bu-bursts of la-la-laughter from the air, from the air . . . la-la-laughter; a fat man with his mustaches dripping with stew lost his breath from laughing; and a one-eyed man laughed till he urinated and beat his head against the wall like a goat; while the blind men complained that they couldn't sleep with such a row going on, and the Mosquito, who was legless as well as blind, cried out that only sodomites could amuse themselves in such a fashion.

No one paid any attention to the blind men's protests and the Mosquito's remark was not even heard. Why should anyone listen to his jabber? "Oh yes, I spent my childhood in the artillery barracks, and the mules and officers kicked me into shape and made a man of me—a man who could work like a horse, which was useful when I had to pull a barrel organ through the streets! Oh yes, and I lost my sight when I was on the booze, the devil knows how, and my right leg on another booze-up, the devil knows when, and the other in another booze-up, knocked down by a car the devil knows where!"

The beggars spread a rumor among the people of the town that the Zany went mad whenever anyone mentioned his mother. The poor wretch used to run through the streets, squares, courtyards and markets, trying to get away from people shouting "Mother!" at him from every side and at any hour of the day, like a malediction from the sky. He tried to take refuge in houses, but was chased out again by dogs or servants. They drove him out of churches, shops, and everywhere else, indifferent to his utter exhaustion and the plea for pity in his uncomprehending eyes.

The town that his exhaustion had made so large—so immensely large —seemed to shrink in the face of his despair. Nights of terror were followed by days of persecution, during which he was hounded by people who were not content to shout, "On Sunday you'll marry your Mother, my little Zany—your old woman!" but beat him and tore his clothes as well. Pursued by children, he would take refuge in the poorer quarters, but there his fate was even worse; there everyone lived on the verge of destitution, and insults were not enough—they threw stones, dead rats, and empty tins at him as he ran away in terror.

One day he came to the Cathedral Porch from the suburbs just as the Angelus was ringing, without his hat, with a wound in his forehead, and trailing the tail of a kite which had been fastened to him as a joke. Everything frightened him: the shadows of the walls, dogs trotting by, leaves falling from the trees, and the irregular rumbling of wheels. When he arrived at the Porch it was almost dark and the beggars were sitting with their faces to the wall counting their earnings. Flatfoot was quarreling with the Mosquito, the deaf-mute was feeling her inexplicably swollen belly, and the blind woman was hanging from a hook in her dreams, covered in flies, like a piece of meat at the butcher's.

The idiot fell on the ground as if dead; he had not closed his eyes for nights, he had not been able to rest his feet for days. The beggars were silently scratching their fleabites but could not sleep; they listened for the footsteps of the police going to and fro in the dimly lit square and the click of the sentinels presenting arms, as they stood at attention like ghosts in their striped ponchos at the windows of the neighboring barracks, keeping their nightly watch over the President of the Republic. No one knew where he was, for he occupied several houses in the outskirts of the town; nor how he slept—some said beside the telephone with a whip in his hand; nor when—his friends declared he never slept at all.

A figure advanced toward the Porch of Our Lord. The beggars curled themselves up like worms. The creak of military boots was answered by the sinister hoot of a bird from the dark, navigable, bottomless night.

Flatfoot opened his eyes (a menacing threat as of the end of the world weighed upon the air) and said to the owl, "Hoo-hoo! Do your worst! I wish you neither good nor ill, but the devil take you all the same!"

The Mosquito groped for his face with his hands. The air was tense, as though an earthquake were brewing. The Widower crossed himself as he sat among the blind men. Only the Zany slept like a log, snoring for once.

The new arrival stopped; his face lit up with a smile. Going up to the idiot on tiptoe he shouted jeeringly at him, "Mother!"

That was all. Torn from the ground by the cry, the Zany flung himself upon his tormentor, and, without giving him time to get at his weapons, thrust his fingers into his eyes, tore at his nose with his teeth, and jabbed his private parts with his knees, till he fell to the ground motionless.

The beggars shut their eyes in horror, the owl flew by once more, and the Zany fled away down the shadowy streets in a paroxysm of mad terror.

Some blind force had put an end to the life of Colonel José Parrales Sonriente, known as "the man with the little mule."

It was nearly dawn.

3

ALEJO CARPENTIER

Like his friend Miguel Angel Asturias, the Cuban Alejo Carpentier rediscovered Latin America in the Paris of the twenties. But in his case, the rediscovery was of a more deliberate character. Whereas Asturias could rely on a family tradition that went back to both the Mayas and the conquistadores, Carpentier is the son of European immigrants who has consciously set about the business of becoming a representative Latin American writer. Up to a point, he has succeeded.

Carpentier was born in Havana in 1904, but his first language was French. (Even today, he speaks Spanish with a distinctly Gallic r.) His father was a French architect, his mother a Russian who had studied medicine in Switzerland. In 1914, the family moved to Europe, and after a journey through Russia, Austria, and Belgium, settled in France. Carpentier attended secondary school there and did not return to his native land until the early 1920s, to study architecture. He never graduated, but has always retained a critical interest in his father's profession. He also studied music, and became a scholar in that field as well.

His approach to Spanish as a literary instrument was, initially, similar to that of a Conrad or a Nabokov in English: he used words as if having first exhausted every available dictionary. With some other young writers, he founded in 1927 a little magazine, *Review of Advance,* whose title suggests its avant-garde tendencies. He returned to France in 1928, after spending forty days in jail for his activities in opposition to the Machado dictatorship. In his flight from Cuba he was helped by the surrealist poet Robert Desnos.

In Paris, Carpentier sided with Desnos's faction at the time of the ideological split with Breton (see Introduction to this part). It was around this time also that he met Asturias and Uslar Pietri. They helped him launch a new literary journal, *The Magnet,* which published one single but important issue in 1931.

Carpentier did not return to Cuba until the outbreak of World War II in 1939. But his long sojourn in Paris had given him a cause. Not only had he had the chance for firsthand acquaintance with and participation in the avant-garde, he had also discovered a great common mission for Latin American intellectuals: to integrate the different national cultures into a truly continental unity; to recapture the fabulous past and update it; to preserve whatever was still meaningful and valuable in the collapsing cultures of the West. The widespread nihilism of the day, and his reading of Spengler's *Decline of the West* (translated into Spanish in 1932), served to convince him that the future of man lay in the New World.

In coming to this stage of his thinking, Carpentier passed through three basic experiences or phases in his development. In the first, he sought a formula for the new Latin American novel in an ill-advised mixture of socialist realism and Afro-Cuban folklore—*Ecué-Yamba-O!* (1933) was the chief tangible outcome of this phase, and one that he later disowned. The second was a scholarly investigation of music in Cuba (published as a book in 1946), which helped him to see from the inside and in colorful detail the essential fabric of his country's culture. The third was the writing of several stories in which he played with time and personal identity while developing a precise, poetic Spanish. He did not collect these stories, however, until 1958, in a volume called *War on Time*. By that date, they looked doubly anachronistic—because they had been preceded by Borges's more dazzling fictions (selection 1), and because Carpentier himself was by that time writing in a different vein. These stories remain, nonetheless, among the best he has ever written, as witness the one selected here. In "Journey Back to the Source," written in 1944, Carpentier used a device anticipated by Plato in one of his dialogues: to present a man's life in reverse order, from the unbirth which is death to the undeath which is birth.

Carpentier's literary apprenticeship was completed in 1949, when he published *The Kingdom of This World*. It is a short historical chronicle, inspired by a visit to Haiti with Louis Jouvet's theatrical troupe. As he related in a preface to the book, he discovered there the "marvelous reality" of Latin America—a land in which the frontiers between dream and reality are permanently blurred because the real is fabulous and the fabulous real. This notion was not entirely original with him: Breton, for one, had preceded him in discovering, on a 1938 visit, that Mexico was the "elective land of surrealism." Carpentier, however, was apparently unwilling to acknowledge his debt to surrealism, on the one hand, and to Spengler's prophetic vision, on the other. He omitted any reference to the philosopher and attacked surrealism as lacking the underpinnings of a coherent faith. He had faith instead, he declared, in Latin America's destiny.

This stance, although it won a measure of favor among more complaisant readers, was not really very sound. Why was the real necessarily more "marvelous" in Latin America than anywhere else? Wasn't there a substantial element of wishful thinking in such a view? A few years later, Carpentier implicitly repudiated the preface by eliminating it from a 1954 French translation of the book—perhaps guessing (no doubt correctly) that Left Bank scrutiny would not have been kind to it. In 1962, however, he again reversed himself and wrote a longer version of the preface to lead off a slim volume of his essays. By then, his thesis looked even weaker.

Whatever Carpentier's failings as a theoretician, there is no question that his literary craftsmanship steadily improved. After 1949 he published five more novels, in which he experimented with different formats: the romance (*The Lost Steps,* 1953); the political chronicle (*The Chase,* 1956); the historical novel (*Explosion in a Cathedral,* 1962, and *Baroque Concert,* 1974); and the satire (*The Recourse to Method,* 1974). In all these books he continued to experiment with narrative structure and to develop his personal view of history.

With the triumph of the Cuban Revolution in 1959, Carpentier found not just a cause but a coherent program of action. He has dutifully participated in his country's cultural activities under the new regime, and since 1966 has held the post of cultural attaché at the Cuban consulate in Paris.

Journey Back to the Source

From "Viaje a la semilla," translated by Frances Partridge, in War of Time *(New York: Knopf, 1970), pp. 105–31.*

"What d'you want, Pop?"

Again and again came the question, from high up on the scaffolding. But the old man made no reply. He moved from one place to another, prying into corners and uttering a lengthy monologue of incomprehensible remarks. The tiles had already been taken down, and now covered the dead flower beds with their mosaic of baked clay. Overhead, blocks of masonry were being loosened with picks and sent rolling down wooden gutters in an avalanche of lime and plaster. And through the crenelations that were one by one indenting the walls, were appearing—denuded of their privacy—oval or square ceilings, cornices, garlands, dentils, astragals, and paper hanging from the walls like old skins being sloughed by a snake.

Witnessing the demolition, a Ceres with a broken nose and discolored peplum, her headdress of corn veined with black, stood in the back yard above her fountain of crumbling grotesques. Visited by shafts of sunlight piercing the shadows, the gray fish in the basin yawned in the warm weed-covered water, watching with round eyes the black silhouettes of the workmen against the brilliance of the sky as they diminished the centuries-old height of the house. The old man had sat down at the foot of the statue, resting his chin on his stick. He watched buckets filled with precious fragments ascending and descending. Muted sounds from the street could be heard, while overhead, against a basic rhythm of steel on stone, the pulleys screeched unpleasantly in chorus, like harsh-voiced birds.

The clock struck five. The cornices and entablatures were depopulated. Nothing was left behind but stepladders, ready for tomorrow's onslaught. The air grew cooler, now that it was disburdened of sweat, oaths, creaking ropes, axles crying out for the oil can, and the slapping of hands on greasy torsos. Dusk had settled earlier on the dismantled house. The shadows had enfolded it just at that moment when the now-fallen upper balustrade used to enrich the façade by capturing the sun's last beams. Ceres tightened her lips. For the first time the rooms would sleep unshuttered, gazing onto a landscape of rubble.

Contradicting their natural propensities, several capitals lay in the grass, their acanthus leaves asserting their vegetable status. A creeper stretched adventurous tendrils toward an Ionic scroll, attracted by its air of kinship. When night fell, the house was closer to the ground. Upstairs, the frame of a door still stood erect, slabs of darkness suspended from its dislocated hinges.

II

Then the old Negro, who had not stirred, began making strange movements with his stick, whirling it around above a graveyard of paving stones.

The white and black marble squares flew to the floors and covered them. Stones leaped up and unerringly filled the gaps in the walls. The nail-studded walnut doors fitted themselves into their frames, while the screws rapidly twisted back into the holes in the hinges. In the dead flower beds, the fragments of the tile were lifted by the thrust of growing flowers and joined together, raising a sonorous whirlwind of clay, to fall like rain on the framework of the roof. The house grew, once more assuming its normal proportions, modestly clothed. Ceres became less gray. There were more fish in the fountain. And the gurgling water summoned forgotten begonias back to life.

The old man inserted a key into the lock of the front door and began to open the windows. His heels made a hollow sound. When he lighted the lamps, a yellow tremor ran over the oil paint of the family portraits, and people dressed in black talked softly in all the corridors, to the rhythm of spoons stirring cups of chocolate.

Don Marcial, Marqués de Capellanías, lay on his deathbed, his breast blazing with decorations, while four tapers with long beards of melted wax kept guard over him.

III

The candles lengthened slowly, gradually guttering less and less. When they had reached full size, the nun extinguished them and took away the light. The wicks whitened, throwing off red sparks. The house emptied itself of visitors and their carriages drove away in the darkness. Don Marcial fingered an invisible keyboard and opened his eyes.

The confused heaps of rafters gradually went back into place. Medicine bottles, tassels from brocades, the scapulary beside the bed, daguerreotypes, and iron palm leaves from the grille emerged from the mists. When the doctor shook his head with an expression of professional gloom, the invalid felt better. He slept for several hours and awoke under the black beetle-browed gaze of Father Anastasio. What had begun as a candid, detailed confession of his many sins grew gradually more reticent, painful and full of evasions. After all, what right had the Carmelite to interfere in his life?

Suddenly Don Marcial found himself thrown into the middle of the room. Relieved of the pressure on his temples, he stood up with surprising agility. The naked woman who had been stretching herself on the brocade coverlet began to look for her petticoats and bodices, and soon afterward disappeared in a rustle of silk and a waft of perfume. In the closed carriage downstairs an envelope full of gold coins was lying on the brass-studded seat.

Don Marcial was not feeling well. When he straightened his cravat before the pier glass he saw that his face was congested. He went downstairs to his study where lawyers—attorneys and their clerks—were waiting for him to arrange for the sale of the house by auction. All his efforts had been in vain. His property would go to the highest bidder, to the rhythm of a hammer striking the table. He bowed, and they left him alone. He thought how mysterious were written words: those black threads weaving and unweaving, and covering large sheets of paper with a filigree of estimates; weaving and unweaving contracts, oaths, agreements, evidence, declarations, names, titles, dates, lands, trees, and stones; a tangled skein of threads, drawn from the inkpot to ensnare the legs of any man who took a path disapproved of by the law; a noose around his neck to stifle free speech at its first dreaded sound. He had been betrayed by his signature; it had handed him over to the nets and labyrinths of documents. Thus constricted, the man of flesh and blood had become a man of paper.

It was dawn. The dining-room clock had just struck six in the evening.

IV

The months of mourning passed under the shadow of ever-increasing remorse. At first the idea of bringing a woman to his room had seemed quite reasonable. But little by little the desire excited by a new body gave way to increasing scruples, which ended as self-torment. One night, Don Marcial beat himself with a strap till the blood came, only to experience even intenser desire, though it was of short duration.

It was at this time that the Marquesa returned one afternoon from a drive along the banks of the Almendares. The manes of the horses harnessed to her carriage were damp with solely their own sweat. Yet they spent the rest of the day kicking the wooden walls of their stable as if maddened by the stillness of the low-hanging clouds.

At dusk, a jar full of water broke in the Marquesa's bathroom. Then the May rains came and overflowed the lake. And the old Negress who unhappily was a maroon and kept pigeons under her bed wandered through the patio, muttering to herself, "Never trust rivers, my girl; never trust anything green and flowing!" Not a day passed without water making its presence felt. But in the end that presence amounted to no more than a cup spilled over a Paris dress after the anniversary ball given by the Governor of the Colony.

Many relatives reappeared. Many friends came back again. The chandeliers in the great drawing room glittered with brilliant lights. The cracks in the façade were closing up, one by one. The piano became a clavichord. The palm trees lost some of their rings. The creepers let go of the upper cornice. The dark circles around Ceres's eyes disappeared, and the capitals of the columns looked as if they had been freshly carved. Marcial was more ardent now, and often passed whole afternoons embracing the Marquesa. Crow's-feet, frowns, and double chins vanished, and flesh grew firm again. One day the smell of fresh paint filled the house.

V

Their embarrassment was real. Each night the leaves of the screens opened a little farther, and skirts fell to the floor in obscurer corners of the room, revealing yet more barriers of lace. At last the Marquesa blew out the lamps. Only Marcial's voice was heard in the darkness.

They left for the sugar plantation in a long procession of carriages— sorrel hindquarters, silver bits, and varnished leather gleamed in the sunshine. But among the pasqueflowers empurpling the arcades leading up to the house, they realized that they scarcely knew each other. Marcial gave permission for a performance of native dancers and drummers, by way of entertainment during those days impregnated with the smells of eau de cologne, of baths spiced with benzoin, of unloosened hair and sheets taken from closets and unfolded to let a bunch of vetiver drop onto the tiled floor. The steam of cane juice and the sound of the Angelus mingled on the breeze. The vultures flew low, heralding a sparse shower, whose first large echoing drops were absorbed by tiles so dry that they gave off a diapason like copper.

After a dawn prolonged by an inexpert embrace, they returned together to the city with their misunderstandings settled and the wound healed. The Marquesa changed her traveling dress for a wedding gown and the married pair went to church according to custom, to regain their freedom. Relations and friends received their presents back again, and they all set off for home with jingling brass and a display of splendid trappings. Marcial went on visiting María de las Mercedes for a while, until the day when the rings were taken to the goldsmiths to have their inscriptions removed. For Marcial, a new life was beginning. In the house with the high grilles, an Italian Venus was set up in place of Ceres, and the grotesques in the fountain were thrown into almost imperceptibly sharper relief because the lamps were still glowing when dawn colored the sky.

VI

One night, after drinking heavily and being sickened by the stale tobacco smoke left behind by his friends, Marcial had the strange sensation that all the clocks in the house were striking five, then half past four, then four, then half past three. . . . It was as if he had become dimly aware of other possibilities. Just as, when exhausted by sleeplessness, one may believe that one could walk on the ceiling, with the floor for a ceiling and the furniture firmly fixed between the beams. It was only a fleeting impression, and did not leave the smallest trace on his mind, for he was not much given to meditation at the time.

And a splendid evening party was given in the music room on the day he achieved minority. He was delighted to know that his signature was no longer legally valid, and that worm-eaten registers and documents would now vanish from his world. He had reached the point at which courts of justice were no longer to be feared, because his bodily existence was ignored by the law. After getting tipsy on noble wines, the young people took down from the wall a guitar inlaid with mother-of-pearl, a psaltery, and a serpent. Someone wound up the clock that played the *ranz des vaches* and the "Ballad of the Scottish Lakes." Someone else blew on a hunting horn that had been lying curled in copper sleep on the crimson felt lining of the showcase, beside a transverse flute brought from Aranjuez. Marcial, who was boldly making love to Señora de Campoflorido, joined in the cacophony, and tried to pick out the tune of "Trípili-Trápala" on the piano, to a discordant accompaniment in the bass.

Then they all trooped upstairs to the attic, remembering that the liveries and clothes of the Capellanías family had been stored away under its peeling beams. On shelves frosted with camphor lay court dresses, an ambassador's sword, several padded military jackets, the vestment of a dignitary of the Church, and some long cassocks with damask buttons and damp stains among their folds. The dark shadows of the attic were variegated with the colors of amaranthine ribbons, yellow crinolines, faded tunics, and velvet flowers. A picaresque *chispero*'s costume and hair net trimmed with tassels, once made for a carnival masquerade, was greeted with applause. Señora de Campoflorido swathed her powdered shoulders in a shawl the color of a Creole's skin, once worn by a certain ancestress on an evening of important family decisions in hopes of reviving the sleeping ardor of some rich trustee of a convent of Clares.

As soon as they were dressed up, the young people went back to the music room. Marcial, who was wearing an alderman's hat, struck the floor three times with a stick and announced that they would begin with a waltz, a dance mothers thought terribly improper for young ladies because they had to allow themselves to be taken round the waist, with a man's hand resting on the busks of the stays they had all had made according to the latest model in the *Jardin des Modes.* The doorways were blocked by maidservants, stableboys, and waiters, who had come from remote outbuildings and stifling basements to enjoy the boisterous fun. Afterward they played blindman's buff and hide-and-seek. Hidden behind a Chinese screen with Señora de Campoflorido, Marcial planted a kiss on her neck, and received in return a scented handkerchief whose Brussels lace still retained the sweet warmth of her low-necked bodice.

And when the girls left in the fading light of dusk, to return to castles and towers silhouetted in dark gray against the sea, the young men went to the dance hall, where alluring *mulatas* in heavy bracelets were strutting about without ever losing their high-heeled shoes, even in the frenzy of the guaracha. And as it was carnival time, the members of the Arara Chapter Three Eyes Band were raising thunder on their drums behind the wall in a patio planted with pomegranate trees. Climbing onto tables and stools, Marcial and his friends applauded the gracefulness of a Negress with graying hair, who had recovered her beauty and almost become desirable as she danced, looking over her shoulder with an expression of proud disdain.

VII

The visits of Don Abundio, the family notary and executor, were more frequent now. He used to sit gravely down beside Marcial's bed, and let his acana-wood cane drop to the floor so as to wake him up in good time. Opening his eyes, Marcial saw an alpaca frock coat covered with dandruff, its sleeves shiny from collecting securities and rents. All that was left in the end was an adequate pension, calculated to put a stop to all wild extravagance. It was at this time that Marcial wanted to enter the Royal Seminary of San Carlos.

After doing only moderately well in his examinations, he attended courses of lectures, but understood less and less of his master's explanations. The world of his ideas was gradually growing emptier. What had once been a general assembly of peplums, doublets, ruffs, and periwigs, of controversialists and debaters, now looked as lifeless as a museum of wax figures. Marcial contented himself with a scholastic analysis of the systems, and accepted everything he found in a book as the truth. The words "Lion," "Ostrich," "Whale," "Jaguar" were printed under the copper-plate engravings in his natural history book. Just as "Aristotle," "St. Thomas," "Bacon," and "Descartes" headed pages black with boring, close-printed accounts of different interpretations of the universe. Bit by bit, Marcial stopped trying to learn these things, and felt relieved of a heavy burden. His mind grew gay and lively, understanding things in a purely instinctive way. Why think about the prism, when the clear winter light brought out all the details in the fortresses guarding the port? An apple falling from a tree tempted one to bite it—that was all. A foot in a bathtub was merely a foot in a bathtub. The day he left the seminary he forgot all about his books. A gnomon was back in the category of goblins, a spectrum a synonym for a phantom, and an octandrian an animal armed with spines.

More than once he had hurried off with a troubled heart to visit the women who whispered behind blue doors under the town walls. The memory of one of them, who wore embroidered slippers and a sprig of sweet basil behind her ear, pursued him on hot evenings like the toothache. But one day his confessor's anger and threats reduced him to terrified tears. He threw himself for the last time between those infernal sheets, and then forever renounced his detours through unfrequented streets and that last-minute faintheartedness which sent him home in a rage, turning his back on a certain crack in the pavement—the signal, when he was walking with head bent, that he must turn and enter the perfumed threshold.

Now he was undergoing a spiritual crisis, peopled by religious images, paschal lambs, china doves, Virgins in heavenly blue cloaks, gold paper stars, the three Magi, angels with wings like swans, the Ass, the Ox, and a terrible Saint Denis, who appeared to him in his dreams with a great space between his shoulders, walking hesitantly as if looking for something he had lost. When he blundered into the bed, Marcial would start awake and reach for his rosary of silver beads. The lampwicks, in their bowls of oil, cast a sad light on the holy images as their colors returned to them.

VIII

The furniture was growing taller. It was becoming more difficult for him to rest his arms on the dining table. The fronts of the cupboards with their carved cornices were getting broader. The Moors on the staircase stretched their torsos upward, bringing their torches closer to the banisters on the landing. Armchairs were deeper, and rocking chairs tended to fall over backward. It was no longer necessary to bend one's knees when lying at the bottom of the bath with its marble rings.

One morning when he was reading a licentious book, Marcial suddenly felt a desire to play with the lead soldiers lying asleep in their wooden boxes. He put the book back in its hiding place under the washbasin, and opened a drawer sealed with cobwebs. His schoolroom table was too small to hold such a large army. So Marcial sat on the floor and set out his grenadiers in rows of eight. Next came the officers on horseback, surrounding the color sergeant; and behind, the artillery with their cannon, gun sponges, and linstocks. Bringing up the rear were fifes and tabors escorted by drummers. The mortars were fitted with a spring, so that one could shoot glass marbles to a distance of more than a yard.

Bang! . . . Bang! . . . Bang!

Down fell horses, down fell standard-bearers, down fell drummers. Eligio the Negro had to call him three times before he could be persuaded to go to wash his hands and descend to the dining room.

After that day, Marcial made a habit of sitting on the tiled floor. When he realized the advantages of this position, he was surprised that he had not thought of it before. Grown-up people had a passion for velvet cushions, which made them sweat too much. Some of them smelled like a notary—like Don Abundio—because they had not discovered how cool it was to lie at full length on a marble floor at all seasons of the year. Only from the floor could all the angles and perspectives of a room be grasped properly. There were beautiful grains in the wood, mysterious insect paths, and shadowy corners that could not be seen from a man's height. When it rained, Marcial hid himself under the clavichord. Every clap of thunder made the sound box vibrate, and set all the notes to singing. Shafts of lightning fell from the sky, creating a vault of cascading arpeggios— the organ, the wind in the pines, and the crickets' mandolin.

IX

That morning they locked him in his room. He heard whispering all over the house, and the luncheon they brought him was too delicious for a weekday. There were six pastries from the confectioner's in the Alameda— whereas even on Sundays after Mass he was only allowed two. He amused himself by looking at the engravings in a travel book, until an increasing buzz of sound coming under the door made him look out between the blinds. Some men dressed all in black were arriving, bearing a brass-handled coffin. He was on the verge of tears, but at this moment Melchor the groom appeared in his room, his boots echoing on the floor and his teeth flashing in a smile. They began to play chess. Melchor was a knight. He was the king. Using the tiles on the floor as a chess-board, he moved from one square to the next, while Melchor had to jump one forward and two sideways, or vice versa. The game went on until after dusk, when the fire brigade went by.

When he got up, he went to kiss his father's hand as he lay ill in bed. The Marqués was feeling better, and talked to his son in his usual serious and edifying manner. His "Yes, Father's" and "No, Father's" were fitted between the beads of a rosary of questions, like the responses of an acolyte during Mass. Marcial respected the Marqués, but for reasons that no one could possibly have guessed. He respected him because he was tall, because when he went out to a ball his breast glittered with decorations; because he envied him the saber and gold braid he wore as an officer in the militia; because at Christmas time, on a bet, he had eaten a whole turkey stuffed with almonds and raisins; because he had once seized one of the *mulatas* who were sweeping out the rotunda and had carried her in his arms to his room—no doubt intending to whip her. Hidden behind a curtain, Marcial watched her come out soon afterward, in tears and with her dress unfastened, and he was pleased that she had been punished, as she was the one who always emptied the jam pots before putting them back in the cupboard.

His father was a terrible and magnanimous being, and it was his duty to love him more than anyone except God. To Marcial he was more godlike even than God because his gifts were tangible, everyday ones. But he preferred the God in heaven because he was less of a nuisance.

X

When the furniture had grown a little taller still, and Marcial knew better than anyone what was under the beds, cupboards, and cabinets, he had a great secret, which he kept to himself: life had no charms except when Melchor the groom was with him. Not God, nor his father, nor the golden bishop in the Corpus Christi procession was as important as Melchor.

Melchor had come from a very long distance away. He was descended from conquered princes. In his kingdom there were elephants, hippopotamuses, tigers, and giraffes, and men did not sit working, like Don Abundio, in dark rooms full of papers. They lived by outdoing the animals in cunning. One of them had pulled the great crocodile out of the blue lake after first skewering him on a pike concealed inside the closely packed bodies of twelve roast geese. Melchor knew songs that were easy to learn because the words had no meaning and were constantly repeated. He stole sweetmeats from the kitchens; at night he used to escape through the stable door, and once he threw stones at the police before disappearing into the darkness of the Calle de la Amargura.

On wet days he used to put his boots to dry beside the kitchen stove. Marcial wished he had feet big enough to fill boots like those. His right-hand boot was called Calambín; the left one Calambán. This man who could tame unbroken horses by simply seizing their lips between two fingers, this fine gentleman in velvet and spurs who wore such tall hats, also understood about the coolness of marble floors in summer, and used to hide fruits or a cake, snatched from trays destined for the drawing room, behind the furniture. Marcial and Melchor shared a secret store of sweets and almonds, which they saluted with *"Urí, urí, urá"* and shouts of conspiratorial laughter. They had both explored the house from top to bottom, and were the only ones who knew that beneath the stables there was a small cellar full of Dutch bottles, or that in an unused loft over the maids' rooms was a broken glass case containing twelve dusty butterflies that were losing their wings.

XI

When Marcial got into the habit of breaking things, he forgot Melchor and made friends with the dogs. There were several in the house. The large one with stripes like a tiger; the basset trailing its teats on the ground; the greyhound that had grown too old to play; the poodle that was chased by the others at certain times and had to be shut up by the maids.

Marcial liked Canelo best because he carried off shoes from the bed-rooms and dug up the rose trees in the patio. Always black with coal dust or covered with red earth, he devoured the dinners of all the other dogs, whined without cause, and hid stolen bones under the fountain. And now and again he would suck dry a new laid egg and send the hen flying with a sharp blow from his muzzle. Everyone kicked Canelo. But when they took him away, Marcial made himself ill with grief. And the dog returned in triumph, wagging his tail, from somewhere beyond the poorhouse where he had been abandoned, and regained his place in the house, which the other dogs, for all their skill in hunting, or vigilance when keeping guard, could never fill.

Canelo and Marcial used to urinate side by side. Sometimes they chose the Persian carpet in the drawing room, spreading dark, cloudlike shapes over its pile. This usually cost them a thrashing. But thrashings were less painful than grown-up people realized. On the other hand, they gave a splendid excuse for setting up a concerted howling and arousing the pity of the neighbors. When the cross-eyed woman from the top flat called his father a "brute," Marcial looked at Canelo with smiling eyes. They shed a few more tears so as to be given a biscuit, and afterward all was forgotten. They both used to eat earth, roll on the ground, drink out of the goldfish basin, and take refuge in the scented shade under the sweet-basil bushes. During the hottest hours of the day quite a crowd filled the moist flower beds. There would be the gray goose with her pouch hanging between her bandy-legs; the old rooster with his naked rump; the little lizard who kept saying *"Urí, urá"* and shooting a pink ribbon out of his throat; the melancholy snake, born in a town where there were no females; and the mouse that blocked its hole with a turtle's egg. One day someone pointed out the dog to Marcial.

"Bow-wow," Marcial said.

He was talking his own language. He had attained the ultimate liberty. He was beginning to want to reach with his hands things that were out of reach.

XII

Hunger, thirst, heat, pain, cold. Hardly had Marcial reduced his field of perception to these essential realities when he renounced the light that accompanied them. He did not know his own name. The unpleasantness of the christening over, he had no desire for smells, sounds, or even sights. His hands caressed delectable forms. He was a purely sensory and tactile being. The universe penetrated him through his pores. Then he shut his eyes—they saw nothing but nebulous giants—and entered a warm, damp body full of shadows: a dying body. Clothed in this body's substance, he slipped toward life.

But now time passed more quickly, rarefying the final hours. The minutes sounded like cards slipping from beneath a dealer's thumb.

Birds returned to their eggs in a whirlwind of feathers. Fish congealed into roe, leaving a snowfall of scales at the bottom of their pond. The palm trees folded their fronds and disappeared into the earth like shut fans. Stems were reabsorbing their leaves, and the earth reclaimed everything that was its own. Thunder rumbled through the arcades. Hairs began growing from antelope-skin gloves. Woolen blankets were unraveling and turning into the fleece of sheep in distant pastures. Cupboards, cabinets, beds, crucifixes, tables, and blinds disappeared into the darkness in search of their ancient roots beneath the forest trees. Everything that had been fastened with nails was disintegrating. A brigantine, anchored no one knew where, sped back to Italy carrying the marble from the floors and fountain. Suits of armor, ironwork, keys, copper cooking pots, the horses' bits from the stables, were melting and forming a swelling river of metal running into the earth through roofless channels. Everything was undergoing metamorphosis and being restored to its original state. Clay returned to clay, leaving a desert where the house had once stood.

XIII

When the workmen came back at dawn to go on with the demolition of the house, they found their task completed. Someone had carried off the statue of Ceres and sold it to an antique dealer the previous evening. After complaining to their trade union, the men went and sat on the seats in the municipal park. Then one of them remembered some vague story about a Marquesa de Capellanías who had been drowned one evening in May among the arum lilies in the Almendares. But no one paid any attention to his story, because the sun was traveling from east to west, and the hours growing on the right-hand side of the clock must be spun out by idleness—for they are the ones that inevitably lead to death.

4

ARTURO USLAR PIETRI

Although an adherent of the avant-garde, the Venezuelan Arturo Uslar Pietri has long been, like the novelists of the Mexican Revolution (see Part Three, 10, 14), actively involved in politics. He also shares with one of them, Martín Luis Guzmán, a preoccupation with contemporary history, and since 1962 has been at work on a trilogy whose first volume is *Portrait in Geography*, about the fight for freedom in the Venezuela of the 1940s and '50s.

Born in Caracas in 1906, Uslar Pietri is a descendant of European career officers who joined Bolívar's army and fought for independence. In 1929 he graduated, with a degree in the social sciences, from the Central University of Caracas. Later, as cultural attaché at the Embassy in Paris, he came into contact with the avant-garde and had the chance to meet Asturias and Carpentier. Before returning to Caracas in 1935 he strengthened his links with an Italian group called the "900," one of whose central tenets was the doctrine of magical realism. Uslar Pietri was probably one of the first to apply this doctrine in a Latin American context, as a means of defining, in 1948, the style of various Venezuelan storytellers. By then, he was teaching at Columbia University in New York, having been forced to leave his native country for political reasons.

In 1950 he returned to Venezuela, where he met Carpentier again. They collaborated in some literary ventures, but Uslar Pietri was then becoming more and more attracted to politics. Even so, this preoccupation does not seem to have seriously impeded his literary output, which has been, before and since, substantial.

His first two books were collections of short stories; in 1931 he published his first novel, *The Red Lances,* a brilliant reconstruction of the wars of independence from the point of view of the wild cavalrymen of the plains. The real hero is a Spaniard who fought savagely against Bolívar's forces. In 1947, Uslar Pietri published two books: *The Way to El Dorado,* a novel on the mad exploits of the tyrant Lope de Aguirre in his search for the golden land, and a third volume of short stories, *Thirty Men and Their Shadows.*

Although he has been recognized as a historical novelist of high distinction, it is primarily on his short stories that Uslar Pietri's reputation rests. The story here excerpted belongs to the 1947 collection. It is a very elaborate presentation, from the victim's own point of view, of his hours of waiting before he is subjected to a brutal flogging. While its content is clearly political, the story avoids all editorializing and instead achieves its effects through the expressionistic use of beating drums. The drums, which hold an irresistible fascination for the protagonist, come to symbolize the beating of the prisoners—the skins of the drums, their own tortured skins; the rhythm of the drums, a pulsating, aural torture that from the very beginning dominates the narrative. More effectively than by any overt description, the text manages to convey its message through its own varied texture—changes in narrative pace, the recurrence of leitmotivs, the obsessively repeated images. With Asturias and Uslar Pietri, Latin American political fiction moves into another dimension without losing its characteristically brutal impact.

The Drum Dance

From "El baile de tambor," translated by G. Alfred Mayer, in Odyssey, vol. 2, no. 3 (September 1962), pp. 60–68.

They threw him down on the brick floor of the cell and shut the door. Everything was dark. The bricks were cool and it felt good to be lying on them. To be calm and quiet. To let himself slide down into sleep without being suddenly surprised.

The heavy footsteps of the provost marshal were going away. They were Ño Gaspar's steps, who was bowlegged and square-shouldered as a sack of cocoa beans, with his white sandals, his shirt unbuttoned at the throat, his chest crossed by the shoulder belt of yellow silk for the rooster's-tale saber.

The sound of the drums came into the cell, a harsh, infinite, unchanging rhythm—the tenor drum clear and the bass husky—and you could imagine in the darkness the sound of the blacks' feet, beating up the dust in the square.

A few smoking lamps that streaked rays of light across the sweaty faces of the blacks in the darkness hung from the leafy saman trees.

That's where Ño Gaspar had found him. He had kept coming closer and closer, slowly, timidly, sticking to the side of a wall, hiding behind a tree, away from the lights. But his feet shuffled to the rhythm and he chewed the vibrant tune between his teeth. He started to dance by himself. And then, without knowing how, he was dancing with the colored girl, her eyes, laughter, fragrance, on fire in the dark.

"Wow, Soledad, we're dancing together."

"Wow, Hilario, you're back."

But just then, or a little later, or much later, Ño Gaspar got there. He didn't have to see him to know it was he. He knew his voice, knew his steps, could feel him coming. He knew that he had come.

"So, Hilario. I knew you were going to come back of your own accord. That you were going to be caught easy. When the search parties went to look for you, I sent them for the hell of it. I know my men. And there it is. You came all by yourself."

They tied his hands behind his back quickly with a piece of rope. The drum dance did not stop but many of those present got wind of what was happening and began to come over to them.

"It's Hilario."

"Yeah. The peon from El Manteco."

"He deserted from the camp in Caucagua."

"They're going to skin him for sure."

He let them lead him away without putting up a fight. From the darkness the eyes of the blacks converged on him. As he passed under the lamps you could see how emaciated he was, his skin had become discolored and leathery, his lips cracked, his eyes sunken, dull.

The provost marshal himself was led to observe,

"You're a sack of bones, Hilario. There's not enough meat on you for a meatball. Ah, the black boy was so solid."

But he said nothing. He hardly seemed to see. He only heard in snatches, confusedly. The voices of some of the women:

"Poor thing. Letting himself get caught that way!"

"He's all bones. He won't be able to stand the whip."

He wasn't sure if he was hearing all that or just imagining it, as he went from the square that was full of the drumbeat, into the dark entry hall of Headquarters, and, too weak to resist the push they gave him, fell onto the bricks of the cell.

Strangled by the rope, his wrists were pounding like the drum, almost with the same beat. He was thirsty. He pressed his dry lips against a damp brick.

He had known that all this was going to happen. He had thought about it an infinite number of times. He had constantly imagined it while he hid, starving, in the forest and came down at night to drink at the river or steal from the farms. He had known it since the day he had run away from camp.

He would have to come back to town and Ño Gaspar would come to get him and tie his hands behind his back, as he had them now, as he had them when Ño Gaspar tied them on recruiting day.

"So that you'll know what's good for you and become a man."

But he felt like sleeping. To make up for all those days and nights in the bush. He felt peaceful there on the bricks.

He pressed his face to the floor and couldn't feel his own weight.

"I feel sort of light."

He could no longer hear the drum. It must be very late at night. But he could sort of feel the weight of the houses resting on the ground. They weren't many. The six on their lots around the square. There were more corrals than farmhouses. But he felt how they weighed down the ground. And he could feel the sleepy, dark water of the river Tuy sliding near or far off. And the wind passing over the roofs, and the trees and the water, and he stroked the dirt on the ground. The wind sped faster than the Tuy toward the sea.

He also seemed to be sliding along and floating.

But suddenly he felt as if he had fallen and he opened his eyes in the darkness.

"And now all that's left is Corporal Cirguelo's whip," he said between his teeth, and he felt a chill.

While he had been in camp he had seen a deserter flogged.

"Taiiiiin . . . shun!" The officer roared. The company came to attention.

It was time for the punishment. Long before daybreak. Corporal Cirguelo and an assistant prepared the whips. They had placed the deserter in front of the company. They had pulled down his pants. It was as cold then as now. They had tied his hands and, put into a crouching position, they had stuck guns down through his arms and his hams, as a brace.

The corporal shoved him with his foot until he came to rest on his side, and before he swung his whip the band started right off playing the "turkey trot" so that they wouldn't hear the cries of the man they were "skinning."

One lash, two lashes, three lashes. The soldiers in the company groaned at each stroke, but the screams of the one being punished could not be heard because the band was playing the trot without stopping and as loud as possible. The black boy, Hilario, was humming it.

"Tara rara rarah, the turkey."

"Tara rara rarah, the gobbler."

Before turning him on his other side to continue, they threw a bucket of salt water on the flayed cheek.

Corporal Cirguelo swung his whip. Now you could hardly hear the groans of the punished soldier.

"Tara rara rarah, the turkey."

Now he couldn't get the catchy tune of the "turkey trot" out of his head. Corporal Cirguelo wore long sideburns and had a gold-capped tooth. He must still be there at the barracks in Caucagua.

Next morning the search party would come to take him. They would put him on a boat on the river. Without untying his hands. They would land him ashore again. When they passed by the houses the people would come out to see him.

"It's a deserter they're taking in."

They would enter Caucagua. Late in the afternoon. Through the back street. They would go by the Islander's general store. And there, around the corner, was the camp. And there, at the door or outside, corporal Cirguelo would no doubt be waiting.

There was a lot of walking to do. Before they got there. They had to take him out of here. Go down the river to the coast. Spend the morning. Time to sleep in the boat. To see, from the bottom where he would be lying, the treetops turning over in the sky. Tie up again. People would come to the river-bank. It would be very late afternoon. And the questions would begin again.

"How did they catch him?"

"Where was he hiding?"

"Did the search party find him?"

And that word that they were going to repeat, were repeating just as he had been repeating it so many times: The skinning. They're going to skin him. He can't get out of the skinning. One hundred lashes. Ah good skinning. Two hundred lashes on each cheek. A skinning for a complete man. Corporal Cirguelo's gold-capped tooth. Tara, rara, rarah, the turkey.

He couldn't get that out of his head from the time he ran away from camp. From the time he had seen that other deserter flogged. From the time he had seen them pick him up sagging and wobbly as a rag-doll effigy of Judas.

And now, lying on the floor of the cell he felt so helpless, without any strength. He wouldn't be able to resist the blows. He wouldn't even be able to resist half of them. One, sang the corporal. Two. Three. The first ones burned like a live coal. Then the bleeding would begin. And then it was as if they were tearing off strips of flesh little by little. Then it began to hurt inside. Thirty, Thirty-one. Along his guts. His spleen. His lungs. Sixty-six. Sixty-seven. And that's where the groaning started. Where they stayed on. Where they went away. Where they began to feel numb.

The brick on which his cheek rested was hot now. He dragged himself farther along the ground until he lay on a cool piece of floor. Everything was still dark and quiet. He started to listen. Not even the wind was going by now. But somewhere in the distance a dog had barked.

Far beyond the guardhouse, the building, the square. The barking came from somewhere outside the village. Somewhere near the river. The forest. The night. The solitude.

"Oh damn."

The barking was coming from the forest. Who could ever catch him now if he were there again. He used to hear the dogs barking far away like that whenever he peered out of the bushes on a slope and saw a farm in a clearing on a little hill. Hunger brought him out of the forest at night. He had learned to walk noiselessly and stop to listen like the deer. To cock his ear into the wind. Sometimes he heard something, would hide in a cluster of corn, and see the men in the search party going by with machetes, guns, and blankets slung diagonally across chest and shoulder.

When a dog scented him and barked, he had to stop. He would lose sight of the farm again and go back into the forest. He ate guavas and roots. Sometimes he got dizzy from hunger. Sometimes he managed to approach a farm without a dog's barking, grabbed everything there was to eat on the stove, and scampered away.

He had never actually gone far from the village. If he appeared some-where else, where he was a stranger, they could discover him. He kept on foraging through the woods near the waterfalls. He would look at the river from a distance. The Tuy rolled along quietly. Sometimes a canoe passed and he recognized some of the peons from where he was.

"Oh damn."

Sometimes, after drinking on his stomach at the river's edge, he released a dry leaf to see it go down the current and remained watching it in a sort of daze until the cry of a *guacharo* in the forest or the babble of a flock of parrots crossing the sky shook him out of it.

He could see the village from certain points. The saman trees in the square, the church, Headquarters, the long street. People at the door of the general store. If he were there where his eyes were, where that man was, leaning against the door. Wouldn't that cause a stir!

"Wow. Here's Hilario."

"The deserter."

"Grab him!"

But he was far off among those trees where the wind made noise. At night all you could see were the lights flickering in the darkness. The village seemed farther away and smaller.

He hadn't kept track of how long he had been in the forest. He was becoming thinner. His skin was getting lighter. He was changing from black to a greenish color, like the alligator's tail. He was less nimble as he walked. He got tired faster when he climbed. He lost his breath and had to rest awhile. Doubled over, breathing hard, he would sit there looking at his feet and hands. They were bonier and more skinny. The palms of his hands were purplish and his nails yellow. There were nights when he didn't have the strength to go near the farms. He would stay under a tree, chattering with the cold. All that was left of his trousers were rags. But it was very cold. If he heard a sound, he was too weak to get up. It could be an animal. It could be a search party. If it was the search party they would capture him. He didn't have the will to resist or even listen. He would remain there for a while, worried, waiting, but the sound was not repeated and he sighed, at ease.

Instead of going farther away, the more ill and weaker he felt, he kept coming closer to town. Every once in a while he would think, "If they catch me now, I won't be able to resist the whip. I won't survive the whip."

But something inside him made him feel that distant, inevitable thing that kept coming dangerously closer.

On two or three occasions, he had gone so far as to follow the riverbank up to the first houses in town. He had even dared sneak into a yard to steal a piece of beef hanging out to dry in the sun.

Someday they would catch him. If it pleased God.

"Oh damn!"

He neither sleeps nor stays awake. He feels the floor turning warm under his body. His whole body throbbing without stopping, on the bricks. A cold tickling sensation in his hands, strangled by the rope behind his back. His bones aching with the sweet pain of a fever. He closes his eyes hard in order to sleep. Vague sparks pass through them. Red spots, rushing through. His pulse keeps on knocking and shaking him without relief.

Prrrm. Prrrrrm. Prrrrrmpumpum. Prrrrrmpumpum. Pum. Pumpum. Like the drum. Sometimes clear like the tenor, sometimes thick and husky like the bass. Like the drum.

Even from the river he could already hear it like that. From the time he started to sneak nearer, in the shadow of the first houses. He hadn't heard the drum for a long time. All he had heard was the sound of the branches, dogs barking, the songs of birds. But not the hot beat of the drum. As he crouched low, hiding, he beat on the ground with his foot and his hand. Dum, dum, dum dum, dum dum. It was like a hot wave of water going around his body.

He was near the lights in the square now and he heard the heavy rhythm of the steps. The shadow of the blacks moved as one solid mass. The lights seemed to go up and down under the branches of the saman trees.

Under the protection of a wall he has drawn near the square. Something like a feverish tremor carries him along with the drum. Everything sounds inside and outside his head like the drumskin pounded by the black fists. He is all worked up. Everything comes and goes with the drum. Women. Lights. The names of things. His own name which calls and calls him without stopping.

Hilario, it says. Hilario, it repeats. Hilario, the drum. Hilario the shadows. Hilario, Hilarito, Hilarion. Larito, larion. Larito, ito, ito, ito. The rhythm resounds. Everything makes him shake. Sounds and resounds. Booms in the darkness. Booms.

Everything staggers. Tum tum. Tum tum. Hilario staggers. So much darkness. So much night. So much drumming. The drum keeps time in the darkness. Hilario trembles. Hilario shuffles. So many women are shaking in the darkness. Hilario, Hilarito, Hilarion.

Leaping shadows moved past him. They and the drum and the square and the lights. He was in their midst. The rhythm beat in his bones and his eyes. Panting mouths and clouded eyes went by.

And that woman in front of him, brought, carried by the drumbeat. Shaking together with him. Bound to him. Beat together with him.

"Yeah! Yeah! Yeah!"

"Wow, Soledad, we're dancing together!"

"Wow, Hilario, you're back!"

And that's where he felt him coming. Felt his footsteps without seeing him. He could distinguish his footsteps between the drumbeats. Ño Gaspar's steps. The heavy, solid, sure step. He recognized his step without turning his head.

He could count them. One. A moment went by. Two. He was coming closer. All you could hear was the footstep of Ño Gaspar the provost marshal. You couldn't hear the drum or the dance. All you could hear was that footstep.

The door squeaked. His eyes were open. From the brick floor he noticed the cell filled with the ashes of dawn and, in the doorway, tall and broad, Ño Gaspar, and behind Ño Gaspar the faces, the blankets, the guns, and the machetes of the men in the search party.

5

JUAN CARLOS ONETTI

Despite his obvious professionalism, Juan Carlos Onetti experienced vast and protracted difficulties in achieving the recognition he deserved. This notwithstanding the fact that he did all the right things: in the early forties he left provincial Montevideo and went to work in Buenos Aires; he had practically all his books issued by leading Argentine publishers, and nearly always dedicated them to influential people; he never missed an important literary competition, and was always available to a small and select group of followers who wrote constantly about him. And yet, he lived for nearly fifteen years in Latin America's most important literary center as if under a curse of invisibility. His books failed to attract notice; in competitions, he always got second prize or perhaps honorable mention, never top honors. He was past fifty when at last the curse seemed to lift, and all over Latin America the best writers began to discover him. Today he stands as one of the acknowledged masters of the new novel. Overall, however, his career has been as marked by frustration and disappointment as the lives of his forlorn characters. One is tempted to see it as designed by a God who shares Onetti's own distinctly black sense of humor.

He was born in Montevideo in 1909, of mixed Brazilian and Uruguayan origins. He amuses himself by supposing that his family is of Irish descent and that the name was originally spelled "O'Nety"; his putative Irish ancestor is alleged to have come from Gibraltar to Uruguay in the 1850s, at a time of fierce civil war. Perhaps it is this ethnic background (or at least his belief in it) that was responsible for Onetti's early interest in British and North American literature.

Onetti never completed secondary school and spent his adolescence and early youth in odd jobs such as night porter, waiter, and ticket-seller at the National Soccer Stadium. Although he began to write rather early, he took his time about publishing his work. He lived in Buenos Aires from 1930 to 1934, where he tried to support himself through writing movie reviews and publishing a few short stories. But he failed to make a living, and returned to Montevideo.

In 1939, Onetti joined the staff of a new weekly, *Marcha,* which was to become the most influential of its kind in Latin America. He headed the magazine's literature section until he moved again to Buenos Aires in 1941. This time he remained for fourteen years, working at a news agency and for various periodicals, while publishing four more novels (his first had appeared earlier, in 1939) and a handful of short stories, and finding himself generally ignored by Argentine intellectual circles. Since his return to Montevideo in 1955, he has worked for several newspapers, as well as the city government. He has published two more novels and several volumes of short stories, and is currently at work on another novel.

As a writer, Onetti belongs among the literary progeny of Dostoevsky. His central concern has always been with the absurdities of human existence, with the sadomasochistic games human beings play with themselves and others, with defeat, corruption, death. But whereas in Dostoevsky there also exist more affirmative possibilities, such as the visionary faith embodied in certain characters, in Onetti the only stance permitted seems to be a kind of hopeless defiance. His protagonists are always scapegoats—the *pharmakoi* of Greek tragedy—but obsessed with a lost, disintegrated Christian faith; Onetti peoples his novels with the "insulted and injured," but strictly excludes the Alyoshas and Myshkins. In him the influence of Dostoevsky has been modified by a generous dose of avant-garde nihilism, and especially by the desperate cynicism of Louis Ferdinand Céline's *Voyage to the End of the Night.*

From this work Onetti also learned how to make literary use of a street vernacular, which in his own case was the distinctive River Plate slang—the invention of a polyglot lumpenproletariat made up of poor Spaniards and Italians, a few Jews from Central Europe, and assorted pimps and whores from southern France. It proved to be an extraordinarily effective instrument for the expression of anger, resentment, and hopelessness. It was the product of a society of immigrants who had failed to discover El Dorado and instead found themselves thrown into the squalid tenements of Buenos Aires and Montevideo, facing the muddy River Plate. Some tango lyrics and music-hall songs had earlier captured the *Angst* of these lost souls before the Argentine Roberto Arlt in the thirties used the slang with devastating effect to present a picture of the Buenos Aires of his time. The work of Onetti represented a continuation and consummation of that of Arlt.

Onetti's deep involvement with the embittered, frustrated souls in his charge was matched by his concern with problems of technique—with narrative structure, with point of view, with the production of a totally coherent fictional world. The novels he published before 1950 reflected this exploration of expressive possibilities. The first, *The Pit* (1939), was a short, lyrical, and cynical account of some masturbatory fantasies of the protagonist. The second, *No Man's Land* (1941), presented a calculatedly distorted picture of Buenos Aires using a technique similar to that adopted by Dos Passos in *Manhattan Transfer*, though Onetti's vision was less conventional. The third novel, *Deadline: Tonight* (1943), was a hallucinatory portrayal of a besieged city, based on tales and anecdotes Onetti had heard from refugees of the Spanish civil war. The presiding influence here was Faulkner; the atmosphere and feeling were totally River Plate, despite Onetti's efforts at Spanish local color.

It was with his fourth novel, *The Short Life* (1950), that Onetti truly began to emerge as one of the masters of the new Latin American narrative. This long, morose, complex work presents the adventures and experiences of its protagonist at three different levels of reality. In everyday life he is a modest Buenos Aires workingman. But in his imagination he assumes two other identities: that of a pimp next door, which he enacts with some success, and that of a doctor in an imaginary small town called Santa María. The narrative switches smoothly back and forth from one level to the next. At the end, the unexpected happens: the protagonist becomes involved in a murder and takes refuge in Santa María.

In this novel, Onetti successfully applied in a long narrative the themes and techniques used by Borges in his short fiction (selection 1), and the book prefigured not only Onetti's works to come but also Adolfo Bioy Casares's *The Dream of Heroes*, Julio Cortázar's *Hopscotch*, and Ernesto Sabato's *About Heroes and Tombs* (Part Five, 3, 4, 5).

For Onetti, *The Short Life* was the beginning of a whole cycle of novels and tales that came to be known collectively as the "Santa María Saga." With a Faulknerian sense of the intricacies of cyclical narrative, he developed a group of characters whose destinies cross and recross each other in the most unexpected patterns. The best books of the cycle are *The Shipyard* (1961), which records the final struggle against fate of Junta Larsen, the most promethean of Onetti's *pharmakoi;* and *The Bodysnatcher* (1964), which relates in a mock-heroic tone an earlier adventure of the same Junta: the time he attempted to run a brothel of weary whores in Santa María.

Perhaps the best short story of the cycle is the first of the two presented here. Its central figure is an old wrestler, engaged in a desperate struggle to preserve a measure of dignity in a corrupt and wretched world. The title, "Jacob and the Other," alludes to the Biblical story of Jacob wrestling with the angel, and, more broadly, to the theme of the endless night battle within every human being. The story was presented to the important international competition organized in 1960 by *Life*. True to form, it won only an honorable mention from the Latin American jury—hardly very rewarding for a writer of fifty-one. Like his protagonists, it would seem, Onetti is a *pharmakos.*

In the second story, "A Dream Come True," Onetti offers yet another version of the *pharmakos*. A middle-aged woman hires a disreputable stage director to help her to dramatize a dream she once had—a dream in which inexplicably, for the first time, she found herself happy. Here the author uses the same device carried to perfection in "Jacob and the Other": the unreliable narrator, the observer who tells everything and understands almost nothing. Only at the very end does the narrator realize the true nature of the woman's longing, her search for a mystical, transcendent happiness.

Set within the sordid small-town milieu of practically all his tales and novels, the story reveals the range of Onetti's obsessions and concerns. It was written in the forties, after *The Pit* and before *The Short Life*, and centers on the same type of protagonist, who suffers life as a tragic fate and escapes from it only in dream and imagination. That experience, that suffering, Onetti subtly implies, is very likely shared by the reader, another character obsessed by dreams.

In its corrosive humor, its compassionate approach to the human predicament, and its elaborate, almost solemn narrative style, "A Dream Come True" is a highly characteristic and effective expression of Onetti's despairing, yet somehow naïve vision of the world. It is a superb embodiment in little of his art.

Jacob and the Other

From "Jacob y el otro," translated by Izaak A. Langnas, in Prize Stories from Latin America (Garden City: Doubleday, 1963), pp. 319–59.

The Doctor's Story

Half the town must have been present last night at the Apollo Cinema, seeing the thing and participating in the tumultuous finale. I was having a boring time at the club's poker table and intervened only when the porter gave me an urgent message from the hospital. The club has only one telephone line, but by the time I left the booth everybody knew more about the news than I. I returned to the table to cash my chips and to pay my losses.

Burmestein hadn't moved. He sucked at his cigar a little more and told me in his smooth and unctuous voice, "Forgive me, but if I were you, I'd stay and exploit your lucky streak. After all, you can just as well sign the death certificate here!"

"Not yet, it seems," I replied and tried to laugh. I looked at my hands as they handled the chips and the money: they were calm, rather tired. I had slept barely a couple of hours the previous night, but that had already become almost a habit; I had drunk two cognacs tonight and mineral water with my dinner.

The people at the hospital knew my car and remembered all its diseases. And so an ambulance was waiting for me at the club entrance. I sat down next to the Galician driver and heard only his greeting: he remained silent—out of respect or emotion—and waited for me to begin the conversation. I started smoking and did not speak until we turned the Tabarez curve and the ambulance entered the spring night of the cement highway, white and windy, cool and mild, with disorderly clouds grazing the mill and the high trees.

"Herminio," I asked him, "what is the diagnosis?"

I saw the joy the Galician was trying to conceal and imagined the inward sigh with which he celebrated this return to the habitual, to the old sacred rites. He started talking, in his most humble and astute tones. I realized that the case was serious or lost.

"I barely saw him, doctor. I lifted him from the theater into the ambulance and took him to the hospital at ninety or a hundred because young Fernández was telling me to hurry and also because it was my duty. I helped to take him out, and right away they ordered me to fetch you at the club."

"Fernández, hm. But who is on duty?"

"Doctor Rius, doctor."

"Why doesn't Rius operate?" I asked him, raising my voice.

"Well," Herminio replied and took his time avoiding a puddle full of bright water, "he must have got ready to operate at once, I say. But if he has you at his side. . . ."

"You loaded and unloaded him. That's enough. What's the diagnosis?"

"What a doctor!" the Galician exclaimed with an affectionate smile. We were beginning to see the lights of the hospital, the whiteness of its walls under the moon. "He didn't move or moan, he started to swell like a balloon, ribs in the lung, a shinbone laid bare, almost certain concussion. But he hit a couple of chairs with his back when he fell and, if you forgive my opinion, it's the backbone that'll decide. Whether it's broken or not."

"Will he die or won't he? You've never been wrong, Herminio." (He had been wrong many times, but always with some good excuse.)

"This time I won't talk," he said, shaking his head as he braked.

I changed clothes and was starting to wash my hands when Rius came in.

"If you want to operate," he said, "I'll have everything ready in two minutes. I've done little or nothing so far because there's nothing to be done. Morphine, of course, to keep him—and us—quiet. And if you want to know where to start, I'd advise you to toss a coin."

"Is there that much?"

"Multiple trauma, deep coma, pallor, filiform, pulse, great polypnoea, cyanosis. The right hemithorax doesn't breathe. Collapsed. Crepitation and angulation of the sixth rib on the right. Dullness in the right pulmonary base with hypersonority in the pulmonary apex. The coma is getting deeper all the time, and the syndrome of acute anemia is becoming accentuated. Is that enough? I would leave him in peace."

It was then that I resorted to my worn-out phrase of mediocre heroicity, to the legend that surrounds me as the lettering of a coin or medal encircles a portrait, and which may possibly stick to my name some years after my death. But that night I was no longer twenty-five or thirty; I was old and tired, and the phrase so often repeated was, to Rius, no more than a familiar joke. I said it with a nostalgia for my lost faith, as I was putting on my gloves. I repeated it and heard myself saying it, like a child that pronounces an absurd magical formula that gives him permission to enter a game or stay in it: "My patients die on the table."

Rius laughed as usual, gave my arm a friendly squeeze, and left. But almost immediately, as I was trying to locate a damaged pipe that leaked into the washbasins, he looked in again to tell me:

"There's a piece missing in the picture I gave you, my friend. I didn't tell you about the woman. I don't know who she is, she kicked or tried to kick the 'corpse-to-be' in the movie theater and then pushed her way to the ambulance to spit at him as the Galician and Fernández were putting him in. I was on duty there and had her thrown out; but she swore she'd come back tomorrow because she had a right to see the dead man—maybe to spit on him at leisure."

I worked with Rius till five in the morning and then sent out for a container of coffee to help us wait. At seven, Fernández came into the office with the suspicious face that God makes him put on to confront important events. On such occasions, his narrow and childish face turns his eyes into slits, leans forward a little, and says through his watchful mouth, "Somebody's robbing me and life is nothing but a conspiracy to cheat me."

He moved toward the table and remained there standing, white and twisted, without a word.

Rius stopped tinkering with the grafts, did not look at him, and grabbed the last sandwich from the plate. Then he wiped his lips with a napkin and asked of the iron inkpot, with its eagle and its two dried-up inkholes, "Already?"

Fernández breathed audibly and put a hand on the table. We turned our heads and saw his suspicion and his confusion, his thinness and his weariness. Idiotized by lack of food and sleep, the boy drew himself up to remain true to his mania for changing the order of things, of the world in which we can understand one another.

"The woman is in the corridor, sitting on a bench, with a thermos and a maté gourd. They forgot all about her and let her in. She says she doesn't mind waiting, she must see him. That man."

"Yes, my boy," Rius said slowly, and I recognized in his voice the malignity that comes of nights of fatigue, the needling that he administers so skillfully. "Did she bring flowers, at least? Winter is over and every ditch of Santa María must be full of *yuyos*. I'd like to push her face in, and I'll ask the chief's permission in a moment for a trip around the corridors. But meanwhile that mare of a woman can visit the body, throw it a flower, spit on it, and throw it another flower."

I was the chief, and so I asked, "What happened?"

Fernández gave a fleeting caress to his lean face, discovered without too much exertion that it contained all the bones promised him by his reading of Testut, and then looked at me as if I were responsible for all the tricks and deceits that jumped out of nowhere to surprise him with mysterious regularity. He discarded Rius without hatred and without violence, kept his suspicious eyes glued to my face and recited, "Improved pulse, respiration, and cyanosis. Sporadically recovers consciousness."

This was much better than I had expected to hear at seven in the morning. But I couldn't be quite sure yet, and so I just thanked him with a nod and took my turn looking at the bronzed eagle of the inkstand.

"Dimas arrived a while ago," Fernández said. "I gave him all the details. May I go?"

"Yes, of course." Rius had thrown himself against the back of his armchair and looked at me with the beginning of a smile. Perhaps he had never seen me so old, perhaps he had never loved me as much as he did that spring morning—or maybe he was trying to find out who I was and why he loved me.

"No, my friend," he said when we were alone again. "With me you can play any farce you like—but not the farce of modesty, of indifference, the kind of garbage that's put into sober words like: 'I have once again only done my duty.' Well, chief, you did it. If that animal hasn't croaked yet, it won't. They advised you at the club to do nothing but sign his death certificate—that's what I would have done, with a lot of morphine, of course, if you hadn't happened to be in Santa María—and now I advise you to give that character a certificate of immortality. With a quiet conscience and with a signature endorsed by Doctor Rius. Do it, chief. And then steal yourself a sleeping-pill cocktail from the lab and go to sleep for twenty-four hours. I'll take care of the judge and the police. I also promise you to take care of the spitting sessions of the lady who's stoking up on maté in the corridor."

He got up and shook my hand, only once, but pausing to transmit the weight and the warmth of his own.

"Okay," I told him. "You'll decide if it's necessary to wake me."

While removing my surgical gown, with a slowness and dignity not entirely produced by weariness, I admitted to myself that the success of the operation, of all operations for that matter, mattered to me as much as the fulfillment of an old and unrealizable dream of mine: to repair my old car with my own hands—and forever. But I couldn't tell this to Rius because he would understand without effort and with enthusiasm; nor could I tell it to Fernández because, fortunately, he could never believe me.

So I kept my mouth shut and, on the way back in the ambulance, heard out with equanimity the clumsily put praises of the Galician Herminio. With my silence, I accepted before history that the resurrection that had just occurred at the Santa María Hospital could not have been achieved by the doctors of the capital itself.

I decided that my car could spend another night outside the club and made the ambulance take me home. The morning, furiously white, smelled of honeysuckle, and there was already a breath of the river in the air.

"They threw stones and said they'd burn the theater down," the Gali-cian said when we reached the plaza. "But the police came and they only threw stones, as I've already told you."

Before taking my pills I realized that I could never know the whole truth of that story. With patience and luck on my side I might find out half of it, the half that concerned the people of the town. But I had to resign myself to the fact that the other half would remain forever out of my reach. It was brought here by the two strangers who would, in their different ways, carry it out again, forever unknown.

At that very moment, with the glass of water in my hand, I recalled that I had first got involved in this story a week earlier, on a warm and cloudy Sunday, while I was watching people coming and going on the plaza from a window of the hotel bar.

The lively, charming man and the moribund giant made their way diagonally across the plaza and the first yellowish sunlight of spring. The smaller of the two was carrying a wreath, the little wreath of a distant relative for a modest wake. They advanced indifferent to the curiosity aroused by the slow beast nearly six and a half feet tall: unhurried but resolute, the lively one marched along with an inherent dignity, as if he were flanked by soldiers in gala uniform and some high personage and a stand, decorated with flags and filled with solemn men and old women, were expecting him. The word spread that they had laid the wreath at the foot of the Brausen monument, to the accompaniment of children's jeers and a few stones.

From then on, the tracks became somewhat tangled. The smaller man, the ambassador, went into the Berne to rent a room, to take an apéritif, and to discuss prices without passion, lifting his hat to anyone in sight and offering deep bows and cheap invitations. He was about forty to forty-five, of medium height, broad-chested; he had been born to convince, to create the mild and humid climate in which friendship flourishes and hopes are born. He had also been born for happiness, or at least for obstinately believing in happiness, against all odds, against life itself and its errors. He had been born, above all and most important of all, to impose quotas of happiness on all possible kinds of people. And all this with a natural and invincible shrewdness, never neglecting his personal purposes or worrying unduly over the uncontrollable future of others.

At noon he called at the editorial offices of *El Liberal*. He returned in the afternoon to see the people from the sports section and get some free publicity. He unwrapped a scrapbook of yellowing photographs and newspaper cuttings, with big headlines in foreign languages, and exhibited diplomas and documents reinforced at the edges with Scotch tape. He made his smile, his unwearying and uncompromising love, float above the ancient memories, the passing years, melancholy, and failure.

"Right now he's better than ever. Maybe he weighs a kilo or two more. This is, of course, why we're on this grand tour of South America. Next year, at the Palais de Glace, he'll regain his title. Nobody can beat him, in Europe or in America. And how could we possibly skip Santa María on a tour that is a prologue to a world championship? Ah, Santa María! What a coast, what a beach, what air, what culture!"

His voice had an Italian tone, but not exactly. There was always, in his vowels and his *s*'s, a sound that could not be localized, a friendly contact with the complicated surface of the globe. He traversed the newspaper building from top to bottom, played with the linotypes, hugged the typesetters, improvised astonishment while standing under the rotary press. The next day he obtained his first headline, cool but unpaid: FORMER WORLD WRESTLING CHAMPION IN SANTA MARÍA. He called at the editorial office every night of the week, and the space devoted to Jacob van Oppen grew bigger every day, until the Saturday of the challenge and the fight.

At noon that Sunday when I saw them parading across the plaza, the moribund giant spent half an hour in church, kneeling before the new altar of the Immaculate Conception. They say he went to confession, and some people swear they saw him beating his chest—presumably before he emerged and hesitatingly pushed his enormous baby face, wet with tears, into the gilded light outside the church.

The Narrator's Story

The visiting cards read: "Comendatore Orsini," and the restless and talkative man handed them out, generously, all over town. A few are still preserved, some decorated with autographs and adjectives.

From that first—and last—Sunday, Orsini rented the hall of the Apollo Cinema for training sessions, with a peso admission charged on Monday and Tuesday, half a peso on Wednesday, and two pesos on Thursday and Friday, when the challenge was picked up and the curiosity and the local patriotism of Santa María began to fill the Apollo. It was that Sunday, too, that the announcement of the challenge was posted on the new plaza, with proper permission from the municipal authorities. On an old photograph, the former World Wrestling Champion of All Weights exhibited his biceps and his gold belt, while aggressive red letters spelled out the challenge: 500 PESOS 500 to whoever enters the ring and is not pinned by Jacob van Oppen in three minutes.

Just a line below the challenge was forgotten; an announcement promised exhibition bouts of Greco-Roman wrestling between the world champion —he would regain his title within a year—and the best athletes of Santa María.

Orsini and the giant had entered South America through Colombia and were now descending it by way of Peru, Ecuador, and Bolivia. The challenge had been picked up in only a few places, and the giant could always dispose of it in a matter of seconds, with the first clinch.

The posters evoked nights of heat and noise, theaters and big tents, audiences composed mostly of Indians and drunks, shouts of admiration, and laughter. The referee lifted his arm, van Oppen went back to his sadness and thought anxiously of the bottle of rotgut waiting in his hotel room, as Orsini was making his smiling progress under the white lights of the ring, drying his forehead with a handkerchief that was even whiter.

"Ladies and gentlemen . . ."—this was the moment for giving thanks, for talking of unforgettable memories, for shouting *vivas!* to the country and to the city. For months now these memories were forming for the two of them an image of South America: sometime, some night, within a year, when they already would be far away, they would be able to recall it without difficulty, with the aid of only three or four repeated moments of devotion.

On Tuesday or Wednesday Orsini took the champion in his car to the Berne, after an almost deserted training session. The tour had become a routine, and estimates of pesos to be earned differed little from pesos actually earned. But Orsini still felt he had to keep the giant under his wing, for mutual benefit. Van Oppen sat down on the bed and drank from the bottle; Orsini gently took it away from him and fetched from the bathroom the plastic glass he used to give his dentures a morning rinse. And he repeated, in friendship, the old cliché: "No morality without discipline." He spoke French as he spoke Spanish; his accent was never definitely Italian. "The bottle is here and nobody wants to steal it from you. But drinking with a glass makes all the difference. There is discipline, there is chivalry."

The giant turned his head to look at him: his blue eyes were turbid and he seemed to see instead with his half-opened mouth. "Dysnoea again, black anguish," thought Orsini. "Best for him to get drunk and sleep it off till tomorrow." He filled the glass with rum, took a swallow, and stretched out his hand to van Oppen. But the beast bent down to take off his shoes and then—second symptom—got up and examined the room. First, with his hands in his belt, he looked at the beds, the useless floor rug, the table, and the ceiling; then he walked around to test with his shoulder the resistance of the doors leading to the corridor and the bathroom, and of the window with the blocked view.

"Now it's starting all over again," Orsini continued. "Last time it was in Guayaquil. It must be a cyclical affair, but I don't understand the cycle. Some night he'll strangle me and not because he hates me—but just because I happen to be at hand. He knows, surely he knows, that I am his only friend."

The barefoot giant slowly returned to the center of the room. His shoulders were bent slightly forward and his face wore a sneering and contemptuous smile. Orsini sat down at the flimsy table and dipped his tongue into the glass of rum.

"*Gott,*" said van Oppen and began to sway as if he were listening to some distant and interrupted music. He wore the black knitted shirt, too tight for him, and the *vaquero* pants Orsini had bought him in Quito. "No. Where am I? What am I doing here?" With his enormous feet gripping the floor, he moved his body and stared at the wall above Orsini's head.

"I'm waiting. Always I find myself in a hotel room in a land of stinking niggers and always waiting. Gimme the glass. I'm not afraid; for that's the worst thing about it—nobody ever comes."

Orsini filled the glass and rose to give it to him. He examined his face, the hysteria in his voice, touched his moving shoulder. "Not yet," he thought. "But almost."

The giant emptied the glass and coughed without bending his head.

"Nobody," he said. "Footwork. Flexions. Holds. Lewis. To Lewis!—at least he was a man and lived like one. Gymnastics is not a man, wrestling is not a man, all this is not a man. A hotel room, a gymnasium, filthy Indians. It's pure hell, Orsini."

Orsini made another calculation and rose again with the rum bottle. He filled the glass van Oppen was clutching to his belly and passed his hand over the giant's shoulder and cheek.

"Nobody," said van Oppen. "Nobody!" he shouted. His eyes turned desperate, then raging. But he emptied the glass with a wise and merry smile.

"Now," thought Orsini. He grabbed the bottle and started pushing against the giant's thigh with his hip, to guide him toward the bath.

"A few more months, a few weeks," thought Orsini. "And then it's over. They'll all come later and we will be with them. We'll go to the other side."

Sprawling on the bed, the giant drank from the bottle and snorted, shaking his head. Orsini lit the table lamp and turned off the ceiling light. He sat down again at the table, adjusted his voice, and sang gently:

> *"Vor der Kaserne*
> *vor dem grossen Tor*
> *steht eine Laterne*
> *Und steht sie noch davor*
> *wenn wir uns einmal wierdersehen,*
> *bei der Laterne wollen wir stehen*
> *wie einst, Lilli Marlene*
> *wie einst, Lilli Marlen."*

He sang the whole song and was halfway through it again when van Oppen put the bottle on the floor and started crying. Then Orsini got up with a sigh and an affectionate insult and walked on tiptoe to the door and the passage. And as on nights of glory he descended the Berne staircase, drying his forehead with a spotless handkerchief.

He walked downstairs without meeting anyone on whom he could bestow a smile or a lift of his hat; but his face remained affable, on guard. The woman, who had waited for hours with determination and without impatience, was sunk in the leather armchair of the lobby, paying no attention to the magazines on the low table and smoking one cigarette after another. She got up and confronted him. Prince Orsini had no escape, nor was he looking for one. He heard his name, raised his hat to the lady, and bent down to kiss her hand. He wondered what favor he could grant her and was ready to grant her whatever she requested. She was small, intrepid, and young. Her complexion was quite dark, her small nose hooked, her eyes very bright and cold. "Jewish or something like that," thought Orsini. "She's pretty." Suddenly the prince heard a language so concise as to be almost incomprehensible, unheard of.

"That poster in the plaza, the ads in the paper. Five hundred pesos. My fiancé will fight the champion. But today or tomorrow, that's Wednesday, you'll have to deposit the money at the Bank or *El Liberal.*"

"Signorina," the prince said with a smile and swayed with a disconsolate gesture, "fight the champion? You'll lose your fiancé. And I would be so sad to see a pretty young lady like you . . ."

But she, looking even smaller and more determined, effortlessly defied the gallantry of a man in his fifties.

"Tonight I'll go to *El Liberal* to take up the challenge. I saw the champion at Mass. He's old. We need the five hundred pesos to get married. My fiancé is twenty and I'm twenty-two. He owns the Porfilio store. Come and see him."

"But señorita," said the prince with a wider smile. "Your fiancé, a fortunate man if you'll permit me to say so, is twenty. What has he done so far? Buying and selling."

"He has also lived in the country."

"The country," the prince hummed the word with ecstasy. "But the champion has dedicated his whole life to this, to fighting. What if he is a few years older than your fiancé? I fully agree, señorita."

"Thirty, at least," she said. She felt no need to smile, relying on the coldness of her eyes. "I saw him."

"But these were the years he devoted to learning how to break, without an effort, arms and ribs, how to remove, gently, a collarbone from its proper place, how to dislocate a leg. And since you have a fiancé of twenty, and healthy . . ."

"You issued a challenge. Five hundred pesos for three minutes. I'll go to *El Liberal* tonight, Mr. . . ."

"Prince Orsini," said the prince.

She nodded her head, without wasting any time for sneers. She was small, compact, pretty, and hard as iron.

"I am happy for Santa María," the prince smiled and bowed. "It will be a great sporting spectacle. But you, señorita, are you going to the newspaper in the name of your fiancé?"

"Yes, he gave me a paper. Go and see him. The Porfilio store. They call him the Turk. But he's a Syrian. He has the document."

The prince understood that it wouldn't be right to kiss her hand again.

"Well," he joked. "First a spinster, then a widow. After Saturday. A very sad destiny, señorita."

She offered him her hand and walked toward the hotel door. She was hard as a lance and had barely enough charm to make the prince look at her back. Suddenly she stopped and returned.

"A spinster, no, because with these five hundred pesos we'll get married. A widow neither, because that champion of yours is very old. He's bigger than Mario but could never beat him. I saw him."

"Agreed. You saw him leaving the church after Mass. But I assure you that when things really get going he becomes a wild beast and I swear to you that he knows his trade. World Champion of All Weights, señorita."

"Well," she repeated with a sudden weariness. "As I told you, the Porfilio Brothers store. Tonight I'll go to *El Liberal;* but you will find me tomorrow, as always, at the store."

"Señorita. . . ." He kissed her hand again.

The woman was clearly looking for a deal. And so Orsini went to the restaurant and ordered a dish of meat and spaghetti. Later he worked on his accounts and, sucking at his gold-ringed cigarette mouthpiece, kept a watch on the sleep, grunts, and movements of Jacob van Oppen.

About to fall asleep above the silence of the plaza, he granted himself a twenty-four hours' vacation. It wasn't advisable to hurry his visit to the Turk. Moreover, as he put it to himself while turning off the light and interpreting the snores of the giant, "I have suffered enough, O Lord; we have suffered enough. I see no reason for hurry."

The next day Orsini took care of the champion's awakening, brought him aspirins and hot water. He listened with satisfaction to van Oppen's curses under the shower and observed with joy the transformation of his rude noises into an almost submarine version of *Ich hatte einen Kameraden.* Like all other men, he decided to lie, to lie to himself and to trust his luck. He organized van Oppen's morning, the slow walk through the town, his enormous torso covered by the knitted woolen sweater bearing in front a giant blue *C,* the letter which spelled out—in all alphabets and in all languages—the words WORLD WRESTLING CHAM-PION OF ALL WEIGHTS. Orsini accompanied him, at a lively step, as far as the streets that descended toward the Promenade. There, for the benefit of the few curious onlookers of eight o'clock in the morning, he repeated a scene from the old farce. He stopped to raise his hat and wipe his forehead, to smile like a good loser, and to give Jacob van Oppen a pat on the back.

"What a man!" he murmured to no one in particular. His head turned away, his arms lowered, his mouth snapping for air, repeated for the benefit of all of Santa María, "What a man!"

Van Oppen kept walking toward the Promenade at the same moderate speed, his shoulders hunched toward the future, his jaw hanging. Then he took the street to the cannery and braved the astonishment of fishermen, loafers, and ferry employees: he was too big for anyone to make fun of him.

But the sneers, though never spoken aloud, hovered all around Orsini that day, around his clothes, his manners, his inadequate education. However, he had made a bet with himself to be happy that day, and so only good and pleasant things could get through to him. He held what he would later call press confer-ences at the offices of *El Liberal,* at the Berne, and at the Plaza; he drank and chatted with the curious and the idle, told anecdotes and atrocious lies, exhibited once again his yellowing and fragile press cuttings. There had been a time, no doubt about it, when things really were that way: van Oppen, world champion, young, with an irresistible bolt grip, with tours that were not exiles, besieged by offers that could be rejected. The words and pictures in the newspapers, though discolored and outdated, tenaciously refused to become ashes and offered irrefutable proofs. Never quite drunk, Orsini believed after the fifth or sixth glass that the testimonies of the past were a guarantee of the future. He needed no change of personality to dwell comfortably in an impossible paradise. He had been born a man of fifty, cynical, kindly, a friend of life, waiting for things to happen to him. All that was needed for the miracle was a transformation of van Oppen, his return to the years before the war, to his bulgeless stomach, sparkling skin, and needle-cold shower in the mornings.

Yes, the future Mrs. Turk—a charming and obstinate woman, with all due respect—had been at *El Liberal* to pick up the challenge. The head of the Sports Section already had photos of Mario doing his gymnastics, but only by paying for them with a speech on democracy, free press, and freedom of information. On patriotism, too, Sports Section added.

"And the Turk would have knocked our heads off, mine and the photographer's, if his bride hadn't intervened and calmed him with a couple of words. They had been muttering to each other in the rear of the store, and then the Turk came out, not so big, I think, as van Oppen, but much more of a brute, more dangerous. Well, you know more about these things than I."

"I understand," smiled the prince. "Poor boy. He's not the first." And he let his sadness float over the olives and potato chips of the Berne.

"The man was fighting mad but got himself under control, put on his short fishing pants, and started doing his gymnastics out in the open. He did everything that Humberto, our photographer, asked of him or invented for him, and all this only to get his revenge and get even for the shock we had given him. And she was there too, sitting on a barrel like his mother or his teacher, smoking, not saying a word, but watching him all the time. And when one thinks that she's less than five feet tall and weighs less than ninety pounds. . . ."

"I know the lady," Orsini agreed nostalgically. "And I have seen so many cases. . . . Ah, human personality is a mysterious thing; it doesn't come from muscles."

"It's not for publication, of course," said Sports Section. "But will you make the deposit?"

"The deposit?" the prince opened his hands in a pious gesture. "This afternoon or tomorrow morning. It depends on the bank. How do you feel about tomorrow morning at your office? It'll be good publicity and free at that. To hold van Oppen for three minutes. . . . As I always say"—and here he showed his golden molars and called the waiter—"sport is one thing and business another. What can one do, what can we do when a candidate for suicide suddenly appears at the end of our training tour. And when—what's worse—he gets help."

*   *   *

Life had always been difficult and beautiful and unique, and Prince Orsini did not have the five hundred pesos. He understood the woman and there was an adjective at the tip of his tongue to define her and to enshrine her in his past, but then he began to think of the man whom the woman represented and fronted for, the Turk who had accepted the challenge. And so he said goodbye to happiness and the easy life. He checked the champion's mood and pulse, then told him a lie and, at nightfall, started walking toward the Porfilio Brothers store with the yellow scrapbook under his arm.

First the worm-eaten ombú tree, then the lamp that hung from it and produced a circle of intimidated light. Suddenly, barking dogs and contending shouts: "Go away!" "Quiet!" "Down!" Orsini crossed the first light, saw the round and watery moon, reached the store sign, and made a respectful entry. A man wearing rope sandals and ballooned country pants was finishing his gin by the counter. He left and they were alone: he—Prince Orsini—the Turk and the woman.

"Good evening, señorita," Orsini smiled and bowed. The woman was sitting on a straw-backed chair, knitting; she withdrew her eyes from the needles to look at him and—perhaps—to smile. "Baby clothes," Orsini thought indignantly. "She's pregnant, she's preparing her baby's layette, that's why she wants to get married, that's why she wants to rob me of five hundred pesos."

He walked straight toward the man who had stopped filling paper bags with maté and was waiting for him stolidly across the counter.

"That's the one I told you about," the woman stated. "The manager."

"Manager and friend," Orsini corrected. "After so many years . . ."

He shook the man's stiffly opened hand and raised his arm to pat him on the back.

"At your orders," said the storekeeper and lifted his thick black whiskers to show his teeth.

"Pleased to meet you, very pleased to meet you." But he had already breathed the sour and deathly smell of defeat, had calculated the Turk's unspent youth, the perfect manner in which his hundred kilos were distributed over his body. "There isn't one surplus gram of fat here, not one gram of intelligence or sensitivity; there is no hope. Three minutes: poor Jacob van Oppen!"

"I've come about these five hundred pesos," Orsini started, testing the density of the air, the poorness of the light, the hostility of the couple. "It's not against me; it's against life," he thought. "I have come here to set your minds at rest. Tomorrow, as soon as I receive a money order from the capital, I'll make the deposit at *El Liberal.* But I'd also like to talk of other things."

"Haven't we already talked about everything?" the woman asked. She was too small for the shaky straw-backed chair; her shiny knitting needles were too big for her. She could be good or evil; now she had chosen to be implacable, to make up for some long and obscure delay, to take revenge. In the light of the lamp, the shape of her nose was perfect and her bright eyes shone like glass.

"That's quite true, señorita. I don't want to say anything I haven't already said before. But I thought it my duty to say it directly. To tell the truth to Señor Mario." He smiled while repeating his greeting with his head; his truculence barely vibrated, deep and muted. "And that's why, *patrón*, I'd like you to serve drinks for three. It's on me of course; have whatever you like."

"He doesn't drink," said the woman without hurry and without lifting her eyes from her knitting, nestling in her aura of ice and irony.

The hairy beast behind the counter finished sealing a package of maté and turned around slowly to look at the woman. "Gorilla chest; two centimeters of forehead; never had any expression in his eyes," Orsini noted. "Never really thought, suffered, or imagined that tomorrow might bring a surprise or not come at all."

"Adriana," the Turk muttered and remained motionless until she turned her eyes toward him. "Adriana, vermouth I do take."

She gave him a rapid smile and shrugged her shoulders. The Turk pursed his lips to drink the vermouth in small swallows. The prince, his heavy green hat tilted backward, was leaning over the counter, touching the wrapping of his scrapbook. Looking for inspiration and sympathy, he talked of crops, rains, and droughts, of farming methods and means of transport, of Europe's aging beauty and of America's youth. He improvised, distributing prophecies and hopes, while the Turk nodded silent agreement.

"The Apollo was full this afternoon," the prince launched a sudden attack. "As soon as it became known that you've picked up the challenge, everybody wanted to see the champion training. I don't want him bothered too much so I raised the entrance price; but the public still insists on paying it. And now," he said while starting to unwrap the scrapbook, "I'd like you to take a little look at this." He caressed the leather cover and lifted it. "It's almost all words, but the photographs help. Look, it's quite clear: world champion, gold belt."

"Former world champion," the woman corrected out of the crackling of her straw-backed chair.

"But señorita," Orsini said without turning, exclusively for the Turk's benefit, as he flipped the pages of decaying clippings, "he'll be champion again before six months are out. A false decision, the International Wrestling Federation has already intervened. . . . Look at the headlines, eight columns, front pages, look at the photographs. See, that's a world champion: nobody in this world can beat him. Nobody can hold him for three minutes and not be pinned. Why! One minute against him would be a miracle. The champion of Europe couldn't do it; the champion of the United States couldn't do it either. I'm talking to you seriously, man to man; I've come to see you because, as soon as I spoke to the señorita, I understood the problem, the situation."

"Adriana," the Turk reminded him.

"That's it," said the prince. "I understood everything. But there is always a solution. If you climb into the Apollo ring on Saturday . . . Jacob van Oppen is my friend, and his friendship has only one limit: it disappears when the bell rings and he starts fighting. Then he is no longer my friend, no longer an ordinary man: he is the world champion, he has to win and he knows how."

Dozens of salesmen had stopped their Fords outside the Porfilio Brothers store, to smile at its late owners or at Mario, to have a drink, to show samples, catalogues, and lists, to sell sugar, rice, wine, and maize. But what Orsini was trying to sell to the Turk between smiles, friendly pats on the back, and compassionate pleas, was a strange and difficult merchandise: fear. Alerted by the presence of the woman and counseled by his memories and instincts, he limited himself to selling prudence and tried to make a deal.

The Turk still had half a glass of vermouth left; he lifted it to wet his small pink lips, without drinking.

"It's five hundred pesos," said Adriana from her chair. "And it's time to close."

"You said . . ." the Turk started. His voice and thought tried to understand, to be calm, to free themselves from three generations of stupidity and greed. "Adriana, I'll have to take down the maté first. You said that if I climb into the ring at the Apollo on Saturday . . ."

"I said this: if you get into the ring, the champion will break you some ribs or other bones; he'll have you pinned in half a minute. There'll be no five hundred pesos then—though you may well have to spend more than that on doctors. And who'll take care of your business while you're at the hospital? And on top of it all, you'll lose your reputation and the whole town will laugh at you." Orsini felt that the time had come for pause and meditation; he asked for another gin, tried to fathom the Turk's stolid face and anxious movements, and heard a sardonic little laugh from the woman, who had dropped her knitting on her thighs.

Orsini took a sip of gin and started to wrap up the rickety scrapbook. The Turk was smelling the vermouth and trying to think.

"I don't mean to say," the prince murmured in a low distracted voice, whose tone was that of an epilogue accepted by both parties, "I don't mean to say that you may not be stronger than Jacob van Oppen. I know much about these things; I have dedicated my life and my money to the discovery of strong men. Moreover, as Señorita Adriana so intelligently reminded me, you are much younger than the champion. More youth, more vigor: I'm prepared to put this in writing. If the champion—just to take an example—bought this store, he'd be out begging in the streets in six months. While you, on the other hand, will be a rich man in less than two years. Because you, my friend Mario, know about business and the champion doesn't." The scrapbook was already wrapped; he put it on the counter and leaned on it to get on with his drink and the conversation. "In exactly the same way, the champion knows how to break bones, how to bend your knees and your waist backward so he can pin you on the 'mat.' That's how it's put—or, at least, that's how they used to put it. On the rug. Everybody to his trade."

The woman had risen to put out a lamp in the corner; she was now standing with her knitting between her stomach and the counter, small and hard, not looking at either man.

The Turk examined her face and then grunted. "You said that if I didn't climb into the ring at the Apollo on Saturday . . ."

"I said?" Orsini asked with surprise. "I think that I offered you some advice. But, in any case, if you withdraw your acceptance of the challenge, we might agree on something, a compensation. We could talk."

"How much?" asked the Turk.

The woman lifted a hand and dug her nails into the beast's hairy arm; when the man turned his face to look at her, she said, "Five hundred pesos, no more and no less, right? And we're not going to lose them. If you don't show up on Saturday, all Santa María will know that you're a coward. I'll tell them, house by house and person by person."

She spoke without passion. Still sticking her nails into the Turk's arms, she spoke to him with patience and good humor, as a mother speaks to the child she reprimands and threatens.

"One moment," said Orsini. He raised a hand and used the other to lift the glass of gin to his mouth until it was empty. "I have thought of that, too. The comments that people, that the town will make if you don't turn up on Saturday." He smiled at the two hostile faces and his tone became more cautious. "For example . . . let us suppose that you do turn up and climb into the ring. Don't try to provoke the champion: that would be fatal for what we're planning. You climb into the ring, realize with the first clinch that the champion knows his job and let him pin you, cleanly, without a scratch."

The woman was again digging her nails into the giant hairy arm; the Turk removed her with a bark.

"I understand," he said then. "I go in and I lose. How much?"

Suddenly Orsini accepted what he had suspected from the beginning of the meeting: whatever agreement he might reach with the Turk, the stubborn little woman would wipe it out before the night was over. He realized without any room for doubt that Jacob van Oppen was doomed to fight the Turk on Saturday.

"How much?" he murmured while adjusting the scrapbook under his arm. "Let's say a hundred, a hundred and fifty pesos. You climb into the ring . . ."

The woman moved a step away from the counter and stuck the needles into the ball of wool. She was looking at the earth and cement floor and her voice sounded tranquil and drowsy. "We need five hundred pesos and he will win them for us on Saturday, with no tricks and no deals. There's nobody stronger, nobody can bend him backward. Least of all that exhausted old man, whatever champion he may have been in his day. Shall we close?"

"I've got to take down the maté," the Turk said again.

"Well, so that's that. Take out what I owe you and give me a last glass." He put a ten-peso note on the counter and lit a cigarette. "We'll celebrate, and you'll be my guests."

But the woman relit the corner lamp and sat down again in the straw-backed chair, picked up her knitting, and smoked a cigarette; and the Turk served only one glass of gin. Then he started with a yawn to carry the bags of maté, piled up against the wall, toward the cellar trapdoor.

Without knowing why, Orsini tossed a visiting card on the counter. He stayed in the store ten minutes more, watching with clouded eyes, perspiring, the Turk's methodical handling of the maté bags. He saw him moving them with the same ease, with as much visible effort as he, Prince Orsini, would use to move a box of cigarettes or a bottle.

"Poor Jacob van Oppen," Orsini meditated. "To grow old is all right for me. But he was born to be always twenty; and it's not he who is twenty now but that giant son-of-a-bitch who is wrapped round the little finger of the fetus in her belly. He's twenty, the animal, nobody can take it away from him to give it back afterward, and he'll be twenty on Saturday night at the Apollo."

From the editorial office of *El Liberal,* almost elbow to elbow with the Sports Section, Orsini made a telephone call to the capital to ask for an urgent remittance of a thousand pesos. To escape the operator's curiosity, he used the direct line; he told loud lies for the benefit of the editorial office, now occupied by thin and bewhiskered youths and a girl smoking through a cigarette holder. It was seven in the evening; he almost made some coarse comments in reply to the obvious hesitation of the man who was listening to him from a distant telephone in some room that couldn't be imagined, making grimaces of disagreement in some cubicle of the capital, on an October evening.

He broke off the conversation with a weary and tolerant smile.

"At last," he said, and blew his nose into a linen handkerchief. "Tomorrow morning we'll have the money. Troubles. Tomorrow noon I'll make the deposit in the managing editor's office. The managing editor's office sounds businesslike, right? . . . Ah, there's the boy. If any of you would like some refreshment . . ."

They thanked him, and one typewriter or another stopped its noise, but no one accepted his invitation. Sports Section, with his thick glasses, was bending over a table marking some photographs.

Leaning against a table and smoking a cigarette, Orsini looked at the men bent over their machines and their jobs. He knew that he no longer existed for them, was no longer in the editorial office. "And I won't exist for them tomorrow either," he thought with a touch of sadness and a smile of resignation. Because everything had been postponed until Friday night, and Friday night was just beginning to bud in the fade-out of the sweet and rosy dusk beyond the windows of *El Liberal,* on the river, above the first shadow that wrapped the deep sirens of the barges.

He bridged mistrust and indifference and made Sports Section shake hands with him.

"I hope that tomorrow will be a great night for Santa María; I hope that the best man wins."

But this phrase would not be printed in the newspaper to serve as support for his smiling and benevolent face. From the lobby of the Apollo—Jacob van Oppen, World Champion, Trains Here from 6 to 8 P.M. Entrance: 3 pesos —he heard the murmurs of the public and the thumping of van Oppen's feet on the improvised ring. Van Oppen could no longer fight, break bones, or risk having them broken. But he could skip a rope, indefinitely, without tiring.

Seated in the narrow ticket office, Orsini checked the statement of receipts and expenditures and tallied his accounts. Even without the triumphant Saturday night, seats at five pesos, the visit to Santa María showed some profit. Orsini offered the other man a coffee, counted the money, and put his signature at the foot of the lists.

He remained alone in the dark and smelly office. The rhythmical tapping of van Oppen's feet on the boards could be heard.

"One hundred and ten animals sitting there openmouthed because the champion skips a rope, the way all schoolgirls skip in the playground—and they probably do it better."

He remembered van Oppen as a young man, or at least not yet grown old; he thought of Europe and the United States, of the true Lost World; tried to convince himself that van Oppen was responsible for the passing of the years, his decline, and his repugnant old age, as if these were vices he had freely acquired and accepted. He tried to hate van Oppen in order to protect himself.

"I should have spoken to him before, maybe yesterday or this morning on those walks of his on the Promenade where he minces along like an old woman. Maybe I should have spoken to him out in the open, facing the river, the trees, the sky, all that these Germans call nature. But Friday has come; it is now Friday night."

He gently felt the bank notes in his pocket and got up. Outside, Friday night was waiting for him, punctual and mild. The hundred and ten imbeciles were shouting inside the movie house; the champion had started his last number, the gymnastics session in which all his muscles swelled and overflowed.

Orsini walked slowly toward the hotel, his hands clasped behind his back, looking for details of the town to dismiss and to remember, to mingle them with details of other distant towns, to join them all into a whole and to keep on living.

The hotel bar stretched out till it became the receptionist's counter. Over a drink with much soda the prince planned his battle. To occupy a hill may prove more important than to lose an ammunition dump. He put some money on the counter and asked for his hotel bill.

"It's for tomorrow really, excuse me, but I'd rather have it now and avoid the rush. Tomorrow, as soon as the fight is over, we have to leave by car, at midnight or at dawn. I phoned from *El Liberal* today and they mentioned some new contracts. Everybody wants to see the champion, naturally, before the Antwerp tournament."

He paid the bill with an outsize tip and went up to his room with a bottle of gin under his arm to pack the suitcases. One, old and black, belonged to Jacob and could not be touched; there was also an impressive heap of his belongings on the stage of the Apollo: robes, sweaters, stretcher springs, ropes, fleece-lined boots. But all this could be picked up later on any pretext. He packed his suitcases and those of Jacob's that had not been proclaimed sacred; he was taking a shower, potbellied and determined, when he heard the room door bang. Beyond the noise of the water he heard steps and silence. "It's Friday night," he thought, "and I don't even know whether it's best to get him drunk before or after talking to him. Or maybe before *and* after."

Jacob was sitting on the bed, cross-legged, contemplating with childish joy the trademark on the sole of his shoe: CHAMPION. Somebody, maybe Orsini himself, had once told him as a joke that those shoes were manufactured for the exclusive benefit of van Oppen, to remind people of him and to make thousands upon thousands of strangers pay homage to him with their feet.

Wrapped in his bathrobe, and dripping water, Orsini entered the room, jovial and shrewd. The champion had grabbed the gin bottle and, after taking a drink, continued to contemplate his shoe without listening to Orsini.

"Why did you pack the suitcases? The fight is tomorrow."

"To gain time," said Orsini. "That's why I began to pack them. But afterward . . ."

"Is it at nine? But it always starts late. And after the three minutes I still have to swing the clubs and lift the weights. And also to celebrate."

"All right," Orsini said, looking at the bottle tilted against the champion's mouth, counting the drinks, calculating.

The champion had put away the bottle and was now massaging the white crepe sole of his shoe. He was smiling a mysterious and incredulous smile, as if he were listening to some distant music that he hadn't heard since childhood. Suddenly he became serious, took in both hands the foot bearing the allusive trademark, and lowered it slowly until the sole was resting on the narrow rug by the bed. Orsini saw the short, dry grimace that had replaced the vanished smile; he hesitatingly moved toward the champion's bed and lifted the bottle. While pretending to drink, he could estimate that there were still two thirds of a liter of gin left.

Motionless, collapsed, with his elbows leaning on his knees, the champion prayed, "Verdammt, verdammt, verdammt."

Without making a noise, Orsini moved his feet from the ground and with his back to the champion, yawning, took out a gun from his jacket hanging from a chair and put it in a pocket of his bathrobe. Then he sat on his bed and waited. He had never needed the gun, not even to threaten Jacob. But the years had taught him to anticipate the champion's actions and reactions, to estimate his violence, his degree of madness, and also the exact point of the compass at which madness began.

"Verdammt," Jacob kept praying. He filled his lungs with air and rose to his feet. He joined his hands at the nape of his neck and dipped from the waist, hard, bending his chest first right, then left toward the midriff.

"Verdammt!" he shouted as if looking at somebody who challenged him, then remade his distrustful smile and began to undress. Orsini lit a cigarette and put a hand into his bathrobe pocket, his knuckles resting against the coolness of the gun. The champion took off his sweater, his undershirt, his pants, and the shoes with his trademark; he threw them all into the corner between the wall and the closet, where they formed a pile on the floor.

Leaning against the bed and the pillow, Orsini tried to remember other outbursts, other prologues, and match them against what he saw. "Nobody said we should go. Who told you we must go tonight?"

Jacob was wearing only his wrestling trunks. He lifted the bottle and drank half its remaining contents. Then, keeping up his smile of mystery, allusions, and memories, began to do gymnastic exercises, stretching and bending his arms while bending his knees to squat.

"All this flesh," Orsini thought with his finger on the trigger of the gun, "the same muscles, or bigger, as twenty years ago; a little more fat on the belly, the loins, the midriff. White, timid enemy of the sun, gringo, and womanish. But these arms and these legs are as strong as ever, maybe stronger. The years didn't pass him by; but they always come, search, and find a place to enter and to stay. We were all promised old age and death, sudden or by inches. This poor devil didn't believe these promises; and to that extent the result is unjust."

Illuminated by Friday's last light and by the lamp Orsini had lit in the bathroom, the giant was shining with sweat. He finished his gymnastics session by lying down flat on his back and lifting himself up on his arms. Then he gave a short and slow salute with his head to the pile of clothes by the closet. Panting, he took another drink from the bottle, lifted it into the ash-colored air, and moved toward Orsini's bed without stopping to look at it. He remained standing, enormous and sweating, breathing with much effort and noise, with an open-mouthed expression of fury from end to end. He kept looking at the bottle, looking for explanations from its label, rounded and secret.

"Champion," Orsini said, withdrawing but not touching the wall, raising a leg to get an easier grip on his gun. "Champion, we must order another bottle. We must start celebrating right away."

"Celebrating? But I always win."

"Yes, the champion always wins. And he'll also win in Europe."

Orsini raised himself from the bed and maneuvered his legs until he was seated, his hand still in his bathrobe pocket.

In front of him, Jacob's enormous contracted muscles were expanding. "There have never been better legs than his," Orsini thought with fear and sadness. "All he needs to knock me out is to bring down the bottle; it takes a lot less than a minute to crush a man's head with the bottom of a bottle." He got up slowly and limped away, showing a bland paternal smile all the way to the opposite corner of the room. He leaned against the table and remained for a moment with his eyes ajar, muttering to himself a Catholic and magical formula.

Jacob hadn't moved. He remained standing by the bed, now with his back toward it, the bottle still in the air. The room was almost dusky now, and the bathroom light was weak and yellowish.

Maneuvering with his left hand, Orsini lit a cigarette. "I have never pushed him that far," he thought.

"We can celebrate now, champion. We'll celebrate till dawn and at four we'll take the bus. Goodbye, Santa María. Goodbye and thanks, you didn't treat us too badly."

White, magnified by the shadow, Jacob slowly put down the arm with the bottle and clinked the glass against his knee.

"We're going away, champion," Orsini added. "He's thinking about it now, and let's hope he'll understand it in less than three minutes."

Jacob turned his body around as if he were in a salt-water pool and doubled up to sit on the bed. His hair, scanty but still untouched by gray, showed through the dark the tilt of his head.

"We have contracts, genuine contracts," Orsini continued, "if we go south. But it must be at once, it must be by the four-o'clock bus. I made a phone call from the newspaper office this afternoon, champion. I called a manager in the capital."

"Today. Today is Friday," said Jacob slowly and without drunkenness in his voice. "So the fight is tomorrow night. We can't leave at four."

"There is no fight, champion. There are no problems. We go at four; but first we celebrate. I'll order another bottle right away."

"No," said Jacob.

Again Orsini leaned motionless against the table. His pity for the champion, so exacerbated and long-suffering in the last few months, turned into pity for Prince Orsini, condemned to a nurse's life of coddling, lying, and boredom with this creature whom fate assigned him to earn a living. Then his pity became depersonalized, almost universal. "Here, in a South American hole that has a name only because someone wanted to comply with the local custom of baptizing any heap of houses. He, more lost and exhausted than I; I, older, gayer, and more intelligent than he, watching him with a gun that may or may not shoot, determined to threaten him with it but certain that I'll never pull the trigger. Pity human existence, pity whoever arranges things in this clumsy and absurd manner. Pity the people I have had to cheat so that I could keep alive. Pity the Turk of the store and his fiancée, all those who don't really have the privilege of choice."

From far away, disjointed, the sound of the conservatory piano reached them; in spite of the hour, one could feel the heat rising in the room, in the tree-lined streets.

"I don't understand," said Jacob. "Today is Friday. If that lunatic no longer wants to accept the challenge I still have to do my exhibition, seats at five pesos."

"That lunatic . . ." Orsini started, passing from pity to fury and anger. "No, it's us. We aren't interested in the challenge. We leave at four."

"The man wants to fight? He hasn't backed out?"

"The man wants to fight and he won't be allowed to back out. But we go away."

"Without a fight, before tomorrow?"

"Champion," said Orsini. Jacob's bent head moved in a negative gesture.

"I'm staying. Tomorrow at nine I'll be waiting in the ring. Will I wait alone?"

"Champion," Orsini repeated while approaching the bed; he affectionately touched Jacob's shoulder and lifted the bottle for a small drink. "We leave."

"Not me," said the giant and began to rise, to grow. "I'll be alone in the ring. Give me half the money and go. Tell me why you want to run away and why you want me to run away, too."

Forgetting about the gun without ceasing to grip it, Orsini spoke against the arch formed by the champion's ribs.

"Because there are contracts waiting for us. And that business tomorrow is not a fight; it's only a silly challenge."

Without betraying his uneasiness, Orsini moved away toward the window, toward Jacob's bed. He didn't dare turn on the light; he had no fight in him to win with smiles and gestures.

He preferred the shadow and persuasion by tones of voice. "Maybe it would be best to end it all here and now. I have always been lucky; something has always turned up and it was often better than what I lost. Don't look behind you; just leave him like an elephant without a master."

"But the challenge was ours," Jacob's voice was saying, surprised, almost laughing. "We always issue it. Three minutes. In the newspapers, in the plazas. Money for holding out three minutes. And I always won. Jacob van Oppen always wins."

"Always," Orsini repeated. He suddenly felt weak and weary; he put the gun on the bed and put his hands together between his naked knees. "The champion always wins. But also always, every single time, I first take a look at the man who accepts the challenge. Three minutes without being pinned to the carpet," he recited. "And nobody lasted more than half a minute and I knew it in advance." He thought while saying this, "And, of course, I can't tell him that I sometimes made successful threats to some contenders and that I bribed others to last less than thirty seconds. But maybe I'll have to tell him after all." Aloud he went on, "And now, too, I have done my duty. I went to see the man who picked up the challenge, I weighed him and measured him. With my eyes. That's why I packed the suitcases and that's why I think we should take the four-o'clock bus."

Van Oppen had stretched himself out on the floor, his head leaning against the wall, between the night table and the bathroom light.

"I don't understand it. You mean that he, that small-town storekeeper who never saw a real fight, will beat Jacob van Oppen?"

"Nobody can beat the champion in a fight," said Orsini patiently. "But this is not a fight."

"Ah, it's a challenge!" Jacob exclaimed.

"That's it. A challenge. Five hundred pesos to whoever will remain on his feet for three minutes. I've seen the man." Here Orsini paused and lit another cigarette. He was calm and disinterested: this was like telling a story to a child to make him go to sleep, or like singing "Lilli Marlene."

"And that one will hold me three minutes?" van Oppen sneered.

"Yes, he will. He's a beast. Twenty years, hundred and ten kilos—it's only my estimate, but I'm never wrong."

Jacob doubled up his feet till he was sitting on the floor. Orsini heard him breathe.

"Twenty," said the champion. "I, too, was twenty once, and not as strong as now; I knew less."

"Twenty," repeated the prince, turning his yawn into a sigh.

"And that's all? That's all there is to it? And how many men of twenty have I pinned in less than twenty seconds? And why should that hick last three minutes?"

"It's like this," Orsini thought with the cigarette in his mouth, "it's as simple and terrible as to discover all of a sudden that a woman doesn't rouse us, to remain impotent and to know that explanations won't do any good, won't even provide relief; as simple and terrible as to tell the truth to a sick man. Everything is simple when it happens to others, when we remain alien to it and can understand, sympathize, and repeat advice."

The conservatory piano had disappeared into the heat of the inky night; there was the chirping of crickets, and, much farther away, a jazz record was turning.

"He'll hold me for three minutes?" Jacob insisted. "I saw him too. I saw his picture in the paper. A good body to move barrels."

"No," Orsini replied with sincerity and serenity. "No one can resist the world champion for three minutes."

"I don't understand," said Jacob. "Then I don't understand. Is there anything more to it?"

"Yes." Orsini was speaking smoothly and indifferently as if the matter were unimportant. "When we finish this training tour, it'll be all different. It will also be necessary to give up alcohol. But today, tomorrow, Saturday night in Santa María—or whatever the name of this hole—Jacob van Oppen cannot clinch and hold a clinch for more than a minute. Van Oppen's chest cannot; his lungs cannot. And that beast won't be thrown in a minute. That's why we have to take the four-o'clock bus. The suitcases are packed and I've paid the hotel bill. It's all settled."

Orsini heard the grunt and the cough to his left and was measuring the silence in the room. He picked up the gun again and warmed it against his knees.

"After all," he thought, "it is strange that I should make so many evasions, take so many precautions. He knows it better than I and for some time now. But maybe this is why I chose the evasions and looked for precautions. And here I am, at my age, as pitiable and ridiculous as if I had told a woman that we were through and was waiting for her reaction, her tears, and her threats."

Jacob had moved back; but the band of light from the bathroom revealed, on his backward-tilted head, the shine of tears. Orsini, still gripping the gun, walked to the phone to order another bottle. He grazed in passing the champion's closely cropped hair and returned to the bed. Raising his legs, he could feel the heavy roundness of his belly against his thighs. A panting noise reached him from the seated man, as if van Oppen had come to the aftermath of a long training session or the end of a very long and difficult fight.

"It's not his heart," Orsini reminded himself, "nor his lungs. It's everything: a six foot six of a man who has begun to grow old."

"No, no," he said aloud. "Only a rest on the road. In a matter of months, it'll all be like before again. Quality, that is what really matters, what can never be lost. Even if one wants to lose it, or tries to. Because there are periods of suicide in every man's life. But they are overcome, forgotten." The dance music had grown louder as the night advanced. Orsini's voice vibrated with satisfaction and lingered in his throat and palate.

There was a knock on the door and the prince moved silently to receive the tray with the bottle, glasses, and ice. He put it down on the table and chose to sit down on a chair to continue the vigil and the lesson of optimism.

The champion had sat down in the shadow, on the floor, leaning against the wall; his breathing could no longer be heard and he existed for Orsini only by virtue of his undoubted and enormous crouching presence.

"Ah yes, quality," the prince resumed his theme. "Who has it? One is born with it or dies without it. It's not for nothing that everybody finds himself a nickname, stupid and comical, a few funny words to be put on the posters. THE BUFFALO OF ARKANSAS, THE GRINDER OF LIÈGE, THE MIURA BULL OF GRANADA. But Jacob van Oppen is simply called 'World Champion.' That's all. That's quality."

Orsini's speech faded into silence and weariness.

The prince filled a glass, tasted it with his tongue, and rose to carry it to the champion.

"Orsini," said Jacob. "My friend Prince Orsini."

Van Oppen's big hands lay heavily on his knees, like the teeth of a trap; the knees supported his bent head. Orsini put the glass on the floor after touching the giant's neck and back with it.

He was adjusting his position with a grimace, weariness attacking his midriff, when he suddenly felt fingers encircling his ankle and nailing him to the floor. He heard Jacob's voice, slow and gay, lazy and serene: "And now the prince will drink the whole glass at one go."

Orsini threw himself back to keep his balance. "That's all I needed: that the beast should think I want to drug him or poison him." He stooped slowly, picked up the glass, and drank it rapidly, feeling the grip of Jacob's fingers weakening on his ankle.

"All right, champion?" he asked. Now he could see the other's eye, a scrap of his lifted smile.

"All right, prince. Now a full glass for me."

With his legs apart and trying not to stumble, Orsini returned to the table and refilled the glass. He leaned against it to light a cigarette and saw, with the small flame of the lighter, that his fingers were trembling with hate. He came back with the glass, the cigarette in his mouth, a finger on the trigger of the gun concealed in his bathrobe. He crossed the yellow band of light and saw Jacob on his feet, white and enormous, swaying gently.

"Your health, champion," said Orsini, offering the drink with his left hand.

"Your health," Jacob's voice repeated from above, with a trace of excitement. "I knew they would come. I went to the church to pray that they would come."

"Yes," said Orsini.

There was a pause, the champion sighed, the night brought them shouts and applause from the distant dance hall, a tug sounded its siren thrice on the river.

"And now," Jacob pronounced the words with some difficulty, "the prince will take another drink at one go. We're both drunk. But I don't drink tonight because it's Friday. The prince has a gun."

For a second, with the glass in the air and contemplating Jacob's navel, the prince invented for himself a life story of perpetual humiliation, savored the taste of disgust, and knew that the giant wasn't even challenging him but was only offering him a target for the gun in his pocket.

"Yes," he said a second later, spat out the cigarette, and took another drink of gin. His stomach rose to his chest as he threw the empty glass on the bed and laboriously moved back to place the gun on the table.

Van Oppen hadn't moved; he was still swaying in the dusk, with a sneering slowness, as if he were performing the classical gymnastic exercises to strengthen his waist muscles.

"We must both be crazy," said Orsini. His memories, the weak heat of the summer's night pressing against the window, his plans for the future were all of no use to him.

" 'Lilli Marlene,' please," Jacob advised.

Leaning on the table, Orsini put away the cigarette he was about to light. He sang with a muted voice, with one last hope, as if he had never done anything but hum those imbecile lyrics, that easy tune, as if he had never done anything else to earn a living. He felt older than ever, shrunk and potbellied, a stranger to himself.

There was a silence and then the champion said, "Thanks!" Feeling sleepy and weak, fumbling with the cigarette he had left on the table by the gun, Orsini saw the big whitish body approach him, relieved of its age by the dusk.

"Thanks," van Oppen repeated, almost touching him. "One more time."

Stunned and indifferent, Orsini thought to himself, "It's no longer a cradle song, it no longer makes him get drunk, weep, and sleep." He cleared his voice again and started, "Vor der Kaserne, vor dem grossen Tor. . . ."

Without needing to move his body, the champion lifted an arm from his hip and struck Orsini's jaw with his open hand. An old tradition stopped him from using his fists, except in desperate circumstances. He held up the prince's body with his other arm and stretched him out on the bed.

The heat of the night and of the fiesta had made people open their windows. The jazz for dancing now seemed to originate from the hotel itself, from the center of the darkened room.

The Prince's Story

It was a town rising from the river in September, give or take five inches south of the equator. I woke up, with no pain, in the hotel-room morning filled with light and heat. Jacob was massaging my stomach and laughing to speed on its way a stream of insults that culminated in a single one that he repeated until I could no longer pretend to be asleep and drew myself up.

"Old pig," he was saying in his purest German, maybe in Prussian.

The sun was already licking the leg of the table and I thought sadly that nothing could be saved from the wreck. At least—I began to remember—that's what I should think, and my expression and my words should adjust themselves to this sadness. Van Oppen must have foreseen something of this because he made me drink a glass of orange juice and put a lighted cigarette in my mouth.

"Old pig," he said, as he filled his lungs with smoke.

It was Saturday morning and we were still in Santa María. I moved my head, looked at him, and made a rapid balance sheet of his smile, his gaiety, and his friendship. He had put on his expensive gray suit and his antelope-skin shoes; a Stetson hat was tilted against the nape of his neck. I suddenly thought that he was right, that life was always right in the end, that defeats and victories didn't matter.

"Yes," I said, withdrawing my hand from his, "I am an old pig. The years pass and things get worse and worse. Is there a fight today?"

"Yes," he nodded enthusiastically. "I told you they would come back and they did."

I sucked at my cigarette and stretched myself out on the bed. It was enough to see the smile to realize that Jacob had won, even if he had his spine broken that hot Saturday night, as anyone could foresee. He had to win in three minutes; but I was getting more money. I sat up in the bed and kneaded my jaw.

"The fight is on," I said, "the champion decides. Unfortunately, the manager no longer has anything to say. But neither a bottle nor a blow can abolish facts."

Van Oppen began to laugh and his hat fell on the bed.

"Neither a bottle nor a blow," I insisted. "The fact still remains that, as of now, the champion hasn't enough wind to support a fight, a real effort, for more than a minute. That's a fact. The champion won't be able to throw the Turk. The champion will die a mysterious death at the fifty-ninth second. The autopsy will tell. I believe we agree, at least, on that."

"Yes, we agree on that. No more than one minute," van Oppen assented, sounding young and gay again. The morning was now filling the entire room, and I felt humiliated by my sleepiness, by my objections, by my bathrobe weighed down by the unloaded gun.

"And the fact is," I said slowly, as if trying to take revenge, "that we haven't got the five hundred pesos. Of course, everybody agrees, the Turk can't win. But we still have to deposit the five hundred and it's already Saturday. All we have left is the bus money and enough for a week in the capital. After that, we're in God's hands."

Jacob picked up his hat and started to laugh again. He was shaking his head like a father sitting on a park bench with his diffident little son.

"Money," he said without asking. "Money for the deposit? Five hundred pesos?"

He passed me another lighted cigarette and put his left foot, the more sensitive one, on the little table. He undid the knot of the gray shoe, took it off, and came over to show me a roll of green bank notes. It was real money. He gave me five ten-dollar bills and could not resist showing off:

"More?"

"No," I said. "It's more than enough."

A lot of money went back to the shoe: between three and five hundred dollars.

And so I changed the money at noon. Since the champion had disappeared—his initialed sweater did not show up that morning for the trot down the Promenade—I went to the Plaza Restaurant and ate like a gentleman, something I hadn't done for a long time. I had a coffee, prepared on my table, the appropriate liqueurs and a cigar, very dry but smokable.

I finished off the luncheon with a tip usually lavished by drunkards or crooks and called the hotel. The champion wasn't there; the rest of the afternoon was cool and gay; Santa María was going to have a great evening. I left the newspaper's telephone number with the receptionist so that Jacob could call me about our going to the Apollo together and a little while later sat down at the *El Liberal* morgue with Sports Section and two more faces. I showed them the money.

"So that there should be no doubt. But I'd prefer to hand it out in the ring—whether van Oppen dies of a syncope or has to make a contribution to the Turk's wake."

We played poker—I lost and won—until they informed me that van Oppen was already at the Apollo. It was still more than half an hour before nine; but we put on our jackets and piled into some old cars to drive the few town blocks that separated us from the cinema, giving the occasion an accent of carnival, of the ridiculous.

I went in through the back door and made my way to the room, littered with newspapers and photographs and furiously invaded by smells of urine and rancid paste. There I found Jacob. Wearing his sky-blue trunks—the color chosen in honor of Santa María—and his world-championship belt that glittered like gold, he was doing setting-up exercises. One look at him, at his childish, clean, and expressionless eyes, at the short curve of his smile, was enough to convince me that he didn't want to talk to me, that he wanted no prologues, nothing that would separate him from what he was determined to be and to remember.

I sat down on a bench, without bothering to listen whether or not he answered my greeting, and lit a cigarette. Now, at this moment, in a few minutes, the story would reach its grand finale. The story of the world's wrestling champion. But there would be other stories, too—and an explanation for *El Liberal*, for Santa María, for the neighboring towns.

"A passing physical indisposition" looked better to me than "excessive training blamed for Champion's failure." But they wouldn't print the capital *C* tomorrow, nor the ambiguous headline. Van Oppen was still doing his setting-up exercises, and I lit another cigarette from the first to neutralize the odor of ammonia, not forgetting that clean air is the first condition of a gymnasium.

Jacob was bobbing up and down as if he were alone in the room. He moved his arms horizontally and seemed both thinner and heavier. Through the loathsome smell, to which his sweat added its contribution, I tried to hear him breathe. The noises from the theater also penetrated into the stinking room. Maybe the champion had wind for a minute and a half, but never for two or three. The Turk would remain standing until the bell rang, with his furious black mustache, with the chaste knee-length pants that I expected him to wear (and I wasn't wrong), with his small, hard fiancée howling with triumph and rage near the Apollo stage and its threadbare rug that I insisted on calling "the mat." There was no hope left, we would never rescue the five hundred pesos. The noises of the impatient mob that filled the theater grew louder and louder.

"We must go now," I said to the corpse doing its calisthenics. It was exactly nine by my watch; I left the bad smell behind me and walked through darkened corridors to the ticket office. By quarter past nine I had checked and signed the accounts. I returned to the smelly room—the roar indicated that van Oppen was already in the ring—and took off my jacket, after depositing the money in a pocket of my trousers. Then I made my way back through the corridors, reached the theater, and went up on the stage. They showered me with applause and insults, which I acknowledged with nods and smiles, knowing that at least seventy of those present hadn't paid for their tickets. In any case, I would never get my fifty percent from them.

I took off Jacob's robe, crossed the ring to salute the Turk, and had time for only two more clown's tricks.

The bell rang and it became impossible not to breathe and understand the odor of the crowd that filled the Apollo. The bell rang and I left Jacob alone, much more alone and finally so than I had left him at so many other daybreaks, on street corners, and in bars, when I began to feel sleepy or bored. The bad thing was that when I left him to occupy my special seat that night I felt neither sleepy nor bored. The first bell was to clear the ring; the second to start the fight. Greased, almost young, without showing his weary weight, Jacob circled, crouching, until he reached the center of the ring and waited with an expectant smile.

Jacob opened his arms and waited for the Turk, who seemed to have grown bigger in the meantime. He waited with a smile until he came close, then made a step back and advanced again for the clinch. Against all rules, he kept his arms up for ten seconds. Then he steadied his legs and turned; he put one hand on the challenger's back and the other, and his forearm as well, against a thigh. I didn't understand this and never understood it for the exact half a minute that the fight lasted. Then I saw that the Turk was flying from the ring, sailing with an effort through the howls of the people of Santa María and disappearing into the darkness of the back rows.

He had flown with his big mustache, with his legs flexing absurdly to find support and stability in the dirty air. I saw him sail close to the roof, among the searchlights, maneuvering with his arms. The fight hadn't lasted fifty seconds yet and the champion had won—or hadn't, depending on the way you looked at it. I climbed into the ring to help him with the robe. Jacob was smiling like a child; he didn't hear the shouts and the insults of the public, the growing clamor. He was sweating, but not much, and as soon as I heard him breathe I knew that his fatigue came from nerves, not from physical weariness.

Pieces of wood and empty bottles were now thrown into the ring; I had my speech ready and the exaggerated smile for foreigners. But the missiles kept flying and I couldn't be heard above the din.

Then the cops moved in with enthusiasm, as if they had never done anything else from the day they got their jobs. Directed or not, they scattered and organized themselves properly and started knocking heads with their flashing nightsticks until all that were left in the Apollo were the champion, the referee, and I in the ring; the cops in the hall; and the poor half-dead boy of twenty, hanging over two chairs. It was then that the little woman, the fiancée, appeared from God knows where—I know even less than others—at the side of the Turk. She started to spit on the loser and to kick him, while I congratulated Jacob with all due modesty and the nurses or doctors carrying the stretcher appeared in the doorway.

A Dream Come True

From "Un sueño realizado," translated by Inés de Torres Kinnell, in Doors and Mirrors: Fiction and Poetry from Spanish America (1920–1970), *selected and edited by Hortense Carpentier and Janet Brof, pp. 190–203.*

The joke had been thought up by Blanes; he used to come into my office when I had one—or into the café when times were bad—and motionless on the rug, leaning a fist on my desk, his bright-colored tie fastened to his shirt by a gold clip and his square clean-shaven head whose dark eyes seemed unable to fix on anything for more than a minute, soon blurring as if Blanes were falling asleep or remembered some pure moment of love in his life, doubtless imaginary, his head stripped of any superfluous detail leaning back against a wall covered with photos and posters, he would hear me out and then comment, mouthing each word: "Of course, you've ruined yourself producing *Hamlet*." Or else, "Yes, we know you've always martyred yourself for art and if it weren't for your insane love of *Hamlet* . . ." While I spent all these years putting up with those God-forsaken people, authors and actors, actresses and theater-owners, reviewers and my own family, friends, plus all their mistresses, all that time losing and making money that only God and I knew would again be lost the following season, existing with that drop of water falling on one's bare skull, that jab in the ribs, that bittersweet taste, that scoffing from Blanes that I couldn't quite understand.

"Yes, of course. You've been driven to acts of madness by that boundless love of *Hamlet* . . ."

If I had asked him what he meant the first time, if I had confessed that I knew no more about *Hamlet* than how to figure the cost of a play starting with its first reading, the joke would have ended right there. But I feared the endless digs my question would spark and I merely grimaced and sent him off. And so I was able to live twenty years without knowing what *Hamlet* was, without reading it, but reading in Blanes' face and the rocking of his head that *Hamlet* was art, pure art, great art and knowing also, although it slowly came to me unawares, that the play also had something to do with an actor or an actress, in this case it was always an actress wearing tight black clothes over absurd hips, a skull, a cemetery, a duel, vengeance, and a young girl who drowns. As well as with W. Shakespeare.

This is why now, only now, with my blond wig parted in the middle, which I wear even to bed, my false teeth which fit so poorly I lisp and babble like a baby, in the library of this rest home for penniless theatrical types, which they refer to by a more pretentious name, I found the book, very small and bound in dark blue with the word *Hamlet* inlaid in gold. I sank down into an armchair without opening the book, resolved never to open it or read one single line, thinking about Blanes, how in this way I could take revenge on him for his joke and remembering the evening Blanes came searching for me in that provincial hotel and after listening to me while he smoked and looked up at the ceiling or at the people wandering into the lounge, opened his lips in order to say, right in front of that poor madwoman:

"It's unbelievable. A man like you who went bankrupt producing *Hamlet* . . ."

I had asked him over to the hotel to offer him a role in some crazy one-nighter titled, I believe, "Dream Come True." The cast of that insane play called for some anonymous young man and Blanes was the only one who could play it since, when the woman came to see me, he and I were the only two left, the rest of the company having escaped to Buenos Aires.

The woman had stopped by the hotel at noon, but as I was asleep she returned at the hour the midday siesta ended in that hot province, when I had found the coolest corner of the dining room where I was eating some breaded cutlet and drinking some white wine—the only drinkable kind around. When I first spotted her, motionless within the hot curtained archway, her eyes widening in the darkened dining room, and after the waiter pointed out my table and she made a straight line for it, her skirt whirling the dust up, I had no idea what lay within that woman, no idea of that thing like a white and flabby ribbon of madness that she unravelled, gently tugging at it like some bandage on the wound of past, lonely years, which she now came to bind me in, like some mummy, me and a few of those days spent in that boring place, crowded with fat and drab people. But something in her smile even then made me uneasy, and I couldn't stop staring at her little uneven teeth which recalled some child asleep and breathing with its mouth open. Her hair, almost totally gray, was braided and wrapped around her head and her clothes were out-of-date, somehow befitting someone or something younger than herself. Her skirt, which reached down to her bootlike shoes, was long and dark and floated out as she walked, settling again only to tremble once more at her next step. Her tight-fitting blouse had lace on it and a large cameo was pinned between her uplifted, young breasts; finally the blouse and skirt were both joined and divided by a rose at her waist, probably artificial, now that I think of it, a flower with a huge center and drooping on a stiff stem which seemed to threaten her stomach.

The woman was around fifty years old. What was impossible to forget, what I feel even now as I remember her walking towards my corner in the dining room, was that feeling of a young girl belonging to some past century who had fallen asleep and had just now awakened, her hair a bit rumpled, barely aged, but one who could at any time, in an instant, become her age and silently collapse before me, consumed by those innumerable days. Her smile was ugly to look at, for while it expressed her ignorance of standing on the edge of aging and sudden death, yet it understood—or at least those bared teeth expressed—the hideous decay that threatened her. It was all there, in the half-light of the dining room. I awkwardly settled my silverware beside my plate and stood up.

"Are you Mr. Langman, the theater producer?"

I nodded, smiled and asked her to join me. She refused to order anything. With the table now separating us, I glanced at the whole shape of her mouth and the lightly painted lips, from whose very center her voice hummed out, with a slight Castilian accent, slipping out between the unmatched teeth. Her small quiet eyes, widening to see better, revealed nothing to me. I could only wait for her to speak, and I thought that whatever kind of woman and life her words evoked would fit her strange appearance, and then the strangeness would disappear.

"I wanted to talk to you about a play," she said. "I mean I have a play . . ."

I thought she'd go on but she stopped and paused for me to say something, smiling and waiting for my words in an unshakable silence. She waited very calmly, her hands folded on her lap. I pushed my plate aside and ordered coffee. I offered her a cigaret but she motioned with her head and smiled, meaning she didn't smoke. I lit mine and began talking, trying to shake her off, gently, but at once and permanently, even though I felt compelled, I don't know why, to behave slyly.

"Madame, I'm so sorry. It's quite difficult, you know. Is this your first play? Yes? Of course. And what is the name of your work?"

"No, it has no name," she answered. "It's so hard to explain. It's not what you think. Of course, one could call it *The Dream, The Dream Come True, A Dream Come True.*"

By now, I was certain she was mad and I felt more self-confident. "Good. *A Dream Come True.* Not bad. Titles are very important. I've always had, you might say, a personal yet selfless interest in giving a hand to beginners. Yes, to instill new values in our national theater. I need not mention that gratitude is the last thing I reap. Madame, there are many who took their first step on our major stages, thanks to me, many who now pocket unbelievable royalties from their plays in our capital city and yearly walk off with some prize. No longer do they remember how they came almost begging, to me . . ."

Even the young busboy standing way off in the corner of the dining room near the icebox, trying to fight off the flies and heat with his dishcloth, could see that my words meant nothing to that strange creature. Turning away from the warmth of my coffee cup, I threw her one last look, and said: "The point is, Madame, you've probably heard that our season here has been a catastrophe. We've had to close down and I've just stayed on in order to settle a few personal matters. I'll also be leaving for Buenos Aires next week. I was wrong, that's all. Even though I gave in and gave them a season of farces, this place isn't ready for us—you see what has happened. So . . . Now, well, we could do one thing, Madame. If you would give me a copy of your play, I'll see whether in Buenos Aires . . . Is it three acts?" I now played her game and fell silent, forcing her to say something. I leaned over, slowly rubbing the tip of my cigaret against the ashtray. She blinked.

"What?"

"Your play, Madame. *A Dream Come True.* Are there three acts?"

"No, there are no acts."

"Well, scenes. Yes, it's the new thing now . . ."

"I don't have a copy. It's nothing I've written . . ." she went on. The time had come to leave.

"I'll give you my Buenos Aires address and when you get it written down . . ."

Her body sagged and hunched over, but her head lifted and I saw the same smile. I paused, positive that she would now go, but a moment later she brushed her hand over her face and continued. "No, it's not what you think. The thing is a moment, you could call it a scene, and nothing happens. Like this moment, here in this dining room, might be acted, I'd leave and that would be all. No," she went on, "there really isn't any plot, just some people on a street, some houses and two cars that go by. I'm there and a man, and some woman who comes out of the doorway of a store across the street and gives him a glass of beer. There's no one else, just us three. The man crosses the street towards the woman with the pitcher of beer and then crosses back and sits down near me at the same table he was at in the beginning."

She was silent for a moment and then smiling, neither at me nor at the half-opened linen cabinet behind me in the wall, she concluded: "Do you understand?"

I sidestepped again, remembering something about experimental theater, mentioning it and explaining how impossible it was to do anything like real art in such a place as we now found ourselves. No one would go to the theater to see something like her play. Perhaps I alone in the entire province was capable of understanding the meaning of her work, the sense behind the action, the car symbolism and the woman who offers a "tumbler" of beer to the man who crosses the street and then comes back to her, "near you, Madame."

She stared at me and there was something in her expression that reminded me of the way Blanes looked when he had to ask me for money and then talk of *Hamlet*: a hint of pity but mainly scorn and dislike.

"That's not the point, Mr. Langman," she said. "Only I wish to see it, no one else, no audience. Myself and the actors, nothing more. I wish to see it once. But that one performance must be done just as I will describe it to you and you must do just as I say, nothing else. Agreed? Well then, please tell me how much it may cost and I shall pay you."

It was hopeless to continue babbling on about experimental drama or similar stuff, face to face with this madwoman who now opened her purse and pulled out two fifty-peso bills. "With this you can hire the actors and take care of our preliminary expenses; later on you can let me know how much more you need." So, I, starving for money, unable to escape that damned hole until someone in Buenos Aires answered my letters and mailed me some pesos, put on my best smile, nodded several times and folded the bills carefully before putting them away in my jacket pocket.

"Don't worry, Madame. I believe I understand the sort of thing you . . ." As I spoke I couldn't look at her; I was remembering Blanes, how I hated seeing that same humiliating scorn on her face. "I'll take care of the matter this very afternoon and if we could meet again . . . tonight? Yes, right here. By then we'll have our leading man and you can explain the scene in greater detail and we'll get it all arranged; just how *Dream, A Dream Come True . . .?*"

Maybe she was simply mad or maybe she also knew, as I knew, that I was incapable of taking off with her hundred pesos, because she didn't ask for a receipt, it didn't seem to cross her mind, and after shaking my hand, she left. She moved out of that dining room with her skirt swirling and braking against the motion of each step, walking tall and out into the heat of the street as one returning to the warmth of a sleep which had lasted countless years and which had shielded her tainted youth from collapsing into rot.

I found Blanes in some dark, messy room, whose brick walls showed through the paint, sprawled behind some green plants, in the damp heat of the late afternoon. The hundred pesos were still in my pocket; until I found Blanes, until I got him to help me give that madwoman her money's worth, I wasn't going to spend one cent of it. I woke him up and waited patiently while he bathed, shaved, lay down and then once more got up to drink a glass of milk which meant he had gotten drunk the night before. Collapsing once again on his bed, he lit a cigaret, still refusing to listen and even after I had pulled up the remains of some dresser chair I'd been sitting in and leaned forward seriously, prepared to present my plan, he stopped me, saying: "First, take a look at that ceiling."

The ceiling, held up by two or three moldy beams, was made of mud tiles and long dried-up bamboo of unknown origin.

"Okay. Let's have it," he said.

I described the whole thing but Blanes kept on interrupting, laughing, insisting it was either all a lie I had made up or else someone had sent the woman as a joke. Then he asked me to explain all of it and the matter was finally settled when I offered half of whatever was left over after expenses. I told him that I really didn't know what the deal was, what it involved nor what the hell that woman wanted from us, but the fifty pesos were ours and now we could either both take off for Buenos Aires, or at least I could go alone if he chose to stay and go on sleeping. He laughed, quieted down and then asked for twenty out of the fifty pesos I told him I had received. So right there I was forced to hand over ten, something I soon regretted because that evening when he appeared in the dining room of the hotel, he was already drunk. Leaning his head over a little plate of ice and smiling, he said: "You never learn, do you? The millionaire patron of B.A. or anywhere in the world where a whisper of art is heard. A man, bankrupted a hundred times staging *Hamlet*, is now gambling everything on an unknown genius—in a corset."

But when she arrived, when that woman appeared from behind my shoulders, all dressed in black, veiled, a small umbrella hooked on her wrist and a watch hanging from a gold chain around her neck, and stretching her hand out to Blanes said hello with that special smile, gentler under those electric lights, he stopped nagging me and said: "Ah, Madame, the very gods have guided you to Langman. A man who has sacrificed hundreds of thousands just to give us *Hamlet* in its true form."

Now, as she looked from one to the other, it seemed she was the one mocking; then she became thoughtful and said she was in a hurry, that she would explain everything until the smallest doubt was cleared up and would only return when everything was ready. Beneath the soft yet clear light, the woman's face and everything that glowed on her body, parts of her dress, the nails on one ungloved hand, the umbrella handle, the watch on its chain, all seemed to return to some reality, protected against suffering the brilliant sunshine. It all made me feel relatively relaxed and throughout the rest of the evening I ceased thinking of her as mad, I forgot the pervading odor of fraud in the whole business, and I felt quite calm as if we were in the middle of some every-day, normal business matter. In fact, there was little for me to worry about now that Blanes was there, acting polite, still drinking, and talking to her as if they had already met several times, ordering her a whiskey which she changed for a cup of linden tea. So that finally, whatever she had come to tell me, she ended up telling him, and I made no objection: with Blanes as the leading man the more he understood of the play, the better it would all work out. The woman's instructions were the following (her voice sounded different as she talked to Blanes and although she never looked at him but spoke with her eyes lowered, I felt she was speaking to him in a very private way, as if confessing to something intimate to her life, which I had heard already but which had to be repeated, as when you stand in an office asking for a passport, something like that).

"The set must show houses and sidewalks, but all thrown together, the way it is in a big city, all shoved one on top of the other. I come out, that is, the woman I'm playing comes out of a house and sits down on the curb, near a green table. Near the table, a man is sitting on a kitchen bench. That's your part. He's wearing a knit shirt and a cap. Across the street there's a vegetable store with crates of tomatoes beside the door. Just then a car crosses the stage, and the man, that's you, gets up to cross the street and I'm afraid, thinking the car will hit you. But you get across before the car passes and reach the other side just as a woman comes out, dressed to go walking, and carrying a glass of beer in one hand. You then drink it all down and come right back just as another car speeds by, this time from the opposite direction. Once again, you get across just in time and sit down on the bench. Meanwhile, I've lain down on the curb like a child, and you come and lean over a little and caress my head."

The play was easy enough to stage but I mentioned that now after having thought it through I felt only one problem remained: that third character, that woman who leaves her house for a walk with a glass of beer.

"Pitcher," she told me. "It's an earthenware pitcher with a handle and a cover."

Blanes nodded and said to her, "Of course, it has some design on it—painted on."

She answered yes and it seemed as if his words had calmed her; she looked content, with that expression of happiness that only women get, a look that makes me want to discreetly close my eyes and not look. We discussed the other woman again and finally Blanes stretched out his hand and said he had everything he needed and there was nothing further for us to worry about. I decided that insanity was contagious because when I asked Blanes whom he had in mind for the woman's role, he answered "La Rivas," and even though I had never known anyone by that name, I caught Blanes glaring at me and said nothing. As it turned out, everything was arranged, settled by the two of them, and there was no need for me to think any further about it. I went right off and found the theater owner, who rented us the place two days for the price of one after I gave him my word that no one but the actors would be admitted.

The next day I got hold of some sort of electrician who, for a day's wage of six pesos, helped me paint and move around the scenery. By nightfall, after working nearly fifteen hours, everything was ready. Sweating and in shirtsleeves, I was having some beer and sandwiches while listening with one ear to the man retelling some local gossip. He paused and then continued:

"Your friend was in good hands today. This afternoon he was with that lady you were with last night at the hotel. Nothing is private around here. She isn't from this area; they say she's here during the summers. I don't like to meddle but I saw them going into a hotel. Yes, I understand, you also live in a hotel. But the one they went into this afternoon was different . . . You know the kind I mean?"

A bit later Blanes arrived and I mentioned the famous actress Rivas was still missing and the business of the cars had to be organized since only one was available. It belonged to the man who had been helping me and for a few pesos he was willing to rent it out and drive it. Actually I had already figured out a solution since the car was an old beaten-up convertible, and all one had to do was drive it by first with the top down and afterwards with the top up, or vice versa. Blanes was silent; he was completely drunk and I hadn't the faintest idea where he had gotten the money. Moments later, it struck me that he was probably cynical enough to have accepted money directly from that poor woman. The thought sickened me and I went on eating my sandwich in silence while he walked about drunk and humming as he mimed and leapt around the stage like a photographer, a spy, a boxer, a football player. With his hat tipped back on his head and humming away, he looked everywhere, from every angle, searching for God knows what. I had no stomach for talking to him; with every passing second I felt more and more convinced that he was drunk on money he had practically stolen from that poor sick woman. So after finishing my sandwich, I sent my man out for six more and another bottle of beer. Meanwhile, Blanes had tired of prancing about and he came over and sat down on some crate near me, still drunk but now sentimental, his hands in his pants pockets, his hat on his knees, and looking glassy-eyed at the stage. Nothing was said for a while and I could see that he had aged and that his blond hair was dull and thinning. He hadn't too many years left as a leading man, or for taking women to hotels, or for much else really.

"I haven't wasted my time either," he blurted out.

"Yes, I can imagine," I answered indifferently.

He smiled, became thoughtful, pulled his hat down and got up again. He continued talking, pacing back and forth, as he had often seen me do at my office while dictating a letter to the secretary, surrounded by personally autographed photos.

"I've been checking that woman out," he said. "It turns out she or her family once had money but later she had to teach. Nobody, you know, nobody says she's crazy. Sort of strange, yes. Always has been but not mad. I don't know why I'm talking to you, oh Hamlet's most sad adopted father, with your snout smeared in sandwich butter. Talking about this to you."

"At least," I told him calmly, "I haven't taken up spying into other people's lives. Nor playing the Don Juan with strange women." I wiped my mouth with my handkerchief and turned toward him with a bored look. "And I also don't get drunk on who knows what sort of money."

As he now stood, hands on hips, looking seriously back at me and spouting insults, no one could have guessed that he was thinking about that woman, that he really didn't mean what he was saying, that it was just something to do while he thought about her, something to keep me from guessing his mind was fixed on her. He walked back to me, squatted down and quickly straightened up again holding the bottle of beer and drank it slowly down, his mouth glued to the opening. He walked around the stage a while longer, and then sat down again, the bottle between his feet and his hands covering it.

"I've talked to her and she's told me," he said. "I wanted to know what it was all about. I don't know if you understand it's not just a matter of pocketing some cash. I questioned her about what we have to perform and then I knew she was mad. Do you want to know? The whole thing is a dream she had, get it? But what's really insane is that she says the dream means nothing to her. She doesn't know the man sitting down and wearing the blue shirt, nor the woman with the pitcher, she's never even lived on a street like this idiotic mess you've dreamed up. So, in the end, why? She says that while she was asleep and dreaming she was happy, the word isn't 'happy' exactly, something else. So she wants to see it all again, afresh. It's crazy, but there's some reason in it. Something else I like about it is there's no cheap sex in any of it. When we were going off to bed, she kept stopping on the street—the sky was so blue, it was so hot—she kept grabbing me by the shoulders and lapels and asking if I understood. I still don't. It's something still unclear to her, too, because she never finished explaining it."

At ten on the dot, the woman arrived at the theater, wearing the same black dress with the watch and chain, which to me seemed out of place on that painted slum street and not the thing for lying down on a curbstone while Blanes stroked her hair. But it didn't matter: the theater was empty; only Blanes was involved, still drunk, smoking and dressed in a blue shirt with a gray cap folded down over one ear. He had arrived early with the young woman who was to appear in the doorway of the vegetable store and then give him a pitcher of beer. The girl also seemed wrong for her role, at least as I had imagined it, although the devil alone knew what the role really was. She was sad and thin, badly dressed and made-up, someone Blanes had probably picked up in some cheap little café, taking her off the streets for the night with some absurd story; this was obvious because right away she started strutting around like some great star, and it was pitiful to watch her stretching her arm and holding the pitcher of beer; I felt like throwing her out right then. The moment the other one, the mad one, got there dressed in black, she stood for a while looking at the stage, her hands clasped in front of her and she seemed to me tremendously tall, much taller and thinner than I remembered. Then, without a word to anyone, with that sick smile fainter but still making me bristle, she crossed the stage and hid herself in the wing of scenery from which she was to appear. I don't know why, but my eyes followed her, absorbing the exact shape of her long body, closely outlined by her tight-fitting black dress. I watched her body until the curtain's edge blocked it from my view.

Now it was I who stood stage-center and since everything seemed ready and it was now past ten, I lifted my arms and clapped to signal the actors. But just then, unaware of what was going on exactly, I began to sense that we had gotten ourselves into something I could never speak of, just the way we may know the soul of another and yet find words are useless to describe it. I gestured to them to start, and when I saw Blanes and the girl he had brought begin to move towards their places, I fled into the wings, where the man was already sitting behind the wheel of his ancient car which now began to shudder and quietly rattle. I perched on a crate, hoping to hide, since I wanted nothing more to do with the insanity which was about to begin. I could see how she stepped out of the door of the small run-down house, her body moving like a young girl's, her hair thick, almost gray and loose down her back where it was tied in a knot with some bright-colored ribbon. She was striding out, just the way a young woman does after she has finished setting the table and decides to step outdoors for a moment to quietly watch the end of the day without thinking of anything. I saw her sit down near the bench where Blanes was and rest her head on her hand, her elbow leaning on her knees, letting her fingertips fall on her half-parted lips; her face turned towards some distant point beyond me, beyond even the wall behind me. I saw Blanes get up to cross the street, crossing precisely before the car, with its top up and belching smoke, passed by and quickly disappeared. I saw Blanes' arm and the young woman's in the facing house joined by the pitcher of beer, and saw how the man drank it all down at once, left the pitcher in her hand and saw how she then slowly and without a sound sank back into the doorway. Once more I saw the man in the blue shirt cross the street an instant before a car with its top down raced by and came to a stop near me, its motor shutting off immediately, and as the bluish smoke from the engine cleared, I made out the young woman on the curb, yawning and then lying down on the pavement, her head resting on an arm which hid her hair and with one knee bent. The man in the shirt and cap then leaned over and stroked the young woman's head. He began caressing her, and his hand moved back and forth, catching in her hair, reaching over to stroke her forehead, tightening the bright ribbon holding her hair; he kept on repeating the caresses.

I got down from my crate, heaved a sigh and feeling calmer, quietly crossed the stage. The car man followed, smiling, intimidated, and the thin girl Blanes had brought came out of her doorway to join us. She asked me something, a short question, a single word and I answered without taking my eyes off Blanes, the woman lying down and his hand still stroking her forehead and her thrown-back head, untiring, unaware that the scene was over, that this last thing, caressing her hair, couldn't go on forever. Blanes' body was bent over; he was still stroking her head, stretching his arm so that his fingertips could run down the length of her hair from her forehead to where it spread over her shoulders and her back resting on the ground. The car man was still smiling, he coughed and spat to the side. The girl who had given Blanes the pitcher of beer began walking over to him and the woman. I turned to the owner of the car and told him he could take it away so we could clear out early. I walked over to him, digging into my pocket for a few pesos. Where the others stood on my right, something strange was going on and as I realized this, I bumped into Blanes, who had taken his cap off and stank of liquor, and he jabbed me in the ribs and shouted:

"Don't you realize she's dead, you animal."

I felt alone, broken by the event, and as Blanes paced drunkenly around the stage like some madman and the girl of the pitcher of beer and the car man leaned over the woman, I understood what it was all about, what it was the woman had been searching for, what it was Blanes had stalked the previous evening, rushing back and forth across the stage like one possessed: it was all clear, like one of those things you know as a child but later on find words are useless to explain.

6

VICENTE HUIDOBRO

The worst enemy of Huidobro the poet was Huidobro the poetical theoretician. In defending his poems, he lost his sense of humor and became a bore. He was the first Latin American to play an active role in the French avant-garde (see introduction to this part), but he had higher aspirations. He wanted to be recognized as the first to have proclaimed a new literary ism: creationism. To validate his claim to this purely chronological distinction (the literary equivalent of the feudal "right of the first night"), Huidobro became involved in endless disputes with another aspirant, the French poet Pierre Reverdy, as well as with sundry Hispanic poets and critics. He spent almost all his literary life, in fact, in useless pursuit of such doctrinal originality. Yet he also happened to produce several of the major poems in modern Latin American letters.

Huidobro was born to a wealthy family in Santiago, Chile, in 1893, and received his formal education at a Jesuit school. His real surname was García Fernández, which is the Spanish equivalent of "Smith-Jones." He therefore devised for himself the more euphonious and original name of "Huidobro"—an early indication of his desire for uniqueness, and his passion (perhaps obsession) with words. The doctrine of creationism, whether or not he can legitimately be considered its inventor, clearly reflects this passion; for, briefly put, it consists in the notion that words have and create their own autonomous reality, impinging on and interacting with other realities.

Huidobro's first four volumes of poetry (1911–1914) were undistinguished; overall, they seemed too much like the work of a modernist epigone. While his efforts to predate some of his avant-garde poems have obscured the chronology of his work, according to Huidobro's own account, he had, even before leaving for Europe in 1916, publicly read a manifesto in Santiago in which he proclaimed the poet's independence from nature. He also claimed to have written then and there some graphic poems, or "calligrammes," as Apollinaire called them. Perhaps he did. But as early as 1912, Apollinaire had published his *Aesthetic Meditations,* followed in 1913 by his book on the cubist painters, in which a new critical approach was evident; his graphic poems, moreover, had been printed in various little magazines (though they would not be published in book form until 1918). It is quite possible, then, that Huidobro became well acquainted with Apollinaire's work while still in Santiago. It is hard to know. What is indisputable is that after reaching Paris, he began writing poems in French and publishing them in *Nord-Sud* (North-South), the journal edited by Pierre Reverdy. Huidobro became friends with him, and had his portrait painted by Picasso, Juan Gris, and Robert Delaunay. In 1917, he published his first French book, *Square Horizon,* illustrated by Gris. Two more volumes in French came out the following year: *Tour Eiffel* (with Delaunay's drawings) and *Hallali.*

By that time, however, Huidobro was in Spain, shocking the younger poets out of their modernist diction. He also published in Madrid, in 1918, three volumes of Spanish verse: *Arctic Poems, Equatorials,* and *The Water Mirror.* (According to Huidobro, the last-named work actually had its first edition in Buenos Aires in 1916, *before* his trip to Europe; but no dated copy of such an edition has ever come to light.)

As regards the French verse, it is perhaps not unduly harsh to describe it as like exercises written on the margins of a Berlitz school manual. With some humor, Huidobro himself admitted, years later, that the charm of these pieces was increased by his relative ignorance of French at the time he wrote them. In the Spanish poems, however, one finds occasional proof that Huidobro was, after all, something more than a tireless PR man. One poem proclaimed the need to abandon mimetic art, to start from scratch, and to invent reality through words. One line—"The poet is a small God!"—became Huidobro's motto.

From 1918 until his death thirty years later, Huidobro commuted between Chile and Europe, mainly France and Spain, involving himself in various kinds of warfare: poetical, with Borges and the Spanish ultraists, with his compatriot Neruda, with the Peruvian César Moro; political, with the Chilean electorate, at the time he ran, unsuccessfully, for the presidency of Chile in 1925; with the Spanish fascists, when, along with many other intellectuals, he gave his support to the Spanish Republic. He was even a Marxist of sorts (although he did at times have trouble convincing others of the sincerity of his political views). Although Huidobro's creationism was based on the same cult of metaphor that underlay various other avant-garde theories, his desire to promote the preeminence of his own doctrine drove him on to the attack—on futurism, because its verse was allegedly too extroverted; on ultraism, on the ground that its productions were lacking in the element of surprise or unpredictability; on surrealism, because it was too involved with automatic writing. And withal, this life of vigorous activity, political and polemical, does not seem to have seriously interfered with his creative work, which proceeded apace.

In 1931 Huidobro published his best long poem: *Altazor*, subtitled "Journey in a Parachute." The title is a portmanteau word, the sort of device Joyce was so fond of. It can be divided into *Alt* (alto: high) and *Azor* (goshawk). The poet sees himself as a bird of prey, soaring in the sky. But he is also aware of the dangers of his vocation: the subtitle embodies the prospect of (fatal) descent. What is important in the poem is not the message (expressed long since in the ancient myth of Icarus) but the medium—the writing. Huidobro is preeminently a poet of words. *Altazor* not only contained the most astonishing series of images and tropes in Spanish American poetry; it also creatively manipulated the very structure of words. The flight and eventual fall of the poet-bird are paralleled in the soaring of words and the final disintegration of lines into isolated letters and phonemes. In this challenging work, Huidobro anticipated the anguished (and also joyful) verbal explorations of poets like the Argentine Oliverio Girondo (Part Four, 13), the Mexican Octavio Paz (Five, 1), and even the Brazilian "concrete" poets (Five, 8). Eliot Weinberger's translation of some sections of *Altazor*, as well as of some other poems, effectively captures Huidobro's unique humor, his gift for rhythms and verbal fancy.

Though primarily a poet, Huidobro also wrote several novels. The only successful one, however, was *Satyr, or The Power of Words* (1939), the story of a perfectly innocent man accused of being a child molester. His increasingly desperate efforts to throw off this defamatory label are all in vain, and in the end he is actually driven to rape a young girl—such is "the power of words" to create reality. The novel, though poorly constructed, thus effectively exemplifies the creationistic notion that to name something is to bring it into existence. One might object, of course, that such a thing could only really happen in the world of literature, of words. But it was only to this world that Huidobro belonged.

Altazor and Other Poems

"Alone," a special translation by David Guss of "Solo," from El Ciudadino del Olvido; *all other poems in this selection especially translated by Eliot Weinberger, from* Altazor.

Alone

Alone between night and death alone
Traveling through the heart of eternity
Eating fruit at the center of the void

Night Death
The dead just planted in the infinite
The earth leaves the earth returns

Alone with a star before me
Alone with a great song inside and no star before me

Night and death
Night and death
The night's death spinning through death

So far far away
The world flies off in the wind
And a dog howls in the infinite searching for the lost land

Poem to Make Trees Grow

Salud salud from my solitary sun
Interior night swum like visionary sap
Health health in bridges of dawn and sunset
Likewise from earth and sky and stars and stone
Health in a seat of air
Health in a silent motion
Five limbs seven limbs twelve limbs
Twelve leaves twenty leaves a hundred leaves
Climbs and climbs and climbs
And flaps and swims inside yourself

Climbs in your darkness
Climbs to your skin
Climbs through your mournful climbing walls
Through your weeping
Through your effervescences of perfumed angels
And your respiration of silent rock

A sky for every limb
A star for every leaf
A river to carry memory
And to wash memories from us like distance
A mountain the body of a still butterfly
A rainbow leaving a cloud of dust in its wake
Climbs swims
Climbs through your dark center
Through your air pipes that expand
Through your virtue of love growing stronger

Love the leaves love
The leaves receive the limb's belief
The leaf relives
Love in the fief
Sap swims
Limb swims
And life swims through the ailing
You've got to seize the leaves
Laugh at the sky at its free peak
Five limbs seven limbs twelve limbs
So all the slimmer swimmers swim
Twelve leaves twenty leaves a hundred leaves
And the swimmers swimming
The slimmer swimmers
Swimming life
A mountain to the body of a melancholy tree
A rainbow leaving a cloud of butterflies in its wake
A tree that rises up and blocks the path of death

Alert

Midnight

In the garden
Every shadow is a stream

That noise coming closer is not a car

Over the skies of Paris
Otto von Zeppelin

Sirens sing
In the black waves
And this clarion that calls
Is not the clarion of victory
                              A hundred airplanes
                              Flying around the moon

PUT OUT YOUR PIPE

The shells burst like full-blown roses
And bombs puncture the days

Amputated songs
                    tremble in the branches

Wind contorts the streets

HOW TO PUT OUT THE STAR IN THE POND

Announcement

The smile in the corner of the lips
Where the smiles die
In the night when rocks weep

Such bitter tears
Someone will know the future and its landscape of stars
The words that fill the pain of mourning horizons

The astrologer enters dressed in poems
Like mist from the streams
He speaks and walks like night
On the peak of his words a bird dies

Nothing matters
Love and enigma maintained
He is of another opinion
Only believing in the phosphorus of the unconscious
In the sword of solitude
That cuts our silence in half
That there may be dialogue between air and nothing

Oh night crucified on the wind
Oh night
Good night

Ars Poetica

Let poetry be like a key
That opens a thousand doors.
A leaf falls; something flies overhead;
Let as much as the eyes see be created,
And the soul of the listener tremble.

Invent new worlds and watch your word;
The adjective, when it does not create life, kills.

We are in the age of nerves.
Muscles hang,
Like a memory, in museums,
But we are not the weaker for it:
True vigor
Lives in the head.

Do not sing the rose, O poets!
Make it bloom in the poem.

For us alone
All things live under the sun.

The poet is a little God.

New Year

The dream of Jacob has been realized;
An eye opens in front of the mirror
And the people letting down the screen
Throw off their flesh like an old coat.

The movie 1916
Comes out of a box.

The European War.

Rain on the spectators
And a rumble of tremors.

It's cold.

In the back of the auditorium
An old man has wheeled into the vacuum.

Altazor: Canto III

Break the ligatures of the veins
The loops of respiration and the chains

Of eyes paths of horizons
Flower screened on uniform skies

Soul paved with recollections
Like stars carved by the wind

The sea is a roof of bottles
That dreams in the sailor's memory

The sky is that great whole mane
Woven between the hands of the aeronaut

And the airplane carries a new language
To the mouth of the eternal skies

Chains of glances tie us to the earth
Break them break so many chains

The first man flies to light the sky
Space bursts open in a wound

And the bullet returns to the assassin
Eternally tied to the infinite

Cut all the links
Of river sea or mountain

Of spirit and memory
Of agonizing law and fever dreams

It is the world that turns and follows and whirls
In an ultimate pupil

Tomorrow the countryside
Will follow the galloping horses

The flower will suck the bee
Because the hangar will be a hive

The rainbow will become a bird
And fly singing to its nest

The crows will become planets
And sprout feathers of grass

Leaves will be tepid feathers
Falling from their throats

Glances will be rivers
And the rivers wounds in the legs of space

The flock will be guided to its pastor
So the day can doze drowsy as an airplane

And the tree will rest on the turtledove
While the clouds turn to stone

Because everything is as it is in every eye
Ephemeral and astrological dynasty
Falling from universe to universe

The poet is the manicurist of the language
And even more the magician who inflames and quenches
Stellar words and the cherries of vagabond goodbyes
Far from the hands of the earth
And he invents all that he says
Things that move outside the ordinary world
Let us kill the poet who gluts us

Poetry still and poetry poetry
Poetical poetry poetry
Poetical poetry by poetical poets
Poetry
Too much poetry
From the rainbow to the asshole pianist of the neighborhood
Enough poetry lady enough bambina
It still has bars over its eyes
The game is a game and not an endless prayer
Smiles or laughter and not the pupil's lamps
That wheel from affliction toward the sea

Smile and gossip of the weaver star
Smile of the brain that evokes dead stars
On the mediumistic table of its radiations

Enough lady harp of beautiful images
Of secret illuminated "likes"
Something else something else we are seeking
We know how to dart a kiss like a glance
Plant glances like trees
Cage trees like birds
Water birds like heliotropes
Play a heliotrope like music
Empty music like a sack
Decapitate a sack like a penguin
Cultivate penguins like vineyards
Milk a vineyard like a cow
Unmast cows like schooners
Comb a schooner like a comet
Disembark comets like tourists
Bewitch tourists like snakes
Harvest snakes like almonds
Undress an almond like an athlete
Chop down athletes like cypresses
Light cypresses like lanterns
Nestle lanterns like skylarks
Breathe skylarks like sighs
Embroider sighs like silks
Drain silks like rivers
Hoist a river like a flag
Pluck a flag like a rooster
Quench a rooster like a fire
Row through fires like seas
Reap seas like wheat fields
Chime wheat fields like bells
Bleed bells like lambs
Draw lambs like smiles
Bottle smiles like liquor
Set liquor like jewels
Electrify jewels like twilights
Man twilights like battleships
Unshoe a battleship like a king
Raise kings like dawns
Crucify dawns like prophets
Etc etc etc

Enough sir violin sunk in a wave wave
Everyday wave of misery religion
Of dream on dream possessions of jewels

After the heart eating roses
And the nights of the perfect ruby
The new athlete leaps on the magic track
Frolicking with magnetic words
Hot as the earth when a volcano rises
Hurling the sorceries of his bird-phrases

The ultimate poet agonizes
The bells of the continents chime
The moon dies with the night on its back
The sun pulls the day out of its pocket
The solemn new land opens its eyes
And moves from earth to the stars
The burial of poetry

All the languages are dead
Dead in the hands of the tragic neighbor
We must revive the languages
With raucous laughter
With wagons of giggles
With circuit-breakers in the sentences
And cataclysm in the grammar
Get up and walk
Stretch your legs limber the stiff joints
Fires of laughter for the shivering language
Astral gymnastics for the numb tongues
Get up and walk
Live live like a football
Explode in the mouth of motorcycle diamonds
In the drunkenness of its fireflies
The very vertigo of its liberation
A beautiful madness in the life of the word
A beautiful madness in the zone of language
Adventure clothed in tangible disdains
The adventure of language between two wrecked ships
Precious catastrophe on the rails of verse

And since we must live and not kill ourselves
As long as we live let us play
The simple game of words
Of the pure word and nothing more

Without clean images of jewels
(Words carry too much cargo)
A ritual of words without shadow
An angel game there in the infinite
Word by word
With the light of a star that a collision brings to life
Sparks leap from the collision and then more violent
More enormous the explosion
Passion of the game in space
Without moon-wings and pretense
Single combat between chest and sky
Total dissolution at last of the voice from flesh
Echo of light that bleeds air over the air

Then nothing nothing
Spirit whisper of the wordless phrase

7

CÉSAR VALLEJO

Although César Vallejo spent more time in Paris during the twenties and thirties than any other Latin American poet of his generation, he hardly conformed to the conventional image of the cosmopolitan expatriate. He rejected the avant-garde for political reasons, wrote poems about his memories of Peru, and was totally haunted by his own demons. In bitter, self-imposed exile he produced some of the best poetry in the Spanish language.

Vallejo, born in a small village in 1892, was a half-caste. Both his grandfathers were Spanish priests; both his grandmothers, their native concubines. By his very origins, then, he found himself symbolically placed in the classic colonial situation. But he also took pride in his Indian ancestry. The harsh yet warm memories of childhood would evoke images of a lost paradise to color his poetry. After completing his secondary education in his native province of La Libertad, Vallejo went to Lima to study medicine at the University of San Marcos. In 1912, however, he returned to La Libertad, to take up literary studies in the city of Trujillo, where he obtained a degree in 1915.

At the time Vallejo began his literary career, there was very little left in Peru of the glory of the Incas or the splendor of the viceregal period which Palma (Part Two, 10) had so wittily evoked. The country had been humiliated by neighboring Chile in the war of 1879 and was very slowly being drawn into the modern world through the well-tried formula of army-supported dictatorships. Vallejo's first book of poems, *Black Heralds* (1918), showed him to be still under modernist influence, especially that of the Lugones of *Sentimental Moon Calendar*, and the Herrera y Reissig of the "Orphic" poems (see Three, 5, 6).

By the early twenties, younger poets all over Latin America were receiving the avant-garde message, and Vallejo was no exception. His French was probably poor, but in 1919 a translation of Mallarmé's *Un coup de dès* had been published in a Spanish journal; the same publication included in one of its earlier issues a Dada anthology. Probably Vallejo saw these texts. But before he had the chance to complete a volume of new poetry, two experiences led him to decide to leave Peru for good: his mother died, and in 1920 he got involved in an obscure political uprising in his native province. He was charged with being the intellectual author of the sedition (although, to the contrary, he had actually been trying to help restore order), and spent nearly four months in prison. He was exonerated in 1921, but the experience would loom large in his future poetry.

In 1922 he published the new volume, *Trilce*, which reveals even in its title its avant-garde inspiration. It represents a merger of two Spanish words: *tres* (three) and *dulce* (sweet), and so means "Three Times Sweet." In thus cutting up words and rearranging their component phonemes in unexpected ways, Vallejo was tearing them away from their etymological roots. There was a certain ambivalence in his feelings toward the Spanish language. It was, of course, a legacy from his grandfathers, but at the same time he had something of his Indian brethren's attitude to a language which had been forced down their throats, and had constituted one of the most effective instruments of colonization. He had a similarly unconventional approach to versification. He took the free verse of the avant-garde and freed it as well from logical continuity and academic syntax. The result was a book that produced a radical transformation of Spanish poetry. Compared to it, the verse being written around the same time by Borges or Huidobro (selections 1, 6) sounded tame: they were playfully effective, even brilliant, but not so obsessively committed, like Vallejo, to total transformation.

In 1923, Vallejo left Peru. For the next fifteen years he lived mainly in Paris, where he married a younger French woman, and became involved in the active literary life of expatriate Spanish Americans. These years were hard and Vallejo made them still harder with his desperate pride and a masochistic urge to suffer. Like the Brazilian Lima Barreto (Three, 15) and the Uruguayan Juan Carlos Onetti (Four, 5), he belonged among the spiritual progeny of Dostoevsky. There was in him something of Ivan Karamazov's need to defy and negate God, but there was also a Christ complex that was closely akin to Prince Myshkin's saintliness. Life in Paris, in any event, seems to have provided him with an inexhaustible supply of misery. He had experienced hunger in his native town, he observed, but then it was hunger shared with his loving family; whereas in France he discovered want in the midst of abundance, loneliness among the bitter and brusque Parisians.

Fortunately, he also discovered political solidarity. After two trips to the U.S.S.R. in 1928–29, he wrote fervently about the new Promised Land of socialism. Because of his Communist affiliation, he was expelled from France in 1930. For two years he lived in Spain, in close contact with various left-wing groups. He published in 1931 a Spanish edition of *Trilce* and a proletarian novel, *Tungsten*, about a 1917 strike in a Peruvian mine owned by North Americans. The book followed the dreary socialist realist formula and argued that the intelligentsia ought to be at the service of the workers, the only true revolutionaries. Such articles of faith were already being seriously questioned at the time the novel was published. The articles he contributed to Peruvian newspapers and journals during this period were very thin in substance and showed him following the party line in his attacks against surrealism. He returned to France in 1932, but continued to visit Spain periodically.

At the outbreak of the Civil War, Vallejo helped Neruda to organize the Spanish American Group Committee for the defense of the Republic. He participated in many meetings, in both France and Spain. But he was already seriously ill and died in Paris in 1938.

If his published work during the thirties had been principally political, the poems he wrote and left ready for publication were more than just occasional pieces. They were a distillation of years of anguish, pain, and hunger. They also were the result of an uncompromising attitude toward language, of a search for the hidden structure of verses and poems, of a relentless pursuit of new words to express what was deeply buried inside him. When these poems were published in 1938—in two separate volumes, *Human Poems* and *Spain, Let This Cup Pass from Me*—they placed Vallejo in the vanguard of the avant-garde. Not only were they new and brilliant and extremely poignant, they were also that rare combination, verse that was both politically and poetically committed.

Human Poems

From Poemas Humanos/Human Poems, *translated by Clayton Eshleman* (New York: Grove Press, 1958), *pp. 43–45, 79–117, 207–9, 305–7, 319–21, 323–25.*

Considering coldly, impartially . . .

Considering coldly, impartially,
that man is sad, coughs, and, however,
takes pleasure in his reddened chest;
that the only thing he does is to be made
of days;
that he's a gloomy mammal and combs himself . . .

Considering
that man proceeds softly from work
and reverberates boss, sounds employee;
that the diagram of time
is constant diorama on his medals
and, half open, his eyes have studied
since distant times
his famished mass formula . . .

Understanding easily
that man stops, at times, and thinks
like wanting to cry,
and given to stretching out like an object
makes himself a good carpenter, sweats, kills
and then sings, lunches, buttons up . . .

Considering too
that man is in truth an animal
and notwithstanding turning hits me on the head with his
                                        sadness . . .

Examining, finally,
his opposed chunks, his stool,
his desperation at the end of his atrocious day, rubbing it out . . .

Understanding
that he knows I love him,
that I hate him with affection and to me he is in sum indif-
                                        ferent . . .

Considering his general documents
and scrutinizing that certificate
that proves he was born very teeny . . .

I signal him,
he comes,
and I embrace him, moved.
So what! Moved . . . Moved . . .

Alfonso, I see you watching me . . .

Alfonso, I see you watching me
from the implacable plane where
forever and never lineally dwell.
(That night you slept between your

dream and mine on rue de Ribouté.)
Palpably
your unforgettable cholo hears you walk
in Paris, he feels you become quiet on the phone
and play on the wire your last act to
take weight, to toast
to the depths, to me, to you.

   I still
buy "du vin, du lait, comptant les sous"
under my overcoat, so my soul doesn't see me,
under my overcoat, that same one, dear Alfonso,
and under the simple ray of the compound temple;
I still suffer, and you, no more, never again brother!
(They've told me in all your centuries of pain,
beloved being,
beloved existing,
you made wood zeros. Is that true?)

   In the "boite de nuit" where you played tangos,
your provoked creature playing out its heart,
escorted by yourself, crying
for yourself and for your enormous resemblance to your shadow,

Monsieur Fourgat, the owner, has aged.
Tell it to him? Recount it all? Never again,
Alfonso; no more!

   The hôtel des Ecoles functions as always
and they still buy mandarins;
but I suffer, like I tell you,
sweetly, remembering
what we both suffered in both our deaths,
in the aperture of the double tomb,
of that other tomb with your being
and of this mahogany one with your existing;
I suffer drinking a glass of you, Silva,
just a glass to fix me up, as we used to say,
and afterward, then we'll see. . . .

   The other toast is this, between three,
taciturn, diverse
in wine, in world, in glass, the one we used to toast
more than once to the flesh
and, less than once, to the mind.

Today is even different still;
today I suffer sweet, bitterly,
I drink your blood as to Christ the hard,
I eat your bone as to Christ the soft
because I love you, Alfonso, two by two,
and could almost say so eternally.

The fact is . . .

The fact is the place where I put on my
pants is a house where
I take off my shirt out loud,
where I have floor, soul, a map of my Spain.
Just now I was talking about
me to myself, and put
on a little book a tremendous loaf of bread
and I've then made the move, I've moved,
trying to hum a little, the right
side of life to the left;
later, I've washed my whole body, my belly,
vigorously with dignity;
I've turned over to see what dirties itself,
I've scraped off what brings me so near
and put that map in proper order that
nodded off or wept, I don't know it.

My house, unfortunately, is a house,
a floor fortunately, where with its
inscription my beloved spoon lives,
my dear now letterless skeleton,
the razor, a permanent cigar.
Truthfully, when I think
what life is,
I can't help saying it to Georgette·
so I can eat something pleasant and go out
for the evening, buy myself a good newspaper
and save a day for when there isn't one,
a night too, for when there is
(they put it this way in Peru—I'm sorry);
in the same way I suffer very carefully
so to not shout or cry, since the eyes
possess, independent of one, their poverties,
I mean, their duty, something
that slips away from the soul and falls to the soul.

Having crossed
fifteen years, after, fifteen, and before, fifteen,
one feels, actually, a little foolish,
it's natural, on the other hand, what to do!
And what not to do, that's worse!
Only to live, only to become
what one is among millions
of breads, among thousands of wines, among hundreds of mouths,
between the sun and its beam that's from the moon
and among the Mass, the bread, the wine, and my soul.

Today is Sunday, and so
the idea comes to my head, to my chest the cry
and to my throat, like a big lump.
Today is Sunday, and this
is many centuries old; otherwise
it would be Monday maybe, the idea coming to my heart,
to my brain the cry
and to my throat a terrifying desire to choke
what I now feel,
like a man that I am and that I've suffered.

The Wretched of the Earth

The day's going to come; wind
up your arm, look under
your mattress, stand again
on your head to walk straight.
The day's going to come, put on your coat.

The day's going to come; grip
your large intestine tight in your hand, reflect
before you meditate, for it's awful
when your wretchedness hits and sinks
on and on in you a tooth.

You have to eat, but I keep telling myself
don't grieve, for grief and graveside
sobbing don't belong to the poor;
pull yourself together, remember,
confide in your white thread, smoke, check
your chain and keep it behind your portrait.
The day's going to come, put on your soul.

The day's going to come; they pass,
they've opened up an eye in the hotel
whipping and beating it with a mirror that's yours . . .
are you trembling? It's the remote state of the forehead
and this recent nation of the stomach.
They're still snoring. . . . What universe puts up with this snore!
How your pores hang on, indicting it!
With so many twos, aye! you're so alone!
The day's going to come, put on your dream.

The day's going to come, I repeat
through the oral organ of your silence
and urge you to move further left with hunger
further right with thirst; in any case
stop being poor with the rich,
poker
your cold, for in it is mixed my warmth, beloved victim.
The day's going to come, put on your body.

The day's going to come;
morning, sea, meteor
pursue your weariness with banners,
and through your classic pride, the hyenas
count their steps to the beat of the ass,
the baker's wife thinks about you,
the butcher thinks about you, fingering
the cleaver in which steel
iron and metal are imprisoned; never forget
that during Mass there are no friends.
The day's going to come, put on your sun.

The day comes; double
your breathing, triple
your rancorous good will
and elbow fear, link and emphasis,
for you, as anyone can see in your crotch the evil
being, aye! immortal,
you've dreamed tonight you were living
on nothing and dying from everything. . . .

Sermon on Death

And, finally, passing then into the domain of death
that drills in squadron, former bracket,

paragraph and brace, pieced brace and diaeresis,
for what the Assyrian podium? for what the Christian pulpit?
the intense landmark of the Vandal furniture
or even less this proparoxytonic retreat?

Is it in order to end
tomorrow in prototype of the phallic show,
in diabetes and in white bedpan,
in geometric face and in defunct,
that sermon and almonds are made fundamental,
that there are literally too many potatoes
and this watery specter in which gold burns
and in which the price of snow scalds?
Is it for this we die so much?
Only to die
must we die each instant?
And the paragraph I write?
And the deistic bracket I raise on high?
And the squadron in which my hoof is failed?
And the brace that fits all doors?
And the stranger diaeresis, the hand,
my potato and my flesh and my contradiction under the sheet?

Weird weird me, werewolf of me, lamb-
heart, judicious stallion, O great work horse of me!
Podium, yes, my whole life; pulpit
likewise, my whole death!
These papers a barbaric sermon;
proparoxytonic retreat of this peelable skin.

Of this luck, thoughtful, auriferous, flank-armed,
I'll defend my catch in two moments
with voice and likewise with larynx,
and of the physical smell with which I pray,
and of the instinct for immobility with which I walk,
I shall honor myself while I live—it must be said;
my botflies will swell with pride,
because, at the center, I exist, and to the right
likewise, and, to the left, equally.

Paris, October 1936

From all this I'm the only one who parts.
From this bench I'm off, from my breeches,

from my great situation, from my acts,
from my number split part to part,
from all this I'm the only one who parts.

From the Champs Élysées or as strange
little Moon Street turns around,
my defunction's off, my cradle parts,
and surrounded by people, alone, loose,
my human resemblance turns around
sending out its shadows one by one.

And I remove from everything, for every
thing remains to make my alibi:
my shoe, its buttonhole, likewise its mud—
even the double in the elbow
of my own shirt buttoned up.

Black Stone on a White Stone

I will die in Paris with hard dirty rain,
on a day I now remember.
I will die in Paris—and I don't run—
maybe a Thursday, like today, in autumn.

Thursday, because today, Thursday, when I prose
these lines, I have forced my humeri on
unwillingly and, never like today have I again,
with all my road, seen myself alone.

César Vallejo is dead, they beat him,
everyone, without his doing anything to them;
they hit him hard with a stick and hard

likewise with a rope; witnesses are
the Thursdays and the humerus bones,
the loneliness, the rain, the roads . . .

8

CÉSAR MORO

No other Latin American poet was less Latin American than the Peruvian César Moro. Although he spent only eight years in France (as compared, for instance, to the fifteen of his compatriot Vallejo), Moro became thoroughly French: he participated actively in the work of the surrealist school and wrote his most vigorous poetry in French rather than his native tongue. After his return to Latin America, he became an instructor in French and continued to write the greater part of his verse in that language. Nevertheless, some of the poems he did write in Spanish are among the best of his time. His bilingualism enabled Moro to escape the fate of some other poets who, though born in Latin America, were completely absorbed by French culture—the Cuban José María de Heredia (not to be confused with his cousin and namesake—Part Two, 3) and the Uruguayans Lautréamont, Laforgue, and Supervielle. Unlike these men, Moro also belonged to Spanish American letters.

He was born in Lima in 1903. His real name was Alfredo Quispez Asín, but he remedied Destiny's oversight by adopting a euphonious pseudonym. He went to Paris in 1925, and for the next eight years devoted himself entirely to the assimilation of surrealist ideas and techniques. He translated poets such as Pierre Reverdy, André Breton, and Benjamin Péret; he contributed his own French verse to surrealist periodicals and participated in some of the theoretical polemics of the time. As a great admirer of Reverdy's, Moro sided with him in his dispute with Huidobro (Four, 6). Moro was also interested in painting; he liked de Chirico's work very much, and took part in the reevaluation of Bonnard's paintings.

In 1933 he returned to Lima, where with some friends he founded one of the first Latin American surrealist journals, *The Use of Words*. He attacked indigenism (a literary movement drawing its inspiration and themes from the indigenous Indian culture), which was then having a powerful revival in Peru, and defended the Spanish Republic during the civil war. In 1938 he moved to Mexico, where he resided until 1948. While there he came to be very close to the group of poets called the "contemporáneos," especially to Xavier Villaurrutia (selection 10). He also had a chance to renew his friendship with Breton during the latter's visit to Mexico. Moro helped him and Wolfgang Paalen to organize the First International Exposition of Surrealism. Although Moro admired Breton, he did not share all his views. They disagreed, for example, in their respective assessments of Diego Rivera. Breton valued Rivera's friendship and patronage very highly, while Moro found the famous muralist too equivocal from the political point of view and hardly satisfactory as a painter.

Three small books of poems were the result of these Mexican years: two were in French (*Le Château de grisou*, 1943; *Lettre d'amour*, 1944, perhaps his most important single poem) and one in Spanish, *The Equestrian Tortoise* (begun in 1938, but published after his death by his friend, the French poet André Coyné, in 1957). Another book dating from this period, *Pierre des soleils*, remains unpublished. But the unity of Moro's work transcends the linguistic barrier. His poetry—desperate, hallucinatory, erotic—found in surrealism its central vision: Moro was a homosexual, and he used the double mask of a pseudonym and a foreign language so as to be able to evoke most freely the ravages of desire, the burning theme of love.

In 1948 he returned to Lima to continue his work amid the hostility and derision of his compatriots. He managed to survive by teaching French in secondary schools. One of his students, Mario Vargas Llosa (Five, 17), presented in his first novel, *The Time of the Hero* (1962), a fictionalized but accurate portrait of Moro as a long-suffering teacher whose students endlessly mock and abuse him. But whatever his troubles, he went on writing his unique, carefully wrought verse. A new volume in Spanish, *Trafalgar Square* (1954), was published by a devoted friend, the Argentine poet Enrique Molina (Four, 14); another volume, *Amour à mort*, would only be published posthumously in 1957, by André Coyné. The title contained a bilingual pun, a witty summary of Moro's double allegiance to poetry and desire. It literally means "Love Until Death," but the combination of sounds suggests a repetition of the word "love" in French *(amour)* and Spanish *(amor)*. After Moro's death in 1956, Coyné collected not only the two volumes of verse already mentioned but also a third one of articles and notes. Since then, the elusive, proud, defiant Moro has found an ever-increasing audience.

A Surrealist Poem

From Anthology of Latin American Poetry, *translated by H. R. Hays, pp. 381–83.*

You Come in the Night with the Fabulous Smoke of Your Hair

You appear
Life is certain
The smell of rain is certain
Rain gives birth to you
And makes you knock at my door
O tree
And the city the sea that you sailed upon
And the night opens at your step

And the heart peers out again from afar
Until it reaches your forehead
And sees you glittering like magic
Mountain of gold or of snow
With the fabulous smoke of your hair
With nocturnal beasts in your eyes
And your body of embers
With night that you sprinkle in fragments
With blocks of night that fall from your hands
With the silence that takes fire at your coming
With the upheaval and the surging
With the swaying of houses
And the oscillation of lights and the most solid shadow
And your words a street like a river
So quickly you come and you went away
And you seek to launch my life
And you only prepare my death
And the death from waiting
And the dying from seeing you far away
And the silences and the waiting for time
To live when you come
And you surround me with shadow
And you make me luminous
And you drown me in the phosphorescent sea where you happen
    to be
And where there is no speech but between you and my obscure
    and fearful notion of your being
Star issuing out in the apocalypse
Among howls of tigers and tears
Of joy and moaning forever and forever
Self-solace in the thin air
In which I seek to imprison you
And to roll down the slope of your body
Even to your sparkling feet
Even to the twin constellations of your feet
In the earthly night
That follows you enchained and dumb
Entangled in your blood
Supporting the dark crystal flower of your head
Aquarium enclosing planets and pontifical trains
And the power that makes the world follow afoot and keeps the
    balance of the seas
And your brain of luminous matter
And my endless adherence and the love that is ceaselessly born
And enfolds you

And that your feet travel upon
Opening indelible footprints
Where the history of the world can be read
And the future of the universe
And that luminous binding together of my life
With your existence

9

JOSÉ GOROSTIZA

If most of the Latin American avant-garde looked almost obsessively to France for a model, a group of Mexican poets were among the first
to be attracted as well to the new Spanish and British and North American
poetry. And they had, moreover, solid links with the poetry written at home
since the modernist period. Díaz Mirón and Gutiérrez Nájera, Tablada,
López Velarde, and Alfonso Reyes had already produced work which demonstrated at once their awareness of foreign experiments and their extreme sensitivity to the distinctive nuances and peculiarities of their own national
idiom (see Part Three, 2, 19). After a brief spell of futurism (the local brand
assumed the name of "stridentism"), the Mexican poets made their own way
through the maze of avant-garde tendencies. A new journal, *Contemporaries*
(1928–1931), became the center of their collective efforts to incorporate the
national culture into the modern world. They sought to eliminate the cultural lag so customary in Latin America—to share, immediately and in full,
in the modern experience; they wanted, in brief, to become truly contemporary. Although the group brought together individuals of widely divergent if
not opposing views, all its members shared certain basic assumptions and
common values. Most notably, they were all decisively against "social" or
"committed" poetry; they believed (with Valéry, Jiménez, and Eliot) in a
more detached, dispassionately intellectual approach. Their collective enterprise—one of the most significant in Latin American letters—produced a
new poetry that anticipated the brilliant achievement of Octavio Paz (Five,
1).

A leading member of the group was José Gorostiza. He was born in
Tabasco province in 1901 and by 1920 had completed his formal education. He
later entered the diplomatic service and in different capacities served his country
in London, The Hague, Rome, Managua, Havana, Rio de Janeiro, Florence,

Paris. Gorostiza has so far published only three books. The first, *Songs to Sing in Boats* (1925), made discreet use of folklore and native landscapes; instead of breaking with a tradition, he transcended it. His second volume, *Death Without End* (1939), consisted of a single long poem that reflected and embodied his European, and most particularly his British, experience. Gorostiza had been living since 1927 in London, where he had been exposed to a more metaphysical kind of verse. One notable influence on him was Eliot's rereading of Donne and his own poetic experiments.

The basic problem confronted by the symbolists—what, if any, meaning does life have?—became in his poem the starting point for Gorostiza's own anguished search. He rephrased the question to read: Is there God or Nothingness? To find an answer, he not only had recourse to the best contemporary models but also sought out an appropriate poetic idiom in the verse of the Spanish Golden Age (especially in Garcilaso and Góngora) and in the rhythms of Mexican folk balladry. For this same theme was deeply embedded in Mexican mythology and folklore. D. H. Lawrence's *The Plumed Serpent* (1926) had already familiarized European readers with a cult of death that could be traced back to the Aztecs. Less well known, in spite of Malcolm Lowry's *Under the Volcano* (1946), is the parodical and carnival-spirited confrontation with death that permeates Mexican folklore to this day and which has found a brilliant expression in Posada's macabre cartoons as well as in some of Orozco's and Rivera's murals. More than ten years after the publication of *Death Without End*, Octavio Paz would dissect in his *Labyrinth of Solitude* (1950) this very Mexican funereal language which Gorostiza had carried to perfection in his verse sequence. Combining the total lucidity of Valéry or Jiménez with Eliot's imaginative use of poetic collage, Gorostiza erected a complex structure in which the images of water and a glass served respectively as metaphors for the irrational and the intelligent life. This basic binary opposition was later developed through the confrontation between language and poetry, chaos and permanence. Moving dramatically from abstract formulation and hermetic symbols to colloquialism and even obscenities, Gorostiza succeeded in producing one of the most extraordinary poems in the Spanish language. The ironic conclusion (as life is a young whore, let's go to hell together) has the vitality and daring of the best baroque poetry.

In 1964 a third volume, soberly called *Poetry*, brought together the sum total of Gorostiza's production, including many heretofore unpublished poems. His reticence as a writer, and his austere and rigorously disciplined style, stand in strong contrast to the traditional exuberance of Latin American poets. But in this as in many other respects, Gorostiza is unique.

Death Without End

From Muerte sin fin, *translated by Rachel Benson, in* New Poetry of Mexico, *pp. 161–63.*

Filled with myself, walled up in my skin
by an inapprehensible god that is stifling me,
deceived perhaps
by his radiant atmosphere of light
that hides my drained conscience,
my wings broken into splinters of air,
my listless groping through the mire;
filled with myself—gorged—I discover my essence
in the astonished image of water,
that is only an unwithering cascade,
a tumbling of angels fallen
of their own accord in pure delight,
that has nothing
but a whitened face
half sunken, already, like an agonized laugh
in the thin sheets of the cloud
and the mournful canticles of the sea—
more aftertaste of salt or cumulus whiteness
than lonely haste of foam pursued.
Nevertheless—oh paradox—constrained
by the rigor of the glass that clarifies it,
the water takes shape.
In the glass it sits, sinks deep, and builds,
attains a bitter age of silences
and the graceful repose of a child smiling
in death, that deflowers
a beyond of disbanded
birds.
In the crystal snare that strangles it,
there, as in the water of a mirror,
it recognizes itself;
bound there, drop with drop,
the trope of foam withered in its throat.
What intense nakedness of water,
what water so strongly water,

is dreaming in its iridescent sphere,
already singing a thirst for rigid ice!
But what a provident glass—also—
that swells
like a star ripe with grain,
that flames in heroic promise
like a heart inhabited by happiness,
and that punctually yields up
to the water
a round transparent flower,
a missile eye that attains heights
and a window to luminous cries
over that smoldering liberty
oppressed by white fetters!

10

XAVIER VILLAURRUTIA

Less reticent and somewhat more prolific than José Gorostiza, Xavier
Villaurrutia shared with his compatriot an exalted concept of poetry and a firm
belief in the creative power of intelligence. Like Gorostiza, he initially found in
the journal *Contemporaries* a congenial outlet for his work. But he was also
interested in the theater, to which he devoted a considerable part of his energies.

Villaurrutia was born in Mexico City in 1903 and attended a French
school, which nurtured his familiarity with French literature. Although he started
to study law, he finally dropped out to devote himself completely to literary work.
His first book of poems, *Reflections* (meaning also "Reflexes"), was published in
1926. Intellectual humor, irony, and startling imagery were already his trade-
marks. A long acquaintance with the French avant-garde could easily be detected,
as well as a natural kinship with Jules Supervielle's elusive verse. But Villaurrutia
was also firmly rooted in the Mexican literary tradition. In a sense, his poems
represented an updating of López Velarde's sensitive and ironically provincial
lyrics (Part Three, 19, III).

In 1931, Villaurrutia published a collection of his *Nocturnes*. They
were the first of a series ("Angel-Nocturne," 1936; "Nocturnal Sea," 1937; "Rose
Nocturnal," 1937) in which the symbol of night, either as an object or an
attribute, is invested by the poet with near-magical powers. This verse sequence
was related to not only the *Nocturnes* of the modernist poet Asunción Silva (Part

Three, Introduction) but harked much further back, to the supreme baroque
verse of Sor Juana Inés (Part One, 11, v). Like another of his acknowledged
sources, Saint John of the Cross, Villaurrutia was an erotic poet and a homosexual. Although he avoided scandal by not identifying the love-objects in his poems
too explicitly, he refused to engage in the kind of elaborate deception usually
practiced by his colleagues of similar bent. He preferred to talk about the "chosen
person," or to represent in the guise of angels those beautiful strangers he was
so attracted to.

In the late twenties and early thirties, Villaurrutia did some preliminary
work for the Mexican stage. As a consequence, he received a Rockefeller Foundation scholarship to study theater at Yale University in the 1935–36 academic year.
His residence in New Haven also came to be reflected in some of his strangest
poems, such as "Cemetery in the Snow." It would be included in his next volume,
Nostalgia of Death (1938). In the first part he collected the already known
"Nocturnes"; the rest of the volume consisted of new poems, in which the
familiar topic of "Life Is a Dream" and the romantic concept of the double
played an essential part. A sense of anguish and the absurd alternated in these
poems with the expression of burning desire. In one of the best pieces, "Tenth
Death," Villaurrutia came very close to the metaphysical stance of Rilke, as
expressed in the *Duino Elegies*.

One more volume of poetry was published before his death in 1950;
it was called *Song to Spring and Other Poems* (1948). The presence of God and
a more religious attitude were manifest in this last work. His *Complete Poetry
and Drama* was issued in 1953. Although Villaurrutia wrote many plays and
helped to bring about a revival of Mexican drama, his verse represented his more
fruitful and creative work. He will be remembered as one of the most personal
and tantalizing voices in Latin American poetry.

Nocturnes

From Nostalgia de la muerte, *translated by Dudley Fitts,* Anthology of
Latin American Poetry, *pp. 367–71; and translated by Donald Justice, in*
New Poetry of Mexico, *edited by Octavio Paz et al. (New York: E. P.
Dutton, 1970), pp. 155–59.*

Angel-Nocturne

You would say that the streets flow sweetly in the night.
Lights are not quick enough to reveal the secret,
the secret known to the men who come and go,
for they are all in the secret,

and nothing were gained by dividing it in a thousand pieces
if, on the contrary, it is so sweet to keep it
to share alone with the chosen person.

If everyone should utter, at a given moment,
in one word only, that which he is thinking,
the six letters of DESIRE would form a huge shining scar,
a constellation still older, still more intense than the others.
And that constellation would be like a burning sex
in the deep body of the night,
or rather, like the Twins when, for the first time in their lives,
they looked, face to face, into each other's eyes and embraced each
        other forever.

Suddenly the river of the street is peopled with thirsty beings.
They walk, pause, go on again.
Exchange glances, venture smiles.
They form in casual couples. . . .

There are turning paths and shaded benches,
shores of undefinable deep forms
and sudden hollows of blinding light
and doors that yield to the slightest touch.

The river of the street is deserted for a moment.
But then it seems to rise up from itself
as though it would begin again.
It is left for a moment paralyzed, a panting mute
like the heart between two spasms.

But a new pulsing, a new throbbing
hurls new thirsty beings into the river of the street.
They cross, intercross, go up.
They fly close to the ground.

They swim on foot, so miraculously
that no one would dare to say they are not walking.
These are the Angels.
They have come down to earth
by invisible ladders.
They come from the sea, heaven's mirror,
in ships of smoke and shade,
to fuse and confuse themselves with mortal men,
to abase their brows to women's thighs,
permit other feverish hands to caress their bodies,

other bodies to seek theirs to the point of knowledge
as the lips of the same mouth know each other in closing,
to wear out mouths inactive for so long,
to set free their tongues of fire,
to utter the songs, oaths, and evil words
in which men concentrate the ancient enigma
of flesh, blood, and desire.

They bear assumed names, divinely simple.
They are called Dick or John, Marvin or Louis.
Only in their beauty are they to be distinguished from mortal men.
They walk, pause, go on again.
Exchange glances, venture smiles.
They form in casual couples.
They smile maliciously going up in hotel elevators
where vertical slow flight is still being practiced.
On their naked bodies there are celestial marks:
signs, stars, blue letters.
They drop into beds, sink into the pillows
that make them think for a moment longer of the clouds.
But they close their eyes, the better to yield to the delights of
    their mysterious incarnation,
and when they sleep they dream not of angels but of mortals.

Translated by Dudley Fitts

Rose Nocturnal

to José Gorostiza

I too speak of the rose.
But my rose is neither the cold
    rose
nor the one in a child's skin,
nor the rose which turns
so slowly that its motion
is a mysterious form of stillness.

It is not the thirsty rose,
nor the wound bleeding,
nor the rose crowned with thorns,
nor the rose of the resurrection.

It is not the rose with naked petals,
nor the wax rose,
nor the silken flame,
nor yet the quick-blushing rose.

It is not the banner rose,
nor the secret garden rot,
nor the punctual rose telling the
    hour,
nor the compass rose of the mariner.

No, it is not the rose rose
but the uncreated rose,
the rose submerged,
the nocturnal,
the unsubstantial rose,
the void rose.

It is the rose of touch in darkness,
it is the rose that comes forward
    inflamed,
the rose of rosy nails,

the bud rose of eager fingertips,
the digital rose,
the blind rose.

It is the molded rose of hearing,
the ear rose,
the noise's spiral,
the shell rose always left behind
in the loudest surf of the pillow.

It is the fleshed rose of the mouth,
the rose that, waking, speaks
as though it were sleeping.
It is the half-open rose
from out of which pours shade,
the entrail rose

that folds up and expands,
required, desired, devoured,
it is the labial rose,
the wounded rose.

It is the rose that opens its lids,
the vigilant, wakeful rose,
the shattered rose of insomnia.

It is the rose of smoke,
the ash rose,
the diamond coal's black rose
which, noiseless, drills through
    darkness
and occupies no point in space.

Translated by Donald Justice

Cemetery in the Snow

Nothing is like a cemetery in the snow.
What name is there for the whiteness upon the white?
The sky has let down insensible stones of snow
upon the tombs,
and all that is left now is snow upon snow
like a hand settled on itself forever.

Birds prefer to cut through the sky,
to wound the invisible corridors of the air
so as to leave the snow alone,
which is to leave it intact,
which is to leave it snow.

Because it is not enough to say that a cemetery in the snow
is like a sleep without dreams
or like a few blank eyes.

Though it is something like an insensible and sleeping body,
like one silence fallen upon another
and like the white persistence of oblivion,
nothing is like a cemetery in the snow!

Because the snow is above all silent,
more silent still upon bloodless slabs:
lips that can no longer say a word.

Translated by Donald Justice

11

NICOLÁS GUILLÉN

In complete contrast to the Mexican poets of the *Contemporaries* group, the Cuban Nicolás Guillén believes in "committed" poetry, and has dedicated the largest part of his work to the promotion of socialism and the denunciation of U.S. imperialism. In this, he has sided with poets such as Vallejo and Neruda (selections 7, 12).

Guillén was born in Cuba in 1902, of mixed blood. In one of his most popular poems he sings of his African grandfather as well as the Spanish one. His father was a journalist and politician who was assassinated in 1917, when Nicolás was only fifteen. He attended law school, but had to quit before he got a degree. For a while he worked in a printer's shop and later for various newspapers.

His first volume of verse was published in 1930. Its title, *Son Themes*, refers to the *son*, a type of Afro-Cuban musical composition that helped Guillén to discover a personal rhythm. From the very beginning, his poetry was basically concerned with that obsessive beat, and could appropriately be identified with the artistic and cultural movement later called *Négritude* ("Blackness") by French Caribbean poets. In 1931, Guillén published a second volume, *Songoro Cosongo*, which incorporated African words into its text and developed even further the exploration of new rhythms. A third volume published in 1934, *West Indies Ltd.*, marked the beginning of his anti-imperialist poetry. Using humor and even satire, Guillén put his *son* at the service of his political ideology.

Two more volumes, published in 1937, completed the very significant production of the thirties and made Guillén one of the most popular Latin American poets of the time. The first, *Songs for Soldiers and Tourists*, reiterated the themes of his previous books; the second, *Spain*, showed Guillén joining Vallejo and Neruda in defense of the Spanish Republic. By then, his work had attracted the attention of North American writers such as Langston Hughes, who translated some of his poems into English.

After a period of relative silence, Guillén collected his poetry in a volume, *The Entire Son* (1947), which was published in Buenos Aires and made his work available all over Latin America. His devotion to the socialist cause was acknowledged by the Soviet Union, which awarded him the Stalin Prize in 1953.

The triumph of the Cuban Revolution found him ready with another volume of verse (*The Dove of Popular Flight*, 1958), and determined to join the victors. Since then, he has become the Castro regime's Grand Old Man of Literature, presiding over the Union of Cuban Writers and Artists and editing the official *Cuban Literary Gazette*. New volumes of poetry have been added to the Guillén canon during this period: *Ballad* (1962) and *I Have* (1964).

Although a poet of limited resources and relatively small output, Guillén has excelled in adapting the rhythms of Cuban popular speech and Afro-Cuban music in verse that nonetheless, for all its Caribbean charm, remains essentially in the traditional Spanish mold.

Two Poems

From El Son entero, *translated by Stephan Schwartz,* Mundus Artium, *vol. 3, no. 1 (Winter 1969), pp. 39–41.*

Kiln-stone

Abandoned evening
Whirls destroyed in the rain.
Memories fall from the clouds
Through the windows.
Long exhausted sighs,
Burnt chimeras.
Your body emerges slowly.
Your hands arrive in their orbit.
Of sugar-cane liquor;
Your willing feet sore from dancing,
Your thighs tautened by spasms,
Your mouth an edible
Substance, your open
Caramel waist.

Your golden arms lift with your cruel teeth,
Your eyes betrayed quickly attack,
Your skin laid out ready
For sleep.
Your sudden forest odor, your throat
Screaming (I imagine), dancing
(I guess), moaning (I suppose, I believe);
Your deepened throat
Echoing forbidden words.

A river of promises
falls from your hair
Lingers in your breasts
And finally coils in a sweet pool in your belly

And rapes your flesh filled with nocturnal secrets.
Glowing coal and kiln-stone
In a cool evening of rain and silence.

Arrival

Here we are!
The word comes to us damp from the forests,
An energetic sun rises in our veins.
The fist is strong
and holds the oar.
In a darkened eye the highest palms sleep.
Our cry escapes like a drop of virgin gold.
Our feet,
Broad and tough,
Harden the dust of the abandoned roads
For the passage of our ranks.
We know where the waters are born,
And we love them pushing canoes beneath the red heavens.

Our song
Is like a muscle beneath the soul's skin,
Our simple song.
We bring our smoke to morning,
And fire to the night,
And a knife like a hard lunar stone,
Useful for barbarous flesh;
We bring crocodiles out of the mud,
And the bow which fells,
And the tropical belt,
And the purified spirit.
So friends, here we are!
The city waits with her palaces, delicate
As the combs of a wild hive;
Streets dry as rivers when no rain reaches the mountains,
The houses watch with their locked-eye windows.
The ancients left us milk and honey
And a crown of laurel leaves.
So friends, here we are!
Beneath the sun
Our sweating skins reflect the moist faces of the captured,
And past night, while stars walk in the points of flames,
Our laugh rises over the rivers and birds.

PABLO NERUDA

Neruda's reputation as a political poet, together with his tragic death at the time of the Chilean army's overthrow of President Allende, will doubtless impede for many years to come any attempt to read his poetry as poetry. He himself, moreover, would have firmly rejected any apolitical approach to his verse. From a time just after the outbreak of the Spanish civil war, he devoted his life and his poetry to the defense of the socialist cause as embodied in the Soviet Union and in Chile's Communist Party; and he dutifully fulfilled whatever task the party assigned him. In 1945, he was elected a senator; in 1948, he had to go underground for denouncing President González Videla's anti-Communist campaign; as recently as 1969, he accepted his party's nomination for the presidency, and just as dutifully resigned to pave the way for Allende's Union of the Left. His last dictated words were a condemnation of the President's assassination.

Neruda was a sincere and dedicated politician, in the best tradition of Sarmiento, Acevedo Díaz, and Rómulo Gallegos (see Part Two, 5, 8; Three, 11). But he was also the greatest Latin American poet since Rubén Darío. For political reasons, the Nobel Prize was slow in coming to him. By the time he did receive it, in 1971, his renown was such that he may well be said to have honored the prize, rather than being honored by it.

Neruda was born in a small, rainy town in southern Chile in 1904 and, like Poe, never knew his mother, who died less than two months after his birth. His real name was Ricardo Eliecer Neftalí Reyes. But as his father, a railroad worker, did not want his son to be a poet, Ricardo invented a poetic pseudonym: Pablo Neruda, taken perhaps from Verlaine's Christian name of Paul and the surname of a Czech gothic novelist. The mask or persona invented by Neruda quickly developed into a mature poet.

In 1921 he left his hometown to complete his studies in French literature in Santiago. Instead of graduating, however, he became part of a group of Bohemian poets, in whose company he discovered friendship and free love, anarchism and experimental poetry. Over the next three years, he won a prize for young poets, and published a first, promising volume of verse, *Crepusculario* (a word that suggests both "crepuscular" and "calendar," 1923), followed by what turned out to be the most successful of all his books—*Twenty Love Poems and a Song of Despair* (1924), destined to become the bible of adolescent lovers. At twenty, Neruda proved to be a gifted erotic poet, one still emerging from under the wing of a now-declining modernism, but already displaying some awareness of avant-garde ideas and techniques. Many of the books he published afterward were less original than the poems he was sending to magazines, which would be collected years later.

In 1927, he entered the diplomatic service and was appointed honorary consul in Burma. After brief visits to Buenos Aires, where he met and disagreed with Borges, and to Europe, where he found the Spanish ultraists uncongenial, Neruda settled in Rangoon. In 1928 he was transferred to Ceylon, in 1930 to Batavia (now Jakarta in Java), and in 1931 to Singapore. He returned to Chile, now married to a Dutch-Indonesian woman, in 1932.

The experience of life in the East, a true season in hell, had lasted five years, and it produced a radical change in both the man and the poet. In the East, Neruda found himself practically isolated from everything he knew. His only means of communication with other men was English, a language he never mastered completely. The religious concept of life prevailing in the Orient was completely exotic and alien to him; and he rejected as well the "sahib" mentality of the ruling British. He felt cut off from his mother tongue and claimed in his letters that he could not even remember how to spell it. He sank obsessively into sex and drugs. His only anchor to reality was his poetry—painfully, agonizingly written in months of despair abruptly punctuated by flashes of hallucinatory insight.

Eventually, however, he did discover another anchor of sorts—an interest in English literature which he owed to Andrew Boyd, a young poet then living in the East. Boyd introduced him to the visionary poetry of William Blake— Neruda even translated two of Blake's shorter poems—and also recommended to his Chilean colleague T. S. Eliot's *The Waste Land* and the novels of D. H. Lawrence, with their archetypal themes and characters. Neruda was already well acquainted with the French symbolists, and had read Baudelaire and Rimbaud very thoroughly. He was familiar as well with the work of another visionary poet, Walt Whitman, whom he would later address in his own verse as "Grandfather." It was through his experience of anguish and isolation, and his passionate reading of these authors, that Neruda discovered the hidden springs of his own lyrical power. He returned, via Rimbaud and Whitman, to the ancient concept of the poet as seer.

This inner development bore fruit after his return to Chile in 1932. The following year there appeared, in a minuscule edition of one hundred copies, a collection of verse entitled *Residence on Earth.* It represented a totally new departure for Neruda—and for poetry in the Spanish language, although full recognition of its merit had to await the publication of a second, expanded edition in 1935. In these dazzling and powerful poems, combining symbolism and surrealism, prophetic insight and a sardonically iconoclastic tone, Neruda revolutionized Hispanic verse no less radically than had Darío before him. Some of the poems were deeply rooted in private experience and openly autobiographical, such as "The Widower's Tango" and "Josie Bliss," in which he recorded his passionate affair with a Burmese woman. Others were personal in a more symbolic fashion like "Entrance to Wood," in which he played with the Spanish words for wood *(madera),* matter *(materia),* and mother *(madre),* three words having the same Latin root and similar in sound. A few pieces anticipated in a chilling surrealistic way events yet to come: the "Ode to Federico García Lorca" was written at least a year before the poet's murder.

By the time the second edition appeared in 1935, and began to receive the recognition Neruda himself felt it deserved, he was serving as Chilean consul in Spain; he had found in Madrid the Argentine woman who was to become his second wife, and had been acknowledged as leader by a group of young Spanish poets, which included not only García Lorca but Rafael Alberti and the even younger Miguel Hernández. But the civil war destroyed the bright prospects Neruda had seen before him, for himself and for Spain. García Lorca was assassinated by the Fascists; Neruda was forced to resign his consulship because of his undiplomatic involvement with the Left; Hernández was imprisoned and would eventually die in prison after Franco's victory. While the war was still raging, Neruda wrote one of his most stirring and effective works, *Spain in Our Hearts* (later included in *Third Residence, 1947*). It was printed and published in 1937, in the front lines, by a group of soldiers and writers. With Vallejo's Spanish sequence (selection 7), it marks the high point of political poetry in the language. Neruda was forced to return to Chile in 1938, and thereafter devoted a significant portion of his time to the support of progressive candidates and causes.

In 1940 he was appointed Consul General in Mexico. He found many new and old friends there, but he also became involved in polemics with some apolitical younger poets, was attacked by the Nazis in Cuernavaca, and wrote very committed poems urging the creation of a second front to help the Soviet Union and twice praising the heroic Russian defense of Stalingrad. He returned to Chile in 1943.

On his way home Neruda stopped off in Peru to visit Machu Picchu, the old stone city built by the Incas atop the Andes. He had by then embarked on a major new work about his country; but now, moved by the vastness and monumental scope of these ruins, he decided to transform this projected "General Song of Chile" into a "General Song" of the entire continent. He was still at work on this project when, in 1948, he was impeached by the Chilean Senate for having published an open letter criticizing President González Videla. Neruda was forced to go underground and finally managed to escape to Argentina, disguised by a beard and on horseback, through the forbidding Andes. The book was finally published in 1950, in a special edition as monumental as the ruins that had inspired it. It was printed in Mexico, with illustrations by the muralists Diego Rivera and David Alfaro Siqueiros, and was sold only by subscription. In Chile the Communist Party printed a clandestine popular edition.

The book belongs to the Latin American tradition of celebrating the grandeur of the land, its history and geography—a tradition extending from the baroque poet Balbuena (One, 11) through the quasi-romantics Olmedo and Bello (Two, 3) to the modernist Darío (Three, 4). Neruda, however, added a vital new dimension with his very contemporary reading of Latin America's social, political, and economic realities. The current economic exploitation by U.S. and/or multinational corporations took up as much space in *The General Song* as the genocidal Spanish conquest or the epic struggles for political independence. Published as it was at the height of the Cold War, the book quickly acquired great political significance, and popular editions and translations into several languages began to proliferate. This political aspect of the work tended to obscure its splendid, if occasional, verse—which included one of the greatest poems Neruda ever wrote, "Heights of Macchu Picchu" (Neruda chose to add an extra "c" to "Machu"). A prophetic ode, it was a record of his emergence out of alienation and despair into a liberating solidarity, and a magnificent instance of the solitary voice of the poet becoming the voice of mute, downtrodden millions—the Indians whose ancestors had built the cities of ancient America.

It was from this time on, especially, that Neruda found in the socialist cause an inexhaustible source of poetic inspiration. Some of his later output, it is true, was *merely* political, or occasional, in nature; but other productions attested to the continuing depth and mastery of the mature poet. These latter included such forceful and vigorous works as: *The Captain's Verses* (1952), his first homage to Matilde Urrutia, the Chilean woman who was to become his third wife and most devoted companion; several volumes of *Elementary Odes* (1954–1959), in which he sang in a deceptively simple style of all the objects of his passionate love and devotion; *Estravagaria* (1958), an ironical and idiosyncratic work in which he set aside the canons of an edifying socialist realism to admit the vagaries of life and death; *Memorial of Isla Negra* (1964), a kind of autobiography in verse that contained some of his best autumnal poems.

In these and other works, Neruda demonstrated not only his grasp of social and individual human realities, but his undiminished appetite for life and for the word. Stricken with cancer in the last years of his life, he was being kept alive by a painful and costly treatment when the violence of the 1973 military coup proved too much for him. He died of a heart attack, leaving in the hands of his publisher eight volumes of poetry and his almost completed memoirs.

Neruda's output was immense, perhaps excessively so. Like Victor Hugo (another of his "grandfathers"), he was really too prolific, and in his writing after *The General Song* he did not exercise such care in revision and polishing as perhaps he should have. But such essentially minor reservations aside, there is no question of his place among the greatest poets in any language.

Six Poems

From Residence on Earth, *translated by Donald Walsh (New York: New Directions, 1973), pp. 3–5, 47, 73–77, 85–87, 155–57, 207–9.*

Dead Gallop

Like ashes, like seas peopling themselves,
in the submerged slowness, in the shapelessness,

or as one hears from the crest of the roads
the crossed bells crossing,
having that sound now sundered from the metal,
confused, ponderous, turning to dust
in the very milling of the too-distant forms,
either remembered or not seen,
and the perfume of the plums that rolling on the ground
rot in time, infinitely green.

All that so swift, so living,
yet motionless, like the pulley loose within itself,
those wheels of the motors, in short.
Existing like the dry stitches in the tree's seams,
so silent, all around,
all the limbs mixing their tails.
But from where, through where, on what shore?
The constant, uncertain surrounding, so silent,
like the lilacs around the convent
or death's coming to the tongue of the ox
that stumbles to the ground, guard down, with horns that struggle
    to blow.

Therefore, in the stillness, stopping, to perceive,
then, like an immense fluttering, above,
like dead bees or numbers,
ah, what my pale heart cannot embrace,
in multitudes, in tears scarcely shed,
and human efforts, anguish,
black deeds suddenly discovered
like ice, vast disorder,
oceanic, to me who enter singing,
as if with a sword among the defenseless.

Well, now, what is it made of, that upsurge of doves
that exists between night and time, like a moist ravine?
That sound so prolonged now
that falls lining the roads with stones,
or rather, when only an hour
grows suddenly, stretching without pause.

Within the ring of summer
the great calabash trees once listen,
stretching out their pity-laden plants,
it is made of that, of what with much wooing,
of the fullness, dark with heavy drops.

Ars Poetica

Between shadow and space, between trimmings and damsels,
endowed with a singular heart and sorrowful dreams,
precipitously pallid, withered in the brow
and with a furious widower's mourning for each day of life,
ah, for each invisible water that I drink somnolently
and from every sound that I welcome trembling,
I have the same absent thirst and the same cold fever,
a nascent ear, an indirect anguish,
as if thieves or ghosts were coming,
and in a shell of fixed and profound expanse,
like a humiliated waiter, like a slightly raucous bell,
like an old mirror, like the smell of a solitary house
where the guests come in at night wildly drunk,
and there is a smell of clothes thrown on the floor, and an absence
        of flowers—
possibly in another even less melancholy way—
but the truth is that suddenly the wind that lashes my chest,
the nights of infinite substance fallen in my bedroom,
the noise of a day that burns with sacrifice,
ask me mournfully what prophecy there is in me,
and there is a swarm of objects that call without being answered,
and a ceaseless movement, and a bewildered man.

Ritual of My Legs

For a long time I have stayed looking at my long legs,
with infinite and curious tenderness, with my accustomed passion,
as if they had been the legs of a divine woman,
deeply sunk in the abyss of my thorax:
and, to tell the truth, when time, when time passes
over the earth, over the roof, over my impure head,
and it passes, time passes, and in my bed I do not feel at night
        that a woman is breathing sleeping naked and at my side,
then strange, dark things take the place of the absent one,
vicious, melancholy thoughts
sow heavy possibilities in my bedroom,
and thus, then, I look at my legs as if they belonged to another
        body
and were stuck strongly and gently to my insides.

Like stems or feminine adorable things,
from the knees they rise, cylindrical and thick,

with a disturbed and compact material of existence:
like brutal, thick goddess arms,
like trees monstrously dressed as human beings,
like fatal, immense lips thirsty and tranquil,
they are, there, the best part of my body:
the entirely substantial part, without complicated content
of senses or tracheas or intestines or ganglia:
nothing but the pure, the sweet, and the thick part of my own life,
nothing but form and volume existing,
guarding life, nevertheless, in a complete way.

People cross through the world nowadays
scarcely remembering that they possess a body and life within it,
and there is fear, in the world there is fear of the words that
        designate the body,
and one talks favorably of clothes,
it is possible to speak of trousers, of suits,
and of women's underwear (of "ladies' " stockings and garters)
as if the articles and the suits went completely empty through the
        streets
and a dark and obscene clothes closet occupied the world.

Suits have existence, color, form, design,
and a profound place in our myths, too much of a place,
there is too much furniture and there are too many rooms in the
        world
and my body lives downcast among and beneath so many
        things,
with an obsession of slavery and chains.

Well, my knees, like knots,
private, functional, evident,
separate neatly the halves of my legs:
and really two different worlds, two different sexes
are not so different as the two halves of my legs.

From the knee to the foot a hard form,
mineral, coldly useful, appears,
a creature of bone and persistence,
and the ankles are now nothing but the naked purpose,
exactitude and necessity definitively disposed.

Without sensuality, short and hard, and masculine,
my legs exist, there, and endowed
with muscular groups like complementary animals,

and there too a life, a solid, subtle, sharp life
endures without trembling, waiting and performing.

At my feet ticklish
and hard like the sun, and open like flowers,
and perpetual, magnificent soldiers
in the gray war of space,
everything ends, life definitively ends at my feet,
what is foreign and hostile begins there:
the names of the world, the frontier and the remote,
the substantive and the adjectival too great for my heart
originate there with dense and cold constancy.

Always,
manufactured products, stockings, shoes,
or simply infinite air.
There will be between my feet and the earth
stressing the isolated and solitary part of my being,
something tenaciously involved between my life and the earth,
something openly unconquerable and unfriendly.

The Widower's Tango*

Oh evil one, you must by now have found the letter, you must
    have wept with fury,
and you must have insulted my mother's memory,
calling her rotten bitch and mother of dogs,
you must have drunk alone, all by yourself, your twilight tea,
looking at my old shoes forever empty,
and you won't be able any longer to recall my illnesses, my night
    dreams, my meals,
without cursing me aloud as if I were still there,
complaining about the tropics, about the *corringhis* coolies,
about the poisonous fevers that did me so much harm,
and about the frightful Englishmen that I still hate.

Evil one, really, what an enormous night, what a lonely earth!
I have come again to the solitary bedrooms,
to lunch on cold food in the restaurants, and again
I throw my trousers and shirts upon the floor,
there are no coat hangers in my room, no pictures of anyone on
    the walls.

*Neruda was a widower only to the extent that he thought he had escaped from Josie Bliss, the Burmese girl to whom this poem is addressed. See also the poem entitled "Josie Bliss".—D.D.W.

How much of the darkness in my soul I would give to get you
    back,
and how threatening to me seem the names of the months,
and the word "winter," what a mournful drum sound it has.

Buried next to the coconut tree you will later find
the knife that I hid there for fear that you would kill me,
and now suddenly I should like to smell its kitchen steel
accustomed to the weight of your hand and the shine of your foot:
under the moisture of the earth, among the deaf roots,
of all human languages the poor thing would know only your name,
and the thick earth does not understand your name
made of impenetrable and divine substances.
Just as it afflicts me to think of the clear day of your legs
curled up like still and harsh solar waters,
and the swallow that sleeping and flying lives in your eyes,
and the furious dog that you shelter in your heart,
so too I see the deaths that are between us from now on,
and I breathe in the air ashes and destruction,
the long, solitary space that surrounds me forever.

I would give this giant sea wind for your brusque breath
heard in long nights with no mixture of oblivion,
merging with the atmosphere like the whip with the horse's hide.
And to hear you making water in the darkness, at the back of the
    house,
as if spilling a thin, tremulous, silvery, persistent honey,
how many times would I give up this chorus of shadows that I
    possess,
and the noise of useless swords that is heard in my heart,
and the bloody dove that sits alone on my brow
calling for vanished things, vanished beings,
substances strangely inseparable and lost.

Entrance to Wood

Scarcely with my reason, with my
    fingers,
with slow waters slow inundated,
I fall into the realm of the
    forget-me-nots,
into a tenacious atmosphere of
    mourning,
into a forgotten, decayed room,
into a cluster of bitter clover.

I fall into the shadow, amid
destroyed things,
and I look at spiders, and I graze on
    thickets
of secret inconclusive woods,
and I walk among moist fibers
    torn
from the living being of substance
    and silence.

Gentle matter, oh rose of dry wings,
in my collapse I climb up your petals,
my feet heavy with red fatigue,
and in your harsh cathedral I kneel
beating my lips with an angel.

I am the one facing your worldly
    color,
facing your pale dead swords,
facing your united hearts,
facing your silent multitude.
I am the one facing your wave of
    dying fragrances,
wrapped in autumn and resistance:
I am the one undertaking a funereal
    voyage
among your yellow scars:
I am the one with my sourceless
    laments,
foodless, abandoned, alone,
entering darkened corridors,
reaching your mysterious substance.

I see your dry-currents move,
I see interrupted hands grow,

I hear your oceanic vegetation
rustle shaken by night and fury,
and I feel leaves dying inward,
joining green substances
to your forsaken immobility.

Pores, veins, circles of sweetness,
weight, silent temperature,
arrows piercing your fallen soul,
beings asleep in your thick mouth,
powder of sweet consumed pulp,
ashes filled with extinguished souls,
come to me, to my measureless
    dream,
fall into my bedroom where night
    falls
and endlessly falls like broken water,
and bind me to your life and to your
    death,
and to your docile substances,
to your dead neutral doves,
and let us make fire, and silence, and
    sound,
and let us burn, and be silent, and
    bells.

Josie Bliss

Blue color of exterminated photographs,
blue color with petals and walks to the sea,
definitive name that falls upon the weeks
with a steely blow that kills them.

What dress, what spring crosses by,
what hand endlessly seeks breasts, heads?
The evident smoke of time falls in vain,
in vain the seasons,
the farewells where the smoke falls,
the precipitous events that wait with a sword:
suddenly there is something,
like a confused attack of redskins,
the blood's horizon trembles, there is something,
something is surely shaking the rosebushes.

Blue color of eyelids licked by the night,
stars of unhinged crystal, fragments
of skin and sobbing vines,
color that the river digs smashing on the sand,
blue that has prepared the big drops.

Perhaps I go on existing on a street that the air makes weep
with a determined lugubrious lament so
that all the women dress in dull blue:
I exist in that distributed day,
I exist there like a stone stepped on by an ox,
like a witness without doubt forgotten.

Blue color of the wing of a bird of oblivion,
the sea has completely drenched the feathers,
its degraded acid, its wave of pallid weight
pursues things piled up in the corners of the soul,
and smoke beats in vain against the doors.

There they are, there they are,
the kisses dragged through the dust next to a joyless warship,
there are the vanished smiles, the suits that a hand shakes calling
     to the dawn:
it seems that death's mouth does not want to bite faces, fingers,
     words, eyes:
there they are again like great fish that complete the sky
with their vaguely invincible blue matter.

13

OLIVERIO GIRONDO

Like his Brazilian counterpart, Oswald de Andrade (selection 17), the
Argentine Oliverio Girondo was too successful as a young iconoclast and professional humorist to be taken seriously by his more solemn contemporaries. Besides,
he was, like Andrade, rich and spoiled. But notwithstanding his constant playful-
ness, Girondo's artistic intentions were deadly serious.

He was born in Buenos Aires in 1891, into a wealthy household. Among avant-garde writers, he was one of the first to visit Paris—a distinction he owed to his parents, who took him to see the 1900 Universal Exhibition there when he was only nine. In later years he would claim to have seen Oscar Wilde, walking the streets with the legendary sunflower in one hand. (This was probably another instance of false recollection—by that time, Wilde had had a long spell at Reading Gaol and had probably discarded sunflowers in favor of less conspicuous adornments.) In 1909, after some time spent at the Lycée Louis le Grand in Paris and at Epsom in England, Girondo struck a bargain with his doting parents: he promised to attend law school in Buenos Aires if they promised to send him each year to Europe for his holidays. They kept their side of the bargain. For several summers, the restless Girondo systematically surveyed the continent and some adjacent territories. He even ventured to visit the sources of the Nile. By 1915 he was writing outrageous plays together with a friend, and creating a sort of uproar in Buenos Aires theatrical life.

In 1922 he published in France his first volume of verse, *20 Poems to Be Read in a Trolley Car.* The book was also illustrated by Girondo—a charming and not totally naïve painter—and it contained the kind of poetry Apollinaire and his friends had been producing in the previous decade. It had, however, little or no initial impact in Buenos Aires. It was not until a second edition was published in 1925, this time in Argentina, that Girondo achieved prominence. By this time the ultraists were rampant, with Borges (selection 1) as their acknowledged leader. In that same year, Girondo published a second volume, *Decals,* in a similarly humorous vein. He became deeply involved in the publication of the avant-garde journal *Martín Fierro,* which had little to do with Hernández's poem (Part Two, 7) and which managed to rally under the same banner younger poets like Borges and Girondo and some older masters such as Ricardo Güiraldes and Macedonio Fernández (Three, 13, 19, II).

Girondo, however, did not stay long in Buenos Aires. A compulsive traveler, he spent the next five years going around the world, discovering new lands and cultures, spreading the ultraist credo in various other Latin American countries. He had time, he had money, he belonged to the then fashionable race of tourist aesthetes. In 1931 he returned to Buenos Aires for a while and published two more books: *Scarecrow* (1932) and *Intermoonlude* (1937).

In 1946, after another spell of traveling and his marriage to a fellow poet, Norah Lange, he published a new book, *Our Countryside,* which diverged from the usual ultraist themes but made a characteristically dazzling use of metaphor. By then, Borges was preoccupied with his "magical" short stories, and a new generation of poets had come to the fore in Argentina who were less interested in the humorous or "frivolous" side of literary experimentation and more concerned with the surreal. Girondo nonetheless discovered affinities with them, and suddenly found himself filling the role of Grand Old Man of Letters.

Ten years later he published his last volume of verse. *Into the Moremarrow* (1956) represented a kind of summation of everything Girondo had attempted in poetry, but it was written in a darker vein. The humor now was black. A tragic sense of life, of the decay and corruption of the flesh, permeated every line and effectively corroded the language. Taking every word apart, coining neologisms out of individually recognizable units, or inventing verbal monstrosities that only remotely alluded to some lost models, Girondo here exploded poetry as effectively as if he had detonated an atomic charge into its very marrow. Lines and words had been mutated out of recognition. What he was doing in this last, desperate work had been to some extent attempted by Huidobro in *Altazor* (selection 6), but Girondo went significantly further.

Girondo died in 1967, six years after an accident in which he suffered injuries that made his life almost unbearable. His largely inaccessible works were collected after his death by Enrique Molina in a single 1968 volume, with a long preface by the latter. Molina (14), a younger surrealist poet, had performed sometime earlier a similar rescue operation with César Moro (8). Since then, critics and readers have begun to see Girondo's work in its proper perspective. The translation of some of his poems presented here is only provisional, a desperate attempt to suggest the inexhaustible inventiveness of the original.

Into the Moremarrow

From En la más médula, *especially translated by Eliot Weinberger.*

The Pure No

The no
the novarian no
the cease aryan no
the nooo
the post-mucosmos of animalevolent zero no's that no no no
and nooo
and monoplurally no to the morbid amorpus nooo
nodious no
no deus
no sense no sex no way
the stiff no bones about it nooo in the unisolo amodule
no pores no nodule
nor me nor man nor *mal*
the no no macro dirt
the no greater than all no things
the pure no
the no bull

Sodium Pentothal So What

So what's not gloomy about the lay
the harmony so what the strain
they had possessed
the head-on gasping grasping sub-sucking smacks
the skinquakes
the spiritual scuba
the honeycomb-come so what
coming so what to the finish line
relapsing lapping weighed down so what what larva the tedious
    tongue-twisting in poisonous cubes
so many others others
thirst so what
X's
the dizzy nexus
the taste of so what nakedness
the stubborn stillborn helliday with the kids
the exnubile pros
giving yourself to give to what
the endless accompaniments
the undressed wounds
the pounding impounding
the warping warp in the daily Sing Sing of the blood
the ideonecrococci with their ancestors of dirt
to be so what
or not to be so what
tough luck
the slow summing shrinking
the venereal Avernos
the fish in the nau-sea for what
whosoever so what's whoever
so many sowhats

so what

  so what

    so what

      and yet

14

ENRIQUE MOLINA

Like the Cuban José Lezama Lima (see selection 15), the Argentine Enrique Molina arrived rather late at the avant-garde banquet. Already the impact of confrontation and scandal had been exhausted, and some of the most important Latin American poets were either dead (Vallejo, 7), about to die (Huidobro, 6), or now occupied with less experimental writing (Guillén, 11; Neruda, 12). Only a few, such as César Moro (8) and Oliverio Girondo (13), continued to produce, in solitude and scorn, their uncompromising verse.

Molina, who was nineteen years younger than Girondo and seven years younger than Moro, was attracted to these iconoclasts. He belonged to the so-called "1940 generation" (though 1945 would be a more appropriate date). Poets of this group found the Argentine literary scene dominated by the work of writers such as Lugones (Part Three, 5) and Borges (Four, 1). The young, however, were not terribly interested in them and felt a greater affinity with surrealism. Failing to find much encouragement in Argentina, they were forced to look elsewhere. Molina was one of those most firmly fixed in his determination not to be constricted by his own country's provincialism.

He was born near Buenos Aires in 1910. Lacking Girondo's family fortune, he enlisted in the merchant marine and visited some of the remotest corners of the planet, attempting to practice what many poets, from Whitman to the surrealists, had done only in their dreams: to be a truly cosmopolitan writer, a citizen of the world. But unlike Blaise Cendrars (the poet who exalted the Trans-Siberian Express and the ocean liners cruising the Amazon River), Molina was less interested in compiling a poetic tourist guide than in chasing, like a true surrealist, the magic landscapes of desire. In his first book, *Things and Delirium* (1941), traces of Rimbaud's quest for the invisible ("The poet has to become a seer," he had said in a much quoted letter), as well as Neruda's own residence in hell, were visible through Molina's very determined pursuit of hallucination as an aesthetic discipline. In 1946 he published a second book, *Earthly Passions*, in which he poetically transmuted the landscape of his native town, Bella Vista, on the broad Paraná River, second only to the Amazon in South America. The book's publication coincided with Girondo's new book, *Our Countryside*. This was not by chance: Molina had found in Girondo the only one among his senior Argentine colleagues he could really care about.

A third book came out in 1951, *Errant Habits, or The Roundness of Earth*, in which he began recording his own visionary travels. A fourth volume, *Loving Antipodes* (1961), completed his passionate rendering of an external reality he saw always in magical terms. (By then, he had also come across Moro's poetry and had even helped to print one of the latter's few books written in Spanish, *Trafalgar Square* [1954].) "Poetry is a knife that plunges deeply into reality," Molina said once, and he used verses as surgeons use scalpels. As a true disciple of Breton, Molina was haunted by desire, and in *Loving Antipodes* he collected many of his most outstanding erotic poems, a sample of which is given here.

This last volume attracted the attention of the Mexican poet Octavio Paz (who, though four years younger than Molina, was already widely recognized as a leading writer), and he wrote a very enthusiastic review of it. By this time, the work of the few Latin American surrealist poets—Moro in Lima, Molina in Buenos Aires, Paz himself in Mexico—was finally beginning to get the attention it deserved. However belatedly, surrealism had won acceptance in the New World.

In Molina's next book, *Free Fire* (1962), a slight change could be detected—he seemed to be making a conscious attempt to write in a more popular vein. Perhaps the hopes raised all over Latin America by the Cuban Revolution could account for the change. In the two volumes that followed (*The Beautiful Furies*, 1966; *Monsoon Napalm*, 1968), Molina continued his commitment to the real world without losing his grip on that extra dimension to which he, like all true surrealists, was devoted.

Two Surrealist Poems

From Poemas, *translated by Thomas Hoeksema,* Mundus Artium, *vol. 3, no. 1 (Winter 1969), pp. 43–45.*

Memory

Those violent caresses vanished
No more moons of ceremonial kisses
A cage of madness opens
Spasms of beautiful cats that howl buried alive
And a center of dead images grows in your marrow
Like a true plague. In the shadow
The woman undresses and gets into bed
Her nuptial flight reaches to remotest fires of the sky
He ripens to death by her side
In the warm greenhouse of her smiles near his face that disappears
Never will they revive on their kisses
Along viscid hills in undulating dormitories
Where indelible weeds sprout
Paths full of fishhooks
Clothes pulsate without a body

A portrait with teeth of fire
Smiling through the walls

Who does not respect the wandering of these souls?
Empty embraces joys of failure and of vertigo
That beguile to flay me like the devil
To venerate me with burned countries on my heart . . . ?

Then
From those huge moons that ferment
In the heat of tropical thickets
Full of women's legs
The light from tongues expands
Once more we are lost
Once more we implore idols of pride and desolation
Of brutal sexes
With smiles lost forever
Fragments of landscape
Lips of sacrilege that do not seek help

That do not have help

Descent into Oblivion

Oh! Behold the dead, seated
motionless around Time;
worshiping their pale, eternal fire,
uncanny, solitary their reunion.

There they sit, invaded by false jungles,
inhabited by damp music, tenacious cicadas.
The north wind heavy upon them, their forgotten faces, hazy
    bodies,
rain suddenly and long.

No; do not speak a forgotten language.
Do not pronounce your name.
May their marred, stormy heads not spin with deadly slowness.
May their empty hearts devoured by birds not recognize you.

15

JOSÉ LEZAMA LIMA

For nearly thirty years, until the publication in 1966 of his only novel, *Paradiso*, the Cuban José Lezama Lima was known to only a handful of devoted readers of poetry. His hermetic diction and metaphysical concept of poetry made him one of the most difficult of the avant-garde writers. But *Paradiso* suddenly projected him into fame, distorting his carefully constructed image. The real difficulties of the novel were overlooked by readers eager to get to the very explicit descriptions of homosexual relations. The fact that it was published in Cuba at a time when the Castro regime was conducting a puritanical campaign against homosexuals gave the novel greater prominence and helped to confuse the issues it raised. The book, and Lezama's previous work, had very little to do with hard-core pornography, or even with William Burroughs's more sophisticated treatment of the theme. *Paradiso* was a complex, extraordinarily intricate, highly coded narrative, the prose equivalent of Lezama's arduous volumes of poetry and criticism, which very few readers had ever bothered to peruse. He was born in Havana in 1910 and was, like José Cemí, the protagonist of his novel, a pampered and sickly child, suffering from asthma at an early age. He grew up in a traditional Cuban family, spoiled by his mother and grandmother and in loving conflict with a stern father, a captain in Cuba's army. His poetic vocation led Lezama to a very personal reading of the Spanish baroque poets, the French symbolists, and all the European writers who continued to develop that fruitful tradition well into the twentieth century. Lezama read Góngora and Quevedo while also reading Valéry and Rilke, Claudel and Eliot, the Spanish Jiménez, and the Chilean Neruda. At the same time, he began delving into Plato, browsing through Aquinas and the Bible, deciphering Heidegger's metaphysical interpretation of Hölderlin's verse. Never a scholar in the academic sense, Lezama absorbed everything pell-mell, unsystematically, with no clear awareness of chronology, so that his reading gave him a highly personal, synchronic perspective on Western culture. Lezama was living then in a country in which the books he cared about so desperately were not always available, or available only in faulty translations, in secondhand résumés. Besides, he was too much of a poet to bother with the tedious business of checking and rechecking sources.

Today, any beginner can correct his fanciful spelling of German names or his always imaginative quotations from the French or Latin. But those who approach Lezama with a blue pencil miss the point. What is important in his texts is not their blurred origins but their destination. Out of these bibliographical limitations he built up his own personal encyclopedia of obscure lore, misread philosophy, and dazzling poetic insights. He belonged to a small coterie of young poets and was responsible for several little magazines (*Origins* was the most successful), which brought about a radical change in Cuban poetry, until then almost exclusively dominated by Nicolás Guillén's folkloric and politically committed approach. Relentlessly, Lezama proceeded to write on just the subjects he really cared about, in books with provocative titles: *Death of Narcissus* (1937); *Enemy Rumor* (1941); *Fixity* (1949); *Giver* (1960). In these collections, he developed a new variety of baroque poetry, one less concerned with predictable effects and preoccupied, like Góngora's, with the translation of reality into dense units of verbal allusion. The image was, as in much of avant-garde theory and practice, the key to his system. For Lezama, it was never an isolated artifact, but the pivotal element in a dynamic system that proceeded from allusion into allusion in an elliptical fugue of meanings whose aim was the rendering of a metaphysical reality.

Like Claudel and Eliot, Lezama was a Catholic writer. He shared with them a need to return to the original sources of Western poetry, especially to that period of Christianity which produced both Aquinas's *Summa Theologica* and Dante's *Divine Comedy*. But instead of producing his own poetical *summa*, as did his models, Lezama chose to write a novel, a long autobiographical work that functioned as a parodic (i.e., baroque) reduction of medieval compilations. The obvious models for this enterprise were Joyce's *Ulysses* and Proust's *À la Recherche du temps perdu; Paradiso* had a bit of both.

But Lezama was less interested than they were in psychological or sociological exploration. Although he captured admirably a segment of Cuban society in the period between 1910 and 1930—even to the point of finding space to describe in elaborate detail some delicious Cuban dishes—he was more concerned with the protagonist's poetical destiny than with his general preparation for life. In this context, his sexual experiences, or lack of them, were not to be treated in primarily physical or physiological terms but as symbolic expressions of man's dual essence. Finding in the texts of Aquinas and St. Augustine a precarious foothold, Lezama would recognize in the myth of man's androgynous origin a metaphysical basis for his own view of homosexuality. In the same way, Cemí's poetic hallucinations lead him to initiation through an older poet into the orphic mystery of creation.

Mixing the occult adroitly with a Rabelaisian sense of humor, highly convoluted prose with faulty scholarship, a wild imagination with the most ambitious rethinking of the West's greatest works of literature and philosophy, Lezama produced a truly encyclopedic novel—but an encyclopedic work conceived and executed under almost incredible medieval conditions. The book is Lezama's *one* book. It was a condensation and expansion simultaneously of everything he had attempted previously. It was, in a sense, monstrous—but monstrous in the same way as a number of other landmark achievements in Latin American literature: Sarmiento's *Facundo* (Two, 5) or da Cunha's *Os Sertões* (Two, 16), and (why not?) Borges's *Ficciones* (Four, 1), as well as Sor Juana Inés de la Cruz's *Dream the First* (One, 11). That is, the masterpieces of a totally unclassifiable literature.

Texts in Prose and Verse

From Paradiso, *translated by Gregory Rabassa (New York: Farrar, Straus & Giroux, 1974), pp. 127–34; and from* Poemas, *translated by Elinor Randall,* Tri-Quarterly, *no. 13–14 (Fall–Winter 1968–69), pp. 138–40, and translated by Nathaniel Tarn, vol. 3, no. 1, pp. 47–49.*

Paradiso

Under the three naked bodies which scratched themselves every time the sun pierced their skins, the boat was drifting, with an assurance neither vain nor exaggerated, away from the elemental and tender green of the shallows toward a sandbank that absorbed the shore birds' shadows.

José Eugenio expanded his thirty-year-old chest. He seemed to be smoking the sea breeze. He widened his nostrils, drank in an epic quantity of oxygen, and then let it out through his mouth with slow puffs. The peace and innocent color of the waters awakened a shouting pride in him, one that was natural and savage. Standing in front of him he saw his five-year-old son, skinny, his ribs showing, panting as the breeze grew stronger, and then trembling as he tried to hide it, slyly watching his father as he pretended to breathe normally. José Eugenio Cemí, the Colonel, was rowing as if the wide-open box of his chest were guiding the knife of the prow. The third person in the boat was Captain Rigal's son Néstor, who was a year older than José Cemí, blond and freckled, with Holland-green eyes, who was laughing as he played in the gusty breeze. The Colonel turned to the freckled blond boy and said, "Do you notice anything strange about Joseíto's breathing? Notice how he doesn't breathe the same way you do. It's as if something inside him is limping through the breeze. When he gets that way, I worry, because it seems as if someone is strangling him."

José Cemí pretended not to hear. He dipped one of his hands into the cold water. As if ashamed, he dried it on his steaming swimming trunks, which gave off a light vapor. The Colonel stopped rowing and told the blond boy to go to the bow. Then he began to splash water with his hands, wetting José Cemí too, who laughed, hiding the trouble he was having in breathing.

"I don't think you can learn how to swim by yourself," he said. "So I'm going to teach you today. Now, you jump into the water and hold onto this finger." He held up his forefinger, created for the exercise of authority, strong, like a midget who was an important personage in the Tower of London. The forefinger curled like an anchor and then straightened up like a reed that jumps its moorings but then comes back to root itself in the sand once more.

José Cemí obeyed his father at once. He made the sign of the cross, a custom his mother had taught him, before jumping into the water. And, while the boat moved slowly along, propelled by the rowing of Néstor Rigal, José Cemí clutched his father's forefinger with his whole hand, feeling the resistance of the water as it tightened like a stone against his panting chest.

"You're not afraid any more, now you can learn by yourself," he said. The Colonel withdrew his forefinger just as a small whirlpool formed.

For three or four minutes Cemí's small body disappeared. The sailor on the Yacht Club pier, guardian of the swimmers' fates, dove into the water. Even though the Colonel also dove in to rescue his son, the sailor got there first, recovered José Cemí's sunken body, and laid it in the boat. The Colonel rowed his unconscious son to shore. After they had moved his arms a little, he opened his eyes, looked at his father, whose face by now was distorted with fright and covered with sweat. To lift his father's spirits, he began to laugh, but the Colonel was turning yellow from fatigue and terror. The waiter brought him a whiskey to revive him, and soon his color came back, and he hugged his son, whose breathing had returned to normal. He was patting his father on the back, alarmed now by the other's fright. The Colonel was weeping and José Cemí, to calm him down, began to throw sand at Néstor Rigal, who, caught between tears and laughter, ran screeching along the shore like a sea bird.

Now José Eugenio Cemí was inspecting the works of Morro Castle, which as an engineer he had rebuilt and as its first director he was inaugurating. He brought along his eldest daughter, Violante, the child from whom he withheld none of his affection. His other child came too, José Cemí, in whom the strong salt air had brought on a bronchial wheeze. This clearly annoyed his father, who wanted to show off his strong, forthright, happy children in front of the other officers. Was sickness not a weakness in soldiery? The lesser officers came over bowing, pretending a show of affection, carrying cameras to take pictures of the children sitting on cannons and stone benches, wearing campaign hats. Clearly, José Eugenio Cemí did not like to exhibit a son who was strangling with asthma. He wanted to avoid the tragicomic vulgarity in which they would offer him recipes, potions, herbals. In which they would jubilantly trot out some relative, exhumed like a gold mummy, to flatter the Chief and lessen his potential displeasure. They passed a dark, gaping hole that ended below in rocky caverns where sharks would round off their hypocritical dreams with a whiplash of activity. "That's where they used to throw prisoners in Spanish times," the Chief said to frighten his children, and then he pointed up the fear on their faces with a smile. Many years afterward, he knew that through that hole the garbage had always been thrown out, and for that reason the sharks lurked at the mouth of the castle, to emerge from their dreams to the Babylonian banquet of its detritus. Tons of garbage that had metamorphosed into the sacred silver of scales and tails that seemed to have been polished by Glaucus and his cortege of merry trumpeteers. A motive to sustain many years of nightmares: now I'm going through the bars that guard the tunnel that ends in the underwater caves, I get scratched, I'm bleeding, finally I find a jutting rock into which I can dig my nails; they grow long to save me. From the mouth of the cave the jailers begin to poke long poles with tridents, then the pardon comes, and the awakening. Sometimes I don't find the small stone and I roll down the tunnel until I splash in, but the sleeping sharks float uninterruptedly in the oil of their muscles, given over to high tide and relaxation. At midnight a small boat begins to row toward Cemí. The oarsmen smile and, bringing the lantern close to his face, they recognize him, and begin to dry him off with a cloth that smells of dry scales and the pancreatin of shrimps.

The Chief wanted to show that his son's bronchial deficiency had its compensations. They were standing beside the pool, a great well with a watery gargoyle on each side, faceless, a mixture of storied, century-old stone and brash, new lime, resembling a squirrel that had looked from left to right for so long that a wall had formed, obelisk to his *logos oculos,* the squirrel subsequently disappearing as inessential. He wanted to show off the natatory skills of his daughter Violante, in an improvised swimming pool. In a nearby room she put on her bathing suit, with that joy that the nearness of water brings to children. They think about it briefly, in a melancholy pause, but in the first splash a sheet of water and another of laughter form an instant apex where an otter wags his malicious tail. The pool was not very wide but it had an Avernal depth. One had to start swimming without the sandy shore to sustain one against early timidity. Violante, never taking her eyes off her father, was swimming along the side, when his gestures edged her away from the margins of safety. In the center of the pool she began to swallow water, she sank, reappeared red-faced, spat out a jet of water, and went circling back to the bottom. The Chief leaped into the water as his daughter sank to the bottom of the pool. There she touched the floor, rose from the pressure of the water, and touched again, like a balloon. José Cemí could see his sister, with the pineapple-leaf hair of a tiny gorgon, glassed in at the bottom of the pool. Two aides ran to the frightening submersion with long poles ending in curved tridents for cleaning the bottom of the pool, and began the extraction with a magical opportuneness. Straddling the fork, Violante ascended to the kingdom of the living like a little Eurydice. Blood and leaves covered her legs, the leaves of damp ivy that appeared when the water receded and the calcimined walls turned purple straining to receive the welcome air.

The Chief came out of the water, a confused Poseidon facing the silence of his two aides and son. With his handkerchief he began to clean the blood from her legs, removed the sanguinary, sticky leaves, smoothed her tangled hair, afterward smiling at José Cemí, who was reduced to such bronchial gasping with the scare of his sister's submersion that the Chief had to carry him inside when they reached home. He did not tell Rialta about the incident at the swimming pool as she fluffed the pillows and began to prepare the concoction of guaco and resin, wiping the sweat from his brow. Finally he began to sink into sleep on his pillow. Rialta noticed that his whole body was trembling and that he was raising his hands to his eyes as if to cast off a vision, the tumult of people who wanted to snatch him away from his pillow back into the waves, from his mother into the Avernal depths of the pool.

"The asthma comes from my side. My grandmother never found a cure for that malady," Rialta said.

"And the humidity of the post, crossing the bay at sundown, did the rest," José Eugenio replied. "I take him to the doctors. He shivers and can barely breathe. They don't spend much time looking at him and say asthma, asthma, as if those were unavoidable syllables, and then they go back to their tolu balsam and resin, and those iodides, and that's how he gets those stains on his face that make him look dirty even when he's just come out of the tub. And the iodide loosens his teeth, weakens him, because however much it may help his asthma, it's bad for his growth. He's never well. Even when he doesn't wheeze he seems on guard, waiting for the first symptoms of shortness of breath. He is constantly frightened, like a person waiting for bad news," José Eugenio said, speaking in gulps. His son's illness worried him incessantly, though he hid the fact not to alarm Rialta.

"I have the feeling that his fears, his fondness for Baldovina, and his reliance on her keep him awake nights. He's horrified of ghosts when I tell him: Look at them, there they are, you can almost touch them. Ghosts and death besiege him. If Baldovina isn't next to him, he can't fall asleep. He only sleeps peacefully next to his grandmother and Baldovina. This must be related somehow to the asthma he has day and night. To cure him, we will have to get rid of that anguish. A French doctor told me that if he swallowed a fistful of salt, it would burn up the moisture in his bronchial tubes and he'd be cured. But, in my opinion, the restfulness of the water would do him a world of good. Something that would suddenly make him calm down, a jab to tranquilize him, if that's possible. What I mean is a fright to cure him of all his fears. He has some kind of terror of falling asleep. He turns in his sleep, gets desperate, wants to write on the pillows. He goes to bed peaceful, and he wakes up as if he had arisen from hell. What does he see on that excursion? To him, sleep is like being kidnaped. Heal his nerves, make him sleep, that's what would help him get better. Every dream that he can't confess strangles him, and that's where the asthma comes from.

"The last doctor we saw told us that he'd be cured as he grew up, four or five years more and he'll be all right," Rialta went on. "They say a person with that sickness has a protection the way the jiqui plant has against lightning. It's a protective sickness, like something divine. A person who has it is immunized against all other illnesses. They say it weakens the heart, but in the long run it's better to have that weakness, because if not the pressure will boil up and burst in the little sparrow's brain. The heart may weaken but we hardly notice it because it's one of the organs that tends to repair itself easily to achieve an organic counterpoint. Only neurotics fret over every single beat. Notice that he's never had typhus, or mumps, or flu. When he comes out of his asthma, he's the happiest child of them all. They follow him, come looking for him. He's an expert in arousing affection. He's so friendly-like, as Grandmother Mela says in her Cuban Spanish. She says things like that in a funny way, out of mischief. For example, she says, 'Today's washerwoman-pickup day,' when the Chinese laundryman is coming." Rialta indulged her Cuban tendency toward digression, something José Eugenio, born of a Spanish father, did not show frequently, only when he was disturbed and obfuscated, and then an avalanche of words would serve him as a shield.

He went to the dining room. He took the whole cake of ice from the icebox. He sank the tongs into it. He went to the bathroom, opened the cold-water tap, and began to carry in the pieces of ice. Rialta had guessed his intentions and shut herself up in the farthest room. She did not wish to see, she could not protest. José Eugenio went to get his son, ordered him to get undressed, submerging him then in the icy bathtub where small pieces of ice still floated, bumping into each other, clinging momentarily together and then separating, melting more and more, reduced to irregular figures, an irreducible geometry now as they dissolved completely. The scene had something of an ancient sacrifice about it. Except that the Colonel did not know to which deity he was making the offering. And the mother, shut up in the farthest room, began to weep and pray.

He took his son, absorbed in that polar solution for his illness. "Cold water will cure your nerves. I think it's the only way we can get rid of that sickness. Don't be frightened, afterward we'll give you an alcohol rubdown so the blood will flow back into your bronchial tubes, cleaning out what's stuck there, which is what stops you from breathing right." He kissed him, sensing how disagreeable the curative method was, an emergency cryotherapy applied in a desperate moment.

José Cemí sank into the bathtub, concealing his trembling. His father threw water in his face, then he rubbed his shoulders. The boy was genuinely afraid of this cure. He began to get rigid, purple, his eyes became glassy, he tried to touch things with his toes but he did not have the strength. José Eugenio lifted his son out of his state of suspension. He propped him up on the bathroom chair, and José Cemí's head fell forward, as if all his breath had left him, and his body was bloodless and lacked substance.

"Rialta, Rialta," he shouted, "bring the towel and the alcohol. And a bottle of cognac." He was cornered in the bathroom now, fearing the outcome. Afraid to raise his eyes and face his wife.

Rialta entered the bathroom with the confidence of a woman going to redress her husband's errors. She dried her son and sprinkled his face with cognac. He threw his head back, and his eyes began to sparkle again. He moved his arms and when Rialta saw that he was reviving, to cover up the moment she said, "Don't you want to go to the park? The boys are already there playing. Let's put on a shirt that doesn't have too much starch so it won't bother you, or, better still, since it's late, you can put on your sailor suit so you won't get scratched." The sailor suit gave him the joyous feeling that arrows were being shot at him as he ran, that the suit was his own body being torn to shreds.

His arm fell over one side of his small bed. For moments his arm was pierced, hanging as if he were looking for an invisible salvation in water, a slow, cold sweat coinciding its pauses with his breathing, which was becoming more painful and urgent. Then calm, and his arm drifted back across his chest. In that aquarium of sleep, his breathing released leaf-shaped bubbles that reached the doorway of Grandmother Augusta's house on the Paseo del Prado, where the

Colonel, in uniform, was bowing quickly in greeting. Sweat passed along his arm again, and again he experienced the separation from his father's finger. In his dream just then, a hand was placed over his eyes, then a dark, horned wave swirled onward with him in the middle, disproportionately, unctuously gigantic, like a rug rolled up with a cigarette inside, that later will show an eye burned into the thickness of its weave. Then a broad fish swam up in ingenuous Christmas pinkness, moving its iridescent fins as if combing itself. The fish eyed the forsaken finger v and laughed. Then it took the finger into its mouth and began to afford it protection. Towing him by the finger, it brought him to a patch of floating moss where the carefully calculated rhythm of his new breathing began. Then he no longer saw salvation in the fish, but instead his mother's face.

If, perhaps through some miracle of the pineal gland, we could see inside his dream again, we might observe a starfish contracting and expanding from the nearness of the fish, which then disappeared among giant leaves whose chlorophyll circulated visibly and was transformed into his mother's face. For him every awakening was a discovery of the infinite expansion of each one of the starfish's radiations. When the arc of his breathing and the expansion of the starfish coincided, a white, algal tegument formed that followed the movements of the ocean's sheets.

Dwarfs were disembarking there, elves perhaps, with heads of long gray hair, laughing in the sway. They walked to a wooden house, the kind Canadian huntsmen live in. José Cemí's mother was there too, with her ceremoniousness of a Cuban lady, precise and jovial. She was instructing them where to sit, seemingly in charge of the gastronomic gathering, and then she became almost invisible.

The arm stretched out again and in its twisted tension it almost touched the rosettes of the dream. As the discharge of sweat ran down the channel of his arm, the rosette, in early dawn now, was collecting the dew, allowing the mysterious equivalencies of the dream to shake and cause the brilliantly colored leaves of its pentagon to tremble. He saw his sister Violante descend into the infernal gap of that pool again, seemingly in quest of the center of the earth, the Greeks' hell. Trembling, he went over to the well, the irregular refraction retreating while the swallowing lasted, but now what he saw at the bottom of the hole was always his mother's face, smiling at him, speaking with tranquil courtesy; smiling at everyone, speaking words of calm courtesy.

The dwarfs gesticulated once more, forming confused, absorbed choruses, finally scurrying off in one direction, without noticing the darkness of the door made of unfinished cedar logs. They exploded, scattering the grotesque diversity of their colors, and the door, without any visible propulsion, opened and let them fly off on their small wooden horses. The ones who stayed in the room were those dwarfs who were wearing red jackets with blue taffeta buttons bearing Ottoman inscriptions like the ones that may be seen in the mosaics of Hagia Sophia. They talked with firm familiarity, speaking of matters that included everyone, and some of them, driven by a seductive dancing spirit, practiced a Pythagorean heel-tapping beat, which seemed to be a known prediction, a rhythm that conquered the secrets of the new house.

His hand, after reaching the limit of its pendular extension, rested its palm on the cold tiles, sponging up the damp dew that now at midnight softened their surface like perspiration. His father was no longer there, pressing him down into the improvised icebergs of the bathtub. His mother, who remained standing as if at a baptism, threw warm, aromatic water of the most diverse colors over his head. The dwarfs passed by silently on their way to the dining room, where the malicious subtlety of the lamplight danced over their red jackets, drawing out daggers, quick serpents. They sat down in their assigned places, which they found with ease, as if the numbers had been whispered to them beforehand. Their joy was reflected in their good appetite; their slow movements, their exaggerated ceremony made it easy to see their presence as a strange outpouring in the depths of the dream. On each of the plates a fish appeared, its face enlarged and corroded by the beginning of sleep. The faces of those many-souled fishes reproduced Rialta's visage over and over, supervising his darknesses and fits, softening the others' bad manners and aggressiveness not by means of furious gestures but by running to his side and creating an atmosphere in which his breathing was able to throw off its reins, evaporate out of blood, which from that moment on was peacefully efficient, harmoniously radiating out into the world.

Summons of the Desirer

Full of desire is the man who flees from his mother.
To take leave is to raise a dew for civil marriage with the saliva.
The depth of desire is not measured by the expropriation of the
    fruit.
Desire is to cease from seeing one's mother.
It is the uneventfulness of a day which prolongs itself
and it is night that such absence goes driving down into like a
    knife.
In this absence a tower opens, in that tower a hollow fire dances.
And thus it widens out and the absence of the mother is a sea at
    rest.
But the fugitive fails to see the questioning knife:
it is from the mother, the shuttered windows, that he is escaping.
What has gone down into old blood sounds empty.
The blood is cold when it goes down and is far flung in circulation.
The mother is cold and has served her time.
If death is responsible, the weight is doubled and we are not set
    free.
It is not through the doors where our own loss looks out.
It's in a clearing, through which the mother keeps on walking but
    no longer follows us now.
It's through a clearing: there she blinds herself and leaves us well.
Alas for him who walks that path no longer where the mother no
    longer follows him, alas.

It is not self-ignorance, self-knowledge continues to rage as in her
    time,
but to follow it would be to burn *á deux* in a tree,
and she hungers to clap eyes on the tree like a stone,
a stone inscribed with the rules of ancient games.
Our desire is not to overtake or incorporate a bitter fruition.
Full of desire is the fugitive
and from our head-on collisions with our mothers falls the
    centerpiece planet
and from where do we flee, if it is not from our mothers that we
    flee,
that never wish to play these cards again, go through the night
    again, the night of such unearthly suffering in the sides?

An Obscure Meadow Lures Me

An obscure meadow lures me,
her fast, close-fitting lawns
revolve in me, sleep on my balcony.
They rule her reaches, her indefinite
alabaster dome recreates itself.
On the waters of a mirror,
the voice cut short crossing a hundred paths,
my memory prepares surprise:
fallow deer in the sky, dew, sudden flash.
Without hearing I'm called:
I slowly enter the meadow,
proudly consumed in a new labyrinth.
Illustrious remains:
a hundred heads, bulges, a thousand shows
baring their sky, their silent sunflower.
Strange the surprise in that sky
where unwillingly footfalls turn
and voices swell in its pregnant center.
An obscure meadow goes by.
Between the two, wind or thin paper,
the wind, the wounded wind of this death
this magic death, one and dismissed.
A bird, another bird, no longer tremble.

Boredom of the Second Day

The descent of love consecrated
by a new fervor, by an oil of recent

saps like the waters of a recent rainfall.
Thus the new grape destroys the purple landscapes.

That which comes from other infected blood,
growing like the nomadic leaves,
turns on the consumed with early anger,
just as the oath attracts irreverent wine.

Behind the curtain he sends the other graceless smile
while he revolves in a too puny dish.
His desires moved from the figure to the uncreated Medusa,
not from the palpable to a shadowy turning.

Always a black light falling on a fabric without names.
They talked, but he could see behind the dialogued figure
an entertainment without an appropriate form
that goes from chair to attic leaving the advice untouched.

He talked, embraced the proffered, and he accepted,
but oblique death contains an ultramodern acid.
There's something of Spring congealing in the sigh
and rolling on till it lodges in another solid body.

For his sidelong look that hurdled his established luck,
a fixed smile crowns the second day of his agony.
He pursued the inaccessible, dazzled in simple truths
hidden behind the faces that gave him their mouths.

On reaching the golden chair of partings,
his desires burst into melodious aquatic flowers.
As the sweet gesture of a moire shadow passes,
the dewy leaves propel his flight to the return.

How indolent a death when his crystals touch new echoes;
he sees the coming of uncounted faces on fleeting stairways.
The fleeting rounds itself out in new and transitory verdure;
and so the leaves leap from carpet to larger carpet.

From the moist trunk, a refuge for white birds,
the vegetal flesh returns with its swollen whip.
The smile revives filled suddenly with light
in which a finger points at it a hanging silence.

The same gesture, the smile come from the very spittle
brings to another flesh its thread and secret.

In sweeping flights it falls into the center of the first fabric,
the blindness fades into an endless whirlpool.

Desires circle the body in another escaped body.
The hand which weighs more now than a full fly,
though quiet, would like to hurt the weight imprinted
on the incipient light. Desires like blown leaves.

Now Has No Weight

Now has no weight, the air dissembles,
it leaves us with a fine dust
and this soft fine dust curses
its shadow with a moan.

When crumbling, or smiling, it questions,
and the elves respond with their dew.
The brash, the one who will not come,
submits in the arbor of emptiness.

It says less than the breeze and weighs
on the back like a bell.
The smoke still hovers, the little smoke congeals

the goat that shoulders morning;
from under its bones its glance
puts horns on the thread of Nothing.

The Cords

The cords
holding the copper plate
vibrate, the scuffles of the test
of leaping leaves
climb or smile
at nightfall.
The night, climber of cords,
descends along the cymbals
of foreboding air.
Still the cords do not balance
those saucers of the night.
The left cord,
rubicund marmalade eye,
the outline polished with vinegar,
the seeing testicle of a horse,

open as an eye
on the stroke of noon.
Twelve o'clock,
the belching of phantasmal drumsticks,
on the cold velvet of shipwreck.

16

MANUEL BANDEIRA

Although Manuel Bandeira always emphatically disclaimed any real affiliation with the Brazilian modernist group (see introduction to this part), he nevertheless found himself hailed as the John the Baptist of the movement. A few of his poems were read at the crucial Week of Modern Art in São Paulo, and thereafter he maintained a lively exchange of views with one of the modernist leaders, Mário de Andrade (selection 18). But Bandeira had found his own path to modernism and insisted on following that path. He was, in a sense, the perfect fellow traveler.

He was born in Recife in 1886 and attended primary school in his native town. He was ten when his family moved to Rio de Janeiro, where he attended the Colegio Pedro II. Later he entered the Polytechnical School in São Paulo. A long spell of tuberculosis cut short his architectural studies. After trying several Brazilian health resorts with no significant improvement in his condition, he decided in 1913 to go to Switzerland, to a sanatorium near Davos-Platz. There he met a fellow sufferer, the poet Paul Eluard.

Returning to Brazil via Lisbon in 1914, he failed to publish there his first book of poems, which would come out only three years later. *The Ashes of the Hours,* as it was called, was still within the Parnassian-symbolist tradition. A second book, *Carnival* (1919), already displayed the metrical innovations and the wit that would bring him recognition as precursor of the modernists. Two more books, published during the next decade, helped to establish Bandeira's indisputable supremacy among the younger poets: *The Dissolute Rhythm,* in 1924, at the height of the modernist revolution, and *Libertinism,* in 1930.

An all-pervading irony, feelings of frustration and tedium, and the ever-present memories of childhood were the characteristic features of Bandeira's poetry. His verses were colloquial, and he knew how to blend native words and idioms into the general educated language of poetry. As he was familiar with the masters of Portuguese and Brazilian literature, his innovations did not come from a mere desire to shock; they were deeply rooted in a creative tradition. His visit to Europe had acquainted him with the avant-garde poets, and he was later to find in Apollinaire a challenging model. But he was always his own master, and in his eclecticism sought inspiration in writers as diverse as Jean Cocteau and Sean O'Casey. Although his irony could sometimes take a tragic turn, Bandeira generally shunned the grand scale in theme or expression. Only as a translator (of Shakespeare's *Hamlet* and Schiller's *Mary Stuart*) did he deal with tragedy squarely.

In his next collection of poems, *Morning Star* (1936), he explored another territory in the landscape of Brazilian myth: the black folklore of his native Recife. As his honors and laurels steadily accumulated—he was elected a member of the Brazilian Academy of Letters in 1940, and appointed professor of Spanish American literature at the Federal University of Rio de Janeiro in 1943 —Bandeira continued to publish his witty, yet melancholy verse.

The first edition of Bandeira's *Complete Poetry* came out in 1924; the last edition, in 1967, also included a selection of his very important *Prose*. His autobiography, modestly called *Itinerary of Pasárgada* (1954), reflected a new phase of his ongoing development. In it he explicitly defended a socially conscious, committed poetry—although he himself went on writing in his own established style.

In 1957, for the first time since 1914, Bandeira journeyed to Europe. He visited Holland, England, and France, and was everywhere received as Brazil's leading poet. It was a fitting return for a man who in 1914 had failed to persuade the Lisbon literary establishment that his verses were worth publishing.

Poems

From Poemas, *translated by Dudley Poore*, Anthology of Contemporary Latin American Poetry, *pp. 125–29; translated by Giovanni Pontiero*, New Directions in Prose and Poetry, *no. 20 (New York: New Directions, 1968), p. 33; and especially translated by Thomas Colchie.*

Salute to Recife

RECIFE
Not the Venice of America
Not the Mauritsstad of the merchant adventurers to the West
    Indies
Not the Recife of Levantine peddlers
Not the Recife I learned to love afterward—the Recife of
    libertarian revolutions

But a Recife without history or literature
A Recife remarkable for nothing
The Recife of my childhood

Union Street where I played snap-the-handkerchief and broke the
    windows of Dona Aninha Viegas's house
Totônio Rodrigues was very old and wore his nose-nippers on the
    end of his nose
After dinner the families took their chairs out on the sidewalk
    gossiping, making love, laughing
Children played games in the middle of the street
The boys shouted:
    Will the rabbit come out?
    Or won't he?
In the distance the sleek voices of little girls sang slightly off key:
    Rose tree give me a rose
    Clove tree give me a bud
(Of those roses many a rose
Died in the bud)

Suddenly
        far away in the night
                        a bell
One grown-up person said:
Fire in Santo Antônio!
Another, contradicting him, São José!
Totônio Rodrigues insisted it was in São José.
The men put on their hats and went out smoking
And I was furious because I was a child and could not go to the
    fire

Union Street . . .
What lovely names they had, the streets of my childhood
Street of the Sun
(Nowadays, I fear, it is called after Dr. So-and-so)
Behind our house was the Street of Regretful Longing . . .
    . . . where I went to smoke on the sly
Not far away, on the water front, was the Street of Dawn . . .
    . . . where I went to fish on the sly

Capiberibe
—Capiberibe
There beneath the tangled woods of Caxangá
Bathhouses of straw

One day I saw a young woman bathing without a stitch
I stood still with beating heart
She laughed
           For the first time I was aware

Flood time! The river floods! Slime, dead oxen, uprooted trees
      submerged in the eddies
And in the whirlpools under the railway bridge the reckless
      half-breeds on rafts of banana trees
Novenas
        Riding on horses
I lay in the girl's lap and she began to run her hand through my
      hair
Capiberibe
—Capiberibe
Union Street where every afternoon the Negress with bananas
      went by
             In her gaudy African shawl
And the man who sold stalks of sugar cane
And the peanuts
  which were called midubim and were not roasted
  but boiled
I remember all the street cries:
  Eggs fresh and cheap
  Ten eggs for a pataca
That was long ago. . . .

Life did not come to me through newspapers or books
It came on the lips of the people in the rude language of the
    people
The apt language of the people
For it is they who speak with gusto the Portuguese of Brazil
  To a tune of our own
  What we do
  Is to ape
  The Lusitanian syntax
Life with a parcel of things I did not clearly understand
Countries of whose existence I did not know

Recife . . .
        Union Street . . .
                My grandfather's house . . .

Never did I think it would all come to an end!
Everything there seemed imbued with eternity

Recife . . .
           My grandfather dead . . .

Dead Recife, good Recife, Recife as Brazilian as my grandfather's
    house.

Translated by Dudley Poore

The Cactus

That cactus recalled the desperate gestures of the statuary:
Laocoön grappling with the snakes,
Ugolino struggling with his famished sons.
It also evoked the Northeast drought, the wax palms and wild
    caatingas . . .
It was enormous, even for this land of exceptional fertility.

Uprooted one day by a mighty gale
The cactus toppled astride the road,
Shattered the eaves of the facing houses,
Impeded the transit of carriages, trams, and cars,
Broke the electric cables and for twenty-four hours deprived the
    city of power and light:

It was beautiful, harsh . . . intractable.

Translated by Giovanni Pontiero

Reality and Its Image

The skyscraper rises into the clean air washed by the rain
And descends reflected in the muddy pool of the patio
Between reality and its image, on the dry ground which
    divides them,
Four pigeons parade.

Translated by Giovanni Pontiero

The Sky

The child looks upwards
At the blue sky above.
He lifts his tiny hand
And longs to touch the sky.

Unable to perceive
That the sky is an illusion:
The child thinks that he cannot reach it,
When he holds it in his hand.

Translated by Giovanni Pontiero

Deeply

Yesterday was Saint John's Eve
And I fell asleep
During all the drinks and
    shouts
Blasts of Bengali firecrackers
Voices folk songs and laughter
Circling the blazing bonfires.

Late in the night I woke up
There were no more voices or
    laughter
Some balloons
Passed by wandering
Silently
From time to time some
Noise of a trolly
Tore through the silence
Like a tunnel.

Where were they
The ones who before
Were dancing
Singing
And laughing
Circling the blazing bonfires?

—They were sleeping
They were lying still
Sleeping
Deeply

When I was six
I missed the end of Saint John's
    Feast
Because I fell asleep

Today there are no more voices from
    that time
My grandmother
My grandfather
Totônio Rodrigues
Tomásia
Rosa
All of them
Where are they?

—They're sleeping
They're lying still
Sleeping
Deeply.
                    Translated by Thomas Colchie

The Dead Ox

I feel myself almost drowning
In the troubled waters of a river,
Which divides, subdivides
The present into disaster,
Where a dead ox floats,
    enormous.

Dead ox, dead ox, dead ox.

Trees in the undisturbed
    landscape,
With trees—tall, so remote!—
My soul lingers, my wondering
    soul,

Wondering forever. While my body
    spins,
Spins on with the dead ox.

Dead ox, dead ox, dead ox.

Dead ox, immoderate ox,
Dreadfully ox, dead ox,
Shapeless, senseless, meaningless.
No one knows what you were.
What you are is dead ox.

Dead ox, dead ox, dead ox!
                    Translated by Thomas Colchie

17

OSWALD DE ANDRADE

If Manuel Bandeira (see selection 16) was the John the Baptist of Brazilian modernism, Oswald de Andrade may well be called its Messiah. He was the first to go to Europe and bring back the gospel of the avant-garde; the first to mobilize and galvanize the hitherto dispersed young poets and novelists who were to fill the movement's ranks; the first to produce manifestoes and works that attracted universal attention. He was also the first to be sacrificed.

He was born in São Paulo in 1890, to a family made wealthy by the coffee boom, and led the life of a playboy. In 1912 he visited Europe, where he read Marinetti's futurist writings, and found in the new literature the most congenial climate for his own anarchistic and witty writing. On his return to Brazil, he dutifully attended law school, and managed to graduate in 1919. But his heart lay with literature—and particularly literature as an instrument of social subversion. He joined forces with other young poets and critics and, in 1922, organized the Week of Modern Art in São Paulo. Less important than his public readings from a work in progress (the novel *The Condemned*) were his constant preaching and his active friendship with some of the most promising new authors. An event that had a decisive effect on both men was his meeting with Mário de Andrade (selection 18) (no relation—Andrade is as common a name in Portuguese as Jones in English).

In 1923, Oswald published his first important novel, *Sentimental Memoirs of João Miramar*. Written in the telegraphic style characteristic of the futurists, fragmenting narrative into brief chapters, playing with words, the book has been compared with the experimental works of James Joyce—though the comparison implies rather more ambitious claims for it than are in fact warranted. In its style the novel was actually modeled closely on the poetic prose then being espoused and practiced by such writers as Marinetti and Blaise Cendrars, the kind of prose that in North American literature is associated with certain experiments by Gertrude Stein, the early Hemingway, the early Dos Passos. In its own cultural context, however, the *Sentimental Memoirs* did have a revolutionary impact; for Brazilian prose was at the time still very much in the hands of the Parnassians and symbolists, and Andrade's novel effectively put an end to that type of self-consciously "beautiful" writing. With his use (and abuse) of colloquial language, obscenities, and regional idioms, Andrade liberated Brazilian prose from the long dominance of Portuguese academic standards, from contrived elegance and carefully musical phrasing. His book was a frontal attack on everything Brazilian letters had held sacred until then. It was witty and it was devastating. It was also frivolous, with the kind of frivolity Jean Cocteau and Noel Coward had made popular.

A second trip to Paris reinforced Andrade's contacts with the avant-garde. He published there a new book, *Pau Brasil,* in which he versified fragments of Pero Vaz de Caminha's letter on the discovery of Brazil (Part One, 2) and other early chronicles. The book's title refers to brazilwood, the first product of his native land to attract the interest of the colonizers. It was the author's way of indicating a return to basic sources.

Andrade was at this time occupied with the development of a complete aesthetic doctrine. In a manifesto published in 1928, he preached the victory of primitive man over the culture imported from the Old World and exalted Tupí, the indigenous tongue of Brazil's Indians. Appropriately called *Anthropophagical Manifesto,* it was dated to commemorate one of the first victims of Brazilian cannibals, the Portuguese bishop Sardinha ("Sardine," a fateful name). One of its lines—originally written in English and borrowed (with a slight alteration) from a fellow poet—was: "Tupí or not tupí, that is the question." Through this double emphasis on cannibalism and the native language, Andrade was reacting in a calculatedly outrageous manner against what he considered the repressive and censorious European tradition. He had been reading Frazer, Lévy-Bruhl, and Freud (especially *Totem and Taboo*) and now advocated a return to a primitive, totally utopian state of nature.

He was at work on a second important novel, *Serafim Ponte Grande,* when the 1930 revolution that brought Getulio Vargas to power disrupted his plans completely and made him aware of the brutal realities beneath the complacent bourgeois surface of Brazilian public life. When he published the novel in 1933, he prefaced it with a violently angry statement in which he not only satirized some of his modernist friends but denounced his own participation in the movement. By then he had discovered Marxism and had come to the view that the opposite of the hated bourgeois was not the Bohemian artist but the proletarian. From then on, Andrade devoted his energies to the literary expression of his strong social commitment.

Serafim was nonetheless a complex and contradictory work. The attack on conventional logic and coherence that in *Sentimental Memoirs* was made in terms of syntax and diction was extended here to external structure: each chapter was independently articulated; chronology was not respected; Serafim, the protagonist, died before the end of the book; and there were even several chapters after the one labeled "Epilogue." Language was less fragmented than in the previous novel, but the whole composition suggested the kind of collage the cubists were then popularizing. Andrade's attack on his former modernist colleagues was embodied in the character of Pinto Calcudo, a disciple of Serafim who eventually becomes the novel's main character after Serafim has made an unsuccessful, Pirandellian attempt to expel him from the book. The ending, with all the characters sailing on forever in a kind of phallic version of the medieval Ship of Fools, was expressive of the uselessness and futility of the modernist rebellion; and it constituted as well an attack on Mário de Andrade.

The last years of Oswald's life were devoted, first, to promoting the cause of proletarian literature through boring novels and essays and then, to a venting of his disillusionment on finding that not even Marxism was immune from abuses of power. Always the iconoclast, Oswald died in 1954, completely out of tune with the world and with the movement he had so energetically promoted.

Two Texts

From "Balada do Hotel Esplanada," especially translated by Thomas Colchie; and from Mémorias sentimentais de João Miramar, *especially translated by Jack E. Tomlins.*

Ballad of the Esplanade Hotel

Late last night
I tried
To see if I
Could write
A ballad
Before I got
To my hotel

Long ago
This heart
Had enough
Of life alone
And wants
To stay with you
At the Esplanade

I wished
I could
Cover this paper
With lovely phrases
It's so good
To be
A minstrel

In future
The generations
Passing this way

Will say
It's the hotel
of the minstrel

For inspiration
I open windows
Like magazines
I must construct
The ballad
Of the Esplanade
And end up
Being the minstrel
Of my hotel

But there's no
Poetry in hotels
Even though
They're Grand Hotels
Or Esplanades

There's poetry
In hibiscus
In the hummingbird
In the traitor
In the elevator

(Envoy)	The elevator
	Would bring
Who knows what	Your love
If some day	Up here

Sentimental Memoirs of João Miramar

Port Out to See

Big zinc sheds on the docks bolt upright in the sun
nailed me up like a poster amidst the hubbub of stevedores and
onlookers because the *Santa Marta* would not sail until tropical
nightfall.

The afternoon dived from the heights in the pallor
channeled between springboards of hills and an old fort. And
roustabouts loaded the ship under sacks in a row.

Sailors from the holds secured the cranes and placid
officers attended to last-minute shoulders.

The taut belly of the gangplank externalized the late
visitors, then to hang in abeyance alongside the blond seamen.

Groups crowded the still pier.

Sorrento

Crones sails cicadas
Mists on the Vesuvian sea
Geckoed gardens and golden women
Between walls of garden-path grapes
Of lush orchards
Piedigrotta insects
Gnawing matchboxes in the trousers pocket
White trigonometries
In the blue crepe of Neapolitan waters
Distant city siestas quiet
Amidst scarves thrown over the shoulder
Dotting indigo grays of hillocks

An old Englishman slept with his mouth open
like the blackened mouth of a tunnel beneath civilized
eyeglasses.

Vesuvius awaits eruptive orders from Thomas
Cook & Son.

And a woman in yellow informed a sport-shirted
individual that marriage was an unbreakable contract.

Indifference

Montmartre
And the windmills of the cold
The stairs hurl souls at the bare-loined jazz

My eyes go in search of memories
Like neckties found

Nostalgias of Brazil
Are flies in the soup of my itineraries
São Paulo with its yellow streetcars
And romanticisms under noctambulist trees

The ports of my country are black bananas
Under palm trees
The poets of my country are black
Under banana trees
The banana trees of my country
Are calm palms
Arms of exiled embraces that whistle
And starched skirts
The ring of riches

Brutality garden
Acclimation

Rue de la Paix
My eyes go in search of neckties
Like memories found.

Sal o May

The cabarets of São Paulo are remote
As virtues

Automobiles
And the intelligent signal lights of the roads
One single soldier to police my entire homeland
And the cru-cru of the crickets creates bagpipes
And the toads talk twaddle to easy lady toads
In the obscure alphabet of the swamps
Vowels

Street lamps night lamps
And you appear through a clumsy and legendary fox trot

Delenda lovely Salomé
Oh tawdry dancing girl
Full of ignorant flies and good intentions

The *javá* is a piggish polka with blue dust
But the purple empurples the procession of pink curtains

"I don't give a damn."
"I want to know about that nonsense of waiting
with the revolver on the road."
"That black thug gave her a punch and the
woman took a kick."
"In her belly."
The saxophone persists in an ache of frenzied teeth
Which the maxixe spasms
Between shots and tips
But the open leakage of gas escapes
Into the penitentiary night
"Lord grant us the illumined spongecake of redemption"

The Tieté rolls heaps of bricks
Water-colored and pink.

Translated by Jack E. Tomlins

18

MÁRIO DE ANDRADE

While Oswald de Andrade (selection 17) was the first to open up
Brazilian letters to avant-garde exploration, it was Mário de Andrade who was the
movement's most effective organizer, and who succeeded in producing its most
representative works during its first decade. One might perhaps call him the Saint
Paul of modernism.

He was born in São Paulo in 1893, only two years after Oswald, and
seven years after his good friend Manuel Bandeira (selection 16). He studied at
the Conservatory of Music and Drama and subsequently became a lecturer on

the history of music. He was basically a folklorist, with interests in anthropology and mythology, and had the scholarly training and the patience that Oswald so conspicuously lacked.

His first volume of verse, *There Is a Drop of Blood in Every Poem* (1917), was still in the Parnassian-symbolist vein. But in his second, *Paulicéia Desvairada,* a hallucinatory exaltation of his native city, Mário was already updating his diction and imagery, with Apollinaire, Cendrars, and other European masters as his obvious models. He was, nonetheless, deeply rooted in his native soil. Unlike Oswald, he never felt the attraction of foreign lands and very determinedly refused to move from Brazil. His meeting with Oswald was decisive for his participation in the Week of Modern Art in 1922. There he read some pages from *Paulicéia,* which was published the same year and which attracted the attention of Bandeira, beginning a friendship that lasted until Mário's death in 1945. His relationship with Oswald took a more uneven course. During the twenties they were very close and Mário incorporated some of Oswald's ideas into his writings.

By 1926 he had conceived a novel that would encompass all the myths of Brazil, not excluding the more recent ones introduced by Italian immigrants. This book, *Macunaíma,* published in 1928, took its name from an old Amazonian folk hero whose adventures Mário had discovered in the writings of a German anthropologist. With his imagination as guide, Mário organized the wealth of fragmentary or unconnected myths, plus the African folklore contributed by slaves and the modern immigrant legends, into a vast symphonic narrative with a complex structure that allowed him to reiterate time and again the same cosmic myth. After many adventures and a long and riotous confrontation with an ogre (the Italian-Peruvian Wenceslao Pietro-Pietra), Macunaíma at last achieves apotheosis in his transformation into the constellation of Ursa Major. In the chapter excerpted here, one of Macunaíma's sexual partners, Ci, Queen of the Amazons, is similarly transformed into a constellation. Writing in a totally invented language in which Tupí words and modern Brazilian slang are happily blended, Mário converts Macunaíma—the Hero Without a Character, as he calls him, but also (in Joseph Campbell's Jungian sense) the Hero with a Thousand Faces—into an embodiment of *Homo brasiliensis.* His motto, "Oh, but I'm so sleepy . . . ," can be seen as a national slogan.

So many layers of meaning did the novel have that Mário (an excellent critic too) decided against publishing the two explanatory prefaces he had prepared for the book. Instead, he wrote endless letters to his friends and especially to Bandeira, discussing his intentions. These letters, plus some critical essays he wrote later, including the book-length *The Modernist Movement* (1942), have become the basis for a wealth of exegesis. When the novel was finally published, at the author's expense and in a very modest edition, neither readers nor critics were ready. They were shocked by the obscenity of some situations and dialogue, bored by the seemingly endless shifting of legends, characters, and places, lost in a vocabulary so rich that only the better-trained anthropologists and folklorists could make full sense of it. But the book's vitality ultimately overcame all

objections. It was discovered that it could be enjoyed without necessarily understanding every word, deciphering every myth, identifying every allusion. Like
Ulysses, Macunaíma was self-explanatory, self-illuminating; it taught its readers
how to read it.

Today, the book no longer seems obscene, rambling, or hermetic. On
the contrary, it is generally recognized as the first successful attempt to write an
all-encompassing Brazilian mythical narrative; a book that in many ways made
possible Guimarães Rosa's masterpiece, *Grande Sertão: Verédas* (selection 22).
Eschewing some of Oswald's excesses (cannibalism is just one of the novel's
motifs, and only a comic one), *Macunaíma* has become a classic. Its success today
can be measured by the witty film adaptation produced by Joachim Pedro de
Andrade, in which some of the myths were updated and Macunaíma even
becomes involved with urban guerrillas.

Mário's books after *Pauicéia* and *Macunaíma* were less controversial.
Always the organizer, he brought to fruition in 1944 an edition of his *Complete
Works* in twenty volumes, a fitting monument to a man who as a poet, scholar,
novelist, and short-story writer left a permanent imprint on Brazilian letters.

Two Texts

From Pauicéia Desvairada *(Hallucinated City), translated by Jack E.
Tomlins (Kingston, Tenn.: Vanderbilt University Press, 1968), pp. 29–57;
and* Macunaíma, *especially translated by Barbara Shelby.*

São Bento Street

Triangle,

There are sailing vessels for my shipwrecks!
And the songs of the water-nymph street of São Bento . . .

Between these two leaden waves of leaden houses,
my delights in the asphyxias of the soul!
There is an auction. There is a white-flesh market. Poor rice
    paddies!
Poor breezes without smooth plushes to smooth down!
Pack of dogs . . . Stock Market . . . Gambling . . .

I have no sailing vessels for more shipwrecks!
I've run out of strength! I've run out of breath!
What the hell! There isn't even a dead port!

"Can you dance the tarantella?" "Ach! ja."
They are the californias of a millionaire life
in a harlequin city . . .

The Commercial Club . . . The Spiritual Bakery . . .
But the disillusion of the amorous shady places
puts *majoration temporaire,* 100 percent! . . .

My Madness, be calm!
Put on your raincoat of alsos!
Not for a long time will you arrive
at the textile factory of your ecstasies;
telephone number: Beyond 3991 . . .
Between these two leaden waves of leaden houses,
behold, out there on the far-far-aways of the horizon,
its smokestack of blue sky!

Landscape I

My London of the fine mists!
High summer. The ten thousand million roses of São Paulo.
There is a snow of perfumes in the air.
It is cold, very cold . . .
And the irony of the little seamstresses' legs
looking like ballerinas . . .
The wind is like a razor
in the hands of a Spaniard. Harlequin! . . .
Two hours ago the Sun burned through.
Two hours from now the Sun will burn through.

A St. Boob goes by, singing beneath the plantain trees,
a tra la la . . . The city police! Jail!
Are jails necessary
to preserve civilization?
My heart feels very sad . . .
While the gray of the goose-fleshed streets
chats a lament with the wind . . .

My heart feels very glad!
This cocky little chill
makes me feel like smiling!

And I walk on. And go on feeling,
with the agitated alacrity of the winter chill,
something like the taste of tears in my mouth. . . .

Nocturne

Lights from the Cambucí district on nights of crime . . .
Hot weather! . . . And the lowering thick clouds,
made from the bodies of moths,
rustling on the epidermis of the trees . . .

The trolleys swish like a skyrocket,
clicking their heels on the tracks,
spitting out an orifice into the whitewashed gloom. . . .

In a perfume of heliotropes and puddles
whirls a flower-of-evil. . . . She came from Turkestan;
and she has circles under her eyes that obscure souls. . . .
She has smelted English pounds between her purple fingernails
in the bordellos of Ribeirão Preto. . . .

      Get-a you roast-a yams! . . .

Lights from Cambucí on nights of crime . . .
Hot weather! . . . And the lowering thick clouds,
made from the bodies of moths,
rustling on the epidermis of the trees. . . .

A golden mulatto
with hair like lustrous wedding rings . . .
Guitar! "When I die . . ." A heady scent of vanilla
pivots, falls, and rolls on the ground . . .
In the air undulates the nostalgia of the Bahias.

And the trolleys pass by like a skyrocket,
clicking their heels on the tracks,
wounding an orifice in the whitewashed gloom. . . .

      Get-a you roast-a yams! . . .

Hot weather! . . . Devils in the air
bodies of naked girls carrying . . .
The lassitudes of the unforeseen forevers!
and souls awakening to the hands of embracing lovers!
Idyls under the plantain trees! . . .
And the universal jealousy with magnificent fanfares
in pink skirts and pink neckties! . . .

Balconies in the pulsating caution, where Iracemas blossom
for rendezvous with white warriors . . . White?
So let the dogs bark in the gardens!
No one, no one, no one cares!
They all embark on the Promenade of the Kisses of Adventure!
But I . . . Behind these garden fences of mine with pinwheels of
    jasmine,
remain while the alleyways of Cambucí in the free
of the freedom of parted lips! . . .

Harlequin! Harlequin!
The lowering thick clouds,
made from the bodies of moths,
rustling on the epidermis of the trees . . .
But on these my garden fences with pinwheels of jasmine,
the stars grow delirious in carnages of light,
and my sky is all a skyrocket of tears! . . .

And the trolleys trace like fireworks,
clicking their heels on the tracks,
jetting an orifice into the whitewashed gloom. . . .

Get-a you roast-a yams! . . .

Jungle-Mother Ci *(from Macunaíma)*

One day the four friends were following a trail through the jungle,
thirsty and pining for the flooded riverbanks and forest pools. There wasn't an
ombú tree for miles around, and the scorching rays of Vei, the sun goddess, were
torn to shreds of light by the foliage and clawed the travelers' backs without ever
a letup. Sweat was pouring off them as if they'd been greased with snake oil to
dance for the witch doctor, but they kept on going. Then all at once Macunaíma
stopped and flung out his arm in a huge warning gesture written plain on the
stillness of the night. The others stopped dead in their tracks. They couldn't hear
a thing, but Macunaíma hissed, "There's something there."

Pretty Iriquí stayed behind and sat primping among the roots of a
samaúna tree, while the three brothers crept forward one step at a time. They
had gone a league and a half and Vei was sick and tired of whipping the three
men's backs by the time Macunaíma, the scout, stumbled on a shapely Indian
woman, a *cunhã*, asleep on the ground. It was Ci, Mother of the Forest. He saw
by her dried-up right breast that the girl was one of the tribe of women who lived
by themselves on the shore of a lake called Mirror of the Moon, which was
drained by the Nhamunda River. The *cunhã's* lovely form was etched with vice
and stained blue with jenipap dye.

The hero flung himself on top of her to have some fun, but Ci wasn't in the humor and let fly her *txara,* a three-pronged arrow as sharp and wicked as its name. Macunaíma pulled out his big horn-handled knife, and a terrible battle began. The shouts of the two adversaries resounded under the canopy of leaves and made the small birds shrink with fear. The hero was getting the worst of the fight. His nose was bleeding from a well-aimed blow and Ci's arrow had nicked him in the rear. The devil-woman didn't have a scratch on her, and every time she lifted her hand the hero's body bled in some new place and he let out a horrendous bellow that made the birds shrivel up with fear. When he finally saw he couldn't get the best of the Amazon, the hero turned tail and ran yelling to his brothers, "Come help me or I'm a goner! Come help me or I'm a goner!"

His brothers ran up and grabbed hold of Ci. Maanape twisted her arms behind her back while Jiguê let her have it on the noggin with his redwood spear. And the spirit-woman fell down helpless in the ferns. When the Mother of the Forest was as still as she could be, Macunaíma went up and played with her and the birds came to hail Macunaíma—new Lord of the Virgin Forest!—a cloud of *jandáias,* red macaws, *tuins, coricas,* parakeets, and parrots.

Then the three brothers started out again with their new companion. They crossed the City of Flowers, skirted the River of Bitterness, passed under the Waterfall of Happiness, took the road of Pleasure, and finally reached My Best Beloved Grove in the wooded Venezuelan hills. There Macunaíma settled to rule over the mysterious jungle, while Ci led the women in forays, armed with barbed three-pointed *txaras* like her own.

The hero lived in peace. He lounged in his hammock the livelong day, killing *taioca* ants and smacking his lips over palm wine. When the drink took hold, he sang to the tune of the trickling waterfalls, and as the woods echoed sweetly with the song, the cobras, leeches, ticks, ants, mosquitoes, and the wicked gods were lulled.

Ci came back at nightfall, redolent with resin, bleeding from the battles of the day, and climbed into the hammock she had woven from strands of her own hair. The couple exchanged playful caresses and then looked at each other, laughing. They laughed and couldn't stop and nestled close together. Ci's fragrance made Macunaíma weak and dizzy.

"God Almighty! How sweet you smell, you precious baby!" he murmured with delight, flaring his nostrils wide. Such a delicious dizziness and drowsiness crept over him that sleep was dripping on his eyelids. But Jungle-Mother still hadn't had enough, and giving the hammock a twitch to enfold the two of them, she invited her partner to play with her again. Drugged with sleep and vexation, Macuaíma kept up the game so as not to lose his reputation; but when Ci was satisfied for the time being, she still wanted to laugh and snuggle cozily together.

"Lemme get some sleep!" the hero grumbled, thoroughly out of sorts. And turning his back on her, he would fall asleep. So Jungle-Mother picked up her *txara* and tickled her companion with that. Macunaíma would wake up howling with laughter, twisting and flopping to escape the tickling.

"Stop that, you sassy thing!"

"I won't!"

"Let's go to sleep, honey."

"No, let's play."

"Oh, I'm so sleepy! . . ."

And they'd have themselves another little game.

But on evenings when Macunaíma had drunk more palm wine than he could hold, Ci would find the Emperor of the Virgin Forest sprawled out dead drunk. When they started to play, the hero would forget what he was doing in the middle of the game.

"Well, hero!"

"Well, what!"

"Why don't you go on?"

"Go on with what?"

"Why, thunder and lightning, we're having us a good time and you stop right in the middle!"

"Oh, but I'm so sleepy. . . ."

Macunaíma would be so drunk and tuckered out that he could barely lift a finger, much less anything else. He'd find a soft place in his partner's hair and go happily to sleep.

To wake him up again, Ci resorted to her final, never-failing stratagem. She hunted in the forest until she found a fiery thistle and, taking a leaf of it, scratched an artful itch in the hero's *chui* and her *nalachitchi*. That always did the trick. Macunaíma would become a panting lion and Ci a lioness, and the couple would go on with their ardent, wonderful, abandoned game.

But it was on nights when they didn't sleep at all that they invented the best games for their pleasure. Then all the burning stars poured onto the Earth a torrid oil so hot that no one could resist it, and a breath of fire ran through the jungle. Not even the birds could stay quiet in their nests. They turned their heads restlessly to and fro; they fluttered from branch to branch and finally worked the most prodigious wonder the world had ever seen: they conjured up a black dawn out of nowhere, chirpchirruping as if they'd never stop. The commotion they made was bad enough, but the scorching heat and fumes were even worse.

Macunaíma would jerk the hammock so that Ci would fall out. Then she'd wake up in a rage and loom over him, and that was the start of a new game. And when one pleasure had thoroughly awakened them, they would invent variations on the theme.

Before six months had passed, the Jungle-Mother whelped a scarlet son, and that was the signal for the celebrated quadroons and octoroons to flock from Bahia, Recife, Rio Grande do Norte, and Paraíba to give Jungle-Mother a bow of ribbon dyed a wicked, flaunting crimson to show that now she was the mistress of the scarlet ribbon of all the Christmas Shepherds' pageants. Then they sashayed off again with glee and jubilation, dancing as they went, dancing as if they didn't plan to stop until the Day of Judgment, with crack soccer players in their wake, and soulful serenaders, all the gilded youth. As a brand-new father should,

Macunaíma rested for a month; however, he refused to fast. The little rascal was born with a flat head and Macunaíma made it even flatter by pounding on it every day as he admonished the little lad, "Hurry up and grow, boy, so you can go to São Paulo and make a pile of money for your folks."

All the Indian squaws loved the little rosy baby, and when he was bathed for the first time, they put all the jewels of the tribe in the bath water so the little boy would always be rich. They sent to Bolivia for a pair of scissors and put them under the headboard of the bed with the points open because they knew if they didn't, Tutu Marambá would come and suck the baby's navel and Ci's big toe. Tutu Marambá did come, found the scissors and was fooled, sucked the scissors' eye instead, and went away happy. No one thought about a thing but that baby. They sent to São Paulo for a pair of the famous woolen booties knit by Dona Ana Francisca de Almeida Leite Morais to put on his tiny feet, and to Pernambuco for lace baby dresses in the most beautiful patterns—"Rose of the Alps," "Flower of Guabiroba," "For thee I pine"—all the exquisite hand-iwork of Dona Joaquina Leitao, better known as Quinquina Cacunda. They filtered the finest tamarind juice, prepared and bottled by the Louro Viera sisters of Obidos, for the little boy to get down his worm medicine with. Those were happy times! But one day a *jucurutu* owl lighted on the Emperor's wigwam and let out his ill-omened hoot. Macunaíma was afraid. He shivered, brushed away the mosquitoes, and drank palm wine until he was so drunk he couldn't stand up, to see if he could brush away his fear. He drank and fell asleep and slept all night. And that night the Black Cobra came and sucked Ci's only living breast so hard that not even the first milk was left. And since Macunaíma's brother Jiguê hadn't had a chance to get any of the pretty young *cunhãs* with child, there was no one to be wet nurse to the poor little papoose. Next morning he sucked his mother's breast, sucked again, gave a poisoned little moan, and died.

They laid the little angel in a wide-mouthed earthenware urn carved to look like a land turtle. Then, with much singing and dancing and palm-wine drinking, they buried him in the very center of the village so the swamp demons couldn't eat his eyes out.

When the ceremony was over, Macunaíma's helpmeet, all decked out in her finest ornaments, took from her necklace a famous charm, a green stone called a *muiraquitã*, and, putting it in Macunaíma's hand, climbed up to heaven on a liana. That's where Ci lives now, having herself a high old time in the sky with no ants to bother her, and dressed to the nines—dressed in light, in fact. Now she's a star, Beta in Centaurus.

Next day, when Macunaíma went to visit his son's grave, he saw that a little plant had sprung up from his corpse. The Indians took good care of it, and it turned out to be the guarana. We use the sundried berries of the plant to cure us when we're sick and to quench our thirst when Vei the sun goddess shines too hot.

19

CASSIANO RICARDO

Although Cassiano Ricardo took some time to accept modernism (he was repelled by the alien European viewpoints of the first modernists), he soon became one of the movement's most active devotees, founding groups and participating in polemics. He first joined the Green & Yellow group, which used the colors of the Brazilian flag to underline their opposition to foreign influences. Later he founded the Anta (Tapir) group, which celebrated miscegenation and exalted the authentic indigenous values. Finally, with some faithful friends, he formed another nationalistic group, The Flag, which alluded to the pioneers who opened up the interior of Brazil to trade and the traffic in Indian slaves. (See Part One, 15, for a critical view of these flag carriers.) Always interested in innovation, Ricardo was nevertheless very consistent. He searched for, and finally found, a mode of expression that was at once authentically Brazilian and uniquely personal.

He was born near São Paulo in 1895 and took a degree in law after studying in his native city and in Rio de Janeiro. He had been practicing literary journalism and writing poetry since his teens. After graduating, he worked for some of the most important newspapers in both São Paulo and Rio.

His poetic output was constant. His first volume of verse, *Inside Night* (1915), was in the symbolist mold. Three more volumes in a similar vein were to follow before he discovered modernism. In 1926 he published *Green & Yellow Sketches,* in which the modesty of the word "sketches" was more than compensated for by the pride of parading the national colors. By that time Ricardo and his group had decided to orient modernism against European models and toward a recovery of a lost Brazilian tradition. The next volume he published, *Let's Go Hunting Parrots* (1926), placed heavy stress on local subject matter and vernacular. Two years later, he published one of his most important books, *Martín Cereré,* an epic vision of Brazilian history.

Another volume, *Take It Easy, Crocodile* (1933), was in the same nationalistic vein. (In using the native word "jacaré," instead of the metropolitan Portuguese "crocodilo," Ricardo was underlining the idiomatic effect of the title.) Unfortunately, by then the Revolution of 1930 had given nationalism distinctly sinister undertones. Plinio Salgado, one of the members of the Green & Yellow group, had founded a fascist party whose followers wore green shirts as counterparts of the German brown and the Italian black one. Ricardo's politics were more literary in nature, but he could not help being associated in the minds of many readers with these theatrical conspirators. His own poetry remained devoted to indigenous subjects and attitudes, but beginning in 1943, with *The Blood of the Hours,* it evinced a greater concern for social and human problems. A strong smell of earth emanated from his verse, according to one of his critics.

When in 1957 Ricardo compiled his *Complete Poetry,* many of his admirers discovered that despite the title, he had eliminated a considerable portion of it while drastically rewriting a good part of the rest. Like Borges, Ricardo never considered a text completely finished and was always tinkering with it anew.

His last volumes (*A Day Following Another,* 1947; *The Glass Sky-scraper,* 1956; *Jeremiah Without Tears,* 1964) showed him in a more restrained, more contemplative mood—as witness the poem excerpted here. In another version of this same poem, he included an epigraph from the Portuguese poet Fernando Pessoa ("I could rest because I abdicated") and added a last strophe in which the lines completely disintegrate: "Ah, my father was king/. . . . / . . . . and it wasn't because he had,/. . . . / but only because. . . ." (The dots indicate gaps in the original text.) An allusion to Don Sebastião, the Portuguese king whose body temporarily disappeared in a 1578 battle, giving rise to a legend, helped to place the whole poem in perspective. Here the poet (using the time-honored device one finds in Yeats and Cavafy as well as in Pessoa and Borges) increased the poetical density of his subject by introducing this allusion to the forever lost and always awaited King Sebastião.

My Father Was the King

"*Meu pai foi rei,*" *especially translated by Thomas Colchie, from* Antologia de Moderna Poesia Brasileira, *edited by Fernando Fereira de Loanda (Rio: Orfeu, 1967).*

My Father Was the King

All of them will shout to me
how he never was, he never was.
And they will throw stones at me,
I know they will.
That's the great law of everything.

But my father was the king.
Not because he had
any golden crown,
ridiculous on his head,
but by the great law
of silvery moons.

Yes, my father was once the king.
(The king you are. The king I am.)

Who of us was ever not-king
because of abdicating?

Yes, my father was once the king.
Much more than king
Solomon.
Because it was nothing
like rubies and emeralds,
a scepter in hand,
but just his signature
on an abdication.

Not the king of spades
in a game of cards,
but the king of have-not

after having-once-had-all,
if not a heart
and a bird in hand.

Yes, my father was once the king.
But the king just because he
could say: almighty,
your stars are the drops
of sweat from your voyage,
but I sweat drops of stars
carrying the stones
in my landscape.

King, but not of the sea,
no returning King Sebastian,
but from shouting
this way: ocean,
I cannot be diminished
by your grandeur.
The tears I cried today,
in the hour of abdication,
are more.

King of saying to me
once: listen, tear out
from the body itself
(from some daisy,

a white petal)
the only favor you have
for the sake of someone
you make happy,
without that someone's knowing
even, and you'll be king.
And you'll say: I was once king,
just abdicating.

Yes, my father was once the king!
(The king you are. The king I am.)
Who of us was ever not-king
because of abdicating?

Who of us was ever not-king
because of renouncing
(in anonymous suicide)
what was dearest in life?

All of them will shout to me
how he never was, he never was.
And they will throw stones at me,
I know they will.
That's the great law of everything.
Still it doesn't matter.
Still an abdication
is better than a kingdom.

20

JORGE DE LIMA

Unlike the two Andrades and Cassiano Ricardo (selections 17, 18, 19), Jorge de Lima did not belong to the São Paulo group. He was instead associated initially with the Northeast movement, which followed Gilberto Freyre's teachings and took a more regionalistic view of modernism. Although he wrote often in prose, his work in verse could be seen as the counterpart of what Graciliano Ramos, Lins do Rêgo, and even Jorge Amado were trying to achieve in their

novels (Part Three, 16, 17, 18). But Lima was less interested than they in
the social context of his work and later took a decidedly Catholic line. Jorge
de Lima was born in 1895 in União, Alagoas, and studied humanities in his
native state; then he went to Rio, where he graduated in medicine. He returned home to set up his practice and also became involved in local politics.
In 1930 he moved to Rio for good. He taught Portuguese and Brazilian literature at the Federal and National Universities and became one of the leading
literary figures of the capital.

He began to publish poetry while in his teens. His first book, *Fourteen Alexandrines* (1914), was written in that meter, the favorite of the Parnassians. But as soon as Lima discovered modernism, he switched to the new
style. A book simply called *Poems* (1927) demonstrated his complete mastery
of the new techniques. In 1928 he published his most famous poem, "That
Mulatto Woman." For years his name would be associated with the kind of
poetry Nicolás Guillén (Four, 11) was writing in Cuba: Afro-American, with
a powerful beat and colorful imagery. In *New Poems* (1929), he included
that poem and others of a similar folkloric nature. As late as 1949 he would
still be publishing *Black Poems*.

His first collection of *Selected Poems* (1932) had a unified theme: the
rejection of a civilization that he saw as totally bereft of spiritual values. Five years
later he was converted to Catholicism. Thereafter his poetry showed a sense of
mission. In *The Unseamed Robe* (1938) he not only alluded to Jesus' robe but
also incorporated Biblical symbols and even literal quotations from the holy texts
into the fabric of his own verses. His poetry became dense with religious refer-
ences, difficult, almost hermetic.

With this return to orthodoxy, Lima also returned to traditional forms
in verse. In 1949 he published a *Book of Sonnets*, followed in 1950 by *Twenty
Sonnets*, which proved his complete mastery of the form. He was less successful
in his attempts to write novels. In 1927 he had published *Solomon and the
Women*. Two more novels were published successively in 1934 and 1935: *The
Angel*, a regionalist tale, and *Calunga*, written in a surrealist vein. In 1939 he
published another novel, *The Dark Woman*.

The poem here excerpted presents Lima in his avant-garde phase. It
is a brilliant, irreverent, satirical piece, one of his best.

The Big Mystical Circus

From "O grande circo mystico," translated by Dudley Poore, Anthology of Contemporary Latin American Poetry (New York: New Directions, 1942), pp. 69–73.

The Big Mystical Circus

Frederick Knieps, Physician of the Bed Chamber, to the Empress
    Theresa,
resolved that his son also should be a doctor,
but the youth, having established relations with Agnes, the
    tightrope artist,
married her and founded the circus dynasty of Knieps
with which the newspapers are so much concerned.
Charlotte, the daughter of Frederick, married the clown,
whence sprang Marie and Otto.
Otto married Lily Braun, the celebrated contortionist,
who had a saint's image tattooed on her belly.
The daughter of Lily Braun—she of the tattooed belly—
wanted to enter a convent,
but Otto Frederick Knieps would not consent,
and Margaret continued the circus dynasty
with which the newspapers are so much concerned.
Then Margaret had her body tattooed,
suffering greatly for the love of God,
and caused to be engraved on her rosy skin
the Fourteen Stations of Our Lord's Passion.
No tiger ever attacked her;
the lion Nero, who had already eaten two ventriloquists,
when she entered his cage nude,
wept like a newborn babe.
Her husband, the trapeze artist Ludwig, never could love her
    thereafter,
because the sacred engravings obliterated
both her skin and his desire.
Then the pugilist Rudolph, who was an atheist
and a cruel man, attacked Margaret and violated her.
After this, he was converted and died.

Margaret bore two daughters who are the wonder of Knieps's
　　Great Circus.
But the greatest of miracles is their virginity,
against which bankers and gentlemen with monocles beat in vain;
their levitations, which the audience thinks a fraud;
their chastity, in which nobody believes;
their magic, which the simple-minded say is the devil's;
yet the children believe in them, are their faithful followers, their
　　friends, their devoted worshipers.
Marie and Helène perform nude;
they dance on the wire and so dislocate their limbs
that their arms and legs no longer appear their own.
The spectators shout encore to thighs, encore to breasts, encore to
　　armpits.
Marie and Helène give themselves wholly,
and are shared by cynical men;
but their souls, which nobody sees, they keep pure.
And when they display their limbs in the sight of men,
they display their souls in the sight of God.
With the true history of Knieps's Great Circus
the newspapers are very little concerned.

21

CARLOS DRUMMOND DE ANDRADE

　　　　Brazil's most popular modernist poet, after Manuel Bandeira (see
selection 16), was undoubtedly Carlos Drummond de Andrade. His shy,
ironic mode, his preference for everyday subjects, his alert social consciousness made Drummond (as he was always called by Brazilian critics) one of
the most widely read poets not only in Brazil but in the rest of Latin America as well. A friend of Neruda's, he shared with the Chilean poet a devotion
to the cause of socialism. Drummond knew how to make his verse accessible
to the common man without renouncing the prerogatives of a personal voice.
He was never an epic poet, nor did he ever attempt to write a *General Song*,
as his Chilean friend did, but in the deceptive simplicity of his lyrics, a collective voice could also be heard.
　　　　Drummond was born in 1902 in Itabira, a small town in the mining

district of Minas Gerais, and was brought up on a ranch. But he never really took to rural life. He was educated in Belo Horizonte, the state capital, and in nearby Friburgo. He got a degree in pharmacy, but soon was devoting more of his time to teaching language and practicing journalism. His affiliation with modernism began with some contributions to the "anthropophagic" movement created by Oswald de Andrade (selection 17) (no relation). Drummond's poetry was more detached and objective than Oswald's, and it has proved to be more durable. As a man from the hinterlands, a "mineiro," he was supposed to be more introspective and reserved than the cosmopolitan Paulistas who formed the core of the modernist movement.

In 1930 he published a volume modestly entitled *Some Poetry*. Three years later, he moved to Rio de Janeiro for good. A 1934 volume, *Marsh of Souls*, showed a process of purification in his verse while the ironic effect was intensified. Life was then for Drummond a dark and anguished experience. The poet was searching for a way to escape his own sense of alienation—and the way was shown him by the Second World War. His next volume, *A Feeling for the World* (1940), produced in the face of total war and destruction, reflected a new sense of solidarity which assuaged his private griefs and anxieties. Drummond's predicament had been similar to that of Auden and Neruda when confronted with the realities of the Spanish civil war; and, like them, he discovered in himself a deep feeling for the entire world. But this did not entail any renunciation of his private voice or the cherished memories of childhood so pervasive in books like *Poetry* (1942) and *Confessions of Minas* (1944, a collection of prose chronicles).

In 1945 Drummond published one of his most important books, *The People's Rose*, in which he again managed to express strong political views without descending to mere propaganda. In successive volumes (*Poetry Until Now*, 1948; *Clear Enigma*, 1951; *Pocketguitar*, 1952; *Lessons in Things*, 1962), he continued with the double task of keeping an alert eye on the world while defining his own peculiar vision in a way accessible to all.

Drummond's influence on younger poets, from João Cabral de Melo Neto to the more recent "concretistas" (Part Five, 8), has probably been the most decisive in the Brazilian literature of this century. The sampling of verse that follows can give no more than a general sense of his unique scope and mastery.

Poems

"Traveling in the Family," translated by Elizabeth Bishop, *in* Latin
American Writing Today, *edited by J. M. Cohen (Baltimore: Penguin,
1967), pp. 67–71; "A um hotel em demolição," translated by Thomas
Colchie,* The Hudson Review, *vol. 25, no. 2 (Summer 1972), pp. 186–93;
and two poems, especially translated by Thomas Colchie.*

Traveling in the Family

To Rodrigo M. F. de Andrade

In the desert of Itabira
the shadow of my father
took me by the hand.
So much time lost.
But he didn't say anything.
It was neither day nor night.
A sigh? A passing bird?
But he didn't say anything.

We have come a long way.
Here there was a house.
The mountain used to be bigger.
So many heaped-up dead,
and time gnawing the dead.
And in the ruined houses,
cold disdain and damp.
But he didn't say anything.

The street he used to cross
on horseback, at a gallop.
His watch. His clothes.
His legal documents.
His tales of love affairs.
Opening of tin trunks
and violent memories.
But he didn't say anything.

In the desert of Itabira
things come back to life,

stiflingly, suddenly.
The market of desires
displays its sad treasures;
my urge to run away;
naked women; remorse.
But he didn't say anything.

Stepping on books and letters
we travel in the family.
Marriages; mortgages;
the consumptive cousins;
the mad aunt; my grandmother
betrayed among the slave girls,
rustling silks in the bedroom.
But he didn't say anything.

What cruel, obscure instinct
moved his pallid hand
subtly pushing us
into the forbidden
time, forbidden places?
I looked in his white eyes.
I cried to him: Speak! My voice
shook in the air a moment,
beat on the stones. The shadow
proceeded slowly on
with that pathetic traveling
across the lost kingdom.
But he didn't say anything.

I saw grief, misunderstanding
and more than one old revolt
dividing us in the dark.
The hand I wouldn't kiss,
the crumb that they denied me,
refusal to ask pardon.
Pride. Terror at night.
But he didn't say anything.

Speak speak speak speak.
I pulled him by his coat
that was turning into clay.
By the hands, by the boots
I caught at his strict shadow
and the shadow released itself
with neither haste nor anger.
But he remained silent.

And there were separate silences
deep within his silence.
There was my deaf grandfather
hearing the painted birds
on the ceiling of the church;

my own lack of friends;
and your lack of kisses;
there were our difficult lives
and a great separation
in the little space of the room.

The narrow space of life
crowds me up against you,
and in this ghostly embrace
it's as if I were being burned
completely, with poignant love.
Only now do we know each other!
Eyeglasses, memories, portraits
flow in the river of blood.
Now the waters won't let me
make out your distant face,
distant by seventy years. . . .

I felt that he pardoned me
but he didn't say anything.
The waters cover his mustache,
the family, Itabira, all.

Translated by Elizabeth Bishop

Don't Kill Yourself

Carlos, keep calm, love
is what you're seeing now:
today a kiss, tomorrow no kiss,
day after tomorrow's Sunday
and nobody knows what will happen
Monday.

It's useless to resist
or to commit suicide.
Don't kill yourself. Don't kill yourself!
Keep all of yourself for the nuptials
coming nobody knows when,
that is, if they ever come.

Love, Carlos, tellurion,
spent the night with you,
and now your insides are raising .
an ineffable racket,

prayers,
victrolas,
saints crossing themselves,
ads for better soap,
a racket of which nobody
knows the why or wherefore.

In the meantime you go on your way
vertical, melancholy.
You're the palm tree, you're the cry
nobody heard in the theater
and all the lights went out.
Love in the dark, no, love
in the daylight, is always sad,
sad, Carlos, my boy,
but tell it to nobody,
nobody knows nor shall know.

Translated by Elizabeth Bishop

In the Middle of the Road

In the middle of the road was a stone
was a stone in the middle of the road
was a stone
in the middle of the road was a stone.

I'll never get over that circumstance
in the lifetime of my retinas overtired.
I'll never get over how in the middle of the road
was a stone
was a stone in the middle of the road
in the middle of the road was a stone.

Translated by Thomas Colchie

To a Hotel Scheduled for Demolition

Goodbye, Hotel Avenida.
Your guests await you
on some other horizon.

You were huge and red,
in each room you had
a curious mirror.

In it was reflected
the passage of each figure
and the rest not to be read

even through the cracks
in the door: what one hides,
pulp of self, and shrieks

without making a sound.
And by adding other faces
in continuous succession,

the mirror wore a thousand masks
of Minas Gerais, Rio, and São Pau-
lists: good and bad: faces.

50 image-years
and 50 on folding
bed 50 with trundles

nocturnal and confident
humbly preserving for us
the uric-acid truth.

(But you lived a long time, Hotel, and in your paunch
whatever was noxious would smile in the dust within you.)

The slow and crimson alexandrine decomposed.
Couples coupling together in the whispering
Carioca* smut, streetcars sparksmelling, politicians
politicianing along insipid corridors
Italian starlets, doormen in ecstasy
    elevator
boys in a panic:
how is such voluptuousness to fit itself
into those four flimsy paneled partitions?
Trays go by silverundulating:
Give me some coffee marmalade morning papers I don't care.
The woman was naked in the center of the room and received
me with the appropriate solemnity of traveling deities:
Stellen Sie es auf den Tisch!

No, I was not your room servant, not even some
boy in your network of communications or a
setting in the daily fuss of prandial service.
Then how is it I'm living out your archives
and feeling cheated really that I never was
in your register the way the dead
are in their numbered compartments?

I act out love affairs I never had
but in you were had pell-mell.
The way the snail
of memories oozes on
        down the stairs
from the two-hundred thousand bodies lodged within you
records recordsds recordsdsds recordsdsdsds
dsdsdsdsdsdsdsdsds
137 is buzzing
hurry the man is dying
is it aspirins? a priest he wants?
No, not if he's a priest himself and is praying
for the sake of the sins of this hotel

*Carioca: Rio de Janeiro.

and of any other hotel along the road
which man travels from one to another, which at no
point has beginning or ending;
and is only the road and always always
is populated with gestures and departures
and arrivals and fleeing and mileage.
He prays he dies and in solitude
a faucet
drips
and the shower
showers
and the blue
flame of gas heater hisses in the bath
above Carioca Square in flower in the sun.

(Through the scaffolding I see you
not broken disemboweled defiled
imagining you unharmed
emerging from the marching sambas of the military police, from
                    the howling chorus of fans on the radio
                    broadcast of the world's championship
offering to one and all, Hotel Avenida,
an unfading victory laurel.)

You were Time itself and you presided
over the fevered recognition of fingers
love without any real place in the city
over collusion of swindlers, over the expectancy
of employment, over stagnation of governments
over the life of the nation in terms of the individual
and over mass movements that came spilling their ways
into the monastic arcade that houses your streetcars.

You were the heart of Brazil,
Carioca nostalgias rocked back and forth
in your lap, diamond buyers came to you
entrusting their stones, cattle drovers
grazed their herds on the terrace
and the sticky sweetness of provincial tears
was packed away each instant in envelopes
(blue ones?) into the management's pigeonholes
and you were a lot of coffee and some promissory notes.

What professor professes the Law of Things
in some illusive alcove, lecturing

to cockroaches too busy to listen?
What flute insists upon playing its sonatina
without piano always after curfew hour?
And the manias of the oldest lodgers
who are visited at night by Chief Prefect Passos to discuss
                              the latest urban developments?

And your dead guests
incomparably hotel dead defrauded
of that familial death to which we aspire
as if to some kind of not-dead-death;
the dead who must be dispatched
quickly, so as not to contaminate sheets
and cupboards
with that peculiar chilliness which encompasses them
and there must be no memory in this bed
of whatever is not simply life at Avenida.

Hear the litany of intestinal bubbles?

Balcony of messengers immobile boatmen
newsstand news for never and more
white laundry rooms with fluted remains
bonbonnières *where silver wrappings*
form serenades on feminine lips
telephonic switchboard sullenly aphonic
discothèque *lamentation of slipped discs*
        stationery shops
        conversation corners
Brahma beer best brand for a loving man
and the Bar Nacional's simple amiability is
suddenly resurrecting Mário de Andrade
                What to do with the clock
                what to do with ourselves
                without time without some point
                without counterpoint without
                a measure of extension
                or even an obituary
                while in ashes the
                impatient bison flees
                whom no one's ever held
                by the horns, affliction?
                He marks time mar-
                king-king-king
                and we alone are marked

with all the failures
of repressed loves
clock which I cannot hear
which will not listen
robot of simple smell
tracking the immense
country of motionless touch
the directions I ran
at your command now end
in the crossing of a T
in vague nightmares
in dejected shadows
where all of our intentions
somehow became stratified.

There's no destroying you
the way termites chew up
book earth existence.
Your hands, yes, voraciously
they scrape away at
the tunic of Venus
the large hand the small
this tattooed verse
and everything I've done
to elude you and everything
in the arkademies the
autarchic institutions
historic and astute
which is taught with malice
concerning the evolution of things
oh hotel clockkeeper
god of the cautious man from Minas,
        silence.
        propriety.
But everything you offended
now avenges itself upon you
        deliberately
with the black arts of witchery.
We swallow your windows
stifling the utterance
of splintering glass which
still struggles, throbbing,
for the moment of hope
when in the evening the breeze
of hoping has passed.

Scream of a child being born.

*Please, my poet friend Martins Fontes, can you recite your
odes a little lower while my wife finishes giving birth in the
room above, and the poet did softly sing, but when the baby
came into the world it was the father who was dancing poetry
and asking his poet friend to celebrate before all, guests, maids,
and sparrows alike, with uplifting song the gratifying inspiration.*

*Your night would fall. At the crossroads, there down below,
ragpickers, jacks-of-all-trades, lottery vendors sat swallowing their
prizes with a sip of rum.*

Mujer malvada, yo te mataré! *actors rehearsing in their
rooms?* I will grind your bones to dust, and with your blood
and it I'll make a paste.* *A bunch of trash downstairs.*

Every hotel is flow. A current
passes through walls, carrying the man
his emanations of substance. Every hotel
is dead, is born again; passing; if pigeons
stop over in one, they inhabit what is not to be inhabited
but merely severed. Other houses take hold
and let themselves be possessed or try to, awkwardly.
Space attempts to fix itself. Life becomes spatialized,
models itself on sentimental crystals.
The doors close every blessed night.
You fail to shut yourself, you cannot. Every minute
someone says goodbye to your unfaithful armoires
and the new arrivals already have return tickets in their bags.
220 Fremdenzimmer and you see yourself always empty
and the mirror is reflecting another mirror
and the corridor is leading to another corridor
man when naked indefinitely.

In the heart of Rio de Janeiro
   absence
in the cattle stockade of streetcars
   absence
in the procession of Saturdays
in the rubbing and clanking of carnival groups
   absence
in the arias of Palermo

*English in the original.

in the wail of evening papers
   absence
worm consuming apple
worm consuming worm
self-consuming worm
worm worms worm

and the anxiety of finish, which has no hope
of that velvet termination of old ruins
or the quick burst of death from hydrogen.

You were Amazonian solitude
getting-to-be home
in getting-to-be city where lizards.
        Come on, old Malta
        snap a picture for me
        pulverashen effigimage
        of this obscure place.

        Add a few kiosks
        turn-of-the-century
        no waternymphs or forests
        but pitifully lice-ridden.

        For an inscription
        ITATIAIA CHEESE
        and whatever else spells
        a servile condition.

        For these halls, so ugly
        much more than dirty
        are twisted cells
        molluscoid conches
        of donkey without a tail
        ignorantly in bondage
        and some poor devil
        within, hunger without.

        Old Malta, *s'il vous plaît*,
        get another shot:
        the hotel marquee
        bigger than the Rio Apa.

        Still not struck there
        in your ethereal seat,

Malta, sub-reptitiously,
by that super construction

which looms out of the ground?
Give me your future picture,
since the urgent thing is to

document each successive possession of place up to the final
judgment and even beyond if there is such a thing as three times
three our belief in a supreme bureau of records for fixed properties going beyond the human instant and the pulverization of
the galaxies.

How is it I remember you so completely when
I never placed a single stone upon stone of you?
But your name—AVENIDA—followed the lead
of my verse and was ampler with more

forms than your accommodations contained
(time degraded them and death saves them),
and where the foundation has fallen and the instant
fled I am compromised forever.

I am compromised forever
I who for so many years have been in and out
the Grand Hotel of the World without manager

in which, nothing concrete existing,
—avenida, avenida—I house
tenaciously the secret guest of me.

Translated by Thomas Colchie

22

JOÃO GUIMARÃES ROSA

In João Guimarães Rosa's great novel, *Grande Sertão: Verédas* (1956),
both the regionalist credo of the Northeast group and the avant-garde experimentalism of the Paulista group came to complete fruition. Paradoxically, however,

Guimarães Rosa came from neither the Northeast nor São Paulo; like Carlos Drummond de Andrade, he belonged to the high plateau of Minas Gerais, the mining region that produced in the late eighteenth century one of Brazil's greatest artists, the mulatto sculptor known as *O Aleijadinho* (The Little Cripple). In the same way as the baroque sculptor had taken a European style and made it his own by the wild force of his imagination and his inspired craftsmanship, so Guimarães Rosa skillfully molded avant-garde ideas and techniques in his powerful hands to produce his unique and intricately sculpted masterpiece.

Guimarães Rosa, born in Codisburgo in 1908, belonged to an old patrician family. He studied medicine in Belo Horizonte, and after graduating, set up his practice in a rural area. It has been said that quite frequently he would ask for a story in lieu of payment. Visiting his patients and even working as an army doctor during the 1930 revolution, Guimarães (as he is usually called in Brazil) came to know his state and its people very intimately. He traveled the deserted roads endlessly, became familiar with little, unknown pathways, spent evenings in long conversation with the oral chroniclers of the *sertão*, or backlands. Out of this accumulation of old lore and tireless research in libraries, he would later issue volume after volume of rural tales.

Guimarães had always been attracted to foreign languages and in 1934 went to Rio to embark on a diplomatic career. He was serving in Hamburg on the eve of World War II and was interned for a while in Baden-Baden after Brazil entered the war against Germany. In 1942 he went to Colombia, to serve at the Brazilian embassy in Bogotá. After a two-year stint there, he returned to Europe, and in 1948 was assigned to Paris. The last years of his life were spent on official duty in the Foreign Office in Rio de Janeiro.

Guimarães had been writing steadily since his youth and had even won a first prize in a 1934 poetry competition organized by the Brazilian Academy of Letters. But he had always refused to let the book that won the prize be published in its entirety. His first book to come out was *Sagarana* (1946), a collection of short stories. The title contains an interlingual pun in its incorporation of the Icelandic or Scandinavian word "saga"—Guimarães was thereby linking these rural stories with medieval prose narratives of the exploits of famous kings and warriors. The allusion was ironical, to be sure, yet also appropriate, because the world he was evoking was still feudal in character. The impact of the volume was great. Widely admired among the "happy few," it was totally rejected by others who found it too "difficult." Its publication marked the beginning of what has been called "the Guimarães Rosa revolution." After this book, it was impossible in Brazil to write stories as before.

Ten years later he simultaneously published his great long novel, *Grande Sertão: Verédas,* and a cycle of short novels collected under the ambiguous title *Corpo de baile.* ("Corps de ballet" would be an approximate translation.) From that moment, Guimarães was generally recognized as the greatest Brazilian novelist since Machado de Assis (Part Two, 14). If Machado radically transformed nineteenth-century narrative, Guimarães succeeded in completely revolutionizing the style and diction of twentieth-century narrative. Moving away from the realistic approach of the regionalists, and rejecting as well some of the more frivolous experiments of the Paulista group, Guimarães rediscovered the baroque possibilities of the oral tale. In *Grande Sertão*, the entire narrative unfolds in a single endless monologue by the protagonist, Riobaldo, evoking in minutest detail various pivotal episodes of his youth. He is presumed to be talking to a silent, absorbed listener whom he apparently wishes to persuade or convince, and this need to persuade lends his account a persistent note of dramatic urgency. His narrative, however, is decidedly not realistic in either form or manner; for instead of adopting a conventional, colloquial style of speech and presenting events in a more or less orderly sequence (as would be characteristic, say, of a narrator in regionalist fiction), Riobaldo constantly deforms words to suit his mood or purpose, leaves sentences unfinished, and throughout makes continual detours, and twists and turns backward and forward. His ceaseless telling and retelling of essentially the same story, without ever quite giving away the key to the mystery he is unraveling, exerts a hypnotic effect on his listener (and reader). And the tale he tells has the scope and character of an epic.

Riobaldo is an illegitimate child, brought up in the backlands of Minas, and, now grown, is engaged in a search for his lost father. He has become involved with a band of *jagunços*, the hired gunmen who work for the big landowners. In his search, Riobaldo finds love in the unexpected form of a comrade-in-arms, Diadorim. But he rejects Diadorim's shyly offered affection, and only at the last minute discovers both his origins and Diadorim's well-guarded secret. The tale, set chronologically in the early twentieth century but belonging in spirit to the era of romance, plays tantalizingly with the theme of homosexuality in a way that recalls some of Thomas Mann's masterly exercises. But Guimarães goes even further than the German master. At the very center of the novel he places an episode in which Riobaldo believes he has met the Devil himself. The primeval search for the father, diabolical temptation, frustrated eroticism—all these motifs are so intricately intertwined and interrelated as to make *Grande Sertao: Verédas* one of the most complex works of fiction ever produced in Latin America. The title contains an allusion to Euclides da Cunha's masterpiece, *Os Sertões* (*Rebellion in the Backlands*, Two, 16), also set in the wild regions of Brazil. But instead of attempting to encompass the whole immense *sertão* of Minas in his narrative (as da Cunha had attempted with the smaller Northeast *sertão*), Guimarães presented in his novel only the small trails or pathways, the *verédas*, he knew so well.

In the last years of his life, as if to compensate for the monumental effort of composing *Grande Sertão*, Guimarães wrote only three volumes of short stories: *First Tales* (1962, translated into English as *The Third Bank of the River and Other Stories*), *Tutaméia* (1967), and *These Tales* (1969). The last two collections were published posthumously. He died in 1967, of a heart attack, two days after having been received formally at the Brazilian Academy of Letters. As a doctor, he knew how weak his heart was and had been postponing for years his entry into the Academy. When he finally decided to enter, he meticulously rehearsed the ceremony (as he did with everything) and succeeded in carrying it off brilliantly. Until the very last moment of his life, he was in complete command of his craft, his words, himself.

Of the two texts that follow, the first, "The Third Bank of the River," is a subtle, dense, mysteriously luminous tale of a man who behaves (like some of Melville's and Kafka's creations) in the most unexpected way. The second excerpt, "The Slaughter of the Ponies," is taken from *Grande Sertão* and is one of the episodes eliminated from the U.S. translation. Both texts, brief as they are, exemplify Guimarães Rosa's superlative narrative skills, that mastery of a form in which he had no rivals. He is beyond dispute Latin America's greatest novelist.

Two Texts

From "A terceira margem do rio," translated by Barbara Shelby, The Third Bank of the River and Other Stories (New York: Knopf, 1968), pp. 189–96; and Grande Sertão: Veredas (The Devil to Pay in the Backlands), especially translated by Jack E. Tomlins.

The Third Bank of the River

Father was a reliable, law-abiding, practical man, and had been ever since he was a boy, as various people of good sense testified when I asked them about him. I don't remember that he seemed any crazier or even any moodier than anyone else we knew. He just didn't talk much. It was our mother who gave the orders and scolded us every day—my sister, my brother, and me. Then one day my father ordered a canoe for himself.

He took the matter very seriously. He had the canoe made to his specifications of fine *vinhático* wood; a small one, with a narrow board in the stern as though to leave only enough room for the oarsman. Every bit of it was hand-hewn of special strong wood carefully shaped, fit to last in the water for twenty or thirty years. Mother railed at the idea. How could a man who had never fiddled away his time on such tricks propose to go fishing and hunting now, at his time of life? Father said nothing. Our house was closer to the river then than it is now, less than a quarter of a league away: there rolled the river, great, deep, and silent, always silent. It was so wide that you could hardly see the bank on the other side. I can never forget the day the canoe was ready.

Neither happy nor excited nor downcast, Father pulled his hat well down on his head and said one firm goodbye. He spoke not another word, took neither food nor other supplies, gave no parting advice. We thought Mother would have a fit, but she only blanched white, bit her lip, and said bitterly, "Go or stay; but if you go, don't you ever come back!"

Father left his answer in suspense. He gave me a mild look and motioned me to go aside with him a few steps. I was afraid of Mother's anger, but I obeyed anyway, that time. The turn things had taken gave me the courage to ask, "Father, will you take me with you in that canoe?" But he just gave me a long look in return: gave me his blessing and motioned me to go back. I pretended to go, but instead turned off into a deep woodsy hollow to watch. Father stepped into the canoe, untied it, and began to paddle off. The canoe slipped away, a straight, even shadow like an alligator, slithery, long.

Our father never came back. He hadn't gone anywhere. He stuck to that stretch of the river, staying halfway across, always in the canoe, never to spring out of it, ever again. The strangeness of that truth was enough to dismay us all. What had never been before, was. Our relatives, the neighbors, and all our acquaintances met and took counsel together.

Mother, though, behaved very reasonably, with the result that everybody believed what no one wanted to put into words about our father: that he was mad. Only a few of them thought he might be keeping a vow, or—who could tell?—maybe he was sick with some hideous disease like leprosy, and that was what had made him desert us to live out another life, close to his family and yet far enough away. The news spread by word of mouth, carried by people like travelers and those who lived along the banks of the river, who said of Father that he never landed at spit or cove, by day or by night, but always stuck to the river, lonely and outside human society. Finally, Mother and our relatives realized that the provisions he had hidden in the canoe must be getting low and thought that he would have to either land somewhere and go away from us for good— that seemed the most likely—or repent once and for all and come back home.

But they were wrong. I had made myself responsible for stealing a bit of food for him every day, an idea that had come to me the very first night, when the family had lighted bonfires on the riverbank and in their glare prayed and called out to Father. Every day from then on I went back to the river with a lump of hard brown sugar, some corn bread, or a bunch of bananas. Once, at the end of an hour of waiting that had dragged on and on, I caught sight of Father; he was way off, sitting in the bottom of the canoe as if suspended in the mirror smoothness of the river. He saw me, but he did not paddle over or make any sign. I held up the things to eat and then laid them in a hollowed-out rock in the river bluff, safe from any animals who might nose around and where they would be kept dry in rain or dew. Time after time, day after day, I did the same thing. Much later I had a surprise: Mother knew about my mission but, saying nothing and pretending she didn't, made it easier for me by putting out leftovers where I was sure to find them. Mother almost never showed what she was thinking.

Finally she sent for an uncle of ours, her brother, to help with the farm and with money matters, and she got a tutor for us children. She also arranged for the priest to come in his vestments to the river edge to exorcise Father and call upon him to desist from his sad obsession. Another time, she tried to scare Father by getting two soldiers to come. But none of it was any use. Father passed by at a distance, discernible only dimly through the river haze, going by in the canoe without ever letting anyone go close enough to touch him or even talk to

681 . Two Texts

him. The reporters who went out in a launch and tried to take his picture not long ago failed just like everybody else; Father crossed over to the other bank and steered the canoe into the thick swamp that goes on for miles, part reeds and part brush. Only he knew every hand's breadth of its blackness.

We just had to try to get used to it. But it was hard, and we never really managed. I'm judging by myself, of course. Whether I wanted to or not, my thoughts kept circling back and I found myself thinking of Father. The hard nub of it was that I couldn't begin to understand how he could hold out. Day and night, in bright sunshine or in rainstorms, in muggy heat or in the terrible cold spells in the middle of the year, without shelter or any protection but the old hat on his head, all through the weeks, and months, and years—he marked in no way the passing of his life. Father never landed, never put in at either shore or stopped at any of the river islands or sandbars; and he never again stepped onto grass or solid earth. It was true that in order to catch a little sleep he may have tied up the canoe at some concealed islet spit. But he never lighted a fire on shore, had no lamp or candle, never struck a match again. He did no more than taste food; even the morsels he took from what we left for him along the roots of the fig tree or in the hollow stone at the foot of the cliff could not have been enough to keep him alive. Wasn't he ever sick? And what constant strength he must have had in his arms to maintain himself and the canoe ready for the piling up of the floodwaters where danger rolls on the great current, sweeping the bodies of dead animals and tree trunks downstream—frightening, threatening, crashing into him. And he never spoke another word to a living soul. We never talked about him, either. We only thought of him. Father could never be forgotten; and if, for short periods of time, we pretended to ourselves that we had forgotten, it was only to find ourselves roused suddenly by his memory, startled by it again and again.

My sister married; but Mother would have no festivities. He came into our minds whenever we ate something especially tasty, and when we were wrapped up snugly at night we thought of those bare unsheltered nights of cold, heavy rain, and Father with only his hand and maybe a calabash to bail the storm water out of the canoe. Every so often someone who knew us would remark that I was getting to look more and more like my father. But I knew that now he must be bushy-haired and bearded, his nails long, his body cadaverous and gaunt, burnt black by the sun, hairy as a beast and almost as naked, even with the pieces of clothing we left for him at intervals.

He never felt the need to know anything about us; had he no family affection? But out of love, love and respect, whenever I was praised for something good I had done, I would say, "It was Father who taught me how to do it that way." It wasn't true, exactly, but it was a truthful kind of lie. If he didn't remember us any more and didn't want to know how we were, why didn't he go farther up the river or down it, away to landing places where he would never be found? Only he knew. When my sister had a baby boy, she got it into her head that she must show Father his grandson. All of us went and stood on the bluff. The day was fine and my sister was wearing the white dress she had worn at her wedding. She lifted the baby up in her arms and her husband held a parasol over the two of them. We called and we waited. Our father didn't come. My sister wept; we all cried and hugged one another as we stood there.

After that my sister moved far away with her husband, and my brother decided to go live in the city. Times changed, with the slow swiftness of time. Mother went away too in the end, to live with my sister because she was growing old. I stayed on here, the only one of the family who was left. I could never think of marriage. I stayed where I was, burdened down with all life's cumbrous baggage. I knew Father needed me, as he wandered up and down on the river in the wilderness, even though he never gave a reason for what he had done. When at last I made up my mind that I had to know and finally made a firm attempt to find out, people told me rumor had it that Father might have given some explanation to the man who made the canoe for him. But now the builder was dead; and no one really knew or could recollect any more except that there had been some silly talk in the beginning, when the river was first swollen by such endless torrents of rain that everyone was afraid the world was coming to an end; then they had said that Father might have received a warning, like Noah, and so prepared the canoe ahead of time. I could half-recall the story. I could not even blame my father. And a few first white hairs began to appear on my head.

I was a man whose words were all sorrowful. Why did I feel so guilty, so guilty? Was it because of my father, who made his absence felt always, and because of the river-river-river, the river—flowing forever? I was suffering the onset of old age—this life of mine only postponed the inevitable. I had bed spells, pains in the belly, dizziness, twinges of rheumatism. And he? Why, oh why must he do what he did? He must suffer terribly. Old as he was, was he not bound to weaken in vigor sooner or later and let the canoe overturn or, when the river rose, let it drift unguided for hours downstream, until it finally went over the brink of the loud rushing fall of the cataract, with its wild boiling and death? My heart shrank. He was out there, with none of my easy security. I was guilty of I knew not what, filled with boundless sorrow in the deepest part of me. If I only knew —if only things were otherwise. And then, little by little, the idea came to me.

I could not even wait until next day. Was I crazy? No. In our house, the word *crazy* was not spoken, had never been spoken again in all those years; no one was condemned as crazy. Either no one is crazy, or everyone is. I just went, taking along a sheet to wave with. I was very much in my right mind. I waited. After a long time he appeared; his indistinct bulk took form. He was there, sitting in the stern. He was there, a shout away. I called out several times. And I said the words which were making me say them, the sworn promise, the declaration. I had to force my voice to say, "Father, you're getting old, you've done your part. . . . You can come back now, you don't have to stay any longer. . . . You come back, and I'll do it, right now or whenever you want me to; it's what we both want. I'll take your place in the canoe!" And as I said it my heart beat to the rhythm of what was truest and best in me.

He heard me. He got to his feet. He dipped the paddle in the water, the bow pointed toward me; he had agreed. And suddenly I shuddered deeply, because he had lifted his arm and gestured a greeting—the first, after so many years. And I could not. . . . Panic-stricken, my hair standing on end, I ran, I fled, I left the place behind me in a mad headlong rush. For he seemed to be coming from the hereafter. And I am pleading, pleading, pleading for forgiveness.

I was struck by the solemn ice of fear, and I fell ill. I knew that no one ever heard of him again. Can I be a man, after having thus failed him? I am what never was—the unspeakable. I know it is too late for salvation now, but I am afraid to cut life short in the shallows of the world. At least, when death comes to the body, let them take me and put me in a wretched little canoe, and on the water that flows forever past its unending banks, let me go—down the river, away from the river, into the river—the river.

The Slaughter of the Ponies

"I'll bet they're killing our ponies!"

And the hell of it was, they were. The corral was full up with our mounts and the poor horses were trapped, hardy and blameless as they were; and they, the damned dogs, with no fear either of God or the law in their hearts, outdid themselves to torment and plunder—as if they were tearing our hearts from our bodies—firing into our ponies, to right and left! It made you sick to see such a sight. Bobbing up and down—somehow understanding, without knowing for sure, that the devil had been turned loose in their midst—the horses whirled crazily around and around, galloping in fits and starts. Some of them reared up on their hind legs and pawed the air with their front hoofs, and fell on top of one another, and tumbled in a whirling jumble. And some with their heads held high in the air beat the necks of others, shaking their stiff and prickly manes: they seemed no more than twisted, curved lines! Their whinnying came as it clutched at their hearts: a shrill, brief cry, if neighed out of rage; short also, but deep and hoarse, if neighed out of fear, like the shriek of a wildcat, blasted from flared nostrils. They spun madly about the enclosure, colliding with the stakes as they ran wild, kicking in frenzied welter. What we were seeing was like an infinity of wildly fluttering wings. They raised dust from the very stones! Then they began to fall flat on the ground, their legs widespread, holding up only their jaws or forelocks: their bodies rippled. They began to fall, nearly all of them, and finally all. Those that were slow to die whinnied in pain. From some it was a piercing, snorted groan, almost as if they were speaking. From still others a constrained whine in the teeth, uttered with great difficulty. That whinny was not breathed out as the animal gave up its strength; it was squeezed out as the animal gasped for its final breath.

"Those damned bastards!"

Fafafa was weeping. João Vaqueiro, too. We all had tears in our eyes. No need to try to undo such meaningless cruelty. Nothing could be done, really. Hellbent on destruction, Hermógenes's men killed as they chose: it was just wanton butchery. They even shot down the stray cattle, the steers and cows, which were so tame that at the beginning of the skirmish they'd come up close to the house in search of shelter. Wherever you looked you could see the animals piled up; and now our horses, barely dead, had to be added to the heap. And then we began to shake for sure. Whoever saw or heard of such a pitiful and awful thing as this? There's not time enough to tell it. The fence was high. There was no way for the animals to escape. There was just one, a big bay, that belonged to "Rough-Hands." His name was Sapphire. He stood bolt upright on his hind legs and then hung there, motionless lest he nod for a single moment as he draped himself over the top of the fence, as if he were being weighed in the scale. His fleshy rump was toward us, and then he fell over the edge and went down. We couldn't tell how it turned out. Pure damn meanness! We all swore revenge. There were no more horses moving. They'd all been gunned down.

Such a crime as that demanded that God Incarnate himself should come down to wreak vengeance on the sight before his eyes. We called down curses. Oh, but it is the nature of faith not to see the turmoil unleashed on all sides. I think God sets nothing to rights unless he holds a contract for the full job. God is the rich tillage and we are the sandy soil. We could hardly bear the sound that met our ears: the terrified whinny of massive suffering, the heartrending neigh of agonizing horses, sharp as the very sword of woe. Someone had to go and shoot them out of pity, one by one, and bring an end to their agony, snuff out their pain at the fuse. But we could not do it. If you listen, sir, you'll understand what I mean. The horses were covered with blood and red froth, jostling against one another—some expiring and others not yet so—and their whinnying: it was a protracted and detached sob, a voice from the depths of them that set your hair on end, like the cry of human distress. The ponies were near the end of their suffering, and they could make no sense of their pain. Instead, they begged us for mercy.

"Dammit. I'll go out there and finish the poor devils off!" These were the words that Fafafa bellowed. But we didn't allow him to go, because it would have been sheer folly. If he'd ventured two steps onto the flat, he would have died, riddled with bullets. So we held Fafafa back. We were forced to remain trapped inside the house and fight as best we could from there while that enormous perversity raged outside. You'll never know, sir: the whinny of a horse suffering in that way suddenly grows hoarse and fills with deep gullies, and sometimes they grunt almost like a pig, or their cry goes shrill and frayed and you can feel their rage and their pain in your own skin. You get to thinking they've turned into some new kind of animal, in some unholy way. Your mouth gapes, your hair stands all on end, you can feel the chill of death on you. And when you can hear the mass martyrdom of innocent animals, the thought occurs to you that you are witnessing the end of the world. What crime did the animal commit that he must pay so high a price as this? And there we were in that wilderness. And to think that so pretty and fine, just a short while ago those were our ponies, backland steeds; and now, ripped to shreds as they were, we could not come to their aid. We were not able. What did Hermógenes and his gang want, anyway? For sure, it had been their intention to leave us within earshot of the neighing of the wretched animals, night and day, day and night, night and day, until we could stand it no longer and rushed headlong into the hell of our own madness. You should have seen Zé Bebelo: he was seething in awesome and terrible thought. Like a cart painstakingly freed by oxen from a mudhole, he was suddenly masterly, and gave the command: "Shoot, boys, and keep your aim low."

Volleys on all sides, fired by the rage of compassion. But it did not help matters. We were just wasting our ammunition. The corral was so far away we couldn't reach the horses. With our enemy under cover, we were wasting our salvoes on thin air. And that was the fix we were in: we were totally powerless. It was the hottest part of the day. Then, I got myself on top of our actual situation and I prayed. Do you know how I prayed? Like this it was: that God was all-powerful, but only after we're dead, and I would wait and wait and wait as even the stones wait. "It matters, it doesn't matter, there's no horse whinnying out there, it's not all the horses neighing. The one who's neighing his wretched-ness is Hermógenes, inside his skin, in the darker part of his insides, in the rasping of his guts. Because wretched he will one day be, if I have my way. So from this day forward, from now on, we shall be at odds: he Hermógenes, mine alone to kill—I the lowly soldier and he the storied warrior." From time to time a whinny could be heard. The horses were sweating out their final agony.

We laid hold of Fafafa. Fast hold, as I told you before. Then all of a sudden Marruaz said, "Alert, sentry, keep an eye open." What was it? They it was—would you believe it?—they themselves were shooting the wounded ponies, to put them out of their misery. That's what they were about. "Thanks be to God," Zé Bebelo exclaimed, his face shining, a good man finally at ease.

"Oh, that's their best!" Alaripe yelled, too.

But Fafafa said not a word; he could not. He merely sat down on the ground, his two hands clutching the sides of his face, and he broke down and cried like a baby. He held the respect of every one of us. With all his bravery he wept himself out.

After that, we simply waited. For a while we rested our rifles. No one fired a shot. We gave them sufficient time off to slaughter our poor ponies. Even when the devastation of the final cry trailed off in the air, we were still stunned to silence, for a long time, and a little while longer. Till the sound and the silence, in remembrance of the horses' suffering, dissolved away toward some far-distant point. Then all the hubbub began anew, more savage than ever before. Here, in what I tell you, can be seen the true wilderness that is this world. True that God exists, slow or fast. He exists, but it's as though He exists through the actions of ordinary people: good folks and bad.

There are tremendous things abroad in this world. The wide backlands, that's a powerful weapon. And is God the trigger?

But I'm not telling you everything that happened: I've cut it all in half to avoid telling you twice as much as you may want to hear. Just enough to give you some idea. We were caught between a rock and a hard place. Even I—as you have often had reason to know—who look at the past over and over in a mirror polished a hundredfold, I keep all the facts in my mind, the little ones as well as the big: even I can find no easy way to describe what happened, what we went through, surrounded and beset in that house at Tucanos by Hermógenes and his thugs. Get out! I can't remember how many days and nights it was. I'd say six, but I may be telling a lie. And if I hit on five or four, I may be telling a whopper. I only know it was a long time. It dragged on for years, sometimes I think. And at other times, when I consider the problem in a different light, I think it just flitted by, in the whiz of a minute that seems unreal to me now, like a squabble between two hummingbirds. Now that I'm older and the more those events retreat into the past, my recollection of them alters, takes on a different value. It's been changed and reconstituted and seems now to have been something lovely that happened a long while ago. Now I've got things straight: I think like a river flows. That is, I barely notice the trees along the banks. Who can understand what I'm trying to say? Whatever I wish to say. Past events obey us and those yet to come, also. Is it true that we can analyze properly only the present? No. The present obeys us, too, and that's the way things are. That much I've learned. Am I talking nonsense? As for me, sir, you know this talk is the same as panning for gold. Then, where is the real lamp of God, the plain, unvarnished truth?

The flow of time during those days and nights got choked and snagged in confusion: it was all directed toward one final horror. It was a block of time within time. We were trapped inside that house, which had become an easy target. Do you know how it feels to be trapped like that and have no way out? I don't know how many thousands of shots were fired: it was all echoing around my ears. The shots continued dizzily whining and popping and cracking. With walls and plaster still standing around us, the beams and tiles of another man's ancestral home set themselves up between us and them as our only defense. I can tell you—and I say this to you so you'll truly believe it— that old house protected us grudgingly: creaking with complaint, its dark old rooms fumed. As for me, I got to thinking that they were going to level the whole works, all four corners of the whole damn property. But they didn't. They didn't, as you are soon to see. Because what's going to happen is this: you're going to hear the whole story told. . . .

Part Five

A NEW WRITING

Poetry was the leading literary genre during the avant-garde revolution in Latin American letters (see Introduction to Part Four). By the early 1940's, however, fiction was unmistakably rising to predominance. Poets, both old and new, were still very active, to be sure, and some of the best writing of the last four decades has been produced by Huidobro and Neruda, Bandeira and Drummond de Andrade, Borges and Lezama Lima, Paz and Parra, Ernesto Cardenal and João Cabral de Melo Neto, Enrique Lihn and César Fernández Moreno. But it has been preeminently fiction that has projected Latin American literature onto the global scene. The symbolic date here is 1961, when a group of leading publishers from Europe and the United States awarded the first Formentor Prize *ex aequo* to Samuel Beckett and Jorge Luis Borges. The subsequent publication in several languages of Borges's *Ficciones*, a volume of short stories, not only consolidated his personal reputation but also aroused general interest in the whole new literature that he so brilliantly represented. Soon other writers—Cortázar and García Márquez, Fuentes and Cabrera Infante, Sábato and Guimarães Rosa, Donoso and Manuel Puig, Vargas Llosa and Severo Sarduy—were discovered and translated. The new Latin American novel was no longer the exclusive province of specialists but was recognized and discussed all over the world.

In the mother countries, Spain and Portugal, the emergence of these new writers completed a process which had begun at the turn of the century: the ascendancy of Latin American literature over its European counterparts was now beyond dispute. What Darío and the modernists had initiated (Part Three, 1–7) was completed by Borges and the new novelists. To consolidate their triumph, some writers (Vargas Llosa, García Márquez, Donoso) even moved to Spain or to other parts of Europe (Cortázar and Sarduy to France, Cabrera Infante to England), close to their actual or potential international audience.

It had taken the best part of twenty years to achieve this breakthrough. The first stories of *Ficciones* had been originally published in Buenos Aires in a slim volume, *The Garden of Forking Paths*, in 1941—exactly two decades before the awarding of the Formentor Prize—and the entire collection appeared three years later, in 1944. By 1940 Borges's friend and collaborator, Adolfo Bioy Casares, had already produced his first important novel, *The Invention of Morel*, with a polemical preface by Borges (Five, 3). In 1945, Bioy Casares published a second novel, *A Plan for Escape*, devoted to exploration of the same kind of nightmarish reality. The work of Borges and Bioy Casares was unique in the context of a Latin American novel still excessively preoccupied with the mimetic rendering of reality. Borges and Bioy sought to return fiction to its magical origins. It was in a pivotal essay written in 1932, "Narrative Art and Magic," that Borges had first begun to develop a new theory of fiction, which rejected the dreary simulations of realism and was based on metaphoric and metonymic magic. This theory was later developed and sharpened in his preface to *The Invention of Morel* and was put into practice in both his and Bioy's fiction.

Other, similar attempts to overcome the limitations of realism soon followed. In 1946, the Guatemalan Miguel Angel Asturias published *El Señor Presidente*, a grotesque, parodic novel, often surrealistic in its imagery, about a Central American dictator; three years later, in 1949, he produced another, more ambitious book, *Men of Maize*, in which he used Mayan folklore and myth to develop a fantastical account of the struggle between the Indians and their exploiters in today's Guatemala. Working independently, the Cuban Alejo Carpentier published in 1949 *The Kingdom of This World*, a historical tale about Haiti at the time of the wars of independence, in which a surrealistic vision of reality was counterpointed throughout with ironic commentary on the fatality of history. These were the founding works of the new fiction in Spanish America.

In Brazil (as noted in the introduction to Part Four), the process had started earlier, with the pioneering work being done by Oswald de Andrade and Mário de Andrade (Four, 17, 18). Both the Brazilians and their Spanish American counterparts had been in contact, more or less directly, with the avant-garde movement and were thoroughly familiar with the best of the experimental fiction produced in Europe and the United States in the early twentieth century. The writers that would emerge in Latin America after 1950 would be equally at home with the new writing produced elsewhere in the Western world; they absorbed and developed the new technical discoveries, and used them with total freedom. They learned how to combine French surrealism with pre-Columbian imagery, existentialism with voodoo, Marx with Spengler, Joyce with Borges. No experiment was too outrageous, no innovation too implausible. The result was a fictional literature of inexhaustible vitality.

At least three distinct generational groupings can be identified in the massive body of work produced in the last three decades. The eldest writers—Guimarães Rosa, Onetti, Lezama Lima, and Ernesto Sábato—published their best work in the middle fifties or even in the sixties. But while their books appeared contemporaneously with the best fiction of younger novelists, they were often the result of a process of gestation extending back a decade or more. The Brazilian Guimarães Rosa's *The Devil to Pay in the Backlands* came out in 1956, but it was the culmination of a complex narrative process that had started in the forties (Four, 22). The Uruguayan Onetti's *The Shipyard* and *The Body Snatcher* were both published in the early sixties, but his first important book, *The Short Life,* appeared in 1950 (Four, 5). The Cuban José Lezama Lima's *Paradiso* came out in 1966, but its first chapters had been published in journals in the fifties (Four, 15). The Argentine Ernesto Sabato's *On Heroes and Tombs* was published in 1961, but it was the second volume of a trilogy whose first, *The Tunnel,* had come out in 1948 (Five, 5). Numbered among the younger writers were such figures as the Uruguayan Carlos Martínez Moreno (Five, 6) and the Mexican Juan Rulfo (7), the Argentine Julio Cortázar (4) and the Chilean José Donoso (12), the Brazilian Clarice Lispector (9) and the Mexican Carlos Fuentes (13), the Colombian Gabriel García Márquez (14) and the Cuban Guillermo Cabrera Infante (15).

In the sixties, a third, still younger group began to emerge. Among these, the most prominent were the Peruvian Mario Vargas Llosa (17), the Argentine Manuel Puig (16), the Brazilian Nélida Piñón (10), the Cuban Severo Sarduy (18), the Mexican Gustavo Sáinz (19), and the Cuban Reinaldo Arenas (20). A predominant characteristic of this last group was a concentration on language not just as the writer's instrument but as itself his real subject. Such a concern, of course, had been manifest in some of the older writers years before: Borges, Guimarães Rosa, Lezama Lima, Julio Cortázar, Cabrera Infante were certainly no strangers to this type of verbal exploration. But it is most especially in the newer writers that the essence of a work comes to lie in its textual surface. They may still seem concerned (as witness the work of Vargas Llosa, Manuel Puig, and Nélida Piñón) with presenting a completely new and fresh picture of Latin American society, or else almost fanatically absorbed in the use of prose as a distorting mirror of its own verbal reality (Sarduy, Sáinz, Arenas); the final result is a total awareness of a novel as a literary text. In the best writers of the group, a return to the preoccupations that have dominated Latin American literature in the last fifty years is also evident. The formal distinction between prose and poetry becomes erased in such writing as that of Sarduy. The newest fiction is as concerned with images and rhythms as the most refined poetry produced by Octavio Paz or João Cabral de Melo Neto. The preoccupations of the new Latin American literature are, finally, one.

1

OCTAVIO PAZ

There is no finer representative of the new Latin American literature than the Mexican Octavio Paz. Not only is he one of the leading poets of today, but through his work as essayist and critic he has helped to redefine a truly modern concept of Latin American culture. Deeply rooted in the Hispanic tradition, yet equally at home in European modernism, Paz has used both surrealism and existentialism as means of furthering his passionate quest for an essential Latin American identity. The discovery of the East and a long and fruitful residence in India completed his basic experience. Out of these decisive encounters with the cultures of today, Paz has evolved a pluralistic notion of reality. When he returned to Mexico in 1968, he was able to explore in the long-suppressed but still-vital native cultures the roots of this elusive Latin American identity. In a series of dazzling books of poems and essays, Paz has helped to illuminate the crisis of today's cultures.

Paz was born on the outskirts of Mexico City in 1914; he studied at the National Autonomous University. By 1931 he was already actively participating in the capital's literary life and contributing with his first poems to the movement of poetical renewal promoted by the *Contemporaries* group (see Gorostiza, Part Four, 9). Although these first poems are very derivative, there was already in Paz a firm notion of poetry as an ultimate verbal experience. In 1937 he went to Spain to participate in a writer's conference organized by the beleaguered Spanish Government during the civil war. There he had the chance to meet Vallejo and Neruda, and to visit Madrid, Valencia, and the south of Spain. He had already written a book of political poems (*They Shall Not Pass*, 1936) (although he would later disown it). On his return to Mexico in 1938, he participated in the political activities of a group of Marxist writers. But the Nazi-Soviet pact of that year caused him to break with the Stalinist faction. He had founded upon his return a little magazine, *Workshop*, which was to become very influential, and in 1943 he helped to found one of Mexico's most vigorous literary reviews, *The Prodigal Son*. By then he had already discovered existentialism, through such pioneering Spanish writers as Unamuno, Machado, and José Bergamín, and his poetry was beginning to reflect his quest for absolute experience. On the literary scene, these were the years of an unrelenting feud with the Stalinists over the doctrine of socialist realism. While totally committed as a man to the cause of social justice, Paz never let that commitment blind him to poetry's main task: a commitment to language.

In 1943 he came to the United States on a Guggenheim Fellowship. He remained here (living in the West and later in New York City) for two years —an experience that proved in many ways profound, even shattering. For his discovery of the United States became indirectly a means to the realization of his own national identity; and out of this experience Paz was to write several years later one of his most important books, *The Labyrinth of Solitude* (1950), in which he applied psychosocial analysis to a discovery of the existential roots of Mexican solitude.

In 1945 Paz returned to Mexico and entered the diplomatic service. He was sent to Paris after the Second World War. There he met André Breton and established permanent links with the surrealists. If his U.S. experience had forced Paz into an anguished search for his identity, the Paris experience helped him to liberate in himself the dark forces of the subconscious. His poetry changed radically. The new poems he wrote were collected in 1949 under the title of *Freedom Under Parole*. It was not until 1958, however, that Paz produced the first of his major poems, *Sun Stone*, in which a new reading of the Aztec myths was achieved through surrealistic imagery.

Two more collections completed the metamorphosis: *The Violent Season* (also 1958), which contains some of Paz's most erotic verse, and *Salamander* (1962).

By 1952, Paz had visited the East and discovered the mysterious beauty of India and Japan. In 1962 he was sent to New Delhi as ambassador, and remained there until 1968. In those six years, Paz studied Buddhism and tantrism and found in these Eastern doctrines a key to the understanding of his own private quest. The harmony of contraries, the annihilation of desire through disciplined sexual experiences, the final fusion of the one and the many—these were the Eastern principles that Paz now began to explore in his poems and essays.

Successive volumes of verse—*Blanco* (1966), *Eastern Rampart* (1968), *Renga* (1971)—and several collections of essays—*The Bow and the Lyre* (especially the revised 1967 edition), *Marcel Duchamp* (1968), *Conjunctions and Disjunctions* (1969), *Critique of the Pyramid* (1970), *The Grammatical Simian* (1974), and *The Children of the Mire* (1974)—have demonstrated not only Paz's scope as a thinker and dreamer but his stature as a master stylist. No other writer of today uses the Spanish language with greater skill or power.

It is impossible to illustrate in an excerpt the density, scope, and variety of Paz's work. Perhaps the best way to approach it is through the reading of *Blanco*, a Mallarméan exercise and his most ambitious poem to date. Paz himself has, with characteristic lucidity, explained the poem's basic intentions in a prefatory note:

> *Blanco*, the color white; blank left in writing; void, emptiness; mark to shoot at (blank: the central white spot of a target); aim, object, or desire.
> *Blanco* is a composition which allows the following variant readings:
> (a) in its totality, as a single text;
> (b) the central column, to the exclusion of those to the left and right, is a poem whose theme is that of the passage of the word from silence before speech to silence after it;

(c) the left-hand column is a love poem, divided into four moments, which correspond to the four traditional elements;

(d) the right-hand column is another poem, counterpointing the erotic one and composed of four variations on sensation, perception, imagination, and understanding;

(e) each one of the four parts made up of the two columns can be read, without regard to previous divisions, as a single text: four independent poems;

(f) the central column can be read as six isolated texts and the right- and left-hand columns as eight.

Eliot Weinberger's translation successfully conveys the complexity and verbal mastery of the original.

Blanco

Especially translated by Eliot Weinberger.

By passion the world is
bound, by passion too it
is released.
—The Hevajra Tantra

*Avec ce seul objet dont
le Néant s'honore.*
—Mallarmé

          the causing
                    the casting
          the seedling
                    sleeping
          the word on the tip of the tongue
          unheard   unhearable
                    unequal
          fertile   barren
                    ageless
          the woman buried with eyes open
          innocent   promiscuous
                    the word
          nameless   speechless

Climbing and descending
The mine-shaft ladders:
The deserted language.
A lamp beating
Beneath the skin of the penumbra.
                                A survivor
Among silent confusions,
                        It rises
On a copper stem,
                        Dissolves
In light's foliage:
                Shelter
Of fallen realities.
                    Asleep
Or extinct,
                High on its pole
(Head on a pike)
                    A sunflower
Now burnt light
                    Over a glass
Of shadow.
                In the palm of a fictitious
Hand,
        Flower
Not seen not thought:
                            Heard,
Appears
        Yellow
Chalice of consonants and vowels,
All burning.

on the wall the shadow of the fire   *flame surrounded by lions*
in the fire your shadow and mine   *lioness in the circus of the flames*
                                            soul among sensations

the fire unties and ties you
Bread Grail Coal   *fruits of flares*
            Girl   *the senses open*
you laugh—naked   *in the magnetic night*
in the gardens of the flame

            The passion of the compassionate coal

A pulse beat, an insisting,
Surge of wet syllables.
Without saying a word
My forehead darkens:
A presentiment of language.
Patience patience
(Livingston in the drought)
River rising a little.
Mine is red and scorches
Among flaming sand-heaps:
Castiles of sand, broken playing-cards
And the hieroglyph (water and coal)
On the chest of Mexico fallen.
I am the dust of that earth.
River of blood,
                    River of histories
Of blood,
          Dry river:
Mouth of the source
Gagged
By the anonymous conspiracy
Of bones,
By the grim stone of centuries
And minutes:
                    Language
Is an expiation,
                    Propitiation
To him who does not speak,
                              Entombed,
Assassinated
            Every day,
The countless dead.
                    To speak
While others work
Is to polish bones,
                    To sharpen
Silences
        To transparency,
To undulation,
                The whitecap
To water:

the rivers of your body
country of pulse beats
to enter you
country of closed eyes
water without thoughts
to enter me
entering your body
country of sleepless mirrors
country of waking water
in the sleeping night

the river of bodies
stars infusoria reptiles
torrent of somnambulist cinnabar
surge of the genealogies
games conjugations mimicries
subject and object abject and absolved
river of suns
"the tall beasts with shining skin"
seminal river of the worlds wheeling
the eye that watches it is another river

I watch myself in what I watch
as if to enter through my eyes
into an eye most crystal clear
what I watch watches me

this that I see is my creation
the perception is conception
water of thoughts
I am the creation of what I watch

delta of arms of desire
in a bed of vertigo

water of truth
                    truth of water

Transparency is all that remains

Desert burning
From yellow to flesh color:
The land is a charred language.
There are invisible spines, there are
Thorns in the eyes.
                    Three satiated vultures
On a pink wall.
It has no body or face or soul,
It's everywhere,
Crushing all of us:
                    This sun is unjust.
Anger is mineral.
                    Colors
Are obstinate.
                    Obstinate horizon.
Drumbeats drumbeats drumbeats.
The sky blackens
                    Like this page.
Dispersion of crows.
Imminence of violet violences.
The sands rise,

Dark herds of ash.
The chained trees howl.
Drumbeats drumbeats drumbeats
I pound you sky
                              Land I pound you
Open sky closed land
Flute and drum lightning and thunder
I open you I pound you
                              You open land
Your mouth filled with water
Your body gushes sky
Tremor
          Your belly quakes.
Your seeds explode
                    The word grows green

breaks out scatters *arid undulation*
rises erects itself into an Idol *between arms of sand*
naked like the mind *shines multiplies denies itself*
in the reverberation of desire *is reborn escapes pursues itself*
turning turning *vision of hawk-thought*
around the black idea *goat in the rock cleft*
the fleece of the joining *naked place*
in a naked woman *snapshot of a pulse beat of time*
firefly tangle of presences *real unreal quiet vibrating*
unmoving beneath the sun unmoving *burnt meadow*
the color of the earth *color of sun on the sand*
the grass of my shadow *on the place of the joining*
my hands of rain *darkened by birds*
on your green breasts *holiness*
woman stretched out *made in the image of the world*

        The world bundle of your images

From yellow to red to green,
A pilgrimage to the clarities,
The word gazing out toward blue
Whirls.
          The drunk ring turning,

The five senses turning
About the selfish
Amethyst.
                    Dazzlement:
I don't think, I see
                    —Not what I see,
But the reflections, the thoughts I see.
The precipitations of music,
The crystallized number.
An archipelago of signs.
Air-image,
                    Mouth of truths,
Clarity humbled in a syllable,
Light-image like silence:
I don't think, I see
                    —Not what I think,
The face blank, forgetfulness,
The splendor of the void.
I lose my shadow,
                    I move
Among impalpable forests,
Quick sculptures of the wind,
Endless things,
                    Sharp passages,
I move,
            My steps
                    Dissolve
In a space that evaporates
In thoughts I don't think.

you fall from your body to your shadow *not there but in my eyes*
in an unmoving falling of waterfall *sky and ground joining*
falling from your shadow to your name *untouchable horizon*
you drop through your likenesses *I am your remoteness*
falling from your name to your body *the furthest point of seeing*
in a present that doesn't stop *imaginations of the sand*
you fall in your causing *scattered fables of the wind*
overflowing my body *I am the stela of your erosions*
you divide yourself like language *god space quartered*
dividing me in your divisions *thought altar and knife*
belly theater of blood *axis of the solstices*
arboreal ivy firebrand tongue of coolness *the firmament is male and female*

tremble of earth your buttocks *testimony of the solar testicles*
rain of your heels on my back *the thought phallus the word womb*
jaguar eye in the eyelash thicket *space is body sign thought*
the flesh-colored cleft in the brambles *always two syllables in love*
the black lips of the prophetess *R   i   d   d   l   e*
whole in each part you divide yourself *the spirals transfigurations*
the bodies of the instant are your body *time world is body*
seen touched vanished *thought without body imaginary body*

contemplated by my hearing   *Horizon of stretched music*
smelled by my eyes   *Bridge from color to smell*
caressed by my smelling   *Scent nakedness in the hands of the air*
heard by my tongue   *Song of the flavors*
eaten by my touch   *Feast of mist*

to inhabit your name   *To depopulate your body*
to fall in your scream with you   *House of the wind*

          The unreality of the watched
          Gives reality to the watching.

          In the center
          Of the world of the body of the spirit
          The cleft   The splendor
                    No
          In the whirl of the disappearances
          The whirlwind of the appearances
                    Yes
          The tree of names
                              No
          Is a word
                    Yes
          Is a word
                    They are air nothing
          They are
                    This insect
          Buzzing among the lines
          Of the page
                    Unfinished
                              Unfinishable
          Thought
                    Buzzing

Among these words
                    They are
Your footsteps in the next room
The birds that return
The neem tree that protects us
                    Protects them
Its branches quiet thunder
Put out the lightning
In its foliage the drought drinks water
They are
           This night
                    (This music)
Watch it flow
                    Between your breasts
Falling on your belly
                    White and black
Night spring
                    Jasmine and wing of a crow
Tabla and sitar
                    No and yes
Together
           Two syllables in love
If the world is real
                    The word is unreal
If it is real the word
                    The world
Is the cleft the splendor the whirl
No
    The disappearances and the appearances
                                        Yes
The tree of names
                    Real unreal
Words they are
                    Air they are nothing
Speech
        Unreal
Gives reality to silence
                    Quiet
Is a weave of language
                    Silence
Seal
    Dazzle
            On the forehead
On the lips
           Before evaporating

Appearances and disappearances
Reality and its resurrections
Silence rests in speech

The spirit
Is an invention of the body
The body
Is an invention of the world
The world
Is an invention of the spirit
No   Yes
    Unreality of the watched
Transparency is all that remains
Your footsteps in the next room
The green thunder
                          Ripens
In the foliage of the sky
                          You are naked
Like a syllable
                Like a flame
An island of flames
Passion of compassionate coal
The world
            Bundle of your images
Drowned in the music
                      Your body
Spilled on my body
                    Seen
Dissolved
          Gives reality to the watching

2

NICANOR PARRA

1914 was a vintage year for the new Latin American literature. For in
that year were born the Mexican Octavio Paz, the Chilean Nicanor Parra, and
the Argentines Adolfo Bioy Casares and Julio Cortázar. The first two altered
radically the course of Spanish American poetry; the last two contributed deci-

sively to the revolution in prose fiction begun in the middle thirties by Jorge Luis Borges. But the work produced by each one was as unique and individual as their respective backgrounds and personalities.

To begin with the poets, it is obvious that while Paz had written a kind of "total" poetry—he is a poet in search of the unreachable absolute: absolute void, or absolute stillness—Parra had assiduously avoided such a quest. His is a poetry of destruction and despair. Its predominant mode is an irony that cuts to the bone and becomes tragically grotesque. If Paz, in his all-encompassing vision and his appetite for perfection, approaches the Goethean prototype, Parra is a true child of a century that has produced such practical jokers as Duchamp, Beckett, and Borges. There is another important difference: while Paz began to write in a Mexican context in which the absence of a major poet was evident (the verse of the *Contemporaries* group never really transcended a certain self-conscious delicacy or exquisiteness), Parra was writing in the overwhelming shadow of Neruda (Part Four, 12). In a sense, he became an antipoet in order to negate the exalted conception of the poet that Neruda represented so grandly. The fact that he finally succeeded in creating a viable alternative confirms his unique gifts.

Parra was born in a small town near Chillán, in southern Chile, in 1914; he belonged to a poor family and had a hard time completing his education. He had, however, not only the unusual gift of poetry but another talent that hardly goes hand in hand with the poetic touch—a scientific vocation. He studied mathematics at the University of Chile in Santiago and later completed his studies at Brown University in the United States and at Oxford. He became a teacher of rational mechanics at the Pedagogical Institute in Santiago. His scientific vocation, however, never interfered with his poetry. On the contrary, it gave him an exacting notion of the value of each word, each sign.

His first collection of poems, quaintly called *Untitled Book of Ballads*, was published when he was twenty-three. He won a municipal prize with it, but it was a derivative book, strongly dependent on the prestige of García Lorca's poetry. (Parra would eventually eliminate it from the list of his works and would never authorize a reprint.) The new poetry he began to write in the forties and fifties was vastly different in style.

In the United States, and later in England, Parra discovered Anglo-Saxon modernism, especially the poems of Eliot and Auden. When he returned to Chile in 1951, he had already written the best part of a new book, *Poems and Antipoems*, which he published in 1954. The title suggests a notion already formulated by the Chilean Vicente Huidobro (see Part Four, 6), who in one of his verses had called himself "antipoet and magician." Neruda had already attacked Huidobro's dictum that poets have supernatural powers, and had bluntly stated: "The poet is not a little god." But it was Parra who really beat Huidobro at his own game by actually creating the kind of critical and surrealistic poetry his predecessor had been aiming at. The "antipoem" is a poem in which all the trappings of romantic rhetoric have been drastically exposed and a prosaic diction has taken over the poem. Parra's "prosaism," however, is only the mask of an intense, anguished vision of man and of poetry. Using narrative devices but deflecting the normal expectations of the reader by interrupting and even cutting short the anecdotal flow, Parra "de-constructs" the poem and finally achieves an almost epigrammatic structure that moves from one intense fragment of verbal reality to the next. In later years, Parra has gone even further. In texts that he has collected in English under the title *Emergency Poems* (1972), he has disposed of the metaphors and even the surrealistic association of images he used in his previous books. Only in the sharp cutting and unexpected assemblage of rather banal sentences do the satirical intentions of the poem become evident. His work is now loaded with all kinds of controversial and nonpoetic material—brutal attacks on the political establishment or the Church, blatantly obscene remarks, outrageous assertions.

Parra's deliberately anarchistic rebellion against society, against all social forms and conventions, has gone so far that even his former fellow Marxists have rejected it. He stands now isolated in a proud, defiant attitude. Some of his most recent works, called derisively *Artifacts*, combine visual puns and graphics that owe something to comic strips and satirical cartoons and that produce devastating effects. Parra's well-honed skills in "de-construction" are at the service of the central task to which he has dedicated himself: the subversion and destruction of all conventional notions of reality.

The poems selected here are from *Poems and Antipoems*, his most influential book, and one of the first to successfully introduce into Spanish American poetry a narrative trend. They have been meticulously transposed into English by a host of distinguished American poets—another sign of the interest Parra's poetry has aroused in the larger international context.

Poems and Antipoems

From Poems and Antipoems, *translated by Miller Williams, W. S. Merwin, Lawrence Ferlinghetti, Allen Ginsberg, and Denise Levertov (New York: New Directions, 1967), pp. 3–5, 35–39, 55–61, 69–71, 89, 145–47 and 149.*

Nineteen-Thirty

Nineteen-thirty. Here begins an epoch
With the burning of the dirigible R–101 as it crashes to earth
Wrapped in black swirls of smoke
And in flames they can see from across the canal.
I offer nothing special. I formulate no hypothesis.
I am only a camera swinging over the desert
I am a flying carpet

A recorder of dates and scattered facts
A machine producing a certain number of buttons per minute.

First I point out the bodies of André
And his unfortunate companions
Who waited hidden half a century under the northern snow
To be discovered one day of the year nineteen hundred and thirty
The year in which I locate myself
And am in a certain way situated.
I point to the precise spot where they were overcome by the storm
Here is the sled that led them to the arms of death
The boat full of scientific documents
Of observational instruments
Full of food and countless photographic plates.

I'm at the top of one of the highest peaks of the Himalayas
Kanchenjunga, and skeptically watch the international team
Setting out to scale her, to decipher her mysteries.
I see how the wind throws them back time and again
To where they started
Until desperation and madness take their minds.
I see some slip and fall into the chasm
And others fight among themselves for a few cans of food.

But not everything I see comes down to an expeditionary force:
I am a rolling museum
An encyclopedia forcing a path through the waves.
I record each and every human act.
Only let something happen anywhere on the globe
And a part of me sets itself moving.
That's what my job is.
I give the same attention to a crime as to an act of mercy
I vibrate the same to an idyllic landscape
And the spastic flashes of an electrical storm.
I diminish and exalt nothing
I confine myself to telling what I see.

I see Mahatma Gandhi personally directing
Public demonstrations against the Salt Law
I see the Pope and his Cardinals in a congestion of anger
Out of their minds as if possessed by the devil
Condemning the religious persecutions in Soviet Russia
And I can see Prince Carol returning by plane to Bucharest.
Thousands of Croatian and Slovenian terrorists are executed en
    masse behind my back

I let it happen, I let it pass
I let the assassinations go on quietly
I let General Carmona stick like a barnacle to the throne of
   Portugal.

This was and this is what was the year nineteen hundred and
   thirty
So were exterminated the kulaks in Siberia
So also General Chiang crossed the Yellow River and took Peking
By this means and no other are the predictions of the astrologers
   fulfilled
To the rhythm of the sewing machine of my poor widowed mother
To the rhythm of the rain, the rhythm of my own naked feet
And of my brothers scratching themselves and talking in their
   sleep.

Translated by Miller Williams

The Viper

For years I was doomed to worship a contemptible woman
Sacrifice myself for her, endure endless humiliations and sneers,
Work night and day to feed her and clothe her,
Perform several crimes, commit several misdemeanors,
Practice petty burglary by moonlight,
Forge compromising documents,
For fear of a scornful glance from her bewitching eyes.
During brief phases of understanding we used to meet in parks
And have ourselves photographed together driving a motorboat,
Or we would go to a nightclub
And fling ourselves into an orgy of dancing
That went on until well after dawn.
For years I was under the spell of that woman.
She used to appear in my office completely naked
And perform contortions that defy the imagination,
Simply to draw my poor soul into her orbit
And above all to wring from me my last penny.
She absolutely forbade me to have anything to do with my family.
To get rid of my friends this viper made free with defamatory
   libels
Which she published in a newspaper she owned.
Passionate to the point of delirium, she never let up for an instant,
Commanding me to kiss her on the mouth
And to reply at once to her silly questions
Concerning, among other things, eternity and the afterlife,
Subjects which upset me terribly,

Producing buzzing in my ears, recurrent nausea, sudden fainting
    spells
Which she turned to account with that practical turn of mind that
    distinguished her,
Putting her clothes on without wasting a moment
And clearing out of my apartment, leaving me flat.

This situation dragged on for five years and more.
There were periods when we lived together in a round room
In a plush district near the cemetery, sharing the rent.
(Some nights we had to interrupt our honeymoon
To cope with the rats that streamed in through the window.)
The viper kept a meticulous account book
In which she noted every penny I borrowed from her,
She would not let me use the toothbrush I had given her myself,
And she accused me of having ruined her youth:
With her eyes flashing fire she threatened to take me to court
And make me pay part of the debt within a reasonable period
Since she needed the money to go on with her studies.
Then I had to take to the street and live on public charity,
Sleeping on park benches
Where the police found me time and again, dying,
Among the first leaves of autumn.
Fortunately that state of affairs went no further,
For one time—and again I was in a park,
Posing for a photographer—
A pair of delicious feminine hands suddenly covered my eyes
While a voice that I loved asked me: Who am I?
You are my love, I answered serenely.
My angel! she said nervously.
Let me sit on your knees once again!
It was then that I was able to ponder the fact that she was now
    wearing brief tights.
It was a memorable meeting, though full of discordant notes.
I have bought a plot of land not far from the slaughterhouse, she
    exclaimed.
I plan to build a sort of pyramid there
Where we can spend the rest of our days.
I have finished my studies, I have been admitted to the bar,
I have a tidy bit of capital at my disposal;
Let's go into some lucrative business, we two, my love, she added,
Let's build our nest far from the world.
Enough of your foolishness, I answered, I have no confidence in
    your plans.
Bear in mind that my real wife

Can at any moment leave both of us in the most frightful poverty.
My children are grown up, time has elapsed,
I feel utterly exhausted, let me have a minute's rest,
Get me a little water, woman,
Get me something to eat from somewhere,
I'm starving,
I can't work for you any more,
It's all over between us.

Translated by W. S. Merwin

The Individual's Soliloquy

I'm the individual.
First I lived by a rock
(I scratched some figures on it)
Then I looked for someplace more
    suitable.
I'm the individual.
First I had to get myself food,
Hunt for fish, birds, hunt up wood
(I'd take care of the rest later),
Make a fire,
Wood, wood, where could I find any
    wood,
Some wood to start a little fire,
I'm the individual.
At the time I was asking myself,
Went to a canyon filled with air;
A voice answered me back:
I'm the individual.
So then I started moving to another
    rock,
I also scratched figures there,
Scratched out a river, buffaloes,
I'm the individual.
But I got bored with what I was
    doing,
Fire annoyed me,
I wanted to see more,
I'm the individual.
Went down to a valley watered by a
    river,
There I found what I was looking
    for,
A bunch of savages,

A tribe,
I'm the individual.
I saw they made certain things,
Scratching figures on the rocks,
Making fire, also making fire!
I'm the individual.
They asked me where I came from.
I answered yes, that I had no
    definite plans,
I answered no, that from here on
    out.
O.K.
I then took a stone I found in the
    river
And began working on it,
Polishing it up,
I made it a part of my life.
But it's a long story.
I chopped some trees to sail on
Looking for fish,
Looking for lots of things,
(I'm the individual.)
Till I began getting bored again.
Storms get boring,
Thunder, lightning,
I'm the individual.
O.K.
I began thinking a little bit,
Stupid questions came into my head,
Doubletalk.
So then I began wandering through
    forests,
I came to a tree, then another tree,

I came to a spring,
A hole with a couple of rats in it;
So here I come, I said,
Anybody seen a tribe around here,
Savage people who make fire?
That's how I moved on westward,
Accompanied by others,
Or rather alone,
Believing is seeing, they told me,
I'm the individual.
I saw shapes in the darkness,
Clouds maybe,
Maybe I saw clouds, or sheet
    lightning,
Meanwhile several days had gone by,
I felt as if I were dying;
Invented some machines,
Constructed clocks,
Weapons, vehicles,
I'm the individual.
Hardly had time to bury my dead,
Hardly had time to sow,
I'm the individual.
Years later I conceived a few things,
A few forms,
Crossed frontiers,
And got stuck in a kind of niche,
In a bark that sailed forty days,
Forty nights,
I'm the individual.
Then came the droughts,
Then came the wars,
Colored guys entered the valley,
But I had to keep going,
Had to produce.
Produced science, immutable truths,
Produced tanagras,
Hatched up thousand-page books.

My face got swollen,
Invented a phonograph,
The sewing machine,
The first automobiles began to
    appear,
I'm the individual.
Someone set up planets,
Trees got set up!
But I set up hardware,
Furniture, stationery,
I'm the individual.
Cities also got built,
Highways,
Religious institutions went out of
    fashion,
They looked for joy, they looked for
    happiness,
I'm the individual.
Afterward I devoted myself to travel,
Practicing, practicing languages
Languages,
I'm the individual.
I looked into a keyhole,
Sure, I looked, what am I saying,
    looked,
To get rid of all doubt looked,
Behind the curtains,
I'm the individual.
O.K.
Perhaps I better go back to that
    valley,
To that rock that was home,
And start scratching all over again,
Scratching out everything backward,
The world in reverse.
But it wouldn't make sense.

        Translated by Lawrence Ferlinghetti
            and Allen Ginsberg

Clever Ideas Occur to Me

On a bench in Forest Park
A woman almost drove me crazy,
God, that was a real Walpurgis Night.

We started out with "Usted."
I didn't have very much to say;
She changed the subject every other sentence.
She gives piano lessons at home
Pays her own way at school
Is a mortal enemy of the cigarette
Takes a course in shorthand by correspondence
Thinks about taking a course in obstetrics
Fennel makes her sneeze
She dreams her tonsils are being taken out
Yellow excites her
She plans to spend the holiday in Linares
Had her appendix out a month ago.

Once she fell from a eucalyptus tree

As if this were nothing
She says her brother-in-law is chasing her
Several nights ago he broke into her room.

I recite her a sonnet from Shakespeare.

The truth is I can barely stand her.
I get mad trying to pretend.
Clever ideas occur to me.
I also say something just for something to say.
Everyone follows his own theories.
Why don't we go to a hotel for a while?

—She says she'll have to put it off a week

I take her to her rooming house
In a taxi.
She promises to call.

Translated by Miller Williams

Women

The impossible woman
The woman three yards high
The lady of Carrara marble
Who doesn't drink or smoke
The woman who doesn't want to undress
For fear of becoming pregnant
The untouchable vestal

Who doesn't want to have babies
The woman who breathes through her mouth
The woman who walks virgin to the marriage bed
But then acts like a man
She who undresses out of kindness
Because classical music enchants her
The redhead who lies face down
The one who only surrenders for love
The maiden who peeks with one eye
The one who lets herself be taken
Only on the sofa, at the edge of the abyss
The one who hates the sexual organs
The one who only makes it with her dog
The wife who pretends to be asleep
(Her husband shines a match on her)
The woman who surrenders for no reason
For loneliness, forgetfulness . . .
The one who carries her maidenhead to old age
The nearsighted lady professor
The secretary with sunglasses
The pale miss with spectacles
(She doesn't want anything to do with a phallus)
All these Valkyries
All these respectable matrons
With their labia major and minor
Will drive me out of my mind sooner or later.

Translated by Denise Levertov

Test

What is an antipoet

A dealer in urns and coffins?
A general doubting himself?
A priest who believes in nothing?
A tramp laughing at everything
  even old age and death?
An ill-tempered talker?
A dancer on the edge of the abyss?
A Narcissus in love with the whole world?
A bloody joker
  willfully wretched?
A poet who sleeps in a chair?
An up-to-date alchemist?
A revolutionary of the living room?

A *petit-bourgeois?*
A charlatan?
  A god?
    An innocent?
A peasant of Santiago, Chile?
Underline the sentence that you consider correct.

What is antipoetry?
A tempest in a teacup?
A spot of snow on a rock?
A salad bowl full of human excrement
  as the Franciscan Father believes?
A mirror that tells the truth?
A woman with her legs open?
A punch in the nose
  of the president of the Writers' Society?
(May God save his soul)
A warning to the young poets?

A jet-propelled coffin?
A coffin run by centrifugal force?
A kerosene coffin?
A funeral home without a body?
Put an X beside the definition you consider correct.

Translated by Miller Williams

I Take Back Everything I've Said

Before I go
I'm supposed to get a last wish:
Generous reader
*   burn this book*
It's not at all what I wanted to say
In spite of the fact that it was written with blood
It's not what I wanted to say.

No lot could be sadder than mine
I was defeated by my own shadow:
The words take vengeance against me.

Forgive me, reader, good reader
If I cannot leave you
With a faithful gesture. I leave you
With a forced and sad smile.

Maybe that's all I am
But listen to my last word:
I take back everything I've said.
With the greatest bitterness in the world
I take back everything I've said.

Translated by Miller Williams

3

ADOLFO BIOY CASARES

For too long, the Argentine Adolfo Bioy Casares was regarded only as Borges's best-known disciple and collaborator. But in the last decade, his stature as one of the leading novelists of Latin America has been internationally recognized. A shy, handsome, uncomfortably polite man, Bioy Casares seemed to fit more neatly in a French literary salon or in a decadent European spa than in the rough, highly politicized Latin American scene. His apparently fragile novels talk about impossible love, wittily play with the vagaries of time and substance, are delicately obsessed with carnality and even with animal metamorphoses. Dreams and reality are indistinguishable. A sad, ironical point of view permeates all his writing. Out of such unlikely material, Bioy Casares has produced a unique and original body of work, in which the traces of Borges's influence serve to reveal the originality of his own approach to narrative.

Bioy, born in Buenos Aires in 1914, of a wealthy family, was a very precocious writer. Although he now disowns his first books of short stories and poems, they paved the way for his long quest for expression. By 1935 he had met Borges and had asked him to become his literary mentor. Bioy's first important book, *The Invention of Morel,* was published in 1940, with a highly laudatory preface by Borges. The preface attracted perhaps more attention than the novel —it was one of Borges's major declarations in favor of a nonrealistic, "magical" fiction. But the novel itself was also a landmark. It carried the pastoral-Provençal-romantic tradition of love-winning-against-all-odds one step further: the protagonist falls madly in love with a woman who is only an image on film, and he sacrifices his own life to be able to enter into her imaginary world. The elegant simplicity of the writing and the subtly ironical mode in which Bioy handled the pastoral subject did not detract from the surrealistic quality of its theme. Many years later, Alain Robbe-Grillet would remember *Morel* in writing the screenplay for Alain Resnais's *Last Year at Marienbad* (1961). Bioy's second novel was also set on an island, but this time a very well-known one. Choosing Devil's Island as the novel's locale, Bioy gave expression in *A Plan for Escape* (1945) to some of his obsessive concerns: the impossible love, the metamorphoses of the body and the soul, the magical character of everyday objects. The new novel was a parody of the suspense adventure tale, but also (like *Morel*) a homage to H. G. Wells. In both books it is possible to read, as if in filigree, *The Island of Dr. Moreau.*

For his third novel, Bioy chose a local setting: *The Dream of the Heroes* is set in Buenos Aires in the late twenties and early thirties. It is the story of a man who has the chance to correct the past by literally reliving it. The basic idea is derived from a Borges story, "The Other Death," but the treatment is radically different. The metaphysical notion of time recovered, or rewound, as it were, is less important here than the oedipal configuration of the attempt: double parricide lurks behind its complex plot. Again, love is impossible and desire finally frustrated.

In the last decade Bioy has written two more novels in which the locale is (as in *The Dream*) the poorer sections of Buenos Aires. But the writing is deliberately less brilliant, deliberately toned down, and the magical elements are presented in an ominously casual way. *The Diary of the War of the Pigs* (1969) is located in the near future—a time in which gangs of young people chase and eventually murder the old. Once again, set off against the brutal reality, love—between an aging man and a young woman—introduces the magical element. The second novel, *To Sleep in the Sun* (1973), concerns a man who is desperately in love with his wife but suspects that she has become (literally) a bitch. The Wellsian theme of men transformed into animals that was a haunting, insistent overtone in *A Plan for Escape* and *The Diary of the War of the Pigs* is here rendered explicitly. But instead of a scientific tract, Bioy produces a beautiful parable about the longings and pains of desire.

Several volumes of short stories complete the roster of Bioy's fictional production. The same persistent themes, the same mild ironies, the same neat writing are present in these tales as in his earlier work.

Bioy has also written detective stories in collaboration with Borges, but they belong really to a third persona: neither Borges nor Bioy, "Biorges" is more openly parodic than either of his inventors. And Bioy has, in addition, produced a detective novel with his wife, Silvina Ocampo, herself a distinguished poet. Entitled *Those Who Love, Hate Too* (1946), it is a highly comic parody of the genre.

The story excerpted here is perhaps one of Bioy's best. The setting of this retelling of the famous myth of Orpheus and Eurydice is Buenos Aires in 1943, at the time when the Peronists, to teach a lesson to the wealthy Argentine landowners and bosses, burned down the elegant Jockey Club. As usual in Bioy, external circumstances matter only as the chaotic background for desire. A truly surrealistic passion pervades the story, as it does all his writing. From this point of view, "The Myth of Orpheus and Eurydice" is a perfect summary of his elegant, obsession-ridden, passionate art.

The Myth of Orpheus and Eurydice

From Guirnalda con amores *(Buenos Aires: Emecé, 1958), especially translated by Suzanne Jill Levine.*

How dramatic those days seem, all those days, the mild and the cold ones, the bright and the muddy ones. Then even the most insignificant of us would only have to open a door, as it were, to walk into adventure. We clearly know it was by chance that we passed it up unknowingly, and that instead of becoming heroes we went to the office, wrote books, and made love to women. Because of magic or memory's irresponsibility, we remember it all, even the anguish and infamy that weighed like lead upon our chests, nostalgically, until finally, to react, we have to realize that tyranny doesn't even serve that purpose, since life is continually offering us occasions to test ourselves. Life is as delicate and fleeting as the mercury escaping a broken thermometer. Or perhaps one should compare it, classically, to the flower, symbol of triumphant beauty, which the pure clumsiness of a hand crumples and withers. Many are the warnings: he who looks, shall see, and doubtlessly he must not allow the weight of everyday things to make him, as it does everybody, a bit lazy, a bit unscrupulous, a bit common. There's another philosophy, however, that recommends closing your eyes from time to time. The bad thing would be that, opening them, we'd wake up at an atrocious moment, because life has a perverse tendency to imitate melodrama and a real talent for striking in a not very original but very cowardly way, and with extremely good aim. We barely finish formulating the phrase *That can't happen to me,* and it's already happening. Let nobody be so incredulous as to deny that love can drive you crazy, nor so humble as not to admit the possibility that for his love someone may die. What happened to Silveira is somewhat like a fable. I can see a moral to it, but maybe you will discover another, since all fables and symbols that have not died allow for more than one interpretation.

As to Silveira, I think he was tired of Virginia. They had loved each other for years, and suddenly Silveira discovered that nothing was as barren as a mistress, that he was very lonely and should get married, to have someone to keep him company, to give him children, and that if Virginia wouldn't take him as a husband (she was already married, she already had children), they should break up. How could a man, an Argentine at least, think up such excuses? As if life leads to something! As if you could build with anything but dreams! As if living happy days in harmony was worth so little! The truth is, Silveira began to meet that silly Irma everywhere. Silveira observed, "Maybe it was by comparison, but when I'd come back to Virginia, the scope of her mind and her body itself seemed supernatural to me. I think that if Virginia had spied on my wretched affair with Irma, she would have smiled."

Apparently Silveira didn't realize that our betrayals do not amuse the people who love us. Virginia didn't see anything, but somebody saw and told. Shortly after—April 15, 1953—life dealt one of those blows that I have mentioned. Virginia died that day. I don't know what she died of. Perhaps others find Silveira presumptuous, because he's convinced that his mistress died of love for him. Perhaps others will ask for further evidence: for Silveira, the circumstances in which Virginia got sick, the way in which she refused to follow the doctor's orders were enough. When the news arrived, he couldn't believe it. His first impulse was to run to Virginia's house, like one who has to see to believe. Then immediately he thought that if he didn't take care of his beloved's life, he should at least take care of her memory. He then asked himself if that scruple was not simply hiding a lack of courage to face the husband, the sons and daughters, the brothers and sisters, those who knew and those who only guessed. He hated himself afterward for having such thoughts. "The person I love most in the world has died," he said to himself, "and I'm concerned with this. I should or should not go, but I shouldn't think of my behavior, but of Virginia." He thought of Virginia awhile, and when he looked at the clock, he didn't understand what he was seeing; he listened, looked again, went to the window: he remembered, like a dream, that in that window there first was light, then night. The clock said four thirty and in the window there was light. It was four thirty of the next day, four thirty of the Wednesday on which they buried Virginia at four. At the same moment in which he realized he'd never see her again, he said, "If she is anywhere, I will see her." He moved, like a sleepwalker, toward a bookshelf that was near the bed, and continued saying, "You've got to begin at the beginning. *He who looks in any book finds what he wants.* In any"—he pondered, standing before the spines of his half dozen volumes—"except in these." He thought of some friends who had an excellent library, but he knew that he was not in the mood for visiting; he could also go to the National Library, although going all the way, with that weight upon his soul, to Mexico street . . . "And the Jockey Club library?" he wondered. "Why not? After all I'm a member, and it's just around the corner."

He combed his hair and went out. Maybe because he was weak that afternoon, he found it very noisy. He entered the club by the side door on Tucumán Street. The doorman, an old, blond Spaniard with a goatlike voice, recognized him, delayed him a few moments to politely, solemnly question him about his health, his father, the weather, which he went on to describe as "a strange autumn, it keeps your cold going but it's better, mark my words sir, much better than last year's humidity, which was unhealthy." He entered the corridor, went up two or three steps, past some glass doors, turned to the right, continued down another dark, cool corridor. He drank two gins in the bar. Then he went toward the main hall and, facing the marble staircase, with a Diana on its landing, he stopped; he awoke from his abstraction and walked suspended and attentive, not suspended and attentive because the beauty or splendor dazzled him (let's not exaggerate); suspended for suddenly finding himself so far from the noisy, harsh city outside; attentive to the almost gloomy light of the high electric bulbs, to the symmetrical design of the tiles, to a certain reddish color of the wood, to a certain smell of resins, to the thick rugs and a something that issued from it all and which was as real inside that house as is a mood inside each one of us. He went into the library.

At a table in the back, to the left, he asked for books. The first part of his plan—maybe the rest was vague, but it had a reality for Silveira, who, after some twenty-odd hours of fasting, vigil, meditation on death, was not in a state of complete sanity—the first part of the plan, I repeat, consisted in remembering what men thought of the other world. He didn't hope to get much further into it but he ought to begin in some way; besides he believed that for the very nature of what he was looking for, he wouldn't find it where he looked for it; his plan was to make an effort in one direction, so that the finding would come to him, freely, from another. He became discouraged. Those books, perhaps the highest expression of the human spirit, had not been written for him. After going over lines like: *It is now the hour to get up from our sleep, let us walk through the happy dwelling of the blessed dead, awake and sing, dwellers of the dust, intone hymns before the throne of Glory* (such was the general tone and essence of his readings), he became deeply saddened, felt cold in his bones, was disheartened for the search. He returned the books and, because he was shivering, decided to take a bath.

Poor Silveira was in the Jockey Club and was who knows where. He looked for the furthest elevator: one that he had seen opposite the bar; when he got there, he pressed the call button, put his face near the peephole, and, with impatience, pushed another door, went down a gray, iron, spiral staircase, in such a small well that he had to stoop so as not to hit his head against the steps going up. He entered a large rectangular room, of tile, that seemed like a room at the bottom of a ship, or perhaps on the bottom of the ocean, or on the bottom of a pond of greenish water; against the wall were wardrobes and a long bench of dark, reddish wood; quiet fans, with large propellers, were hanging from the ceiling; dull straw chairs surrounded a table, and some plants made you think of a hothouse. Spread out along the bench, three or four members were getting dressed or undressed, leisurely; one was waiting for his trousers, which they were ironing at the tailor's, and another, wearing shoes, socks, garters, and naked, was combing his hair in front of sinks and mirrors. A man in white appeared with a bathrobe, two towels, a pair of clogs. Silveira got undressed, wrapped himself in the robe, put on the clogs (thinking, "Sooner or later I'll have to try the fungus," a modest joke which entertained him in his sadness), and ran to the baths. In the first shower room, a transom window was open; he discovered a second more sheltered room, full of steam, and of black, white, and brown marble. An attendant pointed to a shower, regulated it, soaped his back, gave him a little bar of soap. Next to one of the showers in front, another attendant was talking with an old man, whom Silveira gazed at with envy, because he wasn't using, like himself, a modest little bar of soap, but rather an enormous wooden bowl, overflowing with pine soap, and a jute brush; on a metallic label on the bowl there was a name engraved—Almirón—which evoked memories of something he had read about the year 1900 and the visit of the Brazilian president Campos Salles.

There is a pleasure in standing still under the shower; another in allowing yourself to soap your body carefully, slowly, and abstractedly. Forgetting everything, Silveira heard, faraway, the showers and the attendant's conversation with the old man. The attendant's voice, sometimes high and almost childlike, other times howling, was peculiar. By the voice, Silveira suddenly recognized the man: one Bernardo, an Italian of slight build and overdressed, whom you would see until recently on fashionable Florida Street, an incredible survivor of the Buenos Aires of forty years ago, with a pearl-gray tiepin, a stiff collar, kid gloves, a malacca cane, striped pants, and spats, and who was, in the good old days, a valet both to Silveira's uncles and to some friends of the family, all of them dead now. The same Bernardo . . . In his vertigo Silveira's thoughts stopped.

Almirón had left the shower; Bernardo passed him the towels, first the Turkish, then the linen one; he accompanied him to the door; there they paused, but the conversation, apparently, did not end, and followed by Bernardo, Almirón continued on his way.

An uproar was heard coming from the dressing room. The attendant ran to see what was happening; after a while he returned and shouted, "They're attacking the club. We've got to run. They'll trap us like rats."

"They're not going to trap me," Silveira replied.

"I'll go help old Bernardo, he's half blind," said the attendant.

Silveira thought, "Then he's not dead." If Bernardo wasn't dead, what he took for certain was a hallucination. Unless, precisely to prepare his mood, they had put a man in that intermediary place who he couldn't say was alive or dead. As to Almirón, how could he still be alive? Already reassured, he went to a door that was at the other end of the room and opened it. The first thing he made out in the mist was the face of an old family servant, named Soldano, dead some years ago in Quilmes. The servant smiled at him affectionately, as if inviting him to come in; Silveira obeyed. Although there was a mist, this was not another bath room.

If someone, the next morning, wanted to get to the club to inquire after Silveira, at the corner of Tucumán and San Martin Streets he would have found people clustered and police who wouldn't let him through. He pretended perhaps (like others did) that he lived in the Claridge, and from the entrance of that hotel contemplated, for the last time, the Jockey Club building, still perfect. A short spiral of smoke came out from somewhere and the hose, directed by the fireman posted on Tucumán toward a wall the fire didn't reach, sprayed little water; but that witness and so many others of us thought that the fire was put out. We were wrong. Very soon the ruins emerged and then the bare ground. Looking at that ground no one would guess the plan of the building; an architect of today, educated in the admiration of the simple and the trim, would be incapable of imagining it, and you yourself, if they asked you up and down how many staircases, including the spiral ones, could he go in there, or through how many bath rooms could Silveira lose his way when he descended to the other world, you couldn't give a definite answer, because in truth there was something magical about that burned house.

4

JULIO CORTÁZAR

Although Cortázar's Latin American reputation is mainly based on his highly experimental novels, it is probably in the field of the short story that he has done his best work. The most famous, of course, is the one that inspired Michelangelo Antonioni's *Blow-up*, but there are at least a dozen that deserve to be included among the highest achievements of the genre.

Cortázar was born in Brussels in 1914, to Argentine parents, and was only four when his family moved to Buenos Aires. The influence of his early experience is manifest in his glottal pronunciation of *r* and his general familiarity with French culture. His father having deserted the family, Cortázar was brought up in a home dominated by women. He studied in Buenos Aires to become a high-school teacher. At eighteen, with a group of friends, he attempted to go to Europe—the dream of any respectable Latin American man of letters. Failing in this, he completed his studies at home and became a teacher of French literature, first in the provinces, later in Buenos Aires. He had always been interested in English literature, and even wrote an immense and never-finished essay on John Keats. Years later he would also translate the complete prose works of Edgar Allan Poe.

His literary life began with a book of poems he published in 1938 under the somewhat Frenchified pseudonym of Julio Denis. Although he continued to write and eventually published some poems under his own name, he soon realized that verse was not his true medium. After an unsuccessful attempt at writing a dramatic prose poem on the myth of the Minotaur (*The Kings*, 1949), he concentrated his efforts on short stories. It was to Borges that he owed the publication of some of his first stories in a magazine, *The Annals of Buenos Aires*. These were fantastic tales in which Borges's own characteristic themes—the double, the labyrinth, the metamorphoses of men into beasts—were presented in a more dreamy, surrealistic style. Cortázar collected these stories in a volume, *Bestiary*, published in 1951; but it went almost unnoticed.

That same year, he finally left Argentina for good. Peronism had made teaching almost impossible, and Cortázar, unlike the majority of Argentine intellectuals, decided not to fight the regime, but to emigrate instead. Many years later, as if to atone for his lack of political commitment at the time, he became a vocal defender of the Cuban Revolution and, more recently, of the Allende regime in Chile. But he has never returned to live in Argentina, where the passing years have seen a succession of military regimes give way to a new Peronist government, which has now yielded in turn to another military regime.

In France, he worked as a translator for UNESCO, and continued to write. He published several volumes of short stories (*End of the Game*, 1956; *The Secret Weapons*, 1959; *Cronopios and Famas*, 1962) and one novel, *The Winners* (1961). These were good, even exciting books, but they did not win wide recognition for their author.

The breakthrough came with *Hopscotch*. Published in 1963, just when the boom for Latin American narrative was gathering force, the novel exploded all over the continent. It was a complex, sophisticated narrative, which attempted to capture a moment in the life of its characters (the transition between Paris and Buenos Aires) and which built up a challenging labyrinthine structure of themes, ideas, and feelings. It was hailed as a masterpiece, and the Mexican writer Carlos Fuentes called Cortázar the Simon Bolívar of Latin American narrative on the ground that he had liberated it from all cant and provincialism.

More sober consideration reveals the book's shortcomings. Although provocative and brilliant in many respects, there is scarcely anything in its elaborate theorizing that is original; the plot lacks interest, the characters do not develop, and the best episodes are really separate short stories embedded in the text (Berthe Trépat's grotesque concert, for instance). Still, *Hopscotch* was and is important for its role in introducing a new dimension into Latin American fiction. Other, similarly experimental novels (Guimarães Rosa's *The Devil to Pay in the Backlands*, 1956; Lezama Lima's *Paradiso*, 1966; Cabrera Infante's *Three Trapped Tigers*, 1967) were more successful in critical terms, but it was *Hopscotch* that really attracted the attention of the reading public. Two subsequent novels (*62. A Model Kit*, 1968; *Manuel's Book*, 1973) were also experimental in character, but shared the same basic limitations.

In 1966, Cortázar published a fifth book of short stories, *All Fires the Fire*. It contains some of his best tales: "The Southern Thruway," which is the unacknowledged source of Godard's film *Weekend;* "Instructions for John Howell"; and "The Other Heaven." This last story, especially—the one that appears here—incorporates the full range of Cortázar's most characteristic themes and concerns. It is set simultaneously in the Buenos Aires of the twenties and the Paris of the 1860s. Moving from one locale to the other, the protagonist is at the same time a shy Argentine boy who does not dare to approach the prostitutes of the Güemes Arcade, and a double who has a satisfying liaison with a French prostitute of the Galerie Vivienne.

The theme of the double and the theme of desire are played against a background of grotesque middle-class values (in Buenos Aires) and the temptations and horrors of vice (in Paris). And the entire text is inscribed into another text: a couple of unidentified quotations from Lautréamont's *Chants de Maldoror* suggest another reading. The Argentine boy, consumed by desire in the Paris of the 1860s, is a double of the Montevidean poet who lived and died in the same neighborhood at that time. Another level of interpretation is suggested by the introduction of yet another character: Laurent, a Jack-the-Ripper kind of murderer who specializes in prostitutes. The sexual transgressions of the protagonist in Paris, the murderous transgressions of Laurent, and the poetic transgressions of Lautréamont are thus connected in an inextricable web of allusions and analogies. The story is unquestionably Cortázar's masterpiece.

The Other Heaven

From All Fires the Fire, *translated by Suzanne Jill Levine (New York: Pantheon, 1973), pp. 128–152.*

Ces yeux ne t'appartiennent
pas . . . où les as-tu pris?
    . . . . , IV, 5.

It would sometimes occur to me that everything would let go, soften, give in, accepting without resistance that you can move like that from one thing to another. I'm saying that this would occur to me, although a stupid hope would like to believe that it might yet occur to me. And that's why, if strolling around the city time and again seems shocking when you have a family and a job, there are times when I keep repeating to myself that there would be time to return to my favorite neighborhood, forget about my work (I'm a stockbroker), and with a little luck find Josiane and stay with her till the next morning.

Who knows how long I've been repeating all this to myself? And it's pitiful, because there was a time when things happened to me when I least thought of them, barely pushing with my shoulder any corner of the air. In any case, it would be enough to become one of those citizens who let themselves get pleasurably carried away by their favorite streets, and almost always my walk ended in the gallery district, perhaps because arcades and galleries have always been my secret country. Here, for example, the Güemes Arcade, an ambiguous territory where, so many years ago, I went to strip off my childhood like a used suit. Around the year 1928, the Güemes Arcade was the treasure cave in which a glimpse of sin and mint drops deliciously mixed, where they cried out the evening editions with crimes on every page, and the lights burned in the basement movie theater where they showed restricted blue movies. The Josianes of those days must have looked at me with faces both maternal and amused, I with a few miserable cents in my pocket, but walking like a man, my hat slouched and my hands in my pockets, smoking a Commander, precisely because my stepfather had predicted that I would end up blind from foreign cigarettes. I especially remember smells and sounds, something like an expectation and an anxiety, the stand where you could buy magazines with naked women and advertisements of false manicures; already then I was sensitive to that false sky of dirty stucco and skylights, to that artificial night which ignored the stupidity of day and the sun outside. With false indifference, I'd peek into the doors of the arcade where the last mystery began, the vague elevators that would lead to the offices of VD doctors and also to the presumed paradises higher up, of women of the town and perverts, as they would call them in the newspapers, with preferably green drinks in cut-glass goblets, with silk gowns and violet kimonos, and the apartments would have the same perfume that came out of the stores, which I thought were so elegant and which sparked an unreachable bazaar of bottles and glass boxes and pink and rachel powder puffs and brushes with transparent handles over the low light of the arcade.

It's still hard for me to cross the Güemes Arcade without feeling ironically tender toward that memory of adolescence at the brink of the fall; the old fascination still persists, and that's why I liked to walk without a fixed destination, knowing that at any moment I would enter the region of the galleries, where any sordid, dusty shop would attract me more than the show windows facing the insolence of the open streets. The Galerie Vivienne, for example, or the Passage des Panoramas with its branches, its short cuts which end in a secondhand book shop or a puzzling travel agency, where perhaps nobody ever even bought a railroad ticket, that world which has chosen a nearer sky, of dirty windows and stucco with allegorical figures that extend their hands to offer garlands, that Galerie Vivienne one step from the daily shame of the Rue Réaumur and of the Bourse (I work at the stock exchange), how much of that district has always been mine, even before I suspected it was already mine when posted on a corner of the Güemes Arcade, counting the few cents I had as a student, I would argue the problem of spending them in an automat or buying a novel and a supply of sour balls in their cellophane bag, with a cigarette that clouded my eyes and, in the bottom of my pocket where my fingers would sometimes rub against it, the little envelope with the rubber bought with false boldness at a drugstore run only by men, and which I would not have the least opportunity of using with so little money and such a childish face?

My fiancée, Irma, cannot understand what I like about wandering around at night downtown or in the southside district, and if she knew how I liked the Güemes Arcade she would not fail to be shocked. For her, as for my mother, there is no better social treat than the drawing-room sofa, where what they call conversation, coffee, and the after-dinner liqueur take place. Irma is the kindest and most generous of women. I would never dream of talking to her about the things that count most for me, and in that way I will at some point be a good husband and a father, whose sons will also be the much desired grandsons of my mother. I suppose it was because of things like this that I ended up meeting Josiane, but not only for that, since I could have met her on the Boulevard

Poissonnière or on the Rue Notre-Dame-des-Victoires, and instead we looked at each other for the first time in deepest Galerie Vivienne, under the plaster figures which the gaslight would fill with trembling (the garlands moved back and forth between the fingers of the dusty muses), and it didn't take long to know that Josiane worked in that district and that it wouldn't be difficult to find her if you were acquainted with the cafés or friendly with the coach drivers. It might have been a coincidence, but having known her there, while it rained in the other world, that of the high garlandless sky of the street, seemed like a sign that went beyond the trivial meeting with any prostitute of the district. Afterward, I learned that, in those days, Josiane never left the gallery, because it was the time when all they talked about were the crimes of Laurent, and the poor thing lived in fear. Some of that terror turned into graceful, almost evasive, gestures, pure desire. I remember her half-greedy, half-suspicious way of looking at me, her questions that faked indifference, my almost unbelieving fascination at finding out that she lived in the heights of the gallery, my insistence upon going up to her garret instead of going to the Rue du Sentier Hotel (where she had friends and felt protected). And her trust later on—how we laughed that night at the very idea that I could be Laurent, and how pretty and sweet Josiane was in her dime-novel garret, with her fear of the strangler roaming around Paris and that way of pressing closer to me as we reviewed the murders of Laurent.

My mother always knows if I haven't slept at home, and although she naturally doesn't say anything, since it would be absurd for her to do so, for one or two days she looks at once offendedly and fearfully at me. I know very well that she'd never think of telling Irma, but just the same the persistence of a maternal right, which is not at all justified now, annoys me, and especially since I will be the one who in the end comes back with a box of candy or a plant for the patio, and since the gift will represent in a very precise and taken-for-granted way the end of the offense, the return to everyday life of the son who still lives in his mother's house. Josiane was, of course, happy when I'd tell her about those episodes, which, once in the gallery district, would become part of our world with the same plainness of their protagonist. Josiane had great feeling for family life, and she was full of respect for institutions and relatives; I'm not big on secrets, but since we had to talk about something and what she had revealed about her life had already been discussed, we would almost inevitably return to my problems as a single man. We had something else in common, and in that, too, I was lucky, since Josiane liked the galleries, perhaps because she lived in one, or because they protected her from cold and rain. (I met her early one winter, with premature snows our galleries and their world gaily ignored.) We got into the habit of taking walks when she had time, when someone—she didn't like to call him by his name —was content enough to let her enjoy herself with her friends for a while. We spoke little of that someone, after I had asked the inevitable questions, and she told the inevitable lies of all mercenary relationships; you took for granted that he was the boss, but he had the good taste not to make himself visible. I got to thinking it didn't annoy him when I kept Josiane company some nights. The Laurent threat lay heavier than ever upon the district after his new crime on the

Rue d'Aboukir, and the poor thing wouldn't have dared to stray from the Galerie Vivienne once night had fallen. It was enough to make one feel grateful to Laurent and the boss; someone else's fears helped me do the rounds of the arcades and cafés with Josiane, discovering that I could be a real friend to a girl with whom I had no deep relationship. We gradually began to realize, through silences, foolish things about that trusted friendship. Her room, for example, the clean little garret that for me had no other reality than being part of the gallery. In the beginning I had gone up for Josiane, and as I couldn't stay because I didn't have the money to pay for a whole night, and someone was waiting for a spotless rendition of accounts, I almost couldn't see what was around me, and much later, when I was about to fall asleep in my shabby room with its illustrated calendar and silver maté gourd as its only luxuries, I wondered about the garret, but couldn't picture it. I saw only Josiane, and that was enough to put me to sleep, as if I still held her in my arms. But with friendship came prerogatives, perhaps the boss's consent, and Josiane managed it many times so that I could spend the night with her, and her room began to fill the gaps of our dialogue, which wasn't always easy; each doll, each picture card, each ornament settled in my memory and helped me to live when it was time to go back to my room or to talk with my mother or Irma about the nation's politics or family sicknesses.

Later there were other things, and among them the vague figure of the one Josiane called the South American, but in the beginning everything seemed centered around the great terror of the district, nourished by what an imaginative newspaperman had called the Saga of Laurent the Strangler. If, in a given moment, I conjure up the image of Josiane, it is to see her enter the Rue des Jeûneurs café with me, settle down on the purple-felt bench, and exchange greetings with friends and regular customers, scattered words which immediately are Laurent, because down by the stock exchange all one talks about is Laurent, and I who have worked the whole day on end, who, between two sessions of quotations, have had to put up with the comments of colleagues and customers on Laurent's latest crime, wonder if that stupid nightmare will end someday, if things will go back to being as I imagine they were before Laurent, or if we will have to suffer his macabre amusements until the end of time. And the most irritating thing (I say to Josiane after ordering the grog we so much need after that cold and snow) is that we don't even know his name. They call him Laurent because a clairvoyant of the Clichy neighborhood has seen in her crystal ball how the murderer wrote his name with a bloody finger, and the newspapermen are careful not to go against the public's instinct. Josiane is no fool, but nobody could convince her that the murderer's name is not Laurent, and it's useless to fight against the eager terror fluttering in her blue eyes, which are now absently looking at a very tall and slightly stoop-shouldered young man, who has just come in and is leaning on the counter and not greeting anyone.

"It's possible," Josiane says, accepting some soothing thought that I must have invented without even thinking. "But meanwhile I have to go up to my room alone, and if the wind blows out the candle between floors . . . The very idea of getting stuck on the stairs in the dark, and that maybe . . ."

"You don't go up alone very often," I laugh.

"You can laugh, but there are bad nights, precisely when it's snowing or raining, and I have to come back at two in the morning . . ."

She continues her description of Laurent crouching on a landing, or still worse, waiting for her in her room which he has gotten into by means of a skeleton key. At the next table Kiki shivers bombastically and lets out little screams which multiply in the mirrors. We, the men, get a big kick out of these theatrical frights, which will help us protect our companions more prestigiously. It's a pleasure to smoke pipes in the café, at that hour when alcohol and tobacco begin to erase the fatigue of work, and the women compare their hats and boas or laugh at nothing; it's a pleasure to kiss Josiane, who has become so pensive looking at the man—almost a boy—whose back is turned to us, and who drinks his absinthe in little sips, leaning his elbow on the counter. It's curious, now that I think of it: with the first image of Josiane that comes to my mind, which is always Josiane on the café bench, a snowy, Laurent night, inevitably comes the one she called the South American, drinking his absinthe with his back to us. I called him the South American, too, because Josiane assured me that he was, and that she knew this through La Rousse, who had gone to bed with him or just about, and all that had happened before Josiane and La Rousse had a fight over corners or hours, which they now regretted with halfway words, because they had been very good friends. According to La Rousse, he had told her that he was South American, although he spoke without the slightest accent; he had told her that before going to bed with her, perhaps to make small talk while he finished untying his shoes.

"It's hard to believe, him almost a boy. . . . Doesn't he look like a schoolboy who's suddenly grown up? Well, you should hear what La Rousse says."

Josiane persisted in her habit of crossing and uncrossing her fingers every time she told an exciting story. She explained the South American's whim to me, nothing so extraordinary after all, La Rousse's flat refusal, the customer's self-possessed exit. I asked her if the South American had ever approached her. Well, no, because he probably knew that La Rousse and she were friends. He knew them well, he lived in the neighborhood, and when Josiane said that, I looked more carefully and saw him pay for his absinthe, throwing a coin into the little pewter dish while he slid over us—and it was as if we ceased to be there for an endless second—a both distant and curiously fixed expression, the face of someone who has immobilized himself in a moment of his dream and refuses to take the step that will return him to wakefulness. After all, an expression like that, although the boy was almost an adolescent and had very beautiful features, could easily lead one back to the recurrent nightmare of Laurent. I didn't lose a minute in suggesting this to Josiane.

"Laurent? Are you crazy? Why Laurent is . . ."

The thing is, nobody knew anything about Laurent, although Kiki and Albert helped us to keep weighing the possibilities to amuse ourselves. The whole theory fell to pieces when the café owner, who miraculously heard everything that was said in the café, reminded us that at least one thing was known about

Laurent: the great strength that enabled him to strangle his victims with one hand only. And that boy, come on . . . Yes, and it was late already and a good time to go home; I would be alone that night, because Josiane would spend it with someone who was already waiting for her in the garret, someone who had the key because he had the right to, and I accompanied her to the first landing so that she wouldn't get scared if the candle went out while she was walking up, and with a sudden great fatigue I watched her go, perhaps happy, although she would have said the opposite, and then I went out into the snowy, icy street and started walking in any direction, until at one point I found as always the road that would take me back to my neighborhood, among people who read the late-night edition of the newspapers or looked out of the trolley-car windows, as if there really were something to see at that hour and on those streets.

It wasn't always easy to get to the gallery district at the moment Josiane was free; so many times I had to wander alone through the arcades, a bit disappointed, until I began to feel that night, too, was my mistress. The moment they turned on the gaslights, things would come alive in our kingdom; the cafés were the stock exchange of idleness and content, you'd drink in the end of the day, the headlines, politics, the Prussians, Laurent, the horse races, in long gulps. I enjoyed having a drink here and another further on, leisurely watching for the moment when I'd spy Josiane's figure in some corner of the galleries or at some bar. If she already had company, a chosen signal would let me know when I could find her alone; other times she simply smiled, and I was left to devote my time to the galleries; those were the explorer's hours, and so I ventured into the farthest regions of the neighborhood, the Galerie Sainte-Foy, for example, and the remote Passage du Caire, but even though any of them attracted me more than the open streets (and there were so many—today it was the Passage des Princes, another time the Passage Verdeau, and so on to infinity), the end of a long tour, which I myself wouldn't have been able to reconstruct, always took me back to the Galerie Vivienne, not so much because of Josiane, although also for her, but for its protective gates, its ancient allegories, its shadows in the corner of the Passage des Petits-Pères, that different world where you didn't have to think about Irma and could live not by regular schedules, but by chance encounters and luck. With so little to hang on to, I can't calculate the time that passed before we casually talked about the South American again; once I thought I saw him coming out of the doorway on the Rue Saint-Marc, wrapped in one of those black student gowns they'd been wearing so much five years back, together with excessively tall top hats, and I was tempted to go and ask him about his origins. The thought of the cold anger with which I would have received an inquiry of that sort prevented me, but Josiane later considered that this had been foolish on my part, perhaps because the South American interested her in her own way, with something of professional offense and a lot of curiosity. She remembered that some nights back she thought she recognized him at a distance in the Galerie Vivienne, which he didn't seem to frequent, however.

"I don't like the way he looks at us," said Josiane. "Before it didn't matter, but ever since that time you talked about Laurent . . ."

"Josiane, when I made that joke we were with Kiki and Albert. Albert is a police informer, as you must know. You think he would let the opportunity go if the idea seemed reasonable to him? Laurent's head is worth a lot of money, dear."

"I don't like his eyes," Josiane insisted. "And besides, he doesn't look at people. He stares, but he doesn't look at you. If he ever comes over to me I'll run like the dickens, I swear to God."

"You're afraid of a boy. Or are all of us South Americans orangutans to you?"

You can already imagine how those dialogues would end. We'd go and have a grog at the café on the Rue des Jeûneurs, we'd wander around the galleries, the theaters on the boulevard, we'd go up to the garret, we'd have a great laugh. There were several weeks—it's so hard to be precise with happiness—when everything made us laugh. Even Badinguet's clumsiness and the fear of the war amused us. It's almost ridiculous to admit that something as disproportionately base as Laurent could crush our happiness, but that's how it was. Laurent killed another woman on the Rue Beauregard—so close, after all—and in the café it was like being at Mass, and Marthe, who had come racing in shouting the news ended in an explosion of hysterical tears which somehow helped us swallow the knot in our throats. That same night the police went through all of us with its finest comb, in every café and every hotel; Josiane went to her boss, and I let her go, knowing that she needed the supreme protection that smoothed away all cares. But since basically that kind of thing made me vaguely sad—the galleries weren't meant for that, shouldn't be for that—I began drinking with Kiki and then with La Rousse, who sought me out as the bridge she needed to make up with Josiane. People drank heartily at our café, and in that hot mist of voices and drink it seemed almost perfect that at midnight the South American sat at a table in the back and ordered his absinthe with that same beautiful and absent and moon-struck expression. At La Rousse's first intimation, I told her that I already knew, and that, after all, the boy wasn't blind and his tastes did not deserve such resentment; we even laughed at La Rousse's make-believe punches when Kiki designed to say that once she had been in his room. Before La Rousse could claw her with a predictable question, I wanted to know what that room was like. "Bah, what does the room matter?" La Rousse said disdainfully, but Kiki was already plunging into a garret on the Rue Notre-Dame-des-Victoires and, like a bad small-town magician, pulling out a gray cat, piles of scribbled papers, a piano which took up too much room, but above all papers, and finally the gray cat again, which, deep down, seemed to be Kiki's favorite memory.

I let her talk, looking all the time toward the table in the back and thinking that after all it would have been so natural to go over to the South American and say a few words to him in Spanish. I was about to do it, and now I'm only one of many who wonder why at some point they didn't do what they felt like doing. Instead, I remained with La Rousse and Kiki, smoking a new pipe and ordering another round of white wine; I don't quite remember what I felt at giving up my impulse, but it was something like prohibition, the feeling that if I defied it I would enter unsure territory. And still I think I did wrong; I was on the verge of an act that would have saved me. Saved me from what? I wonder. But precisely that: saved me from being able only to wonder about it today, and from having no other answer than tobacco smoke and this vague futile hope that follows me on the streets like a mangy dog.

> *Où sont-ils passés, les becs de gaz? Que*
> *sont-elles devenues, les vendeuses d'amour?*
> . . . . , VI, 1.

Little by little I had to convince myself that we had come into bad times and that while Laurent and the Prussian menace worried us that way, life in the galleries would never go back to being what it had been. My mother must have noticed I was depressed, because she advised me to take some tonic, and Irma's parents, who had a chalet on an island in the Paraná, invited me to spend some time there, resting and leading a healthy life. I asked for fifteen days vacation and left unwillingly for the island, enemies from the start with the sun and mosquitoes. The first Saturday, I made up any old pretext and returned to the city; I stumbled along streets where heels sank into the soft asphalt. Of that senseless vagrancy there remains a sudden delicious memory: As I entered the Güemes Arcade once again, the aroma of coffee suddenly enfolded me, its violence already almost forgotten in galleries where the coffee was weak and reheated. I drank two cups, without sugar, tasting and smelling at the same time, scalding myself and happy. All that came after, until the afternoon's end, smelled different—the humid downtown air was full of pockets of fragrance (I returned home on foot, I believe I had promised my mother to dine with her), and in each pocket of air the smells were more raw, more intense—yellow soap, coffee, black tobacco, printing ink, bitter maté, everything smelled pitilessly, and the sun and sky, too, were harder and more urgent. For some hours, I almost begrudgingly forgot the gallery district, but when I again crossed the Güemes Arcade (was it really at the time of the island? Perhaps I am confusing two moments of the same period, it hardly matters, really), it was fruitless to invoke the jolly slap of the coffee. Its smell seemed the same as always, and instead I recognized that sweetish, repugnant mixture of sawdust and stale beer that seem to ooze from the floors of downtown bars, but perhaps it was because, again, I wanted to find Josiane and I even trusted in the fact that the great terror and the snows had reached their end. I think it was in those days that I began to suspect that desire wasn't enough, as before, for things to revolve rhythmically and suggest some of the streets that led to the Galerie Vivienne, but it's also possible that I ended up giving in meekly to the chalet on the island so as not to make Irma sad, so she wouldn't suspect that my only true repose was elsewhere; until I couldn't stand it any longer and went back to the city and walked until I was exhausted, with my shirt sticking to my body, sitting in the bars drinking beer, waiting for I no longer knew what. And when, on leaving the last bar, I saw that I had only to turn the corner to enter my neighborhood, happiness and fatigue and a dark consciousness of failure became one, because it was enough to look into people's faces to realize that the great terror was far from over, it was enough to look into Josiane's eyes on her corner on the Rue d'Uzés and hear her grumble that the boss had decided to protect her personally from a possible attack; I remember that between two kisses I managed to get a glimpse of his figure in the hollow of a doorway, protecting himself from the sleet with a long gray cape.

Josiane was not the kind to resent absences, and I wonder if she was really aware of the passage of time. We returned arm in arm to the Galerie Vivienne, we went up to the garret, but later we realized we weren't happy as before and we vaguely attributed it to all that was upsetting the neighborhood; there would be war, it was inevitable, the men would have to join the ranks (she used these words solemnly, with an ignorant, delightful respect), the people were afraid and angry, the police had been unable to find Laurent. They consoled themselves by guillotining others—that very morning, for instance, they'd execute the poisoner of whom we'd spoken so much in the Rue des Jeûneurs café during the days of the trial, but the terror was still loose in the galleries and arcades; nothing had changed since the last time I saw Josiane, and it hadn't even stopped snowing.

As a consolation, we went for a walk, defying the cold, because Josiane had a coat that had to be admired on a series of corners and doorways where her friends were waiting for customers, blowing on their fingers or sticking their hands into their fur muffs. Seldom had we taken such a long walk along the boulevards, and I ended up suspecting that, above all, we were sensitive to the protection of the lighted show windows; venturing into any of the nearby streets (because Liliane had to see the coat, too, and further on Francine) sank us further and further into alarm, until the coat had been sufficiently exhibited, and I suggested our café, and we ran along the Rue de Croissant until turning the corner and taking refuge in warmth and among our friends. Luckily for all, the idea of war at that hour was dim in people's memories. Nobody thought of repeating the obscene refrains against the Prussians, everything was so good with the full glasses and the brazier's heat and only we, the owner's friends, were left, yes, the same group as always and the good news that La Rousse had apologized to Josiane and that they had made up with kisses and tears and even gifts. It all had a garland quality (but garlands can be funereal, I understood afterward) and that's why, with the snow and Laurent outside, we stayed as long as we could in the café and found out at midnight that it was the owner's fiftieth anniversary of working behind the same counter, and this had to be celebrated. One flower intertwined with the next, and bottles filled the tables, because now the owner was treating everybody, and you couldn't slight such friendship and such dedication to work, and around three thirty in the morning Kiki, completely drunk, ended up singing the best airs of the operettas of the day, while Josiane and La Rousse cried in each other's arms out of happiness and absinthe, and Albert, almost without giving it importance, twined another flower in the garland and suggested ending the night at La Roquette, where they would guillotine the prisoner at six o'clock sharp, and the owner, extremely moved, realized that the party's end was like the apotheosis of fifty years of honorable work and he insisted,

embracing us all and telling us about his dead wife in Languedoc, upon renting
two hackney coaches for the expedition.

    After that, more wine followed, the evocation of several mothers and
outstanding childhood episodes, and an onion soup that Josiane and La Rousse
raised to the sublime in the kitchen, while Albert, the owner, and I swore eternal
friendship and death to the Prussians. The soup and cheeses must have drowned
such vehemence, because we were all almost quiet and even uncomfortable when
the moment came to close the café with an endless noise of bars and chains, and
to climb into the hackney coaches where all the cold in the world seemed to be
waiting for us. It would have been better for us to travel together to keep warm,
but the owner had humanitarian principles when it came to horses, and he got
into the first carriage with La Rousse and Albert, while he entrusted me with Kiki
and Josiane, who, he said, were like daughters to him. After these words had been
toasted to the full with the coach drivers, the spirit returned to our bodies as we
rode toward Popincourt amid mock racing, shouts of encouragement, and a rain
of false whippings. The owner insisted upon getting off at a certain distance,
citing reasons of discretion which I didn't understand, and arm in arm, so as not
to slip on the frozen snow, we walked up the Rue de la Roquette, vaguely lit by
occasional gaslight, among moving shadows which suddenly materialized into top
hats, trotting coaches, and groups of cloaked figures gathering finally in front of
a wide end of the street, beneath the other taller and blacker shadow of the jail.
A secret world touched elbows, passed bottles from hand to hand, repeated a joke
that ran through boisterous laughter and choked shrieks, and there were also
sudden silences and faces lit for a moment by a match, while we kept pushing
ahead, being careful not to separate, as if each knew that only the will of the group
could pardon its presence in that place. The machine was there on its five stone
bases, and the whole apparatus of justice waited motionless in the brief space
between it and the square body of soldiers with their rifles resting on the ground
and fixed bayonets. Josiane stuck her nails into my arm and trembled in such a
way that I spoke of taking her to a café, but there were no cafés in sight, and
she insisted upon staying. Hanging on me and Albert, she jumped from time to
time to get a better view of the machine, stuck her nails in me again, and finally
made me stoop my head until her lips found my mouth and bit me hysterically,
murmuring words I'd seldom heard her say and which boosted my pride, as if
for a moment I had been the boss. But of all of us the only real *aficionado* was
Albert; smoking a cigar, he killed the minutes comparing ceremonies, imagining
the condemned man's final behavior, the stages which at that moment were
taking place inside the prison and which he knew in detail for reasons he didn't
say. At first, I listened eagerly to learn about each and every part of the liturgy,
until slowly, as from beyond him and Josiane and the celebration of the anniversary, something like abandon gradually came over me, the indefinable feeling that
this shouldn't happen in this way, that something was threatening the world of
the galleries and arcades in me, or still worse, that my happiness in that world
had been a deceptive prelude, a snare of flowers, as if one of the plaster figures
had offered me a false garland (and I had thought that night how things were

woven like the flowers on a garland), to little by little fall back to Laurent, to turn away from the innocent intoxication of the Galerie Vivienne and Josiane's garret, slowly moving toward the great terror, the snow, the inevitable war, the apotheosis of the owner's fifty years, the frozen-stiff hackney coaches of dawn, the tense arm of Josiane, who swore she wouldn't look and who was already seeking a place on my chest to hide her face in the final moment. It seemed (and in that moment the gates began to open, and you could hear the commanding voice of the officer of the guard) that somehow this was an end—I wasn't sure of what, because after all I would keep on living, working in the stock market, occasionally seeing Josiane, Albert, and Kiki, who was now beating my shoulder hysterically, and although I didn't want to take my eyes off the gates that were just opening, I had to give her some attention for a moment, and following her at once surprised and mocking stare, I glimpsed almost beside the owner the slightly bent figure of the South American in a black student gown, and curiously I thought that, too, entered into the garland somehow, and it was a little as if a hand had just woven in the flower that would close it before daybreak. And then I didn't think any more, because Josiane pressed against me moaning, and in the shadow which the two gaslights beside the door wavered without driving it away, the white spot of a shirt appeared, floating between two black figures, appearing and disappearing each time a third bulky shadow bent over it with the gestures of a person embracing or advising or saying something in someone's ear or giving him something to kiss, until it moved to one side, and the white spot became clearer, closer, framed by a group of people in top hats and black coats, and there was a sort of accelerated magic trick, an abduction of the white spot by two figures, which, until that moment, had seemed to form part of the machine, a motion of pulling from someone's shoulders a now unnecessary coat, a hurried movement forward, someone's muffled outcry, maybe Josiane's, convulsing against me, maybe from the white spot, which seemed to slide under the framework, where something was unchained with an almost simultaneous cracking and commotion. I thought that Josiane was going to faint; all the weight of her body slipped down mine as the other body must have been slipping toward nothingness, and I stooped to hold her up while an enormous knot of throats unwound in a Mass finale, with the organ resounding on high (but it was a horse that neighed on smelling blood), and the ebbing crowd pushed us amid the military shouting of orders. Over Josiane's hat—she was now crying mercifully against my stomach—I had a glimpse of the excited café owner, Albert, in his glory, and the profile of the South American lost in the imperfect contemplation of the machine, which soldiers' backs and overzealous craftsmen of justice occasionally revealed, in lightning bolts of shadow between arms and overcoats and a general eagerness to move on in search of hot wine and sleep, like ourselves later piling into a coach to go back, remarking on what each thought he had seen, which was not the same, was never the same, and that's why it was worth more, because between the Rue de la Roquette and the stock-exchange district there was time to reconstruct the ceremony, discuss it, catch yourself at contradictions, brag about sharper sight or steadier nerves to the last-minute admiration of our timid companions.

*   *   *

It was not at all strange that in those days my mother found me worse and outspokenly complained of this puzzling indifference which made my poor fiancée suffer and would end up by depriving me of my deceased father's friends' protection, thanks to which I was making my way in stock-exchange circles. The only answer to such words was silence, and to come home a few days later with a new plant or a discount coupon for skeins of wool. Irma was more understanding. She must simply have counted on marriage to one day bring me back to bureaucratic normality, and in those last times I was on the verge of agreeing with her, but it was impossible for me to give up the hope that the great terror would come to its end in the gallery district and that going home would no longer seem an escape, a need for protection which would disappear as soon as my mother would look at me sighing or Irma would serve me coffee with the fiancée spider smile. We were then under military dictatorship in Argentina, one more of the endless series, but the people were excited above all about the imminent outcome of the world war, and almost every day they had demonstrations downtown to celebrate the Allied advance and the liberation of the European capitals, while the police charged against students and women, stores hurriedly lowered their metal curtains, and I, incorporated by the force of things into some group standing in front of the bulletin boards of *La Prensa,* wondered how much longer I could stand poor Irma's inevitable smile and the dampness that soaked my shirt between sessions of quotations. I began to feel that the gallery district was no longer the limit of a desire, as before, when it was enough to walk down any street for everything to revolve softly on any corner, so that I'd effortlessly reach the Place des Victoires, where it was so pleasing to browse around the side streets with their dusty stores and entranceways and, at the most propitious hour, enter the Galerie Vivienne in search of Josiane, unless I'd whimsically prefer to first take in the Passage des Panoramas or the Passage des Princes and return by way of a slightly perverse detour around the stock exchange. Now, instead, without even the consolation of recognizing, as on that morning, the fierce smell of coffee in the Güemes Arcade (it smelled of sawdust, of lye), I began to admit from way back that the gallery district was no longer the port of repose, although I still believed in the possibility of breaking away from my work and Irma, of effortlessly finding Josiane's corner. The desire to return was constantly alluring me; in front of the newspapers' bulletin boards, with my friends, at home in the patio, especially at dusk, when there they'd be turning on the gaslights. But something made me stay with my mother and Irma, a dark certainty that they would not wait for me as before in the gallery district, that the great terror was stronger. I'd walk into the banks and places of business like an automaton, tolerating my daily obligation to buy and sell stocks, listening to the hoofs of police horses charging against the people who were celebrating the Allied victories, and so little did I now believe that I could free myself from all this that when I got to the gallery district I was almost afraid. I felt like a stranger and different than ever before, I took refuge in a doorway and let people and time pass, forced for the first time to accept bit by bit all that had seemed to be mine before—streets and vehicles, clothes and gloves, snow in the patios, and voices in the stores. Until again it was wonderment; it was finding Josiane in the Galerie Colbert and finding out between kisses and leaps that Laurent no longer was, that the whole neighborhood had celebrated the nightmare's end night after night, and everybody had asked for me and a good thing that Laurent finally . . . but where had I been that I didn't know anything about it, and so many things, and so many kisses. Never had I wanted her more and never did we love each other better beneath the ceiling of her room that my hand could touch from the bed. The caresses, the gossip, the delicious inventory of the days, while twilight gradually came over the room. Laurent? A curly-haired Marseillais, a miserable coward who had barricaded himself in the loft of the house, where he had just killed another woman, and desperately had begged for mercy while the police knocked the door down. And his name was Paul, the monster, imagine that, and he had just killed his ninth victim, and they had dragged him to the police van while the whole force of the second district halfheartedly protected him from a crowd that would have torn him to shreds. Josiane already had time to get used to it, to bury Laurent in her memory, which seldom retained images, but for me it was too much, and I couldn't believe it until her joy finally convinced me that there really would be no more Laurent, that we could wander again through the arcades and streets without distrusting doorways. We would have to go out and celebrate the Liberation together, and as it was not snowing now, Josiane wanted to go to the Palais-Royal Rotunda, which we had never frequented in the times of Laurent. I promised myself, while we went singing down the Rue des Petits Champs, that that same night I would take Josiane to the boulevard cabarets, and that we would finish the evening in our café, where, with the help of white wine, I would make all forgive me for such ingratitude and absence.

For a few hours, I drank down the happy time of the galleries, and I became convinced that the end of the great terror would make me healthy and happy again under my sky of stucco and garlands; dancing with Josiane in the Rotunda, I threw off the last oppression of that uncertain interval, I was born again into my better life, so far from Irma's drawing room, the patio at home, the deficient consolation of the Güemes Arcade. Not even later, when, chatting about so many happy things with Kiki and Josiane and the café owner, I learned about the last of the South American, not even then did I suspect that I was living on borrowed time, a last grace; besides, they talked about the South American with a mocking indifference, as if about any of the neighborhood's oddballs, who managed to fill a gap in a conversation where soon more exciting subjects would be born; that the South American had just died in a hotel room was scarcely anything more than some information in passing, and Kiki was already discussing the parties being prepared in a cabaret on La Butte, and it was hard work interrupting her, asking for some detail, hardly knowing why I asked. Through Kiki, I found out some minor things—the South American's name, which after all was a French name, and which I forgot immediately, his sudden illness on the Rue du Faubourg Montmartre, where Kiki had a friend who had told her; his loneliness, the one measly taper burning on the shelves full of books and papers, the gray cat that her friend had picked up, the anger of the hotel manager, to whom they did those things precisely when he was expecting a visit from his in-laws, the anonymous burial, oblivion, the parties in the cabaret on La Butte, the arrest of Paul the Marseillais, the insolence of the Prussians, for whom the time was ripe to give them a lesson they deserved. And out of all that I separated, like one who pulls two dry flowers off a garland, the two deaths which somehow seemed in my eyes symmetrical, the South American's and Laurent's, the one in his hotel room, the other dissolving into nothingness to yield his place to Paul the Marseillais, and they were almost the same death, something erased forever in the neighborhood's memory. That night, I could still believe that everything would continue as before the great terror, and Josiane was again mine in her garret, and when saying goodnight we promised each other parties and excursions when summer arrived. But it was freezing in the streets, and the news of the war required my presence at the stock exchange at nine in the morning; with an effort which I then thought commendable, I refused to think about my reconquered heaven, and after working till dizzy, I lunched with my mother and thanked her for finding me in better form. I spent that week immersed in stock-exchange struggles with no time for anything, running home to take a shower and changing one soaked shirt for another, which in a while was worse. The bomb fell on Hiroshima, and all was confusion among my customers, I had to wage a long battle to save the most committed stocks and to find an advisable direction in that world where each day was a new Nazi defeat and the dictatorship's angry, futile reaction against the irretrievable. When the Germans surrendered, and the people filled the streets of Buenos Aires, I thought I could take a rest, but each morning new problems awaited me: In those weeks, I married Irma after my mother was on the verge of a heart attack, which the whole family blamed me for, perhaps rightly so. Time and again, I wondered why, if the great terror had ended in the gallery district, the moment never came for me to meet Josiane and again take walks beneath our plaster heaven. I suppose work and family obligations contributed to keeping me from it, and I only know that at odd moments I would take a walk along the Güemes Arcade as a consolation, looking vaguely up, drinking coffee and thinking, each time with less conviction, of the afternoons when I had only to wander a while, without fixed destination, to get to my neighborhood and meet up with Josiane on some corner of twilight. I have never wanted to admit that the garland was closed definitively and that I would not meet Josiane again in the arcades and on the boulevards. Some days I get to thinking about the South American, and in that halfhearted rumination I invent a sort of consolation, as if he had killed Laurent and myself with his own death; sensibly I tell myself no, I'm exaggerating, any day now I'll again venture into the gallery district and find Josiane surprised by my long absence. And between one thing and another I stay home drinking maté, listening to Irma, who's expecting in December, and wonder, not too enthusiastically, if at election time I'll vote for Perón or for Tamborini, if I'll vote none of the above and simply stay home drinking maté and looking at Irma and the plants in the patio.

5

ERNESTO SABATO

Although Sabato has achieved the kind of popular success which has consistently eluded Bioy Casares (selection 3) and even Cortázar (4), he has failed to attain the critical reputation they enjoy. Sabato is a more conventional type of novelist, a direct heir of Dostoevsky and Dickens; there is much in his writing that derives from a nineteenth-century concept of the novel as a web of suspenseful plot, strong characterizations, and long moral speeches. All this may seem terribly old-fashioned today, but it still attracts readers. His most famous work, *On Heroes and Tombs,* is one of the most popular contemporary novels in Latin America.

Born in Argentina in 1911, Sabato (like Parra) had scientific training. He went to Paris in the late thirties to study under the Joliot-Curies, but then and there came into contact with surrealism and (unlike Parra) deserted his scientific vocation forever. His first essays were printed in *Sur,* the leading Argentine literary magazine. They were short, brilliant pieces that showed Sabato as a devoted reader of Borges. In 1948 he published his first novel, *The Tunnel,* the confession of a painter who has murdered his mistress. By then, Sabato had abandoned Borges's ironical and intellectual style to follow the then very popular model of the existentialist novel. A kind of Camusian impassivity permeated the story. His second novel, *On Heroes and Tombs,* was not published until 1961. In contrast with the spareness of *The Tunnel,* this was a big, sprawling book that attempted to capture not only today's Argentina but also some of the flavor of its murderous past. A sort of *Mystères de Buenos Aires,* the novel dwelt upon brutal assassination and incest, irredeemable love and madness. The historical episode of the killing of General Lavalle served as an emblem of the whole bloody plot. The novel was episodic and also derivative. Many things already explored more brilliantly by Roberto Arlt and Borges, by Bioy Casares and Onetti, had been put together in a nightmarish, obsessive way. Some chapters were excellent, others survived only through their links with the whole corpus of the novel. One of the most haunting passages, a "Report on the Blind," gives the key to Sabato's power as a narrator. Its force depends on a maniacal concentration on some issues, on the discovery that haunting the reader is a sure way to making him an accomplice in the writing of the book. The gnostic theories introduced at the end of the report had already been explored (in a more sophisticated way) by Borges in some of his stories ("Three Versions of Judas," for instance), but here Sabato uses them mainly to justify the madness of the protagonist.

Sabato's third novel, *Abbadon, the Exterminating Angel* (1974), com-

pletes the trilogy. It is more about the writing of the previous novel and about
the author himself than about his very secondary fictional characters. Using the
book as a mirror, Sabato exposes his own obsessions and creates a powerful if
highly distorted self-portrait.

Report on the Blind

From On Heroes and Tombs, *translated by Stuart M. Gross, in*
Tri-Quarterly, *No. 13–14 (Evanston, Ill.: Northwestern University,
Fall–Winter 1968–69), pp. 95–105.*

Oh, gods of the night!
Oh, gods of darkness, incest and crime,
    melancholy and suicide!
Oh, gods of rats and caverns,
    bats and cockroaches!
Oh, violent, inscrutable gods
    of sleep and death!

When did this begin that now is going to end with my assassination?
This fierce lucidity that I now have is like a beacon and I can direct its intense
beam toward vast regions of my memory: I see faces, rats in a granary, streets
in Buenos Aires or Algiers, prostitutes and sailors; I turn the beam and see more
distant things: a fountain on our country manor, a stifling siesta, birds, and eyes
that I stick nails into. Perhaps there, but who knows: it may be much further
back, in the most remote periods of my earliest infancy. I don't know. Besides,
what does it matter?

I remember perfectly, on the other hand, the beginnings of my system-
atic investigation (the other, that I was unaware of, perhaps the more profound,
what do I know about it?). It was one summer day in 1947 as I passed by Mayo
Plaza in San Martin Street on the sidewalk in front of City Hall. I was going along
thinking when, suddenly, I heard a little bell, a little bell as if somebody were
trying to awaken me from a millennial sleep. I kept walking as I listened to the
little bell that was trying to penetrate the deepest part of my consciousness; I
heard it but I wasn't listening to it. Until suddenly that faint but penetrating and
obsessive sound seemed to reach some sensitive zone of my being, where the skin
of one's self is very thin and abnormally sensitive; and I woke up frightened, as
if facing a sudden perverse danger, as if in the darkness my hands had touched
the cold skin of a snake. In front of me, staring at me fixedly through her hard,
enigmatic face, I saw the blind woman that hawks her wares there. She had

stopped ringing her little bell, as if she had been sounding it for me only, to awaken me from my senseless dreaming, to inform me that my former existence had ended, like a stupid preparatory stage, and that now I must face reality. We remained thus for those moments that do not form a part of time but which give access to eternity; she, motionless, with her abstract face turned toward me, and I, paralyzed, as by an infernal but frigid apparition. Then my consciousness again entered the torrent of time and I fled.

That is how the final stage of my existence began.

From that day on I realized that it wasn't possible to let a single instant more slip by and that I myself must begin the exploration of that shadowy universe.

Several months passed; one day that fall the second decisive encounter occurred. My investigation was in full progress, but my work was delayed by an inexplicable listlessness, which I now think was an insidious fear of the unknown.

I kept watching and studying the blind just the same.

I had always been concerned about them, and on several occasions I had had discussions about their origin, hierarchy, way of life, and zoological status. At that time I was just beginning to piece together my hypothesis about the cold skin, and I had already received insults verbally and by mail from members of societies linked to the world of the blind. With the efficacy, rapidity, and mysterious sources of information that secret societies and sects always have —those societies and sects which invisibly penetrate society and which, without its being known or suspected, continually watch us, follow us, decide our destiny, our failure, and even our death. This is especially true of the blind, who, to the greater misfortune of the unwitting, have normal men and women at their service, partly deceived by the Organization, partly as a result of sentimental, demagogic propaganda, and, finally, to a large extent, through fear of physical and metaphysical torments that it is said are in store for those who dare pry into their secrets. Torments which, I might say in passing, I then felt I had already suffered in part, and the conviction that I would go on receiving them in a more and more subtle and frightful form, doubtless because of my pride, only accentuated my indignation and my determination to carry out my investigations to the very end.

If I were a little smarter, perhaps I could boast of having confirmed through these investigations the hypothesis that I had imagined about the world of the blind since I was a boy, for it was the nightmares and hallucinations of my infancy that brought me my first revelation. Then, as I grew up, my prejudice kept mounting against those usurpers—those moral blackmailers who abound underground because of that in them which links them to the cold-blooded, slipper-skinned animals that live in caves, caverns, cellars, old passageways, drain-pipes, sewers, catch basins, deep crevices, abandoned dripping mines; and, in the case of some, the most powerful, in enormous subterranean caves, sometimes hundreds of yards deep, as can be deduced from unmistakable but hesitant reports by cavern hunters and treasure seekers, sufficiently clear, however, to those familiar with the threats that weigh over those who try to violate the great secret.

Before, when I was younger and less mistrustful, although I was convinced of my theory I hesitated to verify it or even suggest it, because those sentimental prejudices which tyrannize over our emotions kept me from penetrating the defenses that the sect has erected, all the more impenetrable because of their subtlety and invisibility, aided by truisms learned in school and newspapers, respected by the government and the police, propagated by charities, women, and teachers. Those defenses keep us from getting to those shadowy regions where the commonplaces begin to yield more and more, and the truth begins to be suspected.

Many years had to pass for me to be able to penetrate the exterior defenses. And thus, gradually, with a strength as great as it was paradoxical, like the one that in nightmares drives us toward horror, I went on into the forbidden regions where metaphysical obscurity begins to reign, glimpsing here and there, at first, instinctively, like fugitive, equivocal phantoms, then with greater and terrifying precision, a whole world of abominable beings.

Later I will tell you how I achieved that fearful privilege and how after years of search and threats I succeeded in entering the area where a multitude of beings mills around, among which mere blind people are scarcely noticeable.

II

I remember very well that June 14th, a cold rainy day. I was observing the behavior of a blind man who was working the subway to Palermo, a rather short, stocky man, extremely vigorous and very crude, who was running through the cars with ill-restrained violence, forcing pencils on a crowded mass of crushed people. The blind man belligerently pushes his way through the crowd with one hand held out to receive the tributes that, with sacred distrust, the wretched office workers offer to him, while in the other he holds the symbolic pencils—for it is impossible for anyone to live from the sale of such wares, since some people need a couple pencils once a year or even once a month, but nobody, madman or millionaire, buys a dozen a day. So, as is logical and everyone will agree, the pencils are merely a front, something like the blind man's insignia, a kind of privateering commission which distinguishes the blind from other mortals, as does their famous white cane.

I was observing, then, the course of events, ready to follow that individual in order to confirm my theory once and for all. I made innumerable trips between Mayo Plaza and Palermo, trying to hide my presence at the terminals because I was desperately afraid of awakening the sect's suspicions and being turned in as a pickpocket or some other stupid thing just when my days were incalculably valuable. With certain precautions, then, I maintained a close contact with the blind man, and when finally we made the last trip at one thirty, precisely on that June 14th, I was prepared to follow the man to his lair.

In the Mayo Plaza terminal, before the train made its last trip to Palermo, the blind man got off and headed for the exit to San Martin Street.

We began to walk along the street toward Cagallo.

At the corner he turned toward the Bajo.

I had to redouble my precautions, for that lonely winter night the blind man and I were alone on the street, or almost. So I followed him at a safe distance, remembering how well they hear and their instinct that warns them of any danger which threatens their secrets.

The silence and loneliness had that impressive force that they always have in the Banking Quarter, a section much more lonely at night than any other, probably in contrast with the daytime bustle in those streets, the noise, the recurrent confusion, the urgency, the huge crowd that throngs there during office hours. But also, almost surely, because of the sacred solitude that reigns there when Money is quiet. Once the last employees and managers have left, when that preposterous, exhausting task has ended in which a poor devil who receives five thousand pesos monthly manages five million and in which great crowds deposit with infinite precautions pieces of paper with magic properties which other crowds withdraw with similar precautions. A magic, fantastic process, for although they, the believers, think they are practical, realistic people, they accept that dirty old paper where, with great attention, one can make out a kind of absurd promise by virtue of which a man who does not even sign with his own hand promises, in the name of the State, to give I don't know what to the believer in exchange for the piece of paper. The curious thing is that this promise satisfies this individual, for nobody, as far as I know, has ever demanded that the promise be fulfilled; and still more surprising, in place of those dirty pieces of paper usually another cleaner but still more foolish piece is handed back where another man promises that, in exchange for that piece, the believer will be handed *n* number of said dirty old pieces of paper—something like madness squared. And everything representing Something that nobody has ever seen which they say is deposited Somewhere, especially in the United States in vaults of Steel. To begin with, words like *credits* and *fiduciary* indicate that all this is like a religion.

I was saying, then, that these districts, when stripped of the mad multitude of believers at nighttime, are the most deserted of all, for no one lives there at night, nor could he, because of the tremendous solitude of the gigantic temple halls and the great vaults which guard the incredible treasures. Meanwhile (with pills and drugs), the powerful men who control this magic, sleep fitfully harassed by nightmares of financial disasters. Also, for the obvious reason that in these quarters there is no food, nothing that permits the permanent life of human beings, or even that of rats or cockroaches, because of the extreme cleanliness that exists in these redoubts of nothingness, where all is symbolic and papery at best, and those bits of paper, even though they could represent a certain amount of food for moths and other small insects, are guarded in formidable steel enclosures, invulnerable to any race of living things.

Through the total silence, then, that rules in the Banking Quarter, I followed the blind man along Cagallo toward the Bajo. His steps resounded softly, and momentarily took on a more secret and perverse personality.

We went down to Leandro Alem and, after crossing the avenue, headed for the port district.

I redoubled my caution; at moments I thought the blind man could hear my steps and even my nervous breathing.

Now the man was walking with a confidence that seemed terrifying to me, for I discounted the trivial idea that he might not really be blind.

But what astonished me and accentuated my fear was that he turned again toward the left, toward Luna Park. I say it frightened me because it wasn't logical, since, if this had been his plan from the beginning, there was no reason why after crossing the avenue he should have gone off to the right. Since the supposition that he had lost his way was completely inadmissible, taking into account the surety and rapidity with which he moved, the (fearful) hypothesis remained that he had noticed my pursuit, and that he was attempting to throw me off the track. Or, what was infinitely worse, was trying to lead me into a trap.

Nevertheless, the same tendency that induces us to lean out over an abyss led me after the blind man with more and more determination. So, now almost running (it would have been grotesque if it hadn't been dark), an individual with a white cane and a pocketful of pencils was being pursued silently but frantically by another individual, first along Bouchard Street toward the north and then, when the Luna Park building ended, to the right as if to go down to the port district.

I lost sight of him then because, naturally, I was following him about half a block behind.

I hurried desperately, afraid of losing a part of the secret when I almost had it in my hands (as I then thought).

I reached the corner almost running, and turned quickly to the right, just as he had done.

What consternation! The blind man was against the wall, excited, obviously waiting. I couldn't avoid passing in front of him. He grabbed me by the arm with superhuman strength. I felt his breath on my face. The light was very dim and I could hardly make out his expression, but his whole attitude, his panting, his arm which squeezed me like a pincer, his voice—all showed rancor and merciless indignation.

"You've been following me!" he exclaimed in a whisper that was like a shout.

Nauseated—I felt his breath on my face and smelled his moist skin—and frightened, I mumbled monosyllables, I denied it madly and desperately; I said, "Sir, you are wrong," almost fainting from nausea and revulsion.

How could I have given myself away? At what moment? How? It was impossible to admit that with the normal resources of an ordinary human being he could have noted my pursuit. What? Could it be his accomplices—the invisible collaborators that the sect has planted everywhere: maids, women teachers, respectable ladies, librarians, streetcar guards? Who knows? But in this way that morning I confirmed one of my intuitions about the sect.

I thought all this over in a daze while I struggled to free myself from his claws.

I ran away as soon as I could, and for a long time I didn't get up my courage to continue the inquiry. Not only because of fear—fear that I felt to an intolerable extent—but intentionally, for I imagined that nocturnal episode might have set in motion the closest and most dangerous watch over me. I would have to wait months and perhaps years; I would have to throw them off the track; I would have to make them believe that robbery had been the only object of the chase.

After three years another event led me to pick up the track again and finally I succeeded in entering the redoubt of the blind, of those persons that society labels *Non Videntes,* partly because of common sentimentality, but also, almost surely, as a result of that fear which induces many religious sects never to use the name of God.

III

There is a fundamental difference between persons who have lost their sight through disease or accident and those born blind. To this difference I owe my finally having penetrated the redoubt, although I may not have entered their most secret caverns where the great, unknown hierarchs govern the Sect and therefore the World. From that sort of vantage point I was barely able to obtain news, always deceptive and ambiguous, about those monsters and the means they use to dominate the entire universe, I did find out in this way that they achieve and maintain that hegemony, apart from the simple use of ordinary sentimentalism, through anonymous letters, intrigues, spreading epidemics, the control of dreams and nightmares, somnambulism and drugs. It is enough to mention the marijuana and heroin traffic in U.S. secondary schools, where they corrupt eleven- and twelve-year-olds in order to have them at their absolute and unconditional service. The investigation ended, of course, where it really should have begun— at the threshold of the inviolable. As for domination through dreams, nightmares, and black magic, it isn't even worth the trouble to point out that the Sect has at its service for this purpose the whole army of clairvoyants, neighborhood witches, medicine men, faith healers, fortunetellers, and spiritualists. Most of them, the majority, are mere humbugs, but others have authentic powers under the appearance of a certain charlatanism in order to dominate better the world that surrounds them.

If, as they say, God has power over heaven, the Sect has domination over earth and flesh. I don't know whether, in the end, this organization has to give an accounting, early or late, to what might be called the Luminous Power; but, meanwhile, it is obvious that the universe is under their absolute power, the power of life and death which is exercised by plague or revolution, sickness or torture, deceit or false compassion, mystification or anonymous letters, naïve young teachers, and inquisitors.

I am not a theologian nor am I ready to believe that these infernal powers may be explained by any twisted Theodicy. In any event that would be theory or hope. The other, what I have seen and suffered, those are *facts*.

But let's get back to the differences.

On the other hand, let's not. There is still a lot to say about infernal powers, because some credulous person may think that it's a question of a simple metaphor, not of crude reality. The problem of evil always preoccupied me when, since I was very small, I used to put myself beside an anthill armed with a hammer and to start killing insects without rhyme or reason. Panic spread through the survivors who ran aimlessly. Then I hosed them down, a flood. I could imagine the scene inside, the emergency measures, the running, the commands and countermands to save caches of food, eggs, the security of the queens, etc. Finally, with a shovel I upset everything, made big holes, hunted for tunnels, and destroyed frantically, a general catastrophe. Afterward I began to cavil at the general meaning of existence, and to think of our own floods and earthquakes. Thus I kept elaborating a series of theories, for the idea that we were governed by an omnipotent, omniscient, and kind God seemed so contradictory to me that I didn't even believe it could be taken seriously. When I reached the epoch of the band of attackers, I'had already worked out the following possibilities:

1. God does not exist.
2. God exists and is a louse.
3. God exists, but sometimes sleeps—his nightmares are our existence.
4. God exists, but has attacks of madness—those attacks are our existence.
5. God is not omnipresent; he cannot be everywhere—in other worlds? —in other things?
6. God is a poor devil with problems too great for his strength. He struggles with material like an artist with his work. Sometimes, at some moment he gets to be a Goya, but generally he is a fiasco.
7. God was defeated before History by the Prince of Shadows, and, defeated and converted into the supposed devil, he is doubly disparaged, since the calamitous universe is attributed to him.

I didn't invent all these possibilities, although then I believed them. But later I found out that men had been strongly convinced of some of them, especially the hypothesis of the Devil Triumphant. For more than a thousand years courageous, clear-thinking men had to face death and torture for having unveiled the secret. They were dispersed and annihilated, since, as is to be expected, the forces which dominate the world aren't going to balk at trifles when they are willing to do what they do in general. So, poor devils or geniuses, they were tormented alike, burned by the Inquisition, hanged, whole peoples decimated and scattered. From China to Spain the state religions, Christian or Zoroastrian, swept the world clean of any attempt at revelation. And it can be said that in a certain way they achieved their objective. For although some of the sects couldn't be annihilated, they were converted in their turn into sources of falsehood, as happened to the Mohammedans. Let's examine the process: according to the gnostics, the perceptible world was created by a demon called Jehovah. For a long time the Supreme Deity lets him freely run the world, but finally He sends his son to live temporarily in the body of Jesus, in order to free the world in this way from the false teachings of Moses. Now then, Mohammed thought, like some of those gnostics, that Jesus was an ordinary human being, that the Son of God had descended to him at baptism and abandoned him at the Passion, since, otherwise, the famous cry "Oh God, my God, why hast thou forsaken me?" would be inexplicable. So when the Romans and Jews ridicule Jesus, they are ridiculing a kind of phantom. But the serious thing is—and it happens to other rebel sects in a more or less similar manner—that the mystification has not been cleared up but fortified. Because, for the Christian sects which maintain that Jehovah was the Devil and that a new era begins with Jesus, as well as for the Mohammedans, if the Prince of Shadows reigned until Jesus (or until Mohammed), now, on the other hand, defeated, he has returned to Hell. As is understood, this is double mystification—when the big Lie weakens, these poor devils reinforce it.

My conclusion is obvious—the Prince of Shadows keeps on governing. And that government is carried out through the Sacred Sect of the Blind. It is all so clear that I would almost begin laughing if I were not possessed by terror.

6

CARLOS MARTÍNEZ MORENO

A political moralist, the Uruguayan Carlos Martínez Moreno is more concerned with the national destiny of his characters than with the structure of his narratives; he devotes more space to final judgment on their actions than to the complexities of writing. His style is slightly forensic; his aim, to expose the underlying fabric of Uruguayan society hidden beneath the layers of decorous rationalizations and theories. But he is not indifferent to modern techniques, and in some of his books he has used silent monologue and complex time structures to re-create the anguished quest of his characters.

Martínez Moreno was born in one of the oldest towns in Uruguay in 1917 and has spent almost all his life in Montevideo. He was educated at the National University, became a lawyer specializing in criminal cases, and has also worked as a journalist since the early forties, managing to cover with authority such diverse fields as literary and dramatic criticism and current affairs. He belongs to the Generation of '45: a brilliant group of writers that came to the fore in Uruguayan literature after Onetti (see Part Four, 5) had achieved the first breakthrough.

Martínez Moreno has published five volumes of short stories and five long novels. The first, *The Wall* (1963), was a timely account of the revolutionary Cuba of 1959 as seen through the eyes of a law-minded Uruguayan journalist. If it failed as a novel, it was excellent as reporting. The two next novels (*The Other Half*, 1966; *With the First Signs of Dawn*, 1968) were more exclusively concerned with the private passions of their characters. The last two of his novels published to date (*Coca*, 1971; *Earth in the Mouth*, 1974) make use of his legal expertise. *Coca* is about the drug traffic in South America and follows very closely the outlines of a famous real-life case. The second novel is more Dostoevskian: a petty murder among derelicts is explored very thoroughly through the consciousness of the murderers.

In these novels, as in the previous three, Martínez Moreno seems chiefly concerned with discovering what has happened to the ideals of Uruguayan society: a society that was founded on democratic principles and has now succumbed to rule by a harsh military regime. Although politics as such is kept in the background of his novels, Martínez Moreno shows very clearly that it permeates the whole fabric of society. It is not incidental, then, that the action of his last book takes place at the end of the rather short period (1958–1966) in which, after nearly one hundred years of rule by the Colorado Party, the White Party was in power (see Acevedo Díaz, Part Two, 8).

In exploring the destinies of a decadent bourgeoisie, or the impunity of the international drug smugglers or the grotesque world of derelicts, Martínez Moreno is always in fact exploring the same subject: corruption in the fabric of society. The short story excerpted here is also about corruption—a subtler, almost invisible kind.

The Pigeon

From "Paloma," translated by Giovanni Pontiero, in Short Stories in Spanish, edited by Jean Franco (Harmondsworth, England: Penguin Books, 1966), pp. 137–65.

And the dove came in to him
in the evening.
   (Genesis 8: II)

In the harsh light of that Sunday afternoon, roofs and terraces traced their lines against the blue sky, a sky that was almost indigo. Brígido could see the television aerials like horizontal ladders, and in the foreground the chimneys and the clotheslines, the loathsome, weather-beaten rear walls with their patches of soot, the shutters, the end timbers, and the drainpipes.

It was the usual prospect, that remote yet confined corner that he glimpsed from his patio, with the familiar outlines which were broken from time to time by the providential appearance of some skyscraper. The town of Pocitos was growing, but the patio remained unchanged; his Serrato Statute house, the withered lemon tree (white with guano), the pigeon loft which he had had built when he drew his pension.

He rose from his low chair, and the bright yellow straw shone like a solar disk on the fading lines that ran across the red tiling. He put his thermos flask and maté on the arm of his chair and set about adjusting a latch on the door of the nests; but he only did this to try to fill with little tasks, which spent themselves without trace or memory, the void of a lengthy expectation. It was after three o'clock in the afternoon and, judging by the wind, the pigeons should start to arrive at about four, if they had in fact released them at ten o'clock that morning in Paso de los Toros.

The previous evening, he had caught, in the bustle of preparation, the enthusiasm of the new season: the autumn was turning to gold and the first race was being contended. The club was an old house in the southern style, with the four sides of its large patio checkered beneath the skylight. There they started to pile up, murmuring in the shadows, the large cages crammed with pigeons. It was incredible that after the torpor of that wait and the long journey, a creature could then be released to fly with such impetuosity and cross the country within a few hours. There they were, cooing and emitting a warm, even delicate, scent, as they awaited the arrival of the soldiers.

They would load them into trucks and would take them to the station, so that they could travel through the night, colder, and with an ever more powerful stench, toward the platform of their destination.

On those days the club bustled from dusk onward with the animation of a purposeful, enterprising, and ritual task. Office workers by profession, its members seemed joyfully to shed from their shoulders the burden of the whole office routine, as they set about carefully filling out their flight forms—with the delight of a painstaking task. They did it for pleasure; and that was the way they exercised their freedom, however completely it might resemble their monotonous work, their subservient employment, and the aspect of the rest of their working week. It was Saturday afternoon and, lined up at the long tables, as they took down particulars and sorted them into the pigeonholes of the wall cabinets, they shook off the indolence of the previous six days and the boredom of their daily existence, devoting themselves to the only likely pastime in which they could still have the illusion of sport and the fascination of success. "In a city of a million inhabitants, there will always be a hundred madmen who breed pigeons," someone had written in friendly satire; and unwittingly, he had given them a crazy *raison d'être.* The galley slaves used to get together and go out rowing, once they were free.

Around them, above the feverish activity of their bent shoulders, there passed to and fro conjectures, feeding methods, pedigrees, predictions, and forecasts about tomorrow's wind. In the next room, others ringed the pigeons, drawing them gently in the palms of their hands toward the machine that did the marking; and holding them by the breastbone, they subjected their legs, taped and red, to the gray plastic stapler and numbered tube. They then slipped them away one by one, and called out in a loud voice the numbers of the capsules they were using, and this information too was entered on each form. The operation was rapid and harmless, and once it was over the same hand thrust the pigeon, which timidly appeared to represent the struggle behind the thought of victory, toward the cage whose spring door closed with a snap. The hand still retained for a moment its disturbed gesture, a tremulous flutter as if its fingertips were shedding the anxiety with which each fancier attended to the business of marking and releasing his pigeon.

Brígido had always considered as a fetish—he could now hear the ticking of his stop watch, and he touched it with a cautious movement to make sure that it was working properly in its right place—that sealed stop watch which the club hired out on Saturday evenings to those who were racing. It was a chubby apparatus without a dial, mysterious and almost organic, which seemed to have an indefinable yet definite existence. Into its single slot one had to insert the numbered capsule as soon as it had been extracted from the leg of the returning pigeon, and this entry stamped the hour of its arrival. Back at the club on Sunday night, the president of the race lined everyone up, each with his stop watch throbbing in a throbbing hand. He alerted them, and when he clapped his hands they had to press a button on the opposite side from the slot, which registered another time stamp. This allowed them to check their watches, note the subtle differences of those that were fast or slow, and synchronize them. The information thus sorted, they proceeded to work out adjustments. The pigeon loft of Carrasco had so many minutes' start, and that of the Union so many. It was what was bureaucratically referred to as "working out the handicaps." The same faces, haggard from the anxious suspense of the day's events, ill-shaven and reddened by the sun, the light of their eyes imbedded in the flaccid pouches of aging wrinkles, suddenly became dizzy at the confirmation of those deductions, since on that complexity of numbers, more than on the flight itself, their final triumph depended. But once arrived at, the result only drew, amid the general exhaustion, faint, vapid, and perplexed smiles. The final flush of victory was such a dismal thing, in the last analysis, after the days and months in which they had treasured it, nurtured it, and disbelieved.

Through the kitchen shutters, the disheveled head of Elisa suddenly appeared; the change of life had finally spoiled her temper and had made her lose in domestic life every last trace of coquetry, every semblance of tidiness.

"It doesn't look as if we shall be going out today either," she said aggressively, raising her eyes as if she expected the reply from the fragment of empty sky that she could glimpse from the window frame. "Yes, I know, the races are on!"

"It's the first race of the year," Brígido corrected her.

"And the others on these last few Sundays, what were they?"

"Practice flights," he insisted imperturbably.

"Some difference, for heaven's sake!" replied the voice, which was already withdrawing.

She could not be seen, but she was speaking to herself when she uttered, coldly and audibly, "Pigeons, you and your famous pigeons!"

"Famous" was one of her favorite adjectives, into which she went on putting the greatest possible amount of contempt.

Brígido grabbed his thermos with one hand, and with the other he brought toward it the maté, which washed up and down with the swaying tube, as he contemplated it with a puzzled gaze as if for the first time.

In the reproach of every sunny afternoon that they *frittered away* while the Wyllis remained in the garage—as if the availability of the car were a promise of gratuitous diversions—he was now witnessing another display of the same old grudge: no children, no money, no fame.

He was thinking that he too had a bead to add to the rosary—no affection. The mutual understanding expected from the passage of time had not come, and in its place there had settled an uncomfortable estrangement, the fruits of a growing diffidence, which imponderably estranged them, as if each morning they should awake the one more distant from the other, even greater strangers on the pillow they shared. He recalled his years as an office worker on the frontier, which she referred to as "the years of your gall bladder," certain that the illness and its treatment had marked them more deeply than any possible form of understanding or happiness. His first daily impression was in those days an enormous spoon near his left eye, a spoon filled with an oily liquid, and beyond it the disheveled head which had awakened him (in those days she tidied herself upon rising, but nowadays she floated around with her white locks jabbing her sunken cheeks the whole day long) and rebuked him without tenderness.

"Here's a dose of your famous Amerol. It's gone six o'clock."

He had to take it one hour before getting up, take it and then lie on his right side, so that the remedy could take effect.

As a form of revenge, he had christened with the same words—"your famous Amerol"—the old record that she used to play in the evenings, with the shutters opened onto the patio while she swayed in the canvas rocking chair, silently fanning herself in a halo of motionless heat, and felt herself surrounded and penetrated, to the point of drowsiness, by the heavy scent of the jasmine and by the melody of her much loved song.

> In the quiet of the night
> Say it loud for me to hear

> Love me with all your might—
> as I love you.

It was as though across the silence of the night she wanted to communicate with someone, in a relationship which left Brígido himself, seated there in his pajamas with his slippers dangling from his feet over the step of the patio, at once untouched and shut out. Perhaps she was trying vaguely to communicate with someone and the song helped her to express her dissatisfaction with life in that coastal town, her isolation, her solitude, the vast sensation of lost time.

In this sultry quiet, under the stifling aura of the jasmine and toward the distant center of some other night and some other desire, Gardel and Razzano sang, biting off their words into groups of capricious syllables, to emphasize somewhat that trivial mystery into which she let herself be lulled by that record that never cloyed for her:

> In the qui-et of the night
> Say it loud for-me to he-ar
> Love me with-all your might—
> as I love-you.

When it finally stopped scratching and scrabbling in the heart of that anxious message—the needle first hissed and then drizzled over that mythological voice—had anyone ever listened to her, or ever responded to her ever-diminishing faith, her ever-greater languor and dejection, and the bloated senile carnality of her eyelids?

"Your famous Amerol" had an infallible effect. This identification of romantic love with a bile medicine had always irritated her.

He had often postponed the moment of self-judgment, but on that day he knew with clarity that, toward the end of his life, he had only aspired to peace, to a good pension grading and the benefit of retirement. Those first afternoons, upon returning from the accountant's office, while his claim barely progressed in the labyrinth of archives, desks, staircases, offices, and departments, he and Elisa had spread on the dining-room table brochures of travel agencies, maps of lands and fabulous cities, destined to sum up the lives of those who worshiped them without knowing them; and they had discussed and modified their itinerary of Europe, which followed upon the footsteps of friends or diverged from them, with a precarious conjecture like that of the Grand Tour.

The Pensions Office and the transfer to the Appeals Court had gradually killed that illusion eroded by the long passage of time. Europe had finally transformed itself into equal compensatory parts; "improvements for the house" and the construction of a "scientific" pigeon loft with its nests, perches, and drinking troughs; "my library and my cellar" as Brígido was wont to say, apologizing for not possessing other extravagances more fanciful or costly.

The wind was now blowing strongly; they might arrive before four o'clock. He put the thermos and the maté back in their place and pushed open the narrow side door that led to the garage. The Wyllis had not been out since the previous Sunday and it was getting harder to start. The minute that mattered was that of registering the arrival time of the stop watch, but he was impatient to start off as soon as he had done so. The doors of the shed stood open in readiness and the ancient engine began to rumble, in that zinc box which magnified the noise, a good half hour before the pigeon arrived.

Before the pigeon lofts there were the tea chests, and he thought of them as of his black hair and his youth, as of the sinister cackle of joy which an Elisa now dead but then recently satisfied used to utter in his ear.

"Before the pigeon lofts there were the tea chests," he began to narrate his private Genesis. Even the Wyllis did not throb in those days with this horrible knocking of halting valves. "The world was younger then but the breed was not a shadow of what it is today." And this final conviction restored in him a brilliance submerged in the years, a reflection which he had leaned over to pursue in other wells without success.

"The breed then was not a shadow of what it has become today," and the pigeon that was gliding—surely very close—was the peak of this breed. He pressed his foot on the accelerator for a final burst, then silenced that distressing and hellish din. "We're both getting old," he mentally joked with himself and the Wyllis, thinking himself attached to it in inseparable union, because he was in a happy frame of mind with a breed which everyone envied him and that splendid creature which he felt to be ever nearer, flying with the currents of wind that were coming to fade out in his hand.

He had marked the date of his first victory on the original "Tiger Tea" chest where his first pigeons were housed. Time had later tattooed other dates, but time had also brought more and more competitors; and despite the manuals, the diets and refinements of breeding, to win once a year had already come to mean a great deal; and to win the Inaugural Prize had become an event. *In the city of a million inhabitants there are now more than a hundred madmen who breed pigeons.* And Brígido had not won for five years.

He went out once more into the resplendent, and now slightly clouded, air of the familiar Sunday afternoon, that afternoon which swelled into a long maternal metaphor, as if aware that he could assist it to deliver a pigeon mysteriously surging from its womb.

Into the painless void there suddenly slid a panting and pseudo-intimate twanging voice: *"The Danube team deserved this draw, my friends."* They strangled it without allowing it to explain further.

". . . My friends." The office farewell was now framed in the dining room, and there his face floated on a sea of others which he would never see together again. Smiling faces, rows of bottles, and autographs in the margins. Bachelor farewells, retirements, and funerals all have this irreversible quality. But his activities as a pigeon fancier, as stated in the diploma that faced the taut and happy grins of his ex-companions, had brought him other ties, unforeseen acquaintances, and another window on the world.

Through this window, there appeared every Thursday the Indian-like complexion, the chubby and placid face, of Juan Crisólogo Colla. Barely forty, he was already pensioned like himself and had been in charge of the military pigeon lofts. Shining, his hair plastered down, with all the time in the world, Colla used to sit down and talk incessantly. Without any apparent relation to the vapid conversation, his mouth frequently displayed a smile of dazzling white teeth, and then Brígido forgave him the irritating length of his tale. While he had to listen to him with indulgence, Colla sketched the story of a claim, which he had been pursuing for years, to be granted the "military status" his predecessor in the pigeon lofts had enjoyed. When they granted it, he would take steps to have his small retirement allowance increased. The certainty that he still had years of legal action in front of him seemed to warm to a faintly glowing satisfaction that body which stirred between the arms of the chair, and seemed to afford him a *raison d'être* which there would never have been in the arms of love.

Brígido heard mentioned in vague terms well-known celebrities—without ever having seen them—the Chief Accountant who had promised to make a favorable report to the Legal Adviser at the Ministry, who could not understand the case, and the Attorney General, who received Colla in his shirtsleeves and made him sit opposite him, with the obvious kindness of allowing him to explain the problem all over again. And Colla used to carry about with him a dummy file in which these details were assembled to the letter, line by line, and the words broke off, ran on, and turned the page at precisely the same point as in the original. The very stamps and headings of the different departments were sketched in at the exact places, and the whole affair—with sad pretense— parodied life.

Brígido offered him a drink, listing alcohols that those virgin lips forbade themselves without any temptation whatsoever, knowing beforehand that they would finally request a "malt drink."

Colla warmed the glass in his hands, because the coldness of the liquid had once made him faint with a spasm in the throat, and for a moment they believed him dead. His great bovine eyes had popped more than ever on that occasion. And when there was still some of the malt left in the bottle, he placed it on the floor pretending not to notice, and began looking at the pigeons and discussing them.

He knew a lot, Brígido thought. He had the entire collection of the *Racing Pigeon,* and although he did not know English, he would repeat from memory, like the reports in his file, Squills's notes, which he had had translated one day by a friend, a sergeant major who had been on some training courses in the United States.

Sometimes he would bring magazines or books on pigeon fancying under his arm, and that was preferable to seeing him arrive with the papers for his claim to the rank of captain.

He spoke gently of the advantages of the idea of "total celibacy" for

the male birds, and as he listened to him Brígido could not avoid the farcical
zoological sensation that here was an autobiographical eulogy, an embarrassing
reflection on his own chastity.

As if they possessed the cryptic accent of rite or poetry, he would read
the underlined phrases of the manuals which, even in retirement, he treasured
up under his gothic signature. "The pigeon which upon awakening is firm and
light in the hand, whose plumage is compressed, velvet-like and powdery, whose
eyes have a brilliant sparkle, is a specimen in which one can have faith."

His placid eyes looked up beatifically from the page with a sparkle less
aggressive than that of the prized pigeon, as if that awakening feeling might
compensate for his lack of virility, as if the warmth of the pigeon and the malt
were accepted substitutes and life had also breathed into these little clandestine
glories which flowed through his huge frame, functionless and inane, a soothing
consolation and the only one that his senses could bear.

"Amongst us it isn't given any importance, but it has been the obsession of great men," he observed. "Do you know, for instance, that on several
occasions Darwin was President of the Pigeon Societies of London, and he recalls
the fact with pride in *The Origin of Species?*"

Brígido had never read *The Origin of Species,* nor did he believe that
Colla had either. But the *Racing Pigeon* probably reported a great many things.

"In the seventeenth century," Colla went on, "a whole section of
London was burnt down. The pigeons were more faithful to their homes than
the owners themselves and they remained quietly on the rooftops until the end.
When they decided to fly away their wings were scorched and they fell into the
flames."

He stared with a smug air, as if he had learned that from Darwin.

"A certain Mr. Pepys speaks of it," he added.

One day he appeared with a hideous cartoon drawn in charcoal and
gave it to Brígido. Darwin was standing with his noble head and great stiff beard,
wearing a dark overcoat. He was standing erect and holding a shining dove in
his right hand.

One could see that the head had been taken from some engraving,
"with a pantograph," he confessed, but the rest he had drawn from his imagination. He had depicted an oblong lymphatic body like his own, uncomfortably
attired in an ill-defined and obscure garment. The dove blazed in his right hand,
surrounded by a halo like a vulgar lampshade.

Brígido kept the picture behind the sideboard and brought it out early
on Thursday in readiness for the punctual visit of the artist, regimented and
punctilious even when wasting his time.

"But you have taken down the photograph of the banquet which they
gave you," Colla protested, somewhat flattered. "It isn't fair!"

And the banquet went back up on the wall on that very Thursday night,
when Darwin came down.

*   *   *

He could not say if he saw or merely sensed the pigeon in the sky, swooping with the gusts of wind and gliding above his head. He glanced at the watch on his wrist. It was a quarter to four, and it must have flown a marvelous race. It was above the pigeon loft and started to glide again, as if all its intoxication of air were still not enough for it.

It must come down at once! These were precious seconds. But he saw it soar again and give another spin, in circles that were not narrowing.

It must come down! It must come down! To launch a pigeon into flight was like throwing a bottle into the sea, seeking one's way in an unknown and hostile world. And now one moment it was here, and the next it returned to enjoy its gliding!

He therefore ran to the storeroom and came back sporting his seaman's cap (his "admiral's cap," as Elisa sarcastically called it) because that was what he wore to feed the birds, and that was what induced them to come down from the sky or descend from their perches in the cages. He heard a disquieted cooing, the explosion of rapid flights inside the pigeon lofts, but the pigeon stayed on high, exhilarated, abstracted, transfixed in the gusts of wind or dropping on the edge of a wing, to soar high once more, as if its whole being, insensible to what was happening below, only existed in that breastbone which cleft the furrowed and clouded blue.

Trembling, sprinting from one end of the narrow patio to the other, provoking in his wake a muffled fluttering from the caged pigeons, Brígido began to wave his cap, in sweeping, pathetic salutation, in enormous and violently exaggerated gestures, like a comedian in silent films. No use! The pigeon went on tracing circles in the sky, indifferent, unknown, permeated by a sun which now shone only on its wings and no longer onto the confined space where Brígido brandished his cap, where the afternoon began to be blurred with spoilt and murky breath.

It must descend anyhow. These were precious minutes! He racked his brains feverishly, without devising any solution.

Above one of the cages rested the cane which he used to guide the birds to their proper eating places, and he began to brandish that also, while his cap, lopsided and about to fall, balanced for a moment on his head in which there still seethed solutions to the problem.

He groped in his pocket, while the time on the stopwatch went ticking on, and took out his whistle; this was a signal that they always obeyed. He began to blow it harshly, in confused, heart-rending blasts across the startled air.

Unheeding, majestic, flashing in the patches of sunlight and deafened in the depths of the clouds, inaccessible, the pigeon, it seemed, did not listen. He whistled and whistled, blasted the afternoon with signals of command, and deflated like bellows his lungs which only heaved with anguish.

Less remote than the flight of the pigeon, the face of Elisa appeared once more at the window, with the ruffled surprise of a jack-in-the-box. The white locks and wasted cheekbones engendered reckless laughter which matched the farce of the situation.

"It's making you lose the race on your very doorstep," she shouted with indiscernible harshness. "This is the limit!"

"Please!" Brígido cried with an expression that pleaded for something, excitedly and tensely, without naming it, "please!" and his hands drew a long shape in the air, in the same gesture with which they had flourished the cane which creaked on the ground beneath his feet. "Please, come quickly!"

But since Elisa never understood, since she never knew what he was muttering with his actions if it was not also expressed in words, and since he could not hit upon them, panting and frustrated, he detested that face which demanded explanations, and he fled indoors. His admiral's cap, precariously perched above that desperate face, rolled onto the ground, traversing with a fleeting flash the ray of sunlight which faded at the foot of the nests.

It must come down! This was the Inaugural Prize, this was the long-awaited consecration, the justification of everything, of all those endless years! It must descend, his prize specimen, the peak of his breed!

He came running back into the patio and saw it suspended, unheeding, as if someone were holding it hoisted at the end of a thread, a gentle and unattainable kite directly above its landing place. Without losing any time, relying on a steady pulse which his nerves had not as yet affected, he raised his Winchester to his cheek and fired.

When the shot was heard, the pigeon too folded its wings and let itself come down. It let itself come down resplendent in the afternoon, as if it were descending a heavenly ladder or falling from the hand of Darwin. Dully, its body struck the highest rooftop of the pigeon loft and slid down behind it, between the back of the white laths and the bordering wall.

"You're crazy, crazy!" he again heard the comment of Elisa, who had been silent just long enough for the dry clear report of the gunshot to fill the patio.

He laid the Winchester aside, seized the cane, and, crawling on all fours, slipped it through the gap, between the bottom of the pigeon loft and the ground, until he gradually dragged out the pigeon, warm and covered in blood. . . . *A hundred madmen who breed pigeons, but only one who breeds them and kills them, only one who breeds them and kills them!*

"For God's sake, Brígido!" exclaimed Elisa, who as a rule never invoked His name. "What on earth are you doing?"

He felt the warm wetness of its blood in his hand, while, with a rapid movement, he removed the capsule from its leg, which was twisted and drawn up under its wing, and thus, stunned and convulsed, surrounded by the fallen cap, the abandoned gun, and the shouts of his wife, he got up onto his knees out of the dust, *"Oh my God!"* and taking the stopwatch, he pressed in the capsule.

"Beautiful creature," the exaltation within him proclaimed, with a

furious and malignant gasp. *"Beautiful and stupid creature, if I win this race I'll embalm you."*

He stood up and began to run toward the car. Rigid, "firm and light," the pigeon lay lighting up a prematurely blurred corner of the afternoon, its plumage open and its clotting blood brilliant on the dark tiles.

7

JUAN RULFO

The publication of two slim volumes of fiction in the middle fifties has made the Mexican Juan Rulfo's fortune. Since then he has published only a couple of short stories, but his reputation as one of the leading figures of the new Latin American fiction has never been seriously challenged.

Born in a small town near Jalisco in 1918, Rulfo's life was shattered by the Mexican Revolution. His father was murdered when he was only seven. Although he attended school at Guadalajara and began contributing very early to literary magazines, Rulfo knew to the full the bitterness of being an orphan. His grandmother tried to force him into the priesthood; an uncle promised help under the condition that he drop the family name and assume the anonymous "Pérez" (the Spanish equivalent of "Smith"). Rulfo refused both and went to Mexico City, where he survived doing menial jobs until he secured a bureaucratic position. In 1953, after the successful publication of his only book of short stories, *The Burning Plain,* he got a Rockefeller grant to write his novel, *Pedro Páramo,* published in 1956 and an immediate classic.

Rulfo's world is the world of the destitute and decadent province of his birth. In the short stories, the poor peasants predominate, caught in a complex web of hatred, murders, and incest, incessantly telling their stories in a spare, bitterly ironic style of delivery. It is a haunted, tragic world, a world in which the ghost of the past finally corrupts the living, a world impoverished by a revolution that succeeded only in changing the bosses. *Pedro Páramo* embodies and develops the same dark and pessimistic outlook. A narrative composed of short fragments in which various layers of the past alternate and crisscross, it is the story of a quest.

Juan Preciado (a new Telemachus) goes back to his home town to find his father, Pedro Páramo. But he is too late: Páramo has been murdered by another son. The quest has been over before the novel begins. In the middle of the novel we learn that Preciado himself is dead and that his story has been told, after death, to a fellow ghost. Originally the title of the book was supposed to be "The Murmurs": the voices of the dead that permeate the space of the living.

In finally choosing *Pedro Páramo* as a title, Rulfo gave a strong focus to the novel. Now the main character is obviously the father: a larger-than-life feudal landowner who crushes everyone around him under his heel and even manages to come out of the Revolution stronger than ever. His name is symbolic: *Pedro* alludes to Peter, the founder of the Christian church, but also to stone (*piedra* in Spanish); *Páramo* is a wasteland—the wasteland Pedro has created. A powerfully written book, it alternates flashbacks in which Páramo's past is concisely retold with haunting episodes of Preciado's quest. The technique owes much to Faulkner's *As I Lay Dying,* but Rulfo is also deeply indebted to less fashionable novelists: the Finnish Sillampaa, the Russian Korolenko, the Norwegian Knut Hamsun. He shares with them a desperate love for the destitute and offended. To the vast collective fresco of the novel of the Mexican Revolution, Rulfo has added what is perhaps the most brilliant and moving account of the roots of the Mexican tragedy.

"Luvina," the story selected here, is a concentration within a few pages of the hellish nightmare of *Pedro Páramo.*

Luvina

From The Burning Plain and Other Stories, *translated by George D. Schade (Austin: University of Texas Press, 1970), pp. 111–21.*

Of the mountains in the south Luvina is the highest and the rockiest. It's infested with that gray stone they make lime from, but in Luvina they don't make lime from it or get any good out of it. They call it crude stone there, and the hill that climbs up toward Luvina they call the Crude Stone Hill. The sun and the air have taken it on themselves to make it crumble away, so that the earth around there is always white and brilliant, as if it were always sparkling with the morning dew, though this is just pure talk, because in Luvina the days are cold as the nights and the dew thickens in the sky before it can fall to the earth.

And the ground is steep and slashed on all sides by deep barrancas, so deep you can't make out the bottom. They say in Luvina that one's dreams come up from those barrancas; but the only thing I've seen come up out of them was the wind, whistling as if down below they had squeezed it into reed pipes. A wind that doesn't even let the dulcamaras grow: those sad little plants that can live with just a bit of earth, clutching with all their hands at the mountain cliffsides. Only once in a while, where there's a little shade, hidden among the rocks, the *chicalote* blossoms with its white poppies. But the *chicalote* soon withers. Then you hear it scratching the air with its spiny branches, making a noise like a knife on a whetstone.

"You'll be seeing that wind that blows over Luvina. It's dark. They say because it's full of volcano sand; anyway, it's a black air. You'll see it. It takes hold of things in Luvina as if it was going to bite them. And there are lots of days when it takes the roofs off the houses as if they were hats, leaving the bare walls uncovered. Then it scratches like it had nails: you hear it morning and night, hour after hour without stopping, scraping the walls, tearing off strips of earth, digging with its sharp shovel under the doors, until you feel it boiling inside of you as if it was going to remove the hinges of your very bones. You'll see."

The man speaking was quiet for a bit, while he looked outside.

The noise of the river reached them, passing its swollen waters through the fig-tree branches, the noise of the air gently rustling the leaves of the almond trees, and the shouts of the children playing in the small space illumined by the light that came from the store.

The flying ants entered and collided with the oil lamp, falling to the ground with scorched wings. And outside night kept on advancing.

"Hey, Camilo, two more beers!" the man said again. Then he added, "There's another thing, mister. You'll never see a blue sky in Luvina. The whole horizon there is always a dingy color, always clouded over by a dark stain that never goes away. All the hills are bare and treeless, without one green thing to rest your eyes on; everything is wrapped in an ashy smog. You'll see what it's like —those hills silent as if they were dead and Luvina crowning the highest hill with its white houses like a crown of the dead."

The children's shouts came closer until they penetrated the store. That made the man get up, go to the door and yell at them, "Go away! Don't bother us! Keep on playing, but without so much racket."

Then, coming back to the table, he sat down and said, "Well, as I was saying, it doesn't rain much there. In the middle of the year they get a few storms that whip the earth and tear it away, just leaving nothing but the rocks floating above the stony crust. It's good to see then how the clouds crawl heavily about, how they march from one hill to another jumping as if they were inflated bladders, crashing and thundering just as if they were breaking on the edge of the barrancas. But after ten or twelve days they go away and don't come back until the next year, and sometimes they don't come back for several years. No, it doesn't rain much. Hardly at all, so that the earth, besides being all dried up and shriveled like old leather, gets filled with cracks and hard clods of earth like sharp stones, that prick your feet as you walk along, as if the earth itself had grown thorns there. That's what it's like."

He downed his beer, until only bubbles of foam remained in the bottle, then he went on: "Wherever you look in Luvina, it's a very sad place. You're going there, so you'll find out. I would say it's the place where sadness nests. Where smiles are unknown as if people's faces had been frozen. And, if you like, you can see that sadness just any time. The breeze that blows there moves it around but never takes it away. It seems like it was born there. And you can almost taste and feel it, because it's always over you, against you, and because it's heavy, like a large plaster weighing on the living flesh of the heart.

"The people from there say that when the moon is full they clearly see the figure of the wind sweeping along Luvina's streets, bearing behind it a black blanket; but what I always managed to see when there was a moon in Luvina was the image of despair—always.

"But drink up your beer. I see you haven't even tasted it. Go ahead and drink. Or maybe you don't like it warm like that. But that's the only kind we have here. I know it tastes bad, something like burro's piss. Here you get used to it. I swear that there you won't even get this. When you go to Luvina you'll miss it. There all you can drink is a liquor they make from a plant called hojasé, and after the first swallows your head'll be whirling around like crazy, feeling like you had banged it against something. So better drink your beer. I know what I'm talking about."

You could still hear the struggle of the river from outside. The noise of the air. The children playing. It seemed to be still early in the evening.

The man had gone once more to the door and then returned, saying, "It's easy to see things, brought back by memory, from here where there's nothing like it. But when it's about Luvina I don't have any trouble going right on talking to you about what I know. I lived there. I left my life there. I went to that place full of illusions and returned old and worn out. And now you're going there. All right. I seem to remember the beginning. I'll put myself in your place and think. Look, when I got to Luvina the first time—But will you let me have a drink of your beer first? I see you aren't paying any attention to it. And it helps me a lot. It relieves me, makes me feel like my head had been rubbed with camphor oil. Well, I was telling you that when I reached Luvina the first time, the mule driver who took us didn't even want to let his animals rest. As soon as he let us off, he turned half around. 'I'm going back,' he said.

" 'Wait, aren't you going to let your animals take a rest? They are all worn out.'

" 'They'd be in worse shape here,' he said. 'I'd better go back.'

"And away he went, rushing down Crude Stone Hill, spurring his horses on as if he was leaving some place haunted by the devil.

"My wife, my three children, and I stayed there, standing in the middle of the plaza, with all our belongings in our arms. In the middle of that place where all you could hear was the wind—

"Just a plaza, without a single plant to hold back the wind. There we were.

"Then I asked my wife, 'What country are we in, Agripina?'

"And she shrugged her shoulders.

" 'Well, if you don't care, go look for a place where we can eat and spend the night. We'll wait for you here,' I told her.

"She took the youngest child by the hand and left. But she didn't come back.

"At nightfall, when the sun was lighting up just the tops of the mountains, we went to look for her. We walked along Luvina's narrow streets, until we found her in the church, seated right in the middle of that lonely church, with the child asleep between her legs.

" 'What are you doing here, Agripina?'

" 'I came in to pray,' she told us.

" 'Why?' I asked her.

"She shrugged her shoulders.

"Nobody was there to pray to. It was a vacant old shack without any doors, just some open galleries and a roof full of cracks where the air came through like a sieve.

" 'Where's the restaurant?'

" 'There isn't any restaurant.'

" 'And the inn?'

" 'There isn't any inn.'

" 'Did you see anybody? Does anybody live here?' I asked her.

" 'Yes, there across the street. Some women—I can still see them. Look, there behind the cracks in that door I see some eyes shining, watching us. They have been looking over here. Look at them. I see the shining balls of their eyes. But they don't have anything to give us to eat. They told me without sticking out their heads that there was nothing to eat in this town. Then I came in here to pray, to ask God to help us.'

" 'Why didn't you go back to the plaza? We were waiting for you.'

" 'I came in here to pray. I haven't finished yet.'

" 'What country is this, Agripina?'

"And she shrugged her shoulders again.

"That night we settled down to sleep in a corner of the church behind the dismantled altar. Even there the wind reached, but it wasn't quite as strong. We listened to it passing over us with long howls, we listened to it come in and out of the hollow caves of the doors, whipping the crosses of the stations of the cross with its hands full of air—large rough crosses of mesquite wood hanging from the walls the length of the church, tied together with wires that twanged with each gust of wind like the gnashing of teeth.

"The children cried because they were too scared to sleep. And my wife, trying to hold all of them in her arms. Embracing her handful of children. And me, I didn't know what to do.

"A little before dawn the wind calmed down. Then it returned. But there was a moment during that morning when everything was still, as if the sky had joined the earth, crushing all noise with its weight. You could hear the breathing of the children, who now were resting. I listened to my wife's heavy breath there at my side.

" 'What is it?' she said to me.

" 'What's what?' I asked her.

" 'That, that noise.'

" 'It's the silence. Go to sleep. Rest a little bit anyway, because it's going to be day soon.'

"But soon I heard it too. It was like bats flitting through the darkness very close to us. Bats with big wings that grazed against the ground. I got up and the beating of wings was stronger, as if the flock of bats had been frightened and were flying toward the holes of the doors. Then I walked on tiptoe over there, feeling that dull murmur in front of me. I stopped at the door and saw them. I saw all the women of Luvina with their water jugs on their shoulders, their shawls hanging from their heads and their black figures in the black background of the night.

"'What do you want?' I asked them. 'What are you looking for at this time of night?'

"One of them answered, 'We're going for water.'

"I saw them standing in front of me, looking at me. Then, as if they were shadows, they started walking down the street with their black water jugs.

"No, I'll never forget that first night I spent in Luvina.

"Don't you think this deserves another drink? Even if it's just to take away the bad taste of my memories."

"It seems to me you asked me how many years I was in Luvina, didn't you? The truth is, I don't know. I lost the notion of time since the fevers got it all mixed up for me, but it must have been an eternity. Time is very long there. Nobody counts the hours and nobody cares how the years go mounting up. The days begin and end. Then night comes. Just day and night until the day of death, which for them is a hope.

"You must think I'm harping on the same idea. And I am, yes, mister. To be sitting at the threshold of the door, watching the rising and the setting of the sun, raising and lowering your head, until the springs go slack and then everything gets still, timeless, as if you had always lived in eternity. That's what the old folks do there.

"Because only real old folks and those who aren't born yet, as they say, live in Luvina. And weak women, so thin they are just skin and bones. The children born there have all gone away. They hardly see the light of day and they're already grown up. As they say, they jump from their mothers' breasts to the hoe and disappear from Luvina. That's the way it is in Luvina.

"There are just old folks left there and lone women, or with a husband who is off God knows where. They appear every now and then when the storms come I was telling you about; you hear a rustling all through the town when they return and something like a grumbling when they go away again. They leave a sack of provisions for the old folks and plant another child in the bellies of their women, and nobody knows anything more of them until the next year, and sometimes never. It's the custom. There they think that's the way the law is, but it's all the same. The children spend their lives working for their parents as their parents worked for theirs and who knows how many generations back performed this obligation?

"Meanwhile, the old people wait for them and for death, seated in their doorways, their arms hanging slack, moved only by the gratitude of their children. Alone, in that lonely Luvina.

"One day I tried to convince them they should go to another place where the land was good. 'Let's leave here!' I said to them. 'We'll manage somehow to settle somewhere. The government will help us.'

"They listened to me without batting an eyelash, gazing at me from the depths of their eyes from which only a little light came.

" 'You say the government will help us, teacher? Do you know the government?'

"I told them I did.

" 'We know it too. It just happens. But we don't know anything about the government's mother.'

"I told them it was their country. They shook their heads saying no. And they laughed. It was the only time I saw the people of Luvina laugh. They grinned with their toothless mouths and told me no, that the government didn't have a mother.

"And they're right, you know? The lord only remembers them when one of his boys has done something wrong down here. Then he sends to Luvina for him and they kill him. Aside from that, they don't know if the people exist.

" 'You're trying to tell us that we should leave Luvina because you think we've had enough of going hungry without reason,' they said to me. 'But if we leave, who'll bring along our dead ones? They live here and we can't leave them alone.'

"So they're still there. You'll see them now that you're going. Munching on dry mesquite pulp and swallowing their own saliva to keep hunger away. You'll see them pass by like shadows, hugging to the walls of the houses, almost dragged along by the wind.

" 'Don't you hear that wind?' I finally said to them. 'It will finish you off.'

" 'It keeps on blowing as long as it ought to. It's God's will,' they answered me. 'It's bad when it stops blowing. When that happens the sun pours into Luvina and sucks our blood and the little bit of moisture we have in our skin. The wind keeps the sun up above. It's better that way.'

"So I didn't say anything else to them. I left Luvina and I haven't gone back and I don't intend to.

"But look at the way the world keeps turning. You're going there now in a few hours. Maybe it's been fifteen years since they said the same thing to me: 'You're going to San Juan Luvina.'

"In those days I was strong. I was full of ideas—you know how we're all full of ideas. And one goes with the idea of making something of them everywhere. But it didn't work out in Luvina. I made the experiment and it failed.

"San Juan Luvina. That name sounded to me like a name in the heavens. But it's purgatory. A dying place where even the dogs have died off, so there's not a creature to bark at the silence; for as soon as you get used to the strong wind that blows there, all you hear is the silence that reigns in these lonely parts. And that gets you down. Just look at me. What it did to me. You're going there, so you'll soon understand what I mean.

"What do you say we ask this fellow to pour a little mescal? With this beer you have to get up and go all the time and that interrupts our talk a lot. Hey, Camilo, let's have two mescals this time!

"Well, now, as I was telling you—"

But he didn't say anything. He kept staring at a fixed point on the table where the flying ants, now wingless, circled about like naked worms.

Outside you could hear the night advancing. The lap of the water against the fig-tree trunks. The children's shouting, now far away. The stars peering through the small hole of the door.

The man who was staring at the flying ants slumped over the table and fell asleep.

8

FIVE BRAZILIAN POETS

There has been no break in the continuity of Brazilian poetry since modernism (see Part Four, 16–21). On the contrary, the poets who began to publish in the thirties and forties, and even later, seemed to be concerned with continuing and developing the decisive search begun in the twenties by Manuel Bandeira, Mário de Andrade, Oswald de Andrade, and Carlos Drummond de Andrade. Nevertheless, a new style and diction are detectable, a quest for new or renovated forms—the old ballad, popular songs, graphic poems. One of the postmodernist poets—João Cabral de Melo Neto—dominates the scene with his hard, spare, dense lyrics. But others are equally interesting, if not so powerful. By way of suggesting the variety and diversity of the new poetry, the selections that follow have been chosen from the work of representatives of the major styles and tendencies. This is, of course, the merest sampling of the great outpouring of verse in Brazil in the last two decades or so—an outpouring that confirms the ongoing vitality of Brazilian literature.

I / VINICIUS DE MORÃES

Better known for his film scripts and lyrics for popular songs (he is the author of *Black Orpheus* and "The Girl from Ipanema"), Vinicius de Morães is one of Brazil's most versatile writers. He was born in Rio in 1913 and he got a law degree in 1933. In 1938 he went to England on a British Council fellowship and later became an assistant on the Brazilian program of the BBC. In 1943 he entered the diplomatic service and served in Los Angeles, Paris, and Montevideo.

Since 1933 he has published several volumes of verse; a first collection, *Poetical Anthology,* was printed in 1955. But it was his contribution to the success of the Bossa Nova and a 1956 play, on the theme of Orpheus and Eurydice, later transformed into a film by the French filmmaker Marcel Camus, that made Vinicius truly famous. His poems or song lyrics are bittersweet: they tell about love and lust, exalt the inexhaustible beauty of the female body, and explore loneliness and death. The two excerpted here show the two sides of Vinicius's poetry. The first is a satire on a cheap, chromium-plated Hollywood temptress; the other, a sentimental ballad on life and love. In both, Vinicius's unexpected gift for imagery and his irrepressible humor are evident.

Two Poems

Especially translated by Lawrence Böhme.

Passion Story: Hollywood, California

As a preliminary I shall telegraph you a dozen roses
afterward I will take you to eat chop suey
If the afternoon is golden we will lower the top
your hair in the wind will do eighty miles an hour

You will give me a kiss with indelible lipstick
and I will get hold of your thigh as rigid as wood
you will smile at me and I will put on my dark glasses
against the glare from your two thousand enameled teeth

We will chew each one of us a box of gum
and we will go to the movies smelling of peppermint
your head on my shoulder you will dream for two hours
while I amuse myself on your wiry breast

Again in the automobile I will ask if you want to
you will say there's time and will give me a hug
your hunger demands a tossed salad
I will see your face through tomato juice

Like a gentleman I will help you on with your chinchilla
upon leaving I will take note of your nylons "57"

as you walk, something in you squeaks in C sharp
by the way you walk I know you want to dance the rhumba

You will drink twenty whiskeys and get more affectionate
dancing I will feel your legs between mine
you will smell slightly like a washed dog
you possess a hundred hip rotations per minute

Again in the automobile I will ask if you want to
you will say not today, tomorrow you'll be filming
you play the cigarette girl in a night club of ill repute
and there's a scene where you sell a pack to George Raft

I will telegraph you then a sexy orchid
in the office I will wait for you to take your fruit salts
then you get a sudden desire for Italian food
but you want to go to bed soon; you have a headache.

At the door of your house I will ask if you want to
you will tell me not today, it'll give you a tummyache
from far away you wave a subtly acted farewell
upon noticing that my battery has gone dead

Next day I will wait with the car radio turned on
mentally calling you a whore and other names
you will come then to say there is food at home
with an apron on I will open cans and dry dishes

Your mother will ask me if I've been married long
I will say five years and she stops asking
but since we're young we have to have fun
we will go out in the automobile to have a spin

On top of a hill I will ask if you want to
you will tell me nothing doing, you have a pain in your side
nervously my cigarettes smoke themselves up
and I end up hurting my fingers on your girdle

Next day you come in an elastic sweater
moccasin shoes and red bobby sox
I take you out to dance a swift jitterbug
your twenty years leave my thirty-odd ones tired out

On the way out you get an urge to go bowling
you play to perfection, flirting with the fellow next to us

you give him your phone number and ask if I don't mind
I pretend I don't and start up the car

You're crazy for a cold Coca-cola
you drape yourself over me and bite my neck
I lightly stroke my hand on your bony knee
lost suddenly in a great pity

Afterward I ask you if you want to come to my apartment
you kill the question with a passionate kiss
I hit myself on the leg and step on the gas
you pretend to be scared and say that I drive well

What is that perfume which I had promised you?
I buy the Chanel No. 5 and add a sweet message
"Today I'm going to buy you a twenty-dollar dinner"
and if she doesn't want to, I swear I don't know what I'll do to
     her . . .

You come smelling of lilacs and with heels, my God, so high
that I'm left down below feeling completely cowed
you give orders to the waiter for caviar and champagne
afterward you burp softly and say "I beg your pardon"

In the car I absent-mindedly put my hand on your leg
afterward I take you to the top of a hill
On top I take out the ring, I want to marry you
You say that you will only accept after my divorce

I blurt out the words all mixed up and ridiculous
I want to rip off your blouse and chew up your face
you're not at all afraid of my rantings
and you put my finger out of joint with a ju jitsu hold

After, you pull a box of gum out of your pocket
and chew it furiously saying terrible things
What do I think you are, aren't I ashamed
to make such propositions to a single girl

I blurt out an apology and say that I was thinking . . .
you tell me to think less and pat my cheek
you ask for a cigarette and strike the match with your fingernail
and I gape admiringly at such skillfulness

You ask me to take you to eat a salad
but suddenly I get a strange vision
I see you like a goat grazing upon me
and I hate you for ruminating thus on my flesh

And then I go insane, I give you a punch in the face
I destroy your carotid artery with gnashing teeth
I drain you until the blood runs between my fingers
and at last I possess you, dead and disfigured.

Afterward, repentant, I cry over your body
and I bury you in a ditch, my poor sweetheart
I run away but they discover me because of a strand of hair
and six months later I die in the gas chamber.

First Song from "Orfeu da Conceiçao"

So many are the dangers of this life
for those who are in love; especially
when a moon rises suddenly
and is left there in the sky as if forgotten.
And when the moonlight, which acts insanely,
is accompanied by some random song
then one should be very careful
for a woman must be walking near.
A woman must be walking near who is made of music, moonlight,
    and feeling
whom life does not want, for being so perfect.
A woman just like the moon:
so beautiful she only spreads suffering around her
so modest that she's always naked.

II / JOÃO CABRAL DE MELO NETO

The most personal of the new Brazilian poets, João Cabral de Melo
Neto is at the same time deeply rooted in the best traditions of modernist poetry.
He continues Joaquím Cardozo's and Carlos Drummond de Andrade's explorations in a renewed style (see Part Four, 21). His humor is very dry—less exhibi-
tionistic than Parra's (Five, 2) but equally lethal. His best-known work, a 1967
ballad-play called *Severe Death and Life,* combines the harsh popular rhythms
of the Northeast with a precise, meticulous diction to create the most devastating
denunciation of that wretched part of Brazil (see Da Cunha, Two, 16).

João Cabral was born in 1920 in Recife, Pernambuco, to a distinguished family, closely related to Manuel Bandeira (Four, 16) and Gilberto Freyre. He moved to Rio in 1942 and in 1945 entered the diplomatic service and served in Barcelona, London, Seville, Marseille, Madrid, Geneva, Bern, and Asunción (Paraguay). His *Complete Poetry* was published in 1968. A very retiring person, João Cabral is perhaps the first major Brazilian poet to be closely linked to Spanish poets. His residence in Barcelona, where he published some of his early work, enabled him to attain a certain perspective on Brazilian poetry. In 1950 he published one of his most important poems: "The Dog Without Feathers." A haunting, almost ritualistic poem, it develops the classic themes of life as a river that ends in the sea of death, of man as a destitute creature engaged in a blind, unending struggle for survival. But João Cabral's dazzling verbal powers save the poem from any comfortable cliché. It is a hard, obsessive, brilliant composition.

The Dog Without Feathers

From "O Cao sem Plumas," translated by Thomas Colchie, in The Hudson Review, vol. XXIV, no. 1 (Spring 1971), pp. 23–35.

For Joaquim Cardozo, Poet of the Capibaribe

I

(Landscape of the Capibaribe)

The city is entered by the river
the way a street
is entered by a mongrel;
a fruit
by a sword.

The river suggests now
the smooth tongue of a dog,
now the sad stomach of a dog,
now the other river's
dark, filthy fabric
in the eyes of a dog.

That river
is like a dog without feathers—
knew nothing about the blue rain,
about the rose-colored fountains,

about water from a glass of water
about pitcher water,
about fresh water fish,
about the breeze in water.

It knew about crabs
of silt and rustiness.
Knew about mud
like a mucous membrane.
Must have known about octopus.
Knew infallibly
about the febrile woman who
   inhabits oysters.

That river
never opens itself to fish,
to brightness,

to the uneasiness of knives
that there is in fish.
Never opens itself in fish.

Opens itself in flowers
poor and black
like Negroes.
Opens itself in a flora
filthy and so beggarly
the way the Negro beggars are.
Opens itself in mangroves
with leaves, hard and kinky
like a Negro.

Smooth like the belly
of a fecund bitch,
the river grows
without ever bursting.
It gives birth,
the river, fluid and invertebrate,
like a bitch.

And I've never seen it boil
(the way bread,
when fermenting, boils).
In silence,
the river carries its poor fecundity,
pregnant with black land.

Gives itself in silence:
in gelations of black land,
in capes of black land,
in boots or gloves of black land
for the foot or the hand
that immerses itself.

The way at times
it happens with dogs,
the river would seem to stagnate.
Its waters would flow then
more dense and moody;
flow with the motions
dense and moody
of a snake.

It had something, then,
of that stagnation of a cretin.
Something of that stagnation
of the hospital, of the penitentiary,
    of asylums,
of the filthy and suffocating life
(filthy and suffocating clothes)
where it came crawling along.

Something of that stagnation
of corrupted palaces,
eaten
by mist and mistletoe.
Something of that stagnation
of the fat trees
dripping the myriad sugars
of Pernambuco dining rooms,
—where it came crawling along.

(It is there,
but with backs to the river,
that "the great spiritual families" of
    the city
crack the obese eggs
of their prose.
In the roundish peace of kitchens,
how they stir viciously
their cauldrons
of viscous indolence.)

Are those waters
the fruit of some tree?
Why did that water
seem ripe?
Why the flies above it, always,
as if about to land?

Did that river
gush happily somewhere?
Was it a song or a fountain
somewhere?
Why then had its eyes
been painted blue
on maps?

II

(Landscape of the Capibaribe)

Within the landscape
the river flowed
like a sword of heavy liquid.
Like a dog
humble and heavy.

Within the landscape
(flowed)
of men planted in the mud;
of houses of mud
planted in islands
coagulated in the mud;
landscape of amphibians
of mud and mud.

Like the river,
those men
are like dogs without feathers.
(A dog without feathers
is more
than a dog devastated;
is more
than a dog assassinated.
A dog without feathers
is when a tree without voice.
Is when from a bird
its roots in the air.
Is when for something
they scrape so deep
down to what it has not).

The river knew
about those men without feathers.
Knew
about their beards exposed,
about their sorrowful hair
of shrimp and hemp.

It knew as well
about the great warehouses alongside
    the quays,

where all
is an immense door
without doors,
wide open
to the horizons that smell of
    gasoline.

And knew
about the gaunt city of cork,
where rawboned men,
where bridges, rawboned dwellings
(everyone wears
hopsacking clothes)
dry up
to their thickest whitewash crust.

But it understood better
the men without feathers.
These
dry up
even further
beyond their innermost whitewash
    layer;
even further
beyond their straw;
further
beyond the straw of their hat;
further
even
beyond the shirt they have not;
much further beyond the name
even written on the sheet
of the driest paper.

Because it is in those waters
that they are lost
(slowly
and without sharpness).
There they are lost
(the way a needle is not lost).
There they are lost

(the way a clock is not broken).
There they are lost
the way a mirror is not broken.
There they are lost
the way water is lost from spilling:
without the sharp teeth
with which suddenly
in a man is severed
the cord of man.

In that water,
slowly,
they are being lost
in mud; in a mud
which little by little
also knows not speaking:
which little by little
gathers the defunct gestures
of the mud;
the sticky blood,
the paralytic eye
of the mud.

In the landscape of the river
it is hard to know
where the river begins;
where the mud

begins from the river;
where the land
begins from the mud;
where the man,
where the skin
begins from the mud;
where begins the man
in that man.

It is hard to know
whether that man
is no longer
more to this side of the man;
more to this side of the man
at least able to gnaw
the bones of a living;
able to let blood
in the plaza;
able to scream
if the grindstone chews his arm,
able
to have his life chewed
and not just
dissolved
(in that soft water
that softens his bones
the way it softened the stones).

III

(Fable of the Capibaribe)

The city is made fecund
by that sword
which spills itself,
by that
moist gumming of sword.

At the end of the river
the sea stretches
like a shirt or sheet
across its skeletons
of washed sand.

(The way the river was a mongrel
the sea could be a banner

blue and white
unfurled
at the end of the course
—or the mast—of the river.

A banner
which might have had teeth:
since the sea is always
with its teeth and its scour
gnawing its beaches.

A banner
which might have had teeth:
like a pure poet

polishing skeletons,
like a pure rodent,
a pure policeman
elaborating skeletons,
the sea, with great care,
is always once-more-washing
its pure skeleton of sand.

The sea and its incense,
the sea and its acids,
the sea and the mouth of its acids,
the sea and its stomach,
which eats and eats itself,
the sea and its flesh
vitreous, like a statue,
its silence attained
at the cost of always saying
the same thing,
the sea and its so-pure
professor of geometry.)

The river stands in fear of that sea
the way a mongrel
stands in fear of a door momentarily
        open,
the way a beggar fears
the church apparently open.

First,
the sea resists the river.
The sea refuses the river
its white sheets.
The sea refuses itself
to all in the river
which are flowers of land,
image of dog or beggar.

Then,
the sea invades the river.
The sea
wanting
to destroy in the river
its flowers of tumid land,
all in that land
which can grow and burst

like an island,
a fruit.

But before reaching the sea
the river lingers
in mangroves of stagnant water.
The river is joined
by other rivers
in a lagoon, in swamps
where, torpid, life boils.

The river is joined
to other rivers.
Together
all the rivers
prepare for their struggle
of stagnant water,
for their struggle
of stagnant fruit.

(The way the river was a mongrel,
the way the sea was a banner,
those mangroves
are an enormous fruit:

The same mechanism
patient and useful
of a fruit,
the same force
invincible and anonymous
of a fruit
—still producing its sugar,
even after being severed—.

The way drop by drop
until the sugar,
drop by drop
until the crowns of land,
the way drop by drop
until a new plant,
drop by drop
until the sudden islands
emerging happily.)

IV

(Discourse of the Capibaribe)

That river
is in the memory
like a living dog
inside a room.
Like a living dog
inside a pocket.
Like a living dog,
underneath the covers,
under the shirt,
under the skin.

A dog, because it lives,
is sharp.
What is living
does not weaken.
What is living wounds.
Man,
because he lives,
collides with what is living.
To live
is to go into what is living.

What is living
discommodes life's
silence, the sleep, the
        body
that dreamed for itself
clothing cut from cloud.
What is living collides,
has teeth, edges, is heavy.
What is living is heavy
like a dog, a man,
like that river.

The way everything real
is heavy.
That river
is heavy and real.
The way an apple
is heavy.

The way a mongrel
is heavier than an apple.

The way heavier
is the blood of the mongrel
than the mongrel itself.
The way heavier
is a man
than the blood of a mongrel.
The way much heavier
is the blood of a man
than the dream of a man.

Heavy
the way an apple is heavy.
The way an apple
is much heavier
if a man eats it
than if a man sees it.
The way it is even heavier
if famine eats it.
The way it is even much heavier
if unable to eat it
famine sees it.

That river
is heavy
like the most-heavy real.
Heavy
with its heavy landscape,
where famine
spreads its battalions of secret
and intimate ants.

And heavy
with its heavy legend;
with the flow
of its gelations of land;
giving birth
to its islands of black land.

Because much heavier is
the life which unfolds
in more life,
the way a fruit
is heavier
than its flower,
the way the tree
is heavier
than its seed,
the way the flower
is heavier
than its tree,
etc., etc.

Heavy,
because heavier is
the life which is fought
every day,
the day which is gained
every day
(the way a bird is
striving every second
to conquer its flight).

III / LÊDO IVO

In a sense, Lêdo Ivo's poetry goes back to the more playful and satirical style of the twenties. But his powers of parody are more controlled than Oswald de Andrade's (Part Four, 17). He is also less brilliant. As "Didactic Elegy" shows, there is in him something of the satirical power of Vinicius de Morães and of João Cabral's black humor. But a more sentimental tone dominates his verse. Ivo was born in Maceió, in the Northeast of Brazil, in 1920 and moved to Rio to study law and practice journalism. He has published a dozen books since 1945.

Didactic Elegy

From "Elegia didática," especially translated by Thomas Colchie.

Think about the dead young girls, who have given to the earth
    a secret ardently coveted by men,

and about schoolboys who love with the greatest purity the young
        girls
    next door whose sweethearts carry them off into the vast
    shadow of the city.

Think about the children who have never bathed in the sea, but
        who dream
    always of drowning,

and about the poor prostitutes who, after their men have departed,

run to the back of their houses and give themselves half-naked
   to the ineffable.

Think about all those who set out, guided by the stars,

and about those who have died far from the families who detest
   them.

Think about those who have given themselves to death certain that
   no tear

would be reflected in the effulgent sameness of any beloved faces.

Think about those who have never heard a declaration of love

and about the poor who have never had any notion of the
   destructive
  pleasures of slowly possessing.

Think about the rain, falling on mortgaged country homes,

and about the fruits of the small, suburban farms, touched by the
   euphoria
  of the sun in summer.

Think about the impassable streets, closed to the promise of
   journeys,

and about the people who are going to die listening to winds.

Bend to the remembrance of the strange friends of your
   adolescence.

Admit to the depth of your memory the voices that silently
  have been preparing in your heart,

in the years when no certainty of singing assaulted you.

Accept the restlessness of anger from the words that refuse
  your ardent calling

and open your eyes to a Sunday

that might concentrate everyday's expectation.

Think about the ardors of your childhood, coming back to burn
 annually in your memory,

and about those who have not come back, and have mysteriously
  died
 when they might have been disposed to returning.

Think about the ones who are going to be born, tending toward
  the close
 of your night,

and about the men who have dreamed of possessing the morning's
 serenity of trees

and have spent long evenings walking beside the ocean.

Think about the heavens that open themselves daily to planes

and about the strange women whom you have seen on certain
  nights
 and at times appear in your dreams.

Think about the adolescents uncomprehended by parents

who uselessly guard against a woman's calling them,

and about books with pages unturned, and about lamps not
  lighted.

Think about the windows inland, whose great wish is to open onto
  the sea,

and about the look of children abandoned at dawn in the
  foundling boxes
 of asylums.

Think about the women in labor dead on the tables of hospitals,

far from husbands who do not love them, and have in secret
  desired
 their disappearance.

Think about the noisome dogs carried off by dumpcarts,

and about the popular artists, violently transfigured by the
   inspiration

of a samba that a million mouths will sing at carnival.

Then think about the verses that appear in your dreams

but rejoin the clouds at the breaking of dawn.

Think about the laundresses, singing to the sun on the hill towns

and about the paintings in museums never visited.

Think about mouths that have never dominated the savage
      voluptuousness
   of other mouths

and have been aging like untouchable fruits.

Think about hearts that at a certain moment have sensed
      themselves
   pierced by the light of heaven

and have spent the rest of their days in irreparable darkness.

Think about the missing persons, whose dreadful pictures are
      printed
   in the final edition of evening papers

and about the suicides who have not left notes for lack of pencil
   and paper.

Think about the cities which rise up somberly in sight of travelers
   thirsting for clarity,

and about the sidewalks where no one passes in the morning.

Think about tunnels, dark byways torn out to the Other Side,

And about the steps that have never carried anyone on to glory
   and dominion.

Think about the repugnant beds of suspect pensions,

and about old men who always wait for the sleep called death.

Think about clocks which do not mark off lucid day,

and about the bitches dying of thirst, abandoned in the darkness
   by nature herself.

Think about the children who disregard the fugitive gift
   of the last part of springtime,

and about objects forgotten in the sands of beaches during picnics.

Think about the characters in stories, who have followed
   the uncertain destiny of their creators,

and about the moons whose radiance upsets the serenity of
      adolescents.

Think about doors which have never opened to receive a guest,

and about infected creeks which might wish to be the blue shelter
   for windjammers and yachts.

Think about the hands that have always refused alms,

and about the young women whose sweethearts deprave them with
      no pity
   whatsoever.

Then think about the ivy that embraces ancient houses, in
      suffocating
   caresses,

and about the children of former times, who have known nothing
   about Tomorrow.

Think about the great tides between the reefs, awaiting the mute
      cry
   of daybreaks,

and about the eyes of the blind that suck in the clear water of
      music
   from the hurdy-gurdies.

Think about the dead, particularly the anonymous, war dead,
   who rest in unlocatable cemeteries,

and think about the living, ignorant of the cemeteries
    wherein they will repose one day.

Oh! think about everything, about the calm horizons of your days
    from long ago, about the shudder which passes through you
    come nightfall in unfamiliar surroundings.

Think about your infancy transformed into conversations, into
        winds
    and mango trees exploding at the sun

and about the breasts of women who go on aging without
    perceiving it

and think too about the faces of those women, inexorably
        destroyed
    without your look to solicit them.

Think about your parents, who have trusted in you even when you
    were only silence,

and never have imagined your intrigue with the flight of a verse.

Think about your brothers, in your house on Sundays,

and about the courtyard of the schools where you were awakened
    to nevermore.

Think about times in which you have been strolling alone through
        the fields,

and have turned around with the hope that a woman might have
        been
    following you.

Think about the inaccessible young girls on your oldest street,

and about cries which you have heard coming from anonymous
        throats,

and about voices that were clear even in the midst of rainstorms.

Think about everything and everyone, without being afraid that
        fear
    might assault you with the amplitude of the past.

Think about everything and everyone, and after the memories
  have slipped away

soaring like birds and leaves, sand and voices,

full of confidence in life and in the world,

feeling yourself attached to all men and to all things,

bend to the body of the woman you love

or awaken to the triumphant gladness of just one verse.

IV / HAROLDO DE CAMPOS

In 1952 a small group of poets from São Paulo founded the con-
crete-poetry movement. Taking their name from a Provençal word used by
Pound in one of his *Cantos*, they published a first anthology, *Noigandres*,
soon followed by others. The group's members began traveling all over the
world, seeking to give the movement a truly international character. What
the new group aimed at was not at all new; for graphic poetry, that is, poetry
in which the spatial layout or arrangement of the verse is an essential element, was written by the Greeks, became popular in the Middle Ages, and
was rediscovered in the eighteenth century. As part of their illustrious
genealogy, the concretistas could also claim Mallarmé's *Un coup de dès*, as
well as Apollinaire's more playful *Calligrammes* and Pound's and Joyce's exercises in sight and sound. In Latin America, the Chilean Vicente Huidobro
(Part Four, 6) had preceded them by four decades. But what was really new
was the total devotion and single-minded dedication that Décio Pignatari and
Augusto and Haroldo de Campos brought to the task of spreading the new
gospel. They attracted an international audience for their work and even
aroused Octavio Paz's interest (Five, 1). Of the three, the most literary is undoubtedly Haroldo (born in São Paulo, 1929), who is also a distinguished literary critic and translator. The two poems presented here have been rendered into English with his help.

Two Concrete Poems

Translated by Mary Ellen Solt and Marco Guimarães, in Artes
Hispánicas/Hispanic Arts, *vol. 1, 3–4 (New York: The Macmillan
Company; and the University of Indiana, Winter–Spring 1968), pp.
100–104.*

speech
silver

  silence
  gold

    heads
    silver

     tails
     gold

      speech
      silence

     stop

  silver   golden
  silence   speech

        clarity

if
to be born
to die   to be born
to die   to be born to die
      to be reborn to die again to be reborn
           to die again to be reborn
                to die again
                   again

         again
       not to be born
    not to be dead not to be born
not to be dead not to be born not to be dead
          to be born to die to be born
          to die to be born
          to die
          if

V / FRANCISCO ALVIM

The youngest in this group of Brazilian poets, Francisco Alvim, has been placed by critics in the great tradition of such poet-constructors as Carlos Drummond de Andrade and João Cabral de Melo Neto. The economy and precision of his style are evident in these two poems taken from his second book, *Pass Time* (1974). He was born in Rio and still lives there.

Two Poems

From Passatempo, *especially translated by Thomas Colchie and the author.*

A Corridor

An enormous corridor
that I see everybody walking
that everybody sees me walking

An enormous enormous corridor (enormous)
that so many of us walk
I everybody walks

A corridor that walks
I everybody us
A corridor walks (itself)

The Yellow Grin of Fear

Brandishing a sword
of the finest Toledan steel
he broke into the Academy
Heads roll across every floor
it is necessary to safeguard the bread of our children
to respect authority
The very last gospel in their speeches
says how a god wrought us unequally

9

CLARICE LISPECTOR

While no Spanish American female novelist is comparable in stature to her top-ranking male colleagues, in Brazil two of the best novelists of the last decades have been women. Of these, the more renowned is undoubtedly Clarice Lispector.

She was born in the Ukraine in 1917, of Russian parents, and was only two months old when her family moved to Recife, where she spent her childhood. In 1929 she moved to Rio to study law. Having married a diplomat, Mauri Gurgel Valente, she has lived for the best part of her adult years in foreign countries. Her first book, the novel *Close to the Savage Heart,* came out in 1944. By 1960 she had already published two more novels (*The Chandelier,* 1946; *Besieged City,* 1949) and two volumes of short stories (*Some Tales,* 1952; *Family Links,* 1960). But it was not until her fourth novel, *Apple in the Dark* (1961), that Clarice achieved general recognition. The anguished, morose, introspective narrative of a man who may or may not have committed murder, the book was brilliantly written in a style that combined Virginia Woolf's poetic awareness with the French existentialist penchant for endless ruminations about human existence.

A fifth novel, *The Passion According to G.H.* (1964), was even more successful in blending a poetic imagination with a subtle awareness of physical and metaphysical states of anguish. It is shorter, and more concentrated than *Apple in the Dark,* and one of the most powerful novels produced in the sixties. The excerpt published here, in Jack E. Tomlins's skillful translation, shows her writing at her best.

A volume of short stories, *The Foreign Legion,* published in the same year, served to confirm (if confirmation were needed) Lispector's extraordinary narrative gifts.

The Passion According to G.H.

From A Paixão Segundo G.H., *especially translated by Jack E. Tomlins.*

Then the cockroach began to emerge from inside the wardrobe.

At first, a preliminary quiver of the antennae. Then, following the dry filaments, the glistening body began to appear until it had slipped almost completely through the opening of the cabinet. It was brown and it crawled diffidently as if it were carrying a great weight. Now it was nearly totally visible.

I quickly lowered my gaze. As I hid my eyes, I concealed from the cockroach the cunning that had seized me. My heart was pounding almost joyfully. The truth is that unexpectedly I felt that I was in possession of resources —I had never before used my resources—and now at last an entirely new and latent power throbbed in me, and I was in possession of a certain grandeur: the grandeur of courage, as if my very fear had at last invested me with daring. Moments before, I had casually assumed that my feelings were merely of indignation and revulsion, but now I realized—although I had never known it before— that in reality I was at last caught up by a great fear, a fear far greater than I.

This great fear penetrated deeply into me. Turned inward upon myself, like a blind man who listens fixedly to his own attention, for the first time I felt that I was totally committed to an instinct. I trembled with supreme pleasure as if at last I was aware of the grandeur of an instinct that was vile, total, and infinitely sweet; as if at last I were experiencing in my very self a grandeur of far greater magnitude than my own self. For the first time I was drunk with a hatred so pure that it seemed to well up from an underground spring: I was drunk with the desire—justified or otherwise—to kill.

An entire life of civilized refinement—for fifteen centuries I had not fought back, for fifteen centuries I had not killed, for fifteen centuries I had not died—an entire life trapped in propriety now coalesced in me and reverberated like a silent bell whose vibrations I did not require to hear. I simply recognized them. As if for the first time at last I stood face to face with Nature.

A coldly controlled rapacity had seized me, and because it was controlled, it was all power. Up to that point I had never been the mistress of my powers—powers that I did not understand and did not wish to understand—for life had carefully guarded them within me so that one day finally that unknown, joyous, and unconscious substance might be unleashed that was: me, me, whatever that might be.

With no compunctions, stirred by my surrender to whatever evil is, with no compunctions, stirred, grateful, for the first time I was being the stranger that I was. Except that being a stranger to myself would no longer be a hindrance to me; the truth had already gone beyond me: I raised my hand as if to take an oath and with a single blow I slammed the door on the half-protruding body of the cockroach. . . .

At the same time I had also closed my eyes, and I retained that attitude. I was shaking from head to toe. What had I done? Even then perhaps I knew that I was not referring to what I had done to the cockroach but rather to what I had done to myself.

The fact is that during those moments, with my eyes closed, I took cognizance of myself as one does of a flavor: I was imbued with the flavor of steel and verdigris; I was all acid like a metal on the tongue, like a crushed green plant. All my flavor came to my mouth. What had I done to myself? With my heart pounding, my temples throbbing, I had done simply this to myself: I had killed. I had killed! But why that exultation and, more than that, why the deep-rooted acceptance of the exultation? How long, then, had I been capable of killing? No, that was not the question. The question was rather: what had I killed?

The serene woman that I had always been, had she gone mad with pleasure? With my eyes still closed I was quaking with exultation. To have killed: it was so much greater than I, it was as high as the boundless room that contained me. To have killed opened up the aridity of the sands of the room to the damp, at last, at last, as if I had dug and dug with hard and eager fingers until I discovered within myself the drinkable thread of life which, in reality, was the thread of death. I slowly opened my eyes, gently now, in gratitude and diffidence, ashamed of my splendor.

Free of the damp world from which I had at last emerged, I opened my eyes and saw again the great, harsh, bare light; I saw the door of the wardrobe, now closed. And I saw half of the cockroach's body protruding from the door. Jutting forward, erect in the air, a caryatid. But a living caryatid.

At first I did not understand. I gaped in astonishment. Slowly I realized what had happened: I had not slammed the door with sufficient force. I had, however, caught the cockroach in such a way that it could not escape. And I had left it still alive. Alive and staring at me. I quickly looked aside, violently disgusted.

There was still that final blow to deliver. One blow too many? I did not look at it; rather I kept telling myself that I still had one more blow to deliver. I kept repeating it slowly as if each repetition were bound to give the command order to the pulsation of my heart, to the beats which came so slowly as to seem a pain so vague I could barely feel it. And finally I could hear myself, finally I regained control over myself and I lifted my hand high over my head as if all my body, along with the blow of my arm, would slam down on the wardrobe door.

But it was just then that I saw the cockroach's face. It was quite opposite me at the level of my head and eyes. For a moment I stood stock-still with my hand over my head. Then slowly I lowered it. Had it come perhaps an instant sooner, I might not have seen the roach's face. But the truth was that in that split second it was too late: I did see its face. My hand, which had lowered with my decision not to deliver the blow, slowly rose again to the level of my stomach. Had I not withdrawn from that spot, my stomach would have retreated inside my own body. My mouth had gone quite dry, and I passed my tongue, which was also dry, over my rough lips.

It was a shapeless face. The antennae sprouted like mustaches from the sides of the mouth. The brown mouth was clearly outlined. The fine, long mustaches wriggled slowly and dryly. Its black, faceted eyes stared. It was a roach as ancient as a fossilized fish. It was a roach as ancient as salamanders and chimeras and griffins and leviathans. It was as ancient as a legend. I looked at its mouth: there indeed was its real mouth. I had never seen a roach's mouth. To tell the truth, I had never really seen a roach. I had only been repelled by its ancient and ever-present existence. But I had never stood face to face with one, not even in my imagination.

And that is how I came to the discovery that although it is exceedingly compact, it really consists of numberless brown husks or shells, thin as the skin of an onion, as if each one could be lifted away with the fingernail and still there would remain one more shell, and yet one more. Perhaps the shells were its wings, but then it would have to be made of layer after thin layer of wings, compressed to form its compact body. It had a reddish cast. And it was covered with thin cilia. Perhaps the cilia were multiple legs. The threads of the antennae were now quiet, dusty, dry filaments.

The roach has no nose. I stared at it, at its mouth and eyes: it looked like a mulatto woman at the moment of her death. But its eyes were radiant and black. A bride's eyes. Each eye in itself had the appearance of a roach. The eye fringed, dark, lively, and free of dust. And the other eye quite the same. Two roaches encrusted on the one roach, and each eye copied the roach in its entirety.

Each eye copied the roach in its entirety.

I am sorry to have caused you this trouble, I swear it, but the truth is I do not want this for myself. Take the roach away; I do not like what I have seen. There I was, agape and outraged and hesitant: in the presence of the dusty creature that was staring at me. Here is what I saw: what I saw with a queasiness so distressing and so startling and so utterly free of guile. What I saw was life staring back at me.

How else could I describe that horrible, cruel thing that was there— raw material and dry plasma—as I retreated within myself with dry nausea, I slipping centuries and centuries into the slime. It was slime and not even slime long since desiccated but slime still moist and alive. It was a slime in which the roots of my identity writhed with unbearable sluggishness.

Take all this for yourself! I do not wish to be a living person. I feel only loathing and wonder for myself, with thick slime slowly spurting. That was it. That is what it was, then. I had looked at the living roach and in it had discovered the identity of my most profound life. In fierce demolition hard, narrow passage-ways opened up within me.

I looked at it, at the roach. I hated it so hotly that I moved to its side, one with it, because I could not have borne my hostility had I been forced to bear it alone. And suddenly I wailed sharply and that time I heard my wail. It was as if my truest consistency floated to the surface of my being like pus. And I sensed with shock and nausea that "I-being" came from a source in existence long before the human source, and I realized with horror that it was far vaster than the human source.

There opened in me, with the heaviness of great stone doors, the vast life of silence, the same life of silence within which dwelt the stock-still sun, that same life of silence in which dwelt the immobilized roach. And would it no doubt be the same life of silence in me, if I but had the courage to abandon . . . to abandon my feelings? If I had the courage to abandon hope.

Hope of what? For the first time it shocked me to realize that I had based all my hope on becoming that which I was not. Hope—what other name is there for it?—which now for the first time I was to abandon out of courage or mortal curiosity. Would hope, in my former life, have been based on some truth? With childlike amazement, I now doubted.

In order to know what I really had to hope for, would I first have to go beyond my own truth? To what degree had I, up till now, invented one fate, subsisting underground all the while on another fate?

I closed my eyes and waited for the awesome strangeness to pass and waited to see that my labored breathing would no longer be the same as the wail that I had heard as if from the bottom of a deep, dry cistern, just as the roach was a creature from a dry cistern. I still continued to hear, incalculably far away in me, the wail that no longer rose to my throat.

This is madness, I thought with my eyes closed. But I so undeniably felt that birth within the dust that I could do nothing but follow that which I well knew was not madness. It was, my God, a worse truth, the terrible truth. But why terrible? Simply because it contradicted without words everything that I had formerly thought, also without words.

I waited for the awesome strangeness to pass and for health to return. But I recognized, in an effort immemorial of memory, that I had already felt that strangeness before: it was the same that I had experienced when I first saw my own blood outside of me and was startled by it. The blood I saw outside of me, I was surprised and attracted by it: it was mine.

I did not want to reopen my eyes, I did not want to go on seeing. Ordinances and laws, it was necessary not to forget them. It is necessary not to forget that without ordinances and laws there can be no order. It was necessary not to forget them but to defend them in order to defend myself. But the fact is that I could no longer bind myself in.

The first bond had already involuntarily snapped, and I was detached from the law and even went so far as to intuit that I would enter the hell of living matter. What kind of hell awaited me? Still I had to go. I had to descend to the damnation of my soul. I was consumed by curiosity.

Then I opened my eyes all at once and took in the full view of the boundless vastness of the room, that room that pulsated silently, the laboratory of hell. The room, the unknown room. I had at last gone into the room. The entry to this room had only one passageway and it was very narrow: by a roach's standards. The roach that at last filled the room with its now active vibrations, desert rattlesnake vibrations. Through the tortuous passageway I had reached the deep incision in the wall which was that room, and the crevice formed something like a vast natural salon in a cavern.

Naked, as if ready for the entrance of a single person. And whoever entered would be transformed into a "she" or a "he." I was the one whom the room addressed as "she." And I had entered there, I to whom the room had given the dimensions of a she. As if I were also the far side of a cube, the side which cannot be seen because one views it head on.

And in my great expansion I was in the desert. How can I explain it to you? I was in the desert as I never had been before. It was a desert which beckoned to me like the call of a monotonous and distant canticle. I was being lured. I was advancing toward that madness which was ripe with promise. But my fear was that of a being going not toward madness but rather toward a truth. My fear was that I had a truth which I had come no longer to desire, a disgraceful truth which had brought me crawling to the level of a cockroach. My first contacts with truth had always cheapened me.

Hold my hand, because I feel that I am slipping away. I am slipping away once again to the ultimate primeval divine life, I am slipping away to a hell of raw life. Don't let me see because I am near to seeing the nucleus of life, and through the cockroach that even now I see again, through that specimen of quiet living horror, I fear that in that nucleus I shall no longer know what hope is.

The cockroach is pure enticement. Cilia, cilia blinking as if to call. I also, slowly reduced to what there was in me that was irreducible, I also had thousands of cilia blinking and with my cilia I advance, I the protozoan, pure protein. Hold my hand. I have reached the irreducible with the fatality of the tolling bell. I feel that all of this is ancient and vast. I sense in the sluggish cockroach's hieroglyph the orthography of the Orient. And in this desert of great enticements, creatures: I and the living cockroach. Life, my love, is a great enticement wherein everything that exists is likewise enticed. That room which was deserted and therefore primevally alive. I had attained nothingness and nothingness was alive and moist.

I had attained nothingness and nothingness was alive and moist.

It was then—it was then that very slowly, as if from a tube, the crushed cockroach's insides began to ooze. The cockroach's insides, the thick, whitish, and sluggish substance oozed out as if from a toothpaste tube.

Before my eyes, which were attracted as well as repelled, the shape of the cockroach was slowly changing as it grew thicker on the outside. The white substance oozed slowly upward along its sides as if it bore a burden. Immobilized, it supported on its dusty flanks the burden of its own body.

"Scream," I commanded myself quietly. "Scream," I repeated to myself needlessly with a sigh of profound inner repose.

The white thickness stood still now on top of the shells. I looked at the ceiling, resting my eyes a bit, for I felt that they had grown deep and very large. But if I should scream even a single time, perhaps I should never again be able to stop screaming. If I screamed, no one would be able to do a thing more on my behalf. Still, if I never make my needs known, no one will be frightened of me and they will unwittingly help me, but only as long as I do not frighten anyone by revealing that I have disobeyed the rules. If they find out, they will be frightened, we who keep our outcry as an inviolate secret. If I cry out the warning that I am alive, mute and harsh they will drag me away, for they always carry off those who depart the world of possibility, the exceptional being is dragged away, the being who cries out the warning.

I glanced at the ceiling with heavy eyes. It could all be ferociously summed up that it was better never to cry out the first time. The first outcry unleashes all the others, the first outcry at birth unleashes a life. If I should shout, I would awaken thousands of shouting beings who would shriek from the housetops a chorus of outcries and horror. If I should shout, I would unleash the existence—the existence of what? the existence of the world. Reverently I feared the existence of the world for me.

The simple truth is, I swear, that in an experiment that I never want to do again, in an experiment for which I beg myself forgiveness, I was leaving *my* world and going into *the* world. The fact is that I no longer saw myself: I was simply seeing. An entire civilization that had been erected with the certain guaranty that what is seen is immediately conjoined to what is felt, an entire civilization whose very foundation is the need to save oneself—I stood on its ruins. Only he can depart from that civilization whose special function is departure: a scientist is given license, a priest is given permission. But these are not given to a woman who does not even have the guaranty of a title. And I was fleeing, with some disquietude I was fleeing.

If you could know the loneliness of those first steps I took. It was not like the solitude of a person. It was as if I had already died and was taking my first solitary steps in another life. And it was as if they called that solitude glory. And I knew also that it was a kind of glory, and I trembled in that primeval divine glory that not only did I not understand but neither did I want.

Because, you see, I knew that I was entering the brutal, raw glory of nature. Enticed, meanwhile I struggled as best I could against the quicksand that was dragging me down: and every movement I made toward "no, no!"—every movement impelled me forward the more hopelessly. The fact that I lacked the strength to struggle was my only pardon.

I looked about the room that had imprisoned me and sought an exit. Desperately I attempted to escape. I had retreated so deeply into myself that my soul was flattened against the wall. Not even able to stop myself, not even wanting any longer to stop myself, seduced by the certainty of the magnet that attracted me, I withdrew into myself as far as the wall, where I encrusted myself on the sketch of the woman that hung there. I had withdrawn to the marrow of my bones, my ultimate haven. There on the wall I was so naked that I made no shadow.

And the dimensions, they were still the same or at least I sensed that they were. I knew that I had never surpassed that woman on the wall: she and I were the same. And she was totally preserved, a long and fruitful road.

Suddenly my tension snapped like a noise that is interrupted. And the first true silence began to blow. Whatever I had previously seen in my dark and smiling photographs that was serene and vast and foreign—that, for the first time, was outside of me but totally within my reach, incomprehensible but within my reach.

What eased me, as a thirst is quenched, eased me as if all my life I had waited for water, as necessary for my bristling body as cocaine is for the addict who whimpers after it. Finally my body, drenched in silence, was at peace. My easement came from the fact that I fitted into the mute design of the cavern.

Up till that moment I had not totally understood the nature of my struggle because I had been so thoroughly immersed in it. But now, with the silence into which I had at last fallen, I knew that I had struggled, that I had succumbed, and that I had surrendered. And that now I was really in the room. As inside it as a painting inscribed three hundred thousand years on the wall of a cave. And there I was: I fitted inside myself. I was in myself etched on the wall.

The narrow passageway had been difficult for the cockroach to negotiate, and I had slithered with nausea through that body made up of layers of thin shells and mud. And I had ended up, as foul as the roach, by emerging through the roach onto my past, which was my eternal present and my eternal future, and which is today and always on the wall; and my fifteen million daughters, from the past down to me, were also there. My life had been as eternal as death. Life is so eternal that we divide it into stages, and one of them we call death. I had always been in the midst of life. It matters little that, strictly speaking, it was not myself, not what I conventionally call me. I have always been in the midst of life.

I, the neuter body of the cockroach, I with a life which, after all is said and done, does not escape me because at last I see it outside of me—I am the cockroach, I am my leg, I am my hair, I am the streak of brightest light on the plaster of the wall—I am every infernal piece of me—life in me is so persistent that if they cut me in two, the halves of me, like the lizard, will still keep on shuddering and wriggling. I am the silence etched on a wall, and the most ancient of butterflies flutters and comes face to face with me: eternally the same. From birth to death, it is that in me which I call human, and I shall never really die.

But this is not eternity. It is damnation.

How sumptuous this silence is. It has accumulated over centuries. It is the silence of a staring cockroach. The world looks at itself in me. Everything looks at everything, everything lives every other thing. In this desert, things know things. Things know things so well that . . . I shall call this forgiveness, if I shall want to save myself on the human level. It is forgiveness in itself. Forgiveness is an attitude of living matter.

Forgiveness is an attitude of living matter.

You see, my love, you see how, out of fear, I am organizing. You see how I cannot quite rummage about in these basic elements of the laboratory without immediately wishing to organize hope. It is simply that for the time being the metamorphosis of me into me myself makes no sense at all. It is a metamorphosis in which I lose everything that I had, and what I had was I—I have only what I am. And now what am I? I am: standing in the presence of fear. I am: what I have seen. I do not understand and I am afraid to understand. The material of the world frightens me, with its planets and cockroaches.

I who before had lived on loving words or pride or on anything at all. But what an abyss separates the word from its intent, what an abyss separates the word love, and love that does not make human sense—because love is the living substance. Love is the living substance?

What happened to me yesterday? and now? I am confused. I have crossed countless deserts, but have I been caught under some small detail, as under a large boulder?

No, wait, wait: with some relief I must remind you that I have been out of that room since yesterday. I have already left it. I am free and I still have a chance to recover! If I want to. But do I really want to?

What I saw cannot be organized. But if I really want to, right now, I can still translate what I learned into terms more our own, into human terms, and I can still leave unfurnished the hours I spent yesterday. If I still wish to, in our language I can ask myself in another way what happened to me.

And if I ask in that way, I may yet have an answer that would work my recuperation. It would be recuperation to know that: G.H. was a woman who lived well, lived well, lived well, lived in the superstratum of the sands of the world, and the sands had never caved in beneath her feet. The synchronization was so fine that as the sands moved, my feet moved in time with them so that everything was firm and compact. G.H. lived on the upper story of a superstructure, and although it was built in the air it was a solid structure, she herself in the air, like the bees who weave their lives in the air. This had been going on for centuries with the inevitable or casual variations, and it all worked out. It all worked out. At least nothing spoke and no one spoke, no one said the contrary. It all worked out, then.

But it was precisely the slow accumulation of centuries piling up on centuries that, without anyone's taking notice, was making the structure too heavy to stand on air. The structure was slowly becoming saturated with itself. It was growing more and more compact instead of growing more and more delicate. The accumulation of living in a superstructure was growing heavier and heavier, too heavy to be supported in mid-air.

Like a building in which everyone sleeps peacefully without knowing that the foundations are sagging, a building whose girders will give way all unexpectedly in the midst of so much tranquility because the cohesive force is slowly crumbling away at the rate of a millimeter per century. And then, when it is least expected, in an instant as repetitiously vulgar as that of raising a cocktail glass to smiling lips at a ball—then, yesterday, on a sun-drenched day like these at the height of summer, with men working and kitchens steaming and children laughing and a priest struggling to stave off, but to stave off what? Yesterday, with no notice, came the horrible din of solid substance suddenly undermined and crumbling in the debacle.

In the collapse tons fell on tons. And when I, G.H. even on my luggage, I, one of the persons, opened my eyes, I was—not standing on the ruins because even the ruins had been sucked under by the sands—I was on a tranquil plain, countless kilometers beneath what had once been a great city. Things had become once again what they were.

The world had reclaimed its own reality, and, as after a catastrophe, my civilization had come to an end. I was only a historical fact. Everything in me had been reclaimed by the beginning of time and by my own beginning. I had passed on to a first primeval plane. I stood in the silence of the winds and in the age of tin and copper—in the first age of life.

Listen! Before the living cockroach the worst discovery of all was that the world is not human and that we are not human.

No, do not be frightened! To be sure, that which had, up till that moment, saved me from the life of sentiment by which I existed is the fact that the nonhuman is by far the best part of us; it is the thing, the thing-part of us. That is the only reason why, as a false person, I had not, up till then, sunk beneath the sentimentarian and utilitarian structure. My human sentiments were utilitarian, but I had not gone under because the thing-part, which is the substance of God, was too strong and was waiting to reclaim me as its own. The great neutral punishment of life in general is that it may suddenly suck away the sap of life. If it is not granted the force of life itself, then it bursts like a dike—and it comes pure, unalloyed: purely neutral. That was the great danger: when that neutral thing-part does not thoroughly drench a personal life, that life becomes totally and purely neutral.

But why was it precisely in me that the primeval silence reconstituted itself? As if a serene woman had merely been called, and had serenely laid her embroidery aside on the chair, had stood up without a word—abandoning her life, disowning her embroidery, her love, and her mature spirit—without a word that woman had quite serenely gone down on all fours like an animal and dragged herself along the floor with shining, serene eyes: her former life had laid claim to her and she had gone to meet it.

But why me? But why not me? If it had not been me, I never would have learned the truth. But it was me and I did learn: it is as simple as that. What, indeed, had called me: madness or reality?

Life avenged itself on me, and the vengeance consisted merely of my return, nothing more. Every case of madness is one in which something has returned. The possessed, they are not possessed by what comes, but rather by what returns. Sometimes life returns. If everything was shattered in me as the great force passed over me, that was not because the function of the force was to shatter: it merely needed at last to pass over me because it had become far too torrential to be checked or diverted. As it passed, it covered everything in its path. And afterward, as after a flood, a wardrobe, a person, an unhinged window, three pieces of luggage floated to the surface. And that seemed to me to be hell, that destruction of stratum after human archaeological stratum. Hell, because the world no longer held out for me any human meaning, and man had no human meaning. And in a world with neither humanity nor sentiment—I am terrified.

Without a cry I looked at the roach. Seen close up the cockroach is a magnificent object. A bride draped in black jewels. It is quite rare; it seems a unique specimen. Having caught it at the midpoint of the body with the wardrobe door, I had isolated a unique specimen. Only half of its body was showing. The rest, which was not visible, might well be enormous, divided into thousands of houses, behind things and wardrobes. Still, I did not want the part that fell to my lot. Behind the surface of houses—those faded jewels dragging over the floor?

I felt that I was unclean, as the Bible speaks of the unclean. Why was the Bible so preoccupied with the unclean, why did it list unclean, forbidden animals? Why, if, like the others, they had also been created? And why was the unclean forbidden? I had committed the forbidden act of touching the unclean.

I had committed the forbidden act of touching the unclean.

And so unclean was I in that sudden indirect recognition of myself, that I opened my mouth to ask for help. They tell everything in the Bible, they tell everything—but if I truly understand what they are saying, they themselves will call me mad. People just like me had said those things, yet understanding them would spell my downfall.

"Thou shalt not eat of the unclean: of the eagle, neither of the griffin nor of the merlin shalt thou eat." Nor the owl, nor the swan, nor the bat, nor the stork, nor all manner of crow.

I was beginning to know that the unclean animal of the Bible is forbidden because the unclean is the source—for there are things created that were never elaborated and remained always as they were at the moment of their creation, and only they continued to be the source that was still complete. And because they were the source, they could not be eaten, the fruit of good and evil —to eat the substance of life would expel me from a paradise of adornments and condemn me to wander forever with my staff in the desert. Many were they who wandered with a staff in the desert. Worse—it would condemn me to see that the desert is also alive and is moist, to see that everything is alive and made of the same substance.

In order to construct a possible soul—a soul whose head will not devour its own tail—the law commands that one keep only that which feigns life. And the law commands that he who partakes of the unclean do so unwittingly. So he who partakes of the unclean knowing that it is unclean, shall he also know that the unclean is not unclean? Is that the way it goes?

"And all that crawls and is winged shall be unclean and thou shalt not partake of it."

My mouth gaped in shock: to ask for help. Why? Because I did not wish to become as unclean as the cockroach? What ideal caught me up in the sentiment of an idea? Why should I not become unclean, just as I was coming to know myself to my very depths? What did I fear? To become unclean with what?

To become unclean with joy.

Now I understand that what I had begun to feel was joy, what I had not yet recognized or understood. In my mute outcry for help, I was struggling against a vague primeval joy that I did not wish to discern in myself because, although it was vague, nonetheless it was terrible: it was a joy without redemption. I do not know how to explain it to you, but it was a joy without hope.

Oh, don't take your hand away. I promise that perhaps by the end of this impossible account I shall maybe understand, oh perhaps on the way to hell I shall come to find what we require—but don't take your hand away even though I have long since known that the finding must be along the way of what we are, if I succeed in not sinking once and for all into the depths of what we are.

You see, my love, I am already losing the courage to find whatever it is that I must find. I am losing the courage to surrender myself to the way, and I am already promising us that I shall find hope in that hell. Perhaps it is not that ancient hope. Perhaps it cannot even be called hope. I was struggling because I did not want an unknown joy. My future salvation would forbid that as much as the forbidden creature called unclean. And I opened and closed my mouth torturedly to ask for help, because at that time it had not yet occurred to me to invent this hand that I have now invented to hold my own. In yesterday's fear I was alone and I wanted to ask for help against my first dehumanization. Dehumanization is as harrowing as losing all, my love. I opened and closed my mouth to ask for help, but I could not articulate, nor did I know how to articulate, a single syllable.

The truth is that I no longer had words to speak. My torment was that of wishing that I was bidding eternal farewell to something, something was going to die, and I wanted to utter the word that might at least sum up that which was passing away.

Finally I succeeded at least in articulating a thought: "I am asking for help." It occurred to me then that I had no reason to ask for help. I had nothing to ask.

Suddenly there was that. I was beginning to understand that "to ask for" was the last vestige of a world to which one might appeal which, more and more, was receding into the distance. And if I continued to want to ask for something it was so that I might still clutch after the last vestiges of my ancient civilization, to clutch that I might not be dragged down by that which once again laid claim to me. And to which—in a joy without hope—I was quite surrendering. Oh, I wanted to surrender. To have experienced was the beginning of a hell of wanting, wanting, wanting. Was my will to want stronger than my will to salvation?

More and more I had nothing to ask. And I saw, with fascination and horror, the scraps of my putrid mummy wrappings fall aridly to the ground. I witnessed my metamorphosis from a cocoon into a moist larva. My parched wings slowly shrank. And a whole new body, destined to live on the ground, a new body was born.

Without taking my eyes off the cockroach, I bent down until I felt my body touch the bed. Without taking my eyes off the cockroach, I sat down. Now I had to lift my eyes to see it. Now, leaning over its own midsection, it looked me up and down. I had trapped in front of me the world's unclean. I had unearthed the living thing. I had lost my train of thought.

Then, once again, one more thick millimeter of the white substance oozed out.

. . .

Then, once again, one more thick millimeter of the white substance oozed out.

Holy Mary, Mother of God, I offer up my life to you in exchange for your invalidation of that moment yesterday. The cockroach with its insides oozing out looked at me. I do not know whether it could see me. I do not know what a cockroach sees. But the cockroach and I were staring at one another, and neither do I know what a woman sees. But if its eyes could not see me, its existence lent me existence. In the primeval world that I had entered, beings lend existence to other beings as their way of seeing each other. And in that world which I was gradually coming to know, there are various ways to signify the act of seeing: one being might look at another without seeing it, or one might possess the other, or one devour the other, or one simply be in a corner and the other be there too: all these also signify seeing. The cockroach did not see me directly: it was with me, merely. The cockroach did not see me with its eyes, rather with its body.

And I—I saw. There was no way to avoid seeing it. There was no denying: my convictions and my wings were quickly singed and they served no further purpose. I could no longer make denials. I do not know exactly what it was that I could no longer deny, but still I no longer could. And neither could I continue to avail myself of a civilization that would help me deny what I was seeing.

I saw all of it, all of the roach. The cockroach is an ugly, shiny creature. The cockroach is an upside-down creature. No, strictly speaking, it does not have a right side or a wrong side: it is merely that what it exposes, I hide. I turned the visible side of me into my unknown underside. It stared at me. And it was not a face. It was a mask. The mask of a deep-sea diver. That precious gem of rusty hue. The two eyes were alive like two ovaries. It looked at me with the blind fertility of its stare. It fertilized my dead fertility. I wondered whether its eyes were saline. If I touched them—now that I was gradually growing more and more unclean—if I touched them with my mouth, would they taste salty to me? I had already tasted a man's eyes, and from the taste of salt in my mouth I had known that he was crying.

But, when I thought of the saltiness of the cockroach's black eyes, I suddenly recoiled again. My lips pulled back over my teeth: the reptiles who crawl on the face of the earth! In the dull reverberation of light in the room, the cockroach was a small and sluggish crocodile. The dry and vibrant room. The cockroach and I poised on that arid spot as if on the dry crust of some extinct volcano. That desert onto which I had ventured and where I discovered life and the salt of life. Then again the whitish insides of the roach oozed out maybe something less than a millimeter. That time I could just barely sense the slow movement of the stuff. I stared, abstracted and silent.

Never, up till then, had life happened to me in the daytime. Never by sunlight. Only in the depth of my nights had the world slowly whirled. Except that what happened in the darkness of my own night happened also in the very depths of my being, and my own darkness was none other than the darkness of the outside world. And in the morning, when I opened my eyes, the world went on as a surface: the secret of the night quickly dissolved in my mouth along with the taste of a vanishing nightmare. But now life was happening in broad daylight. Undeniable, so that it might be seen. Unless I looked aside. And I could still look aside.

But the truth is that hell had already spirited me away, my love, the hell of my sickly curiosity. I was already selling my human soul because seeing had already begun to consume me with pleasure. I was selling my future. I was selling my salvation. I was selling us.

"I am asking for help," I shouted to myself then suddenly with the silence of those whose mouths are gradually choked with quicksand. "I am asking for help," I thought, sitting there quietly. But at no time did it occur to me to get up and go away, as though that act were already impossible. The cockroach and I had been buried in a mine.

The scales had then only one dish. On that dish was placed my profound denial of cockroaches. But now "denial of cockroaches" was merely words, and I also knew that at the hour of my death I would also be untranslatable by mere words.

I indeed knew of dying, because dying was the future and is imaginable, and I had always had time for imagining. But the instant, this instant—this very present—that is not imaginable. Between the present and myself there is no chasm: it is now in me.

You understand, I knew of dying beforehand, and dying still made no demands on me. But what I had never experienced was impact with the moment called "right now." Today demands of me today itself. I had never before realized that the time of living also has no word. The time of living, my love, was becoming so right now that I pressed my mouth to the substance of life. The time of living is a slow continuum of creaking doors which are endlessly flung open wide. Two large entry doors were opened, and they had never stopped opening. But they opened endlessly onto—onto nothingness?

The time of living is so hellishly inexpressive that it is nothingness. What I called "nothing" was nevertheless so inseparable from me that to me it was . . . I myself? and therefore it was becoming invisible as I was invisible to myself, and it was becoming nothingness. The doors as usual continued to open.

At last, my love, I succumbed. And it became a single now. One all-engulfing present.

10

NÉLIDA PIÑÓN

Up to a point, Nélida Piñòn could be seen as a disciple of Clarice Lispector's. Both writers share an interest in defining and expressing woman's existential condition; both write intricate, anguished novels. But there the similarities end. While Clarice Lispector is closer to Simone de Beauvoir in her quest for a nonreligious experience, in everything Nélida Piñòn writes there is a quest for some lost transcendental faith.

She was born in Rio in 1937, of Spanish parents, and has devoted her life to writing. After a stint as a journalist for *Cadernos Brasileiros* in the sixties and some teaching in a workshop for young writers, she traveled extensively in Europe and the States.

She published two novels (*Map of Gabriel Archangel*, 1961; *Wood Into Cross*, 1963) and a collection of short stories (*The Season of Fruits*, 1966), and then she produced an ambitious panoramic novel, *Founder* (1969), which attempted to explore through four contrasted and parallel plots the destiny of man. Her fourth novel, *House of Passion* (1971), was more successful. With a cast of only four characters, the novel retraced certain basic myths—the gift of a woman in marriage, the physical possession of a virgin woman as symbolizing possession of the earth—in a context in which Catholic ceremonies and older, more primitive rituals clashed, and were ultimately integrated. Despite its allegorical character, the novel is extremely concrete and even "physical" in its details, as the beautiful chapter excerpted here shows. Recently, Piñón published a fifth novel, *Thebes of My Heart* (1974), an even longer and more ambitious work than *Founder*.

House of Passion

From A Casa da Paixão, *especially translated by Gregory Rabassa.*

She had followed her since she was small. Antônia had witnessed her birth, accused her father with a look, cleaned up Marta, lost in the placenta. She smelled sour, then Marta learned to hide her face in the useless breasts, catching the breathing. Later on, she suffered with the decomposition of that body—martyrized skin, as she defined it with surprise—feeling the sex through the dress.

She trailed after Antônia to discover her secret, her lack of submission to any virtue. Her face closed, barely showing her teeth, her words had to be listened to carefully or they would become lost and no one would hear them. Marta would call, "Antônia, food, water, and be quick."

Just to see her run, so that no one would think that she was dead, forgotten among creatures. Antônia seemed to imitate animals in her way of walking, her scarred face, pity all over her, the way she kept her hair created the image. She stinks—Marta said those words and took pity on the animal that served in the house. She couldn't imagine that sex wide open, some man sinking in there like a snake. She feared an Antônia free for such things. A bad-smelling woman could give pleasure the same as a rare species, those skinny, nervous women who can climb walls because they're so agile, truncated lizards. She felt that Antônia's sex was suppurating, she kept repeating it, but not from the illnesses of men, because nature would respond mysteriously and darkly to such evil things.

In the morning Antônia did the milking. She touched the udder of the cow as if she were loving it, making some kind of love on that fallen flesh that recalled a man's machine. Marta blushed at the comparison. Antônia's way of drawing out the milk was more like a beautiful ejaculation.

Then Antônia would lose herself. She liked ant trails, avoiding Marta. And even when they were close to a tree, in the kitchen, because one demanded of the other the displeasing smell of their respective excited skins, they scarcely spoke.

Marta knew that Antônia probably loved her as one loves a table, a chair, small objects, an extravagance that could divide the earth. But Antônia did everything to make Marta forget her. She wouldn't allow herself to be loved even for brief moments. Marta bringing her a flower, she delicately refusing, placing the flower on Marta's own breast. She was not to be rendered homage, she had told her sternly before. Antônia might well confess: my smell doesn't reconcile itself with yours, because she had told her once that to stink was also to survive. From condor to man, from mountains to dust. She'd been born dirty and she was used to it. Greater cleanliness would have transformed her beauty.

The father watched the closeness of the two women, one almost animal excrement, the other the child of his perdition. Understanding that the union of strange beings was a natural end, he too followed his daughter, faithful and dishonored, bearing in his heart the grief that successive discoveries brought out in him. Marta was lost in Antônia—in whom was he also lost?

The father took care that Antônia should not be offended. When he spoke to her he never looked right at her, and he only noticed her when, looking for Marta, he saw Antônia close by. But Marta recognized Antônia as one of the strongest resources in the home. It would be good if she lived longer than her own mother, whose death she had seen close up. Antônia told her that the woman had trembled as she expired, just like a chicken. She made it clear so that Marta would make the vision grow in her breast.

Antônia slept in the barn, in the straw. Marta brought her coffee just one time. And it's not love, she murmured, so that even she wouldn't get her feelings all mixed up. She wanted to surprise the woman, ugly and dirty, in her beast's lair. For a long time she had wanted to plumb the most secret undergrowth of that body, get into its veins like some tiny thing, smell her nauseating stench, the aged flesh, search out her thoughts perhaps.

The woman didn't sense her arrival, not for a moment did her savage routine warn her of the danger. She slept with her clothes on, saving the trouble of any changing. With her legs open, it was possible to put a branch or a rake in through her gates, not to poke or to dig, but to return to hell the production of ardent animals. A free head, Marta felt. A desire to tread on the woman, not to touch her body, her audacity drew back envisioning other deeper contacts, but to dominate her condition and step on her the way one crushes a fallen leaf, rubbish. She could not resist the fruit power, the star power that that singular woman conferred on her. So much so that she was driven by the pretext of bringing her coffee to warm up her perhaps sclerotic veins.

Antônia opened her eyes. She spied Marta, accepting her presence. That creature who surprised her by mistrusting her existence. "Come here, you bitch."

Marta went closer, she too seemed to expose her body to the thorns, the pains, suffering in general. She had invaded Antônia's realm, it seemed proper to her to accept the insult. It was difficult to conquer a peopled territory through the shadows, everything so hostile. She was guided by the woman's smell, fetid, unpleasant, so many substances had decided to concentrate there so that Marta would not be lost. She imagined the woman swallowed up by the depths of the earth, the naked earth in all its splendor. A weighty breathing asking forgiveness because Marta had finally commanded her to exist.

Antônia didn't get up. She enjoyed that freedom for the first time. Marta was so close, almost in the other's hole, that she could barely stand the adventure of that woman. Passing to hatred or killing was not difficult for her. Like squashing a bug, climbing a tree, picking a piece of fruit and flinging it far off. Never forgetting to return the pit to the ground, what a strange thing it produced, because everyone was androgyne, volatile, and concrete, and she inadvertently sucked.

Antônia had to die, she thought one last time. And she went away because of the malignant love, the kind they offered her. She knew she was destined to love unpleasant, forbidden things, the sun then, until she opened her convalescent eyes and chose the more rooted heat of the earth, which was really rooted in the soil of the intestines, so much so that in the midst of pain and wounds Marta had gone off to hunt it, for she never doubted its trail. Heat was man's crystalline destiny. And she lay down beside the woman as if she could make love to a repulsive creature, then to save her own soul.

They were still for a long time. Antônia, with accelerated breathing, an insect speedily registering the quality of the flight, murmured that only Marta understood, saying no, I rescued you from out of the placenta, the red product of marketplace and woods, I extracted you from the vagina of the woman and it would be easy to sink you back where you'd be forgotten, burying your head in the water, or back to the darkness you came out of, but I saved you the way one saves a nervous fish, the scales slide like a razor, the way one chooses what still hasn't been proven, and Antônia murmured those things as if they'd been lying broken among her teeth for many long days, a meal preserved in alcohol, not pieces of a snake kept in liquor, and she shook her head harshly in a way Marta had never seen her act before, Marta, who had learned how to surprise Antônia a long time ago, when, actually, the secret archives of the two had been started, the years then passed, it was on a cold morning, Marta decided to follow her: Antônia went into the henhouse to collect the daily eggs: she and no one else performed that chore: she would fight with anyone who tried to emulate her, even Marta was expelled when she tried to take her place, not caring in her brief fury that Marta, judging herself wronged, would complain to her father: perhaps through her father to understand a sacred wisdom, and because of which he didn't answer, that only Antônia should gather the warm eggs, pushed out of the fragile and hesitant bodies of the hens: and she followed her in the same way that she had followed her into the barn in order to see that woman conciliating sleep, although Antônia had seemed hesitant of late, would have lost the virility that Marta appreciated, without knowing why, Antônia was an androgyne, she wagered in her sex, and she glowed with the invention of what any concept would deny, her origin had doubtless abandoned some island, a native of doubtful sex, tall in stature, long hair, man and woman as it mattered, to adopt the sinuosity of a river, lost on so many frontiers, and Marta was careful so that Antônia in those moments would not produce in her body another birth, as if creating other weapons, suffering the apathy of a new world: she sought secrecy for the intense observation, perhaps Antônia would suddenly raise up a round belly, almost a pregnant creature: she went into the henhouse closing the door, Antônia revealed a certain beauty that Marta never cared to admit, the beauty of the wild boar for those who understand that perfection, and Marta assessed the open face of the woman with a sudden joy, as if she saw not the customarily repugnant old woman before whom she had let herself be burned by the sun that she loved and for whom she always opened her legs in search of greater torment: Antônia calmly gathered the eggs in a basket, acting without any worry of hurting or damaging them, but she looked at the creatures as if they were Marta, to whom she helped give birth, even though the look she cast at Marta was always furtive, one would not imagine that it was close to love and represented it: perhaps Marta condemned Antônia's lust in gathering the eggs, until Antônia, unable any more to bear an affliction that Marta suddenly understood and had accompanied from the beginning, to which a vehement metamorphosis was owed, at the point of suddenly being changed into a fat woman, close to the tearing of her pelvis, scattering fruits into the world in the midst of the pain—she went to where the hen had left among red feathers and delicate blood a newly constructed egg: she contemplated the warm hay, precisely where the creature had put down the basest part of her body, for Marta the most pleasing and burning, to the point of wanting to insert her finger along the same trail that the egg had known, not to feel the warmth that the closed and silent thing preserved, but to reconstruct in some way the apprenticeship of a hen, which Antônia could clarify perhaps under the power of love, she would say, you can be sure, Marta, her giving birth is different, she doesn't do her best the way a woman does, her pains run in opposite directions and there's no indication of the most honorable among them: she pitied the hen, Antônia lost in contemplation of the nest in which the creature had settled her extremities, had only been there long enough for the time of her pain, her placenta was timid, it had excrement, feathers, and a modest line of blood: Antônia picked up the egg, raising it to the level of her face, smelled the swollen thing, newly abandoned in the world, and, after smelling it, she kissed the egg as in a sacrifice, or in full flight, an object almost converted into a winged piece by her own exhalation: unable to bear, however, the love that broke away from that hot, humid thing that one hen among so many others had manufactured there, to the extreme of the old woman's feeling the product of the hen projecting itself in her face, in Antônia's face there was probably excrement, viscera, everything the hen, intimidated by duty, was to place in its making— Antônia was gliding toward the center of the earth where the hen had also been born, all of her species conceived in that way, in a nest covered with hay, feathers, a smell which Antônia absorbed in the end and which now lived in her skin: she stayed there for a long time, stern, until her legs opened wide over the hay and imitated a hen in laying position, Marta had a precise look at everything Antônia was practicing to assimilate the bird, anyone who saw her would not doubt her transcendence as much as the fact that the old woman was abdicating her human form in the pretext of being the hen who gave up the struggle after an enormous effort, her face showed the rigors of procreation, her cheeks trembled, her teeth, she was so dilated by the effort that Marta murmured: let the creature open her womb for the ground: she wanted to go get her, pull Antônia out of her supreme pretension, explain her minor performance, but the old woman was flapping her arms like wings, her mouth was a beak, her crest was fallen, lost among false clouds: even though Marta had not been negligent in the perfection of those instants, Antônia was delirious—and that was always her excuse—no longer bearing the pain, she was acting as if successive eggs were coming out of her shaken vagina, children, chayotes, green, half thorny, she shouted, however, cries just like a hen's, she cackled, a rooster spreading light, telling of dawn, a hen, no doubt, going to fetch with her hands, in that hidden region, the egg fruit of her passion: she stood up quickly, first withdrawing from her buttocks and adopting as her own the same egg that had been there: later on, in the kitchen, Marta pointed to the egg that the old woman held like a child and said, "The prettiest one of the lot, Antônia."

Antônia looked at her as if sliding down a mountain, fainting and tumbling. She asked Marta to stay, just a few minutes. And seeming to be offering

her a bird, a habit never cultivated by them, she fried the egg and made her eat
it: in the same way as she had demanded her body beside hers in the barn and
they stayed that way, quiet and in surrender, so that the woman's respiration
would become stronger than Marta's, when the most profane secrets would be
transmitted: Marta dragged her fingers in order to know some god who existed
by himself, her only responsibility to be proud of the earth, she touched Antônia's
hand and thought that that instrument at least once had been introduced into
the womb of her mother, had not hesitated to draw her from there with life to
give her afterward to the world, or perhaps to return her to the vegetable world,
with which she would be more closely associated, something discreet, but which
came to constitute her own shape: she thought that other responsibilities should
be credited to that hand, a reason to bring it to her body so that it would rest
calmly on her breasts, grown now, rigid when caressed, a natural modesty that
moved her: Antônia rested on Marta's breasts, the earth breathing outside, they
knew, especially Marta, that her thin skin would explode when the milk flooded
it, it would be necessary to want offspring, any kind of offspring, and she a
fertilization of gods: Antônia slipped her hand down and touched her sex and said
with a barbed-wire voice, I'm old, ugly, but your joy will come out of here: Marta
arose, anointed by Antônia's consecration, she still feared that the miracle would
never take place in the end if Antônia weren't capable of foreseeing: they both
tried to transmit the most vehement truths to the innocence of the atmosphere,
for Marta wanted Antônia to take part in her burning: they were enemies and
they loved each other, the egg that fed her that morning would join her flesh with
fury as if she had had it in her tissues until then, that nourishment that Antônia
had abdicated in her favor.

"So, Antônia, is that the joy you promise?"

Antônia sneezed, just like an animal, hairy, ugly, she pretended to sleep
now, obliging Marta to desist in the spectacle that her always smelly body
represented: but when Marta, with some gesture, looked for a kind of untran-
slated light, which had finally arisen, perhaps conquering the end of the night,
giving relief to the house, to the trees, to what was made dark and later lighted,
Antônia still told her, and it was like a threat, "We know about the egg. What
about your sun sex?"

11

TWENTY SPANISH AMERICAN POETS

While the main interest of Latin American readers may seem to be in fiction (see introduction to Part Five), many writers are still very much concerned with poetry. As in Brazil, so in Spanish America, each decade of this century has produced a new crop of distinguished poets. They may come from Argentina or Cuba, from Central America or Chile, from Peru, Venezuela, or Mexico; the varieties of modes and styles, the differences in style and rhetoric, that separate them may be enormous. But all these new poets share one thing: they continue to develop a tradition that began in the late 1880s with Darío and the modernists (Part Three, 1–7), was radically altered by avant-garde experiments (Four, 6–15), and found in such contemporary writers as Huidobro, Vallejo, Borges, Neruda, Paz, and Parra its new masters.

Surrealism, narrative and even epic verse, popular songs, slang and vernacular of all sorts, revolutionary ideologies—all these and more are to be found in the poetry of the last decades. To try to display fully this vast and vastly disparate production would require another book as long as the present one. Instead of attempting such an impossible task, the selection that follows seeks to mount a collage of voices—voices that, in brief compass, unmistakably represent the continuing vitality of Spanish American poetry.

I / ALBERTO GIRRI

An heir to the surrealist tradition, Alberto Girri (Argentina, 1918) is a loner. Since 1946 he has produced a substantial amount of work, developing in a firm and subtle way a passionate, almost tragic, vision of the world. His sensuality is always severely controlled by intelligence. An elegant irony prevents him from becoming sentimental or purely rhetorical. The evidence of his skill and depth can be found in poems such as "Epistle to Hierónymus Bosch," in which the painter's work becomes an emblem of the poet's unique personal vision.

Epistle to Hieronymus Bosch

From Latin American Writing Today, *edited and translated by J. M. Cohen (Baltimore: Penguin Books, 1967).*

How well you knew
all that we children of wrath
did not understand,
the source of that evil
which deforms our substance,
an incorporeal evil which you examined
like one who piles corpses
and with cold scalpel
extracts the madness from their heads,
and from their anatomies
the confusion of the three kingdoms.
Trees with faces
stones that are also plants,
animate and poisonous metals,
an insect astride a bird
and the bird sharpening its knife;
for of this you spoke and shouted,
and in visual form
established that properly joined
we form a single body,
deprived of the great benefit,
withdrawn from love of the seed
that fell on the ground and died,
not its own loss but ours.
But always man,
I, someone else, or you,
man and his nakedness
stupidly rambling through
gardens of fair delights
and the plateaus of hell,
and behind and above
the haywain of the world,
on which everyone snatches anything he can;
his nakedness, not sex,
homesick for the sum of nakedness,

the primal hermaphrodite unity,
the complete being Adam-and-Eve.

Vagabond of the strange,
hand that aspired to consciousness,
may the prayers of your Mass
have mounted straight
like a perfume.

II / ALI CHUMACERO

A classical style, a dark, somber eroticism, an intelligence that illumi-
nates the lines like inner lightning—these are the characteristics of Ali Chumacero's poetry. Born in 1918, Chumacero has been an active participant in Mexico's
literary life. And yet, his is a totally private poetry, the poetry of a man who writes
in the seclusion of his own inner self. The two selections presented here, in
admirable versions by William Carlos Williams, attest to the passion and privacy
of this poetic vision.

Two Poems

Translated by William Carlos Williams, in Evergreen Review, *vol. 2, no. 7
(Winter 1959), pp. 59–61.*

Widower's Monologue

I open the door, return to the familiar mercy
of my own house, where a vague
sense protects me the son who never was
smacking of shipwreck, waves, or a passionate cloak
whose acid summers
cloud the fading face. Archaic refuge
of dead gods fills the region,
and below, the wind breathes, a conscious
gust which fanned my forehead yesterday
still sought in the perturbed present.

I could not speak of sheets, candles, smoke,
nor humility and compassion, calm

at the afternoon's edges, I could not
say "her hands," "her sadness," "our country"
because everything in her name
is lighted by her wounds. Like a signal sprung
of foam, an epitaph, curtains, a bed, rugs,
and destruction moving toward disdain
while the lime triumphs denying her nakedness
the color of emptiness.

Now time, begins, the bitter smile
of the guest who in sleeplessness sings,
waking his anger, within the vile city
the calcined music with curled lip
from indecision
that flows without cease. Star or dolphin, yonder
beneath the wave his foot vanishes,
tunics turned to emblems
sink their burning shows and with ashes
score my own forehead.

The Wanderings of the Tribe

Autumn surrounds the valley, iniquity
overflows, and the hill sacred to splendor
responds in the form of a revenge. The dust measures
and misfortune knows who gallops
where all gallop with the same fury:
constrained attendance on the broken circle
by the son who startles his father gazing
from a window buried in the sand.

Blood of man's victim
besieges doors, cries out, "Here no one lives,"
but the mansion is inhabited by the barbarian who seeks
dignity, yoke of the fatherland
broken, abhorred by memory,
as the husband looks at his wife face to face
and close to the threshold, the intruder
hastens the trembling that precedes misfortune.

Iron and greed, a decisive leprosy
of hatreds that were fed by rapine and deceits
wets the seeds. Brother against brother
comes to the challenge without pity
brings to a pause its stigma against the kingdom of pity:

arrogance goads the leap into the void
that as the wind dies the eagles abandon
their quest like tumbled statues.

Emptied upon the mockery of the crowd
the afternoon defends itself, redoubles its hide
against stones that have lost their foundations.
Her offense is compassion when we pass
from the gilded alcove to the somber one
with the fixity of glowing coals: hardly
a moment, peaceful light as upon
a drunken soldier awaiting his degradation.

We can smile later at our childish furies
giving way to rancor and sometimes envy
before the ruffian who without a word taking leave
descends from the beast
in search of surcease. The play is his:
mask quitting the scene, catastrophe
overtaking love with its delirium and with delight
looses the last remnant of its fury.

Came doubt and the lust for wine,
bodies like daggers, that transform
youth to tyranny: pleasures
and the crew of sin.
A bursting rain of dishonor
a heavy tumult and the nearnesses
were disregarded drums and cries and sobs
to those whom no one calls by the name of "brother."

At last I thought the day calmed
its own profanities. The clouds, contempt,
the site made thunderbolts by love's phrases,
tableware, oil, sweet odors, was all
a cunning propitiation of the enemy,
and I discovered later floating over
the drowned tribes, links of foam tumbling
blindly against the sides of a ship.

III / CÉSAR FERNÁNDEZ MORENO

An extrovert, the Argentine César Fernández Moreno (born in 1919) inherited from his father, the postmodernist poet Baldomero Fernández Moreno (1886–1950), a love for external reality and a gift for singing of it in simple words. To this inheritance he has added his own talent for narrative and for an imaginative use of non-sequiturs. He was slow in discovering and accepting his gifts, but in *Argentine Until Death Do Us Part* (1963) we find an unmistakably personal voice. The title of the poem comes from a patriotic utterance by the almost forgotten poet Carlos Guido y Spano. "Recycling" Guido's old-fashioned rhetoric, Fernández Moreno has written a bittersweet love song to his native country, a celebration of its shortcomings and blemishes as well as its splendors. True love is never blind.

Argentine Until Death Do Us Part

From "Argentina Hasta la Muerte," translated by Harry Never, in Revista de Letras *(Puerto Rico, Universidad de Mayaguez), pp. 122–130.*

Argentino hasta la muerte
he nacido en Buenos Aires
        Guido y Spano

buenos aires was founded twice
i was founded sixteen
you know how many great-grandfathers one has
i acknowledge six spaniards six criollos and three french
the final score is
combined hispanargintino 13 french 3
luckily the french *en principe* are french
if not what would i do being so spanish
brothers i was finally born in this bittersweet insipidly spicy land
        argentina
i was born in chacomus in buenos aires
i was born in many places almost all near water
when my development began my country's ended
a daughter sprang from each of my ears

i died on a beach in vigo
i am born again each time i make love
i shall be born again in paris during a fine rain
because i brothers just like buenos aires
was not here they brought me from europe
they brought me in sections
first one half the other two centuries later
i have then two uneven legs
one walks the hell of indian attacks and smoke
the other a modern wharf on the red river
split thus by time i walk with a limp
and well i'm an argentine

my most historical grandfather was banished by charles the
        bewitched
he ordered him to breathe these airs not those
because this guy according to my uncle mario
scored with a certain lady of the court
contrary to his majesty's prior right
excellent measure of the good king
here the indian princesses weren't a problem
it was thus this grandfather so spanish so gaucho
founded a dynasty of frontier captains
this is to say landowners
that is to say conservative politicians
doña agustina made a good deal
when she married a certain ortiz de rosas
but later the matter got ugly
the veneer started peeling from the mahogany chests
the gas jets were forgotten along with the furbelows
and were overshadowed by the kerosene era
well it's clear down with real mahogany
and up with kerosene that very distinguished combustible
in the end mama was fixed with five hundred acres
and well i'm an argentine

napoleon and an army of french grandfathers
wished to invade spain poor them
and there was one spaniard who let herself be invaded
she was by mine
producing at length a baby girl
who came to marry my closest spanish relative
the grandfather from whom i most descend
the real baldomero
the one who exchanged his vegetable patch in bárcena for a

clothing store on may avenue
he traded and bartered wholesale with ease
buy for such and sell for much
the government controlled without much enthusiasm
this was a new world how easy to live it up
and it was easy to ruin oneself and leave the family in a shack
but it was not so easy to be the father of a great poet
nevertheless he managed
neither was it easy being the son of a great poet
nevertheless i managed
the son by baldomero fernández
a pure blend of the negro girl lópez
she could not be seen
he blocked the horizon
seventy balconies fall on me with every step i take
you will say be done with the old man
but how could i stop being the piebald cub to that tiger
pardon my wealth
i received my grandfather's goods in words
now with my treasure i go crossing the pampa
crossing the deserted streets my pockets filled with precious stones
and well i'm an argentine

thus engendered and conceived
i move like an agile diver at different levels of society
as a conveniently based airplane with no flight restrictions
i have enough confidence in the boy julito
but i'm more at home among the boys who lived in shacks near
     the lagoon
i would lend them my imported bicycle for each to ride once
     around the block
i didn't smoke or use bad words or threaten to go to a bordello
but we all played with the same little marble cubes on the backs of
     our hands
but we all bit the same damask under the same zinc roofs
we were all equal under the law and under the street lamp on the
     corner
that provincial mediator between the gold sky and the dirt street
reaching the heights of the highest leaves on the plantain tree
surrounded by a halo of insects inclined to a rapid death
we were all equal illuminated thus from above
dragging our slippers on the bedspread of summer dust
i am thus in each of these ways
spanish french indian who knows
warrior farmer merchant poet perhaps

rich poor of all classes and of none
and well i'm an argentine

but of which argentine are you talking
what kind of argentine are you if you're not italian
to be a good argentine you have to be jewish
just a minute just a minute i happen to be a moreno
yes i feigned an education at state college
one two three i'm a moreno can't you see
there i discovered the pythagorean theorem and and tony's pizza
isn't it so gennarelli robiglio
and i have known those other argentines with the mark of assyrian
    or taureg
isn't it so grosman paley
and it was all the same we shouted when any woman passed
isn't it so robiglioman grosmicelli
we are all delighted by fruit ice creams and the remembrances of
    the russian princess
we all put a little strength into that pan-american punch of luis
    ángel firpo
but we all ruined our chance in front of wicked billy petrolle
we all got burned with carlitos gardel
and we'll all die humming a cole porter melody
the benny goodman sextet beats in the cavity of our skull
we were all equal before the law and ginger rogers
before the elliptical horizon of her waist
and before the rectangular horizon of a football field
we all prayed from memory that rosary of eleven beads that began
    bosio bidoglio y paternoster
and thus with unction completed by a sharp left jab
we dissolve in the ecstasy of the grandstand
today progress has exchanged the wooden stands for safe and
    contiguous concrete
the crowd comes early to find room within itself
and is imprisoned by itself
there's no alternative but to pee on itself
but the matter doesn't drop it descends harmoniously step by step
    and one can no longer sit how disgusting
and well i'm an argentine

i know quite well the bosses of bureaucracy
and notice i operated a pencil sharpener even a calculator
a promotion for us was as emotional as a final gallop in a western
i'm also a lawyer
two or three argentines aren't

how could one be argentine without a secretary
but nobody ever is at his office
never is because he isn't
please where are they where are the argentines
the doctor is in politics
the worker is marking time
the lawyer is writing poems don't you see him
actually no one has a profession
we are argentines by profession
there are so few ancestors it's very easy to look good
one can do anything under the counter
but suddenly somebody notices
correction *somebody becomes aware and takes notice* argentine says
    things but in a lengthy manner
and thus the stone walls become like thin wooden fences
a guy doesn't have a thing to grab onto except his own tie
you've revived you old blind cock but you've even lost your tongue
what do you think cholito
are you looking for trouble mallarmé
what would become of me without the typewriter
it expresses me best when it makes mistakes
i'm *tirde fatugied* i should say *exashuted*
oh my how does one pronounce certain movie stars
vos usté tú ta te ti corasón corazón qué vas a hacerle hacelle
bla bla bla you don't even know who you are
sock it to me pal keyserling
buddy ortega pass the info
eh bien je suis argentine

you should observe you should note
that i talk a great deal about my great-great-grandfathers
of my education of my social circle of my difficult language
    problems
but i say nothing of my virtues and my vices
but pug nose please
ethics lead logically to politics
i'm not going to give a good time to the rayados or the orejanos
argentine sir
thus we are essentially alive
on our soil we accommodate twenty million inhabitants
we prefer lie-ins to uprisings
you say that to me but you wouldn't dare repeat it
we need to be insulted twice
then we almost come to blows
we need a friend to separate us

but tell him that wherever i find him i'll break his neck
we need good luck to complete our revenge
we like to find not search
let the foreigners look for oil or whatever
but we know how to find things
the important thing is to shrug off responsibility
fellows i'm working a fantastic mine
i hope my date doesn't come
i have a backlog of work
i hope friday is declared a holiday
don't worry leave it all in my hands
tomorrow at seven ten i'll have the matter ready without fail
and then we'll pass from extreme precision to extreme vacuity
wait and we'll see there is time
and when there is no time when time deserts us shrugs us off tired
        of being promised in vain
then comes the great thrashing of labor
or better yet the rich improvisation of a sarcastic country minstrel
in one of those we assert ourselves and why not
and we are moved by the applause of our particular clique
m'y thanks m'y thanks with our hands clasped high above our
        parietals
and well i'm an argentine
and well our land is this way
piles of luxuries natural to native misery
few aborigines that are no longer a problem
handfuls of whites handfuls of grays loose among the miles
or soon found in groups at the edge of a muddy river
but loose nevertheless
each one alone on florida street
how startling if someone should direct a word to us in the subway
thank god football unifies us
politics as such is like football
what else unifies us i don't understand this unity
perhaps some file cabinets
the procedure is simple take one counter place behind it one clerk
a clerk is a man who smokes
and in front of whom spontaneously springs a line
look sir the important thing is to fill out the form
here papers are reality
to go to the papers means to go to reality
flower of metaphysics *papers are papers*
how poetic *papers sing*
how frightening look i'm making an option for you
but later *ay my papers have burned*

at the end of each year with apparent glee
we fling our calendar pages out the window
then we discover they were all blank
our affairs begin impulsively and end with difficulty
there are so many problems in the end all appears as nothing
the portfolio is the real national symbol not the phrygian cap
like sisyphus with his rock each argentine with his portfolio
outside cowhide inside cow problems
argentine trains are pure sham
empty and shining they rush past the stations without stopping at
    one
the alarms only ring when out of order
then in any case no one is alarmed
the police only discover terrorists when they drop their bombs
public buildings have enormous doors
but the public should enter through the concierge's cat entry
enormous steps rising rampantly
but one climbs up the lawn
when someone carries a book he is its author
cadevila is the same as codovilla
and suddenly up leaps jose hernández tapping a malambo with juan
    manuel fangio
five times world champion the greatest of all argentines as if all
    activities were of equal value
but don't tell me about our national sports or argentine literature
don't believe in the general *generally*
believe in the specific *specifically*
believe in some signatures do not believe in any genuine seals
reality has more than twenty-five regulations per page
what good is a paper in the rain

and well i'm an argentine
this is the revered native song i bring here
i'm sorry it will bother you it will bother me too
but sometimes we must approach the reality of the papers
this recrimination comes from me because i'm an argentine
i'm gaucho and understand it
i'm from this group from this place and no other
i'm argentine for better or worse i'm porteño
here i am at the base of the obelisk looking upward pitching
    headlong toward the sacred sky
here i am in this movie putting up with the boor who kicks the
    back of my seat all evening
here i am on this corner dangerously balancing on the edge of the
    curb

while the greedy autos butt their way into street openings
like pigs converging on their maternal breast
while the little houses of one story with balustrades just in case
alternate with skyscrapers on the broad avenues
like childish writing where the letters waver and stagger
buenos aires you have me in prison
and i can't live without your water in my lungs
i can't live without this heat without this cold
i put on a jacket i take off a jacket
i put on a vest a sweater a shirt i take them off i put them on
    again
but i definitely cover myself
above all at three in the afternoon on a summer day in the
    banking district
don't think this is a tropical country
no such luck we are very civilized as nordic as the best
    norwegian . . .

. . . meanwhile my country
yes homeland i'm talking to thee
to thee behind the word
to thou friend sky favorite of the cumulus sky lighted by the arc of
    a rainbow
sky which day by day revives me with deceiving light
sky who afternoon by afternoon sends out your even kiss
sky who night after night intoxicates me
to thou comrade earth who for now allows yourself beneath me
land of cities fronted with sewers embossed with asphalt
land of turbid eddies of rubble and used matches and the
    droppings of large toads
land of countryside swampland on the face of the planet
you my homeland who flies between sky and earth like a bird
    between his two wings
i'm going to tell you what you need
you need many insolent and roguish sons
generations of profligate sons
who'll love you who'll hate you furiously
who'll take you like an inside curve
who'll take you like a cup of hemlock
who'll take you by the waist
i place on thee and only on thee my whole self
to this light i was given and to this light i give myself
and well i'm an argentine

IV / IDEA VILARIÑO

César Vallejo and tango lyrics are Idea Vilariño's incongruous sources of inspiration. Born in Uruguay in 1920, she has produced little, but everything she writes shows an uncanny power of concentration. In developing the tradition of erotic poetry already established in Latin America by Delmira Agustini (see Part Three, 7) and Gabriela Mistral (Three, 19, IV), Vilariño has achieved a tragic vision of love as a devouring, obscene presence, or an even more unbearable absence. A spare, almost laconic style combines the most refined sense of rhythm with a colloquial, even slangy diction to produce some of the most devastating love poems written in Spanish today.

Three Poems

From Poemas, *especially translated by Eliot Weinberger.*

Metamorphosis

Then I'm the pines
I'm the hot sand
A soft breeze
A small bird wandering the sky
Then I'm the night sea surging
Then I'm night
Then I'm not

Poor World

They'll make it fall apart
it's going to fly to pieces
it will burst just like a bubble in the end
or wondrously explode
like a powder keg or just
suddenly be erased
as if a sponge
erased
its place
in space.

Maybe they won't do it
maybe they'll clean it up.
Life will fall like hair and spin around
like a sterile
mortal sphere
or slowly waste away
passing through the sky
like a whole
wide wound
or maybe just like death.

Inca St.

Inca lampposts ruben
climbing the hill
paradise flowers on the ground
the school
1900 and something
the corner the stars.
The garden inca ruben
cold silence steps
twining branches
a fire climbing
cold frigid moon
the stars without number.
Smell of the earth ruben
jasmine and honeysuckle
the red laurels
the ferns the earth
the whitewashed wall
the stars the grates.
Cold ruben the dark
smell of those flowers
of those festivals years.
An ant climbing
inca lampposts ruben's
sky-blue shirt

V / CINTIO VITIER

A Catholic poet, Cintio Vitier (born in Cuba in 1921) began his literary
life as a protégé of José Lezama Lima (Part Four, 15), but soon developed his

own uniquely personal style. In contrast to Lezama's baroque style, Vitier has aimed at producing "a simple song" (the title of a volume of poetry he published in 1956). Even his faith is extremely personal. He is a questioner, and his Catholicism is an affair more of doubt and endless searching for God than of celebration and communion.

Two Poems

From Con Cuba, An Anthology of Cuban Poetry of the Last 60 Years, *edited by Nathaniel Tarn, translated by Tom Raworth and Nathaniel Tarn (London: Cape Goliard, 1969), pp. 33–35.*

The Dispossessed

They are not mine—not the words, not the things.
They have their festivals, their affairs
that are no concern of mine; I await
their signals like the fire
that's in my eyes with dark indifference.
They are not mine—not the weather, not the space
(and even less the substance).
They come and go like birds
through the doorless windows of my house.
Someone is speaking behind this wall.
If he passed through his path would be
toward the other room: the one who speaks
is I, but I don't understand.
Perhaps my life is a hypothesis
whose theorist grew weary,
a story forever interrupted.
I am alone, listening to those phantoms
that come at dusk to stare at me
with pleas that I encompass them:
Would you wish to refuse, to suffer, to swell with pride?
The glance is not mine, I answer them;
to refuse would be ostentatious; to suffer, interminable—
those exploits have nothing to do with me.
But suddenly I can't dissuade them
for I no longer hear my loneliness
and I am full, sated, like the atmosphere
of my own echoing emptiness.

And I keep telling myself the same things:
that I have no idea who I am
or where I live, or when, or why.
Someone talks endlessly in the other room.
Then everything is useless. I am not alone.
These words remain outside, incomprehensible
like the pebbles of the beach.

Translated by Tom Raworth

The Light on Cayo Hueso

A cyclone's satin light,
that same light I saw as a child
on the bridal mornings of fear,
awaited me here—but much poorer,
much more secret, and still sullen,
as if there were no illumination capable
of bringing together our scattered shadows.
Nor could my grandmother come back with that cup
of foaming chocolate beside my bed
to say: Happiness exists, the here and now
is a railway train which shakes the timbers
laden with light and sweetness.

Through the streets I ran, invisible,
crying like an indomitable pine tree,
paring the sunken stone of omens,
silently conversing with the clouds,
to buy a hammer and some nails
with which to bar the house against fear—
and in the end we fled from the sea, one by one,
searching the fields for the cyclone's eye
focused on us, like an animal's, remote and sad.

That light is here, domesticated now,
superficial and flat, established now
in the absolute solitude of the Reef—
pure weather of my being, telling me now:
nothing remains of this; it was nothing,
don't be afraid and don't wait for other weddings,
burn peacefully as I do, sterile and alone,
hope for no more, this is the only glory
guarding, deserving of (the only shelter)
your deserted flower.

Translated by Nathaniel Tarn

VI / ERNESTO CARDENAL

Catholicism and Marxism have been the contrasting sources of Ernesto Cardenal's inspiration. He was born in Nicaragua in 1925. He seemed destined to become a Trappist monk and even stayed for a while in Thomas Merton's seminary in Kentucky. But he returned to Latin America to take holy orders and began a very active life as preacher and poet. Concerned as much with the evils of this world as with the problems of eternal salvation, Cardenal followed Neruda in writing politically committed verse, verse that explores both the past and the present of Latin America to denounce exploitation and genocide. But instead of using only contemporary images of violence and sin, Cardenal also borrows from the Bible the most impressive themes of human frailty and madness. He is at once very much a new and a traditional poet.

Poems

Translated by Eduardo González, Quincy Troupe, and Sergio Mondragón, in Mundus Artium, *vol. 3, no. 1 (Athens, Ohio: Ohio University, Winter 1969), pp. 77–79.*

2 A.M. It is the hour of the Dawn Service and the church
in shadows seems filled with devils.
This is the hour of darkness and of parties.
The hour of my roamings. And my past hits me.
  "And my sin is always before me"

And while we sing the psalms my memories
interrupt my prayer like radios and jukeboxes.
Old movie scenes, nightmares, lonely hours in hotels,
dances, trips, kisses, bars return to me.
And forgotten faces emerge. Sinister things.
The assassinated Somoza steps out of his tomb
(with Sihon, king of the Amorites and Og, king of Bashan).
The lights from the Copacabana shimmering over the bay's dark
    water
which flows from the sewers of Managua.
The absurd talk of drunken nights
which is repeated and repeated like a broken record.

And the cries of roulette wheels and jukeboxes.
            "And my sin is always before me"

It is the hour in which the lights of the brothels and the barrooms
        shine.
The house of Caiaphas is full of people.
The lights in Somoza's palace are lit.
It is the hour in which the Council of War meets
and the experts on torture go down into the dungeons.
The hour of secret police and of spies,
when thieves and adulterers stalk the houses
and corpses are hidden. A body is thrown into the water.
It is the hour when dying men enter into their last agony.
The hour of temptations and the sweat in the Garden.
Outside the first birds sing sadly calling the sun.
It is the hour of darkness.
And the church is cold as if filled with devils,
while in the darkness we keep on singing the psalms.
                        Translated by Eduardo González

suddenly at night, as upon demonic wings
a long long siren urgently sounds like
the horrible scream of the fire engine rings
like the voice of the white ambulance of death
or like the scream of a mare
reverberating shrilly against
the cold sweated flight of the night
coming closer and closer upon the streets
and the houses climbing
climbing the shadows of silences
and descending and growing
growing descending and receding
growing and descending descending
comes the sounds, comes the screams
but there's no fire. Nor do these screams
come from ambulances of death;
            it is only the dictator Somoza passing.
        Translated by Quincy Troupe and Sergio Mondragón

Someone told me you were in love
with another, another man
and so I went to my room

and wrote that article
against the government
for which they then
put me into jail

Translated by Quincy Troupe and Sergio Mondragón

VII / ROBERTO JUARROZ

      Words are the tools of Roberto Juarroz's obstinate struggle against the ambiguities of reality: the existence (or in-existence) of the objects his words allude to is the focus of his concern. Born in Argentina in 1925, Juarroz is a surrealist, and he reflects the near-obsessive concentration on the physical and concrete so characteristic of Argentine poetry. But for him, a physical object is a sign—that is, a word. The poems presented here belong to his fourth, and perhaps most successful, collection to date: the *Fourth Vertical Poetry* (1969). In the elegant and precise translation provided by Eliot Weinberger, they exemplify Juarroz's mastery of word permutations as the entrance key to the more disturbing permutations of "real" life.

Four Poems

From Cuarta poesía vertical *(Buenos Aires: Aditor, 1969), especially translated by Eliot Weinberger, pp. 5–6, 25, 37, and 75.*

I

Life draws a tree
and death draws another.
Life draws a nest
and death copies it.
Life draws a bird
to live in the nest
and death immediately
draws another bird.

A hand that draws nothing
wanders through the drawings
and switches them around.

For example:
the bird of life
lives in the nest of death
in the tree drawn by life.

Sometimes
the hand that draws nothing
erases one drawing in the series.
For example:
the tree of death
holds the nest of death
but no bird lives there.

And other times
the hand that draws nothing
turns itself
into an extra image:
a bird-shape
a tree-shape
a nest-shape.

And then, and only then,
nothing is missing, nothing extra.
For example:
two birds

live in the nest of life
in the tree of death.

Or the tree of life
holds two nests
where only one bird lives.

Or a single bird
lives in a single nest
in the tree of life
and in the tree of death.

II

I'm awake.
I'm asleep.
I'm dreaming I'm awake.
I'm dreaming I'm asleep.
I'm dreaming I'm dreaming.

I'm dreaming I'm dreaming
I'm awake.

I'm dreaming I'm
        dreaming
I'm asleep.
I'm dreaming I'm
        dreaming
I'm dreaming.

I'm awake.

III

Shouts without
resound within.
Or is it
shouts within
resound without?

A stab at a sketch
that doesn't matter
where it begins
where it ends.

IV

An opaque glass at times
disarranges the stuff of the world,
lopping dreams from our glances,
making us touch what we cannot see.

Reality becomes fixed in an insect,
seemingly lost
in a death without features,
in the blank cup of its small history.

Reality drips
the slow drops
that wet the opaque glass,
that wet our fingers.

Reality
is small and cloudy history.

VIII / BLANCA VARELA

Blanca Varela's poetry—a surrealist poetry capable of investing even
the most banal piece of reality with magical qualities—is also a poetry of loneliness and despair. She was born in Peru in 1926 and has produced some very
powerful lyrics, which sing with ironical detachment of the world's contradictions
and follies. But irony never damps the fire of her poetical imagination. Everything
here burns and cries and is passionately involved in a fight for survival.

Three Poems

Translated by Donald Yates, in Mundus Artium, *pp. 87–91.*

The Things I Say Are True

A star crashes in a small plaza and a bird loses its eyes
and falls. Gathered around it, men weep and see the new
season arrive. The river flows and sweeps along in its cold,
confused arms the dark material accumulated by years and
years behind the windows.

A horse dies and his soul flies to heaven smiling with
its big wooden teeth stained by the dew. Later, amidst
the angels, he will sprout black, silky wings for scaring flies.

All is perfect. Being shut up in a small hotel room,
being injured, cast aside and impotent, while outside
the rain falls softly, unexpectedly.

What is it that is coming, that leaps from above and bathes
the leaves with blood and fills the streets with gilded rubbish?

I know I am sick with a heavy illness, filled with a bitter
water, with an inclement fever that whistles and frightens
all who hear it. My friends have left me, my parrot now is
dead, and I cannot prevent people or animals from fleeing
the terrible black radiance my steps leave in the streets.
I must have lunch alone forever. Terrible.

In the Mirror

I explore the flame and do not extinguish it because I love its
    sorrowful heat,
its anguished, soundless tongues,
its plump skin that I pierce with my fingers
to reach the solitary water of such fragile eyelids.

And I sense the wing in the mirrors that return me ever,
as if I were reaping the violent ashes I have thrown to the fish,
as if a dead bird weighed inside my blood and blocked it there,
close to the blazing fire of insects themselves,
to their little bodies,
beautiful beneath liquors dark and rancid,
intimate and nervous in profound pleasures.

Roots of heavy columns of sleep sunk in the forehead,
acrid drops of fallen fruits
that spill out sharp, unfathomable oils.

The Observer

This is the man,
the most noble executor,
I see him bending over,
I see the four walls of his realm,
the weak line of his arms.

Today I live with the stranger
and from without I tell him
to forget time,
not to keep it folded up
in his little school desk drawer,
to watch its flight,
its profound voyager's health,
to follow it from a distance.

IX / JAIME SABINES

Irony that turns against itself, self-pity that quickly becomes self-mockery, a bitter humor—these are the distinctive traits of Jaime Sabines's poetry. He was born in Mexico in 1926 and has sung the charm of his native province and the unbearable sadness of the capital, as well as the long-lost loves that continually return in memory to fuel the desire for tantalizing new loves. In the controlled diction of his beautiful verse, Sabines has established a paradigm of elegance and subtlety difficult to surpass.

Two Poems

Translated by Paul Blackburn, in Evergreen Review, *vol. 2, no. 7 (Winter 1959), pp. 139–40.*

Bach's Music Moves Curtains

In the dull morning
Bach's music moves
    curtains.
A wind with loves
    slips
into streets and hearts.
Shadows, men,
no one knows why
    grow happy
as though God had descended to fructify
them.
Out of the asphalt
golden spiky shoots might have blossomed.
In today's sunlight
    sun softens
and tame light spreads like an oil on the saddened,
    the tired ones.
For the deaf a song extricates itself from
things,

and a terrible gentleness
the unbearable God
    contaminates
men's health, spreading
from one breast to another.
The hour is unending, un-
    seizable, an
eternity lasting the
space of the bat of an
    eye.

(While I have been talking the day
broke in two like a ripe pomegranate.)

Smashed

Smashed
like a plate,
smashed with desires
homesickness, dreams.
I am he who loves Miss So-and-so the 13th day of each month
and he who weeps for the other, and the one before her, when
he thinks of them.

    What a desire for ripe females
    and new tender shoots of women!
    My right arm commands a waist
    and my left arm a head. My
    mouth wants to bite and kiss and
    dry tears. I go
    from gratification to tenderness

in the madman's house
and I light candlesticks
I burn my fingers like resin

and sing from the chest a boast of unintelligible song.

I've gone wrong
got lost, am broken,
have nothing, no one,
I can't speak
can't make love, can

only move or sway while ashes
drop on me,
stones fall on me
and shadows.

X / CARLOS GERMÁN BELLI

Following in the footsteps of César Vallejo (Part Four, 7), but exaggerating even further the contrast between the popular and the baroque style, Carlos Germán Belli has produced a short but impressive body of work. He was born in Peru in 1927. He has sung with bitter hyperbole the miseries of bureaucracy and the shabby splendors of technology. In his poems, man is always caught in a grotesque web of half-truths and half self-deceptions. A touch of Parra's madness (Five, 2) is in him too, but his prosaisms are always ignited by baroque fire.

O Cybernetic Fairy

Translated by Clayton Eshleman, in the Tri-Quarterly Anthology of Contemporary Latin American Literature (New York: E. P. Dutton, 1969), pp. 186–93. Originally published in Tri-Quarterly, nos. 13–14 (Fall–Winter 1968–69), pp. 216–23.

20 poems from *O Hada Cibernetica!*

1

Why have I been moved
from the maternal cloister
to the terrestrial cloister,
instead of being spawned
in water or air or fire?

•2

Although for so many the sky is so much,
for me it's hell,
there I remain at each step leaving
for two straws
my skin yes and even my bones and even my marrow.

3

When the brain is about as big as a grain of sand

Of the books the luminous plectrum
it could be said comes
to be dregs of the rectum,
for after so much reading without raising up
nothing has been held.

4

Someday love
at last I will grasp,
such as it is for my dead fathers:
not inside eyes, nor outside,
invisible, but perpetual,
if not of fire, of air.

5

In this unfinishable fecal valley
I find I am laggard
shinbones, hide, gullet;
but I'm fed contentedly up
having less ties, less weight,
less days forward.

6

(in the manner of Pedro de Quiros)

Not even once are they coveted—
my dwelling, your oak,
my love, yours,
my rebec, your canto,
aye turtledove! is it this way with you too,
how brief, coveted,
how great, scorned?

7

The cold fear because looking at you
I see you more reserved than yesterday angered
makes each of my body's pores
an eye secretly spying;
but Will it be like this forever,
this bristled hide
in a thousand eyes transfigured?

8

Instead of sweet humans
why didn't my fathers exist
as that stone, that elm, that buck,
that apparently do not discern
and never say to each other:
"don't leave this copse
where now you know
from where cometh the boreal, there goeth the austral."

9

An unknown voice told me:
"you won't lie with Phoebe, no, in that meadow,
if with irons they draw you out
from the luminous cloister, my fetus";
and now that in this grim inn
I still find myself after several lustrums,
I ask why was I not hurled
from the highest cliff,
stutterer, cripple, one-arm or squinted.

10

If there's only air in my purse and brain
I then lamentable fix infer
the sales of my ferrous bars
during so many years,
and my voracious reader even,
have been for my lay belly,
in whose unknown heart
they remain converted
first in feces, then in crude dust,
ultimately all in nothing.

11

O pitted my soul pitted
with thousands of Carlos resentful
for not having known the free choice
to arrange their days
throughout all the time of life;
and not one time even
to be able of itself to say
"open the door of the orb
walk wherever you want,

throughout the south or through the north,
behind your austral or behind your septentrional . . . !"

12

Down with the exchanges!

O Cybernetic Fairy!
when with a puff you'll wither the Exchanges
that have me in their clutch,
and free me at last
so that I can then
dedicate myself to look for a woman
sweet as sugar,
soft as silk,
and eat her up in little pieces,
and scream after:
"down with the Exchange of sugar,
down with the Exchange of silk!"

13

If by chance to this orb
sometime at last
the Cybernetic Fairy comes,
we who don't run
through the valley yelling:
"long live wine! long live coupling!"
perhaps not so brief will our passage be,
nor with leisure and love debauched,
for the magic stamen of life,
so copious will it be
like that on which the bird
firmly rests flight,
or its highest boughs the tree,
or the stones their weight.

14

O nutritious bolus, but of dust!,
Who has formed you?
All turns
on the tenuous relation
between death and the hurricane,
which itself rests on that death polishes
the contents of the bodies,

and the hurricane the places
where reside the bodies,
and that afterward they jointly convert
and ensalivate
bodies well as places,
in what an immense and rare
nutritious bolus, but of dust.

15

Papa, mama,
so that I, Pocho and Mario
would always keep in human line,
how both of you struggled
in spite of the incredible Peruvian salaries,
and after so much so alone I say:
"come, death, that I may abandon
this human line,
and never return to it,
and among other lines at last choose
        a cliff face,
        an elm face,
        an owl face."

16

If the nutritious bolus
enters internal space,
leaving in my back
traces of its step,
and the fire balls
in cosmic space
of a sudden cross
pole to pole,
then I inquire:
What nutritious bolus
will perforate my belly,
or what lethal ball
loosing its embers
will wither my ship?

17

O parents, you knew it well:
the insect is intransmutable into man,
but man is transmutable into insect!;
Perhaps you didn't reflect, my parents,

when here on the orb without thinking you killed
an insect—any insect—
you found lodged obscurely
from the woods in the meekest and most distant corner,
so as to not be seen by humans
neither at day nor during the night,
you didn't think, then, that to pass the time
some of your children
would turn themselves into unarmed insects,
even in spite of your thousands of efforts
so that all the time
they might weigh and measure up like humans?

18

On coming out of the belly your shinbone
had not a splinter
of foot nor your gullet
a splinter of tongue,
but Why others foot and morning starred tongue
had from the belly on without decline
in order to walk, in order to speak?
How many spills you've watched
other firm shinbones passing
when between the hunters' whistles a buck swiftly crosses,
even more than the powerful wind that goads you;
and how much talkative tongue
day and night, for two straws,
stirs even though the master doesn't want it,
and you catch on fire, you roast under the leather
seeing that before a shepherdess won't break off
not even one word the gullet.

19

Thus it will be; I confess to you:
I've decided to smooth out the creases
of my guilty soul, so just as
those of the purse in which are kept
a hundred thousand ferrous bars,
and, like Holland cloth, it will be pure, smooth,
although to achieve such white linen
from now on I'll do it excessively
purifying with the growth
of a hump, as invisible as it is big,
that I bear like cargo on my shoulders

along with the terror and the shame
of seeing myself with my victim or dreaming him up;
and although already I suffer my sentence
that is superior to my hurt,
I don't lament it, death, because I want
to come to you really imbedded
in my pain, senseless;
the leather within
                    smooth linen.

20

What to do with this dwelling-place,
this leather,
this brain,
if nobody covets them
a little,
papa
mama;
and I ask if it's been in vain
that I've been loaned
this dwelling-place,
this leather,
this brain,
papa,
mama.

XI / ENRIQUE LIHN

An unwilling spectator of this world's follies, the Chilean Enrique Lihn (born in 1929) both continues and questions the tradition of politically committed verse represented so brilliantly in his own country by Pablo Neruda (Part Four, 12) and Nicanor Parra (Five, 2). But in Lihn, a Catholic feeling of guilt and a morose, masochistic tendency prevent his political stance from sounding too self-congratulatory. He brings anguish to satire, and a sense of his own inadequacy to his criticism of other people and other countries. His verse is characterized by a perpetual clash between deliberate prosaism and brilliant surrealistic images.

Poems

Translated by William Witherup and Serge Echeverría, in New Directions, *no. 23 (1971), pp. 53–65.*

The Defeat

Concentration of images, reveille of the real;
words restore power to the facts; and
        the burning ghost of the new poetry
is an old man who closes his shop for the last time,
outside the walls of a city that has lost the memory
        of its correspondences
with the boulevard Montparnasse,
the reason for dreams and the good sense of mystery.

It has been a long time, really, since I could
        assist with the burial of the last of the first
        of our magicians, but when I was very young
        I knew his heirs.
That shadow, preserved from the impurities of usage,
        was for some an excellent bone
        wrapping—invisible armor, a commonplace
        proof—for others,
        the irony of a lighthouse
that lit up its own storms.
—And now, what do I do—said one of them; and it was not
        a question, since he was almost fifty:
the author of some poems as dark as this desperate
night.

Reality has exposed us;
        me to, especially, the distant nephew
        of the stars that disappeared
by the magic art we can't practice any more
        without becoming guilty of the night;
vanished to the rhythm of fierce revolving gears in a
        great necessary grinding
as if we errant spirits were superfluous.

Reality is what happens, and, in the center of it
and against it, the machine.
I don't regret it for anyone: to each one the torment of
his faltering steps, of his perversity or of his
insignificance.
Not even for me, perhaps, the last one to abandon this
phantom ship because I was drunk
the night before.
This is still an image. The first of those who
preceded me in understanding that one
can't be the last of them without running
the risk of his luck.
Our enemies are too numerous to allow
us the luxury of thinking about our
friends.
Yesterday afternoon they passed her like a flooding
river, the Jesuits having blown
the dam;
in luxurious cars; in great floats
and also on foot to encourage by their example
the ship's masthead of the poor in spirit. For
these the kingdom of Heaven
and, in advance, the sacred horror of the communist
hell, popular capitalism and its
works of charity: bundles of old clothes;
therefore: a small share of existence
under the old satraps.

The machine, the machine.
It isn't one of those from the century's first decades:
mutilation and ecstasy of the best spirits
nor this other one in which two parallel lines cut
opposed by confabulated worlds
with the same obsession to extend to other worlds.
Would a moment of silence survive the war
by the surprise of our dead
since, really, we are modest persons.
It is a machine. . . . I saw it the other day at
the Paolozzi exhibition.
To these remote countries the undertow brings us only
remains of structures distorted by distant
explosions;
the sculptor proceeds with irony canceling the function
of the forms and smelting into one piece

airplane parts and various artifacts;
but we oscillate between innocence and
        ignorance and we couldn't make ourselves an
        idol of our machines but
        a machine of our idols.
What the hell: an undeveloped people,
involutions of usages and customs whose sense
        adapts itself to the times
when prayer was the comfort of the whip
and the god of Spain the same of the angels.
Our lost battles will have sewn
        fear in us;
our victories: the transfer of respect
from the heroes to those they followed in the order
        of rape
and the patriotic speeches.
    What does solemnly poor mean?
        The Century of the Lights
and our century of poor gaslights surprised us
        in shameful attitudes
organizing misery at the parish priest's, in
        the Great Back Yard,
in the struggle for primogeniture and against the
        Protestant dead.
Gentlemen of goatee and mustache, what an excess
        of honorable
statuary cut with the same scissors!
Many of them exactly like the others: the high collar
would save them from the scaffold.
We honor all kinds of tombs, even those
        we should blow to pieces.
Any family album hides the unscrupulous
        businessman beneath a lordly   ·
        appearance, his hands gloved
after having plunged them into the Funds of Bribery.

    Chinemachinema. The mechanism is of an appalling
        simplicity for its manipulators, but,
        who among them
can establish order where the premeditated
        wickedness of chaos always reigned?
Form follows form and a vast deformity
        moves the whole
heavily, in a fatal direction.

I agree: the best engineers serve in all
        the bands, only these exhausted their
        talent
in presenting an old artifact under a new
        appearance
sufficiently known and insufficiently
        recognized
by the cheated victims of their plundering
        who are taught to confuse
        fatality with crime.
    Enough of farces!
It's known that they would use the techniques of the
        miracle and where the planning of
        the miracle is, the countries in which they operate
        on a grand scale and those in which
        partial operation is enough.
This refers to the hopes based
on the honeymoon with the resurrection of European
        colonialism, beneath faces favorable to the New Deal.
    Who is to say no? Over this
        point the parity of opinions and the
        consensus of the steps in the drawing rooms
        of the Palace.
Not even the most scrupulous skeptic would accept his
        omission from the list of invited guests
to a reunion with the Good Old Days.
The ceremony is a national pastime: the parade under
        the soft twilight
of the gala uniforms eaten by larvae.
To fresh air football and the evangelical Sunday:
        sadness of another Garden of Olives in
        which spirit and flesh ruminate, under the
        same yoke, an agony covered with flies
        on the dishes of grass.
    But what can be expected from the barbarians.
Finally we have not replaced all our
        customs with theirs, a curious lack
        of concentration on the model
condemns our copies to a gilded mediocrity;
    and, in any case, the rest of what we have
        agreed to call national dignity
        would be seriously slashed
        should they decide to adopt the air of our de-
        feat to add it to the celebration of the
        triumph, in this remote colony,

of the perpetuation of the cancer of their empire
in the alien guts.
A few hours ago (tonight and last night are
       confused; the triumphant noise of the
       silence of failure)
one of them, with a burning drunkenness,
was enjoying the street carnival on the
       carnival of the bus, a big dirty bastard,
fingers raised in a V for victory: the braids
       of a heavy Anglo-Saxon little girl who
       rode on a fierce stallion with an
       impassive pugnosed face.
The bulldog-man
spun around on his axis like clothes in
       the washer, elbowing the person
       next to him on the chest
       and shouting:
"I'm a North American. I'm a North American."
I wished his world would have sunk.
  It will be said: "an individual case" and the accusing finger
       must point to the impersonal factors
       that move the individuals
       the river where the fish go during their time
       to spawn;
"de la sociologie avant toutes choses," but what a heap
       of obvious facts in those extreme cases
when clarity springs from the very pores of the
       corpus delicti
thrown quickly to the uncultivated land that the
       moon shows in front of the big housing projects.
  It was enough to see that fellow to get
       a panoramic and well-articulated vision,
       the unnecessary statistics in the last plans.
The difference between one Yankee and another
       represents, to us, a margin of
       unpredictable brutality in relation
       with the forces of an occupation said to be
       peaceful,
and a margin, also, for the cultivation of
       personal friendships in a No Man's Land.
The cultivation of friendship is a personal pastime, the
       entertainment of guests,
the moderation between Moors and Christians,
       the cessation of all antagonism

at lunchtime.
In a small country loaded with traditions,
          formality before everything else, and the use
          of psychological violence
only in unusual cases.
The control, at a flagrant distance, of our old
          machine together with the promise of its
          restoration
in the hands of specialized technicians on the base of
          surplus and heavy industry.

   There is no doubt:
of the 60,000 FBI and CIA agents,
          only one or two have shown a thread
of their intent to climb the floats and
          occupy a swaying place
next to these beauties who eclipsed everything in the
          apotheosis of triumph, but the sense
          of our defeat.
It was all clear in spite of so much glitter and the
          brightness of the looks and the fireworks.

   The invisible army of occupation can fight
          while in bloodless retreat
and can afford to take up spring and summer quarters:
          fishing seasons in the southern lakes and
          harvest-time in the metal deserts.
To the Pacific, to the Atlantic the battleships: here
          it isn't necessary to import peace
in the person of snipers and marines.
The iron belt may be loosened a little
on the other side of the Andes and tightened on the
          really strategic places
where the blood burns, bubbles and screams.

   It only seems possible to arouse a struggle
          between democrats and republicans far away from
          home
by using the Bomb on a small scale,
          razing the nurseries in the pastures
of the short, slant-eyed communists. A
          profound claw,
and then the parade of human rags in honor
          of Liberty and Democracy.

This is what keeps strong men busy:
    "the struggle for Peace," one of them says to us
again occupying the panoramic stream
    that face as impenetrable as an expanding
    mushroom;
some iron crevices look at us, through it
    the real army is lost to sight
in its ascending march toward the abysses beyond
    the sky, striped with columns
    white with panic.
The eyelashes sewn where the lids fold are
    heaps of charcoal, and on the first blurred level
    nothing is known of what is going on
    in the other half of the hemisphere.

Military discipline suffers certain faults
    compensated according to the order
    of number and of strength.
Those boys don't march: they walk, each one
    "in the context of their personal liberty"
    —would say one of their myths—as if they
    could be directed by flaming clans in all
    directions.
To the cantina, to the bar, to the bowling alleys or to the
    human catacombs in the flaming
    stadiums.

Under the closing eyes, the erosion in the
    bags of age: arid mountains filled
    with scars.
The message ends in what intends to be a
    call to wisdom but it is a total delirium
    that makes signs behind the threads
    of the Doric columns.
The orator thinks of death, and death, for the first time,
    of herself, with the
    perplexity of a prima donna
    suddenly raped by a horde
    of beasts, in her own home.
It is a death that allows the curious possibility of
    even killing herself
in a hydrogen bath.

This discovery transfigures her: opulent beauty
    of Marilyn Monroe another St. Sebastian for

the sexed hearts that would like
            to recover from the mutilations of the spirit
            in total butchery.
        But Man, The Fearless, The Hard One
only interprets "cleanly" of course to the
            majorities of his people that might
            turn against him, toward another.
No shadow of doubt has crossed that mask:
            the eagle flies high over the Appalachians,
between fifty stars homes of her pride:
the night filled with stars by the obsession of triumph.

    To be chosen by a chosen people
is not a task that can be accomplished exclusively
            on the level of human forces.
Absolute correctness in the addition of myths, such is
            the way of truth, the American Way,
            crossed by the Divines and the Saints
and those who sewed with their bones the time
            of the limitless drama of expansion.

To present a monolithic flank to the opponent, a
            carapace harder than a hundred of his,
            and under the cover veneered with irrational
            gilded symbols, the account book brought up
            to date:
in the Credit: the proconsul's jaw and the whistling
            of the whip on the sentry's boot, the
            multiplication of taxes and the
            sinking of the small provincial
            markets;
in the Debit: the bargaining with charity funds.
    For the exercise of a Manifest Destiny, the
            fatality is a wage in the office,
one would say the object of a special institutionalized cult
            in order to exorcise it.
Masochism is rampant in all of this:
Thanatos, the Blond Beast's love of
            self-destruction, reduced to the gasping of
            the blond Hottentot's struggle of all against all
            during which it has been progressively detached,
            from self-love together with big pieces
            of human substance
until it remained in the partiality of muscles
            and of bones.

On the ballots the threat of the strongest will triumph,
the stabilization of violence under the face of Caesar,
        under penalty of falling in the inflation of the same,
        and in the dominion of small business
that will ruin the Empire's prestige.
It would be best to know it better than the opposition,
but it is still possible to respond to his blind harassment
        with a new Fourth of July speech.
An unparalleled greatness would be the appropriate leitmotiv.
Without parallel: here is a good puzzle for the
        intellectuals disaffected from bread and circus, and
        who haven't succumbed to the voluntary poverty
        of the Venice of the West or to the
        drugs by the Ganges or in the caves
        of the Old World.
History could stop, the Tower of Babel reconstructed
        and the two-headed eagle flame in the sky.

The Good Old Days

And those of us who were sad, without knowing it, once,
        before all history: a divided people
—remotely close—among distinct childhoods.
Those of us who paid with hesitation for our forced
        permanence
in the garden when they closed the house for an hour,
        and received
the tortured remains of love under kind of
        a "holy patience"
or tenderness mixed
with a eucalyptus branch against unhealthy dreams.
"You are your poor mother's only support; you see
        how she sacrifices herself for all of you."
"Now go back and dream with the angels." Those of us
        who spent the superfluous summer
of poor relatives, in docility, under the
        perverse protective look
of the great uncle and lord; those of us who raised our faces
        to see him
giving the order to kill the sick beast with an ax,
        and then dozing
in his murderous sleep perfumed with peaches.
    Fragile, solitary, absent-minded: "I don't know
        what, doctor," but determined
to hide the hands in nocturnal fright, and

                associate ourselves with fear
through urine and to guilt through paternal punishment.
    Those of us who lived in the ignorance of older
                persons added to our own ignorance,
in their fear of night and sex nourished by
                an old bitterness
—remains of food that is thrown to sparrows—
        "You only remember the bad, I am not
        surprised:
it's an old family problem." But no,
        those of us who were
meticulously loved in the one and only possible
        sense of the word
that no one had said in fifty whole years,
        small engraved faces   seals of the alliance.
Yes, really the son of good will, of the
        most hot and rigorous stoicism. But
        isn't this a proof of love, the
        acknowledgment
of the silent grief that envelops all of us?
    It is transmitted, close to the rocking chair and the
        wall clock, this tendency to mutual
        ignorance,
the habit of the cloister in which each one tries,
        all alone, the same bitterness. Those
        of us who promised ourselves
to reveal the secret of generation on our
        birthday: a version limited to the doubt
        over the flight of the stork and the loan
        of obscure words surprised in the
        kitchen, only to this
like giving away a package with medlars, or in the house
        of the miser
the joy of the medicine given for dessert.
        "Han-fun-tan-pater-han"
    Yes, the same curly copy according
        to an ancient custom, riding, with gentle
        seriousness, on the endless knees of the
        paternal grandfather.
(And it is the time for remembering it. Grandfather, grandfather
    who
        according to an ancient custom imposed
        fearful respect among our children
with your single proud presence: the high boots and the
        whiplash for the morning ride

under the poplars.
Boy from snow-covered lands that returned for you
    in the secret of solitary old age
when the elders were now the others and you the man
    who suddenly wept
since no one listened to him returning to his stories.)
    "Han-fun-tan-pater-han"
  The same rider on old knees. "It's not
    more than two years; then it was thought
that he was too sensitive a child."
The first to be surprised by our own
    fits of rage or cruelty

XII / FAYAD JAMIS

A lyric poet with a most subtle touch, the Cuban Fayad Jamis (born 1930) is also a committed poet, as the "Poem in Nanking" shows. But his commitment has in it nothing of the fanatic. Unlike many of his contemporaries, he has not sought a post in the revolutionary Castro regime. His political utterances are free of revolutionary cant and express his own sensitive reactions to a changing world. For him, revolution is also part of the nature he loves, and describes with such precision and imagination.

Poems

Translated by David Ossman and Carl Hagen, in Con Cuba: An
Anthology of Cuban Poetry of the Last 60 Years, *edited by Nathaniel Tarn
(London: Cape Goliard Press, 1969), p. 55.*

The Milky Way

Tonight, the Milky Way falls out of purple sky onto the trees
Wandering cats yellow lamps bread wine
everything traps a secret the streets don't end in that light mist

It works like the silent spider
like the sailboats which go moving the night
it does not stop my heart grows ripe
soaring over the fall of dust and of leaves

Soon snow will cover the sooty earth
through the window I will look at its terrible whiteness
Perhaps the wings of a dove will touch against the pane

Winter will be more beautiful
when your unknown hair
covers the abyss of my pillow

Poem in Nanking

They say
here in Nanking
that in another time
the poets
on mid-October days like these
liked to smell the heavy chrysanthemums
to eat crabs from the turbid Yangtze
and to drink lots of wine

That was in another time

For years and years
the slow powerful river
has carried much gray earth
between the miserable villages and the sea
and the other great river
the river of the people
has been carrying toward the depths of history
the nights of desperation
the walls of injustice
and the rotten trunks where wind murmurs
Now there are chrysanthemums in the hands of the people
The crabs are beautiful and gray in the paintings of Chi Pai-chi
And poets drink the violent wine of earth and of fire
which revolutions blow.

XIII / PABLO ARMANDO FERNÁNDEZ

His frequent use of Biblical imagery hardly conceals in Pablo Armando Fernández's verse his obsessive concern with the changes brought about in Cuba by the revolution. Born in 1930, he is one of many writers deeply affected by Fidel Castro's victory. He has accepted and praised the revolutionary process, yet has not been able to stop wondering, or suffering. His poems reflect his feelings of guilt and pain, of being lost in a reality torn by moral ambiguities. Cain, the symbol of civil discord, looms large in his verses.

Three Poems

From Latin American Writing Today, *edited by J. M. Cohen (Baltimore: Penguin Books, 1967). Translated by John Gibson, Arthur Boyars, and Christopher Middleton.*

Origin of Eggo

What the dead mouths say is that man
came in the change of light.
The boat was his body and his arms two powerful oars.
Alone, through a strait of turbulent waters
man was a light, the dead say;
before all vanished history, and long
before all time to come.
He was going toward the mountain, they say.
He was gazing ahead, he was gazing behind,
and at the profile his powerful hands
had always cut in the air. He went alone,
and the crystal, the gold pouring from his boat,
molded the torso of each created thing,
until the time of his fulfillment.
Along the shore, in the blurred undergrowth,
ashes or smoking carrion, ruins.
And the tale the dead mouths tell is that
the mountain, man himself,
was borne upon the waters.
But when he reached the center of himself
he was no longer a man;
he was primordial tree, its branches countless oars,
its trunk so many boats identical in strength,
joined in a rounded flower of gold.
In front of him, on each side, and behind him
he saw the mountain multiply to an exact number
divided into equal parts,
each one of them whole, but always the same man
who came on the waters and in the change of light.

Abel Reflects

They've painted the store in other colors
which time hungrily devours.
They've brought a new stock of things to sell
and there is no doubt this pleases death,
that this pleases his willing servants
who kept the figs and the apples
from the child's hands,
who kept the clockwork toys
from the child's hands.
The painted store is one more mask
of death.

Denunciation

The informers talk about
the night the cock may crow;
the toad's eyes in the dew;
trucks that go by without stopping;
San Eleuterio or the Virgin of the Vanished;
dreams to guess the lucky number.
The room is the accomplice of the voices,
three boys die on their way.

XIV / HEBERTO PADILLA

Padilla's imprisonment and subsequent confession that he had been a "counterrevolutionary" have tended to obscure the more important fact of his having produced some very effective verse on the anguish of being a committed poet in a revolutionary regime. Padilla was born in Cuba in 1930 and tried hard to follow the revolutionary line. His poems, which voiced restrained criticism of the revolutionary process, testified to his anguish. Apparently, however, the regime was unwilling to tolerate this criticism, and Padilla was finally crushed by the merciless hands of that history he spoke of so ironically in his verse. He sought in effect, perhaps foolishly, to play the role of a loyal dissident. Instead, he became a Cain to his own work, which he has renounced.

Two Poems

Translated by Paul Blackburn, in the New York Review of Books, *vol. 16, no. 10 (New York, June 3, 1971), p. 4.*

Travelers

I have here the garments of opulence,
though more informal, more beautifully scandalous.
> University diplomas, enormous books
> written especially
> for the Sociology Departments
> of prestigious universities which
> have underwritten all the costs.

They manage to get visas quickly.
They get accurate reports on pacifist campaigns.
Protests against the war in Nam. In short,
> they are people who have chosen the sane,
> correct direction for History.

They have taken the plane illegally, i.e., no passport,
but are the most comfortable travelers of the future.
They feel delightfully subversive
and at peace with their consciences.
Their Nikons, Leicas, Rolliflexes (a
> matter of individual taste) gleam
> perfectly competent to handle
> the tropical light, to handle the
> underdevelopment. Notebooks flip

open for objective interviews, although of course,
they do not deny that they feel just slightly illicit,
> partial toward *corazón,*

because they love guerrilla warfare, the rough outdoor life, the
struggle, and the strange Spanish the natives speak, a
language which would dazzle Noam Chomsky, no doubt.

In two or three weeks they've already sufficient experience
> to write a book on the guerrillas,
> > on the struggle within the cities,
> > > on the Cuban character
> > > > (or on all of these subjects)
> > > > > and as well, one would imagine,

on the *specificity* of the slightly insolent, but
exciting sort of Spanish Cubans speak.

These people are very educated, very serious,
                provided with systems and methods, so that
                        it is by no means a rarity that they go back
frustrated by the lack of sexual freedom among the Cubans,
by the *inevitable* puritanism of revolutions, and by that
which, finally, with a certain melancholy, they end up calling
                the gap between theory and practice.
Privately, they confess (not
in their books or at conferences) that
they cut more cane in that field than the best machete-man,
                "a character firmly beset by siesta."
In the field camps, they do not deny, the people preferred to
        dance,
that the *intellectuals* "not politically minded at all"
were capable of preoccupation even with poetry.

The night they get back and go to bed with their wives, they
imagine they have developed super muscles (those cane fields),
and act like Negroes, despicable simply.
Their mistresses (taken generally three years apart)
applaud these unused, now insatiable husbands.
For several days they project slides in darkened living rooms
in which the traveler appears, the hero surrounded by Cubans:
the ICAP guides, skinny and badly dressed, smile
into the camera.
                A mountain of natives
                        hug the hero fraternally.

There are a lot of photos of that ilk throughout the world
of me: I
look like a mountebank. One eye
stares resentfully at the camera,
the other looks anywhere else.
Wives, sons, friends of the energetic traveler look
and suppress their disgust: I'm trapped in
the photo, a caged lion
                roaring against words of importance:
                (Eternity, History).
But I cannot transmogrify
file clerks from universities, nor clarify
        anything. I'm damned.

Important Occasions

We're contemporaries finally
                                                (endangered, blockaded),
of the important countries,
the ones that really count. All
the bombs of the century destroying more than half the world,
                                                suddenly threaten
                                                to blow up
the shining roofs of the Island.

If they were to ask me now:
                "The enemy's opened a beachhead on
                our coasts—poet, what would be
                the perfect strategy to apply the crunch?"
The way an Englishman gets mad, gathering
my brow into a solid scowl, I'd
know how to answer with total exactitude.

In our streets even geography has been overthrown.
Gorky Park in Moscow
                                begins at the corner of Neptuno.
Peking's Avenue of Peace ends
                                at Zanja and Galiano.
From the woods at La Habana
                                furious Congolese troops emerge.
Uncrowned kings stroll along the Rampa boardwalk, their
worthless, lugubrious lions acting as escort,
                                and Cuban kids
stir about in the night like Zambian flowers.

But I haven't come to inventory these wonders, I
am rigging myself out now to enter History.
                Not full dress.
                No tuxedo or swallow-tailed coat.
                No full trappings in the tropics,
                                not even for these
                                huge solemnities.
Must learn comportment (o yes), to say
buenos días, buenas tardes, buenas noches
in two or three languages at least;
as soon as possible I have to get out of this
tiny apartment in which we barely fit, let

my hair grow; and these primitive unfriendly looks of mine,
                                rip off that disguise.
The pile of photographers and newspapermen
                        are due to arrive any minute.
Perhaps it will be necessary to make a speech.
Must one make a splendid speech for such occasions?

If only it were a matter of launching upon the world,
                                        Cuba, my country,
your multitude of jokers suffering from malnutrition, your poets,
it might be possible to
get something done: to change styles, for example,
undertake an epic, put more enthusiasm in our poetry,
describe shimmering landscapes, Cubans singing
under the moon, girls stripped to their skins, shining like
the moon, poets working the cane fields
                        (a handsome picture!) sometimes
stretched out on the beaches resting, writing
in the sand in capital letters:
VENCEREMOS,
        CLARO QUE VENCEREMOS,
            PATRIA O MUERTE.

History's going to save us—we were thinking.
Going to save us—were we dreaming?
It wasn't all just uprisings, barricades, bonfires:
in our heads it was a dress of bubbling foam, a
Rhine maiden with clear eyes, smiling, standing
at the door, hand outstretched
toward a hungry and waiting people.

            But there was no one in the doorway. Nor in the house.
            Instead we stumbled. They shoved us inside. We
            broke our teeth going in, got our jaw smashed.
We found tools and weapons and we
fought, we struggled, we worked and continued
fighting. But it's true, old Marx,
that History is not enough.
                        Important occasions,
                        man makes them.
                        It's a real, live man who does it,
who masters it, who will fight.
History by itself does
        nothing, dear friends.
                    It does absolutely nothing.

XV / GUILLERMO SUCRE

To the abundant and exciting tradition of Venezuelan poetry, Guillermo Sucre (born in 1933) adds an elegance and refinement that goes against the grain of the surrealistic expressiveness of most of his contemporaries. The key word to describe his poetry is transparency: a quality of precision and light which causes every word in his poems to radiate. Too much light can also blind; at times, Sucre's lines reach that blinding intensity. Although the subject matter of his best poems is frankly erotic, Sucre never falls into the trap of carnality. Belonging to the school of Octavio Paz (Part Five, 1), he never forgets that words are signs, not objects, that they allude to actions but do not perform them.

Poems

From La mirada *(Caracas: Monte Avila, 1970), especially translated by Eliot Weinberger.*

I

Suns in the deep woods
Great branches
A giant bird that shrieks
Wounded
      Its wings
           Divided
Into light and shadow
At the beginning and end of the world
Its head erects
With discord and reconciliation
The world opens in your eyelid
And closes
In the fire of divination
Reality is only real
Through your gaze
Cities that hurry time
Streets that bring and take us
In the splendid ruinous air of the seasons
There you unfold

          You unfold
Joy sadness
Doors close in our way
· We are not clear not opaque
We have no refuge but memory
We have no memory but the present
A day is only a day
A sun desire
In the paradise of exile
With no other present but memory
With that flowing language of summer
Which lit your body
Full of eyes algae anemones
In the great rose grey of the sea

II

The end and the beginning
I let the world pass
I speak among suns
Among bodies
A single desire
Unites
Rich as heaven
Cities and seasons
Streets that lead to the same
Hard possession
Solar rose wind-sex .
Savage hydra
A thousand times I bit your thousand lips
I watched your thousand eyes
I made you sea-star
Singing cliff
Through you
I drank every wine
I covered myself with your ashes
Next to your fire
Passionate ivy
You are the blind night
But I see crevices
Narrow passages in the gloom
I left
In light's fury
The earth shining in my eyes
I wore your face

The face of volcanic rock
Dream-eruptions
Forests breathing on my chest
The coasts the beaches
The sands of desire's scripture
The helplessness of what is fleeting
The glory of what is fleeting
A few steps and a glance
Between the stupor and the meeting

III

We are still not in summer
But we are summer
We might have been something else
Another destiny touched us
We are earth made flesh
The sun weaves our dreams
The sea your fragrance
Memory wavers in the sand
Water washes you and you flower
Coral of desire
Your body and the air expand
Cup of transparency
The dry liquor of language quiets us
Solitude pride
Arch of the sky
                    without horizon
Your body creates space
If a bird crosses
A flash of lightning slashes your eyes
The sea lights up
Its white wounds
                    close in your skin
Salt devours and devours us
Splendor blinds and blinds us
That destiny touched us
Touched me watching me
In its shimmer
                    in your glance

XVI / JUAN GELMAN

The iconography of popular heroes and cult figures (film stars, politicians, assassins), tango lyrics, the heated political controversies of the day—all
these form the themes and images of Juan Gelman's verse. Born in Argentina
in 1930, Gelman has produced a small and concentrated body of work. He has
been committed enough to go to jail for the socialist cause he favors, but he has
continued to write verse as his chief contribution to the social change he wants
so desperately.

Theory re Daniela Rocca

Translated by Patrick Morgan, in Tri-Quarterly, *nos. 13–14 (Fall–Winter
1968–69), p. 251.*

theory re daniela rocca

and so it was that daniela had a chat one day with the angels
slightly crumbled upon their gothic bosoms
fatigued by the critical moment but lucid and lubricious
and daniela had noticed their contrary similarities
the doors that open so as to continue living
the doors that close so as to continue living
the doors in general their missions their angles
angles of the fugues the unbelievable fugues
the parallelograms of hate and of love
breaking into daniela to open out onto other doors
with the help of diverse drugs and alcohols
or of signs that lie under the alcohol
or daniela taking off her bras taking off
her breasts widely divided due to exercise
of love in contrary circumstances of the world
crazy daniela rocca the magazines say
of a poor italian woman who it is true
practiced ferocious methods of forgetting
and didn't kill her parents and was charitable
and pissed one day in september under a tree
and was full of grace like Ave Mary.

XVII / JOSÉ EMILIO PACHECO

A poetry of elements, classical in its allusions, romantic in its desperate attempt to grasp something essential and final, José Emilio Pacheco's lyrics are among the most powerful of today's Latin American poetry. Born in Mexico in 1939, he shows himself a disciple of Octavio Paz (Part Five, 1) in producing verse at once sensual and intellectual, verse in which thought does not detract from passion and feeling. The epigraph of the second poem ("What can I hold you with?") is a quotation from a poem written in English by Borges, another of Pacheco's masters.

Two Poems

Translated by Elinor Randall, in Mundus Artium, *vol. 3 (Winter 1969), pp. 129–31; and* Latin American Writing Today, *edited by J. M. Cohen (Baltimore: Penguin Books, 1967), p. 260.*

The Elements of Night

In the minimal empire that summer has corroded
days, faith, foresight, crumble.
In the final valley
destruction gorges itself
on each slow exile described by its flight.

Here sinks the brow of the vanquished.
All predictions
are weightless cities spoiled by ash,
quenched vortices in which the rain extinguishes
the indecipherable history revealed by the lightning.
And the moment
fulfills its deaths,
revives remains.

In the slow corpse of the hours
night deposits its transient poisons;
words, days shatter against the air.

Nothing is restored, nothing gives
greenness to the burnt valleys.
The banished water will not come back to the fountain,
nor the eagle's bones return for its wings.

For that time, fragile as a wall of frost,
allowed the sphinxes their unshakable riddles.

Late, a broken sphere studded with light
it weighs anchor now from the ruins,
its successor, the tableland on fire.

Translated by J. M. Cohen

For Some Time Now

What can I hold you with?

I

Here is the sun with its one lone eye, its spitfire mouth not bored by burning up eternity. Here it is, like a defeated king watching from his throne his vassals' scattering.

Sometimes, the poor sun, herald of the day that injures and offends you, perched on your body, embellishing with light all that was loved.

Today, it does no more than enter through your window and inform you that it's seven o'clock and the expiation of your sentence lies ahead of you: papers floating around the office, smiles the others spit at you, hope, remembering . . . and the word: your enemy, your death, your origins.

II

On your ninth birthday you built a sand castle on the beach. Its moats conversed with the sea; its courtyards sheltered the sun's reverberations; its battlements were incrustations of coral and reflections.

A legion of strangers gathered to admire your work. You saw their paunches eaten by hair, the women's legs nibbled by bloody nights and by desires.

Tired of hearing how perfect your castle was, you went back home, filled with conceit. Twelve years have passed since then, and you return to the beach often, trying to find the remains of that castle.

They blame the ebb and flow of water for its destruction. But the tides are not at fault: you know that someone kicked it down—and that the sea will build it up again sometime.

III

On the world's last day—when there's no longer any hell or time or tomorrow—you'll speak her uncontaminated name, a name untouched by ashes, pardons, fear. Her noble name of utmost purity, like the broken instant that brought her to your side.

IV

The sea is sounding. The ancient lamp of dawn is setting fire to the dark islands' breasts. The great ship founders engulfed by solitude. And on the breakwater wounded by time—standing, like an open minute—the night is lingering.

Beings of the beach wove labyrinths in the shipwreck's eye, soon to be surging waves, a faithful flock of time, some seaweed, a green shore, a girl destroyed who shines and dances when the sun pays her a visit.

V

For some time now, things for you have had the sour taste of what is dying and of what begins. A bitter triumph of your own defeat, you lived each day under the protective covering of unreality. The sick year left you as pledges some days that wall you in, subdue you, some hours that won't return but live their confusion in memory.

You started to die, to realize that mystery is never going to weaken. Awakening is a forest of discovery, a miracle regaining what is lost, destroying what is won. And the future day a wretchedness that finds you alone, inventing and polishing your words.

You keep on walking and traveling across your history. You have been a stranger and alone, for some time now.

Translated by Elinor Randall

XVIII / HOMERO ARIDJIS

A keen eye for reality, a quick response to the physical world, and an all-encompassing sensuality, which includes, of course, words and images—these are the attributes of Homero Aridjis's verse. Aridjis, born in Mexico in 1940 of a Greek father and a Mexican mother, has something of classical precision in his verses, a light that is not only that of the Mexican plateau. In his most ambitious work to date, a lyrical novel called *Persephone* (1967), he has revitalized the Greek myth by setting it in the black-and-white context of today's Mexico.

Five Poems

Translated by Eliot Weinberger, in Mundus Artium, *vol. 3, no. 1 (Winter 1969), pp. 135–39.*

I

On this bridge where time moves immobile
like the rot or joy of being
within the cables
that traverse it end to end
I have seen the bird of innocence pause
a moment from its flight to say goodbye
I have seen in its eyes the fire of light
that burns over the waters like a carpet
or a tongue always larger and more grooved
I have seen in its beak the song and the marvel
that never rise any higher
from the sadness that encloses them like a nook
I have seen the dark and humid mane of the song
always more radiant and more mute
more the color of wind than of love or voice
curving in its beginnings like a wave

On this bridge that has gazed with frozen gaze
(as a loved and dead face gazes
always farther from the word and more elusive)
pass thousands of specters and autos
thousands of things and beings that move toward infinity
like the final station
I have seen the bird of innocence
rest a moment from its eternity
to say goodbye
in a goodbye barely audible   said almost
with a murmur of wings sounding in the silence

II

The chant beneath the   lights up in its flight
    mist   a road

dawn
opens in a bird's nest
the light

the sun
watches the poem
alive now
III

Possess lady the bodies
the colors
the open images of time
where she born at harvest
perpetuates in silence
Possess those who rising
with the same voice
live on in a word

IV

Noon splits the riverbank
in thin halves of sound
pulls from the beast's back
crackling and smoke

all that is wet
the hour has drunk
all that breathes
rests within me

V

May her presence last
may her eyes never die

I say it before her body
I say it in my heart

I rest in her
I live in her day

watched
the fruit
is heavy

moving its shadow
in the tree

like an object in its name
Possess the being
   the hour
   the place
where they gather
irresistibly
to the unity they awaited

the houses and trees
have darkness below
eyes of red earth
drink in the open blue

the light and your look
speak
across this rising river
of shadowless words

a great fruit basket of beings is the
      earth
where my love is one

may her presence last
may her eyes never die

XIX / JAVIER HÉRAUD

Of all the politically committed poets of Latin America, the Peruvian Javier Héraud (1942–1963) is the only one who has paid with his life for maintaining with a weapon what he stated on a typewriter. He was killed when only twenty-one in a fight between guerrilla forces and the Peruvian army. In his best-known poem, "The River" (1960), he gives a new turn to the theme of life as a river. Taking as its starting point a quotation from the Spanish poet Antonio Machado, Héraud dreams about his metamorphosis into a river. The sad ending does not detract from the dream's passion nor from Héraud's sacrifice.

The River

Translated by Paul Blackburn, in The Tri-Quarterly Anthology of Contemporary Latin American Literature *(New York: E. P. Dutton, 1969), pp. 84–86.*

The River
"life runs like a wide river"
   —Antonio Machado

1

I am a river,
I run down over
wide stones
down past
hard rocks
by the path
sketched out by the
wind.
I have my trees
hereabout overshadowed
by the rain.
I am a river,
I flow each moment more
furiously,

more violently,
I run each
moment, then a
bridge catches my
reflection in its
curvature of beams.

2

I am a river,
a river,
a river
crystalline in the
morning.
Sometimes I am

tender and
sweet-natured. I
glide through fertile valleys,
thousands of times I
offer myself
to the flocks and herds to drink,
to gentle people.
Children crowd about me during the
day,
and
at night trembling lovers
sustain their eyes in mine
and thrust their arms
into the dark clarity
of my ghostly waters.

3

I am the river.
But at times I am
wild
and strong,
at times I respect
neither life
nor death.
I run in
bone-breaking cascades,
I run with rage and with
bitterness,
smash against the
stones harder and harder,
I make them one, of
one I make endless
fragments.
The animals
flee,
leap into flight
when I
overrun my banks
grope through fields,
when I sow the slopes
with pebbles,
when
I drown
the houses and pastures,
when

I drown
the doorways and their
hearts,
the bodies and
their
hearts.

4

And it's here when
I most fall headlong.
When I can reach
the hearts, when
I can
catch them by the
blood,
when I can
look at them
from inside.
And my rage turns
mild, and I
turn
tree,
and I stem myself
like a tree,
and I silence myself
like a stone,
I am silent as a
rose without thorns.

5

I am a river.
I am the eternal
river of happiness. I feel
the approaching breezes,
I already feel the wind
on my cheeks,
and my journey across
mountains, rivers,
lakes, and meadows
becomes interminable.

6

I am the river that voyages along the
    banks,
        tree or dry stone

I am the river that voyages along the
    selvage,
        door or heart wide open
I am the river that voyages through
    the pastures,
        flower or cut rose
I am the river that voyages through
    the streets,
        earth or moistened heaven
I am the river that voyages through
    the houses,
        table or hoisted chair
I am the river that voyages inside
    men,
        tree   fruit
        rose   stone
        table   heart
        heart & door
        restored.

7

I am the river that sings
at noon and to the
men,
who sings in front of
their tombs,
he who turns his face
before the sacred riverbeds.

8

I am the sunset river.
I run through the broken
ravines,
through undiscovered villages
forgotten,
through the cities,
thronged by the population
in the display windows.
I am the river, already
I'm crossing meadows,
there are trees all about me
covered with doves,
the trees sing along
with the river,
the trees sing

with my bird-heart,
the rivers sing with my
arms.

9

The hour will come
when I will have to run
into the oceans
let them
mix my clear waters with their
turbulent waters,
when I will have to
silence my sunny song,
when I shall have to still
my fierce cries to the
dawn of all days, that
my eyes grow clear
against the sea.
The day will come, and
in the immense seas, I
shall never again see
my fertile fields,
not see my green
trees,
my imminent wind,
my cloudless sky,
my dark lake,
my sun,
my clouds,
nor will see anything,
anything,
solely the
blue sky,
immense,
and
everything will be melded into
a single flatness of water,
in which one song of one poem more
will be only small rivers that run
    down,
full-bodied rivers that run down to
    join
my new sunny waters,
my new waters of light
extinguished.

Epilogue

I'm only

a sad man who

wastes his words.

XX / ANTONIO CISNEROS

Drawing inspiration from his native country's glorious and murderous past, the Peruvian Antonio Cisneros (born in 1942) has written short, poignant poems on genocide and greed, on the absurd fertilizing of fields by the rotten carcasses of heroes and villains alike. Coming after Neruda's *General Song* (1950), Cisneros's poems succeed in concentrating their point in a few lines, and by harsh economy and brilliant, piercing images, manage to convey the madness of man.

Poems

From The Spider Hangs Too Far from the Ground, *translated by Maureen Ahern, William Rowe, and David Tipton (London: Cape Goliard; New York: Grossman; 1970).*

The Dead Conquerors

1

They came by water
these men with blue flesh
who trailed beards
& never slept
in order to rob each other blind.
Dealers in crosses
& brandy, who
founded their cities
with a temple.

2

During that summer of 1526
the rain tumbled down
on their daily work, & heads
& no one repaired
the rusty old armor.
Black fig trees grew
between the pews & altars,
while on the roof tiles
sparrows broke their beaks
silencing the bells.
Afterward in Peru
no one, though master
in his own house,
could move around
without treading upon the dead,
nor sleep next to white chairs
or swamps

without sharing his bed
with some cancerous relative.

Shit upon by scorpions & spiders
few survived their horses.

Tupac Amaru Relegated

There are liberators
with long sideburns
who saw the dead & wounded brought back
after the battles. Soon their names
were history & the sideburns
growing into their old uniforms
proclaimed them founders of the nation.
Others with less luck have taken up
two pages of text
with four horses & their death.

Three Testimonies of Ayacucho

From a Soldier

After the battle
there was nowhere to pile up
the dead
so dirty & holloweyed, scattered
over the grass like leavings
from this tough fight,
the swollen & yellowed heroes
littered among the stones
& disemboweled horses
were stretched out beneath the dawn.

I mean that dead comrades
are the same
as any other edible meat
after a battle, & soon
a hundred brown birds
flocked upon their corpses
until the grass was clean.

From a Mother

Some soldiers who were drinking brandy
have told me that now this country
is ours.
They also said
I shouldn't wait for my sons.

So I must
exchange the wooden chairs
for a little oil & some bread.
The land is black as dead ants,
the soldiers said it was ours.
But when the rains begin
I'll have to sell
the shoes & ponchos
of my dead sons.

Someday I'll buy a longhaired mule
& go down to my fields
of black earth
to reap the fruit
of these broad dark lands.

From a Mother Again

My sons & the rest of the dead still
belong to the owner of the horses
& the owner of the lands, & the battles.

A few apple trees grow among their bones
& the tough gorse. That's how they fertilize
this dark tilled land.
That's how they serve the owner
of war, hunger & the horses.

12

JOSÉ DONOSO

In awarding the 1962 prize for the year's best Latin American novel to José Donoso's *Coronation*, the Faulkner Foundation was acknowledging the emergence not only of a new writer but of a whole generation; for Donoso was the first of the new novelists to attract international attention.

He was born in Chile in 1924 to a family of lawyers and physicians, and began his studies at an English school in Santiago. In 1949 he went to Princeton University to study English literature for two years, and his first stories were written and published in English there.

Donoso, however, was not destined to become—like Conrad, Nabokov, or Beckett—an expatriate, using an adopted language as his medium in place of his native tongue. While English would always be his second language, the whole of his literary production would be in Spanish. He was, besides, too deeply concerned with unraveling all the threads that compose the fabric of Chilean society. Before visiting the United States, he had spent some months in the south of Chile, working as a shepherd, and later he labored on the docks in Buenos Aires. This varied experience was reflected in two volumes of short stories (*Summer Vacation*, 1955; *Charleston*, 1960) that he published later. His main efforts, however, have been concentrated on the writing of a series of novels that explore Chilean society in depth.

The first, *Coronation*, was originally published in 1957. It focuses on a decadent segment of society: the wealthy though not aristocratic bourgeoisie, whose days are already numbered. An old matron and her prematurely senile grandson are the main characters, and surrounding them is a chorus of servants, old and young, with whom their lives are inextricably linked. Donoso's approach to his subject, however, is decidedly not that of social realism; instead, the action is propelled through a series of grotesque confrontations serving progressively to reveal the underlying oedipal conflict that is the book's central theme. The character of the matron combines the strength and madness of Dickens's Miss Havisham and James's Julienne Bordereaux. The presentation of the lower classes was less successful: although Donoso excelled in his portrayals of the two old servants, he failed to convey adequately the animal magnetism of the younger lovers. But whatever its shortcomings, *Coronation* was unquestionably one of the best new novels of its decade.

Since then, Donoso, continuing his probing analysis of Chilean society, has published three more novels and is now actively working on yet another. *This Sunday* (1965) could be seen as a rewriting, in a less allegorical vein, of *Coronation*. This time the author contrasts two points of view: those of the adult characters, engaged in a deadly struggle based on their conflicting appetites and obsessions, and those of the children, in which everything that happens is metamorphosed into games and allegory. The chapter excerpted here illustrates beautifully how the dangers and horrors of real life can be neutralized by imagination.

In *Hell Has No Limits* (1966), the setting is no longer the big city, but a small-town brothel. It belongs to a young girl, whose father is a pitiful old transvestite; they are both in love with the same young stud. But the most forceful character is the landowner, a feudal chieftain whose whims can bring life or death to all around him. Written in a spare, ironic style, the novel is one of Donoso's best.

The Obscene Bird of Night (1969) returns to Santiago to present on a large canvas the same themes and similar characters. But this time the style is frankly baroque, and there is no attempt at realism. The main character is a man pretending to be a deaf-mute who finds refuge in an asylum for old women. Moving back and forth from that decrepit setting to a fairy-tale palace in which a double of the protagonist is having a kind of nightmarish existence, the novel abolishes the conventions of time and place, individual identity, and authorial point of view. Close in tone and spirit to Hieronymus Bosch or to Luis Buñuel's dream sequences, this book is Donoso's masterpiece.

Legitimate Games

From This Sunday, *translated by Lorraine O'Grady Freeman (New York: Knopf, 1967), pp. 75–87.*

Why did we call them "Sundays" in my grandmother's house? Sundays were short, official, and they required our best behavior, combed hair, and clean hands. Our parents arrived about eleven. They sat down in the rocking chairs on the porch, or on the steps if it was sunny, my mother fixing her nails, my Aunt Meche reading the newspaper, and my Uncle Lucho shearing off the top of the grass to show my father how to use the driver. We had to stay at the disposal of the visitors and the family. After lunch, when they finished their long conversation around the table, or perhaps a little later, we all went home again.

Saturdays were different because they were completely ours. They would deposit us in front of the green wooden gate and my mother and father, my Uncle Lucho and my Aunt Meche would go their own way to do their own things. After our ceremony with the Doll, no one paid attention to us; and the whole of my grandmother's house was open to the whim of our games. After dinner we three boys went up to sleep in the observatory. Gradually my grandfather and my grandmother and the servants turned off the lights in their rooms, leaving the lawn and bushes dark. Then Marta and Magdalena came up in their nightclothes to play with us. I'm sure that my grandmother knew about these forbidden visits, but she never said anything, so as not to spoil the pleasure of our secrecy. It was the kind of pleasure that she understood. She liked what our parents called our "strangeness," and to protect it she wouldn't permit them to give us presents of organized games, like Ping-pong, parcheesi, horse races, dominoes, or other such things.

"I don't want those things to cripple the children's imagination. I want them to learn how to entertain themselves. They're intelligent enough to invent their own games."

When there were no visitors, my grandmother sat on my grandfather's right at the table, and my mother and my Aunt Meche sat beside her. Across from them sat my father and my Uncle Lucho, who spoke about politics while the feminine side of the table discussed things that touched us more immediately.

"That's just like Mother to get complicated about the children's games.

There's nothing she likes better than to complicate her own life and everyone else's."

"Of course . . . You have time, Mamma, and a big house. But imagine us, with a single servant and living in apartments, what absolute hell it would be if the children could disrupt everything with their strange games. You don't have anything else to do."

It wasn't true. My grandmother had a lot to do, with her shantytown and her poor people. We often saw some toothless woman carrying a set of twins who screamed continuously in her arms. She would ring the doorbell and ask to speak with my grandmother. We knew that all week long my grandmother drove her little car from one place to another on errands for her poor people. But, in spite of her preoccupations, she would always take the trouble to look for some completely useless present to give us on Christmas or our saint's day. One year she scoured the entire city, looking for a shop where they would make her little crystal marbles with my name inside: me, the only one in the family and at school who owned such treasures. One time she gave Marta and Magdalena each a dress embroidered with sequins, dance dresses from when she was young. And I will never forget that Christmas, the Christmas she made one gift to all of us: an enormous key with a heavy baroque handle and a shaft of rusty iron, the key to a castle, a treasure house, a monastery, a city, an arsenal. She told us to look all through the house for a lock that it would fit. We spent several Sundays searching without finding anything, until at last we came upon a closet in the basement. The door squeaked when we opened it. My grandmother must have seen even to that detail. And there fell at our feet a cataract of old junk that delighted us because it increased the range of our games instead of distracting us from them.

Antonia was serving the dessert soufflé.

"This new gift is just like Mother."

"She spends her whole life wasting time on such things."

"And afterwards the children can't concentrate in school, and then they get bad marks in tests on useful things, like mathematics."

My Uncle Lucho lost the thread of his political discourse when dessert was served, and as he was a peacemaker he said to my Aunt Meche, "Come now, you're fighting with your mother again."

"You just don't understand, Lucho. It really makes me mad, this new thing she's doing with the children. And don't think for a moment that she was that way with us. She's changed a lot since then. In those days she used to go off on trips or outings and leave *us* home with the servants."

There was a short pause while my grandfather announced that he was going to his study: it was time now to listen to his opera. They both rushed back to the attack as soon as he had left the room.

"No. She was one of the most inconsiderate people you can imagine. She rode roughshod over everyone. Remember that business with Rosita Lara. . . ."

My grandmother stood up mortified. My father and my uncle went out to smoke their cigars in the garden. But we stayed bolted to our seats, listening, playing with the crumbs on the linen tablecloth.

"I don't remember . . ."

"Oh Meche . . . That time I came home and found Rosita Lara in my bath, bathing with my Helena Rubenstein soap that you gave me for my birthday . . ."

My Aunt Meche laughed.

"I set up an awful row with Mother. She said it wasn't like that at all. Rosita had problems with her husband: as soon as he got his pay on Saturdays he'd go out and spend it on another woman. Mother kept advising her to try and hook him back again. Then one fine day, when she got bored with giving her advice and saw that Rosita wasn't doing anything, she brought her home. She made her bathe in my tub with my soap, tinted her hair, gave her a dress, I think it was one of yours, and then she took her to wait for Lara in that seductive getup, across from the building where he worked—so she could take him directly home and give him a fantastic meal that she had taught her to make. Then they would have a siesta. . . ."

"I don't remember a thing."

As soon as we heard the word siesta, we looked around and nudged one another, and then we went running out to meet in the observatory. I don't remember how old we were then, but I know we were very young. And the idea that Rosita Lara, who to us seemed like nothing more than a grumbling old crone who came and cried about her troubles to my grandmother, the idea that *she* would take a siesta with her husband was hilarious. Because the siesta, in general, was something terribly strange, an inexplicable game of the grownups, a part of those things they called "important" because we had no access to them. One afternoon, when I was particularly anxious for them to take me to my grandmother's, I perched on a box on top of a chair to watch my parents' siesta through the transom window of the bathroom. At first I was alarmed; I thought they were victims of an attack that was making them contort themselves half nude in the heated shadow of their bedroom, beneath the sheets. A little later I thought my father was hurting my mother, perhaps killing her, and I considered screaming. But I realized that it wasn't that, that it was only a game, because they kept murmuring words of love. I got down relieved, but frightened with another kind of fear.

The instant I arrived at my grandmother's house that Saturday, I ran up to the observatory and told my cousins everything. They already knew. It wasn't anything special to them.

"My father and mother do that, too."

"But why didn't you tell me before?"

"Because you were innocent."   .

"And now you're not innocent any more."

Magdalena and Alberto had tried to do it together but nothing came of it because they nearly died with laughter. Then they got bored and didn't try it again. And furthermore, a schoolmate explained to Luis that if a brother and sister did what you do to have children, the result would be monsters, like breeding a cat onto a frog, or children with enormous heads, idiotic and depraved. The same thing happened between cousins, so I, too, was disqualified. We came to the conclusion that grownups pretended the things they did during the siesta were important in order to take advantage of us and give us orders, to make us study and obey. Sometimes, Luis or the girls would intentionally ask my Aunt Meche for something just before the siesta. She would get angry. It was evident that she and my Uncle Lucho were going to do something "important" closed off in their bedroom.

My grandmother, on the other hand, was never too busy to do things for us and she never took a siesta. The idea that she might do it with the Doll filled us with horror. Saturdays and Sundays, at least, were entirely ours, and she responded to any call or exigency. Even though she might be shut up with a women's committee in the piano room, she would leave them until we no longer needed her. Only then would she return to her women: four sheets of corrugated iron for Carmen Rojas, I can get them for half price at the factory. A kilo of red wool for Amanda, so she can knit something to sell—let's see if that won't help a little. A letter for Benicia, so she can put her little girl in the school that's run by the same nuns who took care of my mother when she died; she's a smart little thing, we have to help her. And if the women bumped into any of us when they left the house, they would go into ecstasy over our perfection:

"So pretty, little Magdalena, God bless her, the same as Misiá Chepa. And little Marta, so fat and blond, just exactly like Shirley Temple. What a good grandmother you have, dear, may God protect her. When she dies we're going to make her an *animita*, and just you wait and see, she'll be the most miraculous of all."

Often, on a winter Sunday when we returned home, it was already growing dark. From the back seat, I tried to understand my parents' conversation in the front. Beside the stone wall of the river, under the disheveled willows, I used to see a pair of candles burning, protected by a little tin roof, like a tiny chapel. That was an *animita*. My mother explained to me that ignorant people who didn't go to school, as I was going to go next year, believed that when a person was killed suddenly in an accident, or was murdered, and didn't have a chance to confess his sins, his soul would hover over the place where he had died. And if someone burned a candle to him there, then the dead man's soul would go up to Heaven, and he would intercede to God for the person who offered him the candle.

"What is 'intercede'? What is 'God'?"

My father signaled her to keep quiet. He was as scientific as my Uncle Lucho, very modern, and even though it scandalized my grandmother, they wouldn't allow us to be baptized. They forbade anyone to speak to us about religion or to teach us prayers. But my grandmother didn't have any truck with prohibitions: she had us baptized, secretly, my cousins and me, and told us stories of spirits and saints and apparitions. At school our parents arranged for us not to attend classes in religion. And so we were living in the best of two worlds: sharing, on the one hand, our grandmother's terrible secret of having had us baptized, and on the other, taking pleasure in the livid atmosphere, slightly tinged with criminality, that surrounded us for being the only ones who didn't take religion. Full of pride, we told our schoolmates how my grandmother was destined to be a miraculous *animita*. And in some way, it seemed appropriate to us that she, more than anybody, would die in an accident or in a murder, or some other glorious way, not lying in bed, pale and weak, which was the way we knew all grandmothers died. But of course, that was when we were playing that she was going to die, because we knew very well that she never would.

On Saturdays in winter, we spent the long afternoons shut up in the observatory. We listened to the drumming of the rain on the corrugated tin roof, and the trembling of the leaves in the kumquat tree, which never, not even when the acacias were a gray, smoky leaden, threw off their finely detailed leaves. An enormous Brussels carpet faded to the color of sea biscuit, a remnant from another house and another era even more incredibly spacious than the era and house belonging to my grandmother, spread the specters of its medallions and its complicated gourds over the observatory floor. Here we sat, beside the balcony, beyond the wardrobe, between the beds, in a fortification constructed with old, eviscerated volumes. We played a lot at something we called "idealizations." I would say to Magdalena, "You are ideal."

And she would reply, "Why?"

"Because you are the queen of China."

We would turn off all the lights except one on a night table. The kerosene stove around which we sat threw the reflections of its lacy frame onto our faces and a large rosette of light up to the ceiling. In the warm and slightly fetid shadow of the circle we made in the observatory, any transformation was possible. Then Magdalena would poke around in the trunks and boxes to find some old clothes, she would paint her eyes and adorn herself with finery until she was transformed into the queen of China. But we wouldn't be satisfied. And Luis would say, "You are ideal."

"Why?"

"Because you are tall and languid."

Magdalena was very short. But with this demand from Luis, and without leaving off being the queen of China, she had to walk as though she were an extremely tall and languid woman. We criticized her. If at any moment she stopped being Chinese, or stopped being tall and languid in order to fulfill the "you are ideal" which the rest of us demanded, then she had to pay a forfeit. In Magdalena's case this consisted of going to the toolshed and letting Segundo feel her legs. Afterwards she had to tell us everything.

From one of these idealizations Mariola Roncafort was born. We were idealizing Marta, who was then only nine years old. To all our demands for frivolity, for elegance, for demonstrations of love and I don't know how many other things, she who, in spite of her chubbiness had the imagination and sprightliness of an actress, went on giving satisfaction after satisfaction. How she moved her hands, her feet! The languidness of her pose when she leaned against the doorjamb, her ecstasy in lounging on the cushions, smoking as though she were breathing the perfumes of imaginary incense burners, her caricature of exoticism and richness obtained with a few old rags, some old cords with tassels and fringe stolen from an easy chair, and some feathers plucked from a feather duster! We were cold because, to make our kerosene last, we had lowered the flame. We put on coats, shawls, woolen stockings, we protected ourselves with cushions and blankets so that we could go on enjoying our idealization of Marta, even after the flame of the stove went out. She put the lamp from the night table in the middle of the carpet and covered it with reddish paper. Then, dragging along capes and collars, she danced, she loved, she traveled: she was one of those fabulous women whose pictures we saw in the pages of outdated *Vogues*, stretched out among the plants on their Mediterranean loggias. She spoke French without speaking it. She fell in love with a shadow and followed it to Africa to hunt tigers, to Paris to dance, on board yachts and planes, celebrated by everyone, painted by the great painters, haughty, fabulously gowned.

"You are ideal. . . ."

"Why?"

"Because your name is . . ."

Marta faltered. She was floating around the circle she had created in the semidarkness of the observatory. She was searching for an identity, a name, a line that might surround her creation and enclose it, separate it, preserve it. She lifted an eyebrow, stretched out her arm full of bracelets:

"Yolanda . . . María: María Yolanda. Mari-Yola. Mari-ola. Mariola Roncafort . . ."

Then, raising one shoulder and pressing her chin against it, half closing her eyes and advancing through the room with her arm still raised, her lips emitted syllables of infinite contempt, of arrogant satisfaction:

"Ueks, ueks . . . ueks . . ."

What did we hear in that syllable which made us immediately adopt it as a symbol of something, of well-being, of total security, of beauty, of arrogance? It was perfect on the lips of Mariola Roncafort. It illuminated everything, it said everything, even though we didn't know what it was illuminating or what it was saying.

From that day Mariola began to live a very complex and very definite life with us. We stopped playing idealizations, because that game had been nothing more than a form of searching, and we had found. We dedicated ourselves to creating and living the world and the life of Mariola Roncafort. Mariola was a Ueks. And the Ueks were such incredibly beautiful and well-endowed people, so rich and so daring that all other human beings could only love them, admire them, bathe in their light, in the light to which every Saturday, every moment we were together, the five of us, Alberto and Luis and Marta and Magdalena and I, went on adding details that made it ever brighter. Marta was not Mariola. No one was Mariola. She existed only in our conversations, and in spite of the fact that we made cutouts from magazines of Viking boats which she ordered built to navigate among the intricate, discolored medallions of our carpet, her essence remained in our words, our conversations. We built totally white African palaces for her, so she might go there and cure a pulmonary disease. We sketched the details of her necklaces, her airplanes. We built pink castles with volumes of the *Revue des Deux Mondes* on the largest, most important medallion of the carpet, the geographic location of her kingdom. An astronomer and an underwater fisherwoman. A consumptive after they took us to see *La Traviata,* an expressionist ballerina after they took us to see the Ballet Joos. Her adventures with Segundo and the Doll were endless, because she deigned to mix with mortals, too. But her true world was that of the "Ueks," the world of the beautiful, the chosen people. Soon my grandmother and the servants, and I think even Segundo, were using the word *ueks,* which became part of the family vocabulary.

That afternoon, under the ilang-ilang, Antonia told me, "You look very ueks in your new knickers."

And my grandmother said, "Be a little careful about making noise up there. Remember, a very ueks lady is coming for tea."

Soon, around Mariola Roncafort and the world of the Ueks, other worlds began to emerge, other characters. The "Cuecos," for example, whose geographic territory occupied the medallion directly opposite Mariola's on our carpet: they were ugly, backward people, with short, fat legs and wiglets, and they were always unbearably docile. But beneath that soft and stupid exterior, the Cuecos could be, and sometimes were, perverse and intriguing. In the wars that the Ueks fought on the immense central medallion of our carpet, the Cuecos showed themselves cowardly, but bloodthirsty and hypocritical. Their women were excellent wet nurses. The men, first-class cooks. Mariola chose cooks for all her palaces from the land of the Cuecos. This brought her interminable packs of espionage and poisonings and treason and heroic loyalty when the Ueks were at war with the Cuecos.

Soon, there were the "Old Man–Old Men": dedicated, professional men like our fathers. Serious people. Some of them spoke very sternly. They knew everything and smoked cigars. They used to slap each other on the back and say, "Good to see you, old man. And how's your wife? Fine? I'm glad to hear it, old man. Give her my regards. Look, old man, I have a proposition for you that I think you'll find to your advantage. But old man, what are we doing standing here on this street corner. Let's go into this bar, old man, and have a drink."

The Old Man–Old Men invariably told children like us that they looked just like their fathers, with whom as a general rule they had been to school. They knew all the politicians. They called ministers of state and bartenders by their nicknames. Mariola's politicians were always Old Man–Old Men.

Later, we invented other peoples, who took possession of the different medallions of the carpet. The "Seraphim," who were blond and pink-faced and came out first in class and knew everything without anyone telling them, but were silly, without imagination, without daring, as if they were made of foam rubber. And the "Gravel Throats," whose characteristics I don't remember any more. These peoples changed, destroyed one another, conquered and exterminated one another. Only the Ueks, with their queen Mariola, were eternal. And one day we decided that Mariola had to die so that we could transform her into a goddess.

Someone who was unaware that my grandmother did not like us to be given games presented us with a set of Monopoly. The following Saturday we couldn't find it in the house. My grandmother confessed that she had taken it as a present to a man she was visiting in prison, who was on the verge of coming out and who would go mad if she didn't take him something entertaining. Besides, she didn't like us to play with such games. That made us extremely angry because we had planned to introduce our Ueks characters, and the Old Man–Old Men and the Cuecos, into the innocent game of Monopoly and to play it with Mariola, her lovers, and her retainers. We had capes and turbans prepared to dress up in and play, I don't know by what rules or for what stakes. My mother and my Aunt Meche got furious with my grandmother. Typical, they repeated, typical. She had made their childhood impossible with that sort of thing. Always dressing them the way she wanted to, without ever letting them select so much as a ribbon. Obliging them to go to Mass and take Communion in spite of the fact that it never occurred to her to do it herself.

"And in the month of Mary, didn't I always go with you and the servants?"

"Yes, that much you did, because the processions and the flowers and all those things amused you, because they charm you, like witchcraft."

My grandmother's eyes filled with tears. "I have my own religion."

"Oh, isn't that just dandy! Then why couldn't *we* have religions of our own?"

She was speechless for an instant. Then she turned red and suddenly lashed out, "Do you think God is an idiot? Do you think He prefers me to go to church and listen to the foolish things the priests say, wasting my time instead of going to teach those poor women how to delouse their kids? Yes, Meche, how to delouse them, and you're the one who's so leftist. With these ueks hands I teach them how to cook on only a little money, how to knit and sew to help their husbands . . ."

"And you, what have *you* done to help Papa?"

At the other end of the table, fascinated by these accusations against my grandmother, we took advantage of the heat of the discussion to stay and hear the increasing number of things that came to light whenever my mother and my aunt were angry with her. She stopped, sniffing noisily.

"What do *you* two know?"

"He can't even take you anywhere. You're always going out looking like something the cat dragged in."

"What's wrong with this dress?"

"I bet Rosita Lara made it."

"Yes, and what of it? The way you two behave toward me. I can't stand it. I'm going over to Fanny's right now to tell her how you treat me. . . ."

We rose from the table and went haughtily up the stairs to the observatory. We felt that we were the ones who had been offended. Of course, we were happy, even though quietly, because my mother and my Aunt Meche had chastised her the way they chastised us so often. Our empty costumes were in a jumble on the floor. Mariola's army lay decimated on the carpet.

Was something happening at last?

We always wished for something really terrible to happen. There was a reproduction hanging on our wall, a painting in which, as the afternoon fell beneath the shadow of a pine grove, a retinue of youths and maidens were mourning a corpse shrouded in white linen and covered with flowers. We thought how marvelous it would be to cry like that, to kneel down and tear our hair, to sprinkle incense and throw flowers as we faced a really great tragedy beneath a golden sunset. But nothing ever happened if we did not invent it ourselves.

13

CARLOS FUENTES

In 1958, only one year after José Donoso's *Coronation* (Five, 12), the Mexican Carlos Fuentes published a vast, complex fresco of Mexico City, *Where the Air Is Clearer*. With a kind of Dos Passos flourish and a Faulknerian intensity, Fuentes analyzed what had gone wrong with the Mexican Revolution. His diagnosis of the evils stemming from the dominance of the new bourgeoisie was as severe and cynical as that of Mariano Azuela (Part Three, 10) many years earlier. But to this task of political moralist Fuentes brought more precise and acute critical faculties.

He was born in Mexico City in 1928, to a well-to-do family that provided him with an international education. His father was a diplomat, and Fuentes spent his childhood moving from Santiago de Chile (where he studied at the same school as Donoso) to Buenos Aires, and from Washington, D.C., to Geneva, where he finally got a degree in law. He has lived in either Europe or the United States for many years; he is now the Mexican ambassador in Paris.

But his main interest was and is Mexico. His very first book, *The Masked Days* (1954), a collection of short stories, made evident his preoccupation with Mexican reality in all its dimensions. It was a passionate reading of Octavio Paz's *Labyrinth of Solitude* (Five, 1) that gave Fuentes his key to the deciphering of that reality, in the several novels and dozen short stories that he has thus far produced. After a rather unsuccessful realistic novel (*The Good Consciences*, 1959), he returned, in *The Death of Artemio Cruz* (1962), to the many-layered portrayal of postrevolutionary Mexico found in his first novel. The hero, a patriot who has turned into one of the new exploiters, is now dying, and his consciousness is split into three voices (I, you, he), which alternate in narrating a fragmented, nonchronological biography. Borrowing from Orson Welles's *Citizen Kane* as well as from the *nouveau roman,* Fuentes created a very dynamic narrative with a powerful protagonist. If the book now seems too contrived, it is only because subtler narrative structures have been devised by Cortázar and Cabrera Infante (Five, 4, 15) in later novels. Fuentes's fourth novel, *A Change of Skin* (1968), painted an even more crowded fresco of Mexican life, both its decadent present and its unredeemed past. Using as his basic narrative device a trip to Cholula of two ill-assorted couples, Fuentes mixed the Aztec myths with the pop, moddish present and moved the action back and forth from Mexico to Czechoslovakia, from sacrificial rites in a pyramid to the technological horrors of a Nazi concentration camp. The mixture was not always successful, although some of the episodes were among the best Fuentes had ever written. He has also published two short novels—*Aura* (1962), a sort of rewriting of *The Aspern Papers,* in which the past to be recaptured was not literary but historical and the writing was allegorical instead of symbolical; and *Birthday* (1969), an even more allegorical type of rewriting of a similar subject—and two plays. His latest book, an 800-page novel entitled *Terra Nostra* (1975), is his most ambitious work to date.

The selection presented here, "The Doll Queen," is from a second volume of short stories, *Blindman's Song* (1964). The corruption of innocence, the monstrosities that lurk behind the events of everyday life, the confusions of personal identity—these are some of the themes with which Fuentes builds this haunting story.

The Doll Queen

Translated by Agnes Moncy, in The Tri-Quarterly Anthology of Contemporary Latin American Literature *(New York: E. P. Dutton, 1969), pp. 394–409. Orginally published in* Tri-Quarterly.

I came because that intriguing card reminded me of her existence. I found the card in a book I had forgotten about and whose pages had reproduced a ghost of that childlike handwriting. After a long time of not having done so, I was arranging my books. I went from surprise to surprise because some of them, on the highest shelves, had not been read for a long time. For such a long time, in fact, that the edges of the pages had granulated so that a mixture of golden dust and a grayish film fell into my open palms, evoking the varnished finish which certain bodies have, bodies first glimpsed in dreams and then in the disillusioning reality of the first ballet performance to which we are taken. It was a book from my childhood—perhaps from almost everyone's—and it told a series of more or less truculent exemplary stories, which had the virtue of catapulting us onto the knees of our elders to ask them over and over, why? Children who are miserable with their parents; girls who are carried off by so-called gentlemen and come back dishonored, as well as the ones who leave home willingly, the old man who in exchange for an unpaid mortgage demands the hand of the sweetest, saddest girl in the threatened family—why? I don't remember what the answers were. I only know that from between the stained pages there fell fluttering down a white card in Amilamia's atrocious writing: "Amilamia dosint forget her litel friend and look for me here where the pichure shows."

And on the other side was the map of a path starting at an X, which undoubtedly stood for the bench in the park where I—an adolescent rebelling against my tedious and prescribed education—used to forget about my classes and spend several hours reading books which, if not written by me, seemed to have been: how could I doubt that my imagination alone was the source of all those pirates, all those emissaries of the czar, all those boys, a bit younger than myself, who drifted all day long on a barge up and down the great American rivers? Holding on to the arm of the bench as if it were a miraculous saddletree, I did not at first hear the light steps running across the gravel in the garden, then stopping behind me. It was Amilamia, and she would have accompanied me in silence for heaven knows how long if her playful spirit, on that particular afternoon, hadn't prompted her to tickle my ear with the down of a dandelion that she was blowing at me, her mouth full of air, her brow wrinkled.

She asked what my name was, and after considering it with a very serious face, she told me hers with a smile which, if it wasn't candid, neither was it overly rehearsed. I soon realized that Amilamia had found a midway point, as it were, between the ingenuousness of her years and the formulas of adult mimicry which well-brought-up children should know, especially for such solemn occasions as introductions and farewells. Amilamia's seriousness was more of a natural trait, so much so that her moments of spontaneity seemed cultivated by contrast. I would like to recall her as she was on different afternoons, with a succession of fixed images which, taken together, render Amilamia in her entirety. It doesn't cease to surprise me that I can't think of her as she really was, or as she really moved, lightly and curiously, looking this way and that way constantly. I should try to recall her glued to a certain spot forever, as if in an album. Amilamia in the distance, a dot where the hill used to slope from a lake of clover down to the flat meadow where I used to read on the bench: a dot of sun and shadow flowing and a hand waving to me from up there. Amilamia stopped in her race downhill, with her white skirt puffed and her tiny-flowered bloomers held by elastics around her thighs, her mouth open and her eyes half closed because her running stirred up the air; the little girl shedding tears of pleasure. Amilamia sitting under the eucalyptus trees, pretending to cry so that I'd go up to her. Amilamia lying face down with a flower in her hands: the petals of a cattail that—I discovered later—didn't grow in this garden but somewhere else, perhaps in the garden at her house, because the only pocket in her blue-checked apron was often full of those white flowers. Amilamia watching me read, standing with both hands on the bars of that green bench, inquiring with her gray eyes; I remember that she never asked me what I was reading, as if she could discover in my eyes the images born from the pages of the book. Amilamia laughing with pleasure when I picked her up by the waist and made her spin around my head and she seeming to find a new perspective on the world in that slow flight. Amilamia turning her back and saying goodbye with her arm raised and her fingers waving. And Amilamia in the hundreds of poses she used to take around my bench: hanging from her head with her legs in the air and her bloomers puffed out; sitting on the gravel with her legs crossed and her chin resting on the palm of her hand; lying on the grass, her navel bared to the sun; weaving together branches from the trees; drawing animals in the mud with a stick; licking the bars of the bench; hiding under the seat; silently breaking off stray growths from aged trunks; looking fixedly at the horizon over the hill; humming with her eyes closed; imitating the sounds of birds, dogs, cats, hens, horses. All for me, and yet it was nothing. It was her way of being with me, all this that I remember, but it was also her way of being alone in the park. Yes; perhaps I remember her fragmentarily because I alternated between my reading and contemplating the plump-faced little girl with the straight hair whose color changed with the light: now straw-colored, now burnt chestnut. And only now does it occur to me that at the time, Amilamia established the other reference point in my life, the one that created a tension between my own unresolved childhood and the open world, the promised land that was beginning to be mine through books.

Not then. Then I dreamed of the women in my books, the females— the word disturbed me—who disguised themselves as the Queen so as to buy a necklace incognito; the mythological creations—part recognizable beings, part salamanders, white-breasted and damp-wombed—who awaited monarchs in their beds. And thus, imperceptibly, I moved from an indifference toward my infantile company to an acceptance of the little girl's grace and seriousness, and from there to an unexpected rejection of that useless presence. It was finally irritating to me —me, already a fourteen-year-old, to be around that seven-year-old girl who wasn't, then, a memory and nostalgia of it, but the past and its actuality. I had given in to a weakness. We had run together, hand in hand, over the meadow. We had shaken the pines together and gathered the cones, which Amilamia put eagerly into her apron pocket. We had made paper sailboats together and fol-lowed them overjoyed along the edge of the drain. And that afternoon, when we rolled down the hill together, amidst cries of happiness, and fell down together at the bottom, Amilamia on my chest, the little girl's hair in my lips, and when I felt her panting in my ear and her little arms sticky with candy around my neck, I pushed away her arms angrily and let her fall. Amilamia cried, stroking her wounded elbow and knee, and I went back to my bench. Then Amilamia left and the next day returned and without a word, she gave me the piece of paper and disappeared humming into the forest. I couldn't decide whether to tear up the card or keep it between the pages of the book: *Afternoons on the Farm.* Being around Amilamia had even made my reading become childish. She did not come back to the park. After a few days, I left for vacation, and when I came back, it was to the duties of a first-year baccalaureate student. I never saw her again.

II

And now, almost rejecting the image which without being fantastic is unusual, and in being real is more painful, I am going back to that forgotten park, and now, standing in front of the pine grove and eucalyptus trees, I realize how small the foresty spot is, how my memory has insisted on drawing things large enough to permit my imagination to flood it with its waves. For it was here that Strogoff and Huckleberry Finn, Milady de Winter and Geneviève de Brabante were born, talked and died; in this little garden enclosed by rusty lattices, planted scantily with old unkempt trees, hardly decorated by the cement bench, an imitation of a wooden bench, which makes me wonder whether my beautiful forged iron bench, painted green, ever existed, or whether it was part of my orderly retrospective delirium. And the hill . . . how could I believe that this was it, the promontory that Amilamia ran down and climbed up on her daily walks, the steep slope we rolled down together? Barely a mound of fodder, with no more relief than what my memory insists on giving it.

"Look for me here where the pichure shows." This meant that I had to cross the garden, leave the forest behind, go down the mound in three strides, cross that small orchard of hazelnut trees—it was undoubtedly here that the little girl gathered those white petals—open the creaky park gate, and suddenly remember, know, find myself in the street, realize that all those afternoons of my adolescence, as if by a miracle, had managed to make the surrounding city stop beating, do away with that din of horns blowing, bells ringing, shouting, moaning, motors running, radios, cursing. . . . Which was the real magnet, the quiet garden or the feverish city? I wait for the light to change and cross the street without taking my eyes from the red light, which is keeping the traffic in check. I consult Amilamia's paper. In the last analysis, this rudimentary map is the real magnet of the moment I am living, and just to think of it startles me. My life after those lost afternoons I spent when I was fourteen was obliged to follow a disciplined course and now, at twenty-nine, duly graduated, the head of an office, assured of a reasonable income, still single, having no family to support, mildly bored by going to bed with secretaries, scarcely excited by some eventual trip to the country or the beach. I lacked a main interest like the ones I had earlier, in my books, my park, and Amilamia. I head through the street of this flat, gray suburb. One-story houses succeed each other monotonously with their elongated grilled windows and their big front doors, the paint peeling off. The buzzing of various tasks being done hardly breaks the monotony. The screeching of a knife sharpener here, the hammering of a shoemaker there. In the side passages, the neighborhood children play. The music of an organ reaches my ears mixed with the children's singing. I stop a minute to look at them, with the fleeting impression that Amilamia may perhaps be among those groups of children, showing her flowered bloomers with impunity, hanging by her legs from a balcony, addicted as usual to her acrobatic extravagances, with her apron pocket full of white petals. I smile, and for the first time I want to envision the twenty-two-year-old miss who, if she still lives at the address jotted down, will laugh at my memories or perhaps will have forgotten the afternoons spent in the garden.

The house is exactly like the others. The big door, two grilled windows with the shutters closed. One story only, crowned with a fake neoclassic balustrade, most likely disguising the functions of the rooftop: clothes hung out, troughs of water, the servants' room, the poultry yard. Before ringing the doorbell, I want to rid myself of any illusions. Amilamia doesn't live here any more. Why should she have stayed in the same house for fifteen years? Besides, in spite of her premature independence and solitude, she seemed to be a well-bred little girl, well dressed, and this neighborhood is no longer elegant; Amilamia's parents have no doubt moved. But perhaps the new residents know where they are.

I ring the doorbell and wait. I ring again. That's another possibility; there may be no one here. Will I feel the need to look for my little friend again? No, because it will no longer be possible to open a book from my adolescence and happen to come across Amilamia's card. I would go back to my routine, I would forget the moment which had been important only because of its fleeting surprise.

I ring again. I put my ear to the door and am surprised: hoarse and irregular breathing coming from the other side; a heavy panting accompanied by the disagreeable smell of rancid tobacco filters through the cracked boards.

"Good afternoon. Could you please tell me . . . ?"

Upon hearing my voice, the person withdraws with heavy, uncertain steps. I ring the bell again, this time shouting, "Hello! Open up! What's wrong? Can't you hear me?"

I receive no reply. I keep ringing the bell, but with no results. I withdraw from the door without shifting my eyes from the thin slits in the door, as if distance could give me perspective and even the ability to penetrate. Concentrating fixedly on the cursed door, I keep walking backward, cross the street; a sharp cry saves me in time, followed by a horn blown hard and long, while I confusedly look for the person whose voice has just saved me; all I see is the car going down the street and I embrace a lamppost, a handhold which, more than security, offers me a place to lean on as my icy blood rushes into my burning skin and I sweat. I look at the house that was, had been, must have been, Amilamia's. Behind the balustrade, just as I had guessed, there are clothes waving. I don't know what the rest is: slips, pajamas, blouses, I don't know; I see that little blue-checked apron, stiff, clothes-pinned onto the long line that is swaying between an iron bar and a nail in the white wall of the rooftop.

III

At the City Clerk's Office of Deeds they told me that the property was in the name of a Mr. R. Valdivia who rents the house. To whom? That they wouldn't know. Who is Valdivia? He states that he's a businessman. Where does he live? "Who are you?" the young lady asks me with haughty curiosity. I didn't know how to be calm and sure of myself. Sleep hadn't relieved my nervous fatigue. Valdivia. I leave the Clerk's Office; the sun offends me. I associate the repugnance which the foggy sun sieved by low clouds—and therefore more intense—provokes in me with the desire to return to the damp and shady park. No, all it is, is my desire to know whether Amilamia lives in that house and why I'm not admitted there. But what I should reject, and the sooner the better, is the absurd idea that didn't let me get a wink of sleep last night. To have seen the apron drying on the roof, the same one in whose pocket she kept the flowers, and to think because of this that a seven-year-old girl whom I knew fourteen or fifteen years ago still lived in the house . . . She might have a little daughter. Yes. Amilamia, at twenty-two, was the mother of a little girl who perhaps dressed the same way, looked like her, repeated the same games—who knows?—went to the same park. And musing on this I again arrive at the front door of the house. I ring the bell and wait for the hard breathing from the other side of the door. I was wrong. The door is opened by a woman who must not be over fifty. But wrapped in a shawl, dressed in black, and in low-heeled shoes, no make-up, her hair pulled back to the nape of her neck, graying, she seems to have given up any illusion or pretext of youth and she observes me with eyes that are almost cruel, they're so indifferent.

"You wished?"

"Mr. Valdivia sent me." I cough and run my hand through my hair. I should have picked up my briefcase at the office. I realize that without it I won't play the role well.

"Valdivia?" the woman asks me with neither alarm nor interest.

"Yes. The owner of the house."

One thing is clear: the woman won't let anything show in her face. She looks at me fearlessly.

"Oh yes. The owner of the house."

"May I? . . ."

In bad plays I think the traveling salesman sticks his foot in the door to keep them from shutting it in his face. I do this, but the lady steps aside and with a gesture of her hand invites me to come in to what must have been a place to keep the car. To one side is a glass door in a peeling wooden frame. I walk toward it, over the yellow tiles of the entrance patio, and ask again, facing the lady, who is following me in tiny steps, "This way?"

She assents, and for the first time I notice that in her hands she has a three-decade rosary which she doesn't cease to play with. I haven't seen those old rosaries since my childhood and I'd like to remark on it, but the brusque and decided manner in which the lady opens the door impedes any gratuitous conversation. We enter a long and narrow room. The lady hastens to open the shutters but the room is still darkened by four perennial plants growing in porcelain and encrusted-glass flowerpots. The only thing there is in the living room is an old, high-backed wicker sofa and a rocking chair. But it's not the scarcity of furniture or the plants which draw my attention. The lady asks me if I would like to sit down on the sofa before she herself sits in the rocking chair.

At my side, on the wicker sofa, there is an open magazine.

"Mr. Valdivia apologizes for not having come himself."

The lady rocks back and forth without blinking. I look out of the corner of my eye at that comic book.

"He sends his greetings and . . ."

I hesitate, hoping for a reaction from the woman. She keeps rocking. The comic book has been scrawled on with a red crayon.

". . . and he has asked me to inform you that he will have to disturb you for a few days. . . ."

My eyes search quickly.

"The house has to be reassessed for the cadastre. It seems that it hasn't been done since . . . You've been living here for how many years? . . ."

Yes; that red lipstick is under the chair. And if the lady smiles she does so with her slow hands which caress the rosary beads; for a minute I feel there's a joke on me which doesn't quite upset her features. She doesn't answer me this time either.

". . . for fifteen years at least, haven't you?"

She does not affirm. She does not deny. And on her pale thin lips there isn't the slightest trace of lipstick.

". . . you, your husband and . . . ?"

She looks at me fixedly, without varying her expression, almost defying me to continue. We stay silent for a moment, she playing with the rosary, I bent forward with my hands on my knees. I get up.

"So I'll be back this afternoon with the papers. . . ."

The lady assents as she silently picks up the lipstick and the comic book and hides them in the folds of her shawl.

IV

The scene hasn't changed. This afternoon, as I take down imaginary numbers in a notebook and pretend to be interested in establishing the quality of the floorboards and the dimensions of the room, the lady rocks back and forth, rubbing the three decades of her rosary with the cushions of her fingers. I sigh as I finish the supposed inventory of the living room and ask her if we might go to other parts of the house. The lady sits up, bracing her long black arms on the seat of the rocking chair and adjusting her shawl on her narrow and bony shoulders.

She opens the opaque glass door and we enter a dining room that is hardly more furnished. But the table with round, metallic legs, accompanied by four vinyl-covered chairs in nickel frames, doesn't offer even the hint of distinction that the living room furniture had. The other grilled window, with the shutters closed, must at certain times illuminate this bare-walled dining room without a buffet or a mantel. All there is on the table is a plastic bowl of fruit with a cluster of black grapes, two peaches, and a buzzing crown of flies. With her arms crossed and her face inexpressive, the lady stands behind me. I dare to disrupt the order: it is evident that the family rooms will tell me nothing about what I want to know.

"Couldn't we go up to the roof?" I ask. "I think it's the best way to cover the total surface."

The lady looks at me with a spark in her eyes which is sharp, perhaps because it contrasts with the shadows in the dining room.

"What for?" she says finally. "Mr. . . . Valdivia . . . knows very well what the dimensions of the house are."

And those pauses, one before and one after the owner's name, are the first signs that there is something which is disturbing the lady and making her resort to irony out of self-defense.

"I don't know," I make an effort to smile. "Perhaps I would prefer to start at the top and not"—my false smile is slowly dissolving—"from the bottom."

"You'll do as I say," the lady says with her hands joined over the silver cross hanging on her dark stomach.

Before smiling weakly, I force myself to think that my gestures are useless in the shadows; they're not even symbolic. The binding creaks as I open the notebook and continue noting down, with as much speed as possible, without shifting my glance, the numbers and estimates of this job whose fictitious nature —the mild blush on my cheeks, the definite dryness of my tongue—isn't fooling anyone. And as I fill the graphed page with absurd signs, square roots, and algebraic formulas, I ask myself what it is that keeps me from going to the heart of the matter, from asking about Amilamia and leaving with a satisfactory answer. No. And yet I feel sure that even though I would obtain a reply if I took this approach, I wouldn't discover the truth. My thin and silent companion has a silhouette I wouldn't stop to notice in the street, but in this house of coarse furniture and absent inhabitants, it ceases to be an anonymous face in the city and becomes a stereotype of mystery. This is the paradox, and if my memories of Amilamia have once again awakened my craving to imagine things, I will follow the rules of the game, I will wear out appearances and I won't rest until I have found the answer—perhaps a simple and obvious one—behind the unexpected veils the lady drops along the way. Am I attributing some gratuitous strangeness to my reluctant hostess? If I am, I will enjoy my labyrinthine invention more. And the flies buzz around the bowl of fruit, but they light on that damaged spot of the peach, that nibbled-out chunk—I approach it, using my notes as an excuse —where there is an imprint of tiny teeth in the velvety skin and ocher flesh. I don't look toward where the lady is. I pretend that I'm still taking notes. The fruit seems to have been bitten into but not touched. I crouch to get a better look at it, I lean my hands on the table, I pucker my lips as if I wanted to repeat the act of biting it without touching it. I lower my eyes and I see another trace of something next to my feet: it is of two tires which seem to have been bicycle tires, two rubber marks stamped on the faded wooden floor; they go as far as the edge of the table and then head back, more and more faintly, across the floor to where the lady is. . . .

I close my notebook.

"Let's continue, madam."

When I turn toward her I find her standing with her hands on the back of a chair. Seated in front of her is a heavy-shouldered man with an invisible expression in his eyes, coughing from the smoke of his cigarette: his eyes are hidden by his wrinkled, swollen, thick eyelids, similar to the neck of an old turtle, yet nevertheless they seem to follow my movements. The badly shaven cheeks, cracked by hundreds of gray lines, hang from his prominent cheekbones, and his greenish hands are hidden under his armpits. He is wearing a coarse blue shirt, and his curly hair, mussed up, looks like the bottom of a boat covered with barnacles. He doesn't move, and the real sign that he's alive is that hard breathing (as if his breathing had to get through a series of locks made of phlegm, irritation, worn-out organs), which I had already heard between the cracks of the front door.

Ridiculously, I murmur, "Good afternoon . . ."—and I'm ready to forget the whole thing: the mystery, Amilamia, the assessment, the clues. The sight of this asthmatic wolf justifies a quick escape. I repeat "Good afternoon," this time in a tone of farewell. The turtle's mask opens up into an atrocious smile: every pore of that flesh seems to have been made of breakable rubber, rotten oilcloth. He puts out his arm and stops me.

"Valdivia died four years ago," the man says in that suffocated, remote voice, located in his entrails and not in his larynx: a weak, treble voice.

Arrested by that strong, almost painful claw, I tell myself that it's useless to pretend. The wax and rubber faces observing me say nothing, and because of it I can, in spite of everything, pretend for the last time, make believe that I'm talking to myself when I say, "Amilamia . . ."

Yes: the pretending is over for all of us. The fist that pressed against my arm affirms its strength only for a moment; then it relaxes and finally it falls, weak and shaky, before he raises it and takes the wax hand that was on his shoulder; perplexed for the first time, the lady looks at me with eyes that seem to be a wounded bird's, and she cries, and it is a dry moan that doesn't alter the rigid disturbance in her features. The ogres of my mind are suddenly two lonely old people, wounded and abandoned, who can hardly comfort themselves by joining their hands with a shiver that fills me with shame. My imagination brought me into this bare dining room to trespass on the intimacy and secret of two beings who had been expelled from life because of something which I had no right to know about. I have never despised myself so much. I have never had such a crude lack of words. Any gesture I might make would be in vain: should I go up to them, touch them, caress the lady's head, ask to be excused for interfering? I put my notebook in the pocket of my jacket. I cast out of my mind all the clues I had for my detective story: the comic book, the lipstick tube, the nibbled fruit, the bicycle tracks, the blue-checked apron. . . . I decide to leave this house without a word. The old man, behind the thick eyelids, must have noticed me. He says to me in that wheezy voice, "You knew her?"

The natural sound of that past tense which they must use every day is what finishes destroying my illusions. There's the answer. You knew her. How many years? How many years has the world lived without Amilamia, assassinated first by my forgetting her, then revived just yesterday by an impotent, sad memory? When did those serious gray eyes cease to wonder at the delight of an always solitary garden? When did those lips stop pouting or narrowing in that ceremonious seriousness with which—now I understand—Amilamia discovered and consecrated things in a life which, she perhaps intuited, would be brief?

"Yes, we played together in the park. A long time ago."

"How old was she?" he says in an even quieter voice.

"She must have been seven. Yes, not over seven."

Together with her arms, which seem to implore me, the woman raises her voice: "What was she like, sir? Tell us what she was like, please. . . ."

I close my eyes. "Amilamia is a memory for me too. I can only compare her to the things she touched, carried, and discovered in the park. Yes. Now I can see her coming down the hill. No, it's not true that it's hardly a mound. It was a grassy hill and Amilamia had made a path in it with her coming and going and greeted me from the top before coming down, accompanied by music, yes, the music in my eyes, my olfactory paintings, the tastes in my ears, the smells I touched . . . my hallucination . . . are you listening? . . . She came down waving to me, dressed in white, with a blue-checked apron . . . the one you've hung on the rooftop. . . ."

They take my arms and I do not open my eyes.

"What was she like, sir?"

"She had gray eyes and the color of her hair changed with the sun and the shade of the trees. . . ."

They lead me, gently, together; I hear the man's hard breathing, the rosary cross hitting against the woman's body. . . .

"Please tell us. . . ."

"The air made her cry when she ran; she would reach my bench with her cheeks coated with happy tears. . . ."

I keep my eyes closed. We go upstairs now. Two, five, eight, nine, twelve steps. Four hands guide my body.

"What was she like, won't you tell us?"

"She used to sit under the eucalyptus trees and braid the branches and make believe she was crying so that I would leave my book and go to her. . . ."

The hinges creak. The smell kills everything: it disperses the rest of my senses, installs itself like a yellow Mongol on the throne of my hallucination, heavy as a chest, insinuating as the rustle of draped silk, ornamented as a Turkish scepter, opaque as a deep lost vein, brilliant as a dead star. The hands release me. More than the crying, it is the old couple's trembling which surrounds me. I open my eyes slowly: I let the liquid dizziness of my cornea and then the net of my eyelashes discover the room suffocated by that huge battle of perfumes, vapors, and dew from almost red petals. The presence of flowers here is such that they undoubtedly have living skin: sweetness of hedge mustard, nausea of asarabacca, tomb of tuberose, temple of the gardenia; the tiny windowless room lit up by the incandescent flame-nails of heavy sputtering candles projects its dry wax and damp flowers into the heart of the plexus and only from there, from the sun of life, is it possible to revive and contemplate behind the candles and among the dispersed flowers, the accumulation of old toys, colored hoops and wrinkled deflated balloons, old transparent plums, wooden horses with ruined manes, old skates, blind dolls with their wigs torn off, teddy bears emptied of their sawdust, oilcloth ducks riddled with holes, moth-bitten dogs, rotting jump ropes, glass jars full of dried sweets, worn out childish shoes, the tricycle—three wheels? no, two; and not a bicycle's; two parallel wheels, underneath—the worsted leather shoes; and in front of me, within hand's reach, the little coffin resting on blue boxes decorated with paper flowers, life flowers this time, carnations and sunflowers, poppies and tulips, but like the others, the death flowers, part of the same brew made by all the elements of this wintery funeral in which, inside the silver plated coffin and between the black silk sheets and on the white satin mattress, lies that still, serene face framed by a lace cowl, painted pink; eyebrows traced by the thinnest brush, lids closed, real eyelashes, thick ones that cast a slight shadow on the cheeks, which are as healthy as they were in the park. Serious red lips almost pouting the way Amilamia did when she pretended to be mad so that I would go play with her. Hands joined on her breast. A rosary, exactly like the mother's, strangling the cardboard neck. A small white shroud over the immature, clean, docile body.

The old couple has knelt down, sobbing.

I stretch out my hand and graze the porcelain face of my friend. I feel the cold of those drawn-on features, of the doll-queen presiding over the pomp of this royal death chamber. Porcelain, cardboard, and cotton. "Amilamia dosint forget her litel friend and look for me here where the pichure shows."

I remove my fingers from the false corpse. My fingerprints remain on the doll's skin.

And nausea creeps into my stomach, a depository of candle smoke and the stench of asarabacca in the close room. I turn my back on Amilamia's tomb. The lady's hand touches my arm. Her wild eyes don't make her quiet voice tremble: "Don't come back. If you really loved her, don't ever come back."

I touch Amilamia's mother's hand; dizzily I see the old man's head slumped between his knees, and I walk out of the room to the staircase, to the living room, to the patio, to the street.

V

If not a year, at least nine or ten months have passed. The memory of that idolatry no longer scares me. I've forgotten how the flowers smelled and what the icy doll looked like. The real Amilamia has returned to my memory and I have felt, if not happy, healthy again: the park, the live child, my hours of adolescent reading, have conquered the ghosts of a sick cult. The image of life is stronger than the other. I tell myself that I will always live with my real Amilamia, who has triumphed over the caricature of death. And one day I dare to leaf through that graphed notebook where I recorded these false facts for the assessment. And from its pages, again, falls Amilamia's card in her terrible child's writing and with its map of the way from the park to her house. I smile as I pick it up. I bite one of the edges thinking that in spite of everything the poor old people would accept this gift.

I put on my coat and tighten my tie, whistling. Why not go visit them and offer them this piece of paper in their child's handwriting?

I run up to the one-story house. The rain begins to fall in isolated drops; that wet odor of a blessing which seems to stir the soil and hasten the fermentation of everything rooted in the dust springs up at the impact.

I ring the bell. The showers get heavier and I insist. A shrill voice shouts "Coming!" and I wait for the mother to appear with her eternal rosary and receive me. I turn up my coat lapels. The contact with the rain also transforms the smell of my clothes, my body. The door opens.

"What do you want? Oh, how good that you've come!"

The deformed girl in the wheelchair rests her hands on the doorknob and smiles at me in a twisted, inexplicable way. The hunch in her chest converts her dress into a curtain over her body: a white cloth which is nevertheless given a coquettish look by the blue-checked apron. The little woman pulls out a pack of cigarettes from her apron pocket and lights up one quickly, smudging the end of it with the orange lipstick she is wearing. The smoke makes her squint her beautiful gray eyes. She touches up her copper-colored hair, which is like straw and has a permanent, without ceasing to look at me with an inquisitive and desolate but also desirous look, becoming frightened now.

"No, Carlos. Leave. Don't come back."

And at the same time, from within the house, I hear the old man's hard breathing coming closer and closer: "Where are you? You know you're not supposed to answer the door! Get back inside, you infernal creature! Do you want me to spank you again?"

And the rainwater glides down my forehead, my cheeks, my mouth, and the little frightened hands drop the comic book on the wet flagstones.

14

GABRIEL GARCÍA MÁRQUEZ

The international success of *One Hundred Years of Solitude* has been so overwhelming that it has distorted any serious critical consideration of García Márquez's work. He was born in 1928 in a small town on the Caribbean coast of Colombia, a town he would later metamorphose into the fabulous Macondo. García Márquez never completed his law studies but became a successful journalist in his native country, in Europe, and in the United States. In 1954 he won a first prize from the National Association of Writers and Artists with a story called "One Day After Saturday," presented here. One year later he published his first novel, *The Leaf Storm*, a Faulknerian fragment of what would eventually become the Macondo saga. Two more followed: *No One Writes to the Colonel* (1961), a Hemingwayesque novella about an ex-revolutionary waiting in proud destitution for a promised government pension; and *The Evil Hour* (1962), a longer narrative about injustice and violence in a small town, written with concentrated fury.

Also in 1962, he published a volume of short stories, *Big Mama's Funeral*. The title story introduced a fantastic dimension into García Márquez' stylized realism. Big Mama was larger than life, and to come to her carnival-like funeral, His Holiness the Pope took a gondola down the Tiber and flowed through unmapped Mediterranean channels into the Amazonian fluvial system. Hyperbole had begun to weave its way into García Márquez's narrative.

His fourth novel, *One Hundred Years of Solitude* (1967), set realism aside altogether and, combining myths and romance, developed the tall story of a family, cursed from its origin, and the small town in which the members lived and eventually died. A Borgesian concept of time and space allowed García Márquez to compress within the compass of a hundred years an exploration of Colombian realities from a mythical point of view. Extremely successful in the mixture of hyperbole and a concise, brilliant narrative, the book handled its long cast of characters and its adventurous exploits with a vitality that never let the reader down. An almost Rabelaisian gusto for all the excesses of the flesh permeated the narrative. But García Márquez did not forget to reveal the evil in that almost paradisal land. The follies of civil war and the genocide brought about by imperialism were intertwined with the more private affairs of the main characters. The book catapulted García Márquez into instant fame. He deserved it, although many who praised the book did so for the wrong reasons.

Quite recently García Márquez published his long-awaited fifth novel, *The Autumn of the Patriarch* (1975). It contains the obsessive ruminations of a Latin American dictator who has ruled his country for over two hundred years. Using hyperbole as its chief stylistic resource, the novel suffers from its concentration on one single, predictable character. A formidable achievement from the stylistic point of view, *The Autumn of the Patriarch* finally becomes tedious and, despite some brilliant episodes, fails to hold the reader's interest. Obviously, García Márquez has reached a point in his career at which he has to rethink very carefully his future course.

One Day After Saturday

From No One Writes to the Colonel and Other Stories, *translated by J. S. Bernstein (New York: Harper & Row, 1968), pp. 122–45.*

•

The trouble began in July, when Rebecca, an embittered widow who lived in an immense house with two galleries and nine bedrooms, discovered that the screens were torn as if they had been stoned from the street. She made the first discovery in her bedroom and thought that she must speak to Argenida, her servant and confidante since her husband died. Later, moving things around (for a long time Rebecca had done nothing but move things around), she noticed that not only the screens in her bedroom but those in all the rest of the house were torn, too. The widow had an academic sense of authority, inherited perhaps from her paternal great-grandfather, a Creole who in the War of Independence had fought on the side of the Royalists and later made an arduous journey to Spain with the sole purpose of visiting the palace which Charles III built in San Ildefonso. So that when she discovered the state of the other screens, she thought no more about speaking to Argenida about it but, rather, put on her straw hat with the tiny velvet flowers and went to the town hall to make a report about the attack. But when she got there, she saw that the Mayor himself, shirtless, hairy, and with a solidity that seemed bestial to her, was busy repairing the town-hall screens, torn like her own.

Rebecca burst into the dirty and cluttered office, and the first thing she saw was a pile of dead birds on the desk. But she was disconcerted, in part by the heat and in part by the indignation which the destruction of her screens had produced in her, so that she did not have time to shudder at the unheard-of spectacle of the dead birds on the desk. Nor was she scandalized by the evidence of authority degraded, at the top of a stairway, repairing the metal threads of the window with a roll of screening and a screwdriver. She was not thinking now of any other dignity than her own, mocked by her own screens, and her absorption prevented her even from connecting the windows of her house with those of the town hall. She planted herself with discreet solemnity two steps inside the door and, leaning on the long ornate handle of her parasol, said:

"I have to register a complaint."

From the top of the stairway, the Mayor turned his head, flushed from the heat. He showed no emotion before the gratuitous presence of the widow in his office. With gloomy nonchalance he continued untacking the ruined screen, and asked from up above:

"What is the trouble?"

"The boys from the neighborhood broke my screens."

The Mayor took another look at her. He examined her carefully, from the elegant little velvet flowers to her shoes the color of old silver, and it was as if he were seeing her for the first time in his life. He descended with great economy of movement, without taking his eyes off her, and when he reached the bottom, he rested one hand on his belt, motioned with the screwdriver toward the desk, and said:

"It's not the boys, Señora. It's the birds."

And it was then that she connected the dead birds on the desk with the man at the top of the stairs, and with the broken screens of her bedrooms. She shuddered, imagining all the bedrooms in her house full of dead birds.

"The birds!" she exclaimed.

"The birds," the Mayor concurred. "It's strange you haven't noticed, since we've had this problem with the birds breaking windows and dying inside the houses for three days."

When she left the town hall, Rebecca felt ashamed. And a little resentful of Argenida, who dragged all the town gossip into her house and who nevertheless had not spoken to her about the birds. She opened her parasol, dazzled by the brightness of an impending August, and while she walked along the stifling and deserted street she had the impression that the bedrooms of all the houses were giving off a strong and penetrating stench of dead birds.

This was at the end of July, and never in the history of the town had it been so hot. But the inhabitants, alarmed by the death of the birds, did not notice that. Even though the strange phenomenon had not seriously affected the town's activities, the majority were held in suspense by it at the beginning of August. A majority among whom was not numbered His Reverence, Anthony Isabel of the Holy Sacrament of the Altar Castañeda y Montero, the bland parish priest who, at the age of ninety-four, assured people that he had seen the devil on three occasions, and that nevertheless he had only seen two dead birds, without attributing the least importance to them. He found the first one in the sacristy, one Tuesday after Mass, and thought it had been dragged in there by some neighborhood cat. He found the other one on Wednesday, in the veranda of the parish house, and he pushed it with the point of his boot into the street, thinking, Cats shouldn't exist.

But on Friday, when he arrived at the railroad station, he found a third dead bird on the bench he chose to sit down on. It was like a lightning stroke inside him when he grabbed the body by its little legs; he raised it to eye level, turned it over, examined it, and thought astonishedly, Gracious, this is the third one I've found this week.

From that moment on he began to notice what was happening in the town, but in a very inexact way, for Father Anthony Isabel, in part because of his age and in part also because he swore he had seen the devil on three occasions (something which seemed to the town just a bit out of place), was considered by his parishioners as a good man, peaceful and obliging, but with his head habitually in the clouds. He noticed that something was happening with the birds, but even then he didn't believe that it was so important as to deserve a sermon. He was the first one who experienced the smell. He smelled it Friday night, when he woke up alarmed, his light slumber interrupted by a nauseating stench, but he didn't know whether to attribute it to a nightmare or to a new and original trick of the devil's to disturb his sleep. He sniffed all around him, and turned over in bed, thinking that that experience would serve him for a sermon. It could be, he thought, a dramatic sermon on the ability of Satan to infiltrate the human heart through any of the five senses.

When he strolled around the porch the next day before Mass, he heard someone speak for the first time about the dead birds. He was thinking about the sermon, Satan, and the sins which can be committed through the olfactory sense when he heard someone say that the bad nocturnal odor was due to the birds collected during the week; and in his head a confused hodgepodge of evangelical cautions, evil odors, and dead birds took shape. So that on Sunday he had to improvise a long paragraph on Charity, which he himself did not understand very well, and he forgot forever about the relations between the devil and the five senses.

Nevertheless, in some very distant spot in his thinking, those experiences must have remained lurking. That always happened to him, not only in the seminary, more than seventy years before, but in a very particular way after he passed ninety. At the seminary, one very bright afternoon when there was a heavy downpour with no thunder, he was reading a selection from Sophocles in the original. When the rain was over, he looked through the window at the tired field, the newly washed afternoon, and forgot entirely about Greek theater and the classics, which he did not distinguish but, rather, called in a general way, "the little ancients of old." One rainless afternoon, perhaps thirty or forty years later, he was crossing the cobblestone plaza of a town which he was visiting and, without intending to, recited the stanza from Sophocles which he had been reading in the seminary. That same week, he had a long conversation about "the little ancients of old" with the apostolic deputy, a talkative and impressionable old man, who was fond of certain complicated puzzles which he claimed to have invented and which became popular years later under the name of crosswords.

That interview permitted him to recover at one stroke all his old heartfelt love for the Greek classics. At Christmas of that year he received a letter. And if it were not for the fact that by that time he had acquired the solid prestige of being exaggeratedly imaginative, daring in his interpretations, and a little foolish in his sermons, on that occasion they would have made him a bishop.

But he had buried himself in the town long before the War of 1885, and at the time when the birds began dying in the bedrooms it had been a long while since they had asked for him to be replaced by a younger priest, especially when he claimed to have seen the devil. From that time on, they began not paying attention to him, something that he didn't notice in a very clear way in spite of still being able to decipher the tiny characters of his breviary without glasses.

He had always been a man of regular habits. Small, insignificant, with pronounced and solid bones and calm gestures, and a soothing voice for conversation but too soothing for the pulpit. He used to stay in his bedroom until lunchtime daydreaming, carelessly stretched out in a canvas chair and wearing nothing but his long twill trousers with the bottoms tied at the ankles.

He didn't do anything except say Mass. Twice a week he sat in the confessional, but for many years no one confessed. He simply thought that his parishioners were losing the faith because of modern customs, and that's why he would have thought it a very opportune occurrence to have seen the devil on three occasions, although he knew that people gave very little credence to his words and although he was aware that he was not very convincing when he spoke about those experiences. For himself it would not have been a surprise to discover that he was dead, not only during the last five years but also in those extraordinary moments when he found the first two birds. When he found the third, however, he came back to life a little, so that in the last few days he was thinking with appreciable frequency about the dead bird on the station bench.

He lived ten steps from the church in a small house without screens, with a veranda toward the street and two rooms that served as office and bedroom. He considered, perhaps in his moments of lesser lucidity, that it is possible to achieve happiness on earth when it is not very hot, and this idea made him a little confused. He liked to wander through metaphysical obstacle courses. That was what he was doing when he used to sit in the bedroom every morning, with the door ajar, his eyes closed and his muscles tensed. However, he himself did not realize that he had become so subtle in his thinking that for at least three years in his meditative moments he was no longer thinking about anything.

At twelve o'clock sharp a boy crossed the corridor with a sectioned tray, which contained the same things every day: bone broth with a piece of yucca, white rice, meat prepared without onion, fried banana or a corn muffin, and a few lentils which Father Anthony Isabel of the Holy Sacrament of the Altar had never tasted.

The boy put the tray next to the chair where the priest sat, but the priest didn't open his eyes until he no longer heard steps in the corridor. Therefore, in town they thought that the Father took his siesta before lunch (a thing which seemed exceedingly nonsensical) when the truth was that he didn't even sleep normally at night.

Around that time his habits had become less complicated, almost primitive. He lunched without moving from his canvas chair, without taking the food from the tray, without using the dishes or the fork or the knife, but only the same spoon with which he drank his soup. Later he would get up, throw a little water on his head, put on his white soutane dotted with great square patches, and go to the railroad station precisely at the hour when the rest of the town was lying down for its siesta. He had been covering this route for several months, murmuring the prayer which he himself had made up the last time the devil had appeared to him.

One Saturday—nine days after the dead birds began to fall—Father Anthony Isabel of the Holy Sacrament of the Altar was going to the station when a dying bird fell at his feet, directly in front of Rebecca's house. A flash of intuition exploded in his head, and he realized that this bird, contrary to the others, might be saved. He took it in his hands and knocked at Rebecca's door at the moment when she was unhooking her bodice to take her siesta.

In her bedroom, the widow heard the knocking and instinctively turned her glance toward the screens. No bird had got into that bedroom for two days. But the screen was still torn. She had thought it a useless expense to have it repaired as long as the invasion of birds, which kept her nerves on edge, continued. Above the hum of the electric fan, she heard the knocking at the door and remembered with impatience that Argenida was taking a siesta in the bedroom at the end of the corridor. It didn't even occur to her to wonder who might be imposing on her at that hour. She hooked up her bodice again, pushed open the screen door, and walked the length of the corridor, stiff and straight, then crossed the living room, crowded with furniture and decorative objects and, before opening the door, saw through the metal screen that there stood taciturn Father Anthony Isabel, with his eyes closed and a bird in his hands. Before she opened the door, he said, "If we give him a little water and then put him under a dish, I'm sure he'll get well." And when she opened the door, Rebecca thought she'd collapse from fear.

He didn't stay there for more than five minutes. Rebecca thought that it was she who had cut short the meeting. But in reality it had been the priest. If the widow had thought about it at that moment, she would have realized that the priest, in the thirty years he had been living in the town, had never stayed more than five minutes in her house. It seemed to him that amid the profusion of decorations in the living room the concupiscent spirit of the mistress of the house showed itself clearly, in spite of her being related, however distantly, but as everyone was aware, to the Bishop. Furthermore, there had been a legend (or a story) about Rebecca's family which surely, the Father thought, had not reached the episcopal palace, in spite of the fact that Colonel Aureliano Buendía, a cousin of the widow's whom she considered lacking in family affection, had once sworn that the Bishop had not come to the town in this century in order to avoid visiting his relation. In any case, be it history or legend, the truth was that Father Anthony Isabel of the Holy Sacrament of the Altar did not feel at ease in this house, whose only inhabitant had never shown any signs of piety and who confessed only once a year but always replied with evasive answers when he tried to pin her down about the puzzling death of her husband. If he was there now, waiting for her to bring him a glass of water to bathe a dying bird, it was the result of a chance occurrence which he was not responsible for.

While he waited for the widow to return, the priest, seated on a luxurious carved wooden rocker, felt the strange humidity of that house, which had not become peaceful since the time when a pistol shot rang out, more than twenty years before, and José Arcadio Buendía, cousin of the colonel and of his own wife, fell face down amidst the clatter of buckles and spurs on the still-warm leggings which he had just taken off.

When Rebecca burst into the living room again, she saw Father Anthony Isabel seated in the rocker with an air of vagueness that terrified her.

"The life of an animal," said the Father, "is as dear to Our Lord as that of a man."

As he said it, he did not remember José Arcadio Buendía. Nor did the widow recall him. But she was used to not giving any credence to the Father's words ever since he had spoken from the pulpit about the three times the devil had appeared to him. Without paying attention to him she took the bird in her hands, dipped him in the glass of water, and shook him afterward. The Father observed that there was impiety and carelessness in her way of acting, an absolute lack of consideration for the animal's life.

"You don't like birds," he said softly but affirmatively.

The widow raised her eyelids in a gesture of impatience and hostility. "Although I liked them once," she said, "I detest them now that they've taken to dying inside of our houses."

"Many have died," he said implacably. One might have thought that there was a great deal of cleverness in the even tone of his voice.

"All of them," said the widow. And she added, as she squeezed the animal with repugnance and placed him under the dish, "And even that wouldn't bother me if they hadn't torn my screens."

And it seemed to him that he had never known such hardness of heart. A moment later, holding the tiny and defenseless body in his own hand, the priest realized that it had ceased breathing. Then he forgot everything—the humidity of the house, the concupiscence, the unbearable smell of gunpowder on José Arcadio Buendía's body—and he realized the prodigious truth that had surrounded him since the beginning of the week. Right there, while the widow watched him leave the house with a menacing gesture and the dead bird in his hands, he witnessed the marvelous revelation that a rain of dead birds was falling over the town, and that he, the minister of God, the chosen one, who had known happiness when it had not been hot, had forgotten entirely about the Apocalypse.

That day he went to the station, as always, but he was not fully aware of his actions. He knew vaguely that something was happening in the world, but he felt muddled, dumb, unequal to the moment. Seated on the bench in the station, he tried to remember if there was a rain of dead birds in the Apocalypse, but he had forgotten it entirely. Suddenly he thought that his delay at Rebecca's house had made him miss the train, and he stretched his head up over the dusty and broken glass and saw on the clock in the ticket office that it was still twelve minutes to one. When he returned to the bench, he felt as if he were suffocating. At that moment he remembered it was Saturday. He moved his woven palm fan for a while, lost in his dark interior fog. Then he fretted over the buttons on his soutane and the buttons on his boots and over his long, snug, clerical trousers, and he noticed with alarm that he had never in his life been so hot.

Without moving from the bench he unbuttoned the collar of his soutane, took his handkerchief out of his sleeve, and wiped his flushed face, thinking, in a moment of illuminated pathos, that perhaps he was witnessing the unfolding of an earthquake. He had read that somewhere. Nevertheless the sky was clear: a transparent blue sky from which all the birds had mysteriously disappeared. He noticed the color and the transparency, but for a moment forgot about the dead birds. Now he was thinking about something else, about the possibility that a storm would break. Nevertheless the sky was diaphanous and tranquil, as if it were the sky over some other town, distant and different, where he had never felt the heat, and as if they were other eyes, not his own, which were looking at it. Then he looked toward the north, above the roofs of palms and rusted zinc, and saw the slow, silent, rhythmic blot of the buzzards over the dump.

For some mysterious reason, he relived at that moment the emotions he felt one Sunday in the seminary, shortly before taking his minor orders. The rector had given him permission to make use of his private library and he often stayed for hours and hours (especially on Sundays), absorbed in the reading of some yellowed books smelling of old wood, with annotations in Latin in the tiny, angular scrawl of the rector. One Sunday, after he had been reading for the whole day, the rector entered the room and rushed, shocked, to pick up a card that evidently had fallen from the pages of the book he was reading. He observed his superior's confusion with discreet indifference, but he managed to read the card. There was only one sentence, written in purple ink in a clean, straightforward hand: *"Madame Ivette est morte cette nuit."* More than half a century later, seeing a blot of buzzards over a forgotten town, he remembered the somber expression of the rector seated in front of him, purple against the dusk, his breathing imperceptibly quickened.

Shaken by that association, he did not then feel the heat, but rather exactly the reverse, the sting of ice in his groin and in the soles of his feet. He was terrified without knowing what the precise cause of that terror was, tangled in a net of confused ideas, among which it was impossible to distinguish a nauseating sensation, from Satan's hoof stuck in the mud, from a flock of dead birds falling on the world, while he, Anthony Isabel of the Holy Sacrament of the Altar, remained indifferent to that event. Then he straightened up, raised an awed hand, as if to begin a greeting which was lost in the void, and cried out in horror, "The Wandering Jew!"

At that moment the train whistled. For the first time in many years he did not hear it. He saw it pull into the station, surrounded by a dense cloud of smoke, and heard the rain of cinders against the sheets of rusted zinc. But that was like a distant and undecipherable dream from which he did not awaken completely until that afternoon, a little after four, when he put the finishing touches on the imposing sermon he would deliver on Sunday. Eight hours later, he was called to administer extreme unction to a woman.

With the result that the Father did not find out who arrived that afternoon on the train. For a long time he had watched the four cars go by, ramshackle and colorless, and he could not recall anyone's getting off to stay, at least in recent years. Before it was different, when he could spend a whole afternoon watching a train loaded with bananas go by; a hundred and forty cars loaded with fruit, passing endlessly until, well on toward nightfall, the last car passed with a man dangling a green lantern. Then he saw the town on the other side of the track—the lights were on now—and it seemed to him that by merely watching the train pass, it had taken him to another town. Perhaps from that came his habit of being present at the station every day, even after they shot the workers to death and the banana plantations were finished, and with them the hundred-and-forty-car trains, and there was left only that yellow, dusty train which neither brought anyone nor took anyone away.

But that Saturday someone did come. When Father Anthony Isabel of the Holy Sacrament of the Altar left the station, a quiet boy with nothing particular about him except his hunger saw the priest from the window of the last car at the precise moment that he remembered he had not eaten since the previous day. He thought, If there's a priest, there must be a hotel. And he got off the train and crossed the street, which was blistered by the metallic August sun, and entered the cool shade of a house located opposite the station whence issued the sound of a worn gramophone record. His sense of smell, sharpened by his two-day-old hunger, told him that was the hotel. And he went in without seeing the sign "HOTEL MACONDO," a sign which he was never to read in his life.

The proprietress was more than five months pregnant. She was the color of mustard, and looked exactly as her mother had when her mother was pregnant with her. He ordered, "Lunch, as quick as you can," and she, not trying to hurry, served him a bowl of soup with a bare bone and some chopped green banana in it. At that moment the train whistled. Absorbed in the warm and healthful vapor of the soup, he calculated the distance which lay between him and the station, and immediately felt himself invaded by that confused sensation of panic which missing a train produces.

He tried to run. He reached the door, anguished, but he hadn't even taken one step across the threshold when he realized that he didn't have time to make the train. When he returned to the table, he had forgotten his hunger; he saw a girl next to the gramophone who looked at him pitifully, with the horrible expression of a dog wagging his tail. Then, for the first time that whole day, he took off his hat, which his mother had given him two months before, and lodged it between his knees while he finished eating. When he got up from the table, he didn't seem bothered by missing the train, or by the prospect of spending a weekend in a town whose name he would not take the trouble to find out. He sat down in a corner of the room, the bones of his back supported by a hard, straight chair, and stayed there for a long time, not listening to the records until the girl who was picking them out said, "It's cooler on the veranda."

He felt ill. It took an effort to start conversation with strangers. He was afraid to look people in the face, and when he had no recourse but to speak, the words came out different from the way he thought them. "Yes," he replied. And he felt a slight shiver. He tried to rock, forgetting that he was not in a rocker.

"The people who come here pull a chair to the veranda since it's cooler," the girl said. And, listening to her, he realized how anxiously she wanted to talk. He risked a look at her just as she was winding up the gramophone. She seemed to have been sitting there for months, years perhaps, and she showed not the slightest interest in moving from that spot. She was winding up the gramophone but her life was concentrated on him. She was smiling.

"Thank you," he said, trying to get up, to put some ease and spontaneity into his movements. The girl didn't stop looking at him. She said, "They also leave their hats on the hook."

This time he felt a burning in his ears. He shivered, thinking about her way of suggesting things. He felt uncomfortably shut in, and again felt his panic over the missed train. But at that moment the proprietress entered the room.

"What are you doing?" she asked.

"He's pulling a chair onto the veranda, as they all do," the girl said. He thought he perceived a mocking tone in her words.

"Don't bother," said the proprietress. "I'll bring you a stool."

The girl laughed and he left disconcerted. It was hot. An unbroken, dry heat, and he was sweating. The proprietress dragged a wooden stool with a leather seat to the veranda. He was about to follow her when the girl spoke again.

"The bad part about it is that the birds will frighten him," she said.

He managed to see the harsh look when the proprietress turned her eyes on the girl. It was a swift but intense look. "What you should do is be quiet," she said, and turned smiling to him. Then he felt less alone and had the urge to speak.

"What was that she said?" he asked.

"That at this hour of the day dead birds fall onto the veranda," the girl said.

"Those are just some notions of hers," said the proprietress. She bent over to straighten a bouquet of artificial flowers on the little table in the middle of the room. There was a nervous twitch in her fingers.

"Notions of mine, no," the girl said. "You yourself swept two of them up the day before yesterday."

The proprietress looked exasperatedly at her. The girl had a pitiful expression, and an obvious desire to explain everything until not the slightest trace of doubt remained.

"What is happening, sir, is that the day before yesterday some boys left two dead birds in the hall to annoy her, and then they told her that dead birds were falling from the sky. She swallows everything people tell her."

He smiled. The explanation seemed very funny to him; he rubbed his hands and turned to look at the girl, who was observing him in anguish. The gramophone had stopped playing. The proprietress withdrew to the other room, and when he went toward the hall the girl insisted in a low voice:

"I saw them fall. Believe me. Everyone has seen them."

And he thought he understood then her attachment to the gramophone, and the proprietress's exasperation. "Yes," he said sympathetically. And then, moving toward the hall: "I've seen them, too."

It was less hot outside, in the shade of the almond trees. He leaned the stool against the doorframe, threw his head back, and thought of his mother: his mother, exhausted, in her rocker, shooing the chickens with a long broomstick, while she realized for the first time that he was not in the house.

The week before, he could have thought that his life was a smooth straight string, stretching from the rainy dawn during the last civil war when he came into the world between the four mud-and-rush walls of a rural schoolhouse to that June morning on his twenty-second birthday when his mother approached his hammock and gave him a hat with a card: "To my dear son, on his day." At times he shook off the rustiness of his inactivity and felt nostalgic for school, for the blackboard and the map of a country overpopulated by the excrement of the flies, and for the long line of cups hanging on the wall under the names of the children. It wasn't hot there. It was a green, tranquil town, where chickens with ashen long legs entered the schoolroom in order to lay their eggs under the washstand. His mother then was a sad and uncommunicative woman. She would sit at dusk to take the air which had just filtered through the coffee plantations, and say, "Manaure is the most beautiful town in the world." And then, turning toward him, seeing him grow up silently in the hammock: "When you are grown up you'll understand." But he didn't understand anything. He didn't understand at fifteen, already too tall for his age and bursting with that insolent and reckless health which idleness brings. Until his twentieth birthday his life was not essentially different from a few changes of position in his hammock. But around that time his mother, obliged by her rheumatism, left the school she had served for eighteen years, with the result that they went to live in a two-room house with a huge patio, where they raised chickens with ashen legs like those that used to cross the schoolroom.

Caring for the chickens was his first contact with reality. And it had been the only one until the month of July, when his mother thought about her retirement and deemed her son wise enough to undertake to petition for it. He collaborated in an effective way in the preparation of the documents, and even had the necessary tact to convince the parish priest to change his mother's baptismal certificate by six months, since she still wasn't old enough to retire. On Thursday he received the final instructions, scrupulously detailing his mother's teaching experience, and he began the trip to the city with twelve pesos, a change of clothing, the file of documents, and an entirely rudimentary idea of the word "retirement," which he interpreted crudely as a certain sum of money which the government ought to give him so he could set himself up in pig breeding.

Dozing on the hotel veranda, dulled by the sweltering heat, he had not stopped to think about the gravity of his situation. He supposed that the mishap would be resolved the following day, when the train returned, so that now his only worry was to wait until Sunday to resume his trip and forget forever about this town where it was unbearably hot. A little before four, he fell into an uncomfortable and sluggish sleep, thinking while he slept that it was a shame not to have brought his hammock. Then it was that he realized everything, that he had forgotten his bundle of clothes and the documents for the retirement on the train. He woke up with a start, terrified, thinking of his mother, and hemmed in again by panic.

When he dragged his seat back to the dining room, the lights of the town had been lit. He had never seen electric lights, so he was very impressed when he saw the poor spotted bulbs of the hotel. Then he remembered that his mother had spoken to him about them, and he continued dragging the seat toward the dining room, trying to dodge the horseflies which were bumping against the mirrors like bullets. He ate without appetite, confused by the clear evidence of his situation, by the intense heat, by the bitterness of that loneliness which he was suffering for the first time in his life. After nine o'clock he was led to the back of the house to a wooden room papered with newspapers and magazines. At midnight he had sunk into a miasmic and feverish sleep while five blocks away Father Anthony Isabel of the Holy Sacrament of the Altar, lying face down on his cot, was thinking that the evening's experiences reinforced the sermon which he had prepared for seven in the morning. A little before twelve he had crossed the town to administer extreme unction to a woman, and he felt excited and nervous, with the result that he put the sacramental objects next to his cot and lay down to go over his sermon. He stayed that way for several hours, lying face down on the cot until he heard the distant call of a plover at dawn. Then he tried to get up, sat up painfully, stepped on the little bell, and fell headlong on the cold, hard floor of his room.

He had hardly regained consciousness when he felt the trembling sensation that rose up his side. At that instant he was aware of his entire weight: the weight of his body, his sins, and his age all together. He felt against his cheek the solidity of the stone floor which so often when he was preparing his sermons had helped him form a precise idea of the road which leads to hell. "Lord," he murmured, afraid; and he thought, I shall certainly never be able to get up again.

He did not know how long he lay prostrate on the floor, not thinking about anything, without even remembering to pray for a good death. It was as if, in reality, he had been dead for a minute. But when he regained consciousness, he no longer felt pain or fear. He saw the bright ray beneath the door; he heard, far off and sad, the raucous noise of the roosters, and he realized that he was alive and that he remembered the words of his sermon perfectly.

When he drew back the bar of the door, dawn was breaking. He had ceased feeling pain, and it even seemed that the blow had unburdened him of his old age. All the goodness, the misconduct, and the sufferings of the town penetrated his heart when he swallowed the first mouthful of that air which was a blue dampness full of roosters. Then he looked around himself, as if to reconcile himself to the solitude, and saw, in the peaceful shade of the dawn, one, two, three dead birds on the veranda.

For nine minutes he contemplated the three bodies, thinking, in accord with his prepared sermon, that the birds' collective death needed some expiation. Then he walked to the other end of the corridor, picked up the three dead birds, and returned to the pitcher, and one after another threw the birds into the green, still water without knowing exactly the purpose of that action. Three and three are half a dozen, in one week, he thought, and a miraculous flash of lucidity told him that he had begun to experience the greatest day of his life.

At seven the heat began. In the hotel, the only guest was waiting for his breakfast. The gramophone girl had not yet got up. The proprietress approached, and at that moment it seemed as if the seven strokes of the clock's bell were sounding inside her swollen belly.

"So you missed the train," she said in a tone of belated commiseration. And then she brought the breakfast: coffee with milk, a fried egg, and slices of green banana.

He tried to eat, but he wasn't hungry. He was alarmed that the heat had come on. He was sweating buckets. He was suffocating. He had slept poorly, with his clothes on, and now he had a little fever. He felt the panic again, and remembered his mother just as the proprietress came to the table to pick up the dishes, radiant in her new dress with the large green flowers. The proprietress's dress reminded him that it was Sunday.

"Is there a Mass?" he asked.

"Yes, there is," the woman said. "But it's just as if there weren't, because almost nobody goes. The fact is they haven't wanted to send us a new priest."

"And what's wrong with this one?"

"He's about a hundred years old, and he's half crazy," the woman said; she stood motionless, pensive, with all the dishes in one hand. Then she said, "The other day, he swore from the pulpit that he had seen the devil, and since then no one goes to Mass."

So he went to the church, in part because of his desperation and in part out of curiosity to meet a person a hundred years old. He noticed that it was a dead town, with interminable, dusty streets and dark wooden houses with zinc roofs, which seemed uninhabited. That was the town on Sunday: streets without grass, houses with screens, and a deep marvelous sky over a stifling heat. He thought that there was no sign there which would permit one to distinguish Sunday from any other day, and while he walked along the deserted street he remembered his mother: "All the streets in every town lead inevitably to the church or the cemetery." At that moment he came out into a small cobblestoned plaza with a whitewashed building that had a tower and a wooden weathercock on the top, and a clock which had stopped at ten after four.

Without hurrying he crossed the plaza, climbed the three steps of the atrium, and immediately smelled the odor of aged human sweat mixed with the odor of incense, and he went into the warm shade of the almost empty church.

Father Anthony Isabel of the Holy Sacrament of the Altar had just risen to the pulpit. He was about to begin the sermon when he saw a boy enter with his hat on. He saw him examining the almost empty temple with his large, serene, and clear eyes. He saw him sit down in the last pew, his head to one side and his hands on his knees. He noticed that he was a stranger to the town. He had been in town for thirty years, and he could have recognized any of its inhabitants just by his smell. Therefore, he knew that the boy who had just arrived was a stranger. In one intense, brief look, he observed that he was a quiet soul, and a little sad, and that his clothes were dirty and wrinkled. It's as if he had spent a long time sleeping in them, he thought with a feeling that was a combination of repugnance and pity. But then, seeing him in the pew, he felt his heart overflowing with gratitude, and he got ready to deliver what was for him the greatest sermon of his life. Lord, he thought in the meantime, please let him remember his hat so I don't have to throw him out of the temple. And he began his sermon.

At the beginning he spoke without realizing what he was saying. He wasn't even listening to himself. He hardly heard the clear and fluent melody which flowed from a spring dormant in his soul ever since the beginning of the world. He had the confused certainty that his words were flowing forth precisely, opportunely, exactly, in the expected order and place. He felt a warm vapor pressing his innards. But he also knew that his spirit was free of vanity, and that the feeling of pleasure which paralyzed his senses was not pride or defiance or vanity but, rather, the pure rejoicing of his spirit in Our Lord.

In her bedroom, Rebecca felt faint, knowing that within a few moments the heat would become impossible. If she had not felt rooted to the town by a dark fear of novelty, she would have put her odds and ends in a trunk with mothballs and would have gone off into the world, as her great-grandfather did, so she had been told. But she knew inside that she was destined to die in the town, amid those endless corridors and the nine bedrooms, whose screens she thought she would have replaced by translucent glass when the heat stopped. So she would stay there, she decided (and that was a decision she always took when she arranged her clothes in the closet), and she also decided to write "My Eminent Cousin" to send them a young priest, so she could attend church again with her hat with the tiny velvet flowers, and hear a coherent Mass and sensible and edifying sermons again. Tomorrow is Monday, she thought, beginning to think once and for all about the salutation of the letter to the Bishop (a salutation which Colonel Buendía had called frivolous and disrespectful), when Argenida suddenly opened the screened door and shouted:

"Señora, people are saying that the Father has gone crazy in the pulpit!"

The widow turned a not characteristically withered and bitter face toward the door. "He's been crazy for at least five years," she said. And she kept on arranging her clothing, saying:

"He must have seen the devil again."

"It's not the devil this time," said Argenida.

"Then who?" Rebecca asked, prim and indifferent.

"Now he says that he saw the Wandering Jew."

The widow felt her skin crawl. A multitude of confused ideas, among which she could not distinguish her torn screens, the heat, the dead birds, and the plague, passed through her head as she heard those words which she hadn't

remembered since the afternoons of her distant girlhood: "The Wandering Jew."
And then she began to move, enraged, icily, toward where Argenida was watching
her with her mouth open.

"It's true," Rebecca said in a voice which rose from the depths of her
being. "Now I understand why the birds are dying off."

Impelled by terror, she covered herself with a black embroidered shawl
and, in a flash, crossed the long corridor and the living room stuffed with
decorative objects, and the street door, and the two blocks to the church, where
Father Anthony Isabel of the Holy Sacrament of the Altar, transfigured, was
saying, "I swear to you that I saw him. I swear to you that he crossed my path
this morning when I was coming back from administering the holy unction to
the wife of Jonas the carpenter. I swear to you that his face was blackened with
the malediction of the Lord, and that he left a track of burning embers in his
wake."

His sermon broke off, floating in the air. He realized that he couldn't
restrain the trembling of his hands, that his whole body was shaking, and that
a thread of icy sweat was slowly descending his spinal column. He felt ill, feeling
the trembling, and the thirst, and a violent wrenching in his gut, and a noise
which resounded like the bass note of an organ in his belly. Then he realized the
truth.

He saw that there were people in the church, and that Rebecca,
pathetic, showy, her arms open, and her bitter, cold face turned toward the
heavens, was advancing up the central nave. Confusedly he understood what was
happening, and he even had enough lucidity to understand that it would have
been vanity to believe that he was witnessing a miracle. Humbly he rested his
trembling hands on the wooden edge of the pulpit and resumed his speech.

"Then he walked toward me," he said. And this time he heard his own
voice, convincing, impassioned. "He walked toward me and he had emerald eyes,
and shaggy hair, and the smell of a billy goat. And I raised my hand to reproach
him in the name of Our Lord, and I said to him: 'Halt, Sunday has never been
a good day for sacrificing a lamb.'"

When he finished, the heat had set in. That intense, solid, burning heat
of that unforgettable August. But Father Anthony Isabel was no longer aware of
the heat. He knew that there, at his back, the town was again humbled, speechless
with his sermon, but he wasn't even pleased by that. He wasn't even pleased with
the immediate prospect that the wine would relieve his ravaged throat. He felt
uncomfortable and out of place. He felt distracted and he could not concentrate
on the supreme moment of the sacrifice. The same thing had been happening
to him for some time, but now it was a different distraction, because his thoughts
were filled by a definite uneasiness. Then, for the first time in his life, he knew
pride. And just as he had imagined and defined it in his sermons, he felt that
pride was an urge the same as thirst. He closed the tabernacle energetically and
said, "Pythagoras."

The acolyte, a child with a shaven and shiny head, godson of Father
Anthony Isabel, who had named him, approached the altar.

"Take up the offering," said the priest.

The child blinked, turned completely around, and then said in an almost inaudible voice, "I don't know where the plate is."

It was true. It had been months since an offering had been collected.

"Then go find a big bag in the sacristy and collect as much as you can," said the Father.

"And what shall I say?" said the boy.

The Father thoughtfully contemplated his shaven blue skull, with its prominent sutures. Now it was he who blinked:

"Say that it is to expel the Wandering Jew," he said, and he felt as he said it that he was supporting a great weight in his heart. For a moment he heard nothing but the guttering of the candles in the silent temple and his own excited and labored breathing. Then, putting his hand on the acolyte's shoulder, while the acolyte looked at him with his round eyes aghast, he said:

"Then take the money and give it to the boy who was alone at the beginning, and you tell him that it's from the priest, and that he should buy a new hat."

15

GUILLERMO CABRERA INFANTE

Of all the attempted Joycean chronicles of Latin America (Cortázar's *Hopscotch* and Fuentes's *A Change of Skin* are the most successful), only Cabrera Infante's *Three Trapped Tigers* was close enough to the original to justify the comparison. This Cuban novelist (born in 1929) shared with Joyce a purely verbal concept of narrative, an appetite for language in its infinite metamorphoses, an untiring sense of humor, and the knack of turning words around until they produced unexpected discoveries. But it would be wrong to believe that *T.T.T.* was just an exercise in Joycean wordplay. It was firmly rooted in a purely Cuban vernacular, in the sights and sounds of a reality that the revolution has altered forever. In setting his novel on the eve of Castro's victory, Cabrera Infante was attempting to recapture a Cuba that no longer was. This exercise in nostalgia (written in Europe and published in Spain when the author was in self-imposed exile in England) is a masterpiece—at once the saddest and most comic production of the new novel.

Cabrera Infante comes from a proletarian family; his parents were both Communists and had participated actively in the struggle against Batista's dictatorship. His first writings (short stories, movie reviews) showed his gift with words and a mastery of concise, ironic narrative. One of his stories—very much in the line of Hemingway—attracted the attention of Batista's censor for the use of four-letter words in English. With Castro's triumph, Cabrera Infante was appointed editor of the most influential literary magazine of the day, published on Mondays by the newspaper *Revolution*. But soon Cabrera Infante's idyl with the bureaucrats, who had come out of their sanctuaries to join the triumphant revolution, came to an end. The magazine was closed for "shortage of paper," and Cabrera Infante was sent to Brussels as Cuban cultural attaché. From then on, his relations with the regime steadily worsened. In 1965, after the death of his mother, he left Cuba for good. Soon he became a nonperson and, in due course, an enemy of the revolution. It is against this political background that his books ought to be read.

The first two, published when he was still in Cuba, collected his short stories (*In Peace as in War*, 1961) and his film reviews (*A Twentieth Century Job*, 1963). The publication of *Three Trapped Tigers* in 1967 put an end to two years of speculation about what had happened to his first novel. In 1965, it had won the important Seix-Barral Prize for novels (see introduction). The book was then called *A View of Dawn in the Tropics*. Following a pattern already used in compiling his short stories, he mixed fact with fiction in that first version of the novel. Chapters in which the everyday life of the characters was presented alternated with short, poignant vignettes in which the brutal struggle against Batista was described. But Cabrera Infante was dissatisfied with this approach. He decided to eliminate the vignettes and reorder the novel around its fictional core. The result was a similar and yet essentially different book, called *Three Sad Tigers* in the original Spanish. The title contains an allusion to a children's tongue-twister. In translating the book into English with the help of the author, the translators invented a similar pun. The tigers of the title are both sad and trapped. They are in fact four, like the Three Musketeers, and their stories (presented always in their own words) constitute the basis of the book. A fifth character, Bustrófedon, their verbal master and mentor, is never presented directly. All the reader knows about him is what the other characters recall, the jokes they quote, the tongue-twisters he has left behind. A novel with a shifting center, or with a center constantly being displaced, *T.T.T.* is also a novel of frustration. One of its models is Sterne, the master of narrative interruptus. But the central model is Petronius's *Satyricon*, the fragmented fresco of Rome on the eve of its doom. Like that nocturnal book, *T.T.T.* is also about night life. Its characters are equally engaged in a pursuit of some epiphany that constantly eludes them. With built-in sequences of endless monologues by articulate and inarticulate people, one-sided telephone conversations, reports to the psychiatrist, translations of short stories, and puns and other verbal exercises, the book was a collage of voices—the Cuban vernacular at its peak, a few seconds before all the vitality, the music, and the follies of a carefree, corrupt, and sensual society were obliterated by history.

Seven years after the publication of *T.T.T.* in Spanish, Cabrera Infante published another book with the title once used for this one. But the new book was simply a collection of the revolutionary vignettes. It was different: gone were the jokes, the fun, the light touch. It presented the history of Cuba from the eve of Columbus's discovery of the island to the most recent episodes of the fight against Castro and the collective effect of these brief, devastating vignettes was to show that History is a verbal invention, that heroes write it in their own words before historians print it, that the fight against the establishment (any establishment) was the only constant element in a succession of uprisings, conspiracies, and other genocidal activities carried on by Spaniards against Indians, Patriots against Spaniards, Imperialists against Patriots, Revolutionaries against Imperialists, Counterrevolutionaries against Revolutionaries. History (with that capital letter) is just about the writing of history—that is, about the translating into words of what people have done, or say they have done. For a man whose masters are not only Petronius, Sterne, and Joyce but also Mark Twain, Lewis Carroll, and (especially) Borges, such a discovery was inevitable. The writer (Cabrera Infante believes) is just a translator.

The chapter from *T.T.T.* excerpted here shows how words and rhythms from Cuban speech are transformed into a literary monologue by one of the tigers, the drummer E. Ribot, whose French surname can be translated into "Eribó" (an Afro-Cuban deity) or "Senseribó" (words from a popular song). Everything is finally translation.

Three Trapped Tigers

From Three Trapped Tigers, *translated by Donald Gardner and Suzanne Jill Levine with the author (New York: Harper & Row, 1971), pp. 85–117.*

Ekué was sacred and lived in a sacred river. One day Sikán came to the river. The name Sikán perhaps meant curious woman once or just woman. Sikán, just like a woman, was not only curious but indiscreet. But are the curious ever discreet?

Sikán came to the river and heard the sacred sound that only a few men of Efó were permitted to hear. Sikán listened and listened —and then talked. She went and told her father, who didn't believe her because Sikán was the fibber of Efí. Sikán returned to the river and listened again and this time she also saw. She saw Ekué and heard Ekué and told all about Ekué. So that her father would believe her she pursued Ekué with her gourd (which she used to drink water with), and she caught up with Ekué, who wasn't made for running. Sikán brought Ekué back to the village in her gourd of drinking water. Her father believed her now.

When the few men of Efó (their names must not be repeated) came to the river to talk to Ekué they didn't find him. The trees told them that he had been chased and followed, that Sikán had caught him and taken him to Efí in the gourd of water. This was a crime. But to let Ekué talk without stopping up the ears of profane listeners and to tell his secrets and to be a woman (but who else could have done such a thing?), this was more than a crime. It was sacrilege.

Sikán paid with her skin for her blasphemy. She was skinned alive and died. Ekué died too, some say of shame at letting himself be caught by a woman or of mortification when traveling in the gourd. Others say he died of suffocation in the pursuit—he certainly wasn't made for running. But his secret was not lost nor the custom of reunion nor the happiness of knowing that he existed. With his skin they clad the *ekué* that speaks now in the rites for initiates and is magic. The skin of Sikán the Indiscreet was used to dress another drum, which has neither nails nor ties and which has no voice, because she is still suffering the punishment for not holding her tongue. She wears four plumes with the four oldest powers at her four corners. As she is a woman she has to be beautifully adorned, with flowers and necklaces and cowries. But over her drumhead she wears the tongue of a cock as a sign of eternal silence. Nobody touches it and it is unable to talk by itself. It is secret and taboo and it is called *seseribó*.

Rite of Sikán and Ekué
(Essential mystery of Afro-Cuban magic)

On Fridays we don't have a show, so we can take the night off, and that Friday seemed the perfect day to be at the opening night of the summer dance hall at the Sierra. So it was the perfect night for taking a ride up there to hear Beny Moré singing. Besides, Cuba Venegas was making her debut that night, and I just *had* to be there. You know it's me who discovered Cuba, not Christopher Columbus. I heard her the first time at the time when I was just starting to hear again and at that time I was hearing music wherever I went, so my ear was in perfect pitch. I'd given up music for advertising, but I made very little money in that agency, which was more like a regency, and as there was a whole load of new cabarets and night clubs opening up I brushed up my *tumbadora* (a *tumba* is not a tomb, a joke I repeat like a ritual and every time I say it I remember Innasio: Innasio is Ignacio Piñeiro, who wrote that immortal rumba about a rejected lover who seeks revenge by composing this epitaph on his sweetheart's tomb—you got to hear Innasio himself singing it—which is the lyrics of a rumba: *"Don't weep for her, gravedigger / Don't weep, please / She's not my wife, she's a whore / You dig, gravedigger? / If you do, don't weep!"*) and began practicing my drums nonstop and in one week I was making them sing smooth and sweet and suave, so much so I went to see Barreto and told him, "Guillermo, I want to make a comeback," joking of course.

Anyways, Barreto found me work in the second band at the Capri, the one they have playing between two shows, for people to dance to or to trample themselves to death to but in rhythm or to tread on corns in six-eight time. Take your pick.

Anyways, I was listening to someone singing through the window and the voice didn't sound at all bad. The song (it was Frank Domíngues's "Images": you've got to know it, it goes like this: *"Like in a dream, quite unexpectedly you came to me . . ."*) and the voice came up from below and then I saw that behind it was a tall mulatto girl with hair like an Indian, going up to the patio to hang out her washing. You've guessed it: it was Cuba, who was called Gloria Pérez at that time and obviously I hadn't been working in an advertising agency just for fun and I got her to change her name to Cuba Venegas because nobody named Gloria Pérez is going to be a halfways decent singer, so that *mulata* who was once Gloria Pérez is now Cuba Venegas (or the other way around) and as she's in Puerto Rico or Venezuela or someplace like that and I'm not going to gossip about her now, I can tell you this in passing.

Cuba made it in a very short time: the time it took her to leave me for my very good friend Códac, who was the in photographer that year, and then she discarded Códac for Piloto & Vera (Piloto first and then Vera), who've written two or three good songs, among them "Sad Meeting," which Cuba made *her* instant creation. Finally she moved in with and/or onto Walter Socarrás (Floren Cassalis said in his column that they were married: I *know* they weren't married, but as Arturo de Córdova would say, *Eso no tiene la menor importancia*), he's the musician-arranger who took her on tour through Latin America and who was conducting from his piano stool in the Sierra that night. (*Eso no tiene la menor importancia* either.) And so it was that I went to the Sierra to hear Cuba Venegas sing, with that very pretty voice of hers and her lovely face (Cubita Bella, they call her for a joke) and her tremendous stage presence, and to wait for her to see me and make eyes at me and dedicate to me her song "Stop Him on Site," just for fun.

II

So there I was in the Sierra drinking at the bar no less and chatting with Beny. Let me tell you about Beny. Beny is Beny Moré and to talk about him is the same as talking about music, so let me tell you about music. Remembering Beny made me remember a common past, that is music: a *danzón* titled "Isora" in which the *tumbadora* repeats a double beat of the double bass filling the bar and beating the most accomplished dancer, who has to put up with or dive under the swaying mean measure of the rhythm. Chapottín repeats this tricky beat in a record that did the rounds in '53, the offbeat riffs of "Cienfuegos," which is like a *guaguancó* turned into a *son* where the bass fiddle plays a dominant role. Once I asked old Chapo how the hell he did it and he told me it was (long life to the long fingers of Sabino Peñalver) by improvising the choruses when they were cutting the record. Only this way was a circle of happy music made out of the rigid square of Cuban rhythms. I was talking about this with Barreto in Radioprogreso one day after a recording session where he was on drums and I was playing my *tumba* and from time to time I happened to cut

across him. Barreto told me you had to break the mandatory two-two/four-four
beat of Cuban rhythms, and I told him about Beny who, in his songs, made fun
of that four-to-the-bar prison for squares, making the melody glide over the
rhythm, forcing the band to follow him in his flight and making it supple as a
saxophone, as a legato trumpet, as if he were conducting a rubber band. I
remember when I was playing in his *banda gigante,* standing in for the drummer,
who was not only my friend but who had also asked me to take his place as he
wanted the night off to go *dancing!* It was one hell of a job playing behind Beny,
turning his back to the band, singing and making faces at the audience, sending
the melody soaring over the heads of our earthbound instruments and their
dragging feet and then all of a sudden to see him turn and ask you to throw a
bomb at precisely the metronomic moment, right on the spot. *Ese Beny!*

All at once Beny gives me a slap on the shoulder and says, "Hey,
Charlie, that nymphet from your school? She doesn't look your class!" I didn't
know what he was talking about and as you never know what Beny is talking about
I never paid him much attention except when he's making music but then he's
not talking about singing now. However I turned and looked around. Do you
know who I saw? I saw a girl, almost too young for consent, about sixteen, staring
hard at me. It's always dark both inside and outside the Sierra, but I was able
to see her from the bar though she was on the other side, outside, on the patio,
and looking at me through a dark glass panel. She was staring at me all right and
real hard, there was no doubt about it. Besides I could see she was smiling at me
now, so I smiled back and then I left Beny 'xcuse me a moment and went up
to her table. At first I didn't recognize her because she was very tanned and she
had her hair down and looked all woman. She was wearing a white dress, almost
up to the neck in front, but cut very low down the back. Very, very low, so I could
see the whole of her back and a very pretty back it was too. She smiled at me
again and said, "Don't you recognize me?" It was then I recognized her: it was
Vivian Smith-Corona and you don't need me to tell you the meaning of that
double-barreled name. She introduced me to her friends: Havana Yacht Club
types, or Vedado Tennis, or Casino Español. It was a grand table. Not just
because it was the size of three tables put together, but because there were several
millions sitting in those wrought-iron chairs branding asses that were prominent
both physically and socially. Nobody took much notice of me and Vivian playing
the part of a demichaperone, so she was able to talk to me for a while, me standing
and she sitting and as nobody stood me a seat, I said:

—Let's go outside, meaning the street, where there are many people
talking and breathing in the warm dirty fumes of the buses when it's too hot to
stay indoors.

—I can't, she said. —I'm chaperoning tonight.

I didn't know what to do and I hovered over the social gathering
uncertain whether to go or stay.

—Why don't we see each other later? she said, speaking between her
teeth.

I didn't know what exactly she meant by later.

—Later on, she said. —After they've taken me home. Mummy and Daddy are away at the ranch. Come up and see me.

III

Vivian lived in the Focsa building on the twenty-seventh floor, but it wasn't there, not so high up, that I met her for the first time. It was more like a basement where I met her. She came to the Capri one night with Arsenio Cué and my friend Silvestre. I only knew of Cué by name and at a distance at that, but Silvestre was my classmate at high school, until the fourth year, when I left to study drawing at San Alejandro Academy, imagining at the time that my real name was Raphael or Michelangelo or Leonardo and that Bernard Berenson would be putting out a volume of my paintings—living under the influence of Bustrófedon. Cué introduced me to his fiancée or girl friend first, a tall slender girl with hardly any breasts but very good-looking and you could see she knew it. He introduced me to Vivian and finally he introduced them to me. Very sophisticated he was—and a regular ham. He introduced us in English and to show he was a contemporary of the UN building he started talking in French to his sweetheart or fuckiancée or whatever she was. I was expecting him to switch to German or Russian or Italian on the slightest provocation, but he didn't. He went on talking French or English or both languages at once. We local lads were making plenty of noise and the show was under way, but Cué spoke his English-cum-French above the music and the singer's voice and above the din of dining and drinking and dealing that you get in cabarets. They were both deeply absorbed in showing they could speak French and kiss at the same time. Silvestre was watching the show (or rather the chorus girls in the show, freaks all legs and breasts) as though he was seeing it for the first time in his life, neglecting this real beauty at his side for ersatz flesh and roboobs. (Big B. again.) As I knew those dancing cheeks and chicks as well as Vesalius knew his anatomy and as I'm as tough as a Lawrence in this Arabia Deserta of sex, I stayed in my oasis, gazing at Vivian, who was sitting opposite me. She was looking at the show but, like a proper young lady, sat so as not to turn her back on me and as she saw I was staring at her (she *had* to see it because I was almost touching her fully clothed flesh with tactile eyes) she turned around to talk to me.

—What did you say your name was? I didn't catch it.
—That always happens.
—Yes, introductions are like condolences, social whispers.

I was going to contradict her and say that this always happens to me *only*, but I liked her intelligence and more than that, her voice, which was soft and caressing and agreeably low.

—José Pérez is my name, but my friends call me Vincent.

She didn't understand but gave me an odd look. So much so that I felt embarrassed. I explained it was a joke, that I was parodying a parody, that it came from a speech by Vincent van Douglas in *Lust for Life*. She said she hadn't seen it and asked me if it was good and I answered that the painting was great but the picture was lousy, that Kirk van Gugh! painted while he was crying and vice versa and that Anthony Gauquinn was a bouncer in the Saloon de Refusés but anyways she must have the second opinion of my friend Silvestre, a thorough professional (no joke intended). Finally I told her my name, the real one.

—A very nice name, she said. I didn't pursue the matter.

Arsenio Cué must have been listening all the time because he freed himself from one of those eight arms of his fiancée who looked like a squid with bones and said:

—*Pourquoi ne te maries tu?*

Vivian laughed, but it was an automatic laugh, a loud smile from a TV commercial, a mocking grimace.

—Arsen, his fiancée said.

I looked at Arsenio Cué, who was insisting.

—*Mais oui. Pourquoi non?*

Vivian stopped smiling. Arsenio was drunk and went on using not only his voice but his index finger now. So much so that Silvestre left off looking at the show, though only for a moment.

—Arsen, his fiancée said crossly.

—*Pourquoi, alors?*

He was pissed off. There was a persistent note of annoyance in his voice as though I'd been talking to his fiancée and not to Vivian.

—Arson, she was shouting now. Fiancée not Vivian.

—It's pronounced *Arsen,* I told her.

She looked at me, her blue eyes blazing with fury, unloading all the irritation she felt with Cué on me.

—*Ça alors,* she said to me. —*Chéri, viens. Viens! Embrassez-moi.* This was addressed to Arsenio Cué, presumably.

—Oh, dear, Cué said in English and he forgot us all as he buried himself in those bilingual or trilingual collarbones and ulnas.

—What's the matter with them? I asked Vivian.

She looked at them and told me:

—Apparently they want to turn Spanish into a dead language.

We both laughed. I was feeling good and now it wasn't just because of her voice. Silvestre turned away from the show again, looked at us very seriously, and went back to watching the train of bosoms-cum-limbs which was dollying the conga along a fanciful railroad of music and color and scandal. The number was called "The loco motive of love" and it was set to the tune of "The sea legs."

—*"Let's go to the waterfront, let's get back our sea legs,"* Vivian sang pointedly, touching Cué's fiancée on the arm.

—*Qu'est-ce que c'est?*

—Quit French-kissing and come with me, she said.

—Where to? said Cué's fiancée.

—Yes, where? said Cué.

—To the ladies', *chéris.* Vulgo, jane, Vivian said.

—Wanna wo weewee, Cué said. They got up and as soon as they had left Silvestre turned his attentive shoulders to the show, beating the table with his hand and almost shouting:

—She's beddable.

—What! I said.

—She's an easy lay, Silvestre said.

—Who? Cué said.

—Not your girl, the other one, Vivian. She's a beddable lay.

—Ah! I thought that's who you meant, Cué said, and I had never suspected him to be a puritan, but he quickly added, —Because if you meant Sibila (that was the name of Arsenio Cué's fiancée or whatever she was: I'd been trying to remember it all evening) you've got it the wrong way right around, he said, smiling. —I mean you stand correct. She'll go to bed, but with Myselftov, he said, meaning himself, Cué.

—No, Sibila, no, Silvestre said.

—*Sí, Nobila, sí,* said Cué.

They were both pissed.

—I say that she will go to bed, Silvestre said for the third time.

—Every night and in her own bedroom, said Cué, lisping out the words.

—Not go to bed to, I mean go to bed *with,* you fucker!

I thought it bedder to come between them.

—O.K., O.K., Charlie, she'll go to bed and then she'll go to bed. But we'd better pretend we're watching the show or they'll shove us out.

—Show us out, you mean, Silvestre said.

—Shove or show, it's all the shame, Cué said.

—No, it's not the same, said I.

—It's not the same, it's a shame, said Silvestre.

—They'll show us out, Cué said, —but you're the one they'll shove out.

—It's true, Silvestre said. —It's true!

—It's true it's true, said Cué and he burst into tears. Silvestre tried to calm him down, but at that very moment Ana Coluton came onto the stage to do her number and he had no intention of missing that exhibition of legs and tits and woman's wit that was capable of suggesting *almost* everything. The show was just coming to tit's end when Vivian and Sibila returned and Cué was bent over the table and crying copiously.

—What's the matter with him? Vivian asked.

—*Qu'est qu'il y a chéri?* said Sibila, fluttering over her tearful fiancé. But it was Silvestre who answered:

—He (meaning me) is afraid they will throw him (meaning Cué) out. Or voice versa.

—Yes. If he goes on making these scenes, Vivian said, and Silvestre shouted over her, —*Obs*cenes, I call them. They'll throw us all out (and he drew an eccentric circle with his drunken finger as he was speaking) and as for this fellow (and he directed an erratic arrow with his index finger toward me) they'll fire him, poor fellow, and Silvestre burst into tears too.

Vivian tut-tut-tutted in false chagrin and true amusement and Silvestre gave her a hard look and almost lifted the hand with which he had insisted on Vivian's erotic willingness, but he returned to watching one of the chorus girls pass by en route to the street and the oblivion of the night. Cué cried even louder. When I went back to the band Sibila who was also drunk joined him in his tear-letting and I left the tragicomic scene just as their table floated out into a sea of tears (courtesy of Arsenio Cué & Co.). I arrived on the stage just as they were lowering it into a dance floor.

When I start playing I forget everything else. So there I was beating, scraping, rubbing and swooping and plunging and smashing those drums, crossing, counterpointing them, unisoning them, coming in with the bass fiddle and the piano so I could hardly make out the table of my tearful and timorous and laughing friends, because it was in the dark at the back of the room. I went on playing when all at once I saw that Arsenio Cué was dancing on the floor, no longer crying, with Vivian as amused as ever. I had no idea that she danced so well, so much in swing, just like a Cuban. Cué for his part was being led by her as he smoked a king-size cigarette at the end of a black metallic holder and through his dark glasses he was confronting the world, petulant, pedantic, and pathetic. They passed close to me and Vivian smiled at me.

—I like the way you play, *tú*, she said, and the *tú* was like a second smile on top of the first.

They swayed by me a number of times and ended up dancing in my territory. Cué was helplessly drunk and he had taken off his glasses now and was winking at me out of one eye and smiling and then he winked with both eyes, and, I think, he was saying to me, saying in lipspeak, She's beddable, she's beddable. Finally the number came to an end. It was that raveling bolero, "Miénteme." Vivian left the floor first and Cué came up to me and said quite plainly in my ear: —That one really is beddable, and he laughed and pointed at Silvestre, who was slumped over the table, fast asleep, his small Oriental fat body fallen flat like a corpse shrouded in silk: blue against the white tablecloth, his suit looked expensive even from a distance. In the next number Arsenio Cué danced (more or less) with Sibila, who was also drunk and falling all over the place, so that he now seemed by contrast to be dancing better or less badly than before. While I was playing the bongos I noticed that she (Vivian) hadn't taken her eyes off me. I saw her get up. I saw her cross the room and stand near the band.

—I had no idea you played so well, she said when the dance was over.

—Neither good nor bad, I said. —Just well enough to make a living.

—No, you *really* play well. I like it.

She didn't say whether it was the fact that I was playing that she liked or that I played well or that it was me who was playing well. Would she be a music fan? Or a fiend for perfection? Had I given any indication or sign that betrayed my feelings?

—I mean it seriously, she said. —I would like to play like you.

—You don't have to.

She shook her head. Was she friend or fiend? I would soon know.

—Girls who belong in the Yacht Club don't have to play the bongo drums.

—I don't belong in the Yacht Club, she said and left and I didn't know if she had been hurt or hurt herself. Because I went on playing.

I played and played and I saw Arsenio Cué call the waiter and ask for the check and I went on and on and on and I saw him wake up Silvestre and playing I saw the swarthy, skinflint writer get up and begin to go out with Vivian and Sibila supporting his arms and I went on playing as Cué was paying all that money by himself and playing the waiter came back and Cué gave him a tip which must have been a good one judging by the waiter's satisfied face playing and I saw him go away as well and all of them meet up at the door and the doorman opening the crimson curtains and playing they crossed the classy well-lighted gambling saloon and the curtain closed on, behind them playing. They didn't even say so much as bye-bye. But I didn't care because I was playing and I went on playing and I continued to go on playing for a good while longer.

IV

I saw very little of Vivian before that night at the Sierra, but I saw plenty of Arsenio Cué and my friend Silvestre. I don't know why I saw them but I did. One day I was coming out of a rehearsal (I think it was a Saturday afternoon) and I ran into Cué, who was walking by himself, on foot surprisingly, along 21st Street. It was very hot that day and although the clouds had piled up toward the south it didn't look as though it was going to rain, but Cué was wearing a raincoat (an *imper,* he called it) and he was holding his cigarette holder and smoking and walking along with that knock-kneed awkward stride of his and puffing the smoke out through his nostrils, both of them, like a double column of gray fumes floating ostentatiously out above his lips. He reminded me of the reluctant dragon. Not so much reluctant as a reticent dragon behind his sempiternal dark glasses and well-pruned mustache.

—This tropical heat is intolerable, he said by way of greeting me.

—You must be drowning, I said, pointing at his trench coat.

—Coat or no coat, clothes or no clothes, I don't know how the hell anybody can stand this climate.

This was his theme song. It was on this note that he began his sound tracks against the tropics, the country, the people, the music, the Negroes, women and underdevelopment. Everything. It was his Third World Man's Theme. That afternoon he told me that Cuba (not Venegas, the other Cuba) was not a fit hangout for man or beast. Nobody should live here except plants, insects and fungi or any other lower forms of life. The squalid fauna that Christopher Columbus found when he landed proved the point. All that remained now were birds and fish and tourists. All of these could leave the island when they wanted. On finishing his diatribe, he asked me without changing his tone of voice:

—Do you want to come with me to the Focsa?

—What is to be done? I smiled.

—Nothing. Just to take a stroll around the swimming pool.

I didn't know whether to go. I was tired and my fingers were hurting through the Band-Aid and it was hot. It doesn't make you any cooler going dressed to a swimming pool and stopping on the edge, taking care not to get your clothes wet, just to gaze at the swimmers as if they were fish in a fish tank. I had no wish to go even if the fish were mermaids. I shook my head no.

—Vivian will be there, he said.

The swimming pool in the Focsa building was full, mostly with children. We saw Vivian waving at us from the water. All that could be seen of her was her head without a bathing cap, her hair sticking to her skull, face, and neck. She looked like a little girl. But when she got out she wasn't a little girl. She was quite sunburned and there was a taut shine to her shoulders and legs which was very different from the milky white under her black dress the night I met her. Her hair was much more blond also. She asked me for a cigarette and spoke forget-and-forgivingly, letting the bygones be washed away in the alcohol of the night.

—I skindive here every day, morning, afternoon, and evening, wet-nursing really, she said, pointing to the pool, which had more kids than water. When I offered her a light she took my hand and lifted it to her cigarette. She had a long fine-boned hand now wrinkled by the water. It was a hand I liked and I liked it still more for holding my hand while she was lighting her cigarette and that she brought it very close to her thick well-formed lips.

—Too windy, she said. Was she talking about my style?

Cué had gone over to the other side of the pool and was talking with a group of young girls who had recognized him. Were they asking him for his autograph? They were all sitting on the edge of the pool, their feet splashing in the water, their legs wet and glistening. No, they were just talking. Vivian and I went to a concrete bench and sat down at a cement table under a metal sunshade. My feet were planted in a square of green tiles pretending to look like grass. I took the tape off my fingers and crumpled it in my pocket. Vivian was watching me doing it and now I looked at her.

—Cué came to see you and ran away.

She gazed at the swimming pool and at Cué and his harem of damp groupies. She didn't need to point him out, nor would she have done so even if it was necessary.

—No, he didn't come to see me. He came so they could see him.

—Are you in love with him?

She wasn't surprised by the question, she just burst out laughing.

—With Arsen? She laughed some more. —With that face?

—He's not ugly.

—No, he isn't. In fact, there are many girls who consider him pretty. But not as pretty as he thinks he is. Have you seen him without his sunglasses?

—Yes, on the night I met you (was I giving myself away), when I met
you all.

—I mean during the day.

—I don't remember.

It was the truth. I think that once or twice I had seen him when he
was on television. But I hadn't paid any attention to his eyes. I said that to Vivian.

—I don't mean on television. There he's playing a part and it's different. I mean in the street. Take a good look at him next time he takes his glasses
off.

She sipped at her cigarette as though it was an inhalant and let a cloud
of smoke loose from her mouth and nostrils. I broke into her aerosol of tar and
nicotine.

—He's a famous actor.

Before talking she removed a threadworm of tobacco from her lips by
picking it with her fingers and I suddenly realized how in Cuba the men spit out
any dirt that clings to their mouth, while the women pluck it off with a fingernail.

—I could *never* love a man who has eyes like that. Still less an actor.

I didn't say a word but I felt uneasy. Was I an actor? I also asked myself
how my eyes would look in her eyes. Cué returned before I could answer myself.
He looked worried or contented or both things at once.

—Let's go, he said to me, and to Vivian: —It looks like Sibila won't
be coming today.

—I don't know about that. And I noticed or wanted to notice that she
gave an extra degree of pressure to the cigarette when she stubbed it out on the
concrete table. She threw it away into a corner. Then she went back to the pool.
—Goodbye, she said to us both and then, gazing into my eyes, only to me:

—Thank you.

—For what?

—For the cigarette and the match and (adding I think without malice,
though she paused a minute) for the conversation.

I watched Cué walking off seeing nothing of him but the back of his
trench coat. We were leaving the patio when someone started shouting.

—Someone's calling us, I told him. It was a boy who was waving at us
from the water. He must have been signaling Cué because I didn't know him.
Cué turned around. —It's for you, I said.

The boy was making strange gestures with his arms and head and was
shouting Arsenio Quackquackquack. Now I understood. He was imitating a duck,
which can also mean a fag in Cuba. I don't know if Cué understood the allusion,
but I think he did.

—Come on, he said. —Let's go back to the pool. It's Little Brother.
Sibila's, that is.

We went to the edge and Cué shouted to the boy, calling him Tony.
He swam toward us.

—What is it?

He was as young as Vivian and Sibila. He clung onto the side of the pool and I saw he had a gold bracelet around one arm, a dog-tag made of gold. Cué spoke to him slowly, picking his phrases.

—You're the one who's a duck. When you were swimming. Now you're a dead duck. He had understood. I laughed. Cué laughed too. The only one who didn't laugh was Tony, who looked at Cué in terror, his face grimacing with pain. I didn't understand why but I soon found out. Cué crushed the fingers of one of his hands with his foot pressing down on it. Tony cried out and thrust his legs against the side of the pool. Cué let him go and Tony shot off backward, swallowing water, trying to swim with his feet, holding his hand to his mouth, almost in tears. Arsenio Cué was laughing now, smiling on the edge of the pool. I was surprised not so much at what had happened as at the fact that he seemed pleased with himself, gloating over his revenge. But when he left, he was sweating and he took off his glasses to dry his face. As a concession to the heat and the afternoon and the climate, he took off his trench coat too and carried it over his arm.

—Did you see that? he asked.

—Yeh, I said and as I spoke I took the opportunity to have a look at his eyes.

V

I said that this story would have nothing to do with Cuba, and now I'm going to have to give myself the lie because there isn't a thing in my life which doesn't have to do with Cuba, Cuba Venegas I mean. The night I've been talking about I had gone to the Sierra with the pretext of hearing Beny Moré, which is a pretty good pretext because Beny is pretty good himself, but in fact I had gone to see Cuba and Cuba ("the most beautiful singer human eyes have heard," as Floren Cassalis said) is for the eyes what Beny is for the ears: when you go to see her you go to see her.

—Come right on in, Cuba said, talking through the mirror in her dressing room. She was putting on her makeup and had thrown a dressing gown over her stage costume. She was prettier than ever with her pouting lips wet and full and red, and the blue shadow around her eyes which made them bigger and blacker and more brilliant, and her hair styled a little like a mulatto version of Veronica Lake and her legs crossed showing through her gown open up to her thighs, taut and dark and smooth, almost edible.

—What's new with Verónica Laguna? I said. She smiled, so as to show off her large round white teeth which were a row of cowries over her pink gums. They were so even and perfect they looked like dentures.

—Ready for Freddy, she said, widening the corner of her eyes with a black pencil.

—What's the matter?

—With me? I'm sick.

I went up to her and held her by the shoulders, without kissing her or anything. But she was very cool and got up and slipped out of the gown and with the gown out of my hands: she didn't so much slip out of my hands as she was taking me off like a piece of clothing.

—Let's go someplace after the show.
—Can't, she said. —I have the curse.
—Only to Las Vegas, I mean.
—The thing is, I think I'm running a temperature.

I went to the door and balanced in the void that came through it, holding onto the edge of the door with my hands. I had to push myself forward with both my arms to go out, when I heard her calling me.

—I'm sorry, love.

I made some kind of gesture with my head. *Sic transit Gloria Pérez.*

I went to meet Vivian at the Focsa building three hours later. As I was going in the doorman already came toward me, but I heard Vivian calling me. She was sitting in the darkness of the lobby, or rather she was sitting on a sofa in the darkness.

—What's the matter?
—It's that Balbina, the servant, was awake when I went up and I came down to tell you to wait for me here.
—What are you laughing at?
—Balbina wasn't awake, but I knocked over a lamp in the dark and woke her up. I was trying not to wake her, and as a result I woke her up completely and that's not the only thing, I also broke a lamp that Mummy was very fond of.
—The matter is there . . .
—Only the form is lost. Hey, what's with these gross comments?
—You forget I'm a bongo player.
—You're an artist.
—Yes, of the drumheads between the legs.
—That's really dirty. It's the sort of thing Balbina would say.
—The *servant*, I said.
—What's wrong with that? It would be worse if I called her a maid.
—Is she a Negro?
—What are you talking about!
—Is she black or isn't she?
—All right, yes.

I didn't say anything.

—No, she's not black. She's Spanish.
—It's always one or the other.
—You're neither one nor the other.
—You just don't know how right you are, sweetie.
—How about coming outside with me and exchanging a few punches?

She was joking of course and then I saw that behind the evening dress she was still a little girl and I remembered the day I had gone to the Focsa to see if I could see her (it was five in the afternoon) with the pretext of having a bite in the pastry shop. I saw her come in in her school uniform, a school for rich girls, and nobody would have thought of her as being more than thirteen or fourteen as she tried to protect her young body with the schoolbooks she held in front of her and standing there almost bending over forward to cover up for the embarrassment of her full breasts.

—Didn't you know my friends call me Bile the Kid? I said and she laughed back but it was slightly forced, not because she didn't think it was funny but because she wasn't used to laughing out loud and at the same time as she wanted to show me she understood the joke and that she appreciated it and that she was really a common pleb herself, she felt her laughter was vulgar because she was taught to believe that well-bred people don't laugh out loud. If all this sounds complicated it's because it is complicated.

I tried another joke:

—Or Billy the Bilious.

—*Basta!* Once you get started there's no knowing when you'll stop.

—Are we going out or not?

—Yes, let's go out. I'm glad I came down, because the doorman wouldn't have let you in.

—How'll we manage it then?

—Wait for me at the corner of Club 21. I'll join you in a few minutes.

One thing I was sure of was that I didn't feel like going out with her anymore. I can't quite say if it was because of the doorman or if it was because I was convinced we wouldn't get anywhere. There was more than one street to cross between me and Vivian. I left the street of metaphor, crossed the street of reality, and thought about the street of memory, on that same street of the night I had first met Vivian, and where I had run into Silvestre and Cué, who were returning from seeing Vivian and Sibila back to their homes.

—How's the poor man's Gounod? Cué said, showing off his knowledge of music, of European music. —Did you know that Gounod, yes, the Gounod of the "Ave Maria," was a drummer?

—No, I didn't.

—But you know Gunó, no? Silvestre said. He was drunk and falling all over the place.

—Gunonó? I said. —No, who was Gunonó?

—I didn't say Gunonó, I said Gunó.

Arsenio Cué laughed.

—He's pulling your leg lamely, *mon vieux.* I'll bet you a hundred pesos against a cold cigar butt that this fellow knows who Gounod was. He is something of a tin drummer himself, he said. —Like Gounod, alias Gunó.

I hadn't said anything. Not yet. But I would say it, Cué, *mon vieux.*

—Arsenio, I said and I was about to say Silvestre when I heard a belch behind my back and there was Silvestre almost falling over backward—and Silvestre. The duet.

Were they laughing? Was the duet laughing? I would have blown them apart with a belly laugh, with a smile even. Duets are like that. I know because

I'm a musician. There's always a primo and a second fiddle and even in unison they are fragile.

—Silvestre, you know that Cué just laid an egg?

—No kidding? Silvestre said, almost sobering up. —Tell me, tell me.

—I will.

Cué glanced at me. Was he amused?

—Arsenio Monvieux, I've got something very sad to tell you. Gounod never played the drums. The drummer with whom you fuse or confuse him was Hector Berlioz, the author of "Les Valseskyries."

I thought for a minute that Cué wanted to be as drunk as Silvestre and Silvestre as sober as Cué. Or the other way around, as the two of them would say or one or other of the two. If this was the case I happen to know why. Arsenio Cué was in a taxi once and the driver was listening to music on the radio and Silvestre and Cué started discussing whether what they were listening to (it was classical music) was Haydn or Handel, and the driver let them go on talking awhile and then he said:

—Folks, it ain't one nor the other. It's Mozart.

Cué must have betrayed the same surprise in his face then as now.

—How do you know? Cué asked.

—Because the announcer said so.

Cué couldn't let the matter drop.

—Are you, a taxi driver, interested in music?

But the driver had the last word, as usual.

—And you like music, you, a passenger?

Cué didn't know I knew this story a long time before I knew him. Silvestre did, however. It was he who had told me some time ago and now he must have been remembering the incident, and laughing to himself, almost collapsing, doubly intoxicated in body and soul. But Cué was good at getting out of a tight corner. He knew all the stage tricks. He wasn't an actor for nothing. Now he was aping the common Cuban.

—*Mon vieux*, you've just crushed my musical backbone. It's in the drink.

—Tiger's pit, Silvestre said, meaning tiger spit meaning bad rum. Alcohol was turning him into a true disciple of Bustrófedon and instead of a tongue he had tongue twisters.

I saw Cué was looking at me curiously, deliberately. He was conferring with his pard. Top and second bananas. It was burlesque not theater. Oh sweet misery of life.

—Silvestre, I'll lay my paycheck against a spent match that I know what *Vincent* is going to say next.

I gave a start. Not because he said Vincent, he could easily have overheard that one.

—I bet I know what you want to know.

I didn't say a thing. I just stared at him.

—Does he know? Silvestre said.

He knew I knew. He's a cunning bastard. I had seen it from the time I first met him. In any case I couldn't help admiring him.

—See low say, Cué said. He seemed to be talking in some fake American accent and Silvestre laughed or snickered to himself before asking moronically:

—Whawhawhat?

—Keep it to yourself, I told Cué.

—Keep what? Silvestre said. —I don't get you.

—Why? I'm not a *ñáñigo*. I'm not even a silent drum.

—Come on, what you mean? Silvestre said.

—We don't *mean* anything, I said. I don't know if I said it rudely. — Just words.

—Quite the reverse, Cué said. —We do mean, words don't.

—Reverse of what? said Silvestre, ritardando.

—Of everything, Cué said.

—What everything? said Silvestre.

I said nothing.

—Silvestre, Cué said, —this fella (pointing to me) wants to know if it's true or not.

It was a game of cat and mouse. Of mice and cat.

—Is *what* true? said Silvestre. I continued to say nothing. I kept my arms folded mentally and physically.

—If it's true that Vivian is an easy lay or beddable. Or if she isn't. As Trotsky said to Mornard: Take your pick!

—I don't care either way.

—She's an easy lay, Silvestre said, pounding an imaginary table with his fist. —Extremely beddable.

—Oh no, she's not so easy. She's not easy at all, Cué said, sneering at him.

—She is, you fucker, she is, Silvestre said.

—I don't give a fuck either way, I heard myself say wearily.

—Yes you do. And I'll tell you something else. You're getting mixed up with Vivian and she's not a woman. . . .

—She's just a girl, I said.

—What's wrong with that? Silvestre asked. He was almost coherent again.

—No, she isn't just a girl or anything like it, Cué said. He was speaking to me alone now. —That's one thing she ain't. She's a typewriter.

—What you mean? said Silvestre. He was forgetting one of his many maestros, he had drunk so much. —Explain what you mean.

Arsenio Cué, always the actor, looked at Silvestre and then looked at me condescendingly. Finally he spoke:

—Have you ever seen a typewriter in love?

Silvestre seemed to give the matter a moment of thought and then said, —Me, never. I didn't say anything.

—La Smith-Corona is a typewriter. What's in a name? Everything. She's a perfect typewriter. But she's a display typewriter like you see in a window saying please don't touch. She isn't for sale, nobody can buy her, nobody can use her. They are just there to look pretty. Sometimes you don't know if they're for real or just a copy of something real. A dummy typewriter Silvestre would say now if he were capable of saying it.

—I can, of course I can, said Silvestre.

—Let's hear it then.

—A dumb writer.

Cué laughed.

—You're definitely coming on.

Silvestre smiled gratefully.

—Who would fall in love with a typewriter?

—Me, me, Silvestre said.

—In your case that's understandable. But you're not the only one, if you know what I mean, Cué said, looking at me.

Silvestre jettisoned his ballast of laughter and almost keeled over. I didn't say anything. I did nothing except tighten my lips and stare straight into Arsenio Cué's eyes. I think he took a step backward or at least removed his foot. He had stamped on my fingers but he knew that I wasn't Tony. It was Silvestre who spoke, trying to act as peacemaker.

—The point settled, let's go someplace. Do you want to come?

Cué repeated the invitation. It was better that way. I decided that I would also be *sybilized,* as Silvestre would say.

—Where? I said.

—Right here around the corner. To San Michel. To look at the men of wo.

But not as civilized as all that.

—It doesn't appeal to me.

Silvestre seized my arm.

—Come on, don't be silly. With a bit of luck we'll see some of the old familiar faces.

—It's quite likely, Cué said. —You meet all sorts in the night.

—Could be, I said doubtfully. —But it doesn't appeal to me to see the fairies in action.

—Auction is the word, said Silvestre.

—These ones are very gentle, Cué said. —They're followers of Mamma Gandhi. They're passive to a man.

—They don't interest me. Neither passive or active, peaceful or aggressive.

—They call themselves satiaggrahassives.

—Thank you no.

—You don't know who you're missing, said Silvestre.

—This fellahtio here does, Cué said, laughing spitefully.

—No I don't, you cunt! Silvestre said. —I'm going there just for the put-on, that's all.

—What are you going to do then? Cué asked.

I hesitated a moment.

—Mysteriouso as ever.

—I'm going to the Nacional to see some people.

—Some girl. Same boy, said Silvestre. —Don't you ever get bored with seeing Gene Kelly dancing with Cyd Charisse?

Cué laughed. —Oh sweet mystery of love!

Silvestre laughed. They both laughed, then they shook hands. Silvestre went on his way singing, his voice growing fainter, a parody of a song: *"Mister Mystery wants to rule over us / And I just keep on doing what he says / Because I don't want to hear people say / That Mister Mystery wants to rule over us."*

—Ñico Saquito, Arsenio Cué shouted. —Opus Cule de Sax-Kultur 1958.

VI

I didn't go anyplace that night. I stayed where I was standing on the corner under the street light just as I am now. I could have gone to look for a chorus girl after the second show at the Casino Parisien. But that would have meant going on from there to a club and buying drinks, and then going to a hotel and finally waking up in the morning with a tongue like a tombstone, in a strange bed, with a woman who I would hardly be able to recognize because she would have left all her makeup on the sheets and on my body and my mouth, with a knock on the door and a voice off telling me it's time to get up and having to go to the shower by myself and wash and rid myself of the smell of bed and of sex and of sleep, and then wake up that unknown woman, who would speak to me as though we had been married ten years, with the same voice, the same monotonous certainty. Do you love me, sweetie, she'd say, when what she should be doing would be to ask me what my name was, my name which she wouldn't know any more than I would know hers, and so I would say, I love you very much, sweetie.

I was standing there now thinking that playing the bongo drums or the *tumbadora* or just the drums (or Cuban percussion vulgo *timbales* as Cué would say to show how cultivated and brilliant he was and also knowledgeable in sex/folklore) was to be alone, but not to be alone exactly like flying, I thought, I who have never flown in a plane except to Isle of Pines and as a passenger at that, flying, I mean like a pilot, in a plane, seeing the whole countryside flat, one-dimensional beneath one, but knowing that one is enveloped in dimensions and that the machine, the plane, the drums, are the relation which enables one to fly low and see the houses and people or to fly high and see the clouds and to move between the sky and the earth, suspended, without dimension, but in all the dimensions, and there I am swooping and hovering and diving the double drumplane, counterpointing, stabilizing the beat with my feet, measuring the rhythm in my mind, keeping an eye on those interior *clave* sticks which play all the time, playing like against the *claves* although they're not in the band anyway, counting the silences, my silence while I listen to the sound of the band, doing stunts: banging and twirling and looping the loop first with the left-hand drum, then with the right, then with both, imitating a collision, or a nose-dive, playing possum for the cowbell or the trumpet or the bass fiddle, cutting across them without letting on that I'm off beat, making believe I'm cutting across them, returning to the time, moving in line, straightening up the machine and finally touching down: playing games with the music, playing and drawing music out of that double goatskin nailed to a cube or dice of wood, immortalized kid, its kidding bleat turned into music by its skin between the thighs in form of drumheads the balls of music going with the band staying with it and of course so far away from my solitude and from company and from the world: in music. Flying.

Anyway there I was, standing by myself on the night I left Cué and Silvestre walking to the exhibition of ladybirds in the musical cage of the San Michel, when a convertible passed rapidly and I thought I saw Cuba in it, at the back, with a man who may or may not have been my friend Códac and another couple in front, all of them sitting very close to each other. The car drove on and came to a stop. In the gardens of the Nacional and I thought it wasn't her, that it couldn't be her because Cuba must have been at home, already asleep: Cuba needed some sleep: she had to be in bed early: she didn't feel well: she was *sick*, she said: these were my training thoughts when I heard a car coming up N Street and it was the same convertible that had now halted half a block away, in the dark under the elevated car park, and I heard footsteps coming along the sidewalk and toward the corner and passing behind me and I turned around and there was Cuba with a man I didn't know, and I was very pleased that it wasn't Códac. Of course she saw me there. They all went into the Club 21. I didn't do a thing, I didn't even move.

A short time later Cuba came back to where I was. She didn't say anything. She just put a hand on my shoulder. I removed the shoulder and her hand with it. She remained silent, she didn't even move. I didn't look at her. I looked down the street, and, strangely, I was thinking then that Vivian would be arriving and I wanted Cuba to disappear and I believe I made a pretense of suffering a mental agony as strong as a toothache. Or did I really feel it? Cuba slipped away quickly but then turned around and said to me so softly I could hardly hear her:

—Love, forgive me, do.

It could have been the title of a bolero. Of course I didn't tell her.

—Have you been waiting long? Vivian asked me and I thought it was Cuba speaking, because she had arrived almost at the same moment as Cuba had left and I wondered if they had seen each other.

—No.

—You didn't get tired?

—No, it's O.K., really.

—I was afraid you might have left. I had to wait till Balbina fell asleep. She hadn't seen anything.

—No, I wasn't bored. I was smoking and thinking.

—About me?

—Yes, about you.

I was lying. I was thinking about a difficult arrangement we were rehearsing in the evening, when Cuba had turned up.

—You're lying.

She seemed flattered. She had changed the dress she had been wearing at the cabaret for the one she was wearing the day I had first met her. She looked much more a woman, but there was nothing pale and ghostly about her as there had been then. Her hair was tied up in a high coil and she had made herself up freshly. She was almost beautiful. I told her so, leaving out the almost, of course.

—Thank you, she said. —What are we going to do? We're not going to stand here all night, are we?

—Where do you want to go?

—I don't know. You decide.

Where should I take her? It was after three. There were many places open, but which of them would be suitable for a girl from a rich family? A mean well-lighted place like El Chori? The beach was a long way off and I would spend my salary getting there in a taxi. A late-night restaurant like the Club 21? She would already be sick of eating in places like that. Besides, Cuba would be there. A carbaret, a nightclub, a bar perhaps?

—How about San Michel?

I remembered Cué and Silvestre, those identical twits. But I thought that by now the frantic locomotive of love that does not dare reveal its name would have reached the terminus, that the hour of the she-wolf had ended and that there would only be a few couples left—perhaps heterosexual.

—That sounds like a good idea. It's not far.

—That's a euphemism, I said and pointed to the club. —The moon isn't far.

There was almost nobody in the San Michel—which Silvestre called a queendom by the sea—and the long corridor, a colony of sodomites earlier in the evening, was deserted. There were only two couples—a man and a woman near the jukebox and two shy well-adjusted queens in a dark corner. I couldn't count the bartender in because I could never tell if he was a fairy or if he pretended to be one to do better business. He doubled up for the waiter.

—What'll you have?

I asked Vivian. A daiquiri for her. O.K., that makes two of us. We had already drunk three daiquiris abreast when a group of people came in making a lot of noise. Vivian whispered under her breath, "Oh my God, not them!"

—What's the matter?

—They're people from the Bilmor.

They were friends of hers, from her club or from her mother's club or her stepfather's and of course they would recognize her and of course they would come to our table and of course there would be introductions and all the rest. By all the rest I mean smiles and knowing looks and two of the women in the party getting up and saying excuse me to all the western world and then going to la toilette. I whiled away the time completing with my index finger the circles of water left by the glasses and making new circles with the moisture I forced to drip from the glasses with my fingertip. Someone showed compassion and put on a record. It was La Estrella singing "Be Careful, It's My Heart." I thought about that enormous, extraordinary, heroic she-mulatto who held the portable black mike in her hand like a sixth finger, singing in the Saint John (all the nightclubs in Havana now have the names of exotic saints: schism or snobbism?) hardly three blocks from where we were, singing from a pedestal raised above the bar, like a new and monstrous dark goddess, as the wooden horse must have been worshiped in Troy, surrounded by fanatics more than by fans, without mus. accomp., disdainful and triumphant, her devotees hovering around her like white moths in the light, blinded by her countenance, seeing nothing but the luminous flow of her voice because what issued from her professional mouth was the song of the sirens and we, every man in her public, we were so many Ulysseses lashed to the mast of the bar enchanted by that voice which the worms would never have for lunch because here it was singing now on the record, a perfect and ectoplasmic facsimile, dimensionless as a specter, as the flight of a plane, as the Spirit of Saint John, the beat of the drums: this is the original voice and a few blocks away there was only its replica because La Estrella is her voice and it was her voice that I heard and I headed for it flying by no instruments, led blindly by that sound flaring up in the night and hearing her voice, seeing it in the dark, suddenly I said, "La Estrella, lead me to harbor, you are my astrolabe, the north of my diamond needle, my Stella Polaris!" and I must have said it out loud, because I heard people laughing at our table and around us and someone was saying, a girl, I think, "Vivian darling, but you've *changed* your name," and I excused myself and got up and went out to the drumhead. I pissed to the tune of "Be Careful, It's My Heart." Demo: *"Be careful, it's my cock / Not a policeman's club / You're holding in my hand."*

VII

When I returned, Vivian was by herself and drinking her third daiquiri in a row and mine was waiting for me in my place, frozen, almost solid. I drank it straight without speaking and as she had finished hers, I ordered two more and we didn't say a word about the people whom I no longer knew whether they'd been there or if I had dreamed or imagined them. But they had been there, because "Be Careful, It's My Heart" was playing for the third time running and I saw the stains of our vistiors' glasses on the black formica.

I remember that around us the indirect lighting formed a halo of Vivian's blond hair when I began without saying a word to remove the hairpins from her bun. She gazed into my eyes and she was so close she was squinting. I kissed her or she kissed me, I believe it was she who kissed me, because I remember wondering in my drunkenness where that little girl who was hardly as much as seventeen years old had learned how to kiss. I kissed her again and while I was caressing her shoulders with one hand, I was managing to untie her hair with the other. I opened her zipper and slid my hand right down inside below her waist and she•wiggled and twisted, but I don't think I was putting her off at all. She wasn't wearing a bra and that was the first thing that surprised me. We followed the same kiss along and she was biting my lips real hard and saying some nothing or other at the same time. I slid my hand round the side of her back toward her breasts and at last I felt them, small but seeming to bud, to blossom, to develop nipples under my hand. O.K., so maybe I was drunk and just a lousy bongo player, but I can also be an eroticist if I want to. I left my hand where it was, not moving a finger. She was speaking inside my mouth and I felt something salty and thought she had broken my lip. But they were tears.

She slipped away from me and threw back her head and the light fell on her face. It was completely drenched. Some of it was saliva, but the rest was tears.

—Please be good to me, she said.

Then she went on crying and I didn't know what to do. Women who cry always exile me to a state of confusion, and I was drunk which made me even more alien: all the same they alienate me more than the next drink.

—I feel so unhappy, she said.

I thought that she was in love with me and that she knew—she knew *it*—about In Cuba (that's Doña Venegas's wicked name) and I didn't know what to say. Anyway I shut up like a clam. Women who are in love with me ostracize me more than women who cry and more than the next drink. Now as a last banishment she was crying and the waiter came with two extra drinks nobody ordered. I think he wanted to break our clinch. But she went on speaking with the referee there and all. She wasn't exactly a clean fighter, believe me.

—I wish I was dead.

—But what on earth for? I said. —Things aren't at all bad here.

She gazed into my eyes and went on weeping. All the water in the daiquiris was coming out through her eyes.

—I'm sorry, but it's terrible.

—What's terrible?

—*La vida.*

Another good title for a bolero.

—Why?

—You know.

—Why is it terrible?

—Because that's how it is. *Ay!*

I let her go on crying.

—Lend me a handkerchief.

Lend me your tears. I lent her my handkerchief and she dried her tears and the saliva and even blew her nose in it. My only handkerchief. The only one I had for the night, I mean: I have more at home. She didn't give it back. I mean she didn't ever give it back: she must still have it at home or in her handbag. She swallowed the daiquiri in one gulp.

—Forgive me. I'm an idiot.

—You're not an idiot, I said, trying to kiss her. She didn't let me. Instead she pulled up her zipper and straightened her hair.

—I want to tell you something.

—Please do, I said, trying to appear so attentive and understanding and disinterested that I must have looked like the hammiest actor in the world trying to look disinterested and understanding and attentive while speaking to a public that wasn't listening.

—I want to tell you something. Nobody knows about it.

—And nobody else will.

—I want you to swear you'll never tell anyone.

—Of course I won't.

—Above all, that you won't tell Arsen. ●

—I won't tell *any*one. I was sounding now like a drunkard.

—Promise me.

—I promise.

—It's very difficult. But the best thing is to come clean with it. I'm no longer a virgin.

I must have had the same expression as Cué had during the episodes of Haydn, Handel, Mozart & Co., wholesale makers of music and embarrassment.

—It's the truth, she said. I didn't answer.

—I didn't know.

—Nobody does. You and *this* person and myself are the only people who do. He won't tell anyone, of course. But I had to tell it or I would have burst. I had to tell someone and Sibila is my only friend, but she's the last person in the world I'd want to hear about it.

—I won't tell anyone.

She asked me for a cigarette. I gave it to her and put the packet back in my pocket. I didn't feel like smoking. When I offered her a match she hardly brushed my hand, except for the trembling of her hand which communicated itself to mine through clenched and sweaty fingers. Her lips were trembling as well.

—Thanks, she said, blowing the smoke away and without a moment's pause she said, —He is a very mixed-up young boy, very young, very lost, and I wanted to give a meaning to his life. How wrong I was!

I didn't know what to say: the surrendering of virginity as an act of altruism left me absolutely speechless. But who was I to discuss the possible avatars of the Salvation Army? After all, I was only a bongo player.

—*Ay*, Vivian Smith, she said. She never used the Corona and it reminded me of Lorca, who always introduced himself as Federico García. But there was no tone of complaint or even self-reproach in her voice. I believe she wanted to assure herself that she was there and that I wasn't spitting in her face, which I didn't do because for me it was also only a dream. Only not the dream I had longed for.

—Do I know him? I asked, trying not to look either too eager or jealous.

She didn't reply at once. I gazed at her steadily and although it seemed there were fewer lights at the bar, she wasn't crying. But I saw that her eyes were watery. Two tears later she answered.

—You don't know him.

—Are you sure?

I looked her straight in the eyes.

—Oh well, I suppose you do. He was in the swimming pool the day you were there.

I didn't want to, I couldn't believe it!

—Arsenio Cué?

She laughed or tried to laugh or a mixture of both.

—God no! Can you *imagine* Arsen being mixed up for as much as *one* day of his life?

—In that case I don't know him.

—Yes you do. It's Sibila's brother. Tony.

So I did know him after all. But it didn't bother me to know that that cross-eyed driveling shit of a merboy with his crucifix around his neck and identity band on his wrist and all, that this sophomoronic citizen of Miami was Vivian's Number One Mixed-Up Boy. What did bother me was the fact that she said *is*. If she had said was, it would have been a passing incident whether it had happened by chance or if it had been forced on her. This could mean one thing only, that she was in love. I saw Tony in another light now, with different eyes. What could she see in his? Eyes, I mean.

—Ah yes, I said. —I think I know who he is.

I was delighted that Cué had stamped on his hand after all. No, more than that, I wished Tony, like me, could have his little soul on the tip of his fingers.

—Please, *por favor,* don't ever tell anyone. Promise me.

—I promise you.

—Thank you, she said and she clasped my hand neither mechanically nor tenderly, nor with any interest. It was just another thing her hand could do expertly: like lifting it to her face to light a cigarette, for instance. —I am sorry, she said, but she didn't say why she was sorry. —I'm truly sorry.

It had to be true. It was the night when all the world felt sorry for me.

—*Eso no tiene la menor importancia!*

I think my voice sounded a little like Arturo de Córdova but also a little like my own.

—But I'm sorry and I feel bad about it, she said, but she didn't say *why* she *had* felt bad about it. Perhaps it was her telling me that made her feel bad. —Could you please get me another drink.

I tried beckoning the waiter with my finger but to succeed I would have had to go out hunting waiters: it is not as easy as you'd imagine: Frank Buck wouldn't have been able to bring a Cuban waiter back alive. When I turned around to look at her she was crying again. She was swallowing her tears as she spoke.

  —You really won't tell anyone?
  —No, really. Nobody.
  —Please. *Nobody*, but nobody, swear.
  —I will be quiet as the grave.
  "Gravedigger, I plead with you / That for my good you'll sing / Over her grave a requital / Leave her to hell / Let the devil treat her well / Don't cry for her, gravedigger / Don't cry for her! / You just dig." (Chorus)*

16

MANUEL PUIG

  If Cabrera Infante's characters were obsessed by the American cinema and quoted endlessly from its comic-strip dialogue, the characters of the Argentine Manuel Puig are even more obsessed with the romantic dreams that movies generate. For them, Hollywood is more real than the desolate, ugly town in the Pampas they are condemned to, and Rita Hayworth's betrayal of Tyrone Power in Rouben Mamoulian's version of *Blood and Sand* is more moving than the betrayals they commit in their everyday existence. Movies for them are not only a source of verbal or artistic experience—they are the only real life.

  Puig, born in a small town in the Pampas in 1932, attempted college in Buenos Aires, had a spell at Rome's Institute of Cinematography, and worked for a while at Air France's New York office (where he once sold a ticket to Greta Garbo) before finally discovering that the forgotten and despised small-town life he had known as a boy was his only possible source of creative inspiration. In returning in imagination to that ugly world, Puig was not moved simply by nostalgia; he went back home to expose the roots of that alienated society, and he did it the only possible way: by re-creating in minute detail the horrid existence of men and women whose only contact with beauty and romance was in their excursions to the cinema.

  Published in 1968, *Betrayed by Rita Hayworth* took the Argentine reader by surprise. It was too corny for the sophisticated appetites of people trained to decipher Borges, Bioy, and Cortázar (Part Four, 1; Five, 3, 4); it was

*"Requiem Rumba"—Music & lyrics by Ignacio Piñeiro, copyright 1929 (reproduced by kind permission of Musica Ficta, Inc.).

too complex and parodical for the readers of serials, the consumers of soap operas and sentimental movies. Not until the publication of Puig's second novel, *Heartbreak Tango* (1970), did the readers catch up with the author. They finally discovered that Puig had been using melodrama and the style of cheap novelettes to reveal the frustrated dreams of a whole country. It took them some time to recognize him as the first to see through the Argentine's aspiration to a European life-style. The real Argentina was a country that idolized Eva Perón (not only a charismatic leader but also an actress who had made her reputation in historical soap operas) and had fallen twice under the spell of her husband, a pipe-dream demagogue. The serials and the tango lyrics provided the only true education most Argentines had.

If *Betrayed by Rita Hayworth* followed the consecrated formula of the *Bildungsroman* (it was the story of a sensitive, yet treacherous boy, Toto), *Heartbreak Tango* followed another popular model: the serial. The story of Juan Carlos, the small-town Don Juan, and the women who loved him so desperately, was told in installments which progressively revealed the characters' endless frustrations and hopes. But in telling the story primarily through their thoughts and words, and reducing to the minimum the author's participation, Puig was faithful to the spirit, if not always the letter, of melodrama. Passion, lost and irrecoverable, was at the heart of the book. All the lyrics from well-known tangos and boleros, endlessly quoted or sung by the characters, concentrated on that one feeling. If the words were sentimental and cheap, the montage of successive scenes and episodes was merciless in its cumulative effect. Crisscrossing from a pathetic scene to a crudely realistic one, from the heights of frustrated love to the mechanics of fornication, Puig managed to show his characters both from the inside of their dreams and from the outside of their predictable actions.

In his third novel, *The Buenos Aires Affair* (1973), Puig followed another popular formula: the detective story. But he was less concerned with the investigation of what had really happened to the protagonist, the artist Gladys Hebe D'Onofrio, than with the unraveling of a sadomasochistic affair between her and an influential art critic.

In the recycling of such old and tired formulas as the serial and the detective story, Puig has found a uniquely effective technique for the revelation of hidden realities. In exploding his characters' dreams, he has exposed them for what they are—mere fakes, pallid substitutes for the authentic personal experience and feeling denied them by the social alienation from which they suffer. He is at once a moralist and a consummate master in portraying the subtleties and depths of social reality.

What follows is a chapter from *The Buenos Aires Affair.* It contains a transcription of an imaginary interview conducted by the protagonist to serve her own narcissistic needs. The epigraph (as throughout the novel) comes from a famous Hollywood movie: the stuff Gladys's dreams are made of.

The Buenos Aires Affair

From The Buenos Aires Affair, *translated by Suzanne Jill Levine (New York: Dutton, 1976), pp. 98–115.*

NORMA SHEARER *(a young woman whose hair has turned white after a few months in the People's Prison, walks up the platform of the guillotine where she's to be decapitated, suddenly she remembers herself as an enraptured adolescent in the Viennese palace at the time of her prospective engagement to the Dauphin of France):* I'll be queen of France! *(The drums roll, the queen's head falls and the crowd roars with excitement)*

THE DASHING YOUNG DIPLOMAT *(overlooking the savage spectacle from a tower, he lifts his eyes to the sky, then looks at the inscription in the ring that the beautiful Queen of France once gave him, reading it to himself):* "Everything leads to thee."

(from *Marie Antoinette*, Metro-Goldwyn-Mayer)

Buenos Aires, April 1969

My nails, well kept, not long, polished cyclamen pink, healthy and strong, they are filed but not sharp and the sheet's color is impossible to remember in the semidarkness, it covers the designs on the mattress. Perhaps those designs represent plumes of imperial Roman helmets, shields and lances appearing among the thick foliage of certain trees which also appear often in Gobelin tapestries, mattress fabrics with plumes, lances, shields, thick foliage, all in white and blue or white and pink are those fabrics for mattresses, my nails sink slowly into the sheet and push down the fabric which encloses bolts of combed wool. A wool tuft covers each of the stitches that are inserted between slight, even hills, for my nails to sink into? because the fabric yields but the nail's edge doesn't reach the point of cutting, it barely marks the sheet and blowing lightly over the palm of my hand the mouthful of air is warm like the wool and like the air between the two sheets. The thigh and knee run slowly along the sheet toward an edge of the bed which is next to the wall, they stop a moment and return to their place. The skin is somewhat cooler than the warm sheets, and from the skin moving inward the flesh that grows warmer and warmer from contact with the hot bones and the heating unit cannot be touched because it burns, and a proper diet of dairy products gives the organism the calcium it needs for strength. The radiator consists of a geometric net of pipes with hot water running through them, a screw and nut regulates the increasing or decreasing intake of water and through there a constant drop and a muffled sizzle escape, some horns and motor noises from the street traffic pierce the glass of the windows and putting the wristwatch against the ear one can perceive the tick-tock. Closing one's eyes it is also possible to hear a slight panting, no, at this moment the two bodies are at rest. The blood that circulates through his body, and also through mine, fulfills its course at an astonishing speed but in total silence, and at moments at even a greater speed, the heart beats faster than ever and the chest dilates so as not to press on it and to allow the silent—but not therefore cold—blood, at a temperature perhaps higher than that of the skin, to in turn dilate the heart, and already the only thing one can wish for is to rest, such a wave rises from the diaphragm that the filled lungs dislodge the well-earned yawn, the waistline fatigued from quietly pressing for a whole hour toward his vertical body. There are mirages in the desert, at the edge of this unusually wide bed if I close my eyes I don't see Leo Druscovich sleeping, but I hear—if a car in the traffic doesn't blow its horn—his almost imperceptible breathing. If I don't hear that either, without making the slightest noise I can sit up and from this end of the wide almost square bed I can move toward him and touch him. What if he wakes up? Perhaps he will be annoyed because rest is necessary, closed eyes can't see anything. If he continues sleeping and keeps his eyes closed he won't see anything ugly, as if he were blind. What do people think of when they already have everything they want and cannot ask for anything more? The same as in heaven, they don't think of anything and they sleep, they rest, although it would be nice to think of something. What do the people in heaven think? Only of nice things

**Interview that a lady reporter from the Parisian
fashion magazine** Elle **did of Gladys,
according to the latter's imagination
while resting beside sleeping Leo:**

Reporter: To gain your absolute confidence—I know, you are quite shy—I will
allow you to choose the name of this article.
Gladys: I wouldn't know what to say.
R: What do you think of "Gladys Hebe D'Onofrio Is in Heaven"?
G: I consider it a realistic title and to the point. But for your readers we should
use glamorous Hitchcockian language. "The Buenos Aires Affair"
should be the title.
R: Because of your unprecedented talent you have become a star in the world
of the arts in only a few months. Do you believe that you have now
achieved your highest ambition?
G: No, my highest ambition is to fulfill myself as a woman in matters of love,
and what a paradox, in my case my career has led me to love.
R: This is difficult to believe. Don't all career women say just the opposite?
G: Let them say it.
R: My intention is not to argue but to induce you to tell us, the readers of *Elle*,
what a day in the life of the woman of the year is like.

G: I refuse, the most interesting minutes in the day of the life of the woman of the year are too ribald.

R: So that's how it is. Well then, if you don't want to tell us your story, begin by telling us the love story that you would have preferred to live.

G: Impossible. I consider my own love story unequaled.

R: Since you deny us entrance to your inner self, would you be willing to answer our mediocrity test?

G: Yes, I am willing, although in this moment what I'd most desire would be to spread on my skin the Polynesian body perfume that is recommended on an entire page in your magazine, because tonight I want to surprise someone with a new fragrance.

R: What led you to notice our suggestion about a better perfume?

G: The illustration of Polynesian girls, it shows them as fresh as the breeze from the surf, just as the rosebuds that fall upon the wet sand are soft, just as the flaming sunsets of the islands are warm. Pearl essence scent for the body.

R: Exactly. And now the first question: when you have to select a gift, do you tend to buy something that you yourself like, or rather, do you decide on something that the person in question *should* have?

G: I would buy something that I like.

R: Perfect! The supermediocre person would have bought something mentioned some time ago, and the mediocre one, something considered useful. Second question: If in the new fall season the Parisians decide to introduce as the latest fashion the helmet and armor of the Valkyries, would you be the first to put up with an outfit that weighs twenty-five pounds or would you run to buy Chanel's classical *tailleur* or would you rather burst into resounding laughter?

G: I would burst into resounding laughter.

R: Perfect! Mediocrity is not your forte, Gladys Hebe D'Onofrio. Third and last question: if a young friend of yours—a girl fresh out of high school— asks your advice, would you tell her to enter the School of Architecture, travel to Biafra as a voluntary nurse, or set sail for India to study with the Maharishi?

G: Biafra.

R: What a pity. You're saved from the supermediocre, but you didn't choose the Maharishi, which is the fascinating and new thing to do.

G: My average isn't bad, right?

R: Very good.

G: And what do I care? What I do care about is that at eleven this morning iron knuckles knocked on my door. Before opening I asked who it was, thinking it was anybody but him. . . . I met him a few months ago, at a beach where I was trying to recover my health, a nervous breakdown had undermined my constitution. . . . One night I took a walk down by the sea, wearing the model labeled "water panther," bought in New York at the cost of almost a month's salary. There was nobody on the beach, water panther!, bathing suit and evening gown, all in one, black silk lit by acrylic teardrops. I prayed for someone to see me, looking more elegant than ever. The perfect tones of the night, the black of the water, the black of the sky, incandescent dots in the lampposts along the seaside promenade, incandescent dots in the crest of the black waves, in the acrylic drops, in the stars in the sky.

R: And that night you met him, the answer to your prayer.

G: No. That night I felt lonelier than ever. Imprisoned by despair I returned to the cottage and, almost crazed, I had an inspiration. I couldn't sleep, at five the dawn found me on the beach, for the first time picking up the debris that the surf had left on the sand. Flotsam, I only dared to love flotsam, anything else was too much to dare hope for. I returned home and began to talk—in a whisper so as not to wake up mama—with a forgotten slipper, with a bathing cap in shreds, with a torn piece of newspaper, and I started to touch them and to listen to their voices. That was my work of art, to bring together scorned objects to share with them a moment of life, or life itself. That was my work. Between my last painting and this latest production more than ten years had passed. Now I know why I hadn't painted or sculpted in all that time: because oils, temperas, water colors, pastels, clay, easels, all that was precious, luxurious material which I was not allowed to touch, an inferior being is not allowed to use up, waste, play with valuable objects. That's why for years I did nothing, until I discovered those poor fellow creatures who are rejected each morning by the tide. . . .

R: Don't stop.

G: I don't know, it seems that all that followed was a dream, and that I am still as destitute as then.

R: Your reality today is different.

G: Yes, it's true. . . . As I was saying, after that discovery I continued working, until one day the first group of vacationers came to the beach. I had heard that the men wore their hair very long and with them the women bathed bare-breasted. The windows of my makeshift work room faced a pine grove, on a tree branch a young man with a beard and very long hair was watching, listening to my conversation with the flotsam, judging my work. I closed the curtains. The following afternoon three men knocked on my door—they had very long hair—accompanied by two women with—under blouses of fish netting, gauze, knit raffia—their breasts bare. Sometimes, after working the whole day, I'd close my eyes content with what I had done and I'd dare to think that people might see and hear my works and then praise them deliriously. I opened the door and the strangers came in, they asked to see and to listen. Those words of praise I had dreamed of in the solitude of White Beach now burst from the strangers' lips, but this is even more amazing; they repeated adjective for adjective, exactly, all that I had desired to hear. Sitting on my bench, a bench which before had been in the kitchen, and sitting on the floor around me, my first five friends asked me who I was and wondered why they had not met me before. They said that they would have liked to have created my works, and that afternoon we all went down to the sea together. Leo Druscovich, the only thing they regretted was that Leo Druscovich was not with us. Leo Druscovich, who is he?, and they all burst into the most good-natured laughter. "The Tsar of art criticism," nothing less, and in that way it became clear how foreign I was to the artistic movements in Argentina. Beach parties with an open fire till dawn, then happy dreams stretching to midday, there was only one thought that could keep me awake: two girls and three men invited me to stay with them in their tents at night, but they were so much younger than I. Almost two weeks of joy barely disturbed. They left.

R: Is it true that we women eat more when we are pressed by a carnal frustration?

G: Yes, but at this moment I have a hard time remembering how a woman with carnal frustration feels.

R: In those moments of psychopathic gluttony, do you prefer sweet or salty?

G: I don't remember if it was in your magazine that I saw an advertisement of numerous Poitiers canned crêmes, served in crystal cups.

R: My magazine doesn't advertise fattening products. But I seem to remember some fine Baccarat cup with a short figured stem and a wide mouth, filled halfway with honey-colored crême topped with a bunch of cherries: as the finishing touch, a snowy peak of meringue.

G: And the other cup with a rough base is loaded with dark chocolate crême, a simple star made of five peeled almonds on top. And the champagne glass contains four small peaches colored red with angostura bitters and almost drowned in light yellow crême.

R: Different canned crêmes, chocolate, vanilla, praline, mocha, caramel.

G: Also a crême with cordials in it, a recipe of some French monk.

R: Tell me more about Leo Druscovich.

G: Mama was playing canasta that afternoon. I was trying to resume my work again after my companions left. There was a knock on the door. Without ever having seen that man I already knew him: I had imagined him.

R: Why don't you dare say that you had dreamed of him?

G: Because I never have happy dreams, only nightmares. But in the wakefulness of more than one night I had . . . seen him, driving his sports car with the top down, to some night club on the bank of the River Plate, the pool reflecting the orchestra, an icy, crystalline, sea-green pool. He dances with a model who will hold his interest for only a few hours. And days later the wind blows stronger, Leo alone on the open pampas, a thick scarf protects his neck, and what is his windbreaker made of?, neither leather nor corduroy, it must be that rough army material, lined with goatskin. He gets out of the Land-Rover with a double-barreled gun, the smoke from the pipe warms his chest, he needs to escape his urban problems for a few hours, hunting partridges, he has to kill in order to amuse himself. I'll never understand men, and you? do you by any chance understand the pleasure they get from watching boxing? Have you seen the joy on their expectant faces when the boxer's features have been completely transformed into a shapeless mass?

R: That means that men are not afraid of pain like we are, they don't get intimidated so easily, because in the face of danger a real man becomes . . . bigger.

G: Are you sure of that?

R: Please don't stop, continue with your story.

G: Where was I? Ah yes, after having sentenced himself to solitude and the pampa winds for hours, he returns to the city, running away from a neurotic and possessive woman, the wife of his best friend, a ranch-owner. He should have spent the weekend with them, but already the horses have to be hitched to the chaise to take Leo to the not very distant railroad station. And the train moves through the pampas, Leo returns to his prison of cement, traffic, incessant traffic lights and vanity: the capital of the Argentine Republic, Santa María de los Buenos Aires, those Good Airs filled with homicidal gases. Leo, loved by too many women and envied by too many men . . . Thus did I imagine your days and nights, until you entered my life. But it was Saturday, and our hero will dedicate the remaining day of rest—enclosed in his library—to the study of the great figures of the history of art, his great white passion.

R: White passions. Are there purple ones?

G: Yes, the man who likes to make people suffer is excited by rooms without windows, strangled faces are purple. Didn't you know?

R: I'm beginning to understand you, Gladys Hebe D'Onofrio, to such a point that when one day he knocked on your door I know how you would have liked to be attired: simple reminiscences of a Dresden shepherdess, whose lace is no longer wrought in china, the transparent organdy reveals a dark, golden complexion. Transparent wiles of organdy.

G: Only comparable to the formidable guiles of lace . . . Yes it's true, because the attire chosen was white like a camellia.

R: Its fringes, on the other hand, were soaked in almost orange tints.

G: Up until this point you're right. Continue.

R: Proudly free of jewels.

G: Wrong, I would have been ostentatiously covered with them. I opened the door and invited him in.

R: The door of this hotel room?

G: The door of the White Beach cottage. His friends had told him about me and he had come there especially to meet me. Barely looking at me, he asked to see my works. He saw them and heard them, said that I was his choice for representing the country at the next Exhibition in São Paulo. Only then did he look at me fully to catch my predictable Cinderella reaction. I did not outwardly show the slightest emotion, it was not at all difficult to restrain myself, because São Paulo had no importance whatsoever after seeing such a man enter my door. All that mattered after having seen him was to spend the rest of my life near him to be able to look at him. But here's where the conflict comes in, because I can only see Leo in his totality when he looks at me.

R: What is the look of Leo Druscovich like?

G: I don't know, a cyclone sweeps me off the earth and carries me to unknown territories, where I am caught by rays that read one's thoughts, or electrify, or kill, or give life. I don't know.

R: Tell me, I must find out.

G: The peerless critic thought that I was an impassive, dedicated artist, deaf to the flatteries of fortune, and he felt that this doubled his admiration for my works.

R: Repeat to me the words of the critic.

G: "Perhaps you didn't hear me well: I am chairman of the committee that selects the works to be presented at São Paulo and I've just designated you as the official representative of Argentina." I—impassive, with only time to observe how the waves of his hair caressed his bull-like neck—answered that I had heard him the first time. He added, "I don't understand you. Why don't you jump with joy? Why don't you shout?" I looked at his hands to see if he wore an engagement ring, he didn't have one. Thinking that this man—cultured, powerful, master of my artistic destiny, handsome, temperamental, neurotic, mysterious—was still waiting for the ideal companion, thinking all that distracted me and I didn't hear what he said and I didn't answer him. He became annoyed. "I repeat, why aren't you interested in such an opportunity? It could be justified only by your desire to work, to not interrupt your creativity." I had a ready answer: "Yes, that's the reason, I'm working well and I don't want interruptions for the moment." He turned around and disappeared. The slamming of the door made us, me and my works, tremble. As is to be expected, that night I couldn't sleep and dawn had not yet arrived when I went down to the beach in search of refuse for the making of new works. Far out in the ocean the dying lights of fishing boats, on the wet sand rusty tin cans, on the dunes a shadow and a red signal of alarm: a lighted cigarette. I trembled with fear, the shadow moved. It was coming in my direction. Who could be on the beach at that hour but a madman, a lunatic? In my hand was a sharp pebble I had recently picked up, my only weapon. It would have been senseless to run. I began to tremble, I had lost control of my body, the shadow stopped, the light pants were profiled in the distance, the torso was wrapped in a darker material that did not succeed in hiding the brutal strength of bulky muscles. The pebble fell from my trembling hand. Mutely I prayed that this man would let me escape, or that someone would come by on the coastal highway. I looked north and south, the two *sfumato* limits of the highway, not a single vehicle in sight. . . . A strong man needs only his hands to destroy a woman's weak neck, under the pressure of those claws the bones break like cartilage, the skin is torn like paper. Master of the dying female body, that monster with the deformed face—his eyes are mere slits bordered by giant warts—can bring his slimy skin close to hers, and she's already dead from repugnance. . . . All that passed through my mind like dark lightning and the new morning from one moment to the next gave off an almost daylike light. The burning cigarette became less brilliant, the shadow acquired the forms and colors of Leo Druscovich. Strong forms, friendly colors.

R: Like those Nice landscapes of the good Matisse?

G: Translucent, soaked in white. "Can you carry that load back to your house alone? Here, let me help you." During the walk we spoke of the good weather we were having on the coast, at my door he remained silent for a moment, for fear of ridiculous reactions on the part of my mother I didn't mention the possibility of coming in for a hot drink. He stopped looking straight at me. Like a little boy scolded for some mischief, his eyes suddenly became sad and evasive. He took leave of me making a date to have dinner together that very night. I went to bed without taking all that I had gathered on the beach out of the bag. One question kept pressing me: what had he been doing on the beach at that hour? At the end of a short nap I woke up, tense, and in vain tried to get back to sleep. The cause of my insomnia this time couldn't have been more frivolous: for the date that night I literally didn't have anything to wear. My desire would have been to appear radiant with luxury.

R: And what for you is luxury?

G: My idea of luxury among other things means sleeping until noon, wrapped in the linen of light, fine, soft, and fresh sheets. Every day, fresh, newly perfumed sheets.

R: Perfumed?

G: Yes, on a meadow sheets are spread out in the sun which warms them. When they're brought back inside they again take on room temperature, but the heat doesn't leave, it turns into sun perfume.

R: Hmm . . . How did you dress that night?

G: We ate lobster, white wine is the color of amber, so why do they call it that? When I was a little girl, my secret desire was to catch fire in my hand, the little red translucent flames that hot coals give off are fascinating.

R: And the green flames with yellow tips from kerosene heaters?

G: And the little blue tongues all perfectly even from a gas stove? Liquid amber-colored fire in my glass, that night I wanted to inject fire into myself drinking it like him, but it wasn't possible for me because I had taken barbiturates before our meeting. I'm scared of dying one day because of carelessness with drugs.

R: Alcohol and barbiturates, the traffic lights have turned red.

G: The day that preceded that dinner was very long, I consumed a double, a triple dose of tranquilizers. When I reached the restaurant my eyes were almost closing with sleep. He immediately asked me why I looked so tired. I answered that I had spent the whole day creating. I asked him to tell me what his life was like in Buenos Aires, that city I didn't understand. He drank wine, ate very little, and talked, about his projects, about the importance of the Argentine artistic movement. I felt that my eyes were closing, I tried to pay attention to what Leo was saying but besides the fact that my eyelids were heavy, I was hypnotized by his mouth, by his mustache that moved to and fro, the mustache stretched and returned to its place, and his eyes nailed me against the stately high-backed chair, in that large Renaissance dining room.

R: Tell me something about the mouth of that man.

G: I cannot avoid the commonplace: his mouth is sensual.

R: And you were soon asleep.

G: Exactly. While he spoke and looked at me I managed to keep my eyes open, but the moment that he lowered his eyes to prepare a cigar and light it was fatal for me.

R: Who woke you up?

G: The maître. Leo had paid and gone. There was nobody left in the restaurant, a dishwasher came in from the kitchen with a pail of water to put out the flame of the salamander stove.

R: Who took you home?

G: Several days later I received a special delivery letter from Buenos Aires. Without mentioning the incident at the restaurant at all, he asked me if a trip to Buenos Aires to discuss my presentation at São Paulo fitted into my immediate plans. But don't you think that our indiscreet conversation might wake up Leo?

R: Let's speak in a whisper.

G: I wrote to him about my approaching trip to Buenos Aires, without giving a date. Already settled in this hotel, with all my materials carefully put away in storage, I called him on the telephone. Twenty minutes later, someone who had escaped the doorman's watchful eye was knocking on my door. I opened, I was so excited I couldn't speak. All that happened yesterday.

R: How were you dressed?

G: I had just washed my hair, the white towel wrapped like a turban hiding my hair. And that bathrobe which you can now see thrown on the floor, yellow terry cloth, a color that goes well with a tan.

R: And your famous dark glasses, I presume.

G: Neither of us uttered a word. Finally he said, "Let me come in, if they see me in the hallway they'll throw me out." He came in. He embraced me. He kissed me. We continued standing in the room silently kissing several minutes more, we couldn't tear away from each other. Already exhausted by the excitement and joy, I withdrew my mouth and leaned my forehead on his shoulder. The turban came undone and fell to the floor. He tried to kiss me again. I kept moving my face away. He sought my mouth. I resisted. He became inflamed with passion. I struggled to free myself. He imprisoned my hands in his big hands, he bent my arms against my back and held me tighter than ever against him. His strength was much greater but I continued struggling. He began to kiss my neck and with his snout pushed my bathrobe apart until uncovering a shoulder, from there down to my breast. Suddenly his strength tripled, he lifted me in the air and deposited me on the bed. I was exhausted, but did not know how to give in with dignity. I lay still. He took off his jacket and began to undo his tie, without taking his eyes off me. He was so handsome. I closed my eyes to engrave in my memory that look of desire. And I didn't dare open them again. I heard his footsteps going toward the window, the sound of the Venetian blinds falling, his footsteps coming near. When I opened my eyes, his were staring at me, he tried to take off my dark glasses, I begged him not to, he took off my robe, he had a hard time undoing the inside button of the belt. He kissed me, spread my legs, and caressed my most intimate parts. . . . When one tries to take hold of burning red logs sputtering gold sparks, when one tries to catch the highest and most vibrant flame of a bonfire, the pain of the wounds is so great that forgetting all that colorful splendor we flee screaming. But if one is a prisoner, entangled in the bush, held down by those two strong oak branches, or arms? which stop us, all that's left is to wait for the flesh to burn until it is consumed. . . .

R: But why do you stop? What are you thinking of?

G: I remembered something curious. In his arms I thought that if he was so handsome it was thanks to me, who had known how to draw him to perfection at the "Leonardo da Vinci" Institute.

R: Continue.

G: He asked me if I loved him. I was afraid of telling him the truth, that I had adored him since the first moment I saw him. I preferred to say nothing. He smoked a cigarette in silence. He got dressed and left.

R: And today he came back again.

G: When the banging of iron knuckles could be heard, I trembled from head to toe.

R: Of course, but first tell me what you did between yesterday and today.

G: I slept many hours, waking up from one moment to the next with the impression that he was in the room and could become bored if I didn't talk to him or show him something interesting. And besides sleeping I spent a few hours in the bathtub. And this morning I went to the hairdresser.

R: Was your sexual encounter today less or more intense than yesterday's?

G: When I was in San Francisco, it was hard for me to believe that such a stately modern city was built on the ruins and panic of an earthquake.

R: This last question will be as difficult for me to put to you as easy as it will be for you to answer. How should I phrase it? . . . A man, when walking on the street, or when in a living room, or in the most intimate conversation, gives an image of himself, which at times does not coincide with the other image projected carnally through the total contact of the boudoir.

G: I understand.

R: You'd better. Does the mental image you had of Leo harmonize or clash with the image of Leo in the flesh?

G: I opened the door and he came in without looking me in the eyes. I asked him if he would have a cup of tea with me. As you can see, in this comfortable hotel each room comes equipped with a cute kitchenette. And guess what, he said yes, and handed me the umbrella and raincoat that I asked for. He inquired if I wanted to go out, to see some exhibition, or some movie. I answered him—with my back turned, busy preparing the tea—that there was nothing that interested me in particular. When I turned around I saw that he was already almost naked in the middle of the room, his pants, jacket, shoes, and vest thrown on the floor. He was unknotting his tie. Such insolence offended me and I ordered him to get dressed immediately. He laughed and took off his jock shorts. I couldn't take my eyes away in time and I saw his stiff phallus, in daylight his dimensions frightened me, I thought of my organs still impaired by the attack the day before, I thought of an illustration in my third- or fourth-grade reader with pictures of dungeons, stocks, racks, the instruments of torture with which the Spaniards martyred the old Argentine patriots of 1810. He threw himself upon me and began kissing me by force. I didn't dare scream for help to the hotel servants. But I continued to refuse him—no man can respect a woman who lets herself be taken by force!, I concluded in my heart of hearts—and I continued fighting until my arms lost their strength. Until then my refusal was of a moral order, my own imposition, but when I felt him dripping sweat I felt real repugnance. This last convulsive shuddering found my body without defenses, the tears flowed and I began to shake like a dead leaf swept by the wind. His hands firmly spread my legs, I begged him in an almost unintelligible murmur not to do it. The rest I remember only vaguely, perhaps it was the fear of suffering that caused me to faint, I only know that when I recovered consciousness and felt him moving rhythmically inside me, I could barely find my own hands—hanging lifelessly over the sides of the bed as if crucified—to hold onto his back, the skin of his back was damp, I felt for a tip of the sheet and dried it. He kissed me tenderly. Our mouths could no longer be separated. I waited for him to be the first to withdraw his lips to then tell him yes, I love him, as he had asked me the afternoon before. But I couldn't utter a word, the pleasure

started to climb from my belly to my throat. I opened my eyes, saw his
eyelashes, his temple, a lock of dark-blond hair.

R: What did you think of in that climactic moment?

G: I didn't think of anything.

R: According to the latest psychoanalytical theories, people who make love
without thinking about anything can consider themselves healthy.

G: Then I'm not a healthy woman, because now I remember that when pleasure
forced me with its silky, strangling hand to close my eyes again, I
thought that heaven existed. That God loved me and that's why he had
rewarded me after so much suffering, with a true love. God asked me
if I was ready for any sacrifice for the love of my future companion. I
answered that of course I was, what's more, it would be my pleasure
to bend under Leo's will.

R: Do you remember the dress you had on at that moment? In heaven, I mean.

G: I believe I was wearing the water-panther outfit, but I couldn't swear to it.

R: Don't you think that we woman are braver than we think? Think of what it
means to lock oneself in a room with a being three times our strength.

G: Strength that he needs to protect his beloved. What would become of us if
in the middle of the jungle his strong arm did not deal the fatal ax blow
upon the crouching leopard?

R: Do you have anything else to tell me before I take leave of you?

G: Yes, that when he wakes up I will tell him . . . that I love him, that from
now on his will shall be mine. Up until now he has judged me as cold
and proud, and that's why he thought so much impetus was necessary.
When he knows me as I am, he will love me even more.

R: He is stirring. Have we awakened him with our conversation? I'm going.
. . .

G: Before you go I want to ask you a question. When will the article you
announced in your magazine, on the so-called roots of feminine beauty,
appear?

R: I have seen the advertisement, but that humbug will not appear in my
magazine.

G: I was charmed by the way the advertisement approached the problem: "Does
your beauty have instinctual or cerebral roots? An existential, physical,
or wardrobe origin? Where does it really stem from? Find out." I want
to know, because ever since I've been feeling beautiful I've been goaded
by curiosity, am I an instinctual or an existential beauty?

17

MARIO VARGAS LLOSA

One of the most successful of the new novelists, the Peruvian Mario Vargas Llosa, is also one of the most traditional. His novels continue and expand on the basic themes of Latin American fiction—the uses and abuses of power, the pervasive paramilitary mentality of society, the genocidal treatment of the Indians—which were the staple fare of nineteenth- and early-twentieth-century novelists. A vast fresco of contemporary Peru is captured in his long, detailed, slightly pompous novels. Vargas Llosa is also a conscientious citizen, who constantly makes public statements about the Latin American political situation. His first novel, *The Time of the Hero*, was publicly burned by the right-wing officers of a Lima college who felt he had insulted their dignity. Recently he was attacked by the left-wing officers who then ruled Peru for being too eloquent in defending the freedom of the press. Like Sartre and Solzhenitsyn, Vargas Llosa believes that the role of the writer is to be the conscience of society.

He was born in Arequipa, Peru, in 1936 and spent most of his childhood in Cochabamba (Bolivia), in Piura (Peru), and in Lima. He was a boarder at the military school whose regime he was later to attack in his first novel; later he attended the University of San Marcos, in Lima, and went to Spain to complete his studies at Madrid University. Since then he has spent more time in Europe (Spain, France, and England) than in Peru. But his novels deal exclusively with his native country. After the success of *The Time of the Hero* (1963), Vargas Llosa published two long novels (*The Green House*, 1966; *Conversation in "The Cathedral,"* 1969), and two short ones (*The Puppies*, 1967; *Pantaleon and the Lady Visitors*, 1973). The setting may be Lima or one of the provinces, or even the equatorial jungle, but the conflicts are always similar. A political moralist, Vargas Llosa never tires of denouncing corruption, violence, and injustice. Although his plots are melodramatic and he is always ready to use any of the most familiar devices of pulp fiction (a secret kept from the protagonist through hundreds of pages, a fatal identity suddenly and brutally revealed, a fate worse than death), he builds his novels with the skill of a master craftsman. He knows his Flaubert by heart and he is sufficiently well acquainted with experimental techniques to construct very elaborate narratives; in fact, his novels are perhaps too meticulously structured. In *The Time of the Hero*, by careful editing of each episode he keeps secret the real identity of one of the main characters. In *The Green House*, he tells simultaneously four or five stories that have happened in different moments of time but in the same place. In *Conversation in "The Cathedral"* he transcribes not only the rather brief conversation of two characters in the bar of the title, but also other dialogues they evoke or silently remember while talking. It is all very complicated, if not really complex.

Despite all these dazzling montage effects, Vargas Llosa is a traditional novelist in his reliance on plot and characterization to keep the reader glued to his pages. He is also a solid narrator. In the pages from *The Green House* excerpted here, he develops a confrontation between one of the protagonists and a rich bully. In the novel, the episode is cut in two and printed with a hiatus of some ten pages. Read as a unity, it shows Vargas Llosa's gift for straightforward narrative.

The Green House

From The Green House, *translated by Gregory Rabassa (New York: Harper & Row, 1969), pp. 252–58 and 271–76.*

This time it really got ugly: the orchestra stopped playing, the champs stood motionless on the dance floor, holding on to their partners, looking at Seminario, and Kid Alejandro said, "That's when the trouble really started, that was when the pistols came out."

"Drunkard!" Wildflower shouted. "He was provoking them all the time. I'm glad he's dead. Troublemaker!"

The Sergeant let go of Sandra, took a step forward, did he think that he was talking to one of his servants, sir? and Seminario, choking, so you like to answer back too, he also took a step, you son of a!, another one, his formidable silhouette wavered on the boards that were bathed in blue, green, and violet light, and he stopped suddenly, his face full of surprise. Sandra's laugh turned into a shriek.

"Lituma was pointing his pistol at him," Chunga said. "He drew it so fast that nobody had noticed, like those young fellows in cowboy movies."

"He had every right to," Wildflower babbled. "He couldn't lower himself any more."

Champs and girls had run over to the bar, the Sergeant and Seminario were sizing each other up with their eyes. Lituma didn't like bullies, sir, they weren't doing anything to him, and he was treating them like servants. He was sorry, but he couldn't act that way, sir.

"Stop blowing smoke in my face, Jocko," Chunga said.

"And did he draw his gun too?" Wildflower asked.

"He only put his hand on his belt," the Kid said. "He was petting it like a puppy."

"He was scared!" Wildflower exclaimed. "Lituma had shown him up."

"I thought that there weren't any men left in my home town," Seminario said. "That all Piurans had turned into sissies and fairies. But we've still got this half-breed. Now all you need to see is who Seminario is."

"Why do they always have to fight, why can't they live in peace and enjoy things together?" Don Anselmo said. "Life could be so nice."

"Who can tell, maestro?" the Kid said. "It might be even more boring and sad than it is now."

"You've shown him up, cousin," Monk said. "Bravo!"

"But don't trust him, buddy," Josefino said. "The minute you look away, he'll go for his gun."

"You don't know who I am," Seminario repeated. "That's why you're being so brave, boy."

"You don't know who I am either," the Sergeant said, "Señor Seminario."

"If you didn't have that pistol, you wouldn't be so brave, boy," Seminario said.

"But the fact is that I do have it," the Sergeant said. "And nobody can treat me like his servant, Señor Seminario."

"And then Chunga came running over and stepped in between. You were the bravest of them all!" Jocko said.

"And you people, why didn't you hold her back?" The harpist's hand tried to touch Chunga, but she drew back in her chair and the old man's fingers only brushed her. "They were armed, Chunguita, it was dangerous."

"Not any more it wasn't, because they'd begun to argue," Chunga said. "A person comes here to have a good time, not to get into fights. The two of you make up, come on over to the bar and have a beer on the house."

She made Lituma put his revolver away, she made them shake hands, and she brought them over to the bar, taking them by the arms, they ought to be ashamed of themselves, behaving like a couple of kids, did they know what they were?, a pair of boobs, come on, come on, why didn't they take out their silly pistols and shoot her, and they laughed, Chunga Chunguita, little mother, little treater, the champs were singing.

"Did they start drinking together even after the insults?" Wildflower asked, surprised.

"Are you sorry they didn't shoot each other down?" Jocko said. "The way you women like to see blood."

"Chunga had invited them," the harp player said. "They couldn't make her mad, girl."

They were leaning on the bar and drinking, good friends, and Seminario pinched Lituma on the cheek, he was the last male in the land, boy, the rest were all cream puffs, cowards, the orchestra started playing a waltz, and the human cluster at the bar broke up, champs and girls went back to the dance floor. Seminario had taken off the Sergeant's cap and was trying it on, how did he look, Chunga?, not as horrible as this half-breed here, of course, but he shouldn't get mad.

"He may be a little fat, but he's not horrible," Wildflower said.

"When he was young, he was as skinny as the Kid," the harpist remembered. "And a regular devil, even worse than his cousins."

"They put three tables together and they all sat down," Jocko said. "The champs, Señor Seminario, his friend, and the girls. It looked as if everything had been settled."

"You could see that it was forced and that it wasn't going to last long," the Kid said.

"Not forced at all," Jocko said. "They were having a good time, and Señor Seminario even sang the champs' theme song. Then they danced and told jokes."

"Was Lituma still dancing with Sandra?" Wildflower asked.

"I don't remember why, but they started arguing again," Chunga said.

"That business about who was more of a man," Jocko said. "Seminario was still on it, that there weren't any men left in Piura any more, and all about his wonderful uncle."

"Don't say anything bad about Chápiro Seminario; he was a great man, Jocko," the harp player said.

"In Narihualá he took care of three thieves with his bare fists, and he brought them back to Piura with their necks tied together," Seminario said.

"He made a bet with some friends that he could still do it, and he came here and won the bet," Chunga said. "At least that's what Poppy said."

"I'm not saying anything against him, maestro," said Jocko. "But it was getting to be too much."

"A Piuran just as great as Admiral Grau," Seminario said. "Go to Huancabamba, Ayabaca, Chulucanas, and there are peasant women all over the place who were proud to have slept with my Uncle Chápiro. He had at least a thousand illegitimate children."

"Was he a Mangache maybe?" Monk asked. "There are a lot of types like that in the district."

And Seminario frowned, your mother's the Mangache, and Monk naturally and very proud of it, and Seminario furious, Chápiro was gentry, he only went to Mangachería once in a while, to have a drink of *chicha* and to lay some half-breed, and Monk hit the table with his fist: he was insulting again, sir. Everything had been going along fine, like among friends, and all of a sudden he was starting to insult the Mangaches, sir, people who said bad things about Mangachería would be sorry.

"He always used to come over to where you were, maestro," the Kid said. "The feeling he used to show when he embraced you. It looked like the meeting of two brothers."

"We'd known each other for such a long time," the harp player said. "I loved Chápiro, I was terribly broken up when he died."

Seminario stopped, euphoric: Chunga should lock the door, that night they'd be in charge, his cotton fields were full, the harp player should come over and talk about Chápiro, what were they waiting for, loaded with cotton, they should lock the door, he was paying.

"And customers who knocked at the door were sent away by the Sergeant," Jocko said.

"That was the big mistake; they shouldn't have stayed alone," the harp player said.

"I'm not a fortuneteller," Chunga said. "When customers pay, they get what they want."

"Of course, Chunguita," the harpist apologized. "I wasn't saying it because of you, but for all of us. Naturally nobody could have guessed."

"Nine o'clock, maestro," the Kid said. "It won't be good for you; let me get a taxi."

"Is it true that you and my uncle used the familiar form with each other?" Seminario asked. "Tell these people about that great Piuran, old man, that man who had no equal."

"The only men left are the ones in the Civil Guard," the Sergeant stated.

"He'd caught Seminario's disease with all the drinks," Jocko said. "He began to talk about maleness too."

The harpist cleared his throat, it was dry, they should give him a drink. Josefino filled a glass, and Don Anselmo blew off the foam before he drank. He stayed with his mouth open, breathing heavily: what people noticed most was Chápiro's energy. And that he was so honest. Seminario grew happy, he embraced the harpist, they should see, they should listen, what had he told them?

"He was a bully and a sad devil, but he had family pride," the Kid conceded.

He used to come in from the country on his horse, the girls would go up to the tower to look at him and they were not allowed up there, but Chápiro drove them half crazy, and Don Anselmo took another small drink, and in Santa María de Nieva Lieutenant Cipriano drove the squaws crazy too, and the Sergeant took a small drink too.

"When the beer got to him, he used to start talking about that Lieutenant," Wildflower said. "He admired him a lot."

The big show-off would come along raising the dust, he would rein in his horse and make it kneel in front of the girls. Life arrived with Chápiro, the ones who were sad became happy, and the happy ones got even happier; and such endurance, he would go upstairs, come down, some more gambling, more drinking, upstairs again, with one girl, with two, and all night like that, and at dawn he would go back to his ranch to work without having slept a wink, he was made of iron, and Don Anselmo asked for more beer, and once he played Russian roulette, the Sergeant pounded his chest and looked around as if waiting for applause. The only one, besides, who always paid his bills, the only one who paid right down to the last cent, money is meant to be spent, he used to say, he was always buying drinks for other people, and on the streets and squares the same tune: Anselmo was the one who brought civilization to Piura. But it wasn't because of any bet, just because he was bored, Lieutenant Cipriano was fed up with the jungle.

"But I heard it was all a lie," Wildflower said, "that his revolver was empty, and that he only did it so the soldiers would respect him more."

And the best of friends, he ran into him in the doorway of the Reina, he embraced him, he'd found out too late, brother, if he'd been in Piura they wouldn't have burned it, Anselmo, he would have put the priest and those Gallinacera women in their place.

"What trouble was Chápiro talking about, harp player?" Seminario asked. "The thing that happened to you?"

It was raining cats and dogs, and he said it's impossible to live like a human here, no women, no movies, if you fell asleep in the woods a tree would grow out of your belly, he was from the coast, they should stick the jungle someplace where the sun didn't shine, they could have it, he couldn't take it any more, and he drew his revolver, he spun the chamber twice, and holding it against his head, he pulled the trigger, Fats said that there weren't any bullets in it, that's a lie, there were and he knew it: the Sergeant pounded his chest again.

"Trouble, Don Anselmo?" Wildflower asked. "Did something happen to you?"

"We were talking about a wonderful fellow, girl," Don Anselmo said. "Chápiro Seminario, an old man who died three years ago."

"Come on, harp player, are you getting to be a fibber?" Monk said. "You wouldn't tell us about the Green House before, and now you are. Go ahead, what was the fire like?"

"Oh, you boys," Don Anselmo said. "Nonsense, foolishness."

"You're turning stubborn on us again, old man," José said. "Just now you were talking about the Green House. Where was it Chápiro was arriving with his horse, then? Who were those girls who came out to see him?"

"He was getting back to his ranch," Don Anselmo said. "And the ones who came out to see him were cotton pickers."

He pounded on the table, the laughter stopped, Chunga brought another round of beer, and Lieutenant Cipriano blew on the barrel of his pistol as peaceful as you want, they saw him and they didn't believe him, and Seminario threw a glass against the wall: Lieutenant Cipriano was a motherfucker, he wasn't going to let that half-breed keep on interrupting.

"Did he insult his mother again?" Wildflower asked, blinking rapidly.

"Not his, but that Lieutenant's," the Kid said.

"You in the name of that Chápiro guy and me in the name of Lieutenant Cipriano," the Sergeant proposed very calmly. "A game of Russian roulette, let's see who's more of a man, Señor Seminario."

"He was drunk and we weren't taking him seriously," Jocko said. "Señor Seminario was laughing, trying to tease him."

But the Sergeant had taken out his gun again, he held it by the barrel and the butt and was struggling to open it. Everybody around him began to look at each other and laugh nervously, to move in their seats, suddenly uncomfortable. Only the harp player kept on drinking, Russian roulette?, between sips, what kind of a thing was that, boys?

"Something to prove whether men are men," the Sergeant said. "You'll see in a minute, old man."

"I could tell that Lituma was serious by his calmness," the Kid said.

His face leaning toward the table, Seminario was silent and still, and his eyes, still quarrelsome, seemed concerned now too. The Sergeant finally got his revolver open, and his fingers were taking out the bullets, standing them up among glasses, bottles, and ashtrays filled with butts. Wildflower sobbed.

"Me, on the other hand, I was taken in by how calm he was," Chunga said. "Or else I would have grabbed his pistol away while he was unloading it."

"What's the matter with you, cop?" Seminario said. "What kind of joke is this?"

His voice was broken, and the Kid agreed, yes, that time he had lost all his push. The harpist put his glass down on the table, sniffed the air, restless, were they really getting ready to fight, boys? They shouldn't do that, they should keep on talking in a friendly way about Chápiro Seminario. But the girls were running away from the table, Rita, Sandra, Maribel, jumping, Poppy, Hydrangea, squealing like birds, and, huddled by the staircase, they were whispering, their eyes wide, very frightened. Jocko and the Kid took the harp player by the arms, almost carried him to the orchestra corner.

"Why didn't they talk to him?" Wildflower stammered. "If you talk to him in a nice way, he understands. Why didn't they try at least."

Chunga tried, he should put that pistol away, who was he trying to scare?

"You heard how he insulted my mother before, Chunguita," Lituma said, "and Lieutenant Cipriano's too, and he doesn't even know him. Let's see if people who go around insulting mothers have cold blood and a steady hand."

"What's the matter, cop?" Seminario roared. "Why all the theatrics?"

And Josefino interrupted him: it was no use hiding it, Señor Seminario, why act drunk?, he should admit that he was afraid, and he was telling him with all due respect.

"And his friend tried to hold them back too," Jocko said. " 'Let's get out of here, brother, don't get mixed up in any fights.' But Seminario had already got his dander up, and he gave him a slap."

"And me another one," Chunga protested. " 'Let me go,' and a dirty word, shit on his mother, 'let me go!' "

"You fucking dyke," Seminario said. "Get away from me or I'll put a hole in you."

Lituma was holding the revolver with the tips of his fingers, the fat-bellied chamber with five openings in front of his eyes, his voice was sparse, didactic: first you looked to make sure that it was empty; that is, that there wasn't any bullet left inside.

"He wasn't talking to us, he was talking to his gun," the Kid said. "That's the impression he gave, Wildflower."

And then Chunga got up, ran across the dance floor, and outside, slamming the door behind her.

"When you need them, they're never around," she said. "I had to go all the way to the Grau monument before I could find a pair of cops."

The Sergeant took a bullet, lifted it delicately, held it up to the light of the blue bulb. You had to pick up the round and insert it in the weapon, and Monk lost control, cousin, enough already, they should go back to Mangachería right now, cousin, and José the same, almost weeping, he shouldn't play around with that pistol, they should do what Monk said, cousin, they should leave.

"I can't forgive them for not telling me what was going on," the harp player said. "The shouting of the Leóns and the girls had me all nervous, but I never imagined, I thought they were mixing it up."

"Who could have guessed anything, maestro," Jocko said. "Seminario had taken his gun out too, he was waving it in Lituma's face, and we were waiting for it to go off at any minute."

Lituma, still so calm, and Monk don't let them, stop them, there was going to be trouble, you, Don Anselmo, he'd listen to you. Like Wildflower, Rita and Maribel were weeping, Sandra he should think about his wife, and José about the child she was expecting, cousin, don't be stubborn, let's go to Mangachería. With a dry sound, the Sergeant brought barrel and butt together: you closed the weapon, calmly, confidently, and everything is all set, Señor Seminario, why was he taking so long in getting ready.

"Like people in love who you talk and you talk to, and it's no use because their heads are in the clouds," the Kid said, with a sigh. "Lituma was fascinated by his pistol."

"And he had all of us fascinated," Jocko said, "and Seminario obeyed him as if he were his peasant. As soon as Lituma said that to him, he opened his pistol and took out all the bullets except one. The poor fellow's fingers were shaking."

"Something inside him probably told him he was going to die," the Kid said.

"That's the way, now put your hand on the chamber without looking and give it a spin, so you won't know where the bullet is, spin it fast, like a roulette wheel," the Sergeant said. "That's why they call it that, harp player, do you see now?"

"Enough talking," Seminario said. "Let's get started, you fucking half-breed."

"That's the fourth time you've insulted me, Señor Seminario," Lituma said.

"It made me shiver to see the way they spun the chambers," Jocko said. "They looked like two kids spinning tops."

"Now you can see what Piurans are like, girl," the harp player said. "Gambling away their lives out of pure pride."

"What do you mean, pride?" Chunga said. "It was because they were drunk and they had to screw up my life."

Lituma took his hand off the chamber, you were supposed to draw lots to see who began, but what difference did that make, he'd invited him, so he raised the pistol, put the mouth of the barrel to his temple, you close your eyes, and he closed his eyes, and you shoot, and he squeezed the trigger: click, and a chattering of teeth. He turned pale, they all turned pale, and he opened his mouth and they all opened their mouths.

"Shut up, Jocko," the Kid said. "Can't you see she's crying."

Don Anselmo petted Wildflower's hair, he handed her his colored handkerchief, girl, she shouldn't cry, it was all over now, what difference did it make, and the Kid lit a cigarette and offered it to her. The Sergeant had put the revolver down on the table and was drinking slowly from an empty glass, but nobody laughed. His face looked as if he had just come out of the water.

"Nothing happened, don't get worried," the Kid begged. "It won't be good for you, maestro. I swear that nothing happened."

"You made me feel something I've never felt before," Monk stammered. "Now I'm begging you, cousin, let's leave."

And José, as if waking up, that was enough, cousin, he'd done something tremendous, from the stairway the buzzing of the girls rose, Sandra was howling, the Kid and Jocko take it easy, maestro, easy, and Seminario pounded the table, quiet, wrathful, God damn it, it's my turn, quiet. He lifted up his revolver, he put it to his temple, he did not close his eyes, his chest puffed up.

"We heard the shot as we were coming into the neighborhood with the cops," Chunga said. "And the shouting. We kicked at the door, the police knocked it down with their rifles, and you didn't open it for us."

"A guy had just been killed, Chunga," the Kid said. "Who was going to be thinking about opening up the door?"

"He fell forward on top of Lituma," Jocko said, "and the force knocked them both down onto the floor. The friend started shouting for them to call Dr. Zevallos, but everybody was paralyzed with fright. And besides it wouldn't have done any good."

"What about him?" Wildflower asked, in a very low voice.

He was looking at the blood that had spattered him, and he was touching himself all over thinking that it must have been his blood, and it did not occur to him to get up, and he was still sitting down feeling himself when the cops came in, holding their rifles, nobody move, keeping everybody covered, nobody move, if anything had happened to the Sergeant, they'd pay for it. But nobody paid any attention to them, and the champs and the girls were running and stumbling over chairs, the harpist was lurching about, he grabbed someone, which one was it, he shook him, another, which one had died, and a cop stood in front of the stairway and made those who wanted to get away come back. Chunga, the Kid, and Jocko leaned over Seminario: face down, still holding his revolver in his hand, and a sticky stain was spreading in his hair. His friend, on his knees, was covering his face with his hands, Lituma was still feeling himself.

"The guards asked, 'What happened, Sergeant; did he give you some trouble and you had to shoot him?'" Jocko said. "And he looked sick to his stomach, saying yes to everything."

"The man committed suicide," Monk said. "We didn't have anything to do with it, please let us leave, our families are waiting for us."

But the guards had bolted the door and were guarding it, their fingers were on the triggers of their rifles, and they were being abusive with their mouths and eyes.

"Be reasonable, be human, please let us leave," José repeated. "They were having their fun, we weren't mixed up in it. Who do you want us to swear it to?"

"Bring a blanket from upstairs, Maribel," Chunga said. "To cover him with."

"You didn't lose your head, Chunga," the Kid said.

"I had to throw it away later, there was no way to get the stains out," Chunga said.

"Funny things can happen," the harp player said. "They live differently, they die differently."

"Who are you talking about, maestro?" the Kid asked.

"The Seminarios," the harpist said. His mouth was open, as if he were going to say something else, but he said nothing.

"I don't think Josefino is going to pick me up," Wildflower said. "It's getting very late."

The door was open and the sun was coming through it like a hungry fire, all the corners of the large room were aglow. Above the roofs of the neighborhood, the sky appeared very high, cloudless, very blue, and the golden rump of the desert could be seen too, and the squat, sparse carob trees.

"We'll take you, girl," the harp player said. "That way you'll save yourself taxi fare."

18

SEVERO SARDUY

The most brilliant new writer to appear after the Cuban Revolution, Severo Sarduy has lived in France since 1962, and his name is generally associated with the Tel Quel group of experimental writers. But Cuba and the Cuban brand of Spanish he uses are his real passion. He was born in Camagüey in 1937, and was only twenty-one when Castro entered Havana. His first novel, *Gestures* (1962), describes in a fragmented, parodic fashion the adventures of a mulatto woman, involved in rehearsing a theatrical production and in carrying on revolutionary activities. Already the influence of the French *nouveau roman* was visible, in a narrative that also showed the influence of the new painting.

Sarduy's second novel, *From Cuba with a Song* (1966), was even more experimental. Very little of conventional narrative is left in this exploration of three of the most important cultures which intermingled to produce a distinctive Cuban culture. The first episode is under the sign of the Chinese; the second, of the black; the third and longest, of the Spanish. The presence of a couple of transvestites, whose metamorphoses are developed with carnivalesque humor, give the novel its overall unity. In the third episode, Sarduy takes a leaf out of Joyce's *Ulysses*. The long voyage from tenth-century Spain to the Cuba of tomorrow is illustrated by the changes in the Spanish language since the Middle Ages. One of the most effective episodes of this journey is the entry of Christ into Havana. Here Sarduy not only parodies the primitive religious faith of the Cuban people but makes Christ a folkloric double of Castro.

Sarduy's third novel, *Cobra* (1972), is even more dazzling. The protagonist, a transvestite from the Pigalle district of Paris, travels east, until he rediscovers the Indian roots of Western culture. The metamorphoses of the main character correspond again to the metamorphoses of language. For language is finally the real, and only, protagonist of Sarduy's novels. There is only language in his books; no significance is hidden behind the surface of signifiers. Each signifier refers to another signifier, which in turn refers to a third, and so on. These tantalizing flights are sustained by a rigorously baroque structure.

Sarduy's most recent book is an essay, *Baroque* (1974), published simultaneously in French and Spanish. It is an attempt to link the roots of baroque art to the scientific discoveries of Kepler, Galileo, and Newton. The substitution of a planetary system based on the circle by a system based on the ellipse (two centers instead of one, and one of the centers empty), corresponds in poetry to the use of the rhetorical figure of the ellipse. The shifting of signifiers in writing corresponds thus to this shifting of the center in the cosmic map. While still in Cuba, Sarduy studied under Lezama Lima (see Part Four, 15); it is through his subsequent development and elaboration of his mentor's concept of the baroque that he has finally achieved his own philosophical stance. What he has found is not the certainty of a God, placed solidly in the center of the universe, as in Lezama, but the certainty of the void created by an elliptical system with one empty center.

In an earlier book—a collection of essays, *Written on a Body* (1969) —Sarduy had previously developed some of his key concepts about literature and transvestitism, literature and transgression, literature and eroticism. An erotic writer who has rediscovered (as Roland Barthes has pointed out) the pleasures of the text, Sarduy is today not only the most experimental of all Latin American writers but also the one who has completely erased the boundaries between prose and poetry. His novels are constructed with the rigor and the fantasy of poems. They are devoted not to the construction of narrative (like those, say, of Vargas Llosa) but to the "deconstruction" of language.

The Entry of Christ into Havana

From From Cuba with a Song, *translated by Suzanne Jill Levine, in* Triple Cross *(New York: Dutton, 1972), pp. 305–328.*

Christ Sets Out from Santiago

Along the naves, tapers in little cups with gilded edges were blinking; in the dark those signs were bat eyes nailed against the altars or swarms of glowworms coming out of a bottle. That light of drizzled sand over Help and Mercy would change them at times into water nymphs, and other times into little candy skulls, depending on how the shadows cut them.

The murmur of crackling wax would join the sound of a rusty clock and this the steps of their bare feet. The feet of the Devout Ones scarcely touched the floor, like a hanged man's feet. Beneath the gravestones they were stepping on, among mushrooms and withered relics, lay eight mitered generations: empty eyes would look at the same archivolts, the identical days would from the lantern yellow the circles of angels in the dome, as light as mist; bundles of bones held in place the gold of the tunics that were incrusted in them, and pressed together, dried cartilage, reliquaries, and chalices.

Heads bowed, Help and Mercy advanced toward the vestry. They went reading the In Memoriam engraved in the marble. They touched dark-green texts with the tip of their forefingers and crossed themselves. They heard a warbling: it was Rita Pla's vocal exercises. When they pushed open the doors, they found her before Bruno, who was raising a baton, her mouth open like someone who's about to spell in the first reading book Acorn Air And.

There was a lukewarm air, of wax, among the closets, and a mustard light among the holy-water pots, censers, and purple puppets with their eyelids on backward. Light filtered through a yellow awning, stretched before the baroque ironwork of the window; the wind stretched it—a drum—blowing it—a sail—. Birds were crossing lines on the cloth, and the trolleycars with their long sparking trolleys, in the background of the orange square, outlined by the iron bars, were gods of codices running with burning rattles.

Mercy opened the little platinum mesh pouch that she wore at her waist and out of it came a swollen key with a double point. She carefully sank it into the lock. The click rang like a bell.

Sprawled in a corner of the display case, elbows folded against his chest and his arms in disks, the Redeemer, foot- and headless, was resting. Hooks came out of his wrists and ankles, and from his neck, cut at the Adam's apple, a great screw. He had neither sex nor knee. A tortoise-shell varnish covered him and on his stomach, pale pink. He was worm-eaten. He smelled of incense and naphthalene. On the wounded side you could see a hinge.

On a slab of white wood, stained with ink from the sign HANDLE WITH CARE, his feet and a hand of ovaled nails were exhibited. The other, which gripped a golden flagstaff, and the head, were found in the back of a drawer among broken candelabrums, little Santa Lucía eyes and scapularies.

They put him together in the twinkling of an eye. Bruno screwed on his head until the two little threads of blood which ran down from his eyes continued into those of his neck. Rita combed his beard and with a beer-drenched curler twisted his wig of blond hemp into several snail-shell curls, which she fastened with a barbed-wire crown. Help perfumed him with her "Attractive and Winning." She took out her string of safety pins. They dressed him in a ruffled slip, crackling with starch, and on top, a blanket of rubies and stones from El Cobre Mountain, and snail shells on a string. In his bullfighter's garb he balanced on his flat feet, in the middle of the vestry.

The Christ Fans stepped back to look at him. When they came forward again, they fell on their knees.

With Green Background and Shouting

"Praised be Jesus Christ our Lord who died on the cross to redeem us!" Help shouted praises till she was hoarse, stretching the e's of "redeem" to the point of choking, catching the impulse in soprano and, poor wretch, ending in bass.

"Have pity on us, ay!" (That was Mercy, and she struck her chest as if she were seized with Saint Vitus's Dance.)

"Long live the King of the Jews and the Cubans!" (That was Rita, and she sobbed with emotion.)

And He, before Bruno, looked at himself in the mirror.

"Look how handsome, look how handsome he is!" shouted a little black girl hanging from the bars of the window.

On the street, cars with loudspeakers passed by; the nasal twang of amplifiers came in along with the crackling of broken glass and screeching of rails.

In the tarnished space of the mirror the small doors opened and the red square of the bonnet, the lace sleeve, the black shirt frills of lively golds appeared: it was the Bishop.

"Oh, my beloved!"—and he patted his stomach.

Through the crack between the shutters you could see a brightness in the naves: the dirty silver of the altars, reddish disks dancing clumsily—copper crosses—.

In the vestry's dampness the faithful were five hanged warriors, going around and around in the same place, dervishes, spinning tops, merry-go-rounds. The grass-green, bottle-green floor of rhombi met the orange walls at sharp angles, forming a cuneiform space where he reigned, duplicated in the river of quicksilver.

"Hurry up, girls, we'll be leaving in a minute!" And the Lord Bishop shook a hand bell that was heard again, far away, returning from the dome.

And he shook a hand bell that was heard again, another time, as if it had sounded in the Kingdom of Death.

"We're leaving!" In the naves a band of cracked drums, water-filled guitars, and muted rattles broke out.

What a hissing of prayers! What a creaking of benches! Chest beatings. Ejaculations. The weepers sounded maracas—they played maracas for this burial —and the hoodmasters their mahogany clavichords. Little devils with palm-leaf skirts and castles of yellow feathers on their heads crowded into the baptistery.

He appeared in the door of the vestry, tottering under a canopy of royal palms held up by Help and Mercy, within a white, white light, as from milk curds. Canticles and cheers. Under his vault of greenery he advanced among purple strips of stained-glass windows, shadows of banner, flags.

The sepulcher awaited Him.

You could hear a flapping of wings, like droves of geese: it was the Black Oblates, they were dressed as angels.

These big Pious Babies were already lined up in the choir aisle, rosy and smelling of Eau de Cologne, in white piqué dresses and carrying large palm-leaf baskets, reciting a rosary of river pebbles and sweating into initialed hankies.

Grumpy dwarfs were stamping their feet behind the altar, wrapped in bunches of red-felt ribbon.

The shrouds were replicas of his face, the standard-bearers' ensigns the color of his blood, the cornets of the Municipal Brass Band the silver of his tomb.

"Long live the King of Alto Songo!"—that was the hotheaded misses of the diocese, who had been tippling as they walked since morning. One of them rattled a maraca.

Electric tapers were lit. Crepe-paper flowers carpeted the route to the sepulcher. Make way, people, here comes the Verb of Santiago! The resurrected, sandpapered king was about to begin the voyage on his aluminum throne. The blood barely stained his nose and eyelids. Why it looked like he was going to laugh!

Now the leader shakes his baton (at his age, that's what he shakes best). And the chorus sings the first Gloria—what a triumph for Bruno! Mercy leaves the pulpy palm leaves on the pulpit staircase. She kisses him, sets him on the sepulcher.

Help shouts, "Ready!" Someone breaks into tears.

The King totters, then takes off, balancing under a rainfall of jasmine. He advances toward the portico, between lamps of green glass. The flame flits over the chalk of his face, the shine of rotten fish. White and green, the rust of nails, flowers of tetanus, opens in his dried hands and pierced feet.

"Here comes the handsomest fellow of Caney county." The children clap hands. And take out their bags of confetti.

Creole gentlemen follow him. You've got to admit, that humble vestry wine sure gives a man poise! They march in unison, foot to foot, their stomachs tucked in by In Excelsis Deo sashes.

The Minstrels march, the precious load on their shoulders: in front, Mercy sets the example in her Prussian-blue rayon cloak with a cushion sewn on the left shoulder, and Rita Pla, a cushion on her right shoulder, struts in such a way that you'd think it's the lantern of The Bakers' Masked Ball that's being carried and not the Victor of Santiago on his tomb. The poor Redeemer up there, he must be eating himself up! At the rear, Help, in the best of her wigs, and Bruno hold the two back handles of the sepulcher. Look in wonder, brethren, at what four pillars carry the Blond of Blonds, at what caryatids fit for a mausoleum, in short, what four legs for a bench!

Already they're down the central nave. At his passing the faithful close their eyes, kneel; trembling, they kiss the carpet where he has passed. And make the sign of the cross. Others run. Push. Touch him. Tear white lilies from his funeral carriage.

Already they're near the portico. From the high altar you can see him from the back, outlined against the blue rectangle of night, shower of light; hands and handkerchiefs raised. The stones from El Cobre shrine, mortuary jewels, are already glittering on his cloak, stirred by the breeze in the square.

"Lower him!" Mercy orders, "or his crown will short-circuit on the bulbs of the tympan!"

The bearers stoop. He's outside. The whole square lights up.

"Raise him again!"

And he ascends, standing erect over the sepulcher, proud as a pimp, hoisting a white flag. Behind, red stones, gold stains: the seal of his face on the Pantocrator of Italian mosaic. A silence. Rosary beads passing through fingers. Candles crackling.

The wind on the terraces, whistling through patio palm trees.

Then bells, the hymn. Gentlemen in drill suits and Panamas come out on their balconies, and little girls in straw hats empty baskets of petals. Cigar smoke sweetens the air in slow rings that will break among the fans. The square is full. The people of Santiago sing.

"Straight on, but *moderato*, gents, *per piacere!*" orders Bruno. And the Blond descends the steps, following a gentle parabola as if on an escalator. The Bishop receives him.

No sooner did he set foot on the ground when beneath the portico appears the sorrowful, ash-moon virgin. They've whitened her with rice powder, "so that she really looks pale," her mouth and cheeks, a heart. Her tears, and her seven daggers, are silver.

He crosses the square. Around him trumpets, the rim of the drums, crashing cymbals, shine. The Bishop makes way for him; covered in his hands, the chalice: over the red cloth of his sleeves, gilded lace. In front walk two acolytes swaying censers. Sinuous ribbons of white smoke. The pale parson drops Latin mumbo jumbo as he goes, and makes crosses in the air with his right hand. Women in black mantillas and high shell combs, and stiff men with candles and branches of lilies, walk on either side.

"Come, people of Santiago, who's more stud than he, and who whiter?" howl the Cornucopias of Craniums, beating their breasts.

HELP *(who has pinched a cloak with a black-and-white fiber hood):* "You leave Santiago to enter Death!"

MERCY *(wielding a shroud in which you see Christ's face in an arrow-pierced heart with the inscription "C loves M."—Christ and Mercy):* "You enter Death to give us Life!"

The old people, bundled up, crowd together on the sidewalks, beneath the greenish halo of the street lamps. Joining hands they watch him go by in his Sunday best, and then withdraw in silence, to kneel on the cushions of the antechamber.

In cracked oil paintings the Virgin shines on her half-moon, against a blackened sky of sugar-mill chimneys, and in the yellowish cardboard of screens a mulatto Christ watches over Santiago: a labyrinth of small sugar plantations and boats.

> Look at them oh crack-footed King,
> because you leave they cannot sing

It's Rita, when they stop in front of City Hall where gentlemen greet him from the gates, waving hats. Little devils jingle bells, dancing on one foot before the sepulcher. Against the white façades, the hoodmasters play their clavichords: black stitches around the holes of their eyes.

Then the procession moves on. Empty terraces, lighted lamps, wicker rocking chairs rocking are left behind, and in the shadows of interiors: burnished clocks, mirrors, opulent pineapple goblets, the ancestral portrait.

In the night's dampness they disappear into poplar groves, into the suburbs.

Now, little by little, they are left alone. In the city the tapers' light has traced a white sign, a chalk omega, two inverted fish joined by a thread. Or perhaps a signature.

So they left the last lots behind, the whistle of the land breeze through the mangrove trees, the streaks of saltpeter on the eaves. When they started moving into the thick night, Bruno made him turn his head so that he'd see the rows of windows slowly disappear. Mercy tells that down his cheeks rolled two big tears, and also down his neck, as far as his shoulder blade.

When they straightened his head he saw before him other greens, the surprise of other birds in the calm, the Cuban peasants: little eyes behind windows, lighter than the royal palm leaves of the shutters, Chinese shadows—but in big Panama hats—in front of carbon lamps. They covered the cracks in their walls with newspapers, passed the latch, and between the planks of their whitewashed doors, they peeped out to see him go by. The huts were boxes of hemp, the cracks small yellow stained-glass windows with printed letters.

They followed the windings of a stream, the highway, they disappeared into the mist of a small forest, among the dark cones of the . . . (and here, the exhaustive enumeration of Cuban trees—horseflesh mahogany, guamá, jiqui oak, the annona tree, and so forth—with their botanical jargon)* . . . until Help and Mercy, Rita and Bruno, "dead tired," left the sepulcher on the grass.

In the early morning—or was it the turning of a rattlesnake among dry leaves, the flapping of an owl?—they heard Him cough. He woke up with stiff elbows and wrists; the joints of his ankles rigid. Well you see, it's just that accustomed as he was to vestry climate, tempered by the sighs and yawns of so many fasters, the dampness had gotten into the sawdust of his bones. His fingers stiffened, one foot hard in the air as if on a step, he was petrified in a goodbye: poorly sewn puppet, raffle picture card. His meeting with the Cuban countryside, with insular space and its glowworms, had brought on arthritis.

They stretched His limbs as much as they could. They put Him through calisthenics, recited an Ex Aegypto Israel. The heat was—listen to Help —"thicker than pea soup." There was something sweetish in the air, as if near a beehive or cane-juice stand.

The followers stretched—the few that were left: at the sight of the jungle the rest had resigned themselves to urban mysticism—shook the hay off their uniforms and cassocks, and ran into the woods to piss.

(Tarnished cornets, and on the drums, dew.)

He felt that something was jolting Him in the knees, that his legs were giving way. A shiver ("Oh Father, have pity on me, you who have gotten me into this mess," he thought). His whole body itched—was it jigger fleas? He promised to scourge himself. He wasn't going to wait much longer. Listen to these morning prayers:

HELP (who was putting the pink back into her cheeks with roucou): Now you carry Him for a while, why it's worse than carrying a chimpanzee piggyback. He's got me crippled.

MERCY (who was bathing in a stream): You poke your own hellfire, you lazybones, ramrod, thick clod. Etc., etc.

Stretching and bending they finally reached a town. What a relief for their swollen feet: the square was paved in cobblestones and dark-green water ran along the juncture of the stones. It overflowed from the broken basin of the fountain.

What a smell of coffee, what nice smoke spiraling out the doorways! Bowls of chipped china on shiny crimson tablecloths, the leaning tables, the stools, piled on top.

The women were doing the foot-scratching dance, coming out in flow-ered slippers, the backs of them worn down: "Oh boy, what a visitor." They

*Phonetic delights never omitted in any Cuban tract, from the Mirror of Patience—1608 —to the present day.

opened their houses. Brought out lamps and hung them on the guacimo trees in the patio, and gave away lumps of pan sugar from their cupboards. Why they combed their hair: to receive him!

The Next Day

An arcade stood facing the village, and another one almost parallel: the shadow of the first on the smooth, windowless façades. These successive arches supported unfinished walls, or ruins, a second portico, and the slope of roofs. On a stoop rested the handle of a coach, and over the shadow of its great wheels, on the adjacent wall, hung carbines, telescopes, pendulums, and perhaps pocket pistols and swords with tortoise-shell hilts. From there the early risers set forth in a throng, with great clamor and large red shawls around their necks. They brought accordions. Graters and maracas. What cute music they scratched! It would split anybody's sides! It was a thick-lipped mulatto with even, scorched kinky hair— Mercy's darling—who was shooting off like this, with his razor-sharp voice:

> I have a little thing that you like
> that you like
> that you like

He wriggled like an eel, with a hand on his hip—what Dahoman rings! —pointing with the other to the object of such elliptic verse.

The aroma of honest-to-goodness coffee—accustomed as he was to that of incense—and that spicy odor emanating from the tables revived Him. He was delighted that they ran behind Him, that they wore down the wood of his feet with kisses, that they perfumed him with *agua-ardiente*. He wanted them to entreat Him, but with guitars and gourds; he wanted angels with royal palms. He thought himself a patriot, a Martí-like orator frozen in the threads of an engraving; He pictured himself in a speechmaking pose, raised to a tricolor tribune, or releasing a fighting cock with his callused hands, its feathers crossing his dried, olive face. He would like you to see a blue sky behind him, and a sun of hard fog, a waning moon, several comets. He had the calling of a redeemer, Blondie did, He liked flags.

Help immediately joined in on the fun, not to mention—which would be knocking your head against Redundance—Rita and Bruno, who didn't have to join it, since they had it in them since birth (according to Mercy).

It wasn't till they were in the store, with the "hurry up, we still have the fringes to put up," that they found out: the one they left slipping on the cobblestones outside in the square was not the object of this great fuss; the people were expecting a new candidate, who had promised "to give the town running water and to build a road that would connect them to their neighbors in nearby towns," to arrive at noon. For him the tournament, the cockfights, the "National" band, the tables of breadsticks and the taffy wrapped in colored papers.

Competition horses in checkered girths came from all over the county.

And on foot, pulling their reins, smiling bowlegged riders already appeared in black and gold or blue and gold colors that reappeared on stirrups and blinders, bringing Guinea hens and Mandarin oranges and shopping bags of limes too.

"May you be struck down with lightning!" Mercy exploded, she was cracking up, already wallowing in corners with some of the band players (according to Help), knocking machetes and spats off the walls.

"God, what am I doing here?"—and she ran toward the portico through the steam of boiled milk, the wake of clean pitchers and the marimbas.

She sensed that the party was leaving her. She saw Bruno call to her, between two openmouthed guitarists, against a background of pots and swords.

In full force she crossed the square, fell on her knees before Christ, and cried on His navel—that's as high as her disheveled head could reach.

"Forgive me, Dear God, I didn't know what I was doing." *(and without any sense of dramatic transition)* Help adds: "Fungus! Pustules on his feet! He's rotting, eek!"

She took one step back, and another, without turning around. She opened her hands, drew them near her eyes, scrutinized the palms:

"And I've touched Him! I'm infected: alcohol!"

And He, to get a good look at her, squeezed his glass pupils, those opaque stones that have been dimmed by so much looking at the top of a locker. He was soaked with dew. Bagasse Christ. One foot was eczematous and green, and in the arch a milky flower, of mushrooms. His nose ran and so did the swollen edge of his eyelids.

"Alcohol, for God's sake!" And she shot off to the store.

"And the best!" answered Bruno who awaited her with open arms in the doorway. And he emptied on her head a glass of rum-on-the-rocks. From there he was dragged away. Help and Mercy, yoked together, pulled Him. He went on foot, tied to a beam, handcuffed. They had taken off his crown and put on a palm-leaf hat because it was drizzling, they had tossed lemon juice on his foot and cologne on his head. So that His sore couldn't be seen, they had surrounded Him with vases of wax flowers. So that the Rotten One emerged from an opaque garden whose leaves the cart's jolting could not shake off. They fell into gutters. Got stuck in bogs.

Mercy was getting eaten up by mosquitoes, but stoically she sang:

> tonight it is raining
> tomorrow will be muddy,

When Help answered her the rain fell thicker:

> poor is the carter
> who pulls this cart

And the Foul One went through the drizzle, his feet among flowered urns, his legs among still flowers. Oh how it burns! Water surrounded him right up to his pustules.

"A bigamist I'll be, but not a fag," he thought. And looked out the corner of his eye at Bruno, who was laughing, envious.

It was because the Two Women were rubbing Him with camphor balls, wrapping Him in blankets, inserting in each armpit "because you see, he had fever on only one side" a vulvous thermometer with filigrees and Roman numerals. They even pleaded with Saint Lazarus to rid Him of galloping leprosy.

They had to cross the rising Jobabo River, and hauled the cart by looping the rope through a ring that moved along a rope tied to a palm tree on each bank. And the last just men kept the balance.

Like a rolling barrel full of stones was the noise of the waters. Red turtles leaped to the beams, held on with their little nails, disappeared into slow eddies. Trout jumped up in rapid flight, flicked their tails, spattered water, and remained gasping between planks.

"They fish themselves, God's creatures! Let's pray He doesn't decide to multiply them now!" (Help)

Below, the current dragged away torn roots, and shrubs with nests.

"And the bluish hands of drowned men, saying goodbye!" (Adds Mercy, who scarcely breathes so as not to move, "not everybody walks on water.") They left the rest of the pilgrimage in Oriente province waving handkerchiefs and sneezing. Rita wanted to catch on to the rope and swim to the other side, but they finally convinced her to stay on land. Bruno left the violin cover and three candelabrums with her, to lighten the load. What a farewell! They could still see her from the other bank, behind the strip of mud, moving the three bronzes like a traffic cop. Then she became a blur with the others. At the landing a gust of wind carried away His hat. Bruno raised Him by the head and planted Him on the grass. Then they saw those plaques of pus that whitened his leg to the waist.

They stuck their ears to his stomach, the Magdalenas auscultated Him. Something was bubbling inside.

MERCY (her eyes popping): "The Evil Disease!"

The sweet felt of their earlobes and the pearls of their earrings rubbing His groin certainly seemed to make Him mighty happy. What a pity there wasn't a camera at hand: he was smiling!

Illustrious shores, but a feeble welcome did He receive from those of Santa María del Puerto del Príncipe.

Listen to those welcomes the Camagüeyan ladies forced on Him, sheltered behind the shutters and rails of their windows:

a. You will leave our towers mute, but the bronze of our many bells will sink your ships. (They had taken Him for a pirate!)

b. Ill wind from a leprosarium, angel of rebels, leader of escaped slaves.

c. Locust of cattle, salting of the water, etc.

He, who in so many Gobelins, on so many night tables: wounded pigeon, gentleman of painted plaster, with eyes of chemical blue like a Mexican doll, He, whose signs—parallel fish, crowns, crosses and nails—embellished the glass of every paperweight and, in cement, worn down by rains, the medallions of every façade,

> He, who appeared in so many family portraits.
> And yet they did not recognize Him.

He scratched what he thought most symbolic of the situation (he already had Cuban habits!) and gave Bruno the "forward march" signal.

The shadows of dates clouded his face, in the black gardens of Las Mercedes, the chandelier of the choir loft's arches. He wanted to lose himself in the labyrinths of the angel makers, among the goldsmith stands and old book stalls. Along the banks of the Tínima River the display cases of Spanish flea markets, beneath the yellow halo of candles, were shining in the mist: Catalan panels with beheaded saints and all the arteries of their necks; paintings of balloons rising with sacks of sand and green ribbons: in the baskets, in smoking jackets, handlebar mustaches, and spectacles, brave Matías Perezes would observe the clouds.

Bruno's Statement

It is here necessary to make note of a fact, so that written evidence shall remain which could serve the authoress in securing either total absolution or perpetual hellfire. Here it is: the Redeemer pointed to one of those balloons. It is well known that ascensions are His weak point.

I bear witness that, with the few pesos she had left, with no hope whatsoever of earning more, and much less in such chaste places, Help offered to get it for Him, perhaps because she had seen new stains on Him and knew that sooner or later she'd recover the gift. Whatever the case may be, she went out to buy it.

Every Venetian blind fell. Every salesman spat on her, threw the door in her face.

The lights went out. I hereby testify that that's how the Camagüeyan tour ended.

They saw black propellers among the palm trees: army helicopters were following them. Clean-shaven young pilots descended to the villages He was going to pass through, to intimidate the people and buy Paloma de Castilla crackers. When the travelers arrived, little men in uniforms would point to them with large pencils and, terrified, take off. Through the plastic bellies of the crafts you could see them gesticulate and open maps.

To bother Him, the pilots powdered Him from above with bread crumbs.

Another rumble. They all stooped down—except Him, naturally, He would have hurt his pustules—but they didn't see anything. It was the subway.

There is no rule without the exception: the herbalists of Ciego de Avila came out to receive him, and with a lot of noise. To entertain Him they brought out wooden serpents coiled around little mirrors, mortars, old pomander boxes with the names of leaves where letters were missing, the covers adorned with Florentine and French landscapes.

Mechanical gargoyles followed them, raising whirlwinds with their helices, five bakelite birds. Curtains of dust surrounded Him. If the three faithfuls would stop, the noise of the motors would decrease and the row of transparent machines would stand still in air, perpendicular to the highway. The whirlwinds would then spread and a spiral of straw would surround them.

If they'd flee to the grottoes of reinforced concrete, or hide by the rivers, in the inns on abandoned piles, the patrol—and the dull buzzing—would escort them, forming a V whose vortex, a craft with two propellers, would plane over His head, like a Holy Spirit Dove.

HELP *(and the motors came on louder):* . . . (she opened and closed her mouth—was she shouting? Gusts of wind stiffened her face. A totally bald pate.)

MERCY: . . . *(with calm gestures)*

Bruno touched them and pointed to the mouth of a subway. They went down the escalator, under the panel SUBWAY. With Him and the cart on their backs they passed through a lunch counter (ay, His toes were already spouting pus, falling off in pieces), the cabarets of River Side (pustules had begun on His other leg and, like a belt of rotting metals, they girded His stomach), corridors with amplifiers; on the radio the twelve o'clock noon gongs, the meowing sopranos on the Chinese programs, and the Candado soap commercials.

They bathed Him in sulphur. They came up in the elevator content, out the other mouth of the subway. Motionless, like a band of scabby turkey buzzards, the helicopters were waiting for them at the exit.

The din of the choppers was breaking Help's eardrums; the corruption of the Corpus Christi, Mercy's heart.

The crafts were not following them at equal distances now, but rather, one by one, they dove down like kingfishers, almost flush with roofs and trees; then a hatch door opened in the plexiglass shell, the copilot peered out a second "like the cuckoo of a clock" (Bruno), and took a flash photograph. The mosquito would then return to his place in the V. The next would come down.

Having reached the cherry orchards of Las Villas, He asked them to abandon him to His fate (he showed them the highway with a flabby hand, and with the other He grabbed on to a trunk), to let Him rot on the marabou.

At night they'd take off His blanket and leave Him in the open—so that the night dew would cool his sores—in the light of the V of blinking headlights. In the morning they'd find Him softened, tearful, pecked at by birds.

They hiked down the Villa Clara hills. In the distance, streaking the pink fields, you could see the black lines of the railroad disappearing under the roofs of the kirschwasser factories, branching off on the other side, crossing the pine groves and fishing villages, or else following the rivers that swept along rafts of white trunks, convoyed by signal flags and toads, until disappearing into the curve of inlets, under the red smoke cloud of the distilleries, among the tanks along the docks.

Near a curve in the road they heard call bells. When they turned the corner, they saw two yellow triangles with red edges light up and a barrier fall before them: blocking the way, an armored train had stopped at the crossing.

The bell stopped. What a silence! (They felt they were being watched.) Suddenly the cars opened, unglued boxes, and down the walls, now ramps, tanks rolled out. From their turrets came nets full of green sponges ("Giant pieces of mint!"—Help), portable radios, tape recorders whose tapes were running.

"Somehow we've got to appeal to the popular devotion!" declared Help, and she stamped the first letter on one buttock.

Let me explain: she was dancing in front of a jukebox, and wildly, pardon me, and enthusiastically composing the Lord's texts on her naked body —which looked as if printed on brown paper. With wooden blocks she engraved golden monograms.

No one had come to receive them in Santa Clara. She tore her clothes in anger, crossed herself, and bought a printing set: (to Him):

> I will make of my body Your book,
> they will read from me!

And Mercy *(to the frightened Villa Clara folk behind cracks—families squeezed into bunches—hidden under their mothers' skirts):*

> Come, children of God:
> Here is the flesh made word!

And Help went wild over burning tambourines and cornets from John Coltrane's band.

They came running, and en masse. At the beat of the drums, Help wriggled from head to toe, and from her navel, which projected an O, to the full stop of her knee, letters gleamed all over her.

He couldn't take His eyes off the oscillating band of texts, nor hold back His feet: he wanted to dance, he knew that dance is the new birth, that after death they'll confront us with the mambo band. What a pity! He couldn't even clap hands. He stretched his arms and felt like His armpits were breaking. He was finished now: his nipples were purple, his chest in welts, his throat burning, He was choking, the ganglia of His neck hurt. If the band came on louder—the needle in the striped grooves—for Him it was like bottles breaking against each other, cornets playing under water.

"What wiggly hips!" (said the faithful). Bruno took some steps around her, looking at her hips as if reading.

"But, what about the helicopters?"

They were there. Watching the show from the boxes. The pilots eating popcorn. Whose bags they threw away when the record was over.

Let's not even talk about Matanzas.

The Entry of Christ into Havana

What a reception in Havana! They were all waiting for Him. His picture was everywhere, endlessly repeated, to the point of ridicule or simply boredom: pasted up, ripped off, pulled apart, nailed on every door, pasted around every pole, decorated with mustaches, with pricks dripping into His mouth, even in colors—oh so blond and beautiful, just like Greta Garbo—not to mention the stained-glass reproductions in the Galiano subway. Wherever you look, He looks back.

Bruno: I'm gonna walk no more: I'm sitting right down. I'm at my wits' end: They take more pictures of him than of the Coca-Cola bottle! Let somebody else carry Him. Here's where I'm staying.

And there he stayed, in a fit of hiccups.

Pictures, taken from above, but at different distances: a black spot, a winding line of the highway, tilled fields; a blond head, toes on a platform, a background of pavement, white locks, and up front His profile; close-up: His eyes. His eyes; white locks, profile; dark spot, highway.

A little black girl came running full steam ahead, with a banner waving in the breeze, white knee socks were all you could see of her tiny legs; she came running full steam ahead, her legs—pistons—were all over the place, her knees chuga-chugachuga—a Hittite lion—holding up high a banner that said INRI. You've finally come, she said, we were waiting for You. Her eyes became moist, she was speechless ("She swooned, in a trance, as if she had seen Paul Anka!" said Help), she thrashed about wildly, out of joy, took a few steps toward Him, and fell.

He didn't have time to pick her up. Two others fell upon Him, more and more kept coming. Weeping and embracing Him. They came down from the hills, beating barrels and drums with sticks rolled up in rags. The women threw open their doors; dazed, they clapped their hands over their mouths; a cry; they dropped to their knees, tried to touch Him, kissed the ground where He passed. The children carried around His image in good-luck charms, in little straw dolls. His name was in all the shop windows. They ate Him in mint candies. They dressed up like Him, wearing little crowns of thorns (their faces white with rice powder) and small blood flowers. It was all so pretty!

They came from every direction, climbed trees to see Him, asked for His autograph.

He coughed and suddenly felt that He was moving forward, the people pushing Him, that He was moving backward, driftwood floating in the tide, that He was moving forward again. Sweating. He had chills. They stepped on His feet. They blew their hot breath, thick fumes of Gold Label rum, into His face; the trumpets of Luyanó in His ears. (The flutists were two jaundiced and baggy-eyed dwarfs, puffy cheeks under black berets.) He felt slimy hands caressing Him, and on His thighs wet mollusk lips. The banners covered His sky, the poles fenced Him in like a palisade of red lances. He was gasping for air. He thrashed His arms in acid fumes. He really wasn't made for the proletariat: the masses stifled Him.

"I'll never make it," He said to Himself. He tightened His eyes, clenched His fists, bit His lips. He wanted to stamp and kick. Spin around with his arms outstretched (and, God willing, with knives in both hands), open a path, escape. His dangling limbs did not obey Him. (Horns, rattles, bells.) His hand shook as if it were throwing dice. He tried to stop it: one foot trembled, or was it the other or His head. His hand moved on its own. His feet. He jumped. His body quivered, a goaded frog. An electric shock ran through Him. He was dancing unwillingly to a rock beat. (Balloons popped out of a balcony, doves from another.)

He listened as if someone were whispering in His ear. At the same time Help and Mercy turned toward Him. Once more (but the racket of brass bands, clapping, hurrahs): stuttering, babbling words ("African angels are speaking to Me," He thought). Without turning His head, He looked in the direction of the voices. Attentive, He heard "red," and right after: "It hurts in the back of my eyes."

He saw Help and Mercy shake their heads, stand still, raise their open hands—restored to the fervor of the catacombs—turn from white to yellow and back again to white. Now two great tears rolled down their cheeks. Now they muttered, sobbing, "A miracle, a miracle."

Then He realized He was speaking.

He heard Himself say, "I am freezing inside."

They wrapped Him in the Madonna's cloak from the main altar in the Church of Carmen. The thick cloth, embroidered with gold leaves hung straight down from His shoulders. Black cords intertwined in the shape of clover leaves and rosettes of pearls ran along its edges.

Each step of the bearers shook His blond head, his waxy eyelids, those sick eyes sank deeper. (From a distance He was the Madonna of a Siennese casket.) They threw flowers, they cheered Him. Without turning His head, with the solemnity of a princess in her Mercedes, He greeted the multitudes on the balconies. Carnations stuck to the garlands and brooches of His cloak.

"Blessed be ye, women, wise if not virgins, who have followed Me through thick and thin." He moved His forearm three times like a piggy-bank black boy who bows and doffs his cap. He suddenly unwound: His hands. They hung limp, like rags. He could not quite touch His eyelids:

"How cold they are, oh God, what a pain in the back of My eyes!" And they took off their cloaks, folded them like sashes, wrapped them around His waist. Or transported by mystical delirium ("May Your fire joyously consume me!" said Help), they padded them, and with the same burlap filled in the gaps of His joints. They covered His hinges. They would have torn out the pupils of their eyes to give Him. They wept with only one eye, so He would not see. They turned violet, their nails black, as if the plague were devouring them.

(Thickness of the sky: terraces of wax.

And there, over the streets, the sea: fixed foam, a strip of sand.) He glided over the mob—carried on their shoulders—swift, blinded by the flash bulbs, followed by the cameras—concave green crossed the lenses. Majestic, He was like a redwood statue unearthed from a river bed: His eye sockets full of crabs, His face rotted, His arms broken, His feet black sponges. Branches and leaves of holy palm trees opened before Him, like seaweed before the hull of a ship.

Posing in place, in order of generations, the families looked down at Him from their balconies. In the foreground, right behind the railing, little boys dressed in white suits and black bow ties were rocking back and forth on their wooden horses, chocolate cigars between their fingers. Little girls in starched dresses held yellow hoops next to their perfectly conical skirts, beach pails, and shovels. Behind them, austere, the fathers with mustaches and goatees, and bouquets of flowers in their hands, the mothers in their fancy curls and bonnets, wrapped in shawls. And in the background, leaning against the doors, grinning at the photographer's birdie, the grandparents, gray-haired, almost dead.

　　The squares: theaters with identical boxes. A parade of toy horses, hoops, bouquets, toy horses.

Such repetition made him dizzy, and the choruses too. Mercy touched His forehead with the back of her hand: It was burning. She pressed the wood and it crumbled. A white halo remaining. He had already rotted right through.

　　"King of the Four Roads, spare our sugar harvest!," shouted a reeling peasant with a bottle of rum in his hand, and he hung from Him, crying. Help tried to protect Him. But it was too late. The peasant had torn off a hand. A wooden stump remained, a splinter, out of which ants came scurrying.

　　The people came from all directions. They pushed. They squeezed together. It was a jungle of slender legs, knotty bamboo shoots supporting puffy buttocks, round like purple caimitos. Their trunks bent, swayed back, rocked by gusts of wind. In their midst, jumping over their wide feet, frightened black boys —little frogs, zigzagged around, fanning themselves.

　　A grandstand had been set up—with bleachers and platforms—and a red damask canopy hung over it, supported by four gilded halberds. Banners waved. Helicopters hovered above the square. From the platforms His followers threw them black balls which opened in midair: flowers of Chinese silk. They floated: black gardens. They fell; on the petals His name was imprinted: incomplete, backward, broken.

The sky was a crumpled piece of paper. A thick tent. Slow waves rolled through it: the ebb tide of a salty marsh. Something in the air was going to break.

　　"Come closer," He said to them. "Look at Me."

　　I am He who gives the Face. The big daddy-o. Mine is the page of the Codex. Mine is the ink and the painted image. Where are you taking Me?

　　But an icy gust ripped open His cloak, tore down the flags.

　　The people trembled. They warmed each other with their breath. Their eyes were wide open. They murmured, "This is the day   terror after death change   rot   House of the Black." They began to weep. They lowered their heads in prayer. They beat their brows. He heard Himself say, "Dear God, have pity on Me."

The families went inside: They closed the shutters. They bolted the doors. They piled up the furniture, and the children on top, against the doors so the wind would not blow them open. They covered the mirrors with sheets.

The storm raged. (The little black boys dropped their fans, clung to people's legs, buried their heads between their knees.) It grew dark. It was when they turned on the lights that they saw, in the lights' flickering cones, the white specks scrawling in the air, then orderly, with the slowness of stars, whirlwinds of sculptured water: it was snowing.

They huddled up under His cloak. They tried to warm Him, "But He was already fucked up," Help said—and on to another prayer. The snow burned Him on the face, another kind of fever. He looked like a prisoner, a drowned man. His eyes were sunken and watery, the lids jaundiced, His lips oozing with pus, His neck bloated. Branches of black veins climbed to His throat. Knots of puffy ganglia, spongy animals, rotting between His bones and hide. When He coughed he felt something was burning inside. When He spat, bloody water stained the handkerchief. He was scarcely breathing, sounding like an asthmatic sucking in air. Hunched over. Gasping. A fish on dry land.

"Come on, You're looking great. You look just like a Virgin of Charity!" (It's Mercy, to make Him happy.)

Parallel furrows in the pavement. A carpet of ceiba flowers. White moss.

And He:

"Of all the spectacles I've seen, none . . ."

A fit of coughing broke His bronchial tubes. A downpour of snowflakes pelted Him ("Tiny bird feathers!" said Help); the whirling propellers scattered them.

"If I should die upon the road, on my grave I want no flowers" (He said). And He tried to smile, to reassure the last of the faithful. But when they beat the drums they sprayed needles of ice.

Smooth, a tin sky covered almost the whole landscape. Bell towers and the arms of windmills jutted out over the red roofs. Open bridges, beached ships run aground: the Almendares River multiplied them. Along the snowy banks, stained at intervals by scaffolds and cranes, dying fish were jumping. Sea gulls swooped down to peck at them.

He tightened His throat. He felt that something was bursting in His neck. A taste of copper, warm salt, came up. He spat blood.

He was now a gargoyle, a snow-white rag. Help, in a fit of tears, passed her hand over His head, dried the sweat from His brow, murmured in His ear, "It will soon be over, have faith, it will soon be over." And Mercy, in a fit of tears, patted Him on the back, kissed His temples, murmured in His ear: "It will soon be over, have faith, it will soon be over."

The snow slanted down. At the eaves, broken spirals, veins of white ink that He saw erased, with each gust of wind, to reappear, each time wider.

In the depths of their sockets, His eyes grew glassy. He did not move them. Help and Mercy dragged Him a few steps; they looked at each other: they turned to shout. His body shook. He was weeping. And when He calmed down:

"Why all this moaning?" He said. "Kicking the bucket is great fun. Life only begins after death, the life."

He was choking.

Cutting through the snow, a coach sped by.

Like zinc, from afar, the Havana lakes. Small covered bridges crossed them. On the shore there were austere towers of fortresses, palaces of cedar, tall dovecotes amidst cherry orchards, the ruins of synagogues, cut off minarets: there Infanta Street, frozen, crosses San Lázaro.

"Let's go, every man for himself!" He heard them shout. He tried to raise His head. Then He saw the grandstand crushed by an avalanche. "Oh God," He moaned. "Why didn't You throw in the towel?" The faithful left the square in groups, under yellow raincoats held over themselves with raised arms. The leaders carried lanterns. Helicopters spotlighted them with their floodlights: dotted lines.

"Who has stayed behind?" (poor thing!)

And They:

"Loyal Ones, Followers, Shadows."

On the façades of colonial palaces the snow-covered capitals, moldings, cement flowers. Closed gates; the blue shadow of the latches extended over the iron. Only half-moons, contorted masks, remained of the medallions with the heads of viceroys. Squirrels fled across the cornices.

Sunken gardens. Silent fountains: the tritons driveled threads of ice.

"Curtains of bread crumbs" (said Help).

"Who up there is shaking His tablecloth?" (said Mercy). One of His hands came loose. Swollen, it fell to the ground; in its palm, a sore.

It stayed there, for a moment, on the white cloth; purple knuckles. Three red drops fell upon it, from the wrist, it was buried by the snow.

The Entry of Christ into Death

He saw quick reddish stains in the snow, copper shadows. The ground moved away from him. He was losing footing. He felt he was entering another space. Burning zone, he heard water through swollen leaves, the sleep of rattle-snakes and birds, the ambush. Behind vines, the frightened flight of mocking-birds. Cascades of moss, thick dark-green mats, fell from the highest fronds, clouding the day. Light tigers carried bleeding ducks in their teeth. He heard His steps in the mud, on damp leaves. With the sound of water among rocks, the strokes of a guitar reached His ear. Then the drums, yes: it was the mambo band, the one that greets us on the other side.

His body became strange to Him: a pile of rotting sticks under the snow. Help and Mercy closed His eyes. He saw himself twisted, a broken gargoyle.

Meanwhile, he crossed reverberating forests, stockades of sugar cane that ended in golden leaves. He was getting close. Already among the sputtering sparks of flowers you could see the musicians. He knew that He was going to dance. That dancing means meeting the Dead.

That if you dance well, you get in.

He saw himself crumble. He fell into pieces, with a moan. Wood falling in water. His bald, leprous head split in two. The empty holes of the eyes, the white, perforated lips, the nose in its bone, the ears plugged with two black clots. And farther on, the forehead, the cold globes of the eyes, the trunk, with an arm that sank into the snow as if looking for something buried. And farther up, the curve of the back. The legs in pieces; the snow buried them.

And the foot that stamped three times, the belch, the first beat. He jumped. Two more steps, two steps. He clapped hands to the rhythm. He did a turn. Holding a white handkerchief. He danced on one foot. The band players shook their little bells near his ear. "Who can beat me?" He said to Himself. And he wiggled His hips. The musicians gathered around him. Twice they suddenly changed the batá beat of the tambourines and twice he caught up to them with a caper. He was blond and handsome. And had white feet. He whirled around. Then the other way. Superimposed on himself. He was blond. He was naked. Holding a white handkerchief. He shouted again. "Sugar!" they shouted to Him. He laughed. He wore gold bracelets. Not as shiny as his eyes.

He didn't know that the snow had stopped. Rivulets of mud cracked the white cloth, creased it at the sewers. It was sunny. Grating rails and throwing off sparks, the trolleys, full, passed by again. The river ran. The ships cast off.

(In the parks the old men chatted.)

Then the Faithful, the Fates, crossed the square. They started picking Him up, searching in the mire. Piece by piece, they wrapped Him in a cloth with loving care. They hurried away.

They were already reaching the portals when, from the helicopters, bullets rained down.

19

GUSTAVO SÁINZ

What Manuel Puig (selection 16) did for the Argentine lower and middle classes, Gustavo Sáinz attempted to do for their Mexican counterparts: to tell their pitiful and comic stories in their own words.

Sáinz was born in Mexico in 1940. He has worked as a journalist and a designer, edited literary and educational journals, and taught a course on contemporary literature at the National Autonomous University of Mexico. But his main concern is the writing of novels, of which he has thus far published three.

The first, *Gazapo* (1965), told the story of a group of Mexican teen-agers through the endless recording and re-recording of their conversations, monologues, and confessions. The language was the real protagonist of the novel, whose plot (the slowest seduction in literature this side of *Pamela*) had very little suspense. Even in the title there was a pun, because *gazapo* means in Spanish a young rabbit, a dissembling knave, and a lie. This plurality of meanings corresponded to the plurality of levels on which the novel could be read. It was an instant success, and the young things in Mexico City immediately recognized themselves in Sáinz's parodic recording.

His second novel, *Obsessive Circular Days* (1969), was not so success-ful. It explored a similar world, but became more involved in a picaresque story of a so-called religious college for girls, which was actually an expensive brothel. Although some of its episodes were extremely funny, the narrative as a whole lost coherence through its multitude of digressions and diversions. Sáinz's third novel, *The Princess of the Iron Palace* (1974), is his most ambitious effort to date. It is a tour de force, consisting of an endless monologue by its protagonist, a salesgirl at a big department store, the Iron Palace, who gets involved with drug addicts, gangsters, and pimps. Using throughout the highly idiosyncratic speech of the protagonist and endlessly introducing small variations in her story, the novel unravels very carefully the world of deceit and make-believe that holds the characters together. Here again, an unsurpassed parodical talent allows Sáinz to produce a wonderfully picaresque reconstruction of a world of parasites, call girls, weekend girls, models, and whores. Yet it is the whole of contemporary Mexican society, with its grossly affluent upper and middle classes, that becomes mirrored in this distorting glass. Sáinz never preaches, but his eye and ear have a deadly accuracy. The protagonist, a sort of updated Molly Bloom, seems too shy at the beginning to tell everything, warts and all, but with time she loosens up a lot. The result is a comic masterpiece.

The Princess of the Iron Palace

•

From La Princesa del Palacio de Hierro, *especially translated by John
Bruce-Novoa.*

So my family went to work fast. As soon as they saw I was going with
him, they forbid me to date, they forbid me to go out at night, a whole lot of
things, you know? So I decided to get myself a job—to have an excuse, you see?
—so I could go out and see him. So I went to work at a place where all I did
was dumb things, you know? Like knocking things over. I'd knock over all the
flower vases. Wow, no, you just can't imagine. I broke everything, just everything.
Because they got me that job through pull, see?, so they couldn't do anything
to me, they couldn't get rid of me. I worked at the Boutique in the Iron Palace.
Exclusive gifts where all the gifts were more than a hundred dollars, way over a
hundred, from two hundred up. So absent-minded me, each time somebody
would come over I'd say, How're you doing, kid, how's things, and up goes my
arm and I'd knock over a thousand-dollar jug. Wow, I did horrible things, you
know. I mean I hooked onto that job so that I could let loose and tell people what
I was going through. All the people that came in, I spilled my troubles to.
Everybody, just everybody. There wasn't a person I didn't rattle off my sufferings
to. I was Miss Popular, can you imagine? I suffered like a dog, because then they
got detectives after us, that is my family did, my uncle. So they put one detective
on me and another on Crazy Valdiosera, my crazy green darling. He was so
good-lookin', so, so good-lookin'. Then they jumped to conclusions, you know?
They made up a report for my family, where they said that good-lookin' lived off
the ladies, that one so and so kept him, that others gave him money, and on top
of that he liked marijuana, a whole lot of things, you know, that I thought were
the biggest lies. Naturally to me they were just the biggest lies ever. God no, I
never believed any of it.

They didn't pay me hardly anything at the Iron Palace, and to beat all,
good-lookin' wanted to reform, see?, and so all of a sudden he's so poor so poor,
just so poor. Well, look, he had bought a car from Gabriel Infante, you know?
But seeing as Gabriel really loved me, you know, and I had quit talking to him,
he was really out to get me. So the first chance he got to screw someone that
mattered to me, which was like screwin' me, he put the screws on good-lookin'.
He screwed him by taking back the car for missing a payment, just because he
was behind in his payments, imagine. Before they repossessed the car, he used
to pick me up. We'd go to his house and buy some two-penny rolls. You know,
those two-penny rolls? That's when we were just starting to be poor, see, because
the idiot wanted to reform. We'd buy rolls for two cents and take them over to

his mother's so she could stuff them with leftovers, just think, and that's what we ate. I remember once we saved a few pennies and he bought me a popsicle for dessert. For dessert, you know. A popsicle. Because we were broke, see, unbelievably cleaned out. Then we were just drinking coffee, because we didn't even have two cents for bread. And then they took the car. Wow! But even before they took it, he would come after me on foot, to save gas. Can you imagine, I worked in the Iron Palace on Durango and he lived in the Colonia del Valle district, about six miles away. Then we'd walk back to his house again, and there, finally, we'd get in the car and he'd take me home. Because he never made me take the bus, you know? Listen, he had to scrape up a dollar or a dollar and a half so he could take me home, and then just as much to go back himself, see? He had to get about three dollars, see? So we started living real cheap, you know. We saved all our money and sometimes he'd buy me a slip, you know, once he bought me some shoes that lasted years and years, see, just so we could get married. Until finally he got a job importing shrimp or something like that. Before I died of hunger.

Look, one day we went to the show at the Paseo Theater. We were broke, but we were so in love and we still had the car, so we went to the Paseo. But I forgot that the Paseo is in the same building where my uncle's office is, see? Just think, the Monster. So we get to the Paseo and good-lookin' goes off to buy some sandwiches, and while he was buying the sandwiches, I was looking at the pictures from the movie. Then I hear my uncle's voice. Let's go, little girl. Because he saw me from his office and came down. We were in the lobby and he says to me, go up to my office and tell Pat to come down here. So I said yes, right away. I couldn't tell him I was with good-lookin', you know. I said yes and was gone. So I go up and can't find Pat, his secretary. And then look, when I go back down he says to me, you better go back up there because I don't want you to see how this son-of-a-bitch is going to fall, right here at my feet, and I warned you, right?, so you better go upstairs. And me: what? Now, yes, right now. And those men over there, and he points to two policemen, when they catch him they're going to shoot him full of holes, so you better go up, right?, then me, just ask me if I went up you know. So I say, you'll have to shoot me first then, because I'm going after him, see? So I start looking for him you know, and they don't make a move to stop me. And look, I go into the candy shop and what?, nothing. I go into the restaurant, the book store, down the hallway to the parking lot, and then I get terribly desperate and scared and worried, you know. I started hunting for him very calm and at the end I was screaming. Yelling for him, you know. I yelled, where are you, where are you, and nothing, see? Good-lookin' was nowhere. And I looked for him in all the little diners along the Paseo de la Reforma and nothing, see. Well finally, I go into Sanborn's to fix my face in the restroom and I find him eating Swiss enchiladas. Can you dig it? In Sanborn's. So like since I had disappeared, he had gone off and was eating. Well, I was really scared and told him to come on, hurry, let's go. And he says, why. And I say to him, hurry, let's go, get in the car and let's go, I said, I'll explain later. So when we get in the car, when we were already driving, I say, guess what happened. So

I told him. So he says, why didn't you tell me before. And he says, I'm going right back there now, and he goes back, see, to hunt for my uncle. So I was scared to death, you know. You can imagine. So me: please, don't go back. Well, finally, he wouldn't listen to me. We go back to look for my uncle and we don't find him, thank God, and so he took me home. I get home and there's my dad, you know. What happened? Well my uncle had called him and look, with my little gift for gab I tell him what had just happened with that rat of an uncle of mine. You're not going to believe it. Tell me what happened, come on, what happened? I say, nothing, look, I was walking along with Tito Caruso, who was dressed like this and like that and uncle mistook him for Crazy Valdiosera. So he went in his office and guess what he did, he shoots at Tito Caruso three times. Well in short, I shuffled the whole thing around on him. So my dad got so mad that he called my uncle and then he absolutely forbids him to bother me again. Then my uncle tried to tell him to listen, that's not true, you know? It was that Crazy Valdiosera. But my dad believed me, you know. Because my dad believed everything I said to him. My uncle was a politician, you know. He was always mixed up in politics and he was a congressman, you know. And all kinds of strange things. Besides he was, how could I put it, really paranoid. He always had the idea someone was after him and that the whole world was out to kill him. So he was always loaded with rifles, machine guns. No joke. He had all the guns in the world. A gun in every pocket. A very strange dude, don't you think? He was really funny, and besides, a nice guy, but when it came to me he was terrible, you know? Because he loved me a whole lot. Until he died, the person he loved most in his whole life was me, you know. He always said that after his kids, the only family he had ever had in his life was me.

But we were talking about the Iron Palace. I hardly made a dime, in the first place, because every time someone came in, I would recommend things we didn't sell. I'd say to them, hey look, why don't you go over to Nieto's. I was . . . Look, I'd say to them, where did I see some cut-crystal ash trays. Look, I was in the exclusive gifts department, they came in to buy some ash trays and I'd tell them, oh, no, but I saw some great ones, what you would call really great, in such and such store, and I'd send them somewhere else, you know, I'd recommend other boutiques. Because I felt I had to be, uh, no, no, not smart, but, how would you say when you're real, you know? I mean, when you tell it like it is, see? When you're getting a commission but you still don't try to make them buy from you, but to make it so they find the best, you know? That's what mattered. Then I'd tell everybody about my tragedy. And then it was just my luck to get sick and like I told you before, I'd get sick. In short, I was a wreck and I never sold a thing. Well, the salary was sixty dollars. Sure, on good weeks, at the most I got up to eighty, a hundred in commissions. So I bought a few things; I was going to marry good-lookin', wasn't I? Well, since it was understood we were going to get married, then I'd buy just anything.

It was so really funny with good-lookin', because with good-lookin', look, we went through hell, you know? You know they even shot at us and things like that, and being poor and all that, you see? But we had one thing, we always,

always, always told each other the truth, especially him, you know, who was the one who was supposed to tell the truth. Then one day he left. Oh yeah, he had had a fight with one of his best friends, Tito, you know him, and he had asked me not to talk to him any more. He was never really a close friend of mine you know. So then he had forbidden me to talk to him, but absolutely not. Then one day he had to go to Merida. It was Christmas time and he had to go to Merida. So he wasn't in Mexico City and his friend Tito Caruso shows up. So he says to me, look, I want to talk to you because, look, all right, then just look what he says to me, oh sweetheart, like look, I really want to be your friend, like please talk to me, like I'm not to blame, and like I don't know what. All right, well sure, if you really want to know the truth, I don't have a thing against you, Valdiosera's the only reason that I quit talking to you. He says to me, all right, I've got a problem, look, since I'm the reason you ever started going out with Crazy Valdiosera anyway, now I feel like I have a moral obligation to tell you what's going on. Look, right now Crazy Valdiosera is in Merida and he went with another girl. When he told me that, right when he said that to me, the bell rang and that meant I had to go to lunch, you know? So look, it was such a shock that I turned around and started walking, and so he started walking after me. Hey, baby, what's wrong? I couldn't even answer him. I went up that little black escalator toward the cafeteria and I couldn't say anything back to him at all. And finally, from down below, he shouted, her name's Leonor Cifuentes! Do you know her? She was a lazy, good-for-nothing hooker. He's with Leonor Cifuentes, he yelled, but that was the last I heard. Right then I was going into the cafeteria and I said to myself, no, I'm not going to eat. I felt really bad, you know? So I went back down. I went to Sanborn's. The head waitress at Sanborn's then was a friend of mine, a lady that really treated me good. So I sat down and she came up and said what's wrong? You look all sad, what's the matter? I said, oh, honey, a horrible thing just happened to me and I don't know what to do. Then she says to me, you don't say. Well yeah, I say, they just told me something terrible about Crazy Valdiosera. Oh, don't worry, like no, don't worry, it's nothing, really. And right then . . . Ah, just look how screwed up this world is, really. I was on my way out of Sanborn's. And I was going to call a close friend of good-lookin', good-lookin's closest, closest, closest friend, this one really is his best friend. I said to him, Vulvo, listen, I absolutely need to talk to you, come pick me up. I'll rush right down there. Right then, look, I was still talking to him and Tito Caruso shows up again. Oh, baby, please, forgive me, I didn't think it would hurt you so much, please forgive me, and I don't know what. I was talking to Tito when Vulvo comes up, because he lived only two blocks away. I say, get out of here, Tito, don't let him see you, because he'll tell Valdiosera that you were the one who told me and I don't want him to know, hide. Then Vulvo comes up and you know, Tito hides and Vulvo comes up, and then he says to me, oh, baby, what's the matter? I told him what was wrong and he said, well listen, it's true, baby, I never wanted to tell you, but listen, it's true, and there's no point in going on thinking that you're going to marry Valdiosera, because it would be a horrible life for you. You're worth more than that, don't be stupid, and then look, he says, you deserve something better. Period. He splits. And so look, he's told me not to be stupid, to break up with him, well, all kinds of things, and with that he splits. And so I go to my counter, because I had to get back to work, and so I get there and my boss says, listen, you look terrible. He says to me, what's the matter with you? He says to me, go straighten yourself up. Take an hour off and fix yourself up, he says to me, look at yourself, you're as white as a ghost. Well, look, I left work and went out again and took a walk. I was going past Sanborn's you know, and I turn my head toward the window and I see him. I saw him and it was as if I had seen, no, no, not even the devil would be bad enough, you know? Like I fly in, furious, really furious, I zoom in. Then I stop. He was with some friends I'd never met. I stop in front of him and say, come outside, because we have something to talk about. That's what I said first. Hey, baby, how are you, sweety, and I don't know what. Outside, I said to him, we have to talk and right now. Well he sticks his hand in his pocket like this, left some money on the table and we went outside. But listen, he took the money out like this, he didn't even see how much he took out, word of honor, he put it on the table and then he went outside. So I say to him, please, tell me who you went to Merida with. Oh, baby! Look, Valdiosera was the kind of guy that if you'd ask him, what did you do yesterday, if I hadn't seen him you know, well I stayed home, he'd say, and then if you kept after him, see, really, what did you do, he would get furious that you would have just kind of doubted him. And that day, oh, baby, what's eating you, what are you talking about? Tell me who you went to Merida with. And so I said, please tell me. Ah, baby, what makes you ask?, nobody, I didn't go nowhere with nobody, and something about the shrimp shipments, and who knows what. Someone been telling you those stories? The dude's the biggest liar ever. So I said to him, look, if you tell me you went to Merida with someone, it won't matter, but if you tell me it isn't true, I'll have to break up with you, because I'll never forgive you for lying to me, I'm never going to be able to forgive you, so I'd rather you tell me who you went with, that is, I already know, but I'd rather hear it straight from your mouth. Well listen, you know he got furious and started yelling at me right there outside Sanborn's, right outside Sanborn's. Remember how before, where the parking lot is now, there was a Paseo Jacarandas? Yeh, it was called Paseo de Jacarandas. And he started yelling at me. That's what I get for being such an ass, well I've been an ass all my life, to try to get you to believe anything, but O.K., believe whatever you want, I don't care, well he told me off but good, you know? In short, I said, well all right, if you want to break up, then we'll break up. I came back in and went back, well, you know, to my place. Three minutes later he calls me on the phone. I answered and, oh yeah, when I came in, my boss was waiting for me, and the man under him, and the floor boss, just everybody. You shouldn't lower yourself by putting up with Mr. Green, because they called him Mr. Green. Because look, he'd show up in green suede shoes, green socks, green pants, green shirt, everything green, but different shades of green. My bosses nicknamed him Mr. Green. It's beneath a girl like you to put up with such vulgarity. Listen, they had been right there and they heard everything Valdiosera said to me. Imagine, and they were really mad, and I hadn't noticed them there. When I came in, they were already waiting to scold me. Just then, the phone rings and it was Mr. Green Valdiosera. And so he says to me I SWEAR THAT I WILL NEVER SPEAK TO YOU AGAIN AS LONG AS I LIVE and if you ever run into me on the street, pretend you don't see me, because I'm not even going to say hello. Shit, and he hangs up on me. He didn't even give me a chance to open my mouth, and then, again. It was him, sure, sure, he said the same things over again, but this time he didn't hang up right away, he waited to listen to what I'd say back. And me, me, forget it, not a word. Then three minutes later, the phone rings again. They were still scolding me. It's that those people have known me since I was a little girl, the people I'm talking about. Then the phone rings again. So look, they were scolding me but to high heaven, you know?, and right then the phone rings again and it was that rat Valdiosera. And he tells me again, but remember, I'm never going to forgive you ever. He tells me off but good again, and shit, if he doesn't hang up on me again. You wouldn't believe how I was, oh, no, no, this can't be. When he called back the third time, I said to him: now listen, you're the one who's going to shut up, because now I'm going to tell you something, I'm the one who's never going to talk to you ever again as long as I live, because you have no class and you're common and I never want to have a thing to do with you ever again. Then I hung up on him. About fifteen minutes go by, you know, and he calls and he says to me, oh, honey baby, please forgive me, sweety, please forgive me, I found out who told you that story, how could you have believed them. Like really fast, you see? The first thing I thought was that Vulvo had seen Tito, you know? And he says to me, how could you have believed them. You know that that person only wants to hurt us, besides you know those kind of people who say things like that, how could you even think of believing them, I found out who told you, it's just that I'm really hurt, how could you believe them, please forgive me, and I don't know what. And I'm such an ass, look how I put my foot in my mouth, I say to him, oh, Crazy, honey, how was I going to know that Tito would come and tell me something like that? And he says to me, I only wanted you to tell me his name, goodbye, and shit, he hangs up, he only wanted to know his name and he hangs up on me, if you please, oh yeah, and he tells me, I'm going to kill him, and I don't know what else; and he hangs up on me. There I am out of my mind, running all over Mexico City trying to find Tito, until I found him and tell him, Tito, Tito, Crazy's going to kill you, he wants to murder you. Hide, hide. Then I told him what happened.

Well, the next day you know, I went to work again and what do you think?, Valdiosera comes strolling up with Tito, and Valdiosera has his arm over Tito's shoulder, imagine, and then they went and looked at all the counters, they looked at all the presents in the place, you know? The flower vases, everything, walking along together with his arm around Tito. They'd ask how much and look at the things front and back and upside down, you know, and they never even looked at me, you know? That if they could be gift-wrapped and how long would it take for I don't know what, and not one look. That's after two-timing me, taming me, I should say killing me, really, you know? They've walked by, you know, they've played a dirty trick on me and then they leave. And that's it. I never saw Crazy Valdiosera again. Well anyway, not until two months later, two or three months later. And he came to tell me that all that time he had been working on the shrimp trucks, because now he was a big bully, rich as hell, and real hip, but more than anything, damn good-lookin', so damn good-lookin'.

20

REINALDO ARENAS

A younger disciple of Lezama Lima (Part Four, 15), the Cuban Reinaldo Arenas shares with Severo Sarduy (Five, 18) not only his enthusiasm for baroque literature but a similar gift for unconventional narrative.

Arenas, born in 1943, won his first literary prize with a novel, *Celestino Before Dawn*, published in 1966 and later renamed *The Pit*. It was a free-flowing narrative of the life and misadventures of a poor rural family in the time of the Batista dictatorship. It was told from the point of view of an idiot son. But while this approach was similar to that used in one section of *The Sound and the Fury,* the general trend of the narrative was more metaphorical than anything Faulkner ever attempted.

Arenas's second novel, *Hallucinations* (1968), was even more experimental. Subtitled "An Account of the Life and Adventures of Friar Servando Teresa de Mier," it used Friar Servando's *Memoirs* (Two, 1) as a starting point; but instead of retelling the friar's life in the usual format of the historical or biographical novel, Arenas rewrote the original text entirely, creating not the biography of a man but the biography of a text. His novel is a commentary, an amplification, a digression, a parody, and a critique of the original *Memoirs.* In some passages he merely quotes Friar Servando, slightly editing his words; in others, he amplifies what the friar mentions only in passing; in still others, he frankly invents. For instance, while in Spain, Friar Servando participates in an allegorical court orgy; while in England, he meets Virginia Woolf's Orlando. Throughout, the original text is adroitly counterpointed by Arenas's. The result is a complex and brilliant rendering of a unique career. Friar Servando comes to life in this novel, and his larger-than-life adventures become truly hallucinatory. Although this novel, too, was awarded a prize in Cuba, it was never printed there. The first Spanish edition came out in Mexico, and was immediately translated into French, English, German, Dutch, Italian, and Portuguese. The reasons for its being censored in Cuba itself have never been made public. It is possible that some of Friar Servando's misfortunes in his fight for freedom had uncomfortable implications from the standpoint of the Cuban government; in parodying the early nineteenth century, Arenas may perhaps have introduced some dangerous contemporary overtones. The fact is, in any event, that since the publication abroad of this second novel, Arenas has become a nonperson in Cuba. His third novel, *The Palace of the Very White Skunks* (1975), has been published so far only in a French translation, not in Spanish. The book continues the family saga of the first novel. This time the main subject of the narrative is not the world of childhood but that of adolescence, and at the novel's close, the end of an era is indicated with the commencement of the Castro guerrillas' struggle against Batista. Though in a less spectacular way than Friar Servando, Arenas too has been conducting a private war—for the right of a novelist to follow where his creative inspiration leads him, for the freedom to write, one of Latin America's most contested rights. He has not yet succeeded, but his name is already one to be reckoned with.

Concerning Los Toribios Prison and the Chaining of the Friar

From Hallucinations, *translated by Gordon Brotherston (New York: Harper & Row, 1971), pp. 184–90.*

The friar was going along in the coach, escorted by a platoon of soldiers. The sun was pulverizing the stones, and you could hear the occasional cries of soldiers about to explode. In this fashion they passed through the two Castiles, making a soup out of age-old bones on the way. They then went over snow fields, which melted away under their feet. They went right across Seville and reached Los Toribios prison. "He's been sentenced to life," the constable said. And the friar went along to the last cell in the prison. And there they started to chain him down. They put a thick chain round his neck; this was the principal chain, which was then wrapped round his waist twice, tied round his feet, and then taken right back up to his neck again. The chain passed in its turn through two iron stanchions which ran down either side of the friar like curbstones, and these stanchions were attached to a thick grid embedded in the floor. The friar consequently had to stay lying down without ever being able to get up. Another chain, not such a thick one, was linked to the principal chain around the friar's waist, went around him several times, and then went straight up to his head, which it encircled like a diadem, and then went back down to his feet and enveloped them in iron; the friar was consequently unable to move his head to one side or the other. At the place where this chain encircled his head they made a little hollow in his skin to accommodate another chain which ran down the length of his body and then coiled itself round his knees. It was wound eight times round each knee and then set off back toward his neck, which it girded ceremoniously, and then descended again to his waist, where it formed a huge knot; the friar consequently was unable to move his knees and he had to breathe lightly since the walls of his stomach were pressed in. Out of this knot of chain came ten further chains of the same thickness (they were fairly thin but very strong). The first of them coiled itself three times around the friar's nose, which was long enough to make this feasible, and then set off for one of his ears, pierced it like an earring, went around it ten times (maybe more: the warders could hardly count), and set off for the other ear, which it encircled nine times, so they say, and from there went and wrapped itself around two of the friar's eyeteeth, threaded its way around all his other teeth, held down his tongue at seven different points and ended up in a knot round his uvula: the friar was consequently unable to speak, or to breathe through his nose; naturally he was unable to smell anything either. The second chain went straight for one of the friar's big toes, wound itself tightly around it, and then began to make fast the other toes on that foot. This done, the chain then began to double back on itself until the whole of the foot became quite metallic without a bit of flesh visible anywhere; the friar was consequently unable to move any of the toes on that foot, and still less the foot itself with its heavy chain mail. The next chain made for the other foot, and did similar things to it; consequently both the friar's feet were immobilized. The fourth chain extended to the prisoner's legs and wove itself between them so that together they looked like a single metal plait; and the veins in his legs were constricted, making it very difficult for his blood to circulate. The chains, however, then came up to the convict's thinning hair, and there separated into thousands of chains, so small they were hardly visible, which had the job of holding down every one of the friar's hairs by the *roots;* thus even the prisoner's hair was fettered and this gave him an awful, other-worldly appearance, which frightened even the warders themselves. The next chain went off in the same direction as the four previous ones and reinforced them in a second set of fastenings; thus the friar was deprived of all hope that one of his bonds might be defective. Let us turn now to the sixth chain. This one had a rather special function: it went straight up to the prisoner's brow and then came down and coiled itself around his testicles, first elaborately girdling one and then moving on to the other. This chain then passed up between the friar's buttocks to the principal chain, and the prisoner was consequently almost unable to perform his natural functions; but luckily they gave him so little food that this was hardly a problem. The next chain also went around his testicles but not at all tightly, and then encircled the priestly penis with a certain zest; once it was completely enchained, this organ looked like a splendid serpent with many well-pronounced rings or markings. The constant friction of the chains caused the friar's imprisoned member to be in a state of permanent erection, and this mortified him greatly. It also meant the eighth chain went in a straight line to that part and moored his penis to his thigh like a guy rope; consequently, if the friar had wanted to move his organ he would have had to move his thigh and in turn move the stanchions, and these would have had in their turn to move the iron grid embedded in the floor, and so move the entire prison. Anyway, the next chain zigzagged all over the prisoner's stomach and made some fine patterns on it, then it made a flourish around each of his thighs and joined them together so thoroughly that they formed a single impenetrable slab, and from there it went and entwined itself decoratively around his toes, and then traveled from each of his feet separated into five slender chains which attached themselves to the fingers of each of his hands; so that the friar's hands and feet were bound and he was prevented from making any movement or sign. But this chain, in its turn, had an extra section destined for the prisoner's eyes, which was divided into innumerable tiny chains that served the purpose of pinning down his eyelashes and each hair of his eyebrows; these chains then descended in very close company and ended up making secure the hair of his already enchained nose; the friar was consequently unable to blink. But the tenth and last chain was left free; it emerged from the same area as the others but it was just left dangling. The idea was that it should serve as a point of geographical reference for the jailers, so they could know more or less where the prisoner's various organs were located. Where his mouth was, for example, for the purpose of giving him food. . . . None of his features could be located however, since his whole face was covered with a crisscross of chains; this led the jailer to order that the convict should be fed only with soup, the soup being thrown on to the chains more or less at the spot where his face might be expected to be, so that the liquid could filter through the net of chains and eventually reach his mouth; but it hardly ever worked out like that. And the friar learned how to imbibe through his nostrils. In the end, a warder (who hated the friar bitterly because when he came to the prison, just before he was chained up, the friar had said to him, "I thought there would be nothing but bulls* at Toribios, but you're plainly a cow"), insisted that the chains were flimsy and inadequate, and a whole new set of them came to supplement the old one, and the whole room was filled with an iron-and-lead ball of excessive proportions, which almost touched the ceiling. By order of the jailer four chains were attached to the great mass of metal under which the friar lay buried, and each one was fixed to the ceiling in different corners of the room, so that viewed in the perpetual twilight of that door- and window-less prison the friar looked like a giant spider lying on its back covered with shiny sticky grease. . . . And what of life inside that suffocating net? Fray Servando had slowly got used to prisons. This one was certainly bad, but not unbearably so. He learned to get air through the net of chains, and he learned to suck in that stale water they threw onto the tangle of metal which covered his face; the soup they served him on Mondays (always in the afternoons) would moisten his face late on a Saturday morning. By the way, when his ferrous cage changed temperature and the chains went from hot to cold, the friar knew when day came and went. Had he stayed shut in there, he would have learned over the years to see through the iron and through the ceiling, to the sky, the sun, and the vultures circling over the prison. . . . He got so thin that even his bones shrank in size and the chains became more bearable, and from time to time he was even able to move his plexus and breathe. . . . But

*Toros: hence an untranslatable pun with "Toribios" (T.N.).

despite the fact that he lay there like an upturned turtle under the constant watch of the guards, despite the whole fleets of ships which arrived with the cargoes of ironmongery that were then piled up on top of his skeletal frame, despite the *rigors* of his enchainment, there was still something missing in that entire infernal ritual. For some reason the imprisonment was always less than total; something was impinging on the mass of chains, rendering them puny and useless: and *incapable of imprisoning.* . . . And the fact is the friar's mind was free. Throwing aside the chains, his thoughts slipped nimbly through the walls and were constantly occupied in planning escape, vengeance, and liberation. His thoughts would elude those bars of iron, sneak out right under the guards' noses, and return, going back in time, to sandy fields and white-painted stony hills, and would stroll through cool *chumberales* and mazelike *chaparrales* and arrive at the city with the tireless bells; and then he was under a bench there watching the girls going by in their ponchos selling tamales and sandals. . . . In other words, their efforts were in vain. The friar came and went as he pleased more freely than ever before, and he escaped from time, went into it and out of it again, unencumbered, as he had never been able to do in days of oppression (all his days had been oppressed). And if it had not been for those hateful chains, which pulled at the corners of his mouth, before encircling each of his teeth and tying down his tongue, one would have seen Servando's smile within that immense apparatus, like a fabulous bird, calm, moved by a kind of imperturbable tenderness. . . . In the meantime the warders became suspicious and afraid: they saw that mass looming in the half-light. They saw it glistening. And they couldn't hear a sound. And they became afraid. And their fear awoke new fears in them. So that on top of those chains more chains were heaped, and a new blanket of chains was placed on top of *them.* But the warders were still frightened by the friar's courage, and by the bestiality of the task they were performing. And so yet further chains were demanded; and two brigs brought them from England. And the whole shiny load was put on top of the junk underneath, which was by now rusty and near to cracking open the walls. The prison was almost caving in under that huge weight; but the warders were still afraid and they gathered in frightened groups in the corridors. And they began to be frightened of their fear. And they huddled into corners and pointed toward the friar's cell. And at night one or other of them would become delirious, and say that there were shouts and noises of chains being torn apart coming from the cell; and that the walls were creaking (this was in fact so). . . . And more brigs arrived with more chains. Though quite a few sank on the way, storms being frequent and their cargo excessively heavy; and this led to the friar being accused on another count of witchcraft and diabolical dealings with the devil, of whom the fearful fretful warders were so frightened. But some of the brigs did make it. And the chains were dragged by countless numbers of the *faithful* along to the *holy* prison where the *accursed* convict lay enchained. And more chains were added to more and more chains. In the end they gave up feeding the friar anything but chains. They worked feverishly: day and night nothing could be heard but chains being hauled up and thrown onto a by now distant body. . . . And the warders didn't stop being afraid. . . . Until the moment came: they heard the creaking with terror and clutching onto one another they ran for shelter in the basement cells. Then they heard the creaking again and kept running. Moments later it was as if the walls, the floors, the whole prison had exploded with a bang. It was the weight of the friar's chains finally bringing down the entire building, which just couldn't take any more. And the iron debris forced its way down through the other debris. The friar descended enchained, amidst falling stones and squeaking fetters that twisted and broke. The great iron mass rolled down from floor to floor, grinding passageways to dust and razing those infernal cells to the ground, until it reached the basement and crushed all the fearful warders to death in one go. When he heard the fetters breaking up the jailer ran off down the hill, but a slab of stone hit him in the neck and arrested him, until the friar in his dizzy progress rolled over him. . . . The prison was thus reduced to rubble. But Fray Servando was still enchained, and as the prison stood on a hill he rolled on, destroying villages and burying whole towns. He passed right through Seville in this fashion, causing the Guadalquivir to overflow, squashing reeds, frogs, birds, and meadows to pulp. Then he proceeded to Madrid and razed it to the ground. On his way back he took in the Escorial and reduced it to a pile of rubble, not leaving a single tree upright. He steamrollered his way over the two Castiles, and then went down to Cadiz and submerged the harbor. Such was the friar's progress, rolling along inside his chains, as they slowly cracked and gave way. Along he rolled, and crossed the Leon mountains. Bound just by the principal chain he tumbled down to the sea. But on the way he encountered one or two precipices, and the chain broke and the stanchions gave way. And the friar fell free onto the waves, which were choppy and did not cease for a moment from hurling crabs against the blank cliffs along the coast. Where they were smashed to pieces.

A Note About the Editor

Emir Rodríguez Monegal was born in Melo, Uruguay, in 1921. Following his undergraduate studies at the Lycée Français in both Montevideo and Rio de Janeiro, he did post-graduate work at Cambridge University. He has been a visiting professor at Harvard and Yale and a visiting scholar at Liverpool University. Since 1969 he has been a Professor at Yale University, becoming Chairman of the Spanish and Portuguese Department in 1973. From 1966 to 1968 he edited *Mundo Nuevo*, a Spanish-language literary monthly published in Paris; he has also edited literary magazines in Uruguay and the United States, and has published widely in South America. His most recent book is *Borges: A Literary Life*, a biographical study of the Argentine writer. Professor Rodríguez Monegal lives in New Haven.

Thomas Colchie was born in 1942. He was educated at Princeton and New York universities, and did postgraduate research in Portugal. He has taught comparative literature at Brooklyn College since 1974, and became an advisory editor of *Review*, the journal of Latin American literature, in 1976. Mr. Colchie is currently at work on the translation of two books, Manuel Puig's *Kiss of the Spider Woman* and Graciliano Ramos's *Memoirs of Prison Life*, as well as on the compilation of an anthology of medieval Portuguese poetry.

A Note on the Type

This book was set, via computer-driven cathode ray tube, in Avanta, an adaptation of Electra, a type face designed by W. A. Dwiggins. The Electra face is a simple and readable type suitable for printing books by present-day processes. It is not based on any historical model, and hence does not echo any particular time or fashion.
Composed by The Haddon Craftsmen, Inc., Scranton, Pennsylvania.

Typography and binding design by Virginia Tan.